MW00650785

A Prehistory
of North America

Mark Q. Sutton

Prentice Hall

Boston   Columbus   Indianapolis   New York   San Francisco   Upper Saddle River
Amsterdam   Cape Town   Dubai   London   Madrid   Milan   Munich   Paris   Montreal   Toronto
Delhi   Mexico City   Sao Paulo   Sydney   Hong Kong   Seoul   Singapore   Taipei   Tokyo

Editorial Director: Craig Campanella
Editor in Chief: Dickson Musslewhite
Publisher: Nancy Roberts
Editorial Project Manager: Nicole Conforti
Editorial Assistant: Nart Varoqua
Director of Marketing: Brandy Dawson
Marketing Manager: Laura Lee Manley
Managing Editor: Maureen Richardson
Project Manager: Annemarie Franklin
Operations Specialist: Sherry Lewis
Cover Design Manager: Jayne Conte
Cover Designer: Bruce Kenselaar
Cover Photo: James Helmer
Manager, Rights and Permissions: Zina Arabia
Manager, Visual Research: Beth Brenzel
Full-Service Project Management: Aptara®, Inc.
Composition: Aptara®, Inc.
Printer/Binder: STP/RRD/Crawfordsville
Cover Printer: STP/RRD/Crawfordsville
Text Font: Minion

Credits and acknowledgments borrowed from other sources and reproduced, with permission, in this textbook appear on p. 403.

Library of Congress Cataloging-in-Publication Data

Sutton, Mark Q.
   A prehistory of North America / Mark Q. Sutton.
      p. cm.
   Includes bibliographical references and index.
   ISBN-13: 978-0-205-34201-3
   ISBN-10: 0-205-34201-9
  1. Prehistoric peoples—North America.   2. Indians of North America—Antiquities.   3. Antiquities, Prehistoric—North America.   4. North America—Antiquities.   I. Title.

   E61.S97 2010
   970.01—dc22   2010040562

10 9 8 7 6 5 4 3 2 1

Prentice Hall
is an imprint of

www.pearsonhighered.com

ISBN 13: 978-0-205-34201-3
ISBN 10:   0-205-34201-9

to my beloved Melinda

CONTENTS

LIST OF MAPS

PREFACE

Over the years, there have been numerous treatments of North American archaeology and prehistory; for example, Haven's *Archaeology of the United States . . .* (1856), Baldwin's *Ancient America . . .* (1871), Thomas's *Introduction to the Study of North American Archaeology* (1898), Willey's *An Introduction to American Archaeology* (1966), encyclopedias (e.g., Gibbon 1998), a guide to prehistoric sites in North America (D. H. Thomas 1994), and a series of textbooks (Meggars 1972; Snow 1976; Jennings 1989; Fiedel 1992; Fagan 2005a; Neusius and Gross 2007; and Snow 2009). Only the latter three texts remain in print and widely available. Thus, it seemed to me, there was room for a new synthetic treatment of North American prehistory (I was unaware of the Nuesius and Gross book when I began this project in 2000), especially one that would include a more complete coverage of western North America and a treatment of the Southwest that followed the Pecos classificatory system still so widely employed there. In large part, these issues led to my desire to do this book. The literature on the archaeology and prehistory of North America is vast, and it was not possible to consider every area or issue upon which there has been material written. I apologize to those whose important contributions were not included.

The purpose of this book is to provide an up-to-date general overview of the prehistory of North America, from initial colonization by native peoples to the time of contact with Europeans, but not including post-contact archaeology. The first chapter very briefly introduces the fields of prehistory and archaeology, and the next two chapters deal with the peopling of the New World and the Paleoindian Period across North America. The following chapters deal with the Holocene prehistory of the various culture areas. Finally, the last chapter very briefly touches on the fate of native groups at contact, primarily to provide some continuity with the present. The treatment of North American prehistory in this book is admittedly very general; there is simply far too much material to present any detailed discussion of anything. I have tried to simplify complex issues and regional chronologies but provide the necessary references to explore those things more fully.

I choose to use culture areas as the basis of the chapters, rather than the even broader regional or topical approaches of some of the other extant books. I understand that culture areas are just heuristic devices, but teaching is the purpose of this book. Culture areas are widely recognized by most researchers and lay people alike, and much of the extant archaeological literature is organized in that same manner. Culture areas are also used by the multivolume *Handbook of North American Indians* published by the Smithsonian Institution and in *An Introduction to Native North America* (Sutton 2008), which can serve as a companion volume to this work. Each chapter provides a definition of the culture area, a discussion of geography, a history of research, and major research themes and then proceeds to provide a discussion of the prehistory of the region.

I tried to order the culture areas in a fashion logical to their archaeology, first dealing with northwestern and western North America since they were the first areas occupied during the Pleistocene. After that, I followed the progression of the diffusion of agriculture into North America, beginning with the Southwest and moving east. The Subarctic is dealt with last (in Chapter 13). I recognize that this is unconventional, but since this was the last region to be colonized by humans, an understanding of its prehistory requires that the surrounding regions be discussed first. This book includes a chapter on California (as does Neusius and Gross 2007), a region too often included in a generic "Far West." This has long befuddled me, as California was one of the most complex and dynamic prehistoric places in North America. The absence of agriculture perhaps makes it less interesting to many archaeologists, but I hope that the next generation of archaeologists will have a greater appreciation of the contribution of California to prehistory. In addition, I think this is the only book that deals specifically with the prehistory of Baja California.

The tone of the book follows a decidedly culture-historical approach. I am a firm believer that we should be pursuing questions of process and explanation, but I also believe that one cannot understand process until one understands time and can track change through time; thus, understanding culture history is the first step in learning about North American prehistory. For most of the book, I use the BP ("before present"; essentially meaning "years ago") system, as I think it is easier to follow than the BC/AD, where the reader has to convert the dates in their head to get years ago. The exception is Chapter 9 on the Southwest. In that region, the BC/AD system is so widely used that I decided to also use it there so that anyone looking into the Southwestern literature would not be confused. I have included the very extensive bibliography generated in doing this research to serve as a tool for the student (who will always have a starting point to research a term paper) and professional alike. I have also included a glossary and have listed some Internet resources in the text.

ACKNOWLEDGMENTS

After ten years of working on this book, I am indebted to many people for their help and encouragement. Colleagues in different regions of North America read over various portions of the text to mitigate my errors of fact and interpretation. I appreciate the kind efforts of Kenneth M. Ames, Brooke S. Arkush, Matthew R. E. Des Lauriers, Jill K. Gardner, Ted Goebel, Albert C. Goodyear, William T. Hildebrandt, Don Laylander, Herbert D. G. Maschner, Rebecca Orfila, Max G. Pavesic, Alexander K. Rogers, Fran Rogers, Barbara Roth, Brad Vierra, and Robert M. Yohe II for their comments and suggestions. In addition, a number of anonymous reviewers solicited by Pearson provided valuable guidance, including Donald E. Miller, Roane State Community College; Brooke Arkush, Weber State University; Kenneth E. Sassaman, University of Florida; John C. Whittaker, Grinnell College; Andrew Mckelson, University of Memphis; Robert Kelly, University of Wyoming; Jason Gonzalez, University of Georgia; Uzi Baram, New College of Florida; and Leslie Cecil, Stephen F. Austin State University.

Dr. Marla Iyasere, then dean of Humanities and Social Sciences at CSU Bakersfield, and Dr. Dan McMillin, then chair of the Department of Sociology and Anthropology, provided overall support and funding for a research assistant to help with this book. That assistance was highly valuable and greatly appreciated. Rebecca Orfila did a great job of chasing down references and keeping things organized, and I very much appreciate her efforts. The staff at the CSU, Bakersfield library, particularly Janet Gonzales, contributed greatly to this project by their hard work in obtaining the many hundreds of references ordered through interlibrary loan. After 2007, the folks at the San Diego State University library provided the same invaluable assistance.

I also appreciate the efforts of a number of colleagues for the help in obtaining and sharing maps and photos, including Jim Adovasio, Mitch Allen, David G. Anderson, Brooke S. Arkush, Jim Barlow, James Bayman, Michael Blake, John Blitz, Richard Ciolek-Torrello, Gary Coupland, Don Dumond, Leslie L. Hartzell, Brian Hayden, James Helmer, Jeff Illingworth, Dennis Jenkins, Kevin T. Jones, Terry L. Jones, Adam King, Henry C. Koerper, Marcel Kornfeld, Michael Kunz, Dana Lepofsky, David B. Madsen, Madonna Moss, Murielle Nagy, Gerry Oetelaar, Richard H. Osborne, Virginia Osborne, Max Pavesic, J. Jefferson Reid, Jennifer Reynolds, Eric W. Ritter, Barbara Roth, Monson Shaver, David Hurst Thomas, Ronald Williamson, and Robert M. Yohe, II.

Finally, I thank the editors at Pearson, especially Nancy Roberts, for her faith and encouragement. Nicole Conforti and Annemarie Franklin at Pearson guided the book through its final production, Maria Piper at Pearson who coordinated the production of the maps, and Tony Moore assisted with editing. I appreciate all of their efforts. I must retain the responsibility for the errors and omissions in this book.

Introduction

As Europeans settlers began to enter the regions west of the Appalachian Mountains, they encountered large, sophisticated, and complex earthworks (Fig. 1.1) in the form of pyramids, conical mounds, and linear mounds, some in geometric forms and others as representations of animals. Some of these mound complexes looked to Europeans like defensive constructs and were called "forts." Early investigations of the mounds revealed some details of their complicated construction, and many contained elaborate burials and exotic materials. It was realized that the construction of the mounds would have required a huge investment in labor, but it was thought that were too few Indians currently living in those regions to have built them. So, who had built these mounds? How could this have been done? What happened to the people who built them? The mystery of the "Moundbuilders" generated considerable public interest and was the subject of a great deal of speculation (see Silverberg 1968; Tooker 1978; Willey and Sabloff 1993:22–28, 39–45).

To some of the people first looking at this question, it seemed impossible that the Indians were responsible, partly due to the racist view that the Indians were not intellectually or culturally capable. Speculation then centered on some sort of a "lost race" of white people—perhaps an old and vanished group of Europeans or one of the Lost Tribes of Israel. Others thought that the mounds had indeed been built by Indians. For many decades, considerable ink was spilled in speculation concerning this issue, but very little actual work was done to uncover the truth behind it. The problem was more than just academic. If whites could be shown to have previously occupied the interior of eastern North America, a much better case could be made for taking the land "back" from the Indians.

By the early 1800s, some actual fieldwork to document and describe some of the many mound sites was beginning to be undertaken. The most important of these was the now classic study of Ephraim G. Squier and Edwin U. Davis (1848), who documented a large number of mound sites in the Mississippi Valley. In the end, they concluded that the mounds had been built by some "lost race" of whites. The "lost race" theory was subsequently rejected by Haven (1856), who wrote the first general summary of the archaeology of the United States. The debate subsequently continued to rage.

GREAT MOUND AT MARIETTA, OHIO.

Chas. Sullivan, del.   *From an Original painting in possession of A. Nye Esq. Marietta.*

FIGURE 1.1   The Marietta Mound in Ohio as it appeared in 1840 (from Squire and Davis 1848: 40). (*Source:* © CORBIS All Rights Reserved.)

By the late 1800s, the discipline of archaeology was beginning to become professional, and some serious archaeological investigations were undertaken, often by the newly formed federal Bureau of Ethnology. The moundbuilder issue was important and popular enough that Congress itself assigned the Bureau to investigate and resolve the problem. Cyrus Thomas was given the task and undertook to develop the necessary evidence in a scientific and objective fashion. Thomas assembled the existing data, undertook new surveys and excavations of some mounds, and concluded that the Indians had built the mounds (Thomas 1894). The "lost race" hypothesis was rapidly discarded, and attitudes about the Indians slowly began to change. Today we know that the mounds were constructed by a number of different Indian groups at various times in the past, some as recently as the early 1700s. One of the moundbuilder sites, Cahokia, is located near the city of St. Louis, covers more than five square miles, and contains more than one hundred mounds, including Monk's Mound, the largest single mound in North America. A video on the Moundbuilders is available at www.archaeologychannel.org, "Legacy of the Mound Builders."

The debate over who built the mounds is instructive. After more than one hundred years of speculation on this relatively simple problem, which had racial and political overtones, a concerted effort by scientific archaeology solved it rather quickly. As a result, attitudes toward the Indians began to improve and an appreciation of the fantastically complex prehistory of North

America began to emerge, along with the realization that a great deal of archaeological work would be required to discover and understand that prehistory.

Today, a great deal of archaeology has been done, and our knowledge of North America's past is vastly greater than it was a hundred years ago. New techniques and approaches have made it possible to investigate things that were undreamed of just a few years ago. Who would have known in the 1930s that we would be able to use radiocarbon to accurately date just about any organic material? Who would have guessed in 1990 that we would be able to determine the genetics of early Americans through DNA analysis? What will we be able to discover ten years from now? As we learn more about the past, old interpretations are discarded and new ones are adopted. New and more interesting questions can be addressed, and the search for the past becomes more and more exciting.

Understanding North America's past is of great archaeological importance. It was one of the last places to be colonized by people and provides a natural laboratory for investigating many anthropological questions. Humans entered North America with one or two basic adaptations— terrestrial hunter-gatherers and/or maritime hunter-gatherers—a relatively short time ago (compared to Old World prehistory), although exactly when people first arrived is still uncertain. Once in North America, people developed a complex array of social and political entities, from hunting and gathering bands to (perhaps) agricultural states. How did this happen? How did such a large and linguistically diverse group of cultures develop in California? What was the role of women in early North American societies? What happened to the ancestral pueblo people in the Southwest? What was the role of warfare in the development of political complexity in the Northwest Coast? Was Cahokia really the center of a state-level society? The number of such questions is seemingly endless, and as we expand our knowledge of the archaeology of North America, we can begin to address them. There is so much more to learn.

THE STUDY OF THE PAST

The study of North America's past is conducted primarily through **archaeology**, the recovery and analysis of the material remains left by past peoples. Archaeology employs a series of techniques to discover, recover, and interpret the past through the study and analysis of the materials found in archaeological sites. In North America, the archaeology of native groups before written records (e.g., prior to contact by Europeans) is generally called prehistoric, the archaeology of native groups just after contact with Europeans is called ethnohistoric, and the archaeology of groups after the time of written records is generally called Historic Archaeology.

Other sources of information employed by archaeologists include the historical record, such as the accounts of explorers, missionaries, and the military. Even in historic times, however, many events were unrecorded, and these events can be elucidated by archaeology. Detailed written descriptions of native peoples, or **ethnographies**, can provide a great deal of information useful to archaeologists. Finally, additional information about the past can be obtained in the oral traditions of native groups (Vansina 1985; Echo-Hawk 2000).

An interpretation, or series of interpretations, of the prehistoric past based on information generated by archaeology is called a **prehistory**. Thus, a prehistory is really an account of what happened in the past based on current information. As more information is obtained through archaeological research, the understanding of prehistory is constantly revised. This is an never-ending process of data acquisition and reinterpretation and is the way all Western science operates.

To begin to construct a prehistory, one begins with some basic understanding of remains through space and time. Once a basic idea of the archaeology of a region has been obtained, the information can be synthesized into definitions and descriptions, known as **culture history**, of the past groups for that region. In conjunction, the delineation of **cultural chronology**, the description and sequences of groups through space and time, is also a major goal. The basic culture histories of most regions of North America are now known.

Archaeological information is generated first through the discovery and description of archaeological materials in archaeological sites—artifacts, ecofacts, and features. A **site** is a distinct geographic locality containing some observable evidence of past human activity, such as broken tools (artifacts) or abandoned houses (features). Material remains, including the artifacts, ecofacts, and features within a site, are distributed in patterns that reflect past behaviors, somewhat like evidence at a crime scene. Some sites may be small and fairly simple, while others may be quite large and extend over broad areas. Large sites often contain distinct areas, or loci (singular: *locus*), within them, such as areas where tools were made or plants were processed. Sites can be classified into many types based on a number of criteria. Three of these are (1) geographic context, such as open sites, rockshelters, and caves, (2) function, such as habitation, storage, and ceremonial, and (3) age, such as Pleistocene or historic.

In many cases, materials will begin to accumulate on a site and a site deposit will develop. Soils that form as the result of human activity are generally called **midden** soils and often contain broken tools, used-up artifacts, plant and animal remains, charcoal and ash from fires, and general household trash, all mixed together and decomposed. Sometimes a midden may contain stratigraphy, which is layers of different materials deposited on top of each other.

All archaeological materials in a site belonging to a particular group or time period constitute a site **component**. All sites contain at least one component, and some contain many. Thus, a site may be said to have "a Clovis component" or a "Middle Woodland component," meaning that part of the site deposit dates from those time periods.

Artifacts are the basic units of archaeological analysis and consist of portable objects made, modified, or used by humans. Examples of artifacts include projectile points (arrowheads), ceramic vessels, grinding stones, baskets, and hammerstones. In addition, the debris left over from the manufacture of tools or other objects is also considered artifacts. Natural materials altered by humans, such as the burned rocks around a hearth, are commonly found in a site but are not considered artifacts.

Native North American peoples utilized a variety of weapons prior to the introduction of firearms and metal knives and blades by Europeans. Among the most common were the spear, harpoon, atlatl and dart (see Fig. 1.2), bow and arrow, and blowgun. These weapons utilized sharp tips, sometimes of wood or bone but often of stone. These "projectile points" (e.g., spear points or arrowheads) are very important artifacts to archaeologists since many are of specific styles that can be placed generally in time.

Ecofacts are the unmodified remains of biological materials used by people, such as the bones of animals killed for food or the remains of plants, such as seeds, charcoal, and pollen. While an unmodified bone from an animal used as food is an ecofact, it would become an artifact if it were made into a tool.

Features are nonportable constructions people manufacture for some purpose. Features occur in a wide variety of forms and sizes, including fire pits (hearths), trails, canals, rock art, and earthworks. Sites can contain many features of various kinds, including hearths, pits, floors, structures, and caches.

The remains of humans themselves are often found in sites and can take a variety of forms. Some human materials, such as baby teeth or even an occasional limb bone, represent body parts lost during life and do not necessarily indicate the presence of a burial. If the dead were interred

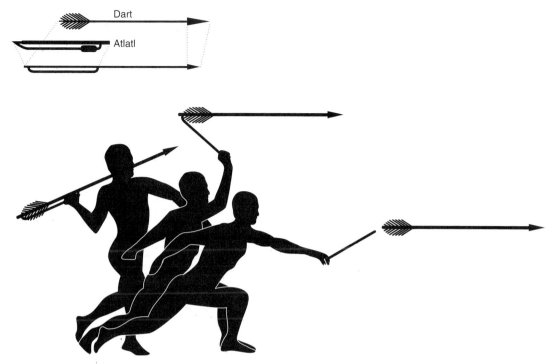

FIGURE 1.2   The atlatl/dart system. The atlatl is a device used to propel a large "arrow-like" dart with greater force and accuracy than an arrow. Nevertheless, the bow and arrow replaced the atlatl/dart across North America.

in a site, the remains would generally occur as either inhumations (burials) or cremations, although naturally mummified remains are sometimes discovered.

Information on sites and their contents is generated through the process of survey and excavation. To find sites, one has to actually go out on the ground and look for them, a process called archaeological survey (or inventory). Some surveys cover large areas and can result in the discovery of large numbers of sites. Much of the archaeology done in the United States today is survey work conducted during environmental studies, a part of archaeology known as cultural resource management (CRM). When a site is discovered in a survey, it is recorded, mapped, described, and assigned a site designation (commonly the state, county, and a number, such as CA-KER-450—the 450th site formally recorded in Kern County, California) so that other researchers know of its existence and an evaluation of its significance can be made.

Some of the sites recorded are investigated further, generally through excavation. Some are selected for excavation due to their importance to a specific research goal or project. Others are excavated because they will be destroyed by some development project, such as a dam or housing tract. Today, an explicit research design—or project plan that outlines why a site is being excavated, the methods used, and the kinds of information sought—is required prior to most excavation work. Excavations can be very small to very extensive, depending on the site itself and the project requirements. It is rare for a site to be completely excavated, as most archaeologists will leave some portion for future research. Many thousands of sites have been excavated across North America, and a huge amount of archaeological information has been generated.

Once archaeological materials and information have been generated, they must be classified and dated. Classification involves assigning artifacts and ecofacts to descriptive and functional categories, such pottery, projectile points, grinding stones, animal remains, and the like. Dating involves assigning an age to materials. In some cases, it is only known whether something is older or younger than something else (relative dating). In other cases, it is possible to assign an actual "year" date to materials (chronometric dating).

The most precise method of dating is dendrochronology (i.e., tree-ring dating), developed in the 1920s. By counting tree rings, archaeologists can determine the exact year a tree was cut down and presumably used for some purpose (Nash 1999). This technique is limited, however, to those areas where wood preserves well and where tree ring sequences have been developed. In North America, the practical use of dendrochronology is limited to the Southwest, but is widely used and highly important there.

The major revolution in dating came in the early 1950s with the development of the radiocarbon technique (see R. E. Taylor 1987; Taylor and Aitken 1997). Using radiocarbon, archaeologists can obtain an age on anything that is organic. Until about 1985, the size of the samples required for "conventional" radiocarbon dating was relatively large (perhaps 100 grams of bone). At that time, a new technique of radiocarbon dating, accelerator mass spectrometry (AMS), was developed that requires much smaller samples (e.g., 1 gram of bone). As a result, much smaller items can be dated, and sensitive materials, such as human bone, can be dated without destroying the entire specimen. Radiocarbon dating can be used on materials between about 50,000 and 150 years old and so is applicable to all of North American prehistory.

Radiocarbon dates (called assays) are reported by giving the calculated age in "radiocarbon years before present" (RCYBP, where the present is AD 1950), listing the standard deviation of the age (the "date" is a statistical number with an error factor), and the lab number. Thus, a standard radiocarbon date would be reported as "1,110 ± 60 RCYBP (UCR-2757)." Radiocarbon years do not directly equate with calendar years, and each date must be calibrated (converted) from radiocarbon years to calendar years. When one reads a radiocarbon date, it is important to know whether date was calibrated—that is, whether it is in radiocarbon years (RCYBP) or calendar years (cal BP).

Archaeologists use a number of reference points for time. Many use the BC/AD system, based on the Gregorian (Christian) calendar, which takes the birth of Christ as its primary referent. The abbreviation AD refers to *Anno Domini*, Latin for "In the Year of Our Lord"; BC means "Before Christ." In this system, a date of AD 700 is actually about 1,300 years ago and a date of 700 BC is actually about 2,700 years ago. In an effort to avoid any religious connotation, some archaeologists now use BCE, "Before the Common Era" instead of BC. Others simply use "years ago," where 700 years ago means 700 years ago. Some will use "BP" (Before Present) to mean years ago, but BP is also commonly used to express radiocarbon dates, which are calculated from AD 1950, and it can be confusing. The Before Present (BP) system is the simplest and is used throughout this book. However, most researchers in the Southwest use the BC/AD system, and that scheme is used in Chapter 9, Southwest

NORTH AMERICA DEFINED

Prior to 1492, Europeans believed the world consisted of Europe, Africa, Asia, and some of the islands of the eastern Pacific. Then Columbus "discovered" the western hemisphere, which Europeans viewed as a "New World" hence, the rest of the world became the "Old World." These terms are still used today.

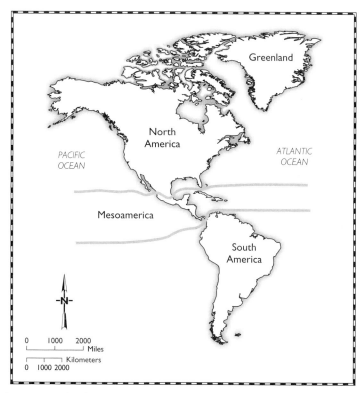

FIGURE 1.3   The New World, showing North, Meso (middle), and South America.

Geographers generally divide the New World into two continents: (1) North America, which extends from the Arctic to the southern boundary of Panama, and (2) South America, which runs from Colombia to the southern tip of Chile (Fig. 1.3). The continent of North America is often further divided into two major regions, North and Central America. In that system, North America consists of the countries of the United States and Canada, while Central America consists of Mexico and all the countries south of and including Panama.

The regions of North America can also be classified by the distribution of native groups in relation to the natural environment. Societies in similar environments tend to be similar to each other, sharing some aspects of economy, politics, and even language, such as the bison hunters of the Plains or fishers of the Northwest Coast. These "culture areas" (first defined by O. Mason [1894]) are based on environments and distributions of groups recorded within the last several hundred years, and ten culture areas are commonly recognized today (Fig. 1.4). While environments and cultures have changed through time, culture areas can still be useful to archaeologists because they denote general geographic regions, can help in the understanding of changing environmental conditions, and can provide a basis of comparison between ethnographic groups and archaeological remains both within and between culture areas (one will note that the boundaries of the culture areas vary even within this book). Following culture areas, North America extends from the Arctic (including Greenland) south into northern Mexico. Mesoamerica (*meso* meaning "middle") is culturally different from North America and extends from northern Mexico south into Panama.

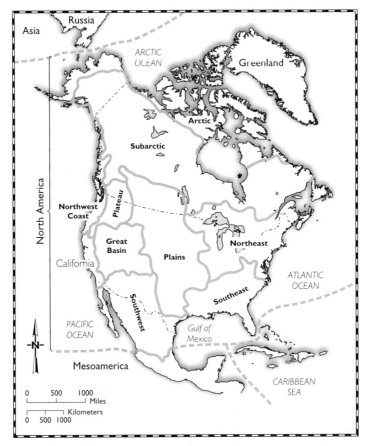

FIGURE 1.4 Culture Areas of North America. Adapted from *Handbook of North American Indian, Vol. 4, History of Indian-White Relations,* W. E. Washburn, ed., p. ix; copyright © 1988 by the Smithsonian Institution. Reprinted with permission of the publisher.

The physical geography of North America is varied. Here, seven general geographic regions are delineated (Fig. 1.5). The Arctic is situated in the far north and is a largely treeless region covered with snow and ice for most of the year. The Subarctic lies to the south and contains a vast, cold, coniferous forest with thousands of lakes. Running north to south through much of western North America are the rugged Rocky Mountains. South of the Subarctic and east of the Mississippi River is an extensive temperate forest, much of which has been cut down in the last 150 years. To the west of the Mississippi River, extending west to the Rocky Mountains, and running north to south along most of North America, is an immense region of grasslands called the Plains. A large desert region occupies much of western North America and includes both the Great Basin and the Southwest. Lastly, the Pacific coast lies along the western boundary of North America and extends from southern Alaska to California, including Baja California.

Much of central North America is drained by the Mississippi River system, which includes the Missouri and Ohio rivers. Other major waterways include the Colorado and Rio Grande in the Southwest, the Columbia on the central Pacific coast, and the system of Great Lakes in the north-central portion of North America. Each of these waterways, along with many others, played important roles in trade, agriculture, and cultural development throughout the human occupation of North America.

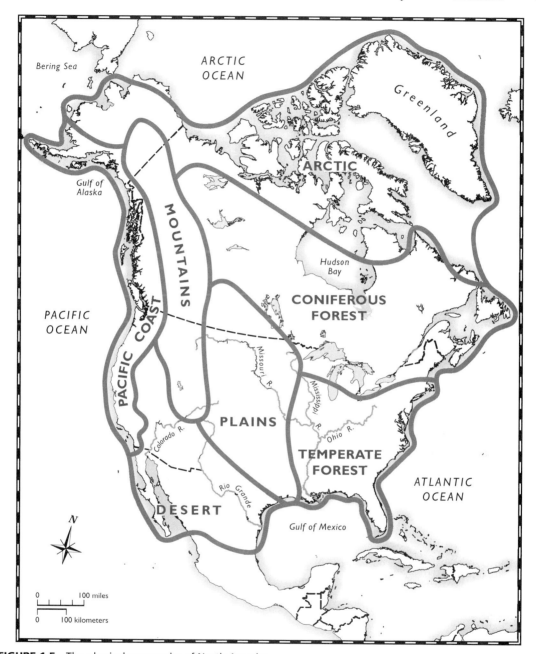

FIGURE 1.5 The physical geography of North America.

The Climate of North America

Climate is the long-term patterns of temperature and precipitation in a given region. Climate affects what kind of plants and animals are present in an area, how much water there is, and how cold or hot it becomes. Throughout time, people have had to adapt to climatic conditions, and as conditions changed, so did human adaptations. Some adaptations can occur very rapidly, and may manifest themselves as changes in technology and social organization. Understanding climatic change through time is important, as it is one of the factors that influences human adaptations (Dincauze 2000).

Climate is commonly used to define broad periods of time. The Pleistocene is essentially the time of glaciers, or the "ice ages," and spanned the time between 1.9 million to 11,000 years ago. The climate of the Pleistocene was dominated by cyclical glacial advances and retreats, becoming cooler and wetter, then warmer and drier, and back. At the height of the last glaciation (called the Wisconsin) about 16,000 years ago, ice covered most of northern North America, with the remainder of the continent being generally cooler and wetter than today. The Holocene, or Recent Period, which we are still in, began when the last glacial period ended about 11,000 years ago (see J. Menzies 2002; Orme 2002). A broad outline of the climate during the Late Pleistocene and Holocene is shown in Table 1.1 (R. B. Dunbar 2000; Scuderi 2002).

TABLE 1.1 Geological Time and Climatic Regimes of North America

Years Ago	Period	Epoch	Glaciers	Climatic Regime[a]	General Climatic Conditions
600			very brief advance	Little Ice Age	brief return to cold
1,000			all but gone	Medieval Climatic Anomaly (MCA)	warmer and drier
4,000			all but gone	Medithermal	similar to today
7,000		HOLOCENE	mostly absent	Altithermal	drier and hotter than today
9,000			in retreat	Anathermal	warming, but cooler and moister than today
11,000			beginning to retreat		
12,000	QUATERNARY		brief resurgence	Younger Dryas	brief return to glacial conditions
14,000			beginning to retreat		warming
16,000			at maximum		colder and wetter
20,000		PLEISTOCENE	advancing		becoming cooler and wetter
25,000			mostly absent		warmer and drier
30,000			near maximum	Wisconsin	colder and wetter
40,000			mostly absent		warmer and drier
45,000			near maximum		colder and wetter
50,000			mostly absent		warmer and drier
55,000			at maximum		cold and wet
1.9 million			N/A	N/A	N/A

[a]Following Antevs (1948)

Obtaining information on past climate, or paleoclimate, is frequently one of the goals of archaeological investigations so that human adaptations can be better understood. Data on paleoclimate are generated from a number of sources, including ice cores, lake cores, packrat middens, pollen profiles, and by using paleontological data, but these data are often fragmentary, making the reconstruction of past climate difficult. As one moves forward in time, the detail of what is known becomes greater, and as more detail has emerged, striking variability in regional climates has become apparent. This is one of the factors responsible for regional difference in societies, past and present. For example, there have been a number of recent episodes when warm water has moved north, disrupting normal weather. These episodes, called El Niño–Southern Oscillation (ENSO) events, are important to understand as they are known to have occurred in the past (see Dunbar 2000:49–60) and are known to have impacted groups in the New World (see Fagan 1999).

BROAD PERIODS IN NORTH AMERICAN PREHISTORY

In organizing North American prehistory, archaeologists generally begin by using three very broad classificatory periods that generally reflect basic economies: Paleoindian, Archaic, and Formative (after Willey and Phillips 1958). **Paleoindian** falls generally within the Late Pleistocene and Early Holocene and reflects an economy that included the exploitation of now extinct megafauna, such as mammoths or large bison. This association has led to the general view that Paleoindians were specialized "big-game hunters." Thus, *Paleoindian* implies a time period but also suggests a type of adaptation and sociopolitical organization. It seems fairly clear, however, that Paleoindians actually practiced a more generalized economy that only included the hunting of megafauna (e.g., Meltzer and Smith 1986; Olsen 1990; Cannon and Meltzer 2004; Byers and Ugan 2005). While the general term *Paleoindian* is commonly used to refer to Pleistocene people in the New World, the emerging possibility that some early Americans may not be related to contemporary Native Americans (see Chapter 2) has resulted in some using the term *Paleoamerican* to refer to these people.

The **Archaic** has been defined in a variety of ways, but it most commonly refers to a generalized hunter-gatherer adaptation postdating the Pleistocene (Willey and Phillips 1958), an "economic pattern in which a wide range of locally available plants and animals are exploited across regional micro-environments by populations familiar with their distribution and seasonality" (Willig and Aikens 1988:5). In essence, the Archaic can be seen as a generalized hunting and gathering adaptation of post-Pleistocene peoples at the band or tribe level of sociopolitical complexity with generally small populations. This very general definition, so widely employed by archaeologist in North America, is really not very useful since it tends to mask the enormous diversity of cultures that fall into its pigeonhole (e.g., Sassaman 2008). In fact, some think the concept is too general and suggest abandoning the term altogether (Simms 1988:41). Despite its flaws, the concept is employed here for the sake of consistency.

The **Formative** is defined herein as an adaptation with a specialty in food production, generally agriculture, first introduced into North America from Mesoamerica about 3,000 years ago. Agriculture was adopted by groups in the Southwest and later diffused east into much of eastern North America. When a hunting and gathering group was initially exposed to domesticated plants and animals, those resources would have formed only a minor aspect of their economy. Some groups eventually became more reliant on crops and decreased their dependence on wild foods. At some threshold, the primary food source of a group would have become crops, making their economy "specialized"; thus, they would be classified as Formative. In theory, food production can provide a base for a large population, which may then develop complex sociopolitical organizations, such as a chiefdom. Thus, being "Formative" implies larger populations and more complex sociopolitical organizations than Archaic groups. Nevertheless, archaeologists in North America do not commonly use the term *Formative* in spite of the fact that they use the concept.

A VERY BRIEF HISTORY OF ARCHAEOLOGY IN NORTH AMERICA

The study of North America's past has a long history, and to comprehend the "state of the art" of what we know today, it is important to understand how we arrived at this point. Below is a very brief summary of the development of North American archaeology, but the reader is directed to one of a number of major treatments on the subject for greater detail (e.g., Meltzer et al. 1986; Trigger 1989; Willey and Sabloff 1993; Patterson 1995; and Kehoe 1998).

Speculation

When Europeans entered the New World, they had many questions about who the native peoples were, where they had come from, and when they had arrived there. At the time, there was very little actual information—but many preconceived notions—available to answer any of these questions. For several hundred years, all of the "work" was purely speculative, done mostly from the comfort of one's home, what Willey and Phillips (1993) called the "Speculative Period." One of the most striking archaeological discoveries of the age was the many large and complex mounds of the Ohio and Mississippi river valleys (see above).

The first problem-oriented archaeological investigation in North America was conducted by Thomas Jefferson. In 1784, before he became president of the United States, Jefferson excavated a mound on his own property in Virginia, carefully recording the stratigraphy and materials recovered, and publishing a report on his results (Jefferson 1797). This was the first scientific archaeological excavation in North America and among the earliest anywhere in the world.

In the early 1800s, mound investigations began, with some being mapped and excavated, albeit crudely. Science was beginning to gain ascendancy in Western thought, and many of the familiar scientific disciplines now taken for granted were born in the mid-nineteenth century. As part of this shift in thinking, those interested in archaeology began to rise from their armchairs and gather field data. By the 1840s, "archaeological writings in which systematic description out-weighed speculation" began to dominate (Willey and Sabloff 1993:8), and one of the first major products of this new approach was the work of Squier and Davis (1848) on the moundbuilder question.

Discovery and Description

By the mid-1800s, archaeology was beginning to become professionalized, and serious efforts to discover the past were begun. The Smithsonian Institution was established in 1846, and the first authoritative treatment of North American archaeology was published in 1856 (Haven 1856). Haven's work set the stage for an "increasingly professional descriptive trend" (Willey and Sabloff 1993:44). More and more purposeful archaeology was being done, and many descriptive reports were being generated.

In the latter half of the nineteenth century, many research institutions and museums were founded, including the Peabody Museum of Archaeology and Ethnology (1866), the American Museum of Natural History (1869), the United States National Museum (1879), the Bureau of Ethnology (1879; renamed the Bureau of American Ethnology in 1894 [see Judd 1967]), and the Museum of the American Indian, Heye Foundation (1916; integrated into the Smithsonian Institution as the National Museum of the American Indian in 1994). In addition, several important scientific journals were established, such as the *American Antiquarian* (1878) and *American*

Anthropologist (1888). Interestingly, however, the Society for American Archaeology and its journal, *American Antiquity*, was not founded until 1934. Each of these entities played important roles in the development of North American archaeology. During this same time, the moundbuilder problem was addressed and settled (Thomas 1894, 1898) and the archaeological remains of the Southwest were discovered.

After 1890, considerable archaeology and anthropology was conducted in the Southwest, and American archaeology developed, at least in part due to these early influences (see D. D. Fowler 2000). Of great interest was the presence of Pueblo peoples living in traditional ways and of the spectacular ruins of the region. Many viewed the Pueblo people as being "more advanced" than other North American Indians, primarily due to the presence of "towns" and large-scale architecture. As a result, the Southwest is probably the best studied region of North America.

Another important issue addressed by late-nineteenth-century archaeologists was the question of when the first people arrived in North America. In the absence of good dating, many postulated that the continent had not been occupied for very long, perhaps only about 4,000 years. Others believed that human occupation might be very old, and, based on the Paleolithic era in Europe, proposed the concept of an "American Paleolithic" dating to the Pleistocene (see D. J. Meltzer 1991). The issue of whether people were in North America during the Pleistocene would have to await further evidence.

Chronologies and Culture Histories

By World War I, archaeology had been firmly established as a scientific tradition, and work had begun across much of the continent. After the war, archaeologists shifted their attention from mere description of sites and artifacts to the construction of regional chronologies and culture histories. Field methods and dating techniques improved with the development of stratigraphic excavations and seriation. Typology became an important focus, and many kinds of artifacts were classified and plotted through space and time for use in chronological sequences. Projectile points became important chronological marker artifacts and remain so today.

The scope and extent of archaeological work expanded between the two World Wars, with research institutes, universities, and museums all participating. Contributing to this effort were the projects undertaken by the Works Progress Administration (WPA), a government program to provide jobs to the unemployed. Using this labor base, government archaeologists conducted many investigations in the United States during the 1930s.

Also during this time, a number of important classificatory concepts appeared. Among the earliest cultural/historical classifications was the Pecos Classification for the Pueblo Southwest (Kidder 1927). The Pecos Classification brought some order to the archaeology of the region and identified the Basketmaker-Pueblo sequence still used today. The concurrent development of precise dating using dendrochronology resulted in a well-dated chronology for the Southwest.

By the 1930s, enough archaeological data had finally been gathered for some regions that the task of developing syntheses of regional prehistory could begin. These syntheses served the important purposes of summarizing what was known up to that time and of illuminating the many gaps in our knowledge. Once identified, people could work to fill in the gaps. A commonly used technique in the construction of culture histories was the use of the direct-historical approach, which was not a new but first formally proposed by Wedel (1938). The idea behind it was that the earliest ethnographic group in an area should be the same as the latest archaeological group, connecting the ethnographic present to the archaeological past. Following this same logic, the use of ethnographic information from other areas as analogs also became common.

The question of the antiquity of humans in the New World took a dramatic turn with the discovery of fluted projectile points in direct association with extinct bison (*Bison antiquus*) at a site near Folsom, New Mexico (Figgins 1927). Skeptics were finally convinced that humans were in the New World during the Pleistocene, although the actual dates of occupation were not yet known.

Just prior to World War II, some archaeologists were beginning to express dissatisfaction with simple description and chronology building, believing that archaeology should contribute something more meaningful to anthropology (e.g., Strong 1936). Other important developments during this time included increasing attention to the interaction between culture and environment (Steward 1938; Kroeber 1939; Wedel 1941a), a change from simply looking at the environment to investigating ecology. The study of settlement patterns was initiated by Willey (1953) with his innovative work in the Viru Valley, Peru, and such work continues. Also, there was an increase in the use of scientific techniques (e.g., dating and remote sensing) and the inclusion of multidisciplinary specialists to archaeological projects, so that more could be learned. In another important work, Willey and Phillips (1958) provided a critical treatment of archaeological method and theory, conceiving of the discipline as operating at the levels of fieldwork, description, and explanation.

Probably one of the most important developments just after World War II was the revolution in dating, particularly the development of the radiocarbon method (see R. E. Taylor 1987). Radiocarbon dating could be used for most sites and on a diversity of samples, allowing many more sites to be dated. This made chronology building much easier and allowed archaeologists to begin to concentrate on other things, such as explanation.

In the "first monographic critique of American archaeology" (Willey and Sabloff 1993:160), Walter Taylor (1948) argued for a more explanatory approach to archaeology, including hypothesis testing. This line of inquiry, called the "conjunctive approach," was not embraced by the discipline during the 1940s, which was still pursuing classification, description, and function. The call for change would have to wait another fifteen years.

Toward Explanation

In the early 1960s, American archaeology began the major theoretical shift from description to explanation. This new approach was called the "New Archaeology" and was championed primarily by Lewis Binford (cf. 1962, 1964; Binford and Binford 1968), who argued that archaeology was a science, that the past was real and knowable, and that archaeology should adopt the scientific method using data to generate hypotheses that could be tested with additional data. Archaeology, Binford argued, should make full use of scientific technology, quantitative techniques, and computers (which were then new). Further, he contended that archaeology should not just describe the record but try to explain it.

The New Archaeology, often called Processual Archaeology, was similar to the conjunctive approach advocated by Walter Taylor (1948) but was better articulated and included a cultural evolutionary perspective adopted from cultural anthropology and biology. The processual approach emphasized research design, hypothesis formation and testing, and the use of the inductive-deductive method, as well as insisting on research into questions of process, not just description. Further, Processual Archaeology stressed the use of developments in middle-range theory, such as ethnographic analogy, ethnoarchaeology, and experimental archaeology.

Processual Archaeology was rapidly adopted by many archaeologists, especially in the United States. Many outside the United States criticized it, although some European archaeologists (e.g., Clarke 1968) made major contributions to the approach. Adopting the method of scientific inquiry meant that specific rules had to be followed, speculation and conjecture had to be testable, and explicit research designs had to be developed and implemented. Several innovative studies conducted in the Southwest, such as those at Carter Ranch (Longacre 1970) and Broken K Pueblo (J. N. Hill 1970), illustrated the potential of Processual Archaeology.

Despite recognition that explanation was the primary objective in archaeology, there still remained a critical need for the discovery, description, and classification of basic data, and the development of culture histories and chronologies remains a major goal in archaeology. Properly described and classified archaeological data are required before any hypotheses, theories, or models of the past can be constructed and tested.

By the 1980s, some archaeologists had become impatient with the apparent lack of results generated by Processual Archaeology. This criticism came at a time when all of science, indeed the entire modern world, was being questioned. The "postmodernists" were critical of all modern things and took a very anti-scientific stance. Some archaeologists (e.g., Shanks and Tilley 1987; Hodder 1991, 1999) adopted this general postmodern view and began to question scientific archaeology. These scholars argued that the past was subjective and that all versions of the past were valid, an approach that became known as "postprocessual archaeology." Many view postprocessualism as a new paradigm, democratizing the past and moving toward a more "humanistic" perspective. Others (e.g., Renfrew 1994:3–4) see postprocessualism as anti-science, advocating a return to an intellectually simpler time.

New Approaches and Methods

At about the same time that postprocessualism appeared, other new theoretical approaches, often lumped together with the postprocessualist approach, were developing. As archaeological theory matured, studies of the past expanded to include the dynamics of power, gender, and inequality and the study of cognitive systems, such as those reflected in rock art. Such work expanded the traditional archaeological horizons to explore the daily lives of people and their systems of relationships.

Concurrently, a number of important technical developments greatly increased the information that could be generated from sites. A new method of radiocarbon dating, accelerator mass spectrometry (AMS), was developed that could date very small samples, meaning more materials could be dated. Advances in chemical analyses (e.g., stable isotopes and proteins) greatly increased the information available from archaeological materials. Such developments have greatly expanded our understanding, such as in the field of past diet and health (e.g., Sobolik 1994; Sutton et al. 2010).

Finally, the application of techniques to recover, isolate, amplify, and identify ancient DNA (aDNA) hold the potential to revolutionize archaeology (e.g., Renfrew 1998). The study of aDNA could be used to address many research questions, including the identification of pathogens in human remains, population migrations, ethnicity and lineage of human remains, the identification of species of food remains, identification of species processed on stone tools, and the identification and tracking of domesticates. As such work continues, a great deal about the past will be learned.

Some Current Issues

North American archaeological theory is healthy, and researchers are pursuing many avenues of investigation. There have, however, been many changes in the way that most archaeology is conducted, and numerous issues and problems "guide" much of the current work. Today, much of the archaeological work in North America is accomplished under the auspices of cultural resource management (CRM). Over the years, various governmental entities (federal, state, and local agencies in Canada, the United States, and Mexico) have enacted legislation requiring that significant archaeological sites be considered (avoided or investigated) prior to development. In the course of CRM work, a great many sites have been discovered, documented, preserved, and managed. The results of CRM studies, generally conducted in response to the needs of managers, are rarely published in the traditional manner (e.g., journals and monographs) and so are sometimes difficult to integrate into other research. Nevertheless, CRM work has made invaluable contributions to the understanding of North American prehistory.

Since about 1980, Native Americans have become much more involved in archaeology, although sometimes in conflict with archaeologists (see Swidler et al. 1997). It is now common for native peoples to be consulted in the course of archaeological projects, and many native groups now provide professional services, such as monitoring and consultation, to archaeological projects. A number of tribes, such as the Navajo in the Southwest, the Nez Perce on the Plateau, and the Dakota on the Plains, have their own CRM programs to do archaeology on tribal lands, some staffed with archaeologists who are themselves Native American.

In addition to CRM programs, tribes are involved in the presentation of the results of archaeological research. For example, the National Museum of the American Indian was created as part of the Smithsonian in 1989 and opened on the National Mall in 2004. This museum, designed by Native American architects and staffed by Native American anthropologists, archaeologists, and curators, brings a unique perspective on the past.

Increasingly, archaeologists are seeking and incorporating Native American perspectives into their research (e.g., Echo-Hawk 2000; Watkins 2005), a practice that serves to expand the way the past is seen. An example of this kind of work was a study undertaken by Janet Spector (see Chapter 14) at the village of Little Rapids, Minnesota (Spector 1991, 1993). Spector involved local descendants of the tribe in her project and discovered that her Native American collaborators had different types of research questions, different ways of viewing the archaeological record, and different overall interpretations. She found that the involvement of members of another culture had fundamentally altered archaeological questions and conclusions.

In 1990, Congress passed the Native American Graves Protection and Repatriation Act of 1990 (NAGPRA). This law requires institutions such as museums and universities holding Native American skeletal remains and associated objects to return such remains to the native groups who lived in the area in historic times. While the law provides for the study of such materials prior to their repatriation, many researchers resist the return of these remains, arguing that the remains are important to science. To many native peoples, the issues are religion (reclaiming their dead), politics (the return of their heritage), and empowerment (ownership and interpretation of the past) (see Bordewich 1996:162–184). Repatriation remains a thorny issue to some but for the most part seems to be progressing smoothly. For additional information on the various issues involved with NAGPRA, see Svingen (1992), Swidler et al. (1997), Peregory (1999), Mihesuah (2000), and Fine-Dare (2002).

Despite various preservation efforts, the archaeological record of North America is fast disappearing. Much of the destruction is due to development, but one of the most detrimental impacts to the archaeological record is looting, sometimes called vandalism or pot hunting (Renfrew 2000; Brodie et al. 2001). Many sites are destroyed by individuals digging into them to obtain "pretty" artifacts for their personal collections or to sell on the black market. Even the collection of arrowheads from the surface of a site, which is technically legal on public lands in the United States, is still very destructive to the archaeological record, as such marker artifacts are often used to date sites.

A major issue in archaeology, past and present, is the failure of archaeologists to publish the results of their work. Archaeology, by its very nature, is destructive, but that damage is mitigated by the publication of the data gathered from a site and the use of that information to interpret the past. This information must be made available to other researchers, and the public, through the publication of a report of the work. Thus, the excavation of a site without publishing the information obtained is tantamount to vandalism. Unfortunately, many site collections have never been analyzed or published, languishing in storage facilities across the country.

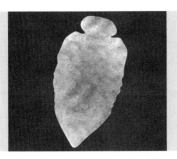

How and When
Peopling the New World

One of the most perplexing issues in North American archaeology is the origins and timing of the peopling of the New World. Ever since the question was first posed in the 1600s, a great deal of effort has been expended searching for an answer. Early explanations regarding origins theorized that the first people in the New World derived from one of the Lost Tribes of Israel, survivors of Atlantis, and immigrants from Egypt (because pyramids had been found in Mexico). It was recognized early on, however, that contemporary Native Americans were visually similar to Asians, and the idea of a migration from Asia across a land bridge was suggested as early as 1637 (Wauchope 1962:85).

In the early 1900s, most archaeologists believed that people had been in North America no longer than about 4,000 years, and this paradigm became entrenched in American archaeology (see Meltzer 1991; Willey and Sabloff 1993). Although a number of sites purportedly dating to the Pleistocene had been found, none were convincing enough to overturn the prevailing paradigm. It was not until the late 1920s, when projectile points were found in direct association with Pleistocene fauna during controlled excavations at several sites (see below), that archaeologists could no longer deny a human presence during the Pleistocene.

After the initial discoveries, many more early sites were found (see Fig. 2.1), and the advent of radiocarbon dating allowed the establishment of a firm chronological record. Over the next forty years, researchers documented and dated a number of Late Pleistocene (commonly called Paleoindian) cultural entities, the earliest being the Clovis Complex (see below and Chapter 3), defined by the presence of a distinctive type of fluted projectile point (Fig. 2.2).

By about 1970, most archaeologists had settled into the belief that pedestrian Clovis hunters followed large game across the Bering Land Bridge (Fig. 2.3) from northeast Asia and entered North America through an ice-free corridor between the two major ice sheets about 13,500 years ago. This theory came to be known as the "Clovis First" model, as it was believed that Clovis hunters were the first migrants into the New World. Questions remained, however, such as (1) how did Clovis people move across North America so fast, and (2) did they cause the extinction

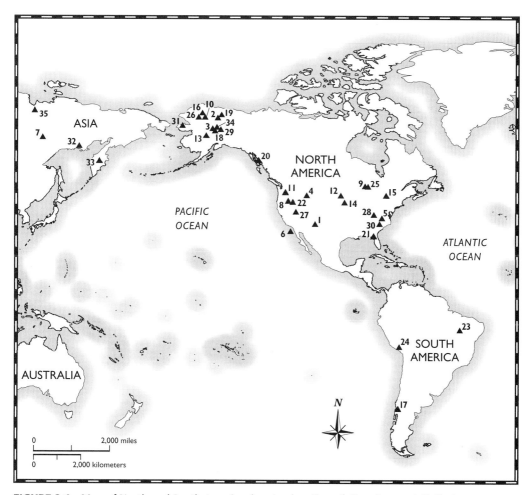

FIGURE 2.1 Map of North and South America showing location of sites discussed: 1) Blackwater Draw; 2) Bluefish Cave; 3) Broken Mammoth; 4) Buhl; 5) Cactus Hill; 6) Daisy Cave; 7) Dyuktai sites; 8) Fort Rock Cave; 9) Hebior; 10) Hilltop; 11) Kennewick; 12) La Sena; 13) Lime Hills; 14) Lovewell; 15) Meadowcroft; 16) Mesa; 17) Monte Verde; 18) Nenana Valley sites; 19) Old Crow; 20) On Your Knees Cave; 21) Page-Ladson; 22) Paisley Cave; 23) Pedra Furada; 24) Quebrada Jaguay and Quebrada Tacahuay; 25) Schaefer; 26) Spein Mountain; 27) Spirit Cave; 28) Saltville; 29) Swan Point; 30) Topper; 31) Trail Creek Cave; 32) Uptar; 33) Ushki; 34) Walker Road; and 35) Yana RHS.

of the Pleistocene megafauna (e.g., G. Haynes 2009)? A few researchers, with an almost religious conviction, believed that people had arrived earlier, perhaps by moving along the coast, but they were not taken seriously by most archaeologists.

In the 1970s and 1980s, various sites were discovered in both North and South America that apparently predated Clovis and could not be easily explained away. In addition, new lines of evidence (linguistic, skeletal, and genetic) were developed and combined with the newly discovered sites to challenge the Clovis First model. These new discoveries reignited the mainstream debate on the peopling of the New World, and the topic again became one of great emotional investment that generated enormous interest (see Wormington 1959; Laughlin and Harper 1979; Ericson et al. 1982; Shutler 1983; Kirk and Szathmary 1985; Mead and Meltzer 1985; Bryan 1986; Carlisle

FIGURE 2.2   Fluted Clovis points from sites in Arizona, Colorado, and New Mexico. (*Source:* National Archives and Records Administration.)

1988; Agenbroad et al. 1990; Bonnichsen and Turnmire 1991, 1999; Dillehay and Meltzer 1991; Meltzer 1993a; Soffer and Praslov 1993; Bonnichsen and Steele 1994; J. V. Wright 1995; F. H. West 1996; Bonnichsen 1999; Dixon 1999, 2001; Dillehay 2000; Echo-Hawk 2000; Fiedel 2000; Lavallée 2000; Adovasio and Page 2002; G. Haynes 2002a; Jablonski 2002; Tankersley 2002).

While it is widely recognized that Clovis was the first successful adaptation in the New World, the idea of the Clovis First model is currently under serious assault (many believe it is already dead; see Bonnichsen et al. [2005]), and a new paradigm shift to a pre-Clovis model may already be underway. Instead of "knowing" what happened, we are back to the same basic questions asked for the last four hundred years: (1) Where did Paleoindians come from?; (2) How did they get into the New World?; (3) How many migrations were there? and (4) When did they arrive?

PLEISTOCENE GEOGRAPHY AND ENVIRONMENT

The westernmost part of North America is separated from the easternmost part of Asia by the Bering Strait, a narrow 55-mile-wide expanse of ocean (see Fig. 2.3). In the middle of the strait lie the Diomede Islands, from which one can see both Asia and North America. The Bering Strait is only about 150 feet deep, and the contemporary Inuit still cross this narrow body of water by boat.

During the Pleistocene, glaciers expanded and sea levels dropped as much as four hundred feet due to the expansion of the glaciers during glacial maximums (Hopkins 1967). This

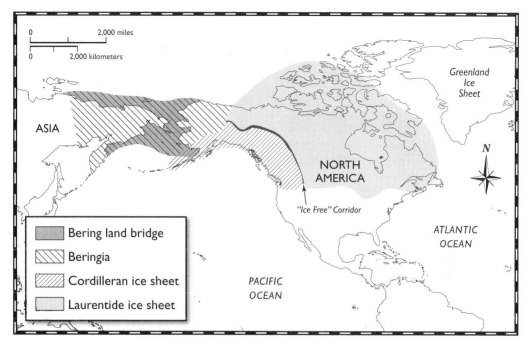

FIGURE 2.3 The geography of northeastern Asia and northern North America at the end of the Pleistocene. Lowered sea levels exposed the land bridge, resulting in the formation of Beringia, with the access to the rest of the New World blocked by the Cordilleran and Laurentide ice sheets. As the ice sheets began to retreat, the "ice-free corridor" developed.

sea level drop exposed the Bering Land Bridge, an immense plain that connected Asia and North America. Southern Alaska became glaciated and formed a barrier that isolated central and northern Alaska from the remainder of North America. This, combined with the exposure of the land bridge, created Beringia (see Fig. 2.3), a geographic entity that included far eastern Asia, the newly exposed land bridge, and central and northern Alaska, much of which remained unglaciated (Elias 2002:10; also see Brigham-Grette et al. 2004). In essence, during the Late Pleistocene, central and northern Alaska and the land bridge became part of Asia (Powers and Hoffecker 1989:283). The land bridge has formed at various times, including between 75,000 and 60,000 years ago and from 25,000 to as late as 11,000 years ago (Elias 2002:11, 13).

Two major ice sheets were present in North America during glacial times (see Fig. 2.3). The Laurentide ice sheet was the largest and covered the majority of northern North America, extending south into what is now the northern United States. The Cordilleran ice sheet originated in the mountains of northwestern North America and joined with the Laurentide sheet to form one vast ice cap.

Beginning sometime about 16,000 years ago, the climate abruptly warmed (a time referred to as the Bølling-Allerød Period) and the glaciers began to retreat. Environmental conditions became quite dynamic, and human adaptations undoubtedly did as well. Beginning about 13,000 years ago, glacial conditions returned for a few hundred years (an event referred to as the Younger Dryas), but the glaciers soon resumed their retreat and the climate warmed dramatically.

FIGURE 2.4   The relative sizes of humans, mammoths (*Mammuthus* sp.)/mastodons (*Mammut americanum*), and large bison (*Bison antiquus*).

Some Important Pleistocene Animals

Several large Pleistocene animals (see Fig. 2.4) are commonly associated with early people in North America but are poorly understood and are briefly discussed below (many others, such as fish, turtles, and dogs are more familiar to most). Mammoths (*Mammuthus* sp.) were large, elephant-like grazers that subsisted on grassland vegetation and ranged over much of North America during the Pleistocene (G. Haynes 1991). The woolly mammoth (*M. primigenius*) lived primarily in Eurasia and Alaska, although some may have lived in the north-central United States (Agenbroad 1984:96: Fig. 3.6). The Columbian mammoth (*M. columbi*) ranged over much of North America south of the ice sheets (Agenbroad 1984:96: Fig. 3.5). Both species became extinct at the end of the Pleistocene some 11,000 years ago.

The other large, elephant-like animal, the American mastodon (*Mammut americanum*), was a browser, living in both grassland and wooded ecozones, particularly spruce forests (King and Saunders 1984:326; G. Haynes 1991) extending all across North America, although the majority of mastodon fossil localities are in the East and Northeast. The American mastodon became extinct by about 11,000 years ago (King and Saunders 1984:325–326), a phenomenon possibly related to the contraction of the spruce forests in eastern North America due to climatic change around that time (King and Saunders 1984:326).

Another large animal that was common during the Pleistocene was bison. Four major species of bison were exploited by humans in North America. The bison probably first encountered by humans in the Pleistocene was the large species, *Bison antiquus* (McDonald 1981:82; adult males weighed about 1,100 kg), with a large subspecies (*B. a. antiquus*) located primarily in the southwestern portion of the continent and a smaller subspecies (*B. a. occidentalis*; about 1,000 kg) on the Plains. Approximately 5,000 years ago, during the warmer and drier middle Holocene, a smaller bison (*B. bison* [about 800 kg]), appeared and replaced both *B. a. antiquus* and *B. a. occidentalis*. *B. bison* then diverged into the two modern subspecies, the plains bison (*B. b. bison*) and the wood bison (*B. b. athabascae*) (McDonald 1981:84, 92–93: Fig. 29; also see discussion in E. Anderson 1984:77).

ISSUES IN DATING

Most of the arguments regarding the various issues of the peopling of the New World are made based on the dating of archaeological materials, primarily using the radiocarbon method. For example, if a site is dated to before Clovis times, it would have major implications. Thus, precise dating is critical to the arguments, and ancient dates must be very solid to be considered valid (see Fiedel 2006). Most organic materials can be dated using the radiocarbon method, and this has proved a huge benefit to archaeology, allowing the placement of many sites and complexes in real time.

The interpretation of a radiocarbon date is not always straightforward. A radiocarbon assay provides the date an organism died, not necessarily when it was used by humans. If a tree died 20,000 RCYBP and its wood was used for firewood 10,000 RCYBP, the date on the charcoal from the hearth would be 20,000 RCYBP, thereby dating when the tree died and not when the fire burned. Archaeologists must be very cautious about what they date and how they interpret those dates. In addition, contamination of radiocarbon samples is always a concern.

In addition, a radiocarbon date is a statistical estimate of time, not a precise measurement, and each assay contains an error factor; for example, 10,500 ± 250 RCYBP. This means that there is a 67 percent probability that the true age of the sample lies between 10,250 and 10,750 RCYBP and a 94 percent probability of the date lies between 10,000 and 11,000 RCYBP. Thus, a date of 10,000 ± 250 RCYBP is about the same as a date of 10,500 ± 250 RCYBP, so radiocarbon dating may not be able to attain a precision greater than about five hundred years (Fiedel 1999a:104). Suites of concordant dates can narrow that gap, but archaeologists must exercise caution in their interpretations.

A third issue related to radiocarbon dating is the calibration of radiocarbon time to calendar time, a process made fairly simple due to the availability of a high-precision calibration curve based on dated tree rings (Stuiver and Braziunas 1993a, b; Stuiver et al. 1998a, 1998b). This curve extends reliably to about 9,000 RCYBP, but the calibration curve for earlier dates is a low-precision line based on a small number of paired uranium/thorium samples and radiocarbon dates on coral (e.g., Bard et al. 1993). While usable (R. E. Taylor et al. 1996), the pre-9,000 RCYBP curve is poorly known and so may be subject to error.

Further, it appears that the radiocarbon calibration curve between 12,500 and 10,000 RCYBP has yielded results that are too young, probably due to fluctuations in the amount of radiocarbon in the atmosphere at that time. Thus, it is possible that calendar time may be 2,000 years earlier (see Fiedel 1999a).

Finally, errors happen and some dates are just bad and unreliable (figuring out which ones is the trick). This is especially true when there is the potential of contamination of the sample. In sum, radiocarbon dating is an important tool, but it must be critically used. In isolation, one or two radiocarbon dates cannot stand alone on important issues.

THE ORIGINS OF NATIVE AMERICANS

To understand the origins of Native Americans, four major questions have to be addressed. First, where, geographically, did the Paleoindians come from? Second, what route or routes were used to enter the New World? Third, how many migrations of people were there? Finally, when did this all happen?

To answer these questions, various lines of evidence continue to be investigated, including archaeological, linguistic, biological, and those related to DNA. Each of these lines of evidence only augments the primary evidentiary line: that is, basic archaeological evidence in the form of sites, tools, food residues, and dates. Ultimately, archaeological data are the key to resolving these issues.

WHERE DID THE PALEOINDIANS COME FROM?

All of the human remains known from the New World are of modern *Homo sapiens* (at least 200,000 years old in the Old World), and there is no evidence that humans evolved independently in the New World. Thus, they must have migrated to the Americas from elsewhere. It has long been recognized that contemporary Native Americans share a number of similarities with people from Asia, and it is widely believed that Paleoindians must have originally migrated from Asia (e.g., Wang et al. 2007). All of the evidence to date continues to support this conclusion, and there is no linguistic or biological data to suggest any other place of origin, although we still do not know the exact location(s) of "homelands" in Asia (or elsewhere).

Linguistic Evidence

The languages spoken by the native peoples of North America are more closely related to those in northeastern Asia than anywhere else (e.g., Greenberg et al. 1986; Greenberg 1987), supporting the idea that migrations into the New World originated in Asia. More recent studies (Cavalli-Sforza 2000; J. Nichols 2002) have confirmed these findings; thus, it is clear that Native American languages originated in northeastern Asia. Based on the sparse linguistic data, it seems premature to attempt to make any definitive statement about the ages of the linguistic groups, the timing of any splits of those groups, and the dating of any migrations based on linguistic data (Goddard and Campbell 1994; J. H. Hill 2005).

Biological Evidence: Morphology

Native Americans share a number of general similarities with Asians, such as straight black hair, general lack of facial and body hair, epicanthic eye folds, and relatively flat faces, among other characteristics (see Crawford 1998:194–238). Skeletal evidence also shows a linkage to Asia. Studies on blood groupings (e.g., Lampl and Blumberg 1979; Szathmary 1979) also show a relatedness between northeast Asians and Native Americans.

Studies of dental traits (Turner 1985, 1987, 1994, 2002) all indicate the relatedness between Native Americans and northeast Asians. There has been some suggestion of a relationship between those two groups and early Europeans (Cavalli-Sforza et al. 1988:6002). This possible link may also be reflected in the DNA data.

Biological Evidence: DNA

A relatively new avenue of investigation into the origins of New World populations is the study of DNA, generally mitochondrial DNA (mtDNA). In this approach, groups of specific mutations (haplogroups or haplotypes) in living peoples are identified and tracked back to their place of geographic origin, and estimates of the time of their divergence are made. Five haplogroups have been identified (A, B, C, D, and X; see discussion in Torroni 2000), leading to a "five founder" model of original genetic material. The recent discovery (Malhi et al. 2007) of a sixth haplogroup, M, suggests that the genetic diversity among colonizing Paleoindians was even greater than once thought. The current genetic evidence links Native American groups to northeastern Asia (e.g., Wang et al. 2007), perhaps even more specifically to Mongolia (Merriwether 2002).

Haplogroup X (M. D. Brown et al. 1998; Malhi and Smith 2002), however, is restricted to groups in North America and has not been positively identified in northeast Asia (Merriwether 2002:302), although it may be present in central Siberia. This finding suggests an additional, although minor, founding mtDNA lineage for New World populations, perhaps one related to a "Caucasoid" population (see discussion in Torroni 2000:84–85). Cavalli-Sforza (2000:38–39) argued that American Indians are most closely related to Asians, then to Europeans, and then to people from Oceania.

Using Y chromosome data, Lell et al. (2002) argued that two major migrations into the New World took place. The first originated in southern central Siberia and gave rise to the predominant genetic type (called Amerind) throughout the New World. A second, later migration originated in the Lower Amur River/Sea of the Okhotsk region of eastern Siberia, contributing to the genetic pool of another linguistic family (called Na-Dene) and some other groups in North and Central America. This conclusion generally supports the movement of the mtDNA haplogroups into the Americas (Lell et al. 2002:204).

Most recently, aDNA data derived from samples of 4,000-year-old human hair recovered from a Saqqaq site in southwestern Greenland (Rasmussen et al. 2010) suggests that Saqqaq people were related to groups in eastern Siberia. Thus, it is possible that a separate migration of Siberians into the New World occurred sometime between 5,500 and 4,000 years ago.

Archaeological Evidence

The archaeology of Beringia is poorly understood, with northeastern Siberia being even less known than Alaska. There are a number of artifact assemblage links between Siberia and Alaska and some linkage between Alaska and the rest of North America, each discussed below. In isolation, none of this evidence is particularly compelling.

HOW DID THE PALEOINDIANS GET INTO THE NEW WORLD?

There are only two ways that people could have migrated: by foot or by boat (see Table 2.1). If by foot, they may have traveled along the Pacific Coast or inland or both (Fig. 2.5). If people moved south from Beringia along the coast, it may be that the rugged nature of the coastline may have required that boats

TABLE 2.1 Summary of Theories of Geographic Origin Regarding the Peopling of the New World

Location	General Path	Method	And Then . . .	Comments
Siberia (Northeastern Asia)	across interior Beringia	on foot	south through the "ice-free corridor"	unlikely: ice-free corridor seems too late
	across interior Beringia	on foot	south after the glaciers melted	unlikely: people were south before ice melted
	following the coast of Beringia	on foot	south around the glaciers	quite possible: increasing evidence
	following the coast of Beringia	by boat	south around the glaciers	quite possible: but so far little direct evidence
Iberia (Europe)	across the North Atlantic following the southern limit of the ice sheets	by boat	into eastern North America	highly improbable: far too difficult, no real evidence
Australia	across the open Pacific Ocean to South America	by boat	then north into the rest of the New World	highly improbable: very difficult, no real evidence

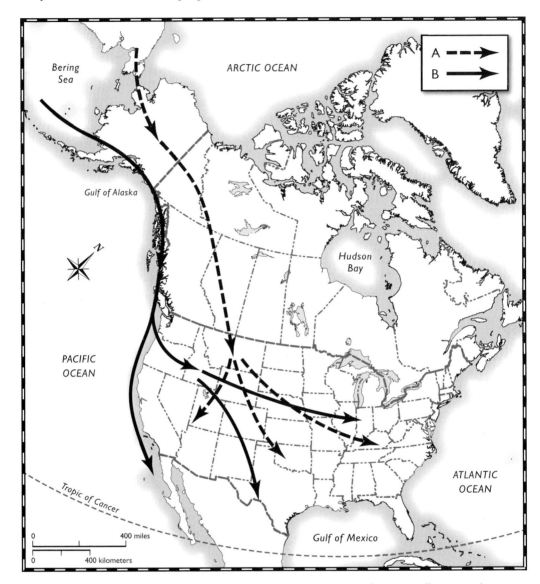

FIGURE 2.5 Alternative routes of migration into the New World. The first generally accepted route (A) was through the "ice-free corridor" onto the northern Plains and then throughout the New World. The other, more recent view (B) is along the coast, with some people heading inland at about the Columbia River with others continuing south along the coast.

be used. Most researchers agree that early people migrated from northeastern Asia, although E. James Dixon (1985) suggested that people first arrived in South America by boat from Australia and migrated north. Others (see below) have suggested that people arrived by boat from western Europe.

A Land Route?

The presence of the Bering Land Bridge connecting Siberia and Alaska is well documented, becoming exposed as sea levels dropped. Once exposed, the land bridge would have been colonized by a succession of plant and animal communities. Insect assemblages from cores (Elias et al. 1996; Alfimov and Berman 2001; Elias 2002) suggest that herbs, grasses, and willows (but no trees) dominated the landscape between 25,000 and 14,000 years ago, subsequently changing to tundra with some small trees between 14,000 and 12,000 years ago and then increasing in alder and spruce trees between 11,000 and 9,000 years ago (Elias 2002:16). In addition, wood for fuel would not have been available in Beringia until after about 13,000 years ago (Hoffecker et al. 1993; Elias 2002:20), although the dung of large herbivores might have been used by people for "firewood" (Rhode et al. 2003). Beginning about 11,000 years ago, sea levels began to rise, eventually inundating the land bridge and cutting off the land route.

A lack of suitable food may have made it difficult for the land bridge to support large mammals before 14,000 years ago (Elias 2002:15), but after that time animals would have been present in an abundance and diversity similar to the modern East African savanna (Elias 2002:17). Large animals included mammoth, mastodon, horse, musk-ox, bison, and caribou. Some of the large animals disappeared from Beringia about 13,400 years ago, but mammoths and mastodons persisted until about 12,900 years ago (Elias 2002:18).

The working model is that when large animals colonized Beringia, hunters followed them on foot. Animals and people would have moved east until they came to the glacial barrier, preventing them not only from moving further east but blocking a southern route as well. Once the glaciers had retreated enough, sometime after 14,000 years ago, people could then have moved south.

AN ICE-FREE CORRIDOR?   As the Cordilleran and Laurentide ice sheets retreated, they would have separated and formed an "ice-free corridor" connecting central Alaska to the northern Plains (see Fig. 2.3). If this corridor formed early enough, people may have used it to move directly into the heart of North America (see Fig. 2.5). This idea was first proposed by Johnston (1933:44; also see C. V. Haynes 1964; Dumond 1980; Catto and Mandryk 1990) and is consistent with the location and age of the Clovis materials on the northern Plains, at one time thought to have witnessed the earliest evidence of human occupation.

Later research (J. M. White et al. 1985; Burns 1990; H. E. Wright 1991; Jackson and Duk-Rodkin 1996; J. Menzies 2002) suggested that any such corridor would have been closed from about 22,000 or 20,000 to about 16,000 or 14,000 years ago. Once the ice began to retreat after 12,000 years ago, an ice-free corridor may have developed (Orme 2002: Fig. 3.1). Even if it existed, an ice-free corridor may not have been suitable for human transit (Fladmark 1979; Mandryk 1990) due to the extreme cold and lack of resources, as it would have taken some time for plants and animals to colonize the newly formed corridor (Driver 1998). In addition, Aoki (1993) argued that demographic modeling does not support the idea that an ice free corridor could have served as a principal route of migration. Thus, it is difficult to envision the ice free corridor as the route by which humans first entered the New World (Mandryk et al. 2001; Mandryk 2005), although some (e.g., Fiedel 2000:81; C. V. Haynes 2005) believe that the corridor was passable during the Late Pleistocene.

A Coastal Route?

If glaciers prevented people from moving south by an inland route into the New World from eastern Beringia until after about 14,000 years ago, an alternative may have been to move along the coast. Sea levels would have been as much as four hundred feet lower before 14,000 years ago, exposing a coastal plain along which people could have traversed (see Fladmark 1979, 1983; Gruhn 1988, 1994; Dixon 1999; Mandryk et al. 2001; Erlandson 2002; Ackerman 2008), although it is not clear whether glaciers extended out onto this coastal plain in the north. It may be that the coastline of northwestern North America was not glaciated after about 13,500 years ago (Fedje 2002:28), allowing people to move south along a continental shelf exposed by lower sea levels (Josenhans et al. 1997; Fedje and Christensen 1999; Fedje and Josenhans 2000; Dixon 2002:25). Such a route may have been sufficiently productive as to be able to support human populations moving south (Fedje et al. 2004; Hall et al. 2004). As sea levels rose at the end of the Pleistocene, sites containing evidence of an early coastal migration or maritime adaptation would have been flooded.

It has been argued that a population movement along the coast may have taken place much earlier than it did inland and may have been done using boats (Dixon 2001, 2002). If the Monte Verde site in Chile (see below) was occupied 15,350 years ago and there is no evidence that a land migration took place that early, so the argument goes, there must have been a coastal or seaborne migration. In support of the coastal argument, its proponents point out that other regions, notably Australia, were colonized before 40,000 years ago by seafaring peoples and that maritime adaptations are known around the world by the Late Pleistocene (e.g., Bednarik 1989; Erlandson 2001).

If people had moved from northeastern Asia along the southern coast of Beringia, and south into the Americas, one would expect to find evidence of some sort of adaptation using maritime resources in coastal northeastern Asia earlier than in the Americas. The earliest known occupation of any kind in far northeast Asia is only about 14,000 years ago (Goebel et al. 2003a:503; Goebel 2004:344; also see Kononenko and Cassidy 2007) and the earliest evidence of a maritime adaptation in that region is from the mid-Holocene (Pitul'ko 1999:430, 432). In addition, it seems necessary that any maritime adaptation would include boats, which would require a very sophisticated and diagnostic technology.

There is no direct evidence of a coastal or maritime adaptation, or of boats, during the Late Pleistocene from Beringia (Yesner 1996:272) or from the western coast of North America, although Erlandson and Moss (1996:295; also see Cassidy et al. 2004; Cassidy 2008; Raab and Cassidy 2009) argued that boats were in use along the western coast of North America by 9,000 or 10,000 years ago.

Currently, the earliest archaeological evidence of a coastal migration along the Northwest coast is from On Your Knees Cave in southeastern Alaska. A bone tool and a human skeleton from the site are dated to about 10,300 years ago (Dixon 2002:26). A video on the On Your Knees Cave site is available at www.archaeologychannel.org, "Kuwoot Yas.Ein: His Spirit Is Looking out from the Cave."

There is evidence of submerged Late Pleistocene sites along the Northwest Coast (Fedje and Josenhans 2000; Fedje 2002; Ackerman 2008), but they remain to be investigated. Further south, several early sites (ca. 13,000 to 11,000 years ago; Erlandson et al. 1999; T. L. Jones et al. 2002) are known along coastal California, suggesting the use of boats and maritime resources at an early date and possible support for a coastal migration route (but see Turner 2003; Fitzgerald and Jones 2003). In addition, recent discoveries at the Quebrada Jaguay (Sandweiss et al. 1998; Sandweiss 2005a, 2005b) and Quebrada Tacahuay (Keefer et al. 1998) sites in Peru suggest that people had developed a maritime adaptation in that region by about 13,000 years ago (earlier than in northeast Asia!). People at these sites exploited fish, sea birds, and shellfish, with little evidence of terrestrial hunting. These coastal occupations are not earlier than inland ones, however, and do not verify a coastal migration hypothesis (Fiedel 2000:60). Submerged early sites no doubt exist all along coastal North America, drowned by rising sea levels.

It seems plausible that people could have migrated along the coast of the Pacific Rim, even quite early, to colonize the Americas. If Late Pleistocene sites do exist on the now-submerged coastal plain of the region (or anywhere else for that matter), they are very difficult to locate and investigate (e.g., Kraft et al. 1983). Nevertheless, research on this possibility continues, and sites on islands along the western coast of North America (e.g., Daisy Cave in California) are currently being investigated. Interestingly, such islands would have been upper mountain regions during the Late Pleistocene, and any Paleoindian sites found there would likely represent a small aspect of the settlement/subsistence patterns of the time (Meighan 1983:445).

Most recently, it has been suggested that the extensive kelp beds that extend from Japan to California may have provided the resource base necessary for a movement of people along the coast in the Late Pleistocene (Erlandson et al. 2007a). Last, there is genetic evidence to suggest that early people settled along the coast and had little gene flow with interior groups (Eshleman et al. 2004), supporting a coastal migration but suggesting a contemporaneous interior migration as well.

HOW MANY MIGRATIONS WERE THERE?

Obviously, at least one migration of people entered the New World from Asia. Some have suggested that a single migration entered eastern Beringia, where the population diverged and gave rise to multiple migrations south of the ice sheets. Others have argued that multiple independent migrations from Asia took place.

Linguistic and Genetic Clues

In theory, different migrations of people into the New World would be detectable in the distribution of languages. Greenberg et al. (1986; Greenberg 1987; also see Ruhlen 1994) classified New World languages into three major linguistic groups—Amerind, Na-Dene, and Eskimo/Aleut—and suggested that three major migrations had taken place, with Amerind first, Na-Dene next, and Eskimo/Aleut last. Critics of the Greenberg classification (e.g., Kaufman and Golla 2000) have argued that the classification of Amerind is flawed and that it does not represent a single linguistic entity and thus does not reflect a single migration. There is general agreement, however, that Na-Dene and Eskimo/Aleut linguistic data do reflect migrations.

Johanna Nichols (2002) defined two major strata of New World languages, an "old" group distributed throughout the New World and a "Pacific Rim" group of more limited distribution. Nichols (2002:278, 288) argued that a migration of "old" languages entered the New World at an early date, followed by the "Pacific Rim" group beginning about 13,000 years ago, meaning that the "old" group had to arrive prior to that time, perhaps by 35,000 years ago (J. Nichols 1990; also see Gruhn 1988; but also see Nettle 1999). Nichols (2002:281) suggested that both linguistic strata originated in northeast Asia, but that the "Pacific Rim" group shared affinities with a number of other linguistic families along the Pacific Rim, including the Asian coast and Melanesia. Nichols (2002:288–289) argued that the Monte Verde (ca. 15,350 years ago) and Clovis peoples (13,200 years ago) must have spoken a language of the "old" group. However, Jane Hill (2005) cautioned that the time depth involved may be beyond current methods of linguistic analysis.

Genetic data (see Schurr [2005] for a summary) have been used to support several models of the number of migrations. Szathmary (1993:216, 1994; also see R. A. Rogers et al. 1992; Merriwether et al. 1995; Stone and Stoneking 1998; Merriwether 2002; D. G. Smith et al. 2005) suggested that a single migration into North America before 25,000 years ago could explain the genetic data if one population (e.g., Amerinds) had moved south of the glaciers before the glacial maximum and was then isolated from groups (e.g., Na-Dene) remaining north of the glaciers until the Holocene. This general model was supported by Forster et al. (1996; also see Wallace and Torroni 1992; Bonatto and Salzano 1997a, 1997b), who maintained that one group carrying the four major DNA haplogroups (A, B, C, and D) initially colonized Beringia by at least 30,000 years ago, with some of those people moving south of the glaciers sometime between 25,000 and 20,000 years ago (when an ice-free corridor was open?) and becoming the Amerinds. The Na-Dene and Eskimo language groups, it was argued, remained in the Alaska region and expanded south after the end of the Pleistocene.

Others (Schurr and Wallace 1999; also see Schurr 2002, 2004a) interpreted the genetic data to reflect two migrations, the first coming to the New World from Asia between 30,000 and 40,000 years ago, and the second (the Na-Dene and Eskimo/Aleut) moving into the New World during the Holocene, after 10,000 years ago. Based on the four identified haplogroups in New World populations, Torroni et al. (1992, 1993; also see Horai et al. 1993, 1996) argued that there were two initial migrations (Haplogroups A, C, and D, followed by Haplogroup B). Following these initial two migrations, the Na-Dene entered, followed by the Eskimo/Aleut. Using Y chromosome data, Lell et al. (2002) arrived at a similar conclusion. The recent discovery of an additional haplogroup (M; Malki et al. 2007) may complicate this issue.

The most succinct interpretation of the genetic data was that of Schurr (2004b). He suggested that there were three migrations—the initial one from south-central Siberia entered between 20,000 and 14,000 years ago and followed a coastal route, and later a second migration entered from the same Siberian region, blending with the people of the first migration. Last, after the last glacial maximum, people from Beringia occupied northern North America and became the Aleut, Eskimo and Na-Dene.

Skeletal Data

Very few skeletal remains of Pleistocene age are known. The earliest may be the recent discovery of a skeleton in the Yucatan in Mexico, radiocarbon dated to about 13,000 years ago (González and Sandoval 2005). However, the analysis of this find in not yet complete. The Buhl burial (Green et al. 1998) and the burial from On Your Knees Cave (Dixon 2002) are also very early.

Studies of skeletal, particularly cranial, morphology support the idea that the first Americans originated in northeastern Asia (Steele and Powell 1993, 1994), but there is a growing body of data that suggests that at least some Late Pleistocene/Early Holocene populations had a cranial morphology different from contemporary Native Americans (Powell and Steele 1992; Steele and Powell 1993, 1994, 2002; Jantz and Owsley 1997, 2001, 2005; Chatters et al. 1999). These skeletons (Table 2.2; also see Dixon 1999: Table 5.1) possess traits suggestive of one or more migrations of people into the New World prior to the migration that gave rise to the contemporary Native American morphology. It is now thought that these early skeletons share traits with populations in Asia (such as the Ainu of Japan) or groups from Polynesia (or even Australia [Neves and Blum 2000, 2001]), suggesting that all these groups shared a common Asian ancestor (González-José et al. 2003).

The most famous of these skeletons is Kennewick Man, an adult male discovered eroding from the bank of the Columbia River (Fig. 2.6) in central Washington in 1996 (see Chatters 1997, 2000, 2001; Chatters et al. 1999). Three radiocarbon dates on bone from the Kennewick Man ($8,410 \pm 60$, $8,410 \pm 40$, and $8,130 \pm 40$ RCYBP) were obtained. The first date of $8,410 \pm 60$ was calibrated to between 8,340 and 9,200 calendar years ago (R. E. Taylor et al. 1998:1172) and firmly established the antiquity of the individual. Kennewick Man lived a difficult life, having suffered a

TABLE 2.2 Early "Morphologically Distinct" Skeletal Remains from North America

Specimen	Location	Radiocarbon Age	Approximate Calendar Age	Reference
Buhl	Idaho	10,675 ± 95 RCYBP	12,500	T. J. Green et al. 1998
Wilson-Leonard	Texas	9,600 to 10,000 RCYBP	11,000	D. G. Steele 1989
Gordon Creek	Colorado	9,700 ± 250 RCYBP 9,400 ± 120 RCYBP	11,000	Breternitz et al. 1971 Swedlund and Anderson 1999
Grimes Point Shelter	Nevada	9,470 ± 60 RCYBP	10,600	Tuohy and Dansie 1997:Table 1
Spirit Cave Mummy	Nevada	9,430 ± 60 RCYBP	10,600	Tuohy and Dansie 1997:Table 1
Spirit Cave Burial No. 1	Nevada	9,300 ± 70 RCYBP	10,500	Tuohy and Dansie 1997:Table 1
Wizards Beach	Nevada	9,225 ± 60 RCYBP	10,500	Tuohy and Dansie 1997:Table 1
Horn Shelter	Texas	9,000 to 10,000 BP	10,200 to 11,400	D. Young 1988:Table 1
Browns Valley	Minnesota	8,700 ± 110 RCYBP	10,000	Jenks 1937; Steele and Powell 1994
Kennewick	Washington	8,410 ± 60 RCYBP	9,200	Chatters 2000
Whitewater Draw	Arizona	8,200 to 10,000 RCYBP	9,000 to 11,400	Waters 1986a

number of chronic injuries, as well as a spear wound to his hip. The wound healed, but the projectile point (a stemmed point dating to the Early Holocene) from the spear remained in his hip. This skeleton has become the focus of a great deal of legal conflict over whether it should be studied or reburied (see D. H. Thomas 2000; Owsley and Jantz 2001; Burke et al. 2008). The courts ruled in 2004 that the skeleton was to be studied, and that work is ongoing.

Other early skeletons with similar morphology include the Buhl burial, dated to 12,500 years ago (Green et al. 1998; also see Neves and Blum 2000). This individual was an 18- to 20-year-old female with substantial tooth wear. Isotopic analysis indicated a diet dominated by terrestrial animals and fish (see Yohe and Woods 2002:21). The Buhl individual is among the earliest known in the New World, but the skeleton was reburied by the local Shoshone-Bannock tribes and is unavailable for further study.

The Spirit Cave mummy was discovered in 1940 (Wheeler 1997) but was not dated until the mid-1990s when its unusual morphology was recognized. The mummy was found to be 10,600 years old (Dansie 1997; Touhy and Dansie 1997) and was discovered wrapped in tule reed mats that were probably made on frames (see Nicholas 1998:724). In addition, two skulls found near Mexico City in 1959 have recently been radiocarbon dated to about 13,000 years ago (T. Stewart 2003:8; Popson 2003:15), essentially Clovis in age. Both apparently exhibit a cranial morphology similar to Kennewick (the full studies have not yet been published). Other examples are listed in Table 2.2.

FIGURE 2.6 View of the Kennewick site along the Columbia River, central Washington. (*Source:* © Tri-City Herald.)

The presence of early crania in both North and South America that are "morphologically distinct" from contemporary Native Americans suggests that a minimum of two migrations took place. Further, Steele and Powell (1999, 2002:112) argued that the early skeletons more closely resemble East Asians than they do modern northeast Asians, suggesting that the population represented by the early skeletons entered the New World from Asia before populations resembling mongoloids (Amerinds) were in northeast Asia to give rise to subsequent migrations. Craniometric data from South America (Powell and Neves 1999; Neves and Blum 2000, 2001; Steele and Powell 2002; Neves et al. 2004) support this general model, although Neves et al. (1996) argued for four migrations. In addition, Neves et al. (1999) suggested that the late populations of Tierra del Fuego, with their distinct cranial morphology, may be a relic population of one of the early migrations. Most recently, it has been suggested that this cranial morphology may have been an adaptive response to new conditions and not indicative of a separate population (Gill 2005).

Some scholars (e.g., Swedlund and Anderson 1999) have argued that cranial morphology is too variable to generalize populations or migrations. In addition, it has been argued, the overall sample size is very small and the results speculative. Irrespective of cranial morphology, early people in North America lived a difficult life (see discussion in Dixon 1999:147–148), with considerable dietary stress, infection, violent nonlethal encounters, many violent or accidental deaths, and a life expectancy in the forties.

Archaeological Evidence

There is surprisingly little archaeological evidence regarding the number of migrations. There was obviously at least one migration, but the archaeological data do not clearly distinguish between potential multiple migrations. There have been some suggestions (see below) that the Nenana and Denali complexes in Alaska represent separate migrations, but the evidence so far is unconvincing.

WHEN DID PEOPLE ARRIVE IN THE NEW WORLD?

The question of when people arrived in the New World is perhaps the most controversial. Taking the perspective that modern Alaska was part of Asia during the Pleistocene (see Fig. 2.3), the real question is, "When did people arrive south of the ice sheets?" The Asian record is of critical importance, however, since people would have had to have been in northeast Asia, then Alaska, then the rest of the New World in that order (at least in theory).

The Clovis First Model

As noted above (also see Chapter 3), the best documented—and for many years believed to be the earliest—culture in the New World is called Clovis, named after a town situated near the archaeological site in New Mexico (Blackwater Draw) where it was first formally defined (E. B. Howard 1935; J. J. Hester 1972; C. V. Haynes 1995). Clovis is also the name of the diagnostic artifact associated with these sites, the Clovis projectile point, seemingly designed for use on a thrusting spear. These points exhibit a unique and sophisticated "fluting" technology found primarily in North America. The Clovis culture has other technological traits, such as bone "wrenches" and beveled bone tools (perhaps used as wedges; Lyman et al. 1998).

Clovis is known from hundreds of sites, many with radiocarbon dated deposits. Clovis sites date between about 13,200 and 12,900 years ago all across North America (although this, too, is debated; see Waters and Stafford 2007a, 2007b; C. V. Haynes et al. 2007). Many of the Clovis sites appear to be places where game, commonly mammoths and mastodons, were killed or processed. As a result, Clovis is often seen as a "big-game hunting" culture.

Clovis appears "suddenly" at the same time (from the perspective of radiocarbon time; see above) all across North America, and there are no generally agreed upon archaeological materials (a "pre-Clovis") that date earlier. Thus, many believe that Clovis represents the material culture of the first immigrants into the New World, and this belief has become known as the "Clovis First" model.

A VERY RAPID COLONIZATION   If Clovis people were the first people (or at least the first major population) to enter North America, they arrived to find a vast region containing a large variety of prey species. Further, if the seemingly sudden appearance of Clovis technology across the continent is real, they must have colonized North America very rapidly. To explain this apparent rapid movement, C. Vance Haynes (1966) proposed that Clovis people entered North America ca. 13,000 years ago, maintained a population growth of 1.3 percent per year, moved at a rate of 6.4 km. per year, and spread across North America in 500 years; well within the dated range of Clovis. Following this, Martin (1973, 1974) suggested a Clovis entry at ca. 13,000 years ago, a population growth of 3.4 percent per year (a rate based on the population growth rate of the *Bounty* mutineers, a founding population on a Pacific island), and a movement of 16 km per year, all of which could explain a population spread across all of North and South America within about 1,000 years.

Both the Haynes and Martin models are very generous in their estimates of population growth for hunter-gatherers. Analogies with ethnographically known migrations suggest population growths closer to 0.5 percent per year and movements closer to 1 km per year. Given these latter numbers, people would have had to have entered North America by 20,000 years ago or earlier to colonize the New World (e.g., Hassan 1981:202; also see Whitley and Dorn 1993:631–633). As noted by Kelly and Todd (1988; Kelly 1996), however, the earliest Americans were unlike any modern hunter-gatherer analogs. Given the lack of archaeological evidence of a 20,000 years ago entry, these early people must have moved faster than contemporary hunter-gatherers.

More recent work generally supports the possibility of a rapid population growth (Fiedel 2000:77, 2005a; Lanata et al. 2008) and rapid dispersal, perhaps using a "leapfrog" method, with "daughter" populations moving some distance away to exploit resources in a new locality (Anderson and Gillam 2002:57–59). In addition, Surovell (2000) suggested that high mobility was compatible with high fertility and would not have impeded a rapid colonization. A cladistic analysis of early Paleoindian projectile points supports this rapid colonization model (Buchanan and Collard 2007). Colonizing new lands is difficult. Population densities would probably have been low, there would have been few "neighbors" to help out, with trading and finding marriage partners being difficult (Kelly and Todd 1988; Meltzer 2002).

A CLOVIS OVERKILL?   Martin (e.g., 1967a, 1967b, 1973, 2002, 2005; also see Agenbroad 1984:103; Alroy 2001; Fiedel and Haynes 2002; G. Haynes 2002b) proposed that as humans entered the New World, they overhunted big game as they moved, causing the extinction of mammoths and mastodons; this became known as the "Pleistocene Overkill" or "Blitzkrieg" model. In essence, Martin proposed that Clovis hunters "ate their way" to Terra del Fuego within a thousand years or so in a continuous front. Martin assumed a uniform environment and distribution of large game, an assumption now known to be flawed. An analysis by James Steele et al. (1998; also see Ranere 2006) took into consideration a much more detailed database of Late Pleistocene ecozones than was available to Martin and concluded that a human dispersal across North America within the Clovis time frame (or even earlier; see Lanata et al. 2008) was possible. In addition, the uneven distribution of fluted points in eastern North America suggests the possibility of a "leapfrog" model of colonization rather than a continuous front (D. G. Anderson 1995b:148; Morse et al. 1996:326), with people perhaps moving from one concentration of megafauna to the next. Most recently, C. Vance Haynes (2005) argued that the Clovis entrance into North America coincided with the extinction of the megafauna, the Clovis drought, and the Younger Dryas, all of which contributed to the demise of the megafauna.

Other researchers do not support the overkill model (e.g., Wesler 1981; S. J. Olsen 1990; Grayson 1991; Grayson and Meltzer 2002, 2003; Guthrie 2003; Cannon and Meltzer 2004; Johnson 2009; J. L. Gill et al. 2009; Meltzer 2009). While it is true that some two-thirds of the large mammal genera in North America became extinct at about the same time that Clovis appeared, many small animals and some plants also became extinct during that same time, and there is little evidence that many of the other large mammal species were hunted by humans. During this same time, the ice age ended and major changes in biotic communities took place. Thus, some believe that the extinctions were due to environmental change (see Stahl 1996; J. L. Gill et al. 2009; Campos et al. 2010) and not human predation, although the human hunting or scavenging of large game probably pushed a few species already on the brink "over the edge." It is also possible, if not likely, that human alteration of the environment (e.g., burning) was a greater threat to Pleistocene fauna than human hunters (e.g., Grayson 2001).

The Pre-Clovis Model

No one questions the presence of Clovis across North America. The real question is this: were people present prior to Clovis? Some of the pre-Clovis supporters think people were in the New World very early (more than 40,000 to 50,000 years earlier than Clovis), while others argue that people were present just a little before Clovis, perhaps just a few thousand years earlier. One argument for a pre-Clovis occupation is that there must have been one, or how else could Clovis appear so suddenly and uniformly? Another general argument is "why not?"; people were present in the Old World for a considerable period of time before Clovis, the land bridge was open at various times during the last 200,000 years, and there was nothing to stop people from migrating to the New World. Indeed, Butzer (1991:141) thought that environmental conditions would have been favorable for people to have entered North America before 30,000 years ago. Of course, just a "why not?" argument does not demonstrate anything.

A VERY EARLY ENTRY   There have been several sites in North America proposed as representing a very early pre-Clovis occupation. In theory, such remains in North America would represent a hypothetical "pre-projectile point" culture (Krieger 1964:42; MacNeish 1976:317), since there is no evidence of any pre-Clovis projectile points. Clovis point technology seems far too sophisticated to just suddenly appear without some technological antecedent.

Great antiquity has been claimed for a number of sites, but all have failed to be verified. In the 1970s, several human skeletons, primarily from California, were assigned Pleistocene ages based mostly on amino acid racemization dating, providing support to claims of an early human presence. Most of these have since been redated by radiocarbon to the Holocene (Taylor et al. 1985: Table 2.1).

A LATER PRE-CLOVIS ENTRY   A number of sites has been discovered that apparently date to within the last 40,000 years or so, supporting the pre-Clovis model. Several are new or marginal, such as bison bones in association with some purported artifacts at a site in Oklahoma dated to 26,000 years old (Wyckoff 1999). Several sites dating before 14,000 years ago are not easily dismissed, however, and have formed the foundation for a growing view that people were present in North America by at least 20,000 years ago. These sites, such as Meadowcroft, Cactus Hill, Topper, Monte Verde, Paisley Cave, and others, are discussed below.

In addition, some believe that Clovis may have originated in North America from a pre-Clovis base. The greatest concentration of known fluted points (Fig. 2.7) is in the Southeast (Anderson et al. 2010; Fig. 1) and it has been argued (e.g., R. J. Mason 1962:246) that the Clovis culture developed in the Southeast and moved north and west. This hypothesis is based purely on the distributions of points, but poor classifications and dating weaken the idea (e.g., Goodyear 1999:437). The other major concentration of fluted points is at Tulare Lake in California (Anderson et al. 2010: Fig. 1; Moratto 2000; but see Rondeau and Hopkins 2008), suggesting the possibility that Clovis originated there and moved east. Morrow and Morrow (1999:227; also see Beck and Jones 2010) argued that fluted point technology developed on the Plains and dispersed rapidly across North America and into South America. In each of these scenarios, some sort of a pre-Clovis, even if just a slightly pre-Clovis, is required. It should be remembered that the spread of Clovis technology does not automatically necessitate an actual population movement, although such a movement is often assumed.

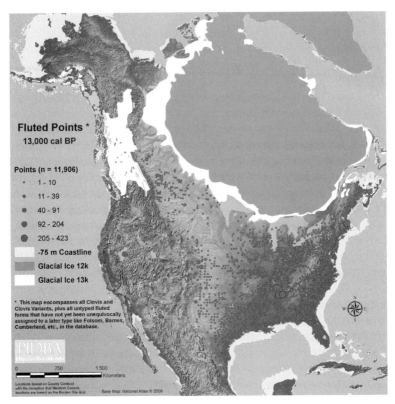

FIGURE 2.7 Map of the distribution of fluted points in North America (from Anderson et al. 2010; image used courtesy Archaeology of Eastern North America, Eastern States Archaeological Federation, and PIDBA [http://pidba.utk.edu/]).

Evaluating the Evidence

The Clovis First model forms a paradigm in American archaeology. A paradigm shift to a pre-Clovis model would require unequivocal evidence. Toth (1991:54; also see Dincauze 1984) proposed four criteria to be met to accept a pre-Clovis occupation: (1) certainty of artifactual or skeletal evidence; (2) solid radiocarbon dating of known cultural or skeletal materials; (3) direct association of artifactual or skeletal materials with radiocarbon dated samples; and (4) a recurrent pattern of sites meeting the first three criteria to guard against a spurious discovery. Similarly, Bonnichsen and Schneider (1999; also see Bonnichsen et al. [2005]) argued that both the Clovis First and pre-Clovis models are theoretically flawed and require more work to adequately develop data expectations for testing.

GENETIC CLUES   Various ideas regarding the number and dating of migrations into the New World have been generated from the genetic data. These ideas derive from the identification of haplogroups and in estimating the rates of mutation and the time it must have taken for those groups to have diverged from their initial occurrences. This requires that the rate of change (a molecular "clock") is known (e.g., Torroni et al. 1994; Meltzer 1995), and many researchers are skeptical about estimates of actual time. If the rate of mutation (the "clock") is slower or faster than assumed, the dates would be wrong.

Recent evidence from the 10,300-year-old skeleton from On Your Knees Cave in British Columbia (Kemp et al. 2007) suggests that there was already considerable genetic diversity by that time, meaning that the "clock" is too fast and that the dating based on genetic data is too early (which would bring it more in line with the archaeological data). In addition, mtDNA studies of Northwest coast groups (Pääbo et al. 1990) indicate that these populations already had significant genetic diversity at the time of their initial migration into the New World.

With these considerations in mind, there have been numerous ideas regarding the timing and number of population movements into the New World. General estimates for the earliest migration are wide ranging and include dates between 40,000 and 30,000 years ago (Schurr and Wallace 1999; also see Schurr 2004a), between 34,000 and 26,000 years ago (Torroni et al. 1992, 1993), between 37,000 and 23,000 years ago (Stone and Stoneking 1998), between 29,000 and 22,000 years ago (Toroni et al. 1994); before 25,000 years ago (Szathmary 1993:216; also see Rogers et al. 1992), at 21,000 years ago (Horai et al. 1993), between 21,000 and 14,000 years ago (Horai et al. 1996; Schurr 2004b), and about 12,000 years ago (Shields et al. 1993). Most believe that the Na-Dene and Eskimo/Aleut entered the New World later, generally during the Early Holocene (see discussion in Torroni 2000; Lell et al. 2002:204).

Both the linguistic and genetic data suggest early (ca. 25,000 to 30,000 years ago) divergences of language families and founding lineages. One must remember that the linguistic and mtDNA evidence only suggests times of population divergence and isolation, and not of actual population movement. If people in North America diverged in northeast Asia at, say, 25,000 years ago, those populations must have migrated to the New World sometime after that date, perhaps considerably later (Merriwether 2002:300).

THE EVIDENCE FROM NORTHEAST ASIA   It is widely accepted that people entered the New World from northeast Asia, either across "mainland" Beringia or by moving along its coast. To do this, two concurrent conditions must have been met: (1) environmental conditions must have been suitable, and (2) people must have been present, probably with some sort of a general "Arctic" adaptation.

Environmental Conditions   During the latter portion of the Pleistocene, glacial conditions fluctuated in northeastern Siberia. The climate became colder at the glacial maximum, woody plants became very scarce, and a lack of fuel may have become a real problem (some sites in the region have combustible shale as fuel in hearths). It is thought, then, that people would have been unable to move east along inland routes during glacial maximums. Paleoclimatic data from northeastern Siberia suggest that the most favorable times for a human migration into the New World were from 40,000 to 23,000 years ago and after about 13,500 years ago (Yi and Clark 1985:12; Goebel 2004:313), although northeastern Siberia does not appear to have been occupied until about 14,000 years ago (Goebel 2002, 2004:344).

The Archaeological Evidence   For many years, it was believed that the earliest archaeological culture in central northeast Asia, the Dyuktai, dated as early as about 35,000 years ago (Michael 1984:22), adding plausibility to the idea of an early entry into North America. The dating of the Dyuktai culture has since been revised to about 16,000 years ago (Goebel 2004:339). It was suggested (Goebel 1999, 2004:344; Pitul'ko 1999:430, 2001:269; Kuzmin 2000:129) that people were present in far northeastern Siberia no earlier than about 14,000 years ago, or perhaps even later, but not earlier than the Late Pleistocene (Pitul'ko 2001:274). There is new evidence of human occupation at the Yana RHS (Rhino Horn Site) site in north-central Siberia dating to about

27,000 years ago, suggesting an Arctic adaptation earlier than believed (Pitul'ko et al. 2004). Bifacial technology and bone foreshafts were also found there.

Dyuktai subsistence included mammoth hunting (Pitul'ko 2001:274) and the technology consisted of microblades (small blades used in composite tools), bifaces, blades, end scrapers, burins, shaft straighteners, bone and ivory points, flaked bone, and unifaces. Dyuktai bifacial technology might be antecedent to the development of Clovis-like fluted technology, but no fluting is known from the Dyuktai culture, and such technology is dated later than 12,700 years ago in northeast Asia (Goebel and Slobodin 1999:143, 147). An artifact thought to have been a fluted point was found at the Uptar site, located along the Sea of Okhotsk in eastern Siberia (King and Slobodin 1996; also see Slobodin 1999:498, 2006:15), hinting at a link between northeastern Siberia and the Clovis technology of North America. However, it is possible that this artifact is just an unfinished, basally thinned, biface dating to the early Holocene (T. Goebel, personal communication 2004) or just an accident (Meltzer 2009:189).

Bifacial technology, but without microblades, is known from Component 7 at the Ushki 1 and 5 sites in Kamchatka (Dikov and Titov 1984; Michael 1984; Dikov 1996; Goebel and Slobodin 1999:138, 147; Slobodin 2006:13). New work at these sites has established the dating of Component 7 beginning about 13,400 years ago (Goebel et al. 2003a:503; Goebel 2004:342), slightly earlier than Dyuktai in Kamchatka. Microblades are known from the higher components 5 and 6 at Ushki and are considered "constituents of the Dyuktai complex" (Dikov 1996:246). Component 6 at Ushki, dated to about 12,200 BP, contained houses and burials.

The 27,000 year age of the Yana RHS site in north-central Siberia (Pitul'ko et al. 2004) is the first evidence that people occupied inland northeast Asia earlier than about 16,000 years ago and opens a possibility that people could have moved across mainland Beringia at that time. Still, the Yana RHS site is far to the west of Beringia, and more such evidence will be required to support the possibility of an early migration into eastern Beringia or the rest of the New World prior to about 16,000 years ago (Hopkins 1996:xix; Goebel 1999; Turner 2002:134).

Finally, Tankersley and Kuzmin (1998:136) noted four distinct patterns in the Late Pleistocene/Early Holocene transition in eastern Siberia. First, the largest game animals became extinct first, followed by progressively smaller species. Second, the frequencies of blade, core, and flake technologies decreased as game animals become smaller. Third, microblade technology appeared as smaller, less gregarious animals became the focus of hunting. Fourth, as subsistence shifted away from large animals, ground stone technologies appeared, presumably for the processing of plant resources. One of the important patterns in this record is that microblade technology appears later than blade technology in northeast Asia.

THE ARCHAEOLOGICAL EVIDENCE FROM ALASKA   During the Pleistocene, much of Alaska formed the eastern portion of Beringia and was essentially far eastern Asia at that time; the "New World" lay to the south of the ice sheets. Thus, it was necessary to traverse Alaska, either along the coast or through the interior, before moving south. Several sites, notably Bluefish Caves (Ackerman 1996a; Cinq-Mars and Morlan 1999), Trail Creek Caves (C. F. West 1996), and Lime Hills (Ackerman 1996b) appear to date to 14,000 years ago (or a bit earlier), indicating that eastern Beringia was inhabited at least by that time (Hamilton and Goebel 1999:156).

Some (e.g., Cinq-Mars and Morlan 1999) have argued that people were in Alaska much earlier, citing materials at Bluefish Caves and Old Crow dated between 25,000 and 40,000 years ago (Irving 1987; also see Irving and Harrington 1973). It is not clear whether the materials from those sites are really artifacts or if they were directly associated with the radiocarbon-dated material (Nelson et al. 1986; Hoffecker et al. 1993:50).

The Nenana Complex   The earliest identified "culture" in eastern Beringia is the Nenana Complex of central Alaska. Nenana technology does not include microblades, and the bifaces have a general similarity to Clovis points but without fluting (Goebel et al. 1991:74; Hoffecker et al. 1993:51). Nenana Complex materials have been found at a number of sites in the Nenana and Tanana river valleys (e.g., the Broken Mammoth [Yesner et al. 1992; Holmes 1996; Yesner 1996] and Walker Road [Goebel et al. 1996] sites) and date between ca. 13,800 and 13,000 years ago, the oldest date being from the Broken Mammoth site (Goebel et al. 2003a:504). At present, there is no direct association between the Nenana Complex and mammoths (a Clovis "trait"), but exploitation of other animals, including bison, caribou, and waterfowl, as well as plants, has been demonstrated. The Nenana Complex is only slightly older than Clovis, leading some to believe that it is the elusive Clovis antecedent (Hamilton and Goebel 1999:156; Hoffecker 2001). It seems that Nenana is related to Component 7 at the Ushki sites in Kamchatka, which is dated to about 13,300 years ago (Slobodin 2001:44; Goebel et al. 2003a:503). It is possible that Nenana represents the initial migration of people into the New World (but see Adovasio and Page 2002:262).

The Denali Complex   The Denali Complex has been identified in the Nenana River Valley and Tanana Basin of central Alaska. Unlike Nenana, Denali includes microblades, wedge-shaped cores, burins, bifacial knives, and microcores (F. H. West 1967; see Powers and Hoffecker 1989; Goebel and Bigelow 1992; Hoffecker et al. 1993:52; Hoffecker 2001). The Denali Complex is younger than Nenana (Goebel et al. 2003a: Fig. 5); however, a date of about 13,700 BP from the Swan Point site (Holmes et al. 1996:320) suggests the possibility of some overlap in time between Nenana and Denali. Denali is similar to Dyuktai in northeast Asia and might be related.

The Mesa Complex   One of the most interesting sites so far discovered in Alaska is the Mesa site (Fig. 2.8), located in north-central Alaska. Some 150 complete or fragmentary lanceolate points were found that look "Clovis" in basic shape (see Fig. 2.9). Most of the dates are around 12,000 years ago, but one hearth was dated to 13,660 years ago (Kunz and Reanier 1994, 1996; Kunz et al. 2003). Several other sites (e.g., Spein Mountain [Ackerman 2001] and Hilltop [Reanier 1995]) are included in the "Mesa Complex," indicating the presence of a substantial Paleoindian occupation in this region (Kunz and Reanier 1994; Bever 2001a). Kunz and Reanier (1996:503) maintained that the Mesa Complex was one of the "most ancient Paleoindian groups" and was ancestral to the Agate Basin Complex on the Plains. It is also possible that the Mesa Complex is related to Paleoindian technologies moving north about 10,000 years ago (Hamilton and Goebel 1999:156).

Discussion   There is no firm evidence of human occupation of eastern Beringia (Alaska) prior to 14,000 years ago (Hamilton and Goebel 1999; Yesner 2001), although the record there is very complex and still poorly understood (Bever 2001b, 2006). The Nenana Complex appears to be the "earliest unequivocally dated cultural occupation" (Goebel et al. 2003a:504) in all of Beringia, although theoretically, there must be earlier materials in Asia that remain undiscovered. Nenana and Denali appear to be separate cultural traditions (Hoffecker 2001:139), with Nenana being a thousand years or so older (Goebel et al. 2003a: Fig. 5), although Dumond (1987a, 2001) argued that they may be a single entity. Nenana and Component 7 at Ushki date to roughly the same time and contain a similar technology, meaning that "biface-and-blade industries occurred across Beringia during and just before the time of Clovis in western North America" (Goebel et al. 2003a:504). When the climate warmed at the end of the Pleistocene, Nenana folks may then have moved south (e.g., Mann et al. 2001), where they developed Clovis technology.

FIGURE 2.8 The Mesa site in northern Alaska. The site is located on top of the mesa. (*Source:* Nature Picture Library.)

A bit later, the microblade technology of the Dyuktai culture appeared in eastern Beringia, occupying the same basic region in central Alaska as Nenana and manifesting itself as Denali (e.g., Goebel et al. 1991:74; Yesner 1996:271; also see Clark 2001). Goebel et al. (2003a:504) argued that this movement represented a second migration from Asia, that of the Na-Dene. Alternatively, Denali people may have evolved directly from Nenana, with the development of a technological adaptation (microblades) in response to the cold of the Younger Dryas (Powers and Hoffecker 1989:284). It may also be that microblade technology developed to exploit smaller animals after the larger ones became extinct (Tankersley and Kuzmin 1998:136).

If Nenana is the Clovis ancestor, where did the Clovis technological trait of fluting originate? A number of fluted points from surface contexts are known in Alaska (e.g., Clark and Clark 1983; Clark 1991a) but remain undated. Clark (1991a; also see Hamilton and Goebel 1999:156) asserted that the fluted points in Alaska (e.g., the Mesa Complex) are not Clovis but had diffused up from the south at some later time. The discovery of mammoth protein residues on fluted points from Beringia (Loy and Dixon 1998) suggests that fluting was early in eastern Beringia (as mammoths were extinct by 10,000 years ago), developed there, and then moved south (also see Morlan 1977:102; Reanier 1995:45; Kunz et al. 2003).

THE NORTH AMERICAN EVIDENCE   Over the years, many sites have been proposed as representing a pre-Clovis occupation in North America. In many cases, the claims have failed scrutiny, but in others they persist.

FIGURE 2.9 Two of the large unfluted points from the Mesa site. Compare to the forms shown in Fig. 2.2. (From: Kunz & Reanier, *Science* 263:660, Fig 2 [1994]. Reprinted with permission from AAAS.)

Meadowcroft Rockshelter   One of the best candidates for a pre-Clovis occupation in North America is Meadowcroft Rockshelter (Fig. 2.10), located in western Pennsylvania. Excavations at Meadowcroft revealed a continuous occupation dating from the Late Pleistocene to ethnographic times (Adovasio et al. 1978, 1982, 1983, 1990, 1999; Adovasio and Carlisle 1988; Adovasio 1993; Adovasio and Pedler 2005). The earliest artifactual assemblage was found in Stratum IIa, radiocarbon dated between about 10,000 and 18,000 years ago (see Adovasio et al. 1982: Table 5.2; Adovasio and Pedler 2004:143–149). The artifacts from this stratum consisted of about a dozen stone tools and a hundred pieces of debitage. Two additional radiocarbon dates of ca. 21,000 and 21,500 years ago were obtained on materials below Stratum IIa. One of the dates was on a piece of "cut bark-like" material thought to be a basketry fragment. If the sample is valid, this represents the earliest dated cultural material in North America.

While there does seem to be a Paleoindian occupation at the site, many archaeologists do not recognize Meadowcroft Rockshelter as having a pre-Clovis component. This disagreement is based on two major issues. The first is the validity of the early radiocarbon dates. Many believe that the radiocarbon samples from Stratum IIa may have been contaminated by old carbon derived from the coal deposits that are ubiquitous in the region, making the dates too old (e.g., C. V. Haynes 1980; Dincauze 1981; Tankersley et al. 1987). Adovasio et al. (1990; Adovasio and Pedler 2005:25) argued that the samples were cleaned of any contamination during laboratory processing

FIGURE 2.10   Excavations underway at Meadowcroft Rockshelter (photo by J. M. Adovasio, Mercyhurst Archaeological Institute; used with permission).

and that the internal consistency of the suite of dates suggests that they are not contaminated, a claim supported by Goldberg and Arpin (1999).

The second major issue is that all of the botanical and faunal materials found at the site represent extant species (Adovasio et al. 1982: Table 5.3). If the materials from Stratum IIa represent a component dating from the Pleistocene, one would have expected to have found the remains of Pleistocene plants and animals, as have been found elsewhere in the region. Adovasio et al. (1980:593) noted, however, that all of the faunal remains from Stratum IIa were too fragmentary to identify and that botanical materials did not preserve well, implying the possibility that Pleistocene species could be present but unidentified.

Other issues include the nondiagnostic forms of the artifacts from Stratum IIa (C. V. Haynes 1980:582) and the possibility that the site may have been below the level of the adjacent creek prior to about 15,000 years ago (C. V. Haynes 1980:583) and so uninhabitable before then. A final, albeit minor, issue is the absence of a Clovis component within the site, although it is possible that Clovis people simply may not have lived there. In combination, however, these factors continue to cast serious doubt on the validity of a pre-Clovis occupation at Meadowcroft Rockshelter.

Pre-Clovis Mammoth Hunting?   Several sites in central North America contain evidence to suggest mammoth hunting by pre-Clovis people about 14,000 years ago. A mammoth from the Schaefer site in Wisconsin (D. J. Joyce 2006) showed bone damage interpreted as butchering marks, and some nondiagnostic stone tools were found in association. A similar situation was found at the Hebior site, also in Wisconsin (Overstreet 2005). Two sites on the central Plains,

FIGURE 2.11 Excavations at the Cactus Hill site, Virginia. Note the various artifacts displayed in the foreground. (*Source:* Kenneth Garrett Photography.)

La Sena in Nebraska and Lovewell in Kansas (Holen 2005), contain mammoths with some bone looking purposefully broken. However, no tools or evidence of butchering was discovered. This evidence appears to be very weak.

Cactus Hill   A Clovis component (Fig. 2.11) was discovered at the Cactus Hill site in Virginia, some fifty miles south of Richmond, Virginia. Excavated in 1993 and 1994 (McAvoy and McAvoy 1997; McAvoy 1997; also see Goodyear 2005), a hearth feature was discovered in the lower reaches of the deposit in Area B (Level 5, Feature 1), was dated to about 12,920 years ago (McAvoy and McAvoy 1997; Table 6.3), and was assigned to a Clovis component. Three inches below "a Clovis working surface" a "hearth-like, amorphous scatter of carbonized wood" (Level 6, Feature 1) was discovered in association with three "blade-like flakes" and dated to 17,000 years ago (McAvoy and McAvoy 1997:169; Table 6.3). These materials were assigned to an "Early Paleoindian" component and suggested the possibility of a pre-Clovis occupation of the site (see Adovasio and Pedler 2004:149–151).

Further excavations at Area B in 1996 revealed additional Clovis-age materials and more artifacts, "a blade core, core blades, and a thin trianguloid biface fragment," below the Clovis layer (McAvoy 1997:194). Three additional radiocarbon dates were obtained on materials from below the Clovis layer (McAvoy 1997: Table 2). A sample of carbonaceous soil from a possible hearth associated with "six core blades" returned a date of about 12,160 years ago. The second sample was obtained on fine charcoal collected from flotation samples from a possible hearth in association with six core blades and returned a date of about 18,700 years ago. The last date (11,250 years ago) was obtained on carbonaceous soil and charcoal particles from beneath a large flake, in association with three core blades and three small flakes. McAvoy (1997:196) suggested the site was first occupied "as early as 15,000 to 16,000 BP," a temporal placement consistent with the materials from Meadowcroft Rockshelter.

There seems no doubt that the Cactus Hill site has a Clovis component, and two early radiocarbon dates (15,060 and 16,670) do suggest the possibility of a pre-Clovis component. However, since the radiocarbon samples were from scattered and mixed charcoal, it is possible that they are not cultural or contaminated. Nevertheless, Haynes (1999a) thought that Cactus Hill might be a valid pre-Clovis site, perhaps related to the Nenana Complex. If so, the pre-Clovis component is 5,000 years earlier than Clovis. Some have used this possibility to link a pre-Clovis occupation in eastern North America to the Solutrean of western Europe (see below). A video on the Cactus Hill site is available at www.archaeologychannel.org, "Ice Age Discoveries: New Evidence (Virginia)."

Topper   A pre-Clovis component has also been claimed for the Topper site in South Carolina with some blade-like flakes and core materials being found about one meter below a Clovis component (Goodyear 2003, 2005; Goodyear and Steffy 2003). The artifacts in question were found in a soil thought to be 2,000 to 4,000 years older than the Clovis component, suggesting that they date between 18,000 and 20,000 years ago (Goodyear 2003:26, 2005:108; Adovasio and Pedler 2004:153–154). However, radiocarbon dates on scattered charcoal from this lower soil are "disappointingly recent" (Fiedel 2000:47). However, recent work at the site (Waters et al. 2009) has supported a pre-Clovis age of the artifacts but has questions whether they are of human origin. A video on the Topper site is available at www.archaeologychannel.org, "They Were Here: Ice Age Humans in South Carolina," and is discussed in an episode of *Time Team America* on PBS.

HIGHLIGHT 2.1

PRE-CLOVIS POOP?

Excavations at Paisley Cave (Fig. 2.12), located in southeastern Oregon along the shore of Pleistocene Lake Chewaucan, had been undertaken since the 1930s (Cressman 1942). A deep deposit contained a record of human occupation dating from the late Pleistocene, but the earliest materials were equivocal and their dating was unclear. In the early 2000s, additional excavations were undertaken by the University of Oregon to attempt to explore the lowest levels of the site and determine their age. In the course of the excavations, fourteen coprolites (preserved feces) were recovered, and based on morphology, size, and color, they appeared to be human. Testing revealed the presence of human aDNA and human hairs within the specimens, and four specimens were dated by radiocarbon to between about 13,000 and 13,800 years ago (Gilbert et al. 2008).

The presence of human coprolites confirms the presence of humans (there being no other reasonable explanation), and the dating supports a pre-Clovis human presence in Oregon, well inland from the coast. While it is always possible that the dating is in error, the fact that four dates were concordant makes this improbable. It is not clear whether this find represents a viable population or a small group of pre-Clovis people who did not survive to successfully colonize the region.

Few Other Sites   Several other sites contain materials that may represent a pre-Clovis occupation. At Fort Rock Cave, Oregon, a radiocarbon date of 15,200 years ago was obtained on charcoal from a level containing some artifacts, including points (Carlson 1983:76; also see Cressman

FIGURE 2.12 Excavations at Paisley Cave, overlooking the Summer Lake Valley (that contained Pleistocene Lake Chewaucan) in southeastern Oregon (photo by Kolby Schnelli, University of Oregon Archaeological Field School Archives; courtesy of Dennis L. Jenkins; used with permission).

1942; Bedwell and Cressman 1971; Bedwell 1973). The connection between the dated materials and the artifacts is dubious, and the associated point styles date no earlier than 12,700 years ago elsewhere (see discussion in Fiedel 2000:51). In the Great Basin, Beck and Jones (2010) argued that the stemmed technology thought to post-date Clovis actually predates it. Although several sites in eastern North America had at one time been claimed as being pre-Clovis in age, none has withstood scrutiny (Morse et al. 1996:323–324). There may also be early materials at the Saltville (SV-2) site in eastern Virginia (McDonald 2000) but this material has not yet been fully evaluated (but see Adovasio and Pedler 2004:151–153; Goodyear 2005). Lastly, there may be some tools associated with a mastodon tusk with possible tool marks at the Page-Ladson site in Florida (Milanich 1994; Webb 2005) but this site remains to be fully evaluated.

The Iberian Connection   There are a large number of Paleoindian sites in eastern North America (Anderson et al. 2010). Although Clovis points have not been demonstrated to be older in eastern North America, the Cactus Hill site may contain a pre-Clovis component. Based on these data, it was suggested (Stanford and Bradley 2002; Bradley and Stanford 2004) that people first entered the New World from northern Europe, crossing the North Atlantic from Iberia, where people had an Upper Paleolithic technology (Solutrean) similar to Clovis, but without fluting. The terminal dates for Solutrean (ca. 18,500 years ago) do not closely overlap with Clovis (ca. 13,500 years ago).

This is not a new idea (e.g., Wilmsen and Roberts 1978:179–180), but it has been argued (e.g., Stanford and Bradley 2002) that the apparent dates of Meadowcroft and Cactus Hill have narrowed the dating gap between the Solutrean and the earliest New World materials sufficiently to reconsider the possibility. There are several seemingly insurmountable problems with the Iberian model (Straus et al. 2005; but see Bradley and Stanford 2006), such as (1) no agreed upon typological similarities occur between the Upper Paleolithic in Europe and North American Paleoindian materials (M. B. Collins 2005), (2) no Solutrean points are known from North America, (3) the purported pre-Clovis materials from Meadowcroft and Cactus Hill are "even less like Solutrean than Clovis" (Meltzer 2002:45), and (4) the genetic and linguistic data show virtually no support for a European origin of Native Americans.

If that were not enough, the migration of people from Europe to North America would have been extraordinarily difficult. To get to North America from Europe would have required that people cross the North Atlantic during the height of the glaciation, traveling from iceberg to iceberg, collecting driftwood, and fishing and hunting; all of this in skin boats against the current. Even the Norse, with a maritime tradition, a much more sophisticated technology, and in better climatic conditions, had a very difficult time crossing the North Atlantic. Straus (2000) argued that a Solutrean migration to North America was unreasonable due to the dissimilarity of Solutrean and Clovis technologies, the gap in dating the two complexes, the lack of any Solutrean maritime technology or adaptation, and the lack of occupational evidence in northern Europe at the time of the proposed migration. In sum, no empirical evidence for the model currently exists (G. A. Clark 2005).

THE SOUTH AMERICAN EVIDENCE   Research into the initial occupation of South America has been ongoing for more than a century (see Lynch [1990] for a review), and many sites dating between 10,000 and 13,000 years ago are known (Lynch 1990:27). In spite of many claims for an occupation that would predate Clovis in North America, the evidence of Pleistocene human occupation in South America presents "only weak or negative indications of early [pre-Clovis] occupation" (Lynch 1990:12; but see Gruhn and Bryan 1991; Lynch 1991; Roosevelt et al. 1996; Gruhn 1997, 2004, 2005). This may be due, at least in part, to a research focus on finding the Pleistocene megafauna and projectile points that mark the earliest occupation of North American but do not occur in South America (Borrero 2006:9). Nevertheless, keeping in mind the coarse resolution of dating, people appear to have arrived in South America at roughly the same time they did in North America (e.g., Roosevelt et al. 1996; L. J. Jackson 2006a), and several South American sites might be earlier than Clovis.

Monte Verde   In the debate about the peopling of the New World, the most important site in South America is Monte Verde, Chile, dated to about 15,350 years ago and interpreted as a brief encampment. A separate locus nearby dated to 33,450 years ago but contained little evidence of human occupation and is not considered a factor in the pre-Clovis debate.

The materials recovered from Monte Verde include tools, features, structure foundations, and food residues (Dillehay 1989, 1997, 2000), including seaweed (Dillehay et al. 2008), all in good stratigraphic context. Features include hearths, a human footprint, and a wishbone-shaped structure of twelve interconnected "rooms" formed from logs and covered with mastodon hides, all of which are "patterned spatially and integrated functionally" (Dillehay and Collins 1991:336). Artifacts from the site include nearly seven hundred stone artifacts, such as projectile points, ground stone implements, hammerstones, debitage, and a number of bone tools and perishable items, such as cordage. Seven of the bone and perishable artifacts were radiocarbon dated between 13,700 and 14,800 years ago. Numerous remains of the usable parts of exotic (from distant sources) botanical species were also found, suggesting a patterned use of these resources (Dillehay and Collins 1991:337).

The claim of pre-Clovis antiquity at Monte Verde prompted critical reviews, and there are many scholars who have considerable doubt whether it is really such an old site. Lynch (1990:26–27) was unconvinced that the artifacts were genuine (meaning that the radiocarbon dates were not cultural), doubted that the fire hearths were cultural (suggesting that the carbon was due to natural decay and not fire), and had "strong doubts" about the site being pre-Clovis. Indeed, Dillehay and Collins (1991:337–338) conceded that only about 3 percent of the stone tools were "unequivocal" tools (with the points being of a style dated to the Holocene; Roosevelt et al. 2002:186), while the remainder were arguable artifacts.

The possible significance of Monte Verde was such that a group of specialists examined the site (Fig. 2.13) and materials and concluded that the artifacts and dates were valid (Meltzer et al. 1997). In spite of this, many archaeologists questioned the validity of the site and its dating (Fiedel 1999b; Haynes 1999b; but also see Collins 1999a; Dillehay et al. 1999). Finally, it was thought that the radiocarbon "reservoir" might be different in the southern hemisphere, making the dates too early, but this seems not to be the case (Taylor et al. 1999). In sum, Monte Verde has been accepted as a valid pre-Clovis site by many archaeologists (e.g., Meltzer 2009:128), but not by all.

Pedra Furada Rockshelter   Another possible early site is Pedra Furada Rockshelter in northeastern Brazil. Features thought to be hearths were radiocarbon dated to about 32,000 years ago and were associated with broken stones believed to be tools (Guidon and Delibrias 1986; Bednarik 1989; also see Guidon and Arnaud 1991). This evidence has been seriously challenged (Lynch 1990; Meltzer et al. 1994) in the belief that the both the "hearths" and "tools" are natural, assertions that have been refuted (Parenti et al. 1994; Guidon et al. 1996). Most recently, calcite

FIGURE 2.13   Archaeologists inspect the Monte Verde site, Chile. (*Source:* Kenneth Garrett/NGS Image Collection.)

deposits covering rock art at the site have been dated by thermoluminescence and electron spin resonance to between 35,000 and 40,000 years ago (Watanabe et al. 2003). Further radiocarbon dating of the hearths have yielded dates in excess of 47,000 years ago (Santos et al. 2003) and have yet to be evaluated.

Discussion   If Monte Verde is valid, then a pre-Clovis presence in South America has been demonstrated and strongly argues for a human presence in North American prior to that occupation. If, not, then there is little else to support a pre-Clovis claim. Indeed, Roosevelt et al. (2002) saw no evidence of a pre-Clovis occupation of South America (or of the New World) but suggested that Clovis may have been only one of a number of adaptations that entered the New World at about the same time (ca. 14,000 years ago). It is difficult to account for the many sites in South America dating to the same basic time as Clovis in North America, even if Clovis people started moving south very rapidly after an entry into North America after ca. 13,500 years ago. It remains possible that a pre-Clovis adaptation quite different than Clovis, and so difficult to associate with Clovis, actually is present in South America but remains unrecognized.

WHERE ARE WE NOW?

Of the four major questions regarding the origins of humans in the New World—from where, by what route(s), how many migrations, and when—we can unequivocally answer only the first. It is clear that migrations into the New World originated from northeast Asia (the Solutrean notwithstanding). The other three questions remain intensely debated. While the linguistic, dental, and genetic data all suggest that New World people diverged fairly early in Asia, those same data do not demonstrate that people actually migrated into the New World at any particular time or times. To address these questions, archaeological data are needed.

The earliest sites currently known in northeast Asia date from about 16,000 years ago. If one accepts a pre-Clovis occupation, particularly in South America (and many archaeologists do), then people must have traversed across North America prior to 16,000 or 17,000 years ago (or earlier) and must have been in northeast Asia sometime prior to that. Unfortunately, there is no evidence of a human occupation in northeastern Asia early enough to support the pre-Clovis model. Actually, given the imprecision of radiocarbon dating, the earliest South American materials may not require a pre-Clovis occupation, but it would require that the initial Clovis people moved south very rapidly, much like the movement of Thule people across the northern Arctic beginning some 700 years ago (Fiedel 2000:79–80).

The suggestion that the earliest people migrating to the New World were maritime adapted is not supported by the archaeological record in coastal northeast Asia or northwestern North America. There is no evidence of a Pleistocene maritime adaptation or of boat technology from these areas. It remains possible that such evidence has been drowned by rising sea levels during the Holocene and remains undiscovered, but this is just speculation. However, the evidence for a coastal migration is building, and if Monte Verde is as early as Clovis, people must (in theory) have moved south very rapidly, such as along the coast (e.g., R. L. Kelly 2003).

There is little direct archaeological evidence for the number of migrations. The presence of early skeletal remains that are "morphologically distinct" from contemporary Native Americans strongly suggests that a minimum of two separate migrations took place, probably at different times (but see Gill 2005).

Is there a pre-Clovis occupation of the New World? Archaeologists appear to have fallen into three major "camps" (Madsen 2004:2): (1) those who believe that Monte Verde and other sites have firmly established a pre-Clovis human presence in the New World; (2) those who ad-here to the Clovis First model; and (3) a large number of archaeologists who maintain that the evidence for a pre-Clovis occupation in the New World is suggestive but not conclusive. Proponents of the pre-Clovis model argue that the Clovis First paradigm prevents objective consideration of an early entry of humans (see Meltzer 1991). Others (e.g., Dincauze 1984) have argued that just because something is possible or is claimed frequently (such as the pre-Clovis model) does not make it true. Nevertheless, there seems to be a growing body of evidence that there was a pre-Clovis presence in the New World (see Bonnichsen et al. 2005; Gilbert et al. 2008; Meltzer 2009). On the other hand, perhaps we do know when people arrived—that is, in Clovis times (R. L. Kelly 2003). In the end, however, the real answer is that we do not yet know. Failure to provide convincing evidence that any specific site is pre-Clovis does not demonstrate an absence of a pre-Clovis occupation, only that a particular site does not demonstrate one. As is the case in all of science, one can only follow the evidence (Meltzer 2009:97).

If there was a pre-Clovis occupation, why is it so difficult to find? Perhaps pre-Clovis populations were too small to have left a record substantial or obvious enough for archaeologists to easily find. However, this issue has not been a problem in finding very small Clovis sites that reflect just a few individuals. Perhaps many pre-Clovis sites have been found but lack diagnostic artifacts and remain undated. While this is possible, it is also speculative. Perhaps geomorphic processes during the Late Pleistocene were erosional, making the preservation of pre-Clovis sites rare. At ca. 11,000 years ago, conditions may have changed to a depositional environment, making site preservation much more common at the same time Clovis appeared. But if this were true, why is it limited to the New World?

Where are the actual remains of the purported pre-Clovis people in the Americas? Why are there no skeletal materials firmly dated to the Pleistocene? Perhaps early immigrants practiced above-ground burial, much like Arctic groups do today (Lynch 1990:13; Crawford 1998:21), with the result that their remains are much more difficult to find. The first people into the New World would have faced a more difficult climate than today and must have had a rather sophisticated toolkit. Why is it so difficult to find? Evidence of Paloeaustralians with a relatively simple toolkit is abundant, despite the fact that fewer archaeologists have worked in Australia for less time (e.g., Fiedel 2006:22).

People in the New World reach "unequivocal archaeological visibility" only during Clovis times (Haynes 1999a). While this does not preclude a pre-Clovis occupation, it seems only reasonable to expect that if humans had arrived earlier in North America, after over 100 years of looking, they would have been found by now (Owen 1984; P. S. Martin 1987; G. A. Clark 1988; Adams et al. 2001). Evidence of Pleistocene occupation is easy to find in the Old World (e.g., Jelnick 1992), but the current evidence does not support an occupation, or at least any substantial occupation that contributed to the development of subsequent New World groups, prior to Clovis times (Jelnick 1992:347).

To accept a pre-Clovis occupation of the New World, it is necessary to believe that people first migrated to the New World during the Old World Upper Paleolithic, but with a barely recognizable Lower Paleolithic technology (the cobble tools claimed for many sites). They must also have traversed difficult territory with that rudimentary technology, subsisted in the New World for millennia without any apparent impact on large animal populations, and lived in places not yet discovered despite an intensive century-long search by archaeologists. Although acceptance of these assumptions requires a significant leap of faith, many are willing to make that leap. At this point, the vast preponderance of evidence suggests an initial entry south of the ice sheets after about 15,000 years ago when the climate began to warm and the ice began to retreat, probably by people with a Clovis technology (see Turner 2002:147).

Of course, there is always the possibility that new discoveries will vindicate the claim for a pre-Clovis entry. Perhaps a few immigrants entered early, failed to prosper (e.g., Meltzer 1989:484), and left a small archaeological footprint, as suggested by Monte Verde and Paisley Cave. If so, a later and much larger migration probably took place during Clovis times, resulting in the unmistakable archaeological record of their presence. It may be useful to recast the question of when these events took place to distinguish between (1) when the first humans arrived in the New World and (2) when the first successful colonization of the New World occurred. This would be a visitation versus colonization issue, much like the Norse/Columbus debate.

Faught (2008) conducted an analysis of radiocarbon dates from many dozens of sites in North and South America. He saw a pattern of very early dates (e.g., Paisley Cave in North America and Monte Verde in South America) that suggested the possibility that people had arrived in the New World at several locations at about the same time, perhaps even from places other than northeastern Asia. This idea, no doubt, will inspire closer examination.

The most recent synthesis of the evidence (Goebel et al. 2008) argued that (1) a single population from Siberia moved into Beringia no earlier than 30,000 years ago, and probably after 22,000 BP, (2) that people moved from Beringia into the Americas no earlier than 16,500 BP, and (3) the colonists likely migrated south along the coast. We shall see if this model survives new data.

A Paleoindian Continent

The Paleoindian Period encompasses the time of the initial human occupation of the New World to the end of the Pleistocene (see Chapter 2). Descriptions of Paleoindian cultures generally begin with Clovis, as a pre-Clovis human presence remains to be adequately demonstrated. Paleoindian cultures have been defined based on a number of criteria, including age (e.g., older than about 10,000 years), association with Pleistocene megafauna (e.g., mammoths or giant bison), and a technology that includes fluted and unfluted lanceolate and stemmed projectile points. The dating of Paleoindian sites has been primarily dependent on radiocarbon determinations and the presence of marker fauna and projectile points. As a result, sites with extinct fauna and Paleoindian hunting equipment are readily recognized and dated, leading to the notion that Paleoindians were "big-game hunters." It may be, however, that Paleoindian sites lacking marker fauna and artifacts and representing activities other than big-game hunting have gone unrecognized due to the lack of "markers." This problem is well understood and is always on the minds of researchers.

The earliest demonstrated Paleoindian culture is Clovis (called "Early Paleoindian" in eastern North America), believed to be present all across North America south of the ice sheets (see Fig. 3.1). Clovis is associated with mammoths and mastodons and is characterized by a particular type of large, fluted, lanceolate projectile point. After Clovis, a number of other, regional Paleoindian complexes appeared, each identified by a different point style. A few of these, such as Folsom on the Plains, retained fluting technology, but that trait was soon lost or discarded. The other regional post-Clovis Paleoindian complexes (see Table 3.1) are defined largely by unfluted lanceolate or stemmed projectile points (but see Beck and Jones 2010). Thus, Clovis appears to be the early base from which the later regional Paleoindian complexes across North America derived.

THE CLOVIS COMPLEX

The characteristic fluted point style known as Clovis (refer to Fig. 2.2) was first identified in 1932 at the Dent site in Colorado (Figgins 1933; also see Brunswig and Pitblado 2007). A few months later, a deposit containing the same style of points associated with mammoth remains was found

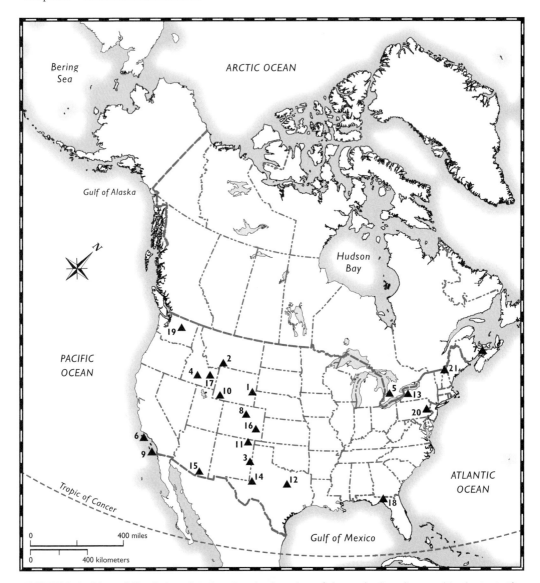

FIGURE 3.1 Map of North America showing the location of the early sites discussed in the text: 1) Agate Basin; 2) Anzick; 3) Blackwater Draw; 4) Buhl; 5) Crowfield; 6) Daisy Cave; 7) Debert; 8) Dent; 9) Eel Point; 10) Fenn; 11) Folsom; 12) Gault; 13) Lamb; 14) Midland; 15) Murray Springs; 16) Olsen-Chubbock; 17) Owl Cave; 18) Page-Ladson; 19) Richey-Roberts; 20) Shawnee Minisink; and 21) Vail.

at the Blackwater Draw site (Howard 1935; Hester 1972; C. V. Haynes 1995) in New Mexico. Blackwater Draw became the type site for the Clovis Culture, so named due to the proximity of the site to the town of Clovis (although some use the term Llano, after the name of the place where Blackwater Draw is located).

The Clovis Culture is characterized by a distinctive large, fluted, lanceolate, projectile point (see Fig. 2.2) probably used on thrusting spears (see C. V. Haynes [2002a] for a general treatment of Clovis). Clovis dates within a very narrow time range, between ca. 13,500 and 12,900 years ago

TABLE 3.1 A General Paleoindian Chronology for North America

Years Ago	Western North America	Central North America (Plains)	Eastern North America	General Environment
8,000	Archaic	Archaic		
9,000		Cody	Archaic	Holocene Environments
10,000	Western Pluvial Lakes Tradition	Plano	Late Paleoindian	Younger Dryas
	Paleocoastal Tradition	Folsom / Mid-land	Middle Paleoindian	
12,000	Clovis			Clovis Drought
13,000				
	Pre-Clovis?			Glacial Conditions

(C. V. Haynes 1992:364; also see Waters and Stafford 2007a, 2007b; Haynes et al. 2007), and hundreds of Clovis sites are known all across North America. In addition, a Clovis site has recently been reported from South America (L. J. Jackson 1995). When animals are found associated with Clovis sites, they are often mammoths, with large bison being the second most associated animal (C. V. Haynes 1993:219). In eastern North America, there is little evidence of big game (e.g., mammoths and bison) and less evidence of big-game hunting during Clovis times (Lepper 1999:378), although such evidence is present at a few sites, such as the Page-Ladson site in Florida (Milanich 1994:47; Purdy 2008).

Environment During Clovis Times

Clovis sites and technology appear immediately after the glaciers began to retreat, presumably the result of people moving south from Beringia as the climate warmed. It is generally thought that Clovis people encountered an environment that was generally cooler and wetter than today.

There is reason to believe that by the time Clovis groups were able to move south past the ice sheets (after about 14,700 years ago), the climate was warmer and drier than it is today and that drought conditions, known as the "Clovis Drought," prevailed (C. V. Haynes 1991, 1993:232; 1999a). Such a drought is not apparent on the southern Plains (Holliday 1997:179, 212) and may have been limited to western North America. This drought may also have had a negative impact on megafauna populations.

At the end of Clovis times, glacial conditions briefly returned during the environmental episode known as the Younger Dryas, at which time the climate became colder and wetter. By that time, many of the large animals hunted by Clovis people had become extinct. Over the next several thousand years, the climate generally became warmer again, and Clovis was replaced by a variety of other Paleoindian groups and adaptations.

Clovis Technology

Clovis technology is very sophisticated and specialized and has no antecedent in the known archaeological record of North America south of the ice sheets, not even in purported pre-Clovis sites (although some see such an antecedent in the Cactus Hill material). Some scholars believe that the Nenana Complex of eastern Alaska is related to Clovis (Hamilton and Goebel 1999:156; Hoffecker 2001). Clovis stone technology is based on the production of blades and flakes for scrapers and gravers and the reduction of bifacial cores for the manufacture of fluted Clovis points (Wilke et al. 1991:245). Other Clovis artifacts include some bone tools, including "wrenches" (perhaps used as shaft-straighteners) and beveled tools used as levers (Lyman et al. 1998), points (Waters et al. 2009), or perhaps foreshafts.

The most sophisticated aspect of Clovis technology is the stone projectile points, particularly the fluting (the removal of channel flakes up the length of the point). The process of fluting is very difficult, and Clovis flintknappers were quite skilled. Once made, the edges along the lower third of the points were typically dulled by grinding, either to strengthen the point base (Titmus and Woods 1991a) or so that sinew used in hafting would not be cut by the edge of the point. Sometimes, the flute scars were scratched, perhaps to increase the efficacy of a hafting adhesive (J. L. Fagan 1984). Fluting made the points thinner, which is thought to have facilitated thrusting between the ribs of large animals. As these large Pleistocene animals became extinct, the need for these specialized tools may have declined, resulting in the "loss" of the sophisticated fluting technology.

Clovis lithic technology shows "a surprising degree of similarity" across North America, "enough to imply considerable historical relatedness" (M. B. Collins 1999b:179), suggesting, based on stone technology, that Clovis was a single entity, although perishable technologies could illuminate greater variability (Lepper 1999:371). There is some broad regional variation in the morphology of large fluted points, with the "classic" parallel-sided Clovis point being called "Western Clovis."

In eastern North America, many of the large fluted points, casually referred to as Clovis, differ from the classic Western Clovis forms in their morphology in that the lower portion of the points are more narrow and their basal indentations are deeper (Goodyear 1999:437). As such, it is possible that the eastern fluted points may date slightly later in time than Western Clovis (Haynes et al. 1984:186; Goodyear 1999:437). This imprecise classification has undoubtedly camouflaged regional technological variations (e.g., Stanford et al. 1999; Tankersley et al. 1999), or even small, separate migrations (Meltzer 1989:484). These morphological and chronological differences between eastern and western forms greatly weaken the argument that Clovis originated in the Southeast (Goodyear 1999:437).

The study of Clovis technology and organization has benefitted from the discovery of perhaps two dozen caches of Clovis materials from the Plains and the Rocky Mountains, including points, bifaces, bone tools, and raw materials. For example, the Anzick site in Montana (Lahren and Bonnichsen 1974; Wilke et al. 1991; Morrow and Fiedel 2006) contained 115 artifacts, including eight finished fluted points, 84 preform blanks and cores, 6 beveled bone tools, and a human burial, dated to about 12,900 years ago (Morrow and Fiedel 2006: Table 7.3). The Richey-Roberts Cache in Washington (Gramly 1993) contained beveled bone tools and many complete, and some very large Clovis points. Unlike the Anzick site, the tools from the Richey-Roberts cache appear to have been used prior to their caching. The Fenn cache, found in the northwestern Plains (Frison and Bradley 1999), contained some 56 artifacts, including numerous points and bifaces (see some of the artifacts at www.pbs.org/wgbh/nova/stoneage/fenn.html). It seems that the many caches represent storage of materials by Clovis people who had been around awhile, knew their landscapes, and expected to return (Kilby and Huckell 2003:7), or were new to the area and were using caches to symbolically transform an unknown landscape into a known one (Gillespie 2007). Ritual behavior is indicated by the discovery of a cache at the Crowfield Early Paleoindian site in southwestern Ontario (Deller et al. 2009). Here, some 182 usable tools appear to have been purposefully destroyed and burned, suggesting some sort of ceremonial behavior (also see Deller and Ellis 2001).

Clovis people went to great lengths to obtain high-quality stone for their points, and specific sources of raw material may have been very important to individual groups of people. The distribution of these raw materials appears to be geographically limited, and it has been suggested that the territories of Clovis groups were defined by the location of quarries (e.g., Jones et al. 2003).

Clovis Adaptations

Clovis is known primarily from sites where animals were killed and butchered (kill sites), so there is relatively little information regarding other aspects of Clovis settlement and subsistence systems. Only a few Clovis camp sites are known, as are the locations of some Clovis-era stone quarries. In addition, several dozen Clovis caches have been found (see above). Kelly and Todd (1988; also see Amick 1996; Tankersley 1998) suggested that Clovis and other Paleoindian groups utilized the land differently than later hunter-gatherers, being more mobile, with larger territories, and movement of entire populations rather than task groups. This would have enabled them able to travel to entirely new areas, increasing their flexibility in times of resource stress.

Clovis kill sites tend to be located in marsh-like areas, perhaps where trapping mammoths was easier (although better preservation in marshes may mean that kill sites in other areas have not been found yet). Thus, there is an association between Clovis and wetland habitats (Grayson 1991; Stanford 1999:281), with water being a key resource (Boldurian and Cotter 1999:115). At these sites, mammoths and large bison appear to have been the major animals exploited. This pattern of Clovis sites in association with kills of large game (mammoths and large bison) has led to the belief that Clovis people had a specialized economy that emphasized big-game hunting. Grayson and Meltzer (2002:348; also see Cannon and Meltzer 2004) argued that there were actually relatively few Clovis sites with unambiguous associations with mammoths, suggesting that "big-game hunting" was actually a minor activity. An analysis of the faunal remains from sixty Paleoindian sites (not limited to Clovis) showed that the species represented at a site were dependent on a variety of factors, including site function (kill vs. camp) and location (grasslands vs. valleys) and generally showed generalized Paleoindian hunting (M. E. Hill 2007).

The few Clovis camps that are known are located in relatively close proximity to kill sites. The Murray Springs Clovis site in Arizona (Fig. 3.1) (Haynes and Huckell 2007) included a mammoth kill and butchering locality in association with a small camp located near a spring. The camp included a Clovis "living floor" with discrete distributions of bones, tools, and other debris. The Gault site in central Texas (Fig. 3.1) (Collins 2002) is an extensive camp and workshop (containing deposits dating from the Late Pleistocene to the Late Prehistoric) situated near springs and a small stream. The remains of mammoths, bison, and horse were found in association with many tools, including Clovis points. In addition, a number of small engraved limestone rocks were also found, providing some insight into Clovis-era expressive culture.

Were Clovis people "big-game hunters" who made a living primarily by hunting mammoths and large bison and driving them to extinction? There is no doubt that Clovis groups utilized big game, but it is also clear that other game was used as well, including deer, rabbit (Gramly 1991: Table 1), and horses (Kooyman et al. 2001, 2006). Some large animals may have been scavenged but others were clearly hunted and killed (Haynes 2002b:396).

Some twenty-five to thirty Clovis kill sites have so far been found, mostly on the Plains and in the Southwest, with little evidence of big-game exploitation east of the Mississippi River. Some scholars (e.g., Meltzer 1993b:305; Cannon and Meltzer 2004) have found no convincing evidence that Clovis people were "specialized big-game hunters," while others (e.g., Waguespack and Surovell 2003; Surovell and Waguespack 2009) argued that they were. It is clear that Clovis people hunted big game, but it is uncertain whether they were specialists in big game.

Meltzer (1993b:305) suggested that Clovis people may have had a generalized economy but took large animals when the opportunity arose, although the opposite may also be possible; a focus on big game and the taking of small game on an opportunistic basis (T. Goebel, personal communication 2004). Clovis people on the southern Plains may have practiced a "broad-spectrum, meat-related," opportunistic foraging pattern (E. Johnson 1991:215), although there are few data on residential or plant procurement/processing sites. Fiedel (2005b) suggested that Clovis people utilized dogs in hunting and as emergency food.

Virtually nothing is known about the use of plants by Clovis people, although plant foods must have played an important role in Paleoindian economies (Dillehay and Rossen 2002). An exception is at the Shawnee Minisink site in Pennsylvania (McNett 1986), where some plant remains, including seeds, plums, and berries, have been recovered.

Our knowledge of the use of plant resources during Clovis times is poor due to several factors: (1) the lack of dated sites other than kill sites, (2) the possibility that plants that did not require processing were used, (3) the possibility that plant processing tools have gone unrecognized, (4) the poor preservation of botanical remains from Clovis sites, and (5) the ongoing assumption that Paleoindians were big-game hunters, with sites having plant processing technology automatically considered to be later in time.

In North America west of the Rocky Mountains, most Clovis materials are surface finds and poorly dated. They are found in a wide variety of environmental settings (Willig 1991, 1996:242; Erlandson and Moss 1996:282), however, suggesting a diversity of adaptations. The general lack of kill sites and the association of many sites with lake and marsh habitats (Willig 1996:242) suggest that the subsistence system was generalized, with exploitation of an assortment of game (e.g., birds, fish, plants, large and small mammals) rather than "megafauna."

Relatively few sites containing Western Clovis materials have been found in the east, suggesting that the Paleoindian materials in the east are later than Western Clovis and that the occupation of the east before about 12,900 years ago was limited (see Curran 1996). Thus, it seems probable that Clovis people entered eastern North America from the west and then moved north and northeast as the ice retreated (Curran 1999:7).

Few data are available regarding the social and political aspects of Clovis groups. The assumption is that they were highly mobile and operated as bands. The patterns of raw material acquisition and use suggest the presence of large group territories. Little is known about Clovis expressive culture, other than the presence of crosshatching on some bone tools, engraving on some stones at the Gault site in Texas (Collins 2002), and the common use of red ochre, thought to reflect some ceremonial function (Roper 1996).

Very few human remains of Clovis age have been found. A partial skeleton of an infant was discovered at the Anzick site in Montana, associated with a cache of Clovis artifacts (Lahren and Bonnichsen 1974; Jones and Bonnichsen 1994; also see Wilke et al. 1991; Morrow and Fiedel 2006). The infant, whose skull was stained with red ochre, was dated to about 12,900 years ago. An analysis of the isotopes in the bone of the infant suggested a diet consistent with mammoth and other animals (but not bison) (Morrow and Fiedel 2006:136).

Another burial dating to Clovis times is the Buhl woman, dated to about 12,500 years ago (Green et al. 1998). This was the primary interment of a 17- to 21-year-old female accompanied by a large stemmed biface, an eyed bone needle, and another bone implement of unknown function. Isotopic analysis suggested that the woman had a diet dominated by terrestrial animals and fish (Green et al. 1998:451; also see Yohe and Woods 2002:21).

HIGHLIGHT 3.1

COMET! A CLOVIS KILLER?

The cause(s) of the extinction of the Pleistocene megafauna, whether by humans or by changing climate, has been hotly debated (see discussions in G. Haynes [2009] and Meltzer [2009]). Many researchers think that environmental condition changes so radically at the end of the Pleistocene that the megafauna could not adjust and so went extinct. Others have posited that Clovis hunters drove the megafauna to extinction then had to adapt to their absence, evolving into later Paleoindian groups. Either way, the megafauna and Clovis hunters disappeared.

However, a new theory has been proposed (Firestone et al. 2007): that a comet impacted just to the north of the Great Lakes region in North America about 12,900 BP. This event, the theory suggests, caused such damage, including continent-wide fires, that many species were wiped out, along with most Clovis people. The resulting "nuclear winter," the argument goes, would have initiated the Younger Dryas, the brief return to glacial conditions, and killed the megafauna and the Clovis people hunting them.

Interestingly, a layer of unknown dark material ("black mats") has long been observed in many Clovis sites, all dating to about the same time as the proposed comet impact (e.g., C. V. Haynes 2008), and containing iridium (found in comets and meteors), lending some support to the idea of impact and resulting fires. Further support for the idea came from stratigraphic data that suggested that most Clovis sites were abandoned at this same basic time and not reoccupied (Kennett and West 2008). However, an analysis of some 1,500 radiocarbon dates from Paleoindian sites (Buchanan et al. 2008) revealed no evidence of a drop in Paleoindian population at 12,900 BP. In addition, Kennett et al. (2009) reported the presence of abundant nanodiamonds, touted as clear evidence of an impact, in soil layers dating to the beginning of the Younger Dryas. Most recently, the evidence for such an impact was reexamined but failed to support the idea (Surovell et al. 2009).

This is an extraordinary claim and will require extraordinary evidence (see Meltzer 2009:55–58) to be convincing. The geological work on this has only just begun, not to mention the archaeological work. It is, however, intriguing and could result in a paradigm shift in Paleoindian studies.

LATER PALEOINDIAN CULTURES

After about 12,900 years ago, classic Clovis disappeared and a variety of new Paleoindian "cultures" appeared, each defined by a new type of projectile point. Each of these Paleoindian entities occupied a much more limited geographic space, but most appear to share some Clovis ancestry. It may be that Clovis was specially adapted for hunting megafauna, and with their demise, regional cultures evolved to their specific regional habitats, each with a slightly different technology and settlement/subsistence pattern.

A Paleocoastal Tradition?

Along the western coast of North America, the earliest sites are slightly later than Clovis but do not share any Clovis traits. These occupations, classified as part of a Paleocoastal Tradition (Moratto 1984:104–109), generally date between 12,000 and 10,000 BP and reflect a maritime orientation. So far, they have been found along the central California coast and on the Channel Islands of Southern California. It is possible that many other such sites were drowned by rising sea levels. Virtually nothing is known about the settlement and subsistence systems of these groups, although it appears that shellfish were a major dietary constituent (Porcasi 2008).

Sites known to date to this time include Daisy Cave (Erlandson et al. 1996), Arlington Springs (Johnson et al. 2002), Cross Creek (Jones et al. 2002; 2008a), and Arlington Point (Erlandson et al. 1999). People at these sites were exploiting a variety of marine resources, such as shellfish, fish, and marine mammals. Further, it has been argued that there is evidence of boat technology from the Eel Point site in that same area dating from ca. 8,000 years ago (Cassidy et al. 2004:109; Raab and Cassidy 2009), and possibly earlier elsewhere (Erlandson and Moss 1996:295).

It seems possible that this Paleocoastal Tradition reflects the hypothesized coastal migration as one of the initial entries of people into North America. In this scenario, Clovis groups would have come south at roughly the same time, but using an interior route and with a completely different adaptation (see Jones et al. 2002).

Paleoindians in Western North America

An extensive system of lakes was present in western North America at the end of the Pleistocene, and many of the higher mountains contained glaciers. As the climate warmed, the glaciers melted and the lake systems began to dry, disappearing by about 9,000 years ago, and much of the interior of western North America became a desert. Sea levels rose during this same time, and much of the exposed coastal plain was flooded.

Of note are the periodic filling and draining of several huge lakes formed by dams of glacial ice. Lake Agassiz covered some 250,000 square miles of the northern Plains region and drained and refilled several times as glaciers advanced and retreated (see Teller and Clayton 1983). At various times, the lake drained east through the Great Lakes or south through the Mississippi River. The lake reached its maximum size about 10,000 years ago and then catastrophically flooded east into the Lake Superior basin. The lake finally disappeared by about 7,500 BP. Another major flood occurred in the Plateau region when glacial Lake Missoula burst through its ice dam and suddenly released some 500 cubic miles of water into the Columbia River, scouring the landscape to the Pacific Ocean (see Highlight 6.2).

In western North America, the Clovis complex (called Western Clovis) was followed by the Western Stemmed Point Tradition, a collection of cultural complexes characterized by crescents and large stemmed, shouldered, and lanceolate points (Willig and Aikens 1988:3). The Western Stemmed Point Tradition, sometimes called the Western Pluvial Lakes Tradition (WPLT; Bedwell 1973; also see T. R. Hester 1973:62–68), generally dates between 11,000 and 9,000 years ago. Most believe that the Western Stemmed Point Tradition is later than Clovis, but others (e.g., Bryan 1988) have argued that stemmed point complexes are at least as old, or even older (Beck and Jones 2010). Western Stemmed point types (Fig. 3.2) include the Windust and Haskett types in the north and the Lake Mojave type in the south. These forms generally date beginning about 11,000 years ago, but some have argued that the Lake Mojave type may be as old as 12,000 years ago (Warren and Crabtree 1986:184).

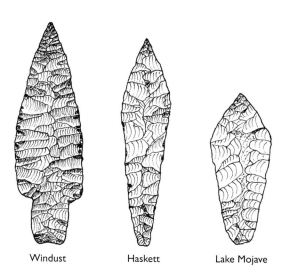

Windust   Haskett   Lake Mojave

FIGURE 3.2 Generalized views of Western Stemmed projectile point types (the longest of the points illustrated here is about 8 cm), drawing by the author.

Materials belonging to the WPLT are commonly associated with lakes or other wetland areas. Some believe that the WPLT should include both fluted and stemmed point forms because they are both found in association with lakes (see Willig and Aikens 1988:28–30), although it seems more likely that the two form a historical continuum (Moratto 1984:103; Basgall and Hall 1991:63; but see Beck and Jones 2010). In Idaho, a Folsom component was found at Owl Cave (S. J. Miller 1982), and some lanceolate point forms are also known (Yohe and Woods 2002), but these occurrences appear related to the Plains rather than the WPLT.

Prior to about 9,000 years ago, western North America was cooler and wetter, with extensive lakes. The correlation of the WPLT materials with mesic habitats suggests a subsistence system that included a breadth of resources from lake margins, such as fish, shellfish, and small game. There is very little evidence of the exploitation of large game during this time, although it is possible that bison were hunted by WPLT people at Tulare Lake in central California (G. L. Fenenga 1991:20).

Paleoindians on the Plains

The best known Paleoindian sequence is from the Plains and Southwest of interior North America. Paleoindian material from the southern Plains has been discussed by V. T. Holliday (1997), from the northern Plains by Frison (1991; also see Kornfeld et al. 2009), and in general by Hofman and Graham (1998; also see J. V. Wright 1995). Clovis ended as the climate returned to glacial conditions (the Younger Dryas), which was a time of considerable environmental change. Ice cores from Greenland now suggest that there was an abrupt warming of the climate at the end of the Pleistocene, perhaps occurring within twenty to fifty years. This would have entailed huge ecological changes, requiring major and rapid cultural changes. However, a new study (Meltzer and Holliday 2010) suggested that climate may not have changed too much on the Plains and that the impact of the Younger Dryas in that region may have been relatively minor.

For the Plains and Southwest, post-Clovis Paleoindian complexes are grouped under "Late Paleoindian," and four major Late Paleoindian complexes, Folsom, Midland, Plano, and Cody, have been defined for the Plains (following Hofman and Graham 1998). A fifth complex, Goshen, has been problematic. Goshen points are very much like Clovis points but are basally thinned, not fluted, and poorly dated. This raises three possibilities: (1) Goshen is slightly earlier than Clovis and is the elusive antecedent, (2) Goshen should be included in Clovis and not considered a separate entity, or (3) Goshen represents a transition from Clovis to Folsom (see Frison 1991, 1999:274–275; Hofman and Graham 1988:96–97; Fiedel 1999a:104).

THE FOLSOM COMPLEX   The Folsom Complex is identified by its characteristic fluted projectile point, smaller and more finely flaked than Clovis. Folsom points were first discovered in 1926 at a site near Folsom, New Mexico (Figgins 1927; also see Meltzer 2006), in direct association with the remains of extinct bison (Fig. 3.3). This discovery finally convinced most archaeologists that people were present in North America during the Pleistocene.

Folsom is slightly younger than Clovis, dating between about 12,900 and 12,200 years ago, although there is some overlap with Clovis in radiocarbon time (Holliday 1997:175; also see C. V. Haynes 1993). Folsom is the only Late Paleoindian culture on the Plains to retain fluting technology, so it seems clear that Folsom is a direct descendent of Clovis. It is thought that the transition from Clovis to Folsom took place rapidly, perhaps within about 100 years (C. V. Haynes 1993:233; R. E. Taylor et al. 1996:524) during a time of drought, at least in Arizona (C. V. Haynes 1993:233–234).

FIGURE 3.3 Folsom point discovered lodged in the ribs of an extinct bison at the Folsom site in 1926. (*Source:* Denver Museum of Nature and Science.)

Folsom technology includes small, fluted points (with a flute that typically covers most of the point), bifacial cores, bifacial knives, end scrapers, and gravers (Amick 1999a; also see Meltzer 2006:247–294). Bone needles and beads are also associated with Folsom technology (Hofman et al. 2000). Folsom use of lithic resources may have been more efficient than Clovis, as tools were apparently repaired and rejuvenated rather than just replaced with new tools (and stone) (Boldurian and Cotter 1999:116). Folsom points appear to have been made from high-quality, nonlocal stone, while other stone tools were made from lower quality, local stone (Amick 1999b:181). Bamforth (2002) argued that these patterns are unsupported by the evidence to date and that Late Paleoindian adaptations were highly variable on the Plains.

Most Folsom sites have been found on the grasslands of the Plains, which is bison (*Bison antiquus occidentalis*) habitat. A few Folsom points have been found east of the Mississippi River but still within bison habitat at that time (Munson 1990). Folsom occurred during the Younger Dryas, a time when the climate briefly returned to glacial conditions, and may have been an "ecological replacement" of Clovis (Boldurian and Cotter 1999:116), with bison replacing mammoths as the primary megafauna game animal. The bison during Folsom times were probably smaller than those of Clovis times (Frison 1991:273).

Like Clovis, Folsom is known primarily from kill sites with associated camp sites (such as the Folsom type site; Meltzer et al. 2002; Meltzer 2006), and few habitation or other types of sites are known. The organization of the known Folsom camps, such as location of food processing, weapon manufacture, and tool maintenance, suggests a general division of labor based on sex and age (Amick 1999b:181; also see Chilton 2005a; Stiger 2006).

The Folsom economy appears to have been focused on communal bison hunting, the same basic system used on the Plains until horses were introduced about three hundred years ago. It seems apparent that Folsom hunters were well organized, had a good knowledge of the terrain, and hunted both all-male and mixed-sex bison herds (McCartney 1990). Bison were generally taken communally throughout most of the year, by driving the animals into arroyos or washes (Todd et al. 1990; Todd 1991). In addition to meat, other edible materials may have been obtained from the stomach contents of bison (Todd 1991:238). These data suggest that storage was not an important aspect of bison utilization (McCartney 1990:119), although Frison (1999:273) believed it likely that cold storage of meat was practiced. In some cases, Folsom hunters killed more animals than they could butcher, not a very "ecological" approach.

While it is clear that Folsom groups hunted bison, they also utilized a diversity of other game, including camels and numerous small animals (Wilmsen and Roberts 1978). Folsom groups probably practiced a pattern of broad-spectrum foraging (Kornfeld 2002) and likely were very mobile with large territories. In spite of this broad economy, Folsom groups may have been dependent on bison herds and may have followed them on their seasonal migrations (Amick 1996:411), with entire groups of people moving from "one kill episode to another" (Hofman 2002:408).

Little is known about Folsom social structure and behavior. Some researchers think that social complexity should have increased from Clovis to Folsom (due to greater specialization toward bison in hunting) and decreased subsequent to Folsom as animal populations became extinct and people were forced to spread out (e.g., Bamforth 1988). Douglas MacDonald (1998) proposed that Folsom groups had small populations, were widely dispersed, highly mobile, and probably had more males than females. This was based on an assumption that bison was the primary resource (and so required more males for hunting) and the "uniform nature of the Folsom toolkit across the Plains" (MacDonald 1998:217). Hints of Folsom ritual behavior are present in a painted bison skull, purposeful piles of bison bones, concentrations of bison skulls, and the use of red ochre (Hofman 2002:409–411).

THE MIDLAND COMPLEX   The Midland Complex was first identified at the Midland site in Texas (Wendorf et al. 1955). Unfluted lanceolate Midland points (see Fig. 3.4) were discovered with a burial thought to precede Folsom. Reanalysis of the stratigraphy suggested that Midland was contemporary with or perhaps slightly younger than Folsom (Holliday and Meltzer 1996:755; Holliday 1997:189). Midland and Folsom are often found together, and it is possible that Midland is an unfluted variant of the Folsom Complex (Hofman and Graham 1998:102). On the other hand, it is possible that Midland is roughly contemporaneous with Folsom and represents a separate group with a similar bison-based economy.

THE PLANO COMPLEX   The Plano Complex represents a series of clearly post-Folsom, Late Paleoindian groups "that had an economic focus during most of the year on bison hunting" (Hofman and Graham 1998:103). These groups are identified by their distinctive unfluted, lanceolate points, including Plainview, Agate Basin, and Hell Gap types (see Fig. 3.4), and generally date between 12,200 and 10,000 years ago.

Plainview is identified by its large, lanceolate point, similar in shape to Clovis but unfluted. Plainview generally dates to about 12,000 years ago (Holliday et al. 1999:444) or a bit earlier (Stanford 1999:310). Frison (1999:275) argued that Plainview points were indistinguishable from Goshen points on the northern Plains and therefore overlapped Clovis in time. Stanford (1999:310) thought that Goshen might be a bit earlier in the north and Plainview a bit later in the south. Thus, the nature and dating of Plainview remains uncertain.

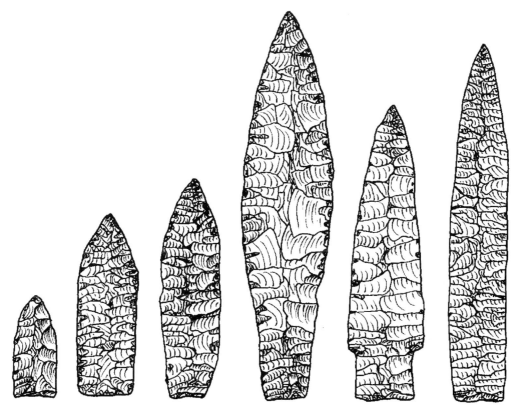

FIGURE 3.4 Generalized views of the projectile points of the Midland, Plano (Plainview, Agate Basin, and Hell Gap), and Cody (Scottsbluff and Eden) complexes (the longest of the points is about 14 cm).

Agate Basin is distinguished by its long, thin lanceolate points dating between about 12,500 and 12,250 years ago (Stanford 1999:312). Excavations at the Agate Basin site (Frison and Stanford 1982) revealed a bison kill locality and associated camp. Agate Basin seems to have developed directly out of Folsom (Frison 1999:276), although the number of bison in the kill sites is greater than Folsom (Stanford 1999:313). The climate during Agate Basin times was somewhat drier than during Folsom times, and Agate Basin people may have moved from the Plains proper to occupy foothill and riverine environments (Stanford 1999:281).

Hell Gap is identified by its stemmed, lanceolate, and broad-bladed points (Stanford 1999:316; also see Larson et al. 2009). Hell Gap dates between 12,000 and 11,500 years ago. Hell Gap is mostly known from the central and northern Plains and probably developed from Agate Basin (Frison 1999:276). Bison hunting was important in Hell Gap times, and communal hunting on a scale larger than other Paleoindian groups took place (Stanford 1999:316).

THE CODY COMPLEX The Cody Complex is characterized by its lanceolate projectile points that have stems, square bases, or both (Stanford 1999:319) and often have parallel flaking patterns (see Fig. 3.4). The points known as Scottsbluff, Eden, and others are included in the Cody Complex. Further, the distinctive "Cody knife" forms a part of the complex. The Cody Complex generally dates between about 12,000 and 10,800 years ago. Environmental conditions at that time seem to have been cooler and wetter, increasing grassland productivity, bison populations, and human carrying capacity (Stanford 1999:325). It seems that by 10,000 years ago, subsistence strategies were different in the mountains than they were on the open Plains, with deer, sheep, and different botanical resources being more important in the mountains and bison on the Plains (Frison and Bonnichsen 1996:306). Indeed, a large net probably used to procure deer-sized game was found in the mountains of Wyoming, dating to about 10,860 years ago (Frison et al. 1986). By the end of Cody times, ca. 8,000 years ago, bison populations may have declined, perhaps due to the effects of the Altithermal, to the point that they were no longer a reliable resource (Frison and Bonnichesen 1996:309).

The Olsen-Chubbock site in Colorado (Wheat 1972) is a typical Cody Complex bison kill site. At this site, a large number of bison (*Bison antiquus occidentalis*) were stampeded into an arroyo, where they were killed and butchered, although many of the animals at the bottom of the pile were not even touched (Fig. 3.5). Numerous Scottsbluff and Eden points were found among the bones, along with debris from processing the animals, manufacturing new tools, and resharpening old tools.

Paleoindians in Eastern North America

In eastern North America, the Paleoindian Period is generally divided into Early, Middle, and Late Paleoindian (Bense 1994; D. G. Anderson 1995a; Goodyear 1999:439), although these divisions

FIGURE 3.5 The remains of bison driven into an arroyo at the Olsen-Chubbock site. (*Source:* University of Colorado Museum, Joe Ben Wheat Photo.)

are problematic (Morse et al. 1996:327). Early Paleoindian, essentially Western Clovis, is relatively rare in eastern North America and was discussed above. Middle Paleoindian is characterized by post-Western Clovis fluted points, and Late Paleoindian is characterized by lanceolate and stemmed point forms.

In the northeast, the ice sheets extended well into the United States at the glacial maximum. Biotic communities just south of the ice sheets probably consisted of belts of tundra-like spruce parklands, conifer forests, and deciduous forests. As the ice began to retreat, these biotic communities began to shift northward. In the Southeast, biotic communities some 10,000 years ago looked much the same as they do today, with forests of oak, hickory, southern pine, and cypress (Ellis et al. 1998:154).

In general, Paleoindian adaptations in the spruce parklands of the north is very poorly known (Carr et al. 2001:86) but may have focused on caribou (Meltzer 1988) or on lowland, postglacial wetland resources (Smith and Laub 2000). The adaptation in the forests to the south was probably more generalized (Meltzer 1988), although game animals may have been scarce, which may have made occupation difficult and may explain why relatively few sites have been found (Fitting 1968; Ritchie 1980). Paleoindians may have been opportunistic, generalized hunters, sometimes hunting megafauna and other times the more familiar species, perhaps deer in the eastern forests and caribou in the northeast (Butzer 1991:140).

In Florida, research indicates that it may have been drier than it is today, perhaps evidence of the "Clovis Drought" in the east. Such conditions would have reduced the number of freshwater sources, making them more critical to both animals and humans. Paleoindian settlement and subsistence systems may have been centered on these "oases" (Neill 1964:17; also see Milanich 1994:40–44; Goodyear 1999:444; also see Purdy 2008). For example, many of the Paleoindian points from Florida have been recovered from areas where such water sources would have been present (Dunbar and Waller 1983:28). Anderson and Faught (2000) suggested that distinct cultural traditions, reflected by regional fluted point styles, emerged in the Southeast at the onset of the Younger Dryas, linking the development of Paleoindian cultures to environmental change.

While classic Western Clovis materials are rare in the east, post-Clovis Paleoindian materials are more common but remain poorly defined and dated (Curran 1996, 1999:6). This Middle Paleoindian Period (ca. 12,900 to 12,500 years ago; Goodyear 1999:439) is characterized by the presence of large fluted points that differ from Clovis by having more waisted bases and deep basal indentations (Goodyear 1999:437). These point types are called a variety of names, including Gainey and Bull Brook in the Northeast, and Cumberland, Ross County, Suwannee, and Redstone in the Southeast.

Many sites dating to Middle Paleoindian times are known in eastern North America and include quarries, habitation sites, kill sites, and caches (Gramly and Funk 1990). Kill sites are rare, but several are large enough to suggest that they were also habitation sites (Curran 1999:4). Based on this, Dincauze (1993:45) proposed that such "big residential" sites served as centers for the early colonization of the region. Encampments such as Debert, Nova Scotia (MacDonald 1968); Vail, Maine (Gramly 1982); and Lamb, New York (Gramly 1999), may be examples of such centers

Middle Paleoindian subsistence in eastern North America was highly variable and included the use of caribou (in the north), deer, hare, fox, fish, and many other species (see Ellis et al. 1998:157–158; Lepper 1999:376). This economic variability may reflect the flexibility of pioneers who took advantage of the many opportunities that were available (Tankersley 1998; Curran 1999:21). The distribution of fluted points in the east, generally in discrete sites in the Northeast and as isolated finds (e.g., Suwannee points) in the Southeast, may reflect environmental variability and regional adaptations (Lepper 1999:362) as well as lithic procurement activities (Tankersley 1995). There is little evidence to suggest that Middle Paleoindian people were specialized hunters, but rather were broad-spectrum generalists (Lepper 1999:378).

The Late Paleoindian Period (ca. 12,500 to 11,900 years ago; Goodyear 1999:440) is characterized by various lanceolate and stemmed point forms. These points are known by a variety of names, including Dalton, Holcombe, Simpson, and Quad (Ellis et al. 1998; Goodyear 1999). Points very similar to those of the Plano and Cody complexes on the Plains are also known (Ellis et al. 1998:Table 1). Dalton is the earliest, most recognized, and widespread of the Late Paleoindian complexes in the east, being represented by almost 1,000 sites (Tuck 1974; McNutt 1996:190; Morse et al. 1996:328; Goodyear 1999). Dalton is also known as Hi-Lo in the Great Lakes region (Stothers and Abel 1991:206; also see L. J. Jackson 2006b; Ellis 2006) and is not contemporaneous with the notched points of the Archaic. The Late Paleoindian Period is the time of the transition between Pleistocene and Holocene environments (Goodyear 1982:392) throughout North America.

THE TRANSITION TO THE ARCHAIC

The Paleoindian Period is generally characterized by the exploitation of extinct megafauna (e.g., mammoths) with a specialized technology (e.g., fluted points). By contrast, the Archaic is viewed as a time when hunter-gatherers practiced a generalized economy. More recent interpretations of Paleoindian subsistence systems (see above) have suggested that Paleoindian adaptation during the Late Pleistocene was very similar to that of the Early Archaic, except that Paleoindians utilized megafauna, whereas the Archaic peoples did not. With the extinction of the megafauna, along with the associated procurement and processing technologies, the adaptation became Archaic, even though the remaining large mammal species were still utilized. Thus, the change from Paleoindian to Archaic economies may reflect merely the loss of megafauna and not a fundamental change in basic economy.

There are some substantial changes that did occur between the Paleoindian and Archaic (Pleistocene/Holocene) times. The climate warmed during the Anathermal (a general period of warming between about 9,000 and 7,000 years ago), resulting in many biotic alterations, such as shifts in the composition and extent of forests, loss of lake systems in the west, rising sea levels, and more. Clearly, Paleoindians had to adapt quickly to such changes, and cultural alterations are evident in the archaeological record. In addition to the obvious changes in projectile point types, artifact assemblages became more diverse and generalized, implying a shift to more broadly based economies. Settlement patterns also changed with people becoming less mobile. Many of the sites throughout North America that contain long records of occupation were inhabited for the first time during the Early Holocene. Populations undoubtedly increased and group territories became more established. The stage was set for the development of the many diverse societies of prehistoric North America.

NEW MIGRATIONS

After the initial migrations of Paleoindians into North America, the Na-Dene and Eskimo/Aleut groups moved into eastern Alaska, probably during the Pleistocene (see Chapter 2). Beginning about 8,000 or 9,000 years ago, the ancestors of the Na-Dene (or Athapaskan) began to move into the previously glaciated Northwest Coast (see Chapter 5) and the western Subarctic (western Canada, see Chapter 13). The eastern portion of the previously glaciated Subarctic (eastern Canada) was occupied at about the same time by Algonquian people moving north from the region of what is now the eastern United States (see Chapter 11).

The Eskimo/Aleut had probably moved into southeastern Alaska during the Early Holocene. The Aleut remained in place, but the Eskimo (the Inuit and Yupik), using a new and sophisticated technology for living in cold climates, moved north to occupy the rest of Alaska (see Chapter 4). Beginning about 4,500 years ago, Paleoarctic groups began moving east and occupied most of the central and eastern Arctic. Sometime after about 1,000 BP, the Inuit moved east, replaced the earlier groups, and eventually occupied Greenland.

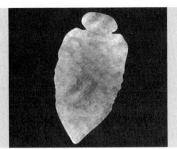

4

Whales and Sleds
The Arctic

To most, the Arctic appears to be a cold and forbidding place with little to offer. Yet it has been occupied since the beginning of North American prehistory by highly skilled peoples able to devise a living with seemingly few resources. Thus, it is a fascinating place where people's spirit, ingenuity, and persistence forged successful adaptations in a difficult environment. In fact, many native peoples, some practicing traditional lifestyles, still persist in the region.

A number of different prehistoric cultural traditions are known in the Arctic, suggesting that different adaptations had been used at different times with different results. In the rather inhospitable region of the eastern Arctic, "peoples and cultures not only survived, but in many cases flourished for 4000 years . . . [and] created highly distinctive regional cultures" (W. W. Fitzhugh 1997:386). Given the extreme conditions and problems of this region, the "occupation of the Arctic is one of the most spectacular achievements of the human species" (Rowley-Conwy 1999:349) and is of great anthropological and archaeological interest.

GEOGRAPHY AND ENVIRONMENT

The North American Arctic (Fig. 4.1) covers about 2 million square miles (see Chester and Oetzel [1998] for a good overview of the geography of the North American Arctic; other Arctic environments are present in Asia and Europe). In general, the Arctic is cold, has relatively little free-flowing water, and has few plants. The region is dominated by the Arctic Ocean to the north, the Bering Strait between Alaska and Asia, and the Bering Sea to the south. The Arctic Ocean has many other named seas, bays, straits, and inlets, as well as many islands (collectively called the Arctic Archipelago), the largest being Greenland. The ocean water is usually subfreezing, but fish and sea mammals are abundant.

Four major geographic regions are defined for the Arctic. The Canadian Shield, which consists mostly of exposed granite bedrock with few hills or mountains, encompasses much of the eastern Arctic to Greenland, and much of it is covered with ice. Several large mountain ranges, such as the Brooks Range in northern Alaska, dominate the western Arctic. The Arctic coastal

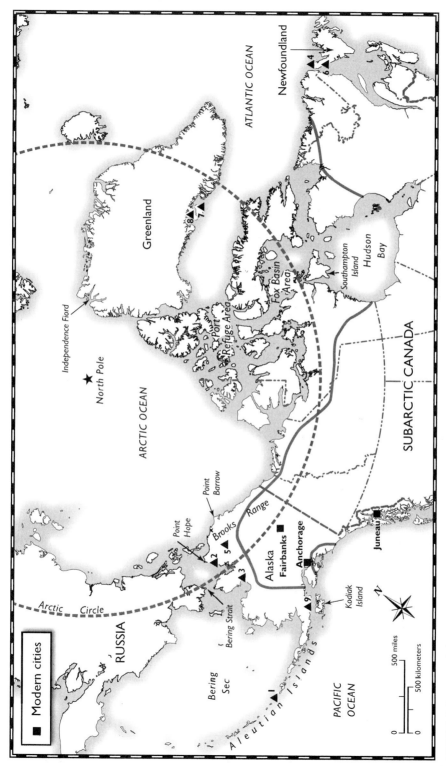

FIGURE 4.1 Map of the Arctic region and the location of places and sites discussed in the text: 1) Anangula; 2) Cape Krusenstern; 3) Denbigh; 4) L'Anse aux Meadows; 5) Onion Portage; 6) Port au Choix; 7) Qeqertasussuk; 8) Qilakitsoq; 9) Ugashik Narrows.

plain stretches from northwestern Alaska east to western Canada. The Aleutian Islands, a series of island chains, run west from southwestern Alaska almost to Asia.

The Arctic receives low levels of solar radiation, much of which is reflected by snow and ice, so the climate is cold year-round. There is relatively little precipitation, and even less evaporation, so much of the Arctic can technically be considered a desert. The Arctic has low biological activity and a small biomass. Vegetation communities are often divided into High Arctic and tundra (Bone 1992:19). The High Arctic is permanently frozen and supports few plants, mostly lichens. The tundra, to the south, supports low-growing vegetation, including dwarf trees, low shrubs, and some grasses, lichens, and mosses. The beginning of the coniferous forest south of the tundra marks the southern boundary of the Arctic. Because there was relatively little vegetation during prehistoric times, it follows that the use of plant resources by prehistoric peoples was limited.

A number of land animals live in the Arctic, including polar, grizzly, and black bears, caribou, musk-ox, many fur-bearing species (e.g., foxes, weasels, and mink), hares and rabbits, and a variety of rodents. Caribou migrate in herds and can be hunted communally. Musk-ox do not migrate and can be hunted year-round. Importantly, when attacked, musk-ox will form a defensive circle and stand in place; thus, they can be easily killed by humans. Marine mammals in the Arctic waters include nineteen species of whales, eight of seal, two of walrus, two of dolphin, and one of porpoise. Over a hundred species of birds nest in the Arctic during the summer, some of which were hunted. Finally, many fish, including salmon, char, trout, pike, smelt, herring, whitefish, halibut, and cod, were caught and consumed.

During the Late Pleistocene and Early Holocene, much of the Arctic, particularly the eastern Arctic, was glaciated and was not occupied by people. It was not until about 5,000 years ago that the eastern Arctic was habitable by people, after the ice had retreated and the region was colonized by plants and animals.

Overall, the Arctic is less biologically diverse than temperate ecosystems, making the Arctic system less stable and more susceptible to major change. Thus, human populations had to be very adaptable to survive in such an unstable system.

A BRIEF HISTORY OF RESEARCH

The Arctic is a fascinating place but a difficult one in which to conduct research. Nevertheless, a surprising amount of archaeological work has been accomplished there. Prior to World War II, much of the work was exploratory, and just the barest outline of a prehistory was developed. After 1945, however, a great deal more research was done (see histories of work in Dekin 1978; H. B. Collins 1984; Harp 1984).

Major institutions working in the Arctic have included the Smithsonian Institution, the Canadian Museum of Civilization, and a number of universities. In Greenland, a province of Denmark, Danish archaeologists have made substantial contributions. On the Asian side of the Arctic, Russian archaeologists have conducted a great deal of research and, since the early 1990s, have been able to coordinate their work with Western scholars to a greater degree. More recently, government archaeologists have become increasingly involved in research as part of development and in conjunction with native groups.

MAJOR THEMES IN ARCTIC PREHISTORY

Perhaps the best known research question in the Arctic is the timing and circumstances involved in the initial settlement of the New World (see Chapter 2). There was at least one migration of people (Amerind) from Asia into the New World (the Arctic) during the Pleistocene, but it is possible that other very early migrations also occurred. It is clear that several other migrations from Asia took place after the Pleistocene, including those of the Na-Dene and the Eskimo/Aleut. It seems that both the Amerind and Na-Dene groups moved south and that the Aleut-Eskimo groups occupied the Arctic.

In addition to the traditional issues revolving around cultural chronology, a central research issue in Arctic archaeology is an understanding of the expansion of peoples into the eastern Arctic, first by Paleoarctic groups about 4,500 years ago and again by the Thule (Inuit) after about 1,000 years ago. Why did Paleoarctic groups move east, and how did they manage to adapt to such a difficult environment without dog sleds and boats, adaptive technology so well known from the ethnographic Inuit? How and why did Paleoarctic groups diverge into the variety of different cultural groups seen in the archaeological record? What happened to those groups? The same basic suite of questions can be asked of the Thule movement east after about 1,000 years ago, except that it is known that the Thule moved into regions already occupied by Paleoarctic peoples. Did the Thule enter after the Paleoarctic peoples had become extinct, or did they forcibly replace or assimilate them? What was the role of changing environmental conditions in all of this?

Much of the research conducted to date in the Arctic has been based on a general core-periphery model (see W. W. Fitzhugh 1997), core areas being central regions of stable resources and occupation (e.g., the mainland Arctic regions) with the peripheries being outlying areas of unstable resources and occupation (e.g., the High Arctic and Greenland). To a great extent, the dynamics of Arctic prehistory has been assumed to be related to expansion and contraction from core areas, generally related to environmental shifts. More recently, topics including biogeography, the role of islands in colonization, population distribution, resource distribution and fluctuation, and abandonment (see W. W. Fitzhugh 1997) have been investigated. A basic chronological sequence is shown in Table 4.1.

PREHISTORY OF THE WESTERN ARCTIC

For the sake of simplicity, the western Arctic is considered herein to consist of coastal Alaska and the Aleutian Islands. This region was occupied from the time of the initial entry of peoples into North America, and its prehistory follows a very different trajectory than the eastern Arctic, which was not occupied at all until after 5,000 BP.

The Paleoindian Period (to ca. 10,000 BP)

It is clear that the first Americans entered the New World through the western Arctic, which during the Pleistocene would have included Beringia. The specifics on the timing and adaptation of the first Americans (presumably of the Amerind linguistic grouping) are not fully understood (see Chapter 2), and it seems likely that at least some of the important Paleoindian sites are now underwater. The Amerind groups apparently moved south and did not permanently occupy the Arctic.

The Paleoarctic Tradition (ca. 10,000 to 4,500 BP)

It is believed that people belonging to the Na-Dene linguistic group followed the Amerind Paleoindians into Alaska, perhaps as early as 12,000 BP, and may have "pushed" the Amerinds south. These new "Paleoarctic" people (see J. V. Wright 1995:53–62) apparently brought with them the Dyuktai Complex (e.g., Goebel et al. 1991:74), a microblade technology that originated in Asia (e.g., Gusev et al. 1999). The Paleoarctic groups occupied central and northern Alaska, probably expanding into southern Alaska after about 10,000 BP, once the glaciers retreated from the area (Yesner 1996:272). (Some researchers refer to Paleoarctic groups as "Paleoeskimo," a very confusing term since they were not Eskimo, who are a linguistic grouping that entered the Arctic later in time.)

TABLE 4.1 A Chronological Sequence for the North American Arctic

Date (BP)	Western Arctic			Eastern Arctic			General Climate
	Aleutians	SW Alaska	W. and N. Alaska	Canada	Greenland	High Arctic	
150	Aleut	Yupik (Western Eskimo)	T H U L E Classic	Inuit			as today
					ABANDONED		colder than today (Little Ice Age)
			Birnirk	Dorset			warmer than today (the MCA)
1,000	Aleutian Tradition	Kodiak Tradition	Punuk				
			N O R T O N Ipiutak		ABANDONED		very cold
2,000			Norton			Independence II	colder than today
			Choris			ABANDONED	
3,000			Arctic SmallTool Tradition	Pre-Dorset	Saqqaq	Independence I	
4,000		Ocean Bay	Arctic Small Tool Tradition				cooling
5,000							
6,000				NOT YET OCCUPIED			warmer than today
7,000							
8,000		Paleoarctic					colder but warming
9,000							
to 10,000		Paleoindian					much colder than today

One of the earliest Paleoarctic sites is Anangula on Umnak Island in the western Aleutians. This site was continuously occupied from about 8,500 to 500 years ago. The technology at Anangula is slightly different than other Paleoarctic sites on the Alaska mainland and is viewed as the first occupation of the region by Paleoarctic people. Others (e.g., Laughlin 1967:447, 1975:515) believe that Anangula represents the initial Aleut occupation of the region and thus the beginning of the Aleutian Tradition (see below). Ackerman (1992) thought that Anangula may be related to earlier materials in central mainland Alaska, such as the Ugashik Narrows site that contained materials that may be related to the Denali Complex (see Chapter 2). This would support the idea that interior peoples moved to the coast sometime about 10,000 BP (Yesner 1996:272; also see Dumond 1987a; Dumond and Bland 1995).

The development of maritime adaptations (a focus on marine resources) in southwestern Alaska is still an open question. Yesner (1998) suggested that maritime adaptations developed rapidly about 6,000 BP as a response to colder conditions limiting terrestrial resources. However, sites such as Anangula, located on an island without major terrestrial resources, indicate that maritime adaptations could have occurred earlier in some areas (B. Fitzhugh 2002:258).

The Ocean Bay Tradition (ca. 7,500 to 4,000 BP)

One of the earliest outgrowths of the generalized Paleoarctic was Ocean Bay, first identified by D. W. Clark (1966, 1979, 1984; B. Fitzhugh 2002:267) on Kodiak Island and on some portions of the mainland in southwestern Alaska. Ocean Bay groups were sea mammal hunters, but by at least 6,000 BP they had a full maritime adaptation. Ocean Bay technology was a core-and-blade flaked-stone tool industry with stemmed points for thrusting spears (or possibly harpoons). Ground slate tools were added later. Ocean Bay villages consisted of small numbers of large structures, and, after 4,500 BP, subterranean sod houses.

Similarities have been noted between the Ocean Bay and Anangula technologies. This led to the hypothesis that Ocean Bay may have been the base on which both the Kodiak and Aleutian traditions developed (Dumond and Bland 1995:412; see below). It is also possible that both the Aleutian and Kodiak traditions derived from the arrival of new groups into the region.

At some point, perhaps 5,000 or 6,000 years ago, peoples speaking the proto-Eskimo/Aleut language moved into western Alaska (others remained in Siberia). These people appear to have quickly moved into the eastern Aleutians by about 6,000 BP (to establish the Aleutian Tradition; see below) and into southwestern Alaska by about 4,000 BP, replacing Ocean Bay groups and establishing the Kodiak Tradition (see below). Laughlin (1967:447, 1975:515; Laughlin et al. 1979) argued that the Eskimo/Aleut migration was earlier, perhaps ca. 9,000 BP. As the sea level rose during the Early Holocene, he suggested, some Eskimo/Aleut groups in southwestern Alaska moved inland to become the Eskimo (Inuit and Yupik linguistic groups) and some stayed on what became islands to become the Aleut (see Dumond 1987b:Fig. 1). Based on nonmetric cranial data, Ossenberg (1994) argued that Eskimoan people showed relatedness to Na-Dene, meaning that Aleut had been effectively isolated from subsequent populations, adding some support to the Laughlin model. Certainly, proto-Eskimo/Aleut diverged into Aleut and Eskimoan by at least 3,000 BP, with Eskimoan later diverging into Yupik (Western Eskimo) and Inuit (Eastern Eskimo). Each of these broad groups occupied different regions, leading to the geographic distribution seen at contact (Dumond 1987b).

The Aleutian Tradition (ca. 6,000 to Contact)

The Aleutian Tradition represents the known prehistory of the Aleut people, initiated by the entry of proto-Eskimo/Aleut peoples into the eastern Aleutian Islands. The dating of the migration is debated, and estimates for the earliest date range from 8,500 BP (the initial occupation of the Anangula site; e.g., Laughlin 1975:515) to 6,000 BP (the appearance of maritime economies) to 4,500 BP (the appearance of groups with clear Aleut traits; e.g., McCartney and Veltre 1999:505), with 6,000 BP most commonly used. Whatever the initial timing, the eastern Aleutians, closest to the Alaskan mainland, were settled first, with the remainder of the Aleutian chain being settled by 3,000 BP (see Veltre 1998). It is unclear whether the Aleutian Tradition was related, at least technologically, to the earlier Paleoarctic and/or Ocean Bay traditions, and there is some thought that the Aleutian Tradition may have developed in relative isolation from the mainland, but with some contact with both mainland Alaska and Asia (see Corbett et al. 1997).

The record of the Aleutian Tradition is poorly known until about 4,500 BP. At this time, the climate began to cool (the Neoglacial), impacting the groups on the Aleutian Islands. A new pattern emerged, one that continued to historic times. This new pattern included the aggregation of populations into larger, permanent villages along the coast with sedentary populations, more elaborate semisubterranean houses with stone walls and multiple rooms, and an intensification of the use of marine resources (Knecht and Davis 2007).

The economy of Aleutian Tradition groups was focused on marine resources. After about 2,200 BP, the use of salmon became important, seen as evidence of Yupik influence (Maschner 1999a:74). By about 2,500 BP, villages became much larger (Maschner 1999a:74) and mortuary practices became more complex. Some secondary burial occurred and in some cases, skulls were even collected and curated. By about 1,500 BP, some wealthy people were purposefully mummified. The practice of mask making began about 2,000 BP (Ray 1967), and bendwood hunting hats, a classic Aleut trait, appeared about 1,000 BP.

Another major change took place about 900 BP. Villages became even larger and house size increased again, with the addition of many attached storage structures. Smaller villages were located in areas thought to be associated with salmon procurement (Maschner 1999b:99). This change may reflect the expansion of the Thule into the Alaska Peninsula, bringing with them ranked corporate social groupings (Maschner 1999a:74). In the end, the late Aleutian Tradition (in essence the Aleut) was one of large, ranked populations in large villages focused on maritime resources (McCartney and Veltre 1999).

Maschner and Jordan (2008) suggested that these sudden and dramatic changes in Aleut society seen at about 4,500 and 900 BP (and perhaps at other times) were the result of catastrophic events, such as climate change (e.g., the Neoglacial), earthquakes, and the movement of new peoples (e.g., the Thule). Thus, dramatic change followed by periods of stability may characterize the development of the Aleut.

The Kodiak Tradition (ca. 4,000 to 200 BP)

The Kodiak Tradition also seems to have had its roots in Ocean Bay, and if the Aleutian Tradition was Aleut, Kodiak was Eskimo. There is some overlap of Kodiak with Ocean Bay groups/sites, arguing for a linkage between the two. Kodiak peoples were sea mammal hunters who also used some land mammals and fish and lived in relatively small, tent-like houses. They mostly used tools of polished slate rather than of flaked stone, an extensive inventory of bone tools, and oil lamps, many of which were highly decorated after about 2,000 BP. A considerable number of local phases have been recognized (see D. W. Clark 1984: Fig. 2, 1998) for the Kodiak Tradition but are typically divided into early (Kachemak, ca. 4,000 to 800 BP) and late (Koniag, ca. 800 to 200 BP) periods.

During Kachemak times (see D. W. Clark 1997), slate tool technology was common, and schooling fish, such as salmon, were mass harvested, as suggested by the presence of nets and processing tools (B. Fitzhugh 2002:267). The first villages were established, along with elaborate ceremonialism and mortuary customs. Warfare is evident toward the end of Kachemak times (due to the Thule?), and both social complexity (social inequality) and storage increased, perhaps in response to large fish surpluses (see B. Fitzhugh 2002:294–298).

By about 800 BP, a number of changes in the artifact inventory occurred, at least in their style (D. W. Clark 1998:179), ushering in the Koniag Period. Composite harpoons, pottery, and communal houses appeared, and whale hunting became the major economic and social activity. Villages became larger and fortified, and wooden body armor appeared. Koniag groups participated in regional trade and interaction until the area was taken over by the Russians ca. 1784. They exist today as the Koniag Eskimo, one of the Yupik groups. If this pattern developed locally (e.g., D. W. Clark 1998:181) it would seem that Eskimoan society originated in the area. If, however, the developments were the result of a migration of Yupik groups into the region from the north (e.g., Dummond 2009:71) then Eskimoan society must have originated to the north.

The Arctic Small Tool Tradition (ca. 4,500 to 2,500 BP)

About 4,500 years ago, or perhaps even as early as 5,000 BP (Dumond and Bland 1995:437), a tool complex dominated by microblades and small burins appeared along the central coast of Alaska. It was originally designated the Denbigh Flint Complex (Giddings 1951, 1964), named from its discovery at the Denbigh site in western Alaska. It was soon realized that the Denbigh complex was widespread in western Alaska, and it was renamed the Arctic Small Tool Tradition (ASTt). Many believe that the ASTt had its origins in Asia, but there is little evidence (see Dumond and Bland 1995:437).

The hallmark of the ASTt is small blades, cores, and burins. The presence of small projectile points in ASTt assemblages suggests that arrows were used, perhaps the first introduction of the bow and arrow into North America from Asia about 5,000 BP (see Blitz 1988). All of the tools are small and standardized, easy to make, easy to carry, and ideal for highly mobile populations (C. Ellis 2008).

Most ASTt sites are small, temporary camps with tent foundations, but several sites with permanent structures are known (Dumond 1987a:82–83). Populations were highly mobile, and they did not use oil lamps because they did not hunt seals. Subsistence was based primarily on caribou and anadromous fish (e.g., salmon), although some terrestrial resources were also used.

The ASTt was relatively widespread across much of Alaska, even expanding into the forests of the Alaskan Subarctic, replacing Archaic Indian groups in that region. Most important, ASTt groups expanded into the eastern Arctic after about 4,500 BP and are the precursors of the early cultures in that region (see below). The ASTt was replaced by the Norton Tradition between about 2,500 and 2,000 years ago, but there are those that believe that Norton is a maritime adapted continuation of the ASTt (e.g., Dumond 1998).

The Norton Tradition (ca. 3,000 to 1,000 BP)

The Norton Tradition appeared along the coast of central Alaska about 3,000 years ago. Norton economies were oriented toward maritime resources, but inland resources remained important (Dumond 2000). It is unclear whether Norton evolved from the preceding ASTt or represents a new group (Dumond 2000). Some of the technological traits of the ASTt continued into the Norton Tradition, but microblades disappeared and new technologies, such as pottery, large points, oil lamps, and slate tools, appeared. Another major change was the beginning of whaling as an important pursuit (Whitridge 2000), and this remained relatively important until the latter part of the tradition. While dogs are present in all Norton Tradition sites, there is no real evidence of dog sleds, suggesting that the function of dogs was limited to hunting assistance and as food. The Norton Tradition is also known for its art in bone and ivory.

The Norton Tradition consists of three major successive phases, Choris, Norton, and Ipiutak (see Anderson 1984:85 90; Dumond and Bland 1995:438–439; Dumond 2000). The Choris Phase (ca. 3,000 to 2,500 BP) is defined by the change in ASTt technology. Microblades were dropped but burins were retained and new technological elements, such as pottery (derived from Asian ceramic traditions), stemmed point forms, slate knives (thought to be used for cutting blubber of sea mammals), and oil lamps (the earliest in the Arctic), were adopted. The earliest whaling is associated with Choris (see Highlight 4.1) and was important along the coast, although Choris groups also occupied interior localities, such as the famous Onion Portage site (see D. D. Anderson 1968, 1988). Some believe it possible that Choris (and the Norton Tradition) dates as early as 3,600 BP (e.g., D. D. Anderson 1984:85).

HIGHLIGHT 4.1

CAPE KRUSENSTERN AND THE OLD WHALING CULTURE

One of the most enigmatic cultures in the Arctic is the Old Whaling Culture, so far identified from only one North American site, at Cape Krusenstern, although a site containing similar materials was found on Wrangle Island in Siberia (see Dumond and Bland 1995:441). Cape Krusenstern is located in north-central Alaska and is now a national monument. The main site at Cape Krusenstern lies atop of a series of 114 parallel beach ridges, formed by a series of sea level drops about 60 years apart over the last 5,000 years or so (Giddings and Anderson 1986; Dumond 2000:13–14). The earliest (highest) beaches (numbers 104 through 80) were occupied by people of the Denbigh Flint Complex. Early Choris remains were found on beaches 78 to 53, Old Whaling on Beach 53, later Choris on beaches 52 to 44, and Norton Phase materials on beaches 44 to 36 (Dumond and Bland 1995:Table VII).

The Old Whaling component at Cape Krusenstern consists of five winter and five summer houses with oil lamps, slate tools, a single toggle harpoon head, seal remains, and abundant whale bone (which is also abundant on the Choris beaches). The Old Whaling Culture is dated between about 3,200 and 3,000 BP (Dumond 2000:14), and some believe that it represents the earliest evidence of routine whaling in the Arctic (see discussion in Ackerman 1998:252–255).

It is odd that Old Whaling would be isolated on a beach between two Choris occupations, as if it suddenly appeared and then disappeared. However, the dating of the beaches has been questioned, and it has been suggested that the beach sequence was misinterpreted, that the Old Whaling component dated to 2,900 BP, and that it was older than any of the Choris beaches (Mason and Ludwig 1990). In addition, there is some question whether the "Old Whalers" actually hunted whales or were just seal hunters who scavenged a whale or two.

Many believe the Old Whaling Culture is a part of early Choris, but others (e.g., Dumond 2000) consider it a separate entity. Others think it is related to early Eskimo (see Ackerman 1984:116), or possibly a very poorly known "early High Arctic adaptation" (Ackerman 1998:259). It also seems possible that it is a misinterpretation of some other cultural phenomenon (such as interior Archaic groups visiting the coast) and that the Old Whaling Culture is not a valid entity.

The Norton Phase (ca. 2,500 to 2,000 BP) is defined by a shift in emphasis toward a focus on marine resources, with interior resources (e.g., caribou and fish) becoming less important.

Settlements of the Norton Phase consisted of relatively large villages located along the coast, although some inland settlements were still occupied. Net sinkers, used for marine fishing, appeared, and pottery (virtually identical to Choris types) continued to be used. Some have called the latter part of the Norton Phase "Near Ipiutak," but that designation is not used here.

The Ipiutak Phase (ca. 2,000 to 1,000 BP) is defined by major changes again. For reasons that are unclear, Ipiutak groups dropped the use of pottery, oil lamps, and ground slate and stopped hunting whales. Seals and walrus became important, and coastal settlements were located where resources were abundant (at least seasonally), although some small Ipiutak settlements were located in the interior for hunting caribou. Of great interest is the earliest use of smelted iron (traded in from Asia, perhaps ultimately from China). Ipiutak groups also adopted elaborate burial customs (O. K. Mason 1998:275), including some burials in coffins with household goods and other burials containing ritual items, suggesting that a segment of the population had special status, perhaps possessing important shamanistic powers.

One of the major Ipiutak sites is located at Point Hope, where more than 650 house pits have been identified. Although this appears to be a huge village, not all the houses were used at the same time, and most researchers now believe that Point Hope represents a series of small settlements occupied over a long period of time (with more than just Ipiutak components), with a population of perhaps two hundred people at any one time (O. K. Mason 1998:274).

Ipiutak may be related to very early Thule (Okvik or Old Bering Sea) along coastal Siberia (see, e.g., D. D. Anderson 1984:88), while others (e.g., Shaw 1998) think that at least some Ipiutak groups may have been related to ethnographic Yupik groups. Still, the answer to the question of the progeny of Ipiutak is quite unclear (see Dumond 2000).

The Thule (ca. 1,500 BP to Contact)

Sometime about 1,500 years ago, a new group speaking Inuit languages related to but separate from the Yupik languages spoken in the other Arctic portions of mainland Alaska arrived in Alaska. The Thule brought with them a new, specialized whale-hunting maritime adaptation (sometimes called the Northern Maritime Tradition). Thule groups later moved into western Alaska, filling a niche in the eastern Arctic vacated by the Ipiutak, who had abandoned whaling about 500 years earlier. Thule did not suddenly replace all Ipiutak groups, who overlapped considerably in time with the Thule (see Gerlach and Mason 1992). This diversity may be due to the development of different polities related to whaling competition (e.g., O. K. Mason 1998). The Thule eventually developed into the ethnographic Inuit.

In addition to a focus on whaling, the Thule are also defined by art styles and a number of technological innovations, including distinctive pottery, drag floats (by ca. 1,400 BP) used in whale and walrus hunting, and sleds pulled by dogs (by ca. 1,000 BP), an innovation that enabled much greater load transport and mobility. The toggle harpoon is also a distinctive Thule marker but is known earlier in Norton and even Dorset in the eastern Arctic (see below). Toggle harpoon heads are more effective in certain circumstances, such as attaching floats to whales and in hunting walrus. Thule pottery appeared in the western Arctic after about 1,000 BP and was used to cook meat rather than plants (see Frink and Harry 2008).

In the western Arctic, the Thule lived along the coast in large, sedentary winter villages of fifteen to twenty-five large semisubterranean houses built of whale bone, stones, skins, and sod (see Savelle 2002), although it is possible that not all of these houses were occupied at the same time and that Thule winter villages were actually much smaller (Park 1997). Hunting walruses, seals, and bowhead whales were the major activities during this time. In the summer, the Thule moved inland, lived in small camps, and exploited fish and caribou, the latter of which were hunted communally (Morrison 1997).

The origin of the Thule is not well known, but they appear to have initially developed some 2,000 years ago on the Siberian side of the Bering Strait, perhaps derived from whale hunting Norton groups in that area. The earliest Thule (the Okvik and Old Bering Sea phases; see Table 4.2) were whale hunters, and by 1,500 BP (the Birnirk Phase) they had moved into western Alaska. A bit later, the Punuk appear to have developed military cadres, who appear to have invaded western Alaska at the expense of non-Birnirk groups, such as the Ipiutak (O. K. Mason 1998, 2009). By about 1,000 BP, Punuk and Birnirk groups seem to have developed into the Classic Thule.

Whaling appears to have fostered increasing competition and developing complexity across the Thule phases in the Bering Sea area. By Punuk times (ca. 1,200 to 700 BP), the size of villages increased and warfare appears to have been rather important, judging by the appearance of body armor of bone, antler, and ivory (e.g., Sheehan 1985:138; also see Maschner and Reedy-Maschner 1998; O. K. Mason 2009).

TABLE 4.2 Summary of Thule Chronology

Phase	Dates (BP)	Geographic Location	Characteristics
Classic Thule	1,000 to present	central to northern Alaska, east across the Arctic to Greenland	open-water hunting of whales and seals from boats, some caribou hunting, winter seal hunting, pottery, dog sleds, large seasonal villages with substantial houses, ethnographic Inuit after contact
Punuk	1,200 to 700	coastal mainland on both sides of the Bering Strait	similar to Old Bering/Okvik Sea, larger population, addition of new art styles, harpoon float equipment appears as whaling increases in importance
Birnirk	1,500 to 1,000	central Alaskan coast, into northern Alaska by 1,200 BP	coastal; hunting of seals, whales, and caribou pottery; sleds (but no dogs); substantial houses but small villages
Old Bering Sea	1,900 to 1,500	coastal eastern Siberia and islands of the Bering Strait	pottery, polished slate tools, toggle harpoon heads, changed carved art tradition, substantial houses
Okvik	2,000 to 1,800	coastal eastern Siberia	pottery, polished slate tools, toggle harpoon heads, carved art tradition, substantial houses

Early (Birnirk) Thule buried at least some of their dead in log-lined tombs. Later (Classic) Thule groups either placed their dead on open platforms or buried them under rock cairns. An analysis of the well-preserved body of an eight-year-old girl found near Point Barrow revealed that she had been chronically ill with emphysema and had starved to death (Zimmerman et al. 2000). Notable was the considerable care given the child in life and in death.

Beginning sometime about 1,000 BP, or perhaps as late as 700 BP, the Classic Thule began a rapid expansion east across the Arctic. The eastern Arctic was occupied by a number of Paleoarctic groups with very different adaptations than the Thule. The reasons for, mechanisms of, and impact of the Thule expansion are not fully understood. The Thule expansion is discussed further below.

PREHISTORY OF THE EASTERN ARCTIC

The eastern Arctic lies east of Alaska and includes all of the islands in the Arctic Ocean as well as Greenland. The whole of the eastern Arctic, northern Alaska, and northern coastal Siberia are currently occupied by the Inuit, but they entered the eastern Arctic less than 1,000 years ago (the Thule expansion, see below). Prior to the Inuit, the eastern Arctic was occupied by a variety of early groups unrelated to the Inuit.

Until about 4,500 BP, the eastern Arctic was covered by ice, making it essentially uninhabitable by humans. Once the ice had retreated sufficiently, sea mammals, land animals, fish, and birds colonized the region, and humans followed (Fig. 4.2). The first humans into the region were essentially ASTt groups from the western Arctic who migrated all the way to Greenland. This population movement happened very rapidly (see Dekin 1976) and on foot, as they did not have boats or dog sleds. The reasons for the migration of these ASTt people into the eastern Arctic are not fully understood but are likely related to population pressure in the west (Maxwell 1985:47–48) and/or to the newly available niche in the east. Like their western ASTt relatives, eastern ASTt groups were predominately oriented to terrestrial resources when they moved east, but their focus gradually shifted to maritime resources, primarily sea mammals.

The very first migrants into the eastern Arctic were ASTt groups carrying an ASTt toolkit. As they moved into different areas, these ASTt groups very rapidly diverged into a variety of expressions (cf. cultures; see Fig. 4.2), each with a unique adaptation that was different from the later Thule pattern; a testament to human adaptability (Bielawski 1988). Few sites contain a complete record of the prehistory of the eastern Arctic (Helmer 1991), but the Port Refuge area in the Canadian High Arctic may have such a record, and work there could lead to a more complete understanding of the cultural chronology and adaptations (McGhee 1976).

The Pre-Dorset (ca. 4,500 to 2,800 BP)

The initial ASTt movement into the eastern Arctic was into coastal regions of Canada, where people hunted caribou, musk-ox, polar bears, hares, birds (Maxwell 1985:88; Milne and Donnelly 2004), as well as seals and walrus (Maxwell 1985:84), with fish, caribou, and seal being the primary game. Large, well-defined tent rings are seen as Pre-Dorset summer houses, while smaller, less-defined foundations may represent winter houses (Ramsden and Murray 1995). This dichotomy in dwellings implies a seasonal movement of settlements, probably from the coast to the interior, a model also supported by the different hunting technologies—harpoons for sea mammals and the bow and arrow, probably for caribou.

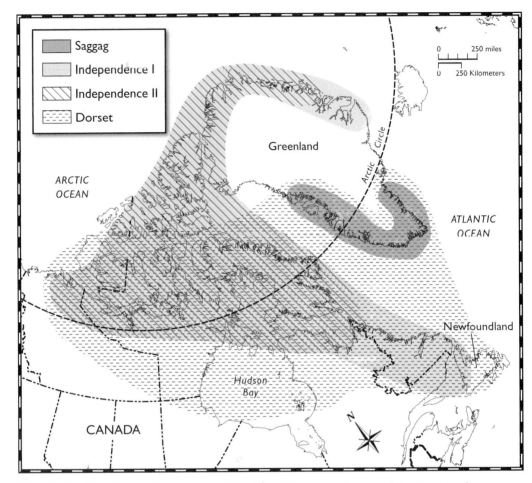

FIGURE 4.2   Map showing the general distribution of the early cultures in the eastern Arctic.

Dogs may have been present, but they were not used to pull sleds. Some art from this time is also known (see Fig. 4.3).

Between 3,500 and 3,000 BP, there seems to have been a decline in the number of people (McGhee 1996:125), perhaps associated with the region becoming colder, and some groups appear to have followed the movement of the tundra to the south, into what are now the forests of the Subarctic, to hunt caribou (Gordon 1996:149). Pre-Dorset likely evolved into Dorset (W. E. Taylor 1968: vii; Nagy 1994), as Dorset is found in the same general area immediately afterward, and traces of the beginning of Dorset art (see Highlight 4.2) can be seen in Pre-Dorset sites.

Saqqaq (Also Known as Sarqaq; ca. 4,500 to 2,800 BP)

The earliest occupation of southern Greenland was by people called Saqqaq (or Sarqaq), thought to related to ASTt-derived groups. Saqqaq was first identified by Meldgaard (1952), and their arrival in Greenland is uncertain, but they were there by at least 3,900 BP (Grønnow 1994). Saqqaq tool assemblages are clearly ASTt, but there are also some similarities to the later Dorset. Møbjerg (1999) noted that bone tools appear about 3,600 BP and suggested that this could reflect the

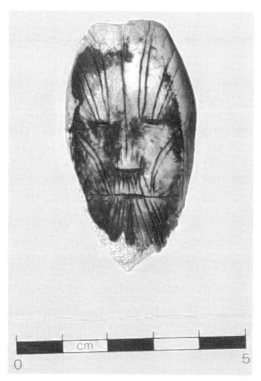

FIGURE 4.3   A small (54 mm high) Pre-Dorset maskette, believed to represent a tattooed woman. (*Source:* "A Face from the Past: An Early Pre-Dorset Ivory Maskette from North Devon Island, N.W.T. by James Helmer, 10(1-2):179–202, Journal Etudes/Inuit/Studies, 1986.)

hunting of walrus and perhaps baleen whales (also see Whitridge 2000). People appear to have hunted marine and terrestrial mammals (Møbjerg 1999:452) and lived in tents.

Saqqaq is very poorly known, but it seems clear that it predates Pre-Dorset (Jensen 2005) but may be part of a "general Pre-Dorset sphere" (Maxwell 1985:103). Saqqaq may have been actually replaced by Pre-Dorset or even Dorset, or it may have developed into early Dorset (Jensen 2005).

New aDNA data derived from samples of 4,000-year-old human hair recovered from the permafrost of the Qeqertasussuk site in southwestern Greenland (Rasmussen et al. 2010) suggests that Saqqaq people were related to groups in eastern Siberia. Thus, it is possible that a separate migration of Siberians into the New World and all the way to Greenland occurred sometime between 5,500 and 4,000 years ago. The implications of this idea have yet to be explored.

Independence I (ca. 4,500 to 3,500 BP)

Beginning about 4,500 BP, people moved into the central High Arctic, including northern Greenland. This pioneering culture was first identified at Independence Fiord in northeastern Greenland (Knuth 1954), and their sites are generally found on relic shorelines twenty-two meters higher than current sea level (raised mostly due to isostatic rebound). Younger materials were found in the same area at lower shorelines, and the older culture was named Independence I, with the younger being called Independence II (see below). Independence I may have been a specialized northern extension of Pre-Dorset (Bielawski 1988:70); recall that a similar argument was made for Saqqaq.

Independence I groups occupied exposed, rocky beaches and were organized into small bands (one to five families) of highly mobile people. Musk-ox was the staple food, but some hares, char (freshwater fish), and migratory waterfowl were also eaten. Interestingly, very few sea mammals were taken. Independence groups had the bow and arrow, tools (burins) for working ivory and wood, and probably used dogs for hunting musk-ox. During the summer, when there was constant daylight for months, hunting was probably good and food plentiful. Meat was stored under rock cairns for the winter, and driftwood was gathered and stored. Independence I people had highly developed sewing skills (McGhee 1996:59–60), and the manufacture and repair of skin items (clothing and tent covers) likely occupied the winter when there was no sun for months. Food probably ran short in the winter, and people must have "semi-hibernated" during that time (McGhee 1996:64). The dependence on musk-ox was so extensive that any variation in their availability could have been disastrous for people.

Independence I houses are rather distinctive. Summer dwellings were substantial skin tents, anchored by rocks. Winter houses were larger, even more substantial wooden-framed, skin-covered structures with a large slab-lined, box-shaped hearth in the center (often, but incorrectly called a "central passage"; see McGhee 1996:50, 54). The center of the house was used for cooking, and people slept on the sides. Some of the house features found in the Saqqaq area (see above) resemble Independence I houses.

Independence I population peaked by about 4,000 BP, declined rapidly, then stabilized. About 3,500 BP, populations suddenly declined again, perhaps due to a cooling climate (Maxwell 1985:117). It is also possible that the overhunting of musk-ox was a factor (Savelle and Dyke 2002). By about 3,000 BP, the High Arctic region was abandoned, to be reoccupied by Independence II groups about 2,500 BP.

Independence II (ca. 2,500 to 2,000 BP)

After being abandoned about 3,000 BP, the High Arctic became warmer again at about 2,500 BP and was reoccupied, this time by groups called Independence II. Independence II was similar to Independence I in many ways, including settlement type and location (at the sixteen-meter shoreline), subsistence, and house types, but the artifacts appear to be more closely related to late Pre-Dorset (Maxwell 1985:119). It began to get colder and by 2,000 BP, the High Arctic region was again abandoned, with settlement shifting to the south.

The Dorset (ca. 2,800 to 700 BP)

The Dorset are perhaps the most intriguing of the early groups in the eastern Arctic. They apparently developed from a Pre-Dorset (ASTt) base in coastal Canada about 2,800 BP and later expanded to occupy all of the eastern Arctic by about 1,500 BP, replacing or absorbing all of the previous early groups. They were first recognized in 1925 as being clearly different from the ethnographic Inuit (Jenness 1925). One of the reasons the Dorset are so interesting is that they initially appeared, compared to the Inuit, to be poorly adapted to the Arctic. They did not use the bow and arrow, dog sleds, or boats, raising the question of how they survived. The Dorset were ultimately replaced by the Thule expanding from the western Arctic.

The origin of the Dorset is still unclear. Some have argued for a direct evolution from Pre-Dorset to Dorset (e.g., W. E. Taylor 1968: vii; Maxwell 1985) and perhaps even the other preceding groups. Some researchers (e.g., Maxwell 1985:167–245) have divided the Dorset into early, middle, late, and terminal phases (but this is not expanded upon here). Dorset sites have wonderful preservation of organic artifacts, due to large, frozen midden accumulations.

Dorset economies were quite different than earlier groups, in that Dorset hunters focused on sea mammals, primarily seals, walrus, and beluga and narwhal whales, with little utilization of terrestrial resources, although birds were important.

Dorset settlements were located along ocean shorelines, where they built large and permanent villages in areas with year-round access to marine mammals. One could argue that this provided the Dorset a more stable way of life, as opposed to a seasonal round of groups continually moving across the landscape (as the Pre-Dorset did). The Dorset did occasionally hunt caribou, but very few Dorset caribou hunting sites are known (Howse 2008).

Early Dorset people lived in skin-covered structures that contained a central hearth, similar to the features found in Independence houses (see above). They may also have used snowhouses, as inferred from the presence of snow knives, large ivory blades used for cutting snow (Maxwell 1985:153). After about 1,400 BP, Dorset houses became much more substantial semisubterranean structures with whalebone supports and tunnel entrances, an innovation designed to keep the houses warmer. These structures are very similar to the later Thule houses, and it is possible that the Thule borrowed the architecture from the Dorset.

After about 1,500 BP, some Dorset groups built longhouses (or hearth rows), structures up to forty-five meters in length that appear to have been more for communal gathering than residential purposes. They may have been associated with communal hunting during the spring and summer (Damkjar 2005). Some of the sites where these longhouse structures have been found also contain many foundations of traditional Dorset tents, suggesting the presence of relatively large numbers of people and supporting the communal nature of the longhouses (Maxwell 1985:157). Longhouse function may have been more complex. Using a core-periphery model, Friesen (2007) suggested that increasing social complexity in Late Dorset was exhibited by a formalization of burial practices in the core (the Foxe Basin of Canada), while the groups on the periphery resisted such complexity by the construction of communal longhouses in an attempt to remain egalitarian.

Another fascinating aspect of the Dorset is their technology. The bow-and-arrow technology of earlier groups was dropped, perhaps since it may have been too cold to hunt caribou. Drilling technology was also dropped (McGhee 1996:142), with holes being scratched into tools. Slate knives, possibly used to skin seals (Renouf and Bell 2008), are known, and the Dorset used steatite vessels and oil lamps to heat their houses. The use of native copper and meteoric iron for some tools began in late Dorset times and continued until contact. There is some evidence that the Dorset had small sleds, but there is no evidence of the use of dogs to pull them. Even though a few dogs were present, the sleds were likely pulled by hand and were used to transport large game animals and even to move large boulders for house foundations.

The Dorset focused on the hunting of maritime resources, but there is little evidence of boats or of the technology of floats or toggle harpoons used from boats, although there is some evidence of kayaks (Maxwell 1985:137). The Dorset apparently hunted seals along shorelines and on sea ice with barbed harpoons, and, in fact, the colder conditions may have provided greater hunting opportunities on ice floes.

Women's roles seem to have involved shared labor among multifamily households, rather than in nuclear families, such as the Inuit. Women may also have functioned as ritual intermediaries between hunters and the souls of animals (see LeMoine 2003). Other hints at Dorset ritual and belief are present in their spectacular artistic tradition (see Highlight 4.2).

HIGHLIGHT 4.2

DORSET ART

Arctic peoples have an artistic tradition that has spanned many thousands of years. Much of Arctic art was everyday art, with form and aesthetics being incorporated into all manufactured items and much of it containing subtle messages. Sculpture was the primary art form, and walrus ivory was the most popular medium for Eskimo sculpture. Bone was the second most popular material, followed by wood and stone. Stone was difficult to carve and was the least used material, although soft steatite was frequently used. Arctic artists were mostly men; more recently, however, Eskimo women have begun creating some outstanding works of art, much of it paintings and drawings, but including some sculpture (see Leroux et al. 1994).

The Dorset had a fabulous art tradition and made considerable use of wood, bone, ivory, antler, and steatite (see Martijn 1964; Graburn 1976; W. W. Fitzhugh 1988; Swinton 1992). Both humans and animals were represented in naturalistic (some carvings clearly show people wearing parkas) and abstract forms, and some figures appear to have been associated with magic and shamanism (McGhee 1996:155; Sutherland 2001), and a number of masks of human faces are known (also see Fig. 4.3).

Three-dimensional Dorset sculpture was very elaborate, and virtually every animal in the Dorset world was depicted. About half of the art is of dangerous animals, including humans and polar bears. Some of the human and polar bear figures have slits on their throats that were filled with red ochre, seemingly representative of violent death.

Some Dorset motifs have been adopted by the Inuit and have carried over into contemporary Inuit art. General reviews of Inuit art are presented in Martijn (1964), Graburn (1976), W. W. Fitzhugh (1988), and Swinton (1992).

Dorset mortuary practices are poorly known, as few of the Dorset deceased have been found. McGhee (1996:147) suggested that the bodies had been placed in the open and left to the elements. A few burials have been found, but they tend to be secondary. Thus, it seems that most of the dead were left to the elements, with some of the bones being later collected and interred. Another hint at Dorset ritual behavior is the distribution of sewing needles. Their presence at some occupation sites and their absence in others may reflect a ritual taboo regarding sewing during certain seasons or activities. As a hypothetical example, it may have been considered unlucky to sew caribou skins during the time caribou were hunted.

Between about 1,800 and 1,500 BP, it was very cold, and the Dorset may have abandoned some areas, with some people perhaps moving south into the Newfoundland region of the Northeast culture area (see Chapter 11) (Maxwell 1985:216). A major Dorset occupation, dating between about 1,900 and 1,200 BP, is known at Port au Choix (aka Phillip's Garden) on the northwestern coast of Newfoundland (see Harp 1976; Renouf and Murray 1999). To date, some sixty-seven Dorset structures have been identified there, and a number of toggle harpoon heads (Tuck 1976:36, Plate 26), generally considered to be Thule markers, have been found. Port au Choix has been interpreted as a seasonal camp (Renouf and Murray 1999:130), where the hunting of seals was the primary activity, although the taking of fish and birds increased in importance through time, suggesting that as time progressed, the site was occupied for longer periods during the year (Hodgetts et al. 2003). There is also evidence that the processing of seal skins was a major activity at the site (Renouf and Bell 2008). By about 1,200 BP, warming sea temperatures may have reduced seal populations in Newfoundland, which, in conjunction with expanding Indian groups (with bow-and-arrow technology; Erwin et al. 2005) from Labrador, may have encouraged the Dorset to leave (Renouf and Bell 2009).

The fate of the Dorset remains obscure. Originally believed to have been gone by the time of the Thule entry (Tuck and Pastore 1985; also see McGhee 1976:39), the Dorset, or at least some of them, appear to have survived well into Thule times. Friesen (2004:690) argued that the Dorset successfully adapted to the climatic changes of 1,000 BP but that they actively tried to avoid the more aggressive Thule and were unable to adapt to the "social and demographic factors stemming from relations with incoming Thule" (Friesen 2004:686). The idea that the Thule contacted the Dorset is supported by the Thule adoption of some Dorset traits, such as certain types of architecture and harpoon head technology. On the other hand, Park (1993) argued that the Thule obtained Dorset harpoon technology by scavenging abandoned Dorset sites.

Biological data provide some illumination of the issue. Data on Thule and Dorset aDNA show that the two populations were different, suggesting replacement and not assimilation (Hayes et al. 2005), although other aDNA data (Helgason et al. 2005) suggest there was some mixture of the two populations. The skeletal data (Ossenberg 2005) also indicate some mixture. Obviously, the question remains unresolved.

A mysterious group on Southampton Island in the eastern Arctic, called the Sadlermuit, could have been a band of surviving Dorset (see Maxwell 1985:244–245). Dental (Shields and Jones 1998) and aDNA (Hayes et al. 2005) data support the idea that the Sadlermuit were related to the Dorset (Shields and Jones 1998), but other analyses (Rowley 1994) and skeletal data (Ossenberg 2005) suggest that the Sadlermuit were related to the Inuit and not to the Dorset. The Sadlermuit isolated themselves from the Inuit, refusing to trade or to marry outside their group, and spoke a "strange" dialect. Unfortunately, they were wiped out by disease in the winter of 1902–1903, before they could be further investigated.

It is also possible that the Dorset had contact with the Norse (Sutherland 2009), which may have resulted in the Dorset being substantially impacted by European diseases (Agger and Maschner 2009). If so, the reduced Dorset populations would have been unable to adapt to changing environmental conditions or to resist the incoming Thule. Surviving and isolated Dorset groups may have been absorbed by the Thule (Appelt and Gulløv 2009).

The Thule Expansion into the Eastern Arctic (ca. 700 to Contact)

By 1,500 BP in the western Arctic (see above), the Thule, with languages quite different from those of the Paleoarctic groups, had developed a specialized whale-hunting adaptation that proved quite successful. Some of the Thule then expanded east and rapidly occupied the entire eastern Arctic (Fig. 4.4). For a considerable time, it was thought that the Thule migration into the eastern Arctic had begun about 1,000 BP and that its primary causal factor was related to a warming trend at that time (the MCA). In warmer times, there would have been less sea ice (recall that less ice was a problem for the seal-hunting Dorset), and the range of the bowhead whale, a major Thule prey, would have expanded east, presumably with Thule hunters in pursuit.

New evidence now suggests that the Thule did not move east until about 700 BP (Friesen and Arnold 2008; McGhee 2009). If so, it would have been at a time when the climate was again cooling, making whale hunting more difficult. If not following whales, then, why did the Thule move? There are a number of possibilities, including the exploitation of new maritime habitats and prey by the very sophisticated Thule (Dumond 2009), a military expansion (O. K. Mason 2009), and an expansion of trade related, perhaps to the arrival of the Norse in Greenland (McGhee 2009).

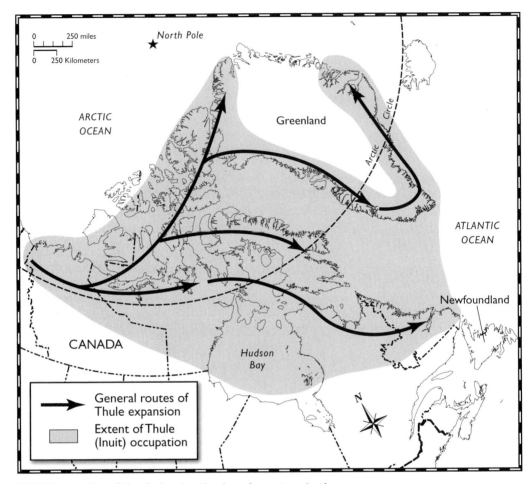

FIGURE 4.4   Map of the Thule migration into the eastern Arctic.

As noted above, it is not yet clear whether the Thule expanded into a region that had been abandoned or whether they actually encountered and replaced existing groups. It is clear that by about 500 BP, the Thule had reached Greenland and encountered the Norse (see Highlight 4.3), although the result of that contact is still debated. The earliest Thule migrants are called "Classic" (or "Pioneering"), but after about 500 BP, they diversified into the many Inuit groups encountered at contact.

HIGHLIGHT 4.3

THE INUIT AND THE NORSE

The earliest documented contact between Europeans and native peoples of the New World was that of the Vikings from Scandinavia, known as the Norse, about 1,000 years ago (McGovern 1980, 1990). Beginning in AD 982, the Norse established several colonies in Greenland. A few years later, in AD 986, a lost Norse ship apparently observed some unknown land west of Greenland, and ten years later, Lief Erikson sailed west to explore this newfound land (hence the place name, Newfoundland). The Norse established a small, short-lived colony at L'Anse aux Meadows in Newfoundland in AD 1004 (A. Ingstad 1985; H. Ingstad 1985). Most Norse contacts with native peoples in North America were probably never very intense or sustained for very long. There is currently no direct evidence of any European diseases in the Arctic prior to 1492, or for any major Norse influences on native cultures, although it is possible that disease brought in by the Norse impacted the Dorset (Agger and Maschner 2009).

Sometime about AD 1200, the Thule (Inuit) expanded east into Greenland and came into contact with the Norse (see McGhee 2009). By about AD 1400, the Norse had abandoned Greenland. What happened? A number of possibilities present themselves (see McGovern 2000). First, there is some evidence of conflict between the Inuit and the Norse, and it may be that the Inuit pushed the Norse out of Greenland by force. If so, it would be a unique case of Native Americans invading an area occupied by Europeans and replacing them. It has been argued that the fighting ability of the native peoples so discouraged the Norse that the European invasion of the New World was delayed by 500 years (McGhee 1984).

Another possibility is that about 650 years ago, the climate became too cold (the Little Ice Age) for the agricultural Norse, who would have just packed up and gone home (e.g., Fagan 2000; Diamond 2005). If this is true, it would illustrate the fate of groups that fail to adapt to changing climatic conditions.

A third possibility has recently been suggested. Perhaps the Norse were actually successful in Greenland and did not need to adopt Inuit practices (see McGovern 2000), but changing economies and trading spheres in other Norse communities to the east in Iceland and Scandinavia led to a collapse of independent Norse colonies, such as the one in Greenland. If even a few people left Greenland due to a loss of trading opportunities, or were lost to conflict with the Inuit (as in the first model), there might have been too few laborers to maintain the colony (Dugmore et al. 2007:19).

The Thule also carried with them several major innovations, including body armor, the bow and arrow, dog sleds, boats, and floats for whale hunting. These were huge advantages and allowed the Thule to move quickly about the landscape, to hunt a wider range of animals at greater distances, and to be more likely to prevail in any military encounter. Toggle harpoon heads appear to have been present across the Arctic since about 3,000 BP, but the Thule used them to greater effect after about 1,000 BP.

The Classic Thule were whale hunters (Fig. 4.5), but as they moved east, they diversified their economy by adding a variety of other prey to their list, including seals, walrus, caribou, musk-ox, fish, and birds. Thus, caribou probably became an important resource after 600 BP (Friesen and Stewart 2004) and perhaps fish as well (Whitridge 2001).

The Classic Thule lived in large, permanent villages with many houses, perhaps reflecting the number of people necessary to crew whaling boats. Thule winter houses were semisubterranean; had tunnel entrances, cold traps, and raised sleeping platforms; and were usually covered by skin (or sometimes sod). Snowhouses were also used for temporary shelter in the winter. Summer houses were small skin tents held down with rocks.

Burial of the dead was uncommon, but when it occurred, the dead were buried on the surface under rock cairns. It is possible that the dead were treated differently by season, buried in cairns in the summer (when they were living on land) and by a different method during the winter (when they were living on the ice, with no available rock) (see Maxwell 1985:289). Eight very

FIGURE 4.5 Ethnographic Inuit in a large open boat with a whale they have successfully killed and moved to shore. Note the large floats on the right side of the picture. This float technology allowed hunters to harpoon a whale, attach floats, and let the whale exhaust itself until it could be killed. (*Source:* Washington State Historical Society.)

well-preserved individuals, six women and two children who died about 525 years ago, were found buried under rock piles at the Qilakitsoq site in western Greenland (Hansen et al. 1991). The analysis of the bodies and associated material culture (they were interred in their clothing and with some tools) revealed information about technology, art, tattooing, last meals, biological relationships between the individuals, and disease.

At about 650 BP, the climate became colder (the Little Ice Age), and much of the northern Arctic was abandoned (see Morrison 1990:111), with the northern groups moving south. In the southern part of the Arctic, villages became smaller and the relatively large population aggregates dispersed, with seasonal rounds to pursue a variety of game. Late Thule reflected the much more mobile lifestyle recorded by ethnographers (e.g., Boas 1888). Thus, the ethnographic Inuit were different than the Classic Thule who entered the region only a few hundred years earlier.

NATIVE ARCTIC CULTURES AT CONTACT

As discussed in Highlight 4.3, the Thule of the eastern Arctic were first contacted by the Norse moving west from Iceland, but these contacts had little lasting impact on the Thule, and the Norse were gone by AD 1300. In the early 1600s, Europeans again entered the eastern Arctic and encountered the Thule (Inuit). Some Inuit were captured and taken to Europe as curiosities, and a few others were killed. The first Europeans in the western Arctic were the Russians, who arrived in Alaska in 1732. They contacted and fought with the Aleut and Yupik groups, finally gaining control of the region in 1804. The United States purchased Alaska from Russia in 1867, and the Russians left the region at that time, although their cultural influences, particularly religion, persist to this day (see Black [1988] for a history of the Russians in Alaska).

After 1840, American whalers became very active in the northern Arctic, where whaling activities reached their peak in about 1900. This intensive hunting depleted whale populations to the point that the native peoples struggled to locate them. In addition, the whaling ships commonly stopped at coastal native villages, where the sailors spread venereal diseases. Although contacted by Europeans in the 1600s in the east and the 1700s in the west, most Arctic groups remained largely unaffected by Old World diseases until the 1800s, after which disease decimated native populations.

Until fairly recently, many Arctic people lived in a largely traditional manner, but after World War II, radical change came to the Arctic. Many military bases were opened, Western material culture became more prevalent, and many people moved to small towns around bases and regional centers, where they now live in Western-style houses that do not stay as warm as traditional housing. Traditional subsistence activities, such as hunting and fishing, are still very important in the economy and social identity of many Arctic people.

For the most part, the governments of both the United States and Canada ignored the native people of the Arctic. There was some effort to build schools, but little other help was provided, and virtually nothing was done to control the effects that development in the region (e.g., mining, lumber, fishing, whaling) had on the native groups. In the United States portion of the Arctic, all groups signed the 1971 Alaska Native Claims Settlement Act (ANCSA). The Canadian government remains in negotiations to settle other native claims (see Crowe 1991). One agreement has resulted in the creation of a new northern Canadian province, Nunavat, which is controlled by the Inuit. Greenland won province status from Denmark in 1979 and now governs itself, and the majority of the members of the Greenlandic legislative assembly are Inuit.

The future looks promising. The Inuit are making an effort to reinvigorate their culture. Native languages are being taught in schools, and the use of native technologies (e.g., clothing, weapons for hunting, dog sleds) and skills is being encouraged. Some Inuit families have even returned to a traditional lifestyle.

Further Reading

There is a considerable literature on the prehistory of the Arctic. The best summaries are present in Dumond (1984, 1987a, 1987b), Maxwell (1985), J. V. Wright (1995), McGhee (1996), and Maschner et al. (2009). The Canadian Museum of Civilization and the University of Alaska publish monographs that deal with the Arctic, and major journals include *Arctic, Arctic Anthropology,* and *Canadian Journal of Archaeology.*

5

Salmon and Potlatches
The Northwest Coast

The Northwest Coast, extending from the Alaskan panhandle south to northwestern California, was home to some of the most complex prehistoric hunter-gatherer societies in North America. The social organizations of these groups fascinated early anthropologists, and some of the earliest ethnographic studies in North America were conducted in that region. Northwest Coast groups lived in an area of such abundant natural resources that many researchers consider the region a "Garden of Eden." They had large populations, were organized into ranked societies, had elaborate art traditions, engaged in considerable warfare, and held slaves (generally war captives). The level of complexity varied among the diverse Northwest Coast groups (e.g., groups in the southern Northwest Coast were clearly less complex; see Erlandson et al. 1998), but all shared the features noted above.

This level of cultural complexity is unusual for hunter-gatherers. Thus, an understanding of Northwest Coast complexity has considerable theoretical importance to anthropology (Maschner 1991; Ames 1994, 2006) for help in understanding the development of complexity in general and among hunter-gatherers in particular. The complexity in the Northwest Coast is an exception to the general rule of complexity among hunter-gatherers and as such has become a critical analogy in the study of complexity.

GEOGRAPHY AND ENVIRONMENT

The Northwest Coast extends along the Pacific coast of North America from Yakutat Bay in southern Alaska over 1,500 miles south to Northern California (Fig. 5.1) (see Suttles 1990b). The culture area is long and narrow, mostly near the coast. High coastal mountains run along the entire length of the Northwest Coast, resulting in a rugged coastline and the formation of a large number of islands, such as Haida Gwaii (formerly the Queen Charlotte Islands) and Vancouver Island. The islands and sinuous coast create many thousands of miles of coastline, much of which provided habitat for many resources. For the purposes of this book, the Northwest Coast is divided into three major regions (following Kroeber 1939; Matson and Coupland 1995; Matson 2003) (see Fig. 5.1). The North Coast extends from Yakutat Bay in Alaska south to the northern tip of Vancouver Island,

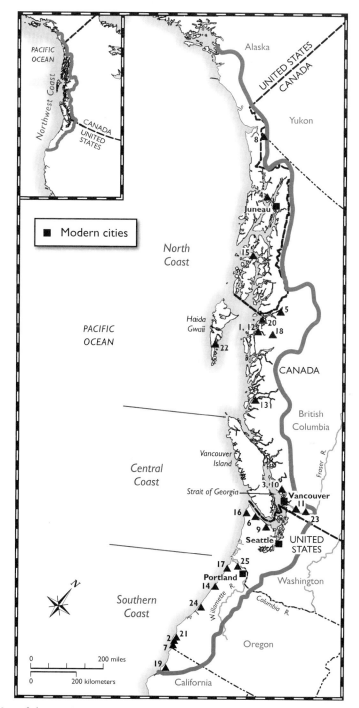

FIGURE 5.1 Map of the Northwest Coast showing the major subregions and the location of places and sites discussed in the text: 1) Boardwalk; 2) Chetlessenten; 3) Glenrose Cannery; 4) Ground Hog Bay 2; 5) Greenville Cemetery; 6) Hoko River; 7) Indian Sands; 8) Kwäddy Dän Ts'inchi; 9) Manis; 10) Marpole; 11) Maurer; 12) McNichol Creek; 13) Namu; 14) Netarts Sandspit Village; 15) On Your Knees Cave; 16) Ozette; 17) Palmrose; 18) Paul Mason (Kitselas Canyon); 19) Point St. George; 20) Prince Rupert Harbour; 21) Raymond's Dune; 22) Richardson Island; 23) Scowlitz; 24) Tahkenitch Landing; 25) Youngs River Complex.

the Central Coast extends from the northern tip of Vancouver Island south to the Columbia River, and the South Coast extends from the Columbia River south to Northern California.

The climate of the Northwest Coast is wet and relatively mild, with cool summers and wet winters. Rainfall is abundant, although it varies from about 40 inches per year in the south to 130 inches a year in the north. As a result of the substantial rainfall, numerous rivers and streams with many bays and estuaries have been formed. The largest rivers in the region are the Fraser and Columbia (see Fig. 5.1).

The ocean environment provided critical resources, including a large variety of marine fish, many species of sea mammals, and abundant shellfish on and near the shore. Virtually all of the Northwest Coast is covered by a temperate rainforest. In the north, the forest is generally made up of spruce, western hemlock, and red cedar, while in the south it consists primarily of Douglas fir and western hemlock. Many species of pine, oak, cedar, and ash, as well as numerous other plants, grow in both types of forest. The mountains and thick forests make it difficult to travel inland. The terrestrial environment contains numerous large and small mammals, many of which were used as food by the prehistoric inhabitants of the region. The critical resource was salmon, which mature in the ocean and then migrate up nearly all of the rivers and streams to spawn. Many aquatic birds that inhabit the region were also hunted, and a few groups hunted whales.

A BRIEF HISTORY OF RESEARCH

Archaeological research along the Northwest Coast (see Carlson 1990; Matson and Coupland 1995:37–47) began later than in other regions of North America. Early anthropological investigations, fathered by Franz Boas, focused so heavily on the ethnography of the extant Northwest Coast groups that little archaeology was conducted, although some influential avocational work was done quite early. The first scientific work in the region was conducted by the Jesup North Pacific Expedition in the late 1800s (Carlson 1990:107). This early archaeology focused on later sites related to extant peoples, so no culture history or chronology was proposed.

A general model of culture history was finally offered (Kroeber 1939), suggesting that people from the interior moved to the coast (now believed to be quite the opposite) and was a beginning point for subsequent work. The advent of radiocarbon dating after 1950 allowed sites and components to be placed in time, and general culture histories were proposed by Charles Borden and Roy Carlson in the 1960s, which were largely dependent on models based on the ethnographic record. By the 1970s, a basic chronology was in place and archaeologists became more interested in ecology and process and on the development of complexity. At this same time, several major regional research efforts were undertaken, such as the North Coast Prehistory Project in Prince Rupert Harbour conducted by the Archaeological Survey of Canada between 1968 and 1974 (see MacDonald and Cybulski 2001; Ames 2005).

Today, as in other areas of North America, cultural resource management is the major impetus for most of the work performed in the region. Importantly, much of the CRM work is now conducted in concert with native groups.

HIGHLIGHT 5.1

GLACIAL DISCOVERIES

One of the very few benefits of global warming and the melting of the glaciers is that archaeological materials frozen in the ice millennia ago are being exposed and discovered.

In southern Alaska, a number of preserved materials have been found, including various artifacts and even people who died on the ice (e.g., Hare et al. 2004; Dixon et al. 2005). The mission now is to find and document the materials before they are lost from exposure to the modern environment.

For example, a projectile point made from antler some 7,300 years ago was found with pine pitch adhesive still preserved (Helwig et al. 2008). Another discovery consisted of the modified feathers of six different bird species, dated to 4,500 BP, indicating use of feathers for weapons (fletching) and perhaps decorative or ceremonial purposes (Dove et al. 2005).

In a discovery reminiscent of the Ice Man in Italy (Sjøvold 1992), the frozen body of a young man who died accidentally on a glacier about 550 years ago was found in northwestern British Columbia (see Beattie et al. 2000). The individual was named Kwädāy Dän Ts'ínchí ("Long Ago Person Found"). Found with him were clothing, a hat, tools, weapons, and food, providing a rare opportunity to link the material culture to a single individual of known age and sex.

MAJOR THEMES IN NORTHWEST COAST PREHISTORY

A number of important research questions apply to the Northwest Coast. First, if the initial migrants into North America took a coastal route (see Chapter 2), they must have come south along the Northwest Coast. Where are their sites (probably underwater), and how did they live? A related issue is that there seems to be a difference between the North Coast and the Central and South coasts during the early Holocene. What does that tell us about the earlier movements of people and subsequent developments? Does it reflect a migration of inland peoples to some portions of the coast and not to others?

There are probably two major research goals for most archaeologists in the Northwest Coast: the building of local and regional chronologies and an understanding the development of complex societies (Ames 2003:19). Researchers are attempting to understand the role of resources, particularly salmon, in the development of economies, when groups adopted village life, how inequality arose, the role of warfare, and the role of surpluses (see Highlight 5.2). Further, the role of salmon dependence and storage is hotly debated and poorly known. There is a tendency to view salmon as *the* enabling resource, a bias that might actually hinder archaeological research.

Most recently, the study of households has become a popular topic (see Ames 2006). The presence of distinct houses and the hope that the artifacts in the houses can be related to specific occupations fuels this work. The elucidation of household organization, craft production, status, and even kinship systems is possible from such studies (such as at Ozette, see Highlight 5.3).

HIGHLIGHT 5.2

THE POTLATCH

In ethnographic times, rank and title were very important to Northwest Coast societies. Individuals were ranked within a family, families within a lineage, lineages within a clan, clans within their moieties, moieties within the village, and villages within the culture. This system was extraordinarily complex, and each ranked entity (from individuals to villages) would mark important events in such a way as to affirm their rank or to increase their rank. These ceremonies were called potlatches.

Potlatches were held for many significant occasions, such as the birth of a child, the onset of puberty, marriages, funerals, the construction of a house, to erase shame, or for changing power alliances. The scale would depend on the significance of the event and who was involved. The group hosting a potlatch would feed, entertain, and offer gifts to the attendees. The wealthier and higher ranked the hosts were, the more they could afford to give away; in Northwest Coast society, sharing and giving wealth away were the traits that made someone rich, not the retention of wealth. On occasion, goods were even purposefully destroyed during a potlatch to impress the attendees with the wealth of the group, and sometimes totem poles were erected to observe the event. Potlatches were also important religious ceremonies where origin stories were reenacted, the world was renewed, and where birth, death, and rebirth were major themes.

Sponsorship of a potlatch also provided the opportunity for social mobility, through the mechanism of a rivalry potlatch. A lower ranked individual or group would challenge an individual or group of higher rank to a potlatch, the winner claiming the rank. To win, the challenger would have to stage a "better" potlatch than that of the challenged. The attendees determined the winner.

Many items were stockpiled in anticipation of presenting a potlatch, including a variety of foods and gifts for all of the guests (which could be in the many hundreds in some cases), as well as numerous items needed for decoration and display. Gifts could include shell money, blankets, wooden boxes, strings of red-headed woodpecker scalps, barrels of fish oil, large obsidian blades, and even slaves. A typical potlatch was held in the largest structure available to the group holding the event, often a large communal house.

The introduction of European trade goods dramatically altered Northwest Coast economies, particularly due to the deaths of many people from disease, which may have escalated potlatching. In fact, some scholars believe that the potlatch was much less intensive (see Codere 1950; Drucker and Heizer 1967; Jonaitis 1991) before contact. Also, it had long been proposed that the potlatch system replaced warfare late in time as a form of competition (Codere 1950), but that was probably not the case (Lovisek 2007).

Using ethnographic analogy and the direct historical approach, archaeologists have assumed that potlatching (or feasting in general) was integral to the development of complex societies along the Northwest Coast after about 3,500 BP (see Carlson 1994:349). But what would a potlatch/feast look like in the archaeological record? One would expect to find evidence of large communal houses, differential treatment of the deceased, considerable quantities of stored food (mostly salmon), elaborate artwork and personal wealth items, labrets (jewelry for pierced lower lips worn by the wealthy), potlatch-specific artifacts (e.g., spoons and masks), and broken and scattered potlatch items in cemeteries. Indeed, these patterns appear in the archaeological record about 3,500 BP.

Last, many of the groups that lived in the Northwest Coast prior to contact still live in the region, and many are actively involved in cultural research. As a result, one of the general research goals is connecting the archaeological materials to ethnographic groups (e.g., the Ozette site, see below). A basic chronological sequence for the Northwest Coast is shown in Table 5.1.

THE PALEOINDIAN PERIOD (TO 10,000 BP)

Cultural manifestations dating from the Paleoindian Period are poorly represented along the Northwest Coast and are generally included in the Northwest Pebble Tool Tradition that includes bifaces and large cobble tools (Ackerman 2008:71). Recall from Chapter 2 that it is possible that

TABLE 5.1 General Chronological Sequences for the Northwest Coast

Date (BP)	General Periods	Regional Sequences			An Alternative Chronology*	General Climate
		Northern Coast	Central Coast	South Coast		
150	Developed Northwest Coast Pattern	Late Period	Gulf of Georgia Phase	Late Holocene	Late Pacific	cooler and wetter
						MCA, warmer
1,000						cooler and wetter
			Marpole Phase		Middle Pacific	
2,000		Middle Period				
			Locarno Beach Phase			
3,000						
	Middle Holocene	Early Period	Charles Phase	Middle Holocene	Early Pacific	
4,000						cooling, but still warm
			Old Cordilleran			
5,000	Early Holocene	North Coast Microblade Tradition		Old Cordilleran		drier and hotter than today
					Archaic	
6,000						
7,000						
8,000						warming, but still cooler and moister than today
9,000						
to 10,000	Paleoindian/Northwest Pebble Tool Tradition				Paleoindian	glacial times

*From Ames and Maschner (1999:66)

the first people moving into North America came south following the coastline. However, 10,000 years ago, sea levels were much lower and the coastline was farther to the west. Thus, many Paleoindian sites, if they still exist, may now be underwater (e.g., Fedje 2002).

Nevertheless, some evidence of a Paleoindian presence has been found. While few occupation sites have been identified, a few isolated Clovis points have been found (Ames and Maschner 1999:65; also see Fedje et al. 2004). The earliest known occupation site is at Ground Hog Bay 2, located in southeastern Alaska. The initial occupation was dated between about 11,000 and 9,800 BP,

at the site, dating between about 9,000 and 6,300 BP, contained bifaces but no microblades. Faunal remains indicated the use of both terrestrial and marine resources.

Further south, along the Lower Columbia River region, the Youngs River Complex is thought to date between 8,000 and 6,000 BP. It may be similar to the Windust materials to the east (see Chapter 6), but it is only known from a few surface sites and there are no firm dates (see Pettigrew 1990; Matson and Coupland 1995:79–80).

Still further south, on the Oregon coast, the known record is also meager, and it has been argued that some early sites could have been lost to erosion and sea level rise (Lyman 1991:33). In addition, few archaeologists have looked for early sites due to their focus on late shell middens. Only two sites dating to Old Cordilleran times are known. The first is Indian Sands (see above), which contained a ca. 8,000 BP component (Moss and Erlandson 1995) with a small deposit of shellfish remains, perhaps the earliest shell midden on the South Coast (Minor 1997). The second is Tahkenitch Landing, dated between 7,000 and 8,000 BP (Minor 1995), although it might date after ca. 6,700 BP (Moss and Erlandson 1998a:19). Minor (1997) argued that the people at Tahkenitch Landing exploited a wide variety of marine fish and birds. These groups probably would have been generalized foragers, exploiting littoral, riverine, and upland resources.

Some have argued (Lyman 1997) that marine resources were utilized in Old Cordilleran times but were not the primary focus of the economy. Minor (1995, 1997) thought that marine resources were a focal point before ca. 5,000 BP. This question remains unresolved, and the antiquity of the maritime adaptation on the South Coast remains unknown (Erlandson et al. 1998).

THE MIDDLE HOLOCENE (CA. 5,000 TO 3,500 BP)

The Middle Holocene, which includes the Early Pacific Period (Ames and Maschner 1999) and Early Period, has been viewed as beginning about 7,000 BP and in full effect by 5,800 BP, when conditions were cooler and wetter than the Early Holocene but hotter and drier than today. However, Moss et al. (2007:515) saw little to support a major change at 5,800 BP and argued that the Early Holocene lasted until about 4,850 BP, when a major climatic change did take place (Moss et al. 2007:493). As we have already seen, the archaeological record prior to about 5,000 BP is quite sparse, but there was a dramatic increase in sites along the Northwest Coast after that time, clearly marking 5,000 BP as an important time.

Sea levels generally stabilized at about 5,000 BP, leading Fladmark (1975) to propose that the related increase in resource availability and reliability led to the development of the complex societies seen in ethnographic times (as discussed below). While environment alone does not "dictate" human cultural response, it clearly does play an important role.

Although present at a few sites prior to about 5,000 BP, shell middens began to appear in many places after that time, suggesting sedentary lifestyles, growing populations, increasing political and social complexity, and the first evidence of warfare (trauma in skeletons). In essence, then, the basic framework of the economic system of the Northwest Coast developed during this time. The appearance of shell middens has often been viewed as representing larger populations exploiting abundant food resources. Interestingly, though, Moss (1993) argued that to the ethnographic Tlingit, shellfish was a lower class food, avoided by people of high status. Thus, there may have been a social aspect of shellfish use in the past. Some of the earliest wet sites, containing perishable artifacts such as basketry, also appear during this time and shed light on the development of the woodworking and textile industries.

Along the North Coast after about 5,000 BP, microblades were dropped and groups evolved into a series of regional cultures with considerable cultural variability. A more sedentary collector strategy was adopted (Fladmark et al. 1990:237), and it appears that local groups focused on local resources (Matson and Coupland 1995:142). Large numbers of bone harpoon tips for fishing and sea mammal hunting have been recovered from archaeological sites, along with ground slate tools for filleting fish (perhaps salmon). Adzes of various sizes for woodworking, including some made of shell, have been present, although not in large numbers. No residential structures are known from the North Coast during this time.

The Middle Holocene component at Namu contained several dozen burials (see Hester and Nelson 1978) that are among the earliest known for the region. Cemeteries are present in the Prince Rupert Harbour area that date to at least 4,500 BP, suggestive of increased sedentism and perhaps even status differentiation (e.g., MacDonald and Cybulski 2001).

North Coast economies were orientated to marine resources, including sea mammals, deep ocean fish, shellfish, and salmon, although some hunting of land animals also occurred. The level of dependence on salmon is unknown, but there is no evidence of large-scale storage of salmon, suggesting that it was not yet the key resource. Coupland (1998) argued that a full-blown maritime adaptation did not appear until about 4,500 BP and that this led to the emergence of the Developed Northwest Coast Pattern (see below), groups that can be tied to the ethnographic cultures. A similar argument was presented by Carlson (2008), who suggested that the maritime adaptation focused on salmon began between 6,000 and 5,000 BP. On Haida Gwaii, the time between about 5,000 BP and contact is called the Graham Tradition (Mackie and Achenson 2005), reflecting the connection of prehistoric materials to the ethnographic Haida.

The archaeology of the Middle Holocene is a little better known along the Central Coast, particularly in the Gulf of Georgia region. Here, research has identified the Charles Phase (ca. 4,500 to 3,300 BP), which was first proposed by Borden (1975:97). There appears to be more sites in the Charles Phase than in the earlier Old Cordilleran times, suggesting a population increase. The economy was broad based, mostly fish and shellfish, but included seals, elk, and deer. There is no evidence for storage, and the role of salmon is unclear. Tools such as flaked stone points and knives, harpoon heads, and carved antler have been found, but no ground slate knives have been identified. There is evidence of some trade in utilitarian and prestige materials (Grier 2003). A few residential structures have appeared, the earliest (ca. 4,800 BP) at the Maurer site on the lower Fraser River (Schaepe 2003), supporting the idea of at least some semipermanent settlements. Some burials are known, but they do not contain grave goods. No actual labrets have been found, but some tooth-wear evidence attests to their use (see Matson and Coupland 1995:117).

Along the South Coast, relatively few sites are known before 3,000 BP (Minor et al. 2001:Table 2). This time has been called the Early Littoral (Lyman 1991), and such sites generally contain materials similar to Charles Phase on the Central Coast. People were generalized foragers, and while sea mammal hunting was important (see Hildebrandt and Jones 2002), it was integrated into an overall economy that focused on terrestrial resources. The Palmrose site on the northern Oregon coast (T. J. Connolly 1992) was occupied as early as 4,000 BP, and its inhabitants focused on a variety of marine and terrestrial resources. The earliest house remains, about 3,200 years old, were documented at the Raymond's Dune site in far southern Oregon (Minor et al. 2001).

THE DEVELOPED NORTHWEST COAST PATTERN (CA. 3,500 TO 200 BP)

By about 3,500 BP, there was a dramatic change in Northwest Coast cultures. During the Late Holocene the climate had become cool and moist (much like today), although there were some fluctuations, such as the Medieval Climatic Anomaly (MCA). This time is also known as the Middle and Late Pacific periods (Ames and Maschner 1999). The use of shellfish dramatically increased, and many large shell middens appeared. Salmon (and other resources, see D. K. Hanson [2008]) apparently became much more important and began to be stored in large quantities, permanent villages with many large houses became common, and complex social institutions developed (see Coupland 1998). These developments are indicated by the exploitation of substantial quantities of salmon, elaborate artwork and personal wealth, the use of labrets and their elaboration through time, differential treatment of the dead, the inferred presence of the potlatch (e.g., potlatch-specific artifacts), broken and scattered potlatch items in cemeteries, and large house structures (see Carlson 1994:349). This reflects a clear increase in complexity and is collectively known as the Developed Northwest Coast Pattern (DNWCP), essentially the beginnings of the complex social groups encountered by Europeans in the 1700s, although not all archaeologists like the DNWCP as an organizational construct.

Why did the DNWCP develop? A large number of archaeological models have been introduced. The first, and perhaps most influential, was proposed by Fladmark (1975), who suggested that prior to about 5,800 BP, dynamic sea levels and climate made the environment unstable. Once sea levels reached their modern positions, productive littoral environments developed and rivers stabilized, with shellfish and salmon becoming predictable and productive. Shellfish began to be used and shell middens appeared. Salmon were available in such quantities that storage technology appeared, people began to live in large villages, and large and complex societies eventually emerged. This is the "Garden of Eden" hypothesis.

The current evidence for the Fladmark model is weak (Moss et al. 2007:494). Shell middens are now known to have occurred earlier than 5,800 BP, even as early as 9,750 BP (Moss et al. 2007: Table 14.1). Sea levels did not stabilize everywhere at that time either, but fluctuated on local scales. For example, sea levels did not stabilize on Haida Gwaii or Vancouver Island until about 2,000 BP due to tectonic uplift, and they were not extensively settled by people until that time (Ames and Maschner 1999:93), an interesting fact that actually supports the basics of the Fladmark model. Further, it is not clear whether salmon actually became more important than other animal resources through time (Butler and Campbell 2004) and whether it was a factor in the development of cultural complexity. Notwithstanding these criticisms, however, there is evidence that sea level did generally stabilize about 5,000 years ago and that there was a dramatic increase in the use of salmon in most places after that time.

More recent models (see discussions in Coupland 1988, 1998; Ames 1994, 2005, 2006; Matson and Coupland 1995:148–154; Ames and Maschner 1999; Moss et al. 2007) have emphasized a number of factors other than resource abundance. For example, a population increase may have resulted in the need to develop more complex social organizations. The relatively brief availability of salmon may have resulted in the intensification of their capture, the development of the technology for storage (salmon can be caught en masse for a short time in the fall and must be stored for use during the remainder of the year), and the location of settlements near important resource areas. Innovations in salmon procurement and storage would have gradually increased their yield, perhaps resulting in the necessity to have managers of knowledge, schedules, labor, equipment, and facilities, leading to the development of an elite class and eventually a stratified society. Eventually, these elites would have gained control (i.e., ownership) of resource localities, creating conditions of competition. Such competition could have been for prestige, for resources, or for resource localities and could have given rise to warfare, which in turn would have led to further increases in social and political complexity.

The role of warfare in the evolution of the DNWCP is also not well understood but most certainly had some role in the development of complex organizations. Warfare was first seen by about 5,000 BP (Maschner 1997) but was sublethal. Warfare was more prevalent and lethal by

3,500 BP, and by about 1,800 BP at least some villages had become fortified. By 1,800 BP, the bow and arrow was in use, wooden and bone body armor was developed in response, and bone points that were effective against armor became abundant (Maschner 1997:277). By 1,100 BP, many defensive sites were being constructed. At the time of contact, warfare was common but may have been less than during prehistoric times. It is possible that potlatching replaced warfare late in time as a form of competition (Codere 1950), although this notion has been challenged (Lovisek 2007).

Slavery may have also played a role in the development of the DNWCP. Slaves were usually war captives, and with the advent of warfare and raiding, Northwest Coast groups obtained and kept slaves for use as laborers and as status symbols (Ames 2001). However, it is possible that slavery did not develop until later, about 1,500 BP (Ames 2001).

Other possible factors in the DNWCP include trade, especially of obsidian, copper, and shell. Trade in obsidian took place as early as ca. 9,500 BP, intensified between 6,000 and 4,000 BP, stabilized about that time, and declined after about 1,500 BP (see Carlson 1994). Large-capacity boats and netsinkers appear at this time, suggesting an expansion of fishing into deeper ocean waters.

It has been suggested (Maschner 1991:932) that beginning about 1,500 BP, the northern Northwest Coast witnessed a major shift in settlement systems from numerous small villages centered on resource-rich areas to fewer but larger villages situated in defensive locations. According to Maschner (1991), this resulted in less emphasis on local resources and greater emphasis on distant but abundant and storable resources, primarily salmon. Such stored resources were controlled by a relatively few powerful individuals and this, coupled with climatic fluctuations, led to the development of ranked society.

By 1,500 BP, the DNWCP was present throughout the Northwest Coast (Matson and Coupland 1995:247). The origins of the DNWCP are not clear (Matson and Coupland 1995:125), but it may have originally emerged from the Northwest Coast Microblade Tradition along the North Coast, likely earlier than on the Central Coast. However, this may simply be because more research has been conducted in the Central Coast.

The DNWCP on the North Coast

The DNWCP appears to be generally earlier on the North Coast than on the Central Coast, beginning perhaps by 3,500 BP (Matson and Coupland 1995:229; Moss 2004). The cultures during this time were relatively homogeneous, but some important regional exceptions were more elaborate. None of the cultural complexes so far investigated are as well known as the Locarno Beach Phase of the Central Coast. The pattern appears to become more complex earlier as one moves south.

Salmon were clearly important during the DNWCP, as evidenced by fish traps (perhaps for large-scale salmon fishing) as early as 5,500 BP (Moss and Erlandson 1998b:Table 1) and fish weirs (see Fig. 5.2) by at least 3,000 BP (Moss and Stuckenrath 1990). In southeast Alaska, artifact styles linked to the ethnographic Tlingit are present by at least 1,600 BP (Moss et al. 1989; Moss 2004).

In the Prince Rupert Harbour area (see Fladmark et al. 1990; Ames 1998, 2005; MacDonald and Cybulski 2001), large and deep shell middens appear after about 3,500 BP, and large winter villages appear by about 3,000 BP, persisting until contact. At the Paul Mason (Kitselas Canyon) site on the Skeena River, dated ca. 3,000 BP, two rows of rectangular houses aligned along a "street" were found (Coupland 1988). The layout of this village (Fig. 5.3) was

FIGURE 5.2   The remains of a wooden fish weir along the Coquille River, Oregon, dating between 1,000 and 500 BP (photo by Madonna L. Moss) .

very similar to the ethnographic pattern, suggesting ranked corporate groups and providing the earliest evidence of settled village life on the Northwest Coast (see Coupland 1985, 1988; Matson and Coupland 1995:183–191). Nearby, a second large village, known as Boardwalk (Stewart and Stewart 2001), also contained a nearly intact village with a single row of houses dating just after the Paul Mason site (ca. 2,500 to 2,000 BP). The site also contained over 100 burials, evidence of warfare and trade (in copper, obsidian, and shell), and faunal remains of mostly terrestrial mammals (Stewart and Stewart 2001). A third large village with two rows of houses was found at the nearby McNichol Creek site (Coupland et al. 1993, 2003) and dates to about 1,600 BP. One of the excavated houses apparently belonged to a chief, who communicated his power through architecture and art (Coupland 2006). McNichol Creek was a small winter-to-summer seasonal village where stored salmon, shellfish, and deer were the primary foods (Stewart and Stewart 2001).

The Namu site (see above), first occupied by about 11,000 BP (Hester and Nelson 1978; Carlson 1996b:97), continued to be occupied until contact, although the occupation was less intensive after about 2,400 BP. Interestingly, the faunal data from Namu indicate a substantial decline in the use of salmon after about 3,800 BP, and especially after about 2,200 BP (Cannon 2002:317). This may indicate periodic failure of salmon runs, possibly indicating that shortage of this vital resource contributed to the development of complex ritual systems and the relocation of winter villages to new locations (Cannon 2002). However, it is not clear that

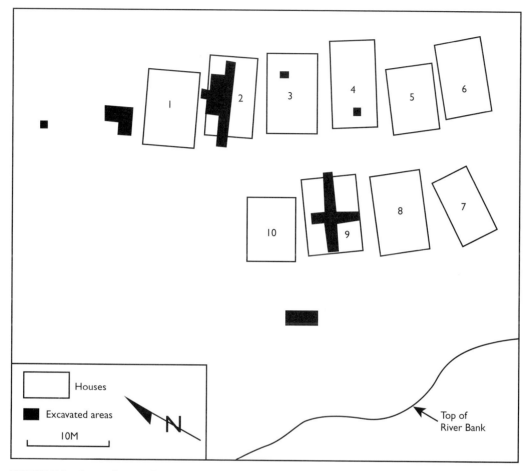

FIGURE 5.3   General map of the house layout at the Paul Mason site. Note the two rows of houses (redrawn from Coupland 1988: Fig. 5.2; used with permission).

salmon productivity changed dramatically through time (Butler and Campbell 2004). It should be cautioned that the absence of salmon (or any other animal) bones in a site could be the result of people processing the animal away from the village, bringing back only the boneless fillets (the "Schlepp Effect"; Daley 1969). Thus, it is often difficult to quantify salmon use through time.

The mortuary patterns of the DNWCP in the Prince Rupert Harbour area are also of importance. After about 2,500 BP, there are clear indications of rank and warfare (Fladmark et al. 1990:234; Archer 2001; Ames 2005:301) and some evidence of postmortem modification of human bones, especially skulls (Cybulski 1978). By about 2,500 BP, labrets were worn almost exclusively by men (Ames and Maschner 1999:189). There are more males than females in the cemeteries that have been investigated, suggestive of warfare (more young males with trauma) and perhaps slavery (slaves, often female, were not buried in cemeteries). Ames (2005:301) identified four "classes" of burial individuals: (1) those without access to cemeteries (whose remains were found elsewhere); (2) those in a cemetery but without grave goods; (3) those in a cemetery with grave goods of worked bone, labrets, and other materials; and (4) those in cemeteries with materials from distant sources, such as copper items, shell beads, and amber. This latter class has only been found at the Boardwalk site and suggests use by high-status people from across the region.

To illustrate, the Greenville Cemetery (Cybulski 1992), north of Prince Rupert Harbour and dating later in time than the Prince Rupert sites, contained many interments, most of which had been buried in boxes. None of the burials had grave offerings of artifacts, although there were a few dog skulls and considerable evidence of food offerings. Dental wear indicated that some of the women had worn labrets (Cybulski 1992:67). The cemetery appears to have been used during two episodes, the first between 1,500 and 1,000 BP and again between 800 and 700 BP. After 700 BP, the mortuary pattern changed to aboveground burial.

The dead at Greenville, and at some other sites in the region, seem to have been buried in a shell midden that contained little evidence of an actual occupation, as no features (e.g., hearths or houses) and few artifacts were found. This suggests several intriguing possibilities (see Cybulski 1992:168; Ames 2005). First, the dead may have been buried in preexisting (earlier) shell deposits (such as at the Scowlitz site; Lepofsky et al. 2000), but that would not explain the paucity of features or artifacts at Greenville. Second, the shell deposits may have been purposefully constructed with soil brought in from a nearby village site or shell processing locality. Third, it is possible that the shell middens developed concurrently as a result of food offerings to the dead. In any case, the shell middens became sacred once they were used for burials (see D. Brown 2003:164).

The DNWCP on the Central Coast

Much of what is known about the DNWCP along the Central Coast comes from sites in and around the Gulf of Georgia, located in the center of that region and including the Fraser River delta (where the city of Vancouver is now located). In general, there are signs of ranked societies on the Central Coast by ca. 3,000 BP, artifacts similar to those used in ethnohistoric contexts appear, prehistoric art motifs are reminiscent of historic societies (see Carlson 1982), and settlement patterns were stable (Cannon 2003), all of which suggests an in situ evolution into the ethnographic groups (rather than population replacements).

Other factors may have also had a profound influence on the evolution of DNWCP groups on the Central Coast. There is evidence of considerable tectonic activity and volcanism at this time, and it is believed that earthquake-generated tsunamis hit the coast and impacted settlements at least six times in the last 3,000 years (Hutchinson and McMillan 1997; Losey 2005a). This could have wiped out entire groups and radically altered the cultural landscape.

Three phases of the DNWCP have been identified in the Gulf of Georgia area, and this general chronology (see Mitchell 1990) is broadly employed here as a framework for the entire Central Coast, although there is considerable regional variation. Each of these phases is discussed below.

THE LOCARNO BEACH PHASE (CA. 3,300 TO 2,500 BP)   The Locarno Beach Phase (see Mitchell 1990:341, 344; Wright 1995) appears to have developed out of the earlier Charles Phase (see above). The artifact inventory includes ground slate tools and an increase in bone tools, labrets, and some carved art. Pithouses are known from several sites, and it is possible that several had plank houses (Johnstone 2003). Both land and sea mammals were captured, and there was an increase in the use of salmon and shellfish. Thus, the Locarno Beach economy was apparently more specialized than that of the Charles Phase.

The most significant change in the Locarno Beach Phase was the transition from a nonstorage to a storage economy. Evidence suggests that salmon were caught in large numbers and processed (filleted and dried) at some other location where the fish bones were discarded. Such a process is indicative of large-scale storage (e.g., Matson and Coupland 1995:166). It may be that through time, shellfish were the staple in the winter but were collected locally, used immediately, and not stored (Croes and Hackenberger 1988). Later, flatfish (e.g., halibut) were obtained in relatively small numbers and were processed and stored. Still later, salmon were taken in large numbers, processed, and stored, completing the shift from nonstorage to storage. This is generally supported by the discoveries at Hoko River (Croes 1995, 2005), where the faunal data suggest that very few land mammals were taken and that flatfish were more important than salmon until about 1,500 BP, when salmon became more important.

Matson and Coupland (1995:183) concluded that the Locarno Beach Phase is the beginning of, but not a fully developed, aspect of the DNWCP. There is evidence of salmon storage and plank houses, but Locarno Beach lacks the other aspects of the DNWCP, such as winter villages, large multifamily houses, or clear evidence of ascribed status. These elements would appear in the subsequent Marpole Phase.

THE MARPOLE PHASE (CA. 2,500 TO 1,200 BP)   The Marpole Phase, named after the Marpole site located within the city of Vancouver, marked the appearance of the fully developed DNWCP (Matson and Coupland 1995; also see Wright 1995). It is reasonably clear that Marpole developed from the preceding Locarno Beach Phase (Burley 1980:39), and the best summary of Marpole was presented by Burley (1980). It was a time of considerable cultural change, characterized by the "widespread appearance of large houses, standardized art forms, and elaborate burials" (Lepofsky et al. 2005:267) and of the first large corporate household units (Coupland 1996:121).

By 2,000 BP, large villages with rows of large rectangular plank houses, probably multifamily households (see Matson and Coupland 1995:208), were present. There was ascribed status (Matson and Coupland 1995:224), abundant art, and a marked dependence on stored fish. The social order included elites, commoners, and slaves. There appears to have been a "reorganization of labor into larger social groups," perhaps associated with the emergence of ranking (Lepofsky et al. 2005:283).

Artifacts of the Marpole Phase consist of flaked stone points and other tools, microblades, and thinner ground slate knives, perhaps reflecting an emphasis on craftsmanship. The use of native copper ornaments continued, and labrets increased in importance. Carved stone art was common, but there was an increased emphasis on wooden art and an increase in the number of woodworking tools, such as adze blades. Such tools would be needed to make planks for houses.

Regional systems, having existed since the early Holocene, appear to have been widely integrated after 2,000 BP (e.g., Grier 2003). Long-distance trade in obsidian declined (Carlson 1994) but remained important (Grier 2003:176), and there was greater use of local obsidian sources, suggesting more local networks. The social and economic networks seen in the Gulf of Georgia late in time seem to have been formed and solidified at this time (Lepofsky et al. 2005).

Mortuary patterns continued to evolve during this time, and there was a shift from interment in shell middens to the use of other treatments, such as inhumation, cremation, or exposure aboveground. Some burials contained grave goods, and skull deformation was a common practice to indicate differential status. No major differences in the mortuary treatment of males and females have been noted (Burchell 2006). An important cemetery is located at the Scowlitz site on Lower Fraser River (Fig. 5.4). This village, with eighteen house depressions, was first occupied about 3,000 BP (Locarno Beach Phase) and was enlarged during the Marpole Phase. About 1,500 BP, occupation of the site ceased and it was used solely as a cemetery, with the dead interred in cairns covered with mounded earth (see Lepofsky et al. 2000). This pattern is different than the contemporaneous Greenville Cemetery to the north, illustrating the differences between the North and Central coasts.

FIGURE 5.4   Excavation of Mound 1 at the Scowlitz site, 1992 (photo by Michael Blake; used with permission).

Several other issues regarding the development of the Marpole Phase and subsequent DNWCP groups are important, along with the aforementioned possibility of tectonic and volcanic activity. First, winters may have been shorter and terrestrial resources may have been more abundant and predictable. This environmental change may have initiated a period of significant forest fires that may have been a factor in the development of Marpole (Lepofsky et al. 2005:267). Second, the bow and arrow diffused into the area by about 1,800 BP. This may have led to an increase in warfare and the development of large sedentary villages, with large houses inhabited by perhaps 20 to 60 people (Maschner 1991:930). Fortified sites also appeared at this time. Third, the abundance of salmon is of great interest at this time. Finney et al. (2002) suggested that Alaskan sockeye salmon populations abruptly declined about 2,100 BP and stayed low until about 1,200 BP. Although this model was based on Alaskan data, it may have been more widespread and could have impacted the entire Northwest Coast. Perhaps not coincidentally, human populations appear to have expanded after 2,500 BP, peaked at about 2,000 BP, declined rapidly until about 1,800 BP (Lepofsky et al. 2005), and began to increase again after about 1,200 BP.

Indeed, it has been suggested that as salmon, the critical resource, decreased, the cultural response was to impose increasing control of this resource (Coupland 1988; D. K. Hansen 2008). This may have led to the replacement of relatively egalitarian social institutions by complex, ranked, corporate groups as a means of maintaining control of the resource.

Population movements may have also been an important aspect of the DNWCP during the Marpole Phase. It has been proposed (Mitchell 1990:357–360; also see McMillan 2003b; Lepofsky et al. 2009) that before 2,500 BP, Salishan groups (ancestral to the Salish) occupied the coasts along the protected waterways of the Puget Sound, Gulf of Georgia, and Queen Charlotte Strait, while Wakashan groups (ancestral to the Kwakiutl and others) occupied the ocean waters of the western half of Vancouver Island. According to this model, at about 2,500 BP and continuing until ca. 150 BP, Wakashan groups expanded north onto Haida Gwaii and then onto the mainland west of the Queen Charlotte Strait, occupying territory previously occupied by Salishan groups. Thus, it is possible that Locarno Beach Phase groups were Salishan and that the Marpole Phase represents incoming Wakashan groups. On the other hand, the stability of settlement patterns suggests an in situ evolution into the ethnographic groups rather than population replacements (Cannon 2003).

THE GULF OF GEORGIA PHASE (CA. 1,200 BP TO CONTACT)   The Gulf of Georgia Phase of the DNWCP on the Central Coast (see Mitchell 1990:346), also known as the Late Period or the Late Pacific Period, is the direct archaeological manifestation of the ethnographic groups in the region. All of the traits of the ethnographic Northwest cultures were present: large permanent villages with substantial plank houses, intensive procurement and storage of salmon and other resources, complex social structures, potlatching/feasting, endemic warfare, and fortified sites (see Schaepe 2006). Most researchers agree that the ethnographic groups can trace their roots directly back to the beginning of the Gulf of Georgia Phase, and perhaps earlier.

One major change related to this phase was in mortuary patterns. Prior to about 700 BP, the dead had been buried in the ground, either in shell middens or in specially constructed mounds. After 700 BP, however, the dead were placed in the open (such as in trees) in order to accelerate decomposition. This change took place all across the Northwest Coast and may represent a fundamental shift in social organization (Lepofsky et al. 2005:273).

A different cultural pattern may have been present on the west side of Vancouver Island, where groups may not have adopted salmon as the primary staple until fairly late, after about 750 years ago. Prior to that time, large settled populations occupied the area but focused on whales, other fish, and fur seals (see McMillan et al. 2008). A similar pattern can be seen at several sites in this region. This suggests that salmon was not always the primary impetus to cultural complexity.

HIGHLIGHT 5.3

OZETTE: THE POMPEII OF THE NORTHWEST COAST

One rainy day 250 years ago, a wall of mud engulfed a coastal village near Ozette in northwestern Washington. The mud moved too quickly for people to pack up their possessions, but not fast enough to kill. Much of the village itself was buried, though, along with all the belongings of the occupants. The mud sealed the buried village, and all of the perishable materials were preserved. The site was discovered in the 1970s, and Richard Dougherty of the University of Washington spent ten years excavating it.

Six large multifamily plank houses (Fig. 5.5) were excavated (see G. C. Wessen 1990: Fig. 2; also see Matson and Coupland 1995:266–267). Each contained a huge quantity and variety of materials, including high-status items, although some houses contained more status items than others. In the houses, these prestige items were found in the corner, where the family of highest status lived (G. C. Wessen 1990:419). The complete excavation and extraordinary preservation allowed an analysis of household production, development, and status (Samuels 2006), a rare opportunity in archaeology.

FIGURE 5.5   Excavation in progress at the Ozette site. Note the wooden house planks. (*Source:* Ruth Kirk with Richard D. Daugherty, Hunters of the Whale, New York: Wiliam Morrow & Company/Addison Wesley, 1974.)

Some 55,000 artifacts, about 30,000 of which were wooden, were recovered. These included a variety of domestic, subsistence, and miscellaneous items, such as toys, games, canoes, decorations, carvings, foods (such as shellfish), and tools for whaling, seal hunting, and ocean fishing (see G. C. Wessen 1988; also see Samuels 2006). A great deal of artistic material was also recovered (see Daugherty and Friedman 1982; G. C. Wessen 1990: Figs. 3–6, 8–4) (also see Fig. 5.6).

FIGURE 5.6   A whale fin effigy carved from cedar wood and inlaid with otter teeth from the Ozette site. (Courtesy of the Library of Congress.)

Ozette is so far unique on the Northwest Coast, although a few other waterlogged sites have been excavated, revealing a great deal about perishable artifacts in different regions (Croes 2003). To learn more about Ozette, visit (www.makah.com). The Archaeology Channel also has a video on Ozette available on the Internet (www.archaeologychannel.org/content/video/ozette1.html).

The DNWCP on the South Coast

On the South Coast, the DNWCP appears only after about 2,500 BP, and this general period of time is sometimes called the Late Littoral (Lyman 1991). Groups practicing a Northwest Coast lifestyle were clearly present along the lower Columbia River (e.g., Pettigrew 1990). As to the north, groups began to live in large villages with large plank houses. Fishing was the primary economic pursuit, and fishing gear (harpoons and hooks) is abundant at archaeological sites of this time. Salmon were taken along most of the waterways, especially the Columbia and Willamette rivers. Along the coast, sea mammals were important, and in all cases, terrestrial resources were significant. The burial data (Lyman 1991:301) and the analysis of households (e.g., Ames et al. 1992; Ellis 2006) suggest the presence of a ranked society. The bow and arrow diffused into the region about 1,700 BP.

A number of relatively late villages are known along the coast of Oregon and Northern California. These include the Netarts Sandspit Village site in Oregon (Losey 2005b), dated between 700 and 300 BP, which features several large multifamily plank houses. The large site of Chetlessenten, located on the far southern Oregon coast (see Erlandson et al. 1997) and occupied from about 400 to 150 BP, contained a shell midden and many large square and rectangular plank houses, some with burials in them. Finally, the Point St. George site in Northern California (Gould 1966) was a very late village. Its excavation and interpretation were guided by ethnographic data, which for the time was cutting-edge work.

NATIVE NORTHWEST COAST CULTURES AT CONTACT

Most Northwest Coast groups have managed to survive, and many still live in their traditional territories, albeit on reservations or reserves, although some groups have no land base. Most live in poverty, although many work seasonally in the lumber and fishing industries. After the ban on potlatching was lifted by the Canadian government in 1951, Northwest Coast peoples began to revive the practice, rediscovering their culture and traditions in the process. Today, some groups have reestablished the system of ranking and potlatching to acknowledge ranks within the community.

Fishing rights continue to be a major issue facing Northwest Coast Indians (see Cohen 1986). They have fought and won many court battles since the late 1800s, but with little effect as the decisions were often ignored by non-Indians. The most significant ruling was in 1974, when Indian fishing rights were affirmed in the *Boldt* decision (reviewed and upheld by the U.S. Supreme Court in 1979), which is being slowly implemented.

In 1998, the Makah tribe in northwestern Washington received permission to resume traditional whale hunting with harpoons and canoes (and large-caliber rifles), an activity that has not been performed since the 1930s. The permit limited the Makah to taking five whales per year, but there was considerable protest over the move by environmental groups, with some employing ships to disrupt the hunt.

Finally, there have been numerous efforts, both private and governmental, to restore totem poles and to rejuvenate early art traditions. In addition, several ancient towns have been reproduced as tourist attractions. The economic potential for the native people of the Northwest Coast from these pursuits is considerable.

Further Reading

There is considerable literature on the prehistory of the Northwest Coast. Nine chapters of the Northwest Coast volume of the *Handbook of North American Indians* (Helm 1981) are devoted to prehistory. The most recent general summaries of Northwest Coast prehistory are present in Matson and Coupland (1995), C. V. Wright (1995), Ames and Maschner (1999), and Ames (2003), although there is a great deal of other literature from specific areas that is more recent. The Canadian Museum of Civilization publishes monographs that deal with the Northwest Coast, and important journals include *Arctic Anthropology* and *Canadian Journal of Archaeology*.

Roots and Pithouses
The Plateau

The Plateau culture area (Fig. 6.1) is located in the northwest corner of the United States and the southwest corner of Canada, inland from the Northwest Coast (D. E. Walker 1998a). People on the Plateau interacted with people in the surrounding culture areas to a considerable extent, and much of Plateau prehistory was influenced by these interactions. Salmon, roots, and large mammals were the key resources on the Plateau and are defining characteristics, much like salmon and sea mammals were on the Northwest Coast. Other major features of Plateau culture area include political complexity, broad kinship ties across groups, institutionalized regional trading networks, and settlements along rivers (D. E. Walker 1998b:3). The adoption of the horse after 1720 dramatically changed Plateau culture (see below).

GEOGRAPHY AND ENVIRONMENT

The Plateau is a region of interior highlands and basins extending from the Great Basin north into southern Canada (see Chatters 1998). It is bounded on the west by the Coast and Cascade ranges and on the east by the Rocky Mountains, and it includes central and northern Idaho, eastern Oregon, eastern Washington, and southern British Columbia. The environment of the Plateau is highly variable and complex, and the coastal mountains form a rainshadow that limits rainfall in the interior. The Plateau is drained by numerous rivers, the largest including the Columbia, Fraser, and Snake.

Based on broad differences in environment (e.g., Hunn 1990a), the Plateau can be split into northern and southern divisions. The Canadian (northern) Plateau is rather mountainous, drained by the Fraser and Thompson rivers, and is mostly covered by forests of pine and fir. The summers are warm and the winters can be extremely cold, with considerable snowfall. The Columbia (southern) Plateau is not quite as mountainous, but there are areas with extensive lava flows. The winters are cold and the summers are hot. The rainshadow effect of the southern Cascade Range limits rainfall to about six inches a year, making the Columbia Plateau relatively arid. Much of the southern Columbia Plateau is covered by sagebrush prairie and mixed short grasslands, and many of the small basins contain marshes.

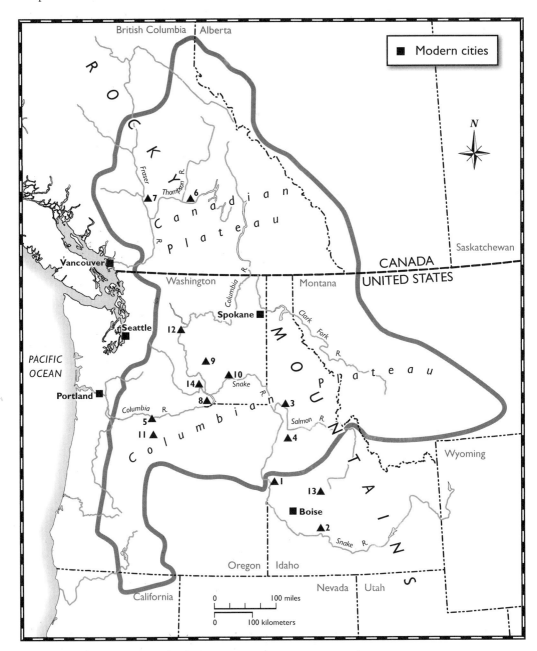

FIGURE 6.1 Map of the Plateau showing the major subregions and location of the sites discussed in the text: 1) Braden; 2) Buhl; 3) Cooper's Ferry; 4) DeMoss; 5) Five Mile Rapids; 6) Gore Creek; 7) Keatley Creek; 8) Kennewick; 9) Lind Coulee; 10) Marmes; 11) Paquet Gulch; 12) Richey-Roberts; 13) Simon; 14) Tsulim.

Food resources on the Plateau include deer, moose, elk, caribou (in the north), bears, mountain sheep, pronghorn, a few bison, rabbits, rodents, birds, and insects. For most of prehistory, salmon was a critical resource. Shellfish were available in large quantities in several of the river systems. Perhaps the most important plants were roots and tubers, particularly camas, although acorns, pine nuts, and various berries were also important. Other plants, including cattail, willow, and hemp, provided materials for basketry, housing, and tools.

Until about 700 years ago, the southern portion of Idaho would have been part of the Plateau culture area. At that time, Numic peoples moved north out of the Great Basin to occupy that area, changing its "affiliation" from Plateau to Great Basin. As a result, the prehistory of southern Idaho was tied to the Plateau until 700 years ago and to the Great Basin after that time.

A BRIEF HISTORY OF RESEARCH

As with many areas in North America, most intensive research on the Plateau began after World War II (see Lohse and Sprague 1998:17–28). Prior to 1945, the majority of information on the regional prehistory was generated by explorers, ethnographers, and amateurs. Only intermittent professional work was conducted, mostly in the United States. After 1933, the University of Oregon began a research program, but that activity dropped markedly during World War II.

After 1945, archaeological research programs were initiated at other universities, notably the University of Washington, the University of British Columbia, and later at Simon Fraser and Washington State universities. The construction of dams in the late 1940s and 1950s resulted in a great deal of excavation at sites affected by those projects (the River Basin Surveys directed by the National Parks Service). By the 1960s, environmental laws in Canada and (later) the United States resulted in archaeology being conducted in advance of many construction projects. By the early 1960s, attempts to synthesize Plateau prehistory had begun, and beginning in the early 1970s, research shifted from being simply descriptive to a focus on explanation and ecology.

By the 1990s, most archaeology done on the Plateau was related to Corps of Engineers development, the largest projects being the work associated with the construction of dams in Washington State (see Lohse and Sprague 1998:24–25). As the political power of the Native Americans increased, they began to put considerable pressure on the government to control archaeological research. Perhaps the most notable example of this is the Kennewick Man case (see Chapter 2). Today, most academic research is focused on the rise of complex societies, the transition between mobile foragers and sedentary collectors (see Highlight 6.1).

HIGHLIGHT 6.1

FORAGERS AND COLLECTORS

Hunter-gatherers are classified in a number of ways, one being how they organize their procurement of resources. Binford (1980) proposed that hunter-gatherers practicing a "forager" strategy generally move people to the resources. They occupy a series of camps as they move about the landscape from resource to resource on a daily basis, rarely storing food and having no permanent home. Thus, foragers "generally have high residential mobility, low-bulk inputs [gathering small quantities of resources at any one time], and regular daily food procurement" (Binford 1980:9).

Hunter-gatherers practicing a collector "strategy" employ specially organized task groups to exploit specific resources, often in bulk, with storage being important (Binford 1980:10). Such tasks groups go out into the landscape to obtain resources and then bring them back to the people. Collectors generally maintain permanent or semipermanent residences (being generally less mobile than foragers), with many smaller activity locations used briefly by specific task groups to obtain resources.

The forager/collector classification is widely used by archaeologists, who tend to view the two strategies as relatively stable and uniform (not Binford's intent). The assignment of a culture to one or the other strategy usually is based on criteria such as having villages (must be a collector) or traveling to resources (must be a forager). In truth, most hunter-gatherers typically employ tactics of both strategies (Sutton 2000), making classification difficult.

MAJOR THEMES IN PLATEAU PREHISTORY

One of the major issues in attempting to understand the whole of Plateau prehistory is related to the focus on large housepit sites dating between 3,000 and 1,000 BP, meaning that much less is known about other time periods. Clearly, greater attention needs to be paid to earlier sites. Early sites may be difficult to find, however, as they may have been destroyed by devastating flooding in the early Holocene (see Highlight 6.2) or buried (and sealed) under volcanic ash.

What was the influence of the surrounding culture areas on the Plateau? It is commonly believed (or assumed) that the Northwest Coast dominated the Plateau, but at least some flaked and ground stone tools are unique to the Plateau (Fladmark 1982:131). It is clear that at least some Northwest Coast groups moved into the Plateau, but it is not known when that occurred or what impact it had on existing groups or adaptations. An understanding of the origin of the Nesikep Tradition of British Columbia (see below) may help elucidate this issue.

One of the primary research issues in the Plateau is to understand the variability in hunter-gatherer adaptations and the rise and fall of complex societies. Large and complex groups developed after about 3,000 years ago, although it is unclear why. The role of climate, changes in resource availability, influences from the coast, trade, and/or other factors in the evolution of these complex cultures are being investigated. In addition, the identification of Plateau ethnographic groups in the archaeological record is a major issue as part of the NAGPRA process.

The Plateau was a culturally diverse region, and there is considerable variation in cultural sequences and development from area to area (Pokotylo and Mitchell 1998:96). Nevertheless, there seems to be a general consensus on a basic outline of Plateau prehistory. This basic chronological sequence is shown in Table 6.1. A longstanding tradition of rock art is also present on the Plateau (e.g., Keyser 1992).

THE PALEOINDIAN PERIOD (CA. 14,000 TO 10,000 BP)

There is relatively little evidence of a Paleoindian occupation of the Plateau. Much of the Canadian Plateau had been under ice until about 11,000 BP, and after the glaciers retreated, it took some time for the area to become habitable. The southern Columbia Plateau, on the other hand, was not glaciated and could have been occupied very early on. Such an occupation may be masked by several factors. First, there were several huge floods in the drainage of the Columbia River at the end of the Pleistocene that might have swept away at least some of the evidence of any Paleoindian occupation in that area (see Highlight 6.2). Second, much of the volcanic activity on the Columbia Plateau occurred in the Early Holocene, resulting in many lava flows and ash

TABLE 6.1 A Chronological Sequence for the Plateau

Date (BP)	Broad Periods[a]	Columbia Plateau[b]	Canadian Plateau[c]	General Climate
200	Late Archaic	Winter Village	Kamloops	as today
				Little Ice Age
		PLATEAU PITHOUSE TRADITION		Medieval Climatic Anomaly
1,000				as today
			Plateau	
2,000	Middle Archaic		Shuswap	
		Pithouse II		cooler and wetter
3,000				
		?	Lochnore	
4,000				
		Pithouse I	Nesikep	
5,000	Early Archaic			warm but cooling
		Cascade		
6,000				
7,000			Cascade	
8,000	Paleoarchaic	Windust		warming, but still cooler and moister than today
9,000				
to 10,000		Paleoindian		colder and wetter than today

[a]Following Andrefsky (2004)

[b]Following Chatters (1995)

[c]Following Rousseau (2004)

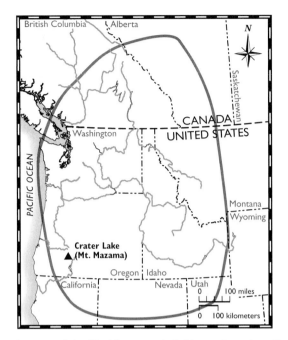

FIGURE 6.2   The general extent of the Mt. Mazama ash fall in northwestern North America.

deposits that probably buried many early sites. The most notable of these events was the eruption of Mt. Mazama in Oregon, an event that created Crater Lake and spread ash across much of the Plateau (Fig. 6.2). The Mt. Mazama eruption had been dated to about 6,700 BP (e.g., Mehringer et al. 1977; Hallett et al. 1997), but more recent work has indicated that the date should be revised to about 7,700 years ago (Zdanowicz et al. 1999; Bacon and Lanphere 2006).

HIGHLIGHT 6.2

THE GREAT MISSOULA FLOODS

As the glaciers retreated at the end of the last ice age, a number of large lakes formed behind dams of ice. One such lake was Lake Missoula, located along the border of Idaho and Montana (see Alt 2001; L. N. Smith 2006). Lake Missoula filled and drained a number of times, depending on whether the glaciers were advancing or retreating. It was a massive lake, as large as several hundred miles long, several thousand feet deep, and containing some five hundred cubic miles of water, more than Lake Erie and Lake Ontario combined.

Between 15,000 and 13,000 years ago, Lake Missoula may have formed and drained some forty times, each time eroding landforms, cutting deep canyons (called coulees), and creating the great "scablands" of southwestern Washington. The floods were sudden as the water burst through the ice dam. During the largest floods, it was estimated that the lake discharged more than ten cubic miles of water an hour, which moved down the canyons at eighty miles an hour. Nothing would have survived the rushing water and ice. A similar flood event occurred in southern Idaho when Utah's ancient Lake Bonneville drained onto the Snake River Plain, some 14,500 years ago.

If early Paleoindians were in the area during those times (and there is no direct evidence that they were), they would have been killed and the evidence of their presence would now be jumbled up in alluvial deposits scattered across Washington and Oregon, making it difficult to detect their presence. A NOVA program on Lake Missoula, "Mystery of the Megaflood," was produced for television (also see http://www.pbs.org/wgbh/nova/ megaflood). It was recently proposed that some of the geographical features formed by the Bonneville flood may have become sacred landscapes to later populations (Pavesic 2007).

The actual evidence of Paleoindians on the Plateau is uncommon but widespread (Pokotylo and Mitchell 1998:82). Several spectacular caches of Clovis material have been found, including the Richey-Roberts Clovis point cache in eastern Washington (Gramly 1993; also see Highlight 3.1) and the Simon Clovis point cache in Idaho (B. R. Butler 1963; Titmus and Woods 1991b). Another cache, this time of stemmed points, was found at the Cooper's Ferry site in northern Idaho and was dated to about 12,000 years old (Davis and Sisson 1998:12). This, coupled with dates between 12,300 and 11,250 BP from Lind Coulee, a Western Stemmed Tradition site in Washington, suggest that stemmed points date earlier than once thought (Craven 2004).

Other evidence of Paleoindian occupation has been found in central Washington (Galm and Gough 2000) and northwestern Idaho (Yohe and Woods 2002:12, 21). Finally, several human burials dating to Paleoindian times have been found on the Plateau, including the Buhl Burial (Green et al. 1998; Neves and Blum 2000) and burials in deposits dated as early as 10,260 BP from Marmes Rockshelter, in eastern Washington (Sheppard et al. 1987).

THE ARCHAIC (CA. 10,000 BP TO CONTACT)

After about 10,000 BP, groups on the Plateau shifted to an Archaic lifestyle—that is, one of generalized hunting and gathering, with the hunting of large mammals, primarily elk and deer, being very important. The Archaic can be divided into the Paleoarchaic, Early Archaic, Middle Archaic, and Late Archaic (Andrefsky 2004; also refer to J. V. Wright 1995), with the Paleoarchaic equating to the Windust Period and the Early Archaic to the Cascade Period. The Windust and Cascade periods are sometimes included in the Old Cordilleran culture of the Northwest Coast (see B. R. Butler 1961; Matson and Coupland 1995:68). The Middle and Late Archaic divisions generally equate to the Plateau Pithouse Tradition.

Windust (ca. 10,000 to 8,000 BP)

The Windust Period (Rice 1972), sometimes called the Early Period (Chatters and Pokotylo 1998:73) or Paleoarchaic (Andrefsky 2004), is characterized by a change from fluted to stemmed projectile points and is part of the Western Stemmed Tradition. Major point types include Windust and Haskett stemmed points (see Fig. 3.3). Few sites dating to Windust times have been found, and the period is poorly known. It is possible that other Windust sites lie undiscovered beneath the Mt. Mazama ash, laid down across the region about 7,700 years ago. The climate was warming after the end of the Pleistocene.

It is believed that Windust people lived in small and mobile groups, exploited a variety of resources (Rice 1972; Chatters and Pokotylo 1998:74; but see Ames 1988), and obtained obsidian from the north (Galm 1994:282). The remains of large mammals, such as bison, elk, deer, and pronghorn, have been found at several early sites, including the Marmes Rockshelter in Washington (Ames et al. 1998:104) and several small caves in Idaho (Henrikson 2003). Salmon appear in the Columbia Plateau by about 9,500 BP, as witnessed by the large number of salmon remains discovered at the Five Mile Rapids site on the Columbia River (V. L. Butler 1993; Ames and Maschner 1999:83; also see Cressman et al. 1960). Further evidence of the use of salmon comes from the Gore Creek skeleton, dated to 8,300 BP (Cybulski et al. 1981:50). Isotopic values from this skeleton indicated that some marine-derived protein, probably salmon, was consumed but was less important in the diet than in more recent inhabitants (Chisholm and Nelson 1983).

Little is known of Windust mortuary patterns. Cremated remains were recovered from the Marmes Rockshelter (Sheppard et al. 1987; Chatters and Pokotylo 1998:74), where numerous individuals were cremated in the same place over decades or perhaps centuries. Several inhumations are also known, including Gore Creek and Kennewick Man (see Chapter 2; Chatters 1997, 2000, 2001; Chatters et al. 1999). Of great interest is the possibility that Kennewick Man could represent a population distinct from other native groups (see Chapter 2).

Cascade (ca. 8,000 to 4,500 BP)

After about 8,000 BP, the climate began to cool slightly, improving the availability of large mammals. At this time, the Cascade period, sometimes called the Middle period (Chatters and Pokotylo 1998:74) or the Early Archaic (Andrefsky 2004), began. It is characterized by leaf-shaped points, called Cascade points, and other technologies that might be related to salmon processing (Andrefsky 2004:28). After the eruption of Mt. Mazama at about 7,700 BP, additional projectile point forms appeared, specifically side-notched points such as Northern Side–notched and Bitterroot types.

During Cascade times, people lived as small groups of mobile hunter-gatherers, practicing a broad-based foraging strategy that was reliant primarily on large mammals. Salmon fishing was clearly important by 6,000 BP but was not primary, and some roots were eaten. Virtually nothing is known of Cascade Period art or ritual. The mortuary pattern was primary inhumation (see Highlight 6.3).

By 7,000 BP, Cascade groups on the Canadian Plateau had adapted to the cooling environment to become the Nesikep Tradition (see below). Sometime about 5,200 BP on the Columbia Plateau, some Cascade groups adopted a new settlement pattern in which they built pithouses and lived in small communities of two or three pithouses during the winter (Pithouse I; Chatters 1995). This resulted in decreased mobility and in the absence of evidence for storage, suggesting that foraging intensified and that resources were relatively easy to obtain. This pattern was abandoned by about 4,200 BP, and the groups again adopted a broad-based foraging pattern.

HIGHLIGHT 6.3

THE WESTERN IDAHO ARCHAIC BURIAL COMPLEX

Data on mortuary practices are relatively rare on the Plateau. However, in western Idaho several small cemeteries were discovered that contained human burials with elaborate grave goods (one cemetery also contained dog remains), called the Western Idaho Archaic Burial Complex (WIABC) (Pavesic 1985). The WIABC is dated between about 6,600 and 4,000 BP (Pavesic 1985; Green et al. 1986; Yohe and Pavesic 2000, 2002). The WIABC cemeteries contain human primary and secondary inhumations (some with red ochre) of both males and females, possible cremations, and, in one instance, purposefully buried dogs. The cemeteries

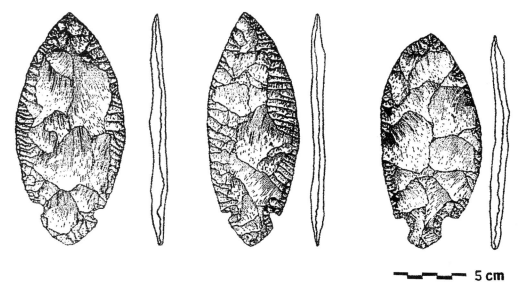

5 cm

FIGURE 6.3 "Turkey-tail" bifaces from the Rosenberger site, a Western Idaho Archaic Burial Complex site in Idaho. (From *Stone Tool Analysis,* by Plew, Woods, Pavesic. ©1985 University of New Mexico Press.)

are typically located on sandy knolls along rivers and do not appear to be associated with habitation sites.

A variety of unusual artifacts was found with some of the human burials. Most notable are various flaked stone items, including large bifacial blades, "turkey-tail" bifaces (Fig. 6.3), large side-notched points, and lanceolate points. In addition, perform blanks, cache bifaces, stone pipes, shell beads, shaft straighteners, bone awls, and hematite crystals were also found (Pavesic and Studebaker 1993; Pavesic 2000). It appears that at least some of the flaked stone artifacts were not used but were produced specifically as burial goods (C. D. Madsen 1997). A study of the source of the obsidian from the DeMoss site shows that local obsidians were used (Hughes and Pavesic 2009).

The latter part of the WIABC is associated with the Midvale Complex, one of the pithouse complexes on the Columbia Plateau (see Meatte 1990:65; Roll and Hackenberger 1998:129). Pavesic (1985:82) originally thought that the WIABC might have been a manifestation of a regional trade network in which obsidian was traded west and other goods were imported from the coast (Yohe and Pavesic 1997; also see Galm 1994:285–286). It is possible that the cemeteries were related to workshops where trade goods were manufactured. A study of isotopic values on human bone from the Braden site suggested that the people were heavily dependent on salmon by 6,600 BP, and the presence of dental caries from burials at the DeMoss site suggested a dependence on camas by 5,900 BP (Yohe and Pavesic 2002).

Nesikep Tradition (ca. 7,000 to 4,500 BP)

On the Canadian Plateau, Cascade groups coalesced into new pattern by about 7,000 BP, one adaptive to an expansion of forests (which are not productive ecozones, especially during cold winters) and a cooling environment (Stryd and Rousseau 1996:187; Rousseau 2004; also refer to Sanger 1967). This pattern lasted until the beginning of the Plateau Pithouse Tradition (see below), but its origins remain unclear. It is possible (e.g., Prentiss and Kuijt 2004a) that Nesikep represents the movement of coastal peoples (the early or proto-Salish) inland, but others (e.g., Rousseau 2004:12) have rejected that notion, believing that the proto-Salish came later. Nesikep is generally divided into early and late periods.

Early Nesikep (ca. 7,000 to 6,000 BP) groups were highly mobile foragers living in small, short-term camps (Rousseau 2004:5). The primary game were large mammals, such as elk and deer, but a number of other resources, including rabbits, birds, fish, freshwater shellfish, and plants, were also used. While salmon were eaten, they were not a primary resource (Stryd and Rousseau 1996:187; Pokotylo and Mitchell 1998:83). Early Nesikep is characterized by lanceolate and corner-notched points, microblades (Stryd and Rousseau 1996:188), and distinctive bifaces (Rousseau 2004:6).

Late Nesikep is called the Lehman Phase (Rousseau and Richards 1988) and dates between about 6,000 and 4,500 BP. The population during Lehman times appears to have been larger than in Early Nesikep times (their sites are larger), but people still lived in small, mobile camps. The Lehman Phase is characterized by the presence of microblades and distinctive side-notched points (Rousseau 2004:11). Lehman groups were broad-spectrum foragers (Rousseau 2004:10), but they focused on hunting deer and elk (Pokotylo and Mitchell 1998:84). While the use of freshwater shellfish increased, there is no evidence of intensive salmon exploitation. Few human remains are known from this time, but isotope values from some burials indicate a primarily terrestrial diet (Cybulski et al. 2007).

By about 5,000 BP, the climate became cooler and wetter with increasing snowfall and an expansion of forests. Salmon had been used since at least 9,000 BP but became a major resource after about 5,000 BP (Plew 1983:59). It appears that at least some Lehman groups began to shift to a semisedentary system of pithouse villages at about this time (called the Lochnore Phase), leading to the initial establishment of the Plateau Pithouse Tradition (see below).

Plateau Pithouse Tradition (ca. 4,500 to 200 BP)

Sometime about 5,000 years ago, some groups on the Plateau began to change from small bands of highly mobile foragers living in small camps to eventually evolve into relatively large populations of semisedentary collectors living in semipermanent villages of more than 100 pithouses. This new way of living is broadly known as the Plateau Pithouse Tradition (PPT), first defined by Richards and Rousseau (1987:49; also see J. V. Wright 1995:851–894). The climate was becoming cooler and the environment became generally more productive. A very general summary of the PPT is presented in Table 6.2, and the various PPT phases on the Columbia and Canadian plateaus are discussed below.

The PPT began modestly, with a few groups of highly mobile foragers focusing their efforts on a smaller number of specific resources (e.g., large game or salmon), thus reducing their need to maintain mobility (Chatters and Pokotylo 1998:75). People spent their winters in small settlements of a few small, deep, generally round pithouses, located in ecotones where a variety of resources could be exploited. By about 4,200 BP, the pithouse way of life was abandoned and people returned to their former pattern of highly mobile foraging, although it is not clear why.

People again adopted a PPT over most of the Plateau after about 3,500 BP, but perhaps a bit earlier on the western Snake River Plain of southern Idaho (T. J. Green 1993:67). This pattern lasted, in various forms, until contact. People shifted from a broadly based forager economy where people lived in small, mobile groups to a collector economy in which a smaller number of specific resources were obtained on a strict schedule (e.g., Chatters 1995:341; Stryd and Rousseau

TABLE 6.2 A General Summary of the Plateau Pithouse Tradition

Dates (BP)	General Traits	Canadian Sequence	Columbia Sequence	General Periods*
200 to 650	small pithouse villages, smaller territories, less-complex social organization, population decline, collector strategy	Kamloops	Winter village	IId
650 to 1,250	abandonment of the very large villages for smaller ones			IIc
1,250 to 1,800	appearance of large winter villages, period of greatest social complexity, large corporate family groups, intensive collectors	Plateau		IIb
1,800 to 2,500	resource depletion, population decline, corporate groups, intensification of collector strategy	Shuswap	Pithouse II	IIa
2,500 to 3,400	small villages, collector strategy, distinctly different than earlier forager groups, appearance of storage facilities, variety of point types, limited trade			I
3,400 to 3,700	no pithouse villages, broad-spectrum mobile foragers	Lochnore		—
3,700 to 5,200	small pithouse villages but occupied by forager groups		Pithouse I	—

*After Prentiss et al. 2005a: Table 2, 55–56

1996:198). People lived in small pithouse communities during the winter and in camps during the summer. Storage became important for the first time. The continual reoccupation of winter sites suggests that the economic system was stable, probably due to the addition of roots to the diet (Chatters and Pokotylo 1998:76; Lepofsky and Peacock 2004).

These PPT groups were logistically organized collectors (sensu Binford 1980) with winter base camps (villages) and smaller summer camps, with resources being procured, processed, and stored based on a seasonal schedule. On the Plateau, these collectors had larger groups, corporate organizations, and less mobility than their predecessors and may have also had social stratification (see B. Hayden et al. 1985).

It is not clear why this greater sedentism, settlement nucleation, and development of the collector strategy occurred, but it may be related to climate changes that involved a reduction in populations of large mammals, creating a focus on salmon resources (Kuijt 1989), or an influx of new people from the coast, or perhaps increasing warfare that forced people to concentrate into protected locales (Chatters 2004). Such factors could have acted as selective pressures on the several different types of semisedentary foragers and collectors that had developed "under conditions of relaxed competition" by about 5,000 BP (recall the contemporaneous Lehman and Lochnore groups on the Canadian Plateau). As conditions changed, increased competition may have selected for the type of collectors characterized by the Plateau Pithouse Tradition (Chatters and Prentiss 2005:46).

By about 2,600 BP, large "Aggregate Pithouse Village Complexes," some with more than 100 houses (though not all occupied at the same time), were established. Larger pithouses also appeared, suggesting larger families, extended families (corporate groups), and/or communal/ritual structures (e.g., Hayden and Adams 2004). Salmon was apparently the primary resource in these villages, but large mammals remained important, and after about 2,500 BP, roots become very important (Lepofsky and Peacock 2004).

It has been suggested (Hayden 1997a) that this pithouse pattern was based on the best fishing spots and specific upland regions being controlled by elite, hereditary, title-holding families, while common families, and perhaps even slaves, had little direct access to resources. It was further argued (Hayden 1997a, 1997b, 2005) that these large villages were politically and economically stable. However, based on data from the Keatley Creek site, Prentiss et al. (2003, 2005b) asserted that this pattern did not emerge until after 1,700 BP and suggested that it was not very stable.

Late in time, after 650 BP, pithouse villages became smaller, populations declined, social complexity waned, and the collector-based economy simplified, perhaps due to a warming of the climate. This late pattern was still fairly complex, however, and reflects the continuity between prehistoric PPT cultures and the ethnographic groups in the region (Hayden 1997a:246).

THE PLATEAU PITHOUSE TRADITION ON THE CANADIAN PLATEAU   On the Canadian Plateau, the PPT is divided into four phases (Stryd and Rousseau 1996:197; Pokotylo and Mitchell 1998; Rousseau 2004). The earliest is the **Lochnore Phase (ca. 5,000 to 3,400 BP)**, represented by collector groups that overlapped with Lehman Phase (Late Nesikep) foragers, suggesting that as the climate cooled at least two separate adaptations coexisted for a time (Pokotylo and Mitchell 1998:84), possibly forming the initial "pool" of adaptations that would later be subjected to selection (e.g., Chatters and Prentiss 2005). It is possible that Lochnore collectors had diverged from the earlier Nesikep Tradition, but they may also represent new peoples that were ultimately ancestral to the ethnographic Athapaskan Interior Salish (Elmendorf 1965; also see Stryd and Rousseau 1996:199, 200; Rousseau 2004:12; Cybulski et al. 2007:72).

The Lochnore Phase is characterized by wide side-notched points, many bone tools, ornaments of marine shell (Stryd and Rousseau 1996:193; also see Galm 1994; Pokotylo and Mitchell 1998:85; Rousseau 2004:14), microblades, and pithouses (Stryd and Rousseau 1996:195). Lochnore people were moderately mobile and lived in small to medium-sized residential camps with small pithouses that were located in resource-rich places. The economy was one of broad-spectrum, opportunistic foraging (Rousseau 2004:14) with evidence of the use of a wide range of animal resources. A focus on salmon and the use of storage facilities is seen for the first time (Stryd and Rousseau 1996:195). Very few human remains have been found, suggesting to some (Stryd and Rousseau 1996:197) that the dead were placed in trees to decompose.

The **Shuswap Phase (ca. 3,400 to 1,800 BP)** emerged as the climate became cooler and wetter. The forest expanded and seems to have forced people and large mammals closer to the rivers, where salmon had increased along with rainfall. Shuswap represents an intensification of the Lochnore pattern, with collecting replacing foraging as the primary economic pattern. Microblade technology was dropped in favor of smaller projectile points, and there was an elaboration of bone and antler technology. The dead were buried in the floors of pithouses (Rousseau 2004:15).

Populations were still fairly small, and people lived in small, semisedentary winter villages with pithouses, and mobility declined. The use of salmon expanded, and storage became more important. Trade with the coast increased (see Galm 1994), and Shuswap groups may have even occasionally visited the Plains (see Rousseau 2004:15–16).

The **Plateau Phase (ca. 1,800 to 1,200 BP)**, also called the Thompson Phase (Pokotylo and Mitchell 1998:88; also see Rousseau 2004:16–19), began as the climate warmed and the forests retreated. It is marked by a rapid population increase and the development of the Aggregate Pithouse Village Complex, with the Keatley Creek site (see Highlight 6.4) being a prime example. Village size increased from an average of two or three pithouses to twenty pithouses, although some had more than a hundred pithouses. Many hundreds of people would have lived in such communities, which represent the "maximum fluorescence of the Canadian Plateau hunter-gatherer-fisher cultures" (Rousseau 2004:19).

HIGHLIGHT 6.4

KEATLEY CREEK

One of the largest pithouse villages on the Canadian Plateau is the Keatley Creek site (Hayden et al. 1996; Hayden 1997b), located on a tributary of the Thompson River. The site (Fig. 6.4) contains some 115 pithouse depressions, some of which are more than twenty meters (sixty-five feet) in diameter. Keatley Creek was first occupied about 3,500 BP and remained relatively small for several thousand years. The large aggregate village "emerged abruptly" about 1,600 BP, accompanied by rapid population growth, and people occupied both small and large houses. There was an increasing preference for larger houses, and by 1,200 BP, the number of occupied houses declined but their size increased, perhaps reflecting the appearance of complex social organizations (e.g., clans). At this time, Keatley Creek

FIGURE 6.4   The Keatley Creek site, note the ubiquitous housepits (photo by Brian Hayden; used with permission).

was home to perhaps forty to sixty household groups (not all of the 115 pithouses were occupied at the same time). After 1,200 BP, the population began to decline and the site was finally abandoned by about 800 BP (Prentiss et al. 2003; Prentiss et al. 2007:320).

The staple foods at Keatley Creek were salmon and roots. Interestingly, salmon productivity declined about 1,200 BP (perhaps due to river blockages; see below), and mammals became more important. The more plentiful pink salmon has generally been assumed to have been the staple species, but only chinook, sockeye, and coho have been identified from the site (Speller et al. 2005). If salmon runs were smaller than originally believed, it is possible that the linkage between control of salmon and increasing social organization was not as strong as previously thought (Speller et al. 2005).

The very large pithouses at Keatley Creek (and at similar sites) are interpreted as multifamily corporate groups; that is, "rich" families (Hayden and Adams 2004:85), although some of the large pithouses were apparently used for ritual purposes (Hayden and Adams 2004). Poor families would have lived in smaller pithouses. Continuity in the use of specific lithic resources suggested that these corporate groups were stable over a long period of time, perhaps 1,000 years (Hayden et al. 1996), and retained rights to the use of specific fishing areas and mountain lithic sources. Further, some of these corporate groups were "non-privileged," suggesting a social hierarchy that included elites and commoners (Hayden 1997a:242). Prentiss et al. (2007) argued that social inequality emerged abruptly at the site during a time of increasing population and resource intensification and that social units may have been clans or clan-like organizations. A pattern similar to that at Keatley Creek can be seen at some other large pithouse villages (e.g., Prentiss et al. 2008).

Sites like Keatley Creek contain a record of the development of complex societies on the Plateau and serve as important laboratories to test various models. Others have been investigated, and a great deal of work remains.

The average Plateau Phase pithouse increased in size to a diameter of about six meters (twenty feet), but some were as large as twenty meters (sixty-five feet). Most pithouses are thought to represent the dwellings of nuclear families (Rousseau 2004:17), but some are larger (perhaps for extended families) and some were square or rectangular. Storage pits also increased in size, and large ovens used for root processing appeared. Roots (Lepofsky and Peacock 2004), salmon, and large mammals were the staples of the economy. Dogs became important at this time, apparently as pack animals to transport salmon up to the villages (Rousseau 2004:19). Mortuary practices are poorly known, but cremation was common (Rousseau 2004:17).

The bow and arrow diffused into the Canadian Plateau about 1,500 BP (Rousseau 2004:17), later than in the Columbia Plateau to the south, and was used concurrently with the atlatl (spear thrower) for several hundred years (Rousseau 2004:17). Bow-and-arrow technology, using small barbed and notched points, may have made the hunting of large mammals easier. The Interior Plateau Art Tradition (see Styrd 1982; Keyser 1992) also began at this time.

Finally, trade seems to have increased dramatically throughout the Plateau (Hayden and Schulting 1997), with an elite class controlling power and wealth. The trade of prestige items may have developed to enhance social position, as seen by the distribution of many exotic items across the region (see Galm 1994).

After about 1,200 BP, large aggregate villages such as Keatley Creek became much smaller, marking the beginning of the **Kamloops Phase (ca. 1,200 to 200 BP)**. The climate had begun to warm by this time, and while the general economic pattern of the previous Plateau Phase continued, populations of both salmon and large mammals declined. Human populations also decreased, so villages contained fewer and smaller pithouses, indicative of less status differentiation. The presence of fewer ovens suggests that roots also became less important (Lepofsky and Peacock 2004:136).

Technology changed to some degree but more in scale than form. Kamloops side-notched arrow points appeared, and the Interior Plateau Art Tradition (see Styrd 1982) became more elaborate. Mortuary patterns were variable, mostly flexed burials in unmarked graves, but some burials under rock cairns have been found (Pokotylo and Mitchell 1998:88; Rousseau 2004:20).

Why did things change at 1,200 BP? One idea is that massive landslides blocked the Fraser River and disrupted the salmon run, resulting in the abandonment of the large pithouse villages (Hayden and Ryder 1991). Others (e.g., Kuijt 2001) argued that the abandonment of the large villages was part of a larger regional process and was not linked to a single landslide or event on the Fraser River. The climate was warming, and it is possible that resources were reduced due to drought and fires (Kuijt and Prentiss 2004).

THE PLATEAU PITHOUSE TRADITION ON THE COLUMBIA PLATEAU   On the Columbia Plateau, the PPT is divided into three phases (Chatters 1995) and followed a similar trajectory to that of the Canadian Plateau with some differences in detail. The earliest PPT division is **Pithouse I (ca. 5,200 to 3,700 BP)**, when some late Cascade foragers began to focus on fewer resources and adopted a less mobile lifestyle (Chatters and Prentiss 2005:56). They constructed relatively small pithouses and lived in very small villages but did not practice storage. Large mammals were the primary game, and while salmon was used, it was not a staple. Pithouse I people appear to have entered an area, over-exploited the local resource base, and then moved on to the next area. It appears that bow-and-arrow technology became important on the Columbia Plateau at about this time (Ames et al. 2010). The Pithouse I adaptation ultimately proved unsustainable, and the population crashed after about 3,900 BP (Chatters 1995:388), and the pithouse villages disappeared by 3,700 BP. The climate had begun to cool at about this time, and the forests expanded, perhaps reducing large mammal populations. The Pithouse I experiment had failed, and people returned to a pattern of highly mobile foraging.

The **Pithouse II (3,400 to 1,800 BP) Period** originated when people once again began to live in small villages of small pithouses. A collector strategy was adopted and salmon was intensively exploited, along with roots and large mammals. Food storage became important for the first time. Populations and village sizes remains relatively small. After about 2,400 BP, the basic collector strategy was intensified, with salmon becoming the staple.

Bison were present and hunted, although they were never very important. The Tsulim site, located in south-central Washington (Chatters et al. 1995), is a bison kill site dated to about 2,100 BP. There, bison were driven into a sand dune "trap" and killed using bow and atlatls. Bison meat was stored in ice caves in southern Idaho as early as 8,000 BP (Henrikson 2003).

The **Winter Village (1,800 to 200 BP) Period** is marked by the appearance of much larger, aggregate villages, although not as large or as complex as those on the Canadian Plateau, although one such village, the Paquet Gulch site in north central Oregon, contained more than 100 pithouses (Jenkins and Connolly 1994). Between about 2,500 and 1,000 BP, the climate was warmer and drier, the forests retreated, and grassland areas developed. Salmon remained the staple, and storage continued to be a critical element of the economy. The appearance of cemeteries may imply the presence of formal territories (Chatters and Pokotylo 1998:78), and inequalities in burials are apparent, suggesting differential status.

Of considerable interest is an apparent increase in violence. Fortified sites appear, some food caches appear to have been "hidden" as if from enemies, and there was a dramatic increase in skeletal injuries (Chatters 2004). This may be related, at least in part, to the presence of the bow and arrow (which made warfare easier) and/or a growing competition for resources. Much more research is required on this issue.

NATIVE PLATEAU CULTURES AT CONTACT

The first contact between Plateau groups and Euroamericans was in 1805, when the American expedition led by Lewis and Clark passed through the region. Some of the Plateau groups had earlier obtained horses from the Plains and appeared to be similar to several of the Plains groups that Lewis and Clark had just observed. Almost immediately, both the British and Americans established trading posts and competed for the fur trade in the region. In 1825, the Hudson's Bay Company became the primary trading company. European diseases seriously impacted Plateau groups.

Plateau groups have been mostly able to maintain their cultures. The various groups reside on 10 reservations in the United States and on 407 reserves in Canada (see Lahren 1998). As at many reservations, problems of unemployment, poor health, alcoholism, and substandard services continue to be problems, although the situation appears to be improving. Most Plateau groups are now involved in logging, tourism and recreation, gambling, and other activities that hopefully will contribute to their long-term success.

Fishing rights continue to be a major issue (see Cohen 1986; Hewes 1998:637–640), most of which were guaranteed by treaty but have often been ignored by government agencies. The Indians have generally been successful in the courts, but most whites have resisted, and tensions still run high. In addition, dam construction has limited some fish runs and destroyed traditional fishing localities.

Further Reading

There are a number of summaries of Plateau prehistory, beginning with the chapters in the handbook (Chatters and Pokotylo 1998; Pokotylo and Mitchell 1998; Ames et al. 1998; and Roll and Hackenberger 1998). Other recent summary works include Chatters (1995), J. V. Wright (1995), and Prentiss et al. (2005a), and a number of books on specific topics include Carlson and Bona (1996) and Prentiss and Kuijt (2004b).

A number of universities now publish archaeological materials in the form of occasional papers. Several important regional journals, including the *Canadian Journal of Archaeology*, *Journal of Northwest Anthropology*, *Idaho Archaeologist*, and *Tebiwa*, contain information on Plateau prehistory.

Acorns and Diversity
California

California (Fig. 7.1) is a region of substantial natural diversity, containing high mountains, deserts, extensive river and lake systems, and coastlines, all coupled with a mild climate. As such, California has always been a popular place to live. Ethnographically, California is characterized by its enormous cultural diversity (some 100 different native groups were recorded at contact), acorn economies, shell bead money, extensive trading systems, large populations, complex sociopolitical organizations, and a general absence of pottery and agriculture (e.g., Kroeber 1925; Heizer and Whipple 1971; Lightfoot and Parrish 2009). California is the only culture area given the same name as the political state, although their borders are not the same (see Fig. 7.1). Parts of the state of California fall within the Great Basin (see Chapter 8) while other areas lie within the Southwest (see Chapter 9) The *Handbook of North American Indians* included Baja California within the Southwest, but for the purposes of this book, it is considered part of California.

California is known for its ubiquitous oak trees, providing acorns that were the focus of the economies of many ethnographic Californian groups (see Highlight 7.1). Other important resources included grass seeds; game such as elk, deer, rabbits, and rodents, fish, birds; and even insects. In coastal habitats, various species of sea mammals, shellfish, and fish were exploited, with some being extremely abundant at certain times and places.

Based on the apparent abundance of acorns, many researchers have viewed California as a sort of "Garden of Eden," a place so bountiful that it could support a large population and where agriculture was "unnecessary." This view can be misleading. Acorns were indeed ubiquitous, productive, storable, and important, but they required a great deal of time and effort to collect and process. In addition, the abundant game noted by Europeans during the nineteenth century may have been the result of a population rise from decreasing hunting pressure subsequent to the huge loss of human populations from European diseases (e.g., Broughton 2002:65; Preston 2002). California may not have been the idyllic place many think it was (also see Raab and Jones 2004).

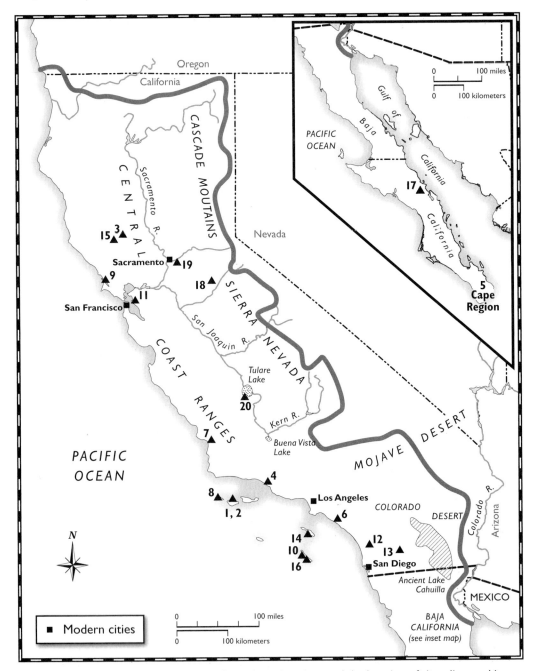

FIGURE 7.1   Map of California showing the major subregions and the location of sites discussed in the text: 1) Arlington Springs; 2) Arlington Point; 3) Borax Lake; 4) Browne; 5) Cape Region; 6) Cogged Stone site; 7) Cross Creek; 8) Daisy Cave; 9) Duncans Point Cave; 10) Eel Point; 11) Emeryville Shellmound; 12) Harris; 13) Indian Hill Rockshelter; 14) Little Harbor; 15) Mostin; 16) Nursery; 17) San Borjitas Cave; 18) Skyrocket; 19) Windmiller; 20) Witt.

HIGHLIGHT 7.1

ACORNS: THE WHEAT OF ANCIENT CALIFORNIA

One of the hallmarks of California Indians over the last 5,000 years or more was the use of acorns for food. Acorns are the nuts from the oak tree (Quercus sp.), some fifteen species of which grow in California. They are plentiful, very nutritious, and easy (but time-consuming) to obtain, and can be stored. Acorns were collected in the fall, stored in granaries, and processed daily as needed. The nut would be removed from the shell, pounded to a powder in a mortar, leached with water to remove the bitter tannic acid, and made into a mush or bread. It would then be eaten alone or with other foods. Most of the work in acorn collection and preparation was apparently done by the women. Archaeologically, mortar and pestle technology is associated with the adoption of acorns, as they generally must be processed in mortars. The appearance of large numbers of mortars and pestles across much of California about 5,000 years ago suggests that acorns were adopted about that time, but perhaps earlier in northwestern California (Hildebrandt 2007:90).

The adoption of acorns as a food staple impacted humans in several ways (e.g., Basgall 1987). First, populations grew, presumably due to an increased food supply. The general health of the population appears to have declined, however, due to dental problems related to tooth wear from the stone grit in the acorn meal from processing and from the increased labor requirements (Leigh 1928; Moodie 1929; Schulz 1981). It also may be that the health of women and children was especially affected. As populations grew, birth spacing may have been shortened, more young women may have died during childbirth, and child mortality may have increased due to the loss of postparturition females (Dickel et al. 1984; also see Bruhns and Stothert 1999:66–70).

Nevertheless, large and relatively complex groups did evolve where resources were abundant, and it has been argued that some California hunter-gatherer groups developed chiefdom-level sociopolitical organizations, leading to the concept of a California Formative (Meighan 1959a). The environmental and cultural factors involved in such a development are of great interest to California archaeologists.

GEOGRAPHY AND ENVIRONMENT

The geography of California is very complex and can be divided into any number of natural regions but is split here into seven broad areas (see Fig. 7.1). The North Coast region is characterized by mountains, thick forests, many rivers, and a rugged coastline with many cliffs and few beaches. The Central Coast is distinguished by relatively low mountains (the Coast Ranges), oak parkland forests, and stretches of both rocky and sandy coastlines. The South Coast, including the Channel Islands, is characterized by a coastal plain, oak parklands, and sandy beaches. Baja California extends an additional thousand miles to the south and is generally arid with a mountainous spine and many sandy beaches.

The Sierra Nevada and Cascade ranges run along the eastern edge of California. The Sierra Nevada are mostly granitic and rugged, with extensive foothills along the western side and an escarpment on the eastern edge. Most of the rainfall of the Sierras falls on the western side, and a large number of rivers flow west into the Central Valley. The Cascade Range, to the north and west of the Sierra Nevada, is generally volcanic and is less rugged than the Sierras. It, too, has many rivers that flow into the Central Valley.

The Central Valley of California lies between the Sierra/Cascade and Coast ranges and stretches some four hundred miles north to south. The Central Valley actually consists of two valleys, the Sacramento in the north and the San Joaquin in the south. The rivers from the Cascades and northern Sierras drain into the Sacramento Valley and into the south-flowing Sacramento River. The rivers from the central and southern Sierras drain into the San Joaquin Valley and into the north-flowing San Joaquin River. One of the largest freshwater lakes in western North America, Tulare Lake, lies in the San Joaquin Valley. The Sacramento and San Joaquin rivers ultimately join south of Sacramento and flow west into the San Francisco Bay. The confluence of these two large rivers forms a delta that contains the largest marsh system in western North America.

To the east of the coastal mountains in Southern California lies the Colorado Desert, an arid region of low elevation and sparse vegetation. Much of this region is dominated by a large north-south trending valley extending from Palm Springs to northern Baja California, called the Coachella Valley at the northern end and the Imperial Valley at the southern end. The Colorado River to the east has occasionally changed its course, flooding the Imperial Valley and creating a large lake, Lake Cahuilla. The Mojave Desert lies to the north of the Colorado Desert, and while it is situated mostly within the modern state of California, it is technically part of the Great Basin and is discussed in Chapter 8.

The climate of California is currently fairly mild but has varied through time. The broad climatic regime of the Anathermal, Altithermal, and Medithermal (see Table 1.1) provides a general guide to California paleoclimate. Between about 1,200 and 700 BP, a major period of warming and drought, called the Medieval Climatic Anomaly (MCA; see Stine 1994), occurred. The MCA affected all of California, along with the rest of the world, creating environmental conditions to which populations adjusted (see Moratto et al. 1978; Jones et al. 1999; Kennett and Kennett 2000; J. K. Gardner 2007).

A BRIEF HISTORY OF RESEARCH

Initial archaeological work was undertaken in California along the Santa Barbara coast in the 1870s, and some preliminary explorations were conducted in other regions during the late nineteenth and early twentieth centuries. With the establishment of the Anthropology Department at the University of California, Berkeley (UC Berkeley) in 1902, Alfred Kroeber and his colleagues began to conduct systematic investigations across the state. Among the earliest stratigraphic excavations anywhere in the world was at the Emeryville Shellmound on the eastern shore of San Francisco Bay (Uhle 1907).

By the late 1930s, work in the delta region of the Central Valley resulted in the creation of a general "early, middle, and late" sequence for central California (Heizer and Fenenga 1939; Lillard et al. 1939), a blueprint that is still employed today (Beardsley 1954a, 1954b; Hughes 1994a). Researchers at UC Berkeley remained active, and after 1945, Robert F. Heizer became a major influence (see T. R. Hester [1982] for a summary of Heizer's contributions). Later, other universities became heavily involved in California archaeology, and those contributions continue.

After 1970, environmental laws required that archaeology be conducted for most state and federal projects, and a huge cultural resource management (CRM) industry developed, employing hundreds of archaeologists in government agencies and private consulting firms. This has resulted in the generation of an overwhelming amount of information.

MAJOR THEMES IN CALIFORNIA PREHISTORY

A number of important research foci dominate California archaeology. First, the questions of when people first arrived in California and how they got there are central to an understanding of the initial colonization of the New World. If people did move down the coast, perhaps even by boats, such evidence should be found in California.

The investigation into the intensification of resources, particularly acorns, after ca. 2,500 BP also remains an important research question. Some believe that intensification was the result of population expansion, while others have proposed that it fueled a population expansion with a parallel increase in sociopolitical complexity. Understanding this process has important anthropological implications.

Finally, efforts to understand the development of complex chiefdoms along the Southern California coast consume a great deal of energy among California archaeologists. The specific mechanisms by which this occurred is of great interest, but of larger importance is a general understanding of the evolution of sociopolitical complexity among hunter-gatherers, both in California and elsewhere in the world.

The prehistory of California is long, diverse, and quite complex. The discussion below is organized by the very broad climatic periods shown in the far left column of Table 7.1, although the bulk of the table provides a basic chronology for each of the natural regions described above.

THE LATE PLEISTOCENE (CA. TO 10,000 BP)

As discussed in Chapter 2, there are four basic models for the initial peopling of the Americas: either by a coastal or inland route, and by Clovis or pre-Clovis people. A number of sites in California have been proposed as representing pre-Clovis occupations, but all either remain unconfirmed, have been disproved (e.g., the supposed 30,000-year-old hearth on Santa Rosa Island [see Orr 1968; Moratto 1984:55]), or redated to the Holocene (Taylor et al. 1985; R. E. Taylor 1991). Thus, there is virtually no evidence of a pre-Clovis occupation of California.

The Clovis Complex

While a few isolated Clovis points are known along the coast, the vast majority of Clovis evidence has been found inland, primarily isolated fluted (Clovis?) points from surface contexts (see Rondeau et al. 2007). Only two major Clovis localities, both along lake margins, have been identified in California: Borax Lake and Tulare Lake. In addition, there may be a Clovis-age component at the Scotts Valley site south of San Francisco (Cartier 1993), and a possible Clovis-age human burial was found at the Mostin site in northwestern California (see discussion in Moratto 1984:99–101), although many believe that the Mostin burial is actually no older than about 6,300 BP (Fredrickson and White 1988:79; White and King 1993:136).

The Borax Lake site was excavated in the late 1930s and 1940s. The Clovis component (called the Post Pattern in that region) contained fluted points and crescents (Harrington 1938, 1948; Willig 1991). Little else is known about these early people from Borax Lake (see M. E. White 2002:448–452).

The second major Clovis locality in California is at Tulare Lake, situated in the central San Joaquin Valley. Clovis points were reported from the surface of the Witt site, located along the southwestern shore of the lake (Riddell and Olsen 1969), but little else was discovered. Additional research at several nearby sites was conducted in the 1990s (see G. L. Fenenga 1991, 1993), but these sites had been plowed and subjected to heavy predation by vandals, to the extent that few artifacts of any kind, much less the projectile points, remained. Studies of the vandal collections have revealed large numbers of Clovis projectile points, blades, crescents, and other flaked stone items from the locality (Wallace and Riddell 1988; W. J. Wallace 1991, 1993:6; West et al. 1991; Wilke 1991). Tulare Lake has one of the highest concentrations of fluted points in North America (Anderson and Faught 1998; but see Rondeau and Hopkins 2008), although most are out of context.

TABLE 7.1 A Chronological Sequence for California[*]

Broad Climatic Regime	Date (BP)	North Coast		Central Coast	South Coast	Sierra Nevada/ Cascade Range	Central Valley	Colorado Desert	General Climate
		Northern	Southern						
Late Holocene	150	Gunther Pattern	Augustine Pattern	Late Period	Del Rey Tradition	Late Period	Late Period	Late Prehistoric	same as today
									warmer
				Middle Period					
	1,000								similar to today
	2,000	Berkeley Pattern				Early Late Period	Middle Period	Late Archaic	
		Mendocino Pattern		Early Period					
Middle Holocene	3,000				Encinitas Tradition	Middle Holocene	Early Period		
	4,000							Early Archaic	
	5,000	Borax Lake Pattern							warmer than today
				Milling-stone					
	6,000					Early Holocene	Early Holocene		
Early Holocene	7,000								
	8,000						Western Pluvial Lakes Tradition	San Dieguito	
Pleistocene-Holocene Transition	9,000			Transitional	San Dieguito				conditions similar to today
Late Pleistocene	to 10,000	Post Pattern (Clovis)			Paleo-coastal?	Paleoindian (Clovis)			colder and wetter than today
				Paleo-coastal?					

[*]A separate sequence for Baja California is presented in Table 7.3.

A Paleocoastal Tradition?

There is a growing body of evidence to suggest that at least some people entered the New World by moving south along the coast (see Chapter 2). A number of very early sites are known along the coasts and islands of central and Southern California, apparently reflecting people with an adaptation and technology separate from Clovis, and possibly reflecting a separate migration.

This early coastal occupation can be classified as a Paleocoastal Tradition (ca. 12,000 to 10,000 BP; see Moratto 1984:104–109), a cultural complex with a maritime focus (e.g., the use of shellfish, fish, and marine mammals), presumably using boats (although the earliest evidence of boat-building technology in the area is dated at only about 8,000 BP [Cassidy et al. 2004:109; Raab and Cassidy 2009; also see Erlandson and Moss 1996:295]). Sites dating to Paleocoastal times (see Erlandson et al. 2007b) along coastal central and Southern California include Daisy Cave (Erlandson et al. 1996), Arlington Springs (Johnson et al. 2002), Cross Creek (Jones et al. 2002; 2008a), Arlington Point (Erlandson et al. 1999), and Eel Point (Raab and Cassidy 2009).

Little is known about Paleocoastal settlement systems. Rising sea levels may have drowned many Paleocoastal sites (Moratto 1984:108; Erlandson et al. 2007b), making it difficult to identify and characterize the period. It is also possible that areas away from the coast were more productive, and thus coastal occupation may have been less common (as was suggested for the North Coast; Hildebrandt and Levulett 1997:144).

THE PLEISTOCENE-HOLOCENE TRANSITION (CA. 10,000 TO 9,000 BP)

Along the coast, the earliest Holocene materials dating to the transition between the Pleistocene and Holocene are poorly understood, although it appears as if maritime adaptation continued. No sites dating to the Pleistocene/Holocene transition are known along the Northern Coast, but a few have been found along the Central Coast (Breschini and Haversat 1991). Some eighty sites have so far been discovered on the Central and Southern coasts that date between 10,000 and 8,000 BP (Erlandson 1994:248; Erlandson et al. 2007b: Table 4.1).

Hildebrandt and Jones (1992, 2002) suggested that the earliest peoples along the coast exterminated coastal fur seal and sea lion populations, ultimately leading to a general abandonment of the coast between 8,000 and 6,500 BP, a pattern seen all along the Pacific Coast (but see Jones and Hildebrandt 1995; Lyman 1995). Hildebrandt and Jones (1992) also argued that the early development of boats enabled the colonization of the Channel Islands and the exploitation of fur seal and sea lion populations residing there; hence, the islands remained occupied during the early Holocene, while the mainland coast apparently did not.

An important early site on the Central Coast is Cross Creek (Fig. 7.2), the oldest shell midden on the mainland coast of western North America, dated between 10,350 and 9,700 BP (Jones et al. 2002). The site assemblage contained many manos and metates, suggesting that the exploitation of small seeds thought to have begun about 8,500 BP along the Southern Coast (the Encinitas Tradition, see below) may have occurred earlier on the Central Coast than previously believed (Jones at al. 2007:135). Jones et al. (2002) argued that the data from Cross Creek suggested a coastal entry (Paleocoastal?) separate from an inland Clovis entry (but see Fitzgerald and Jones 2003; Turner 2003). A second site with possible a Paleocoastal connection is Diablo Canyon (Greenwood 1972), whose early component, dated between 9,300 and 8,900 BP, contained evidence of the use of fish and shellfish (Greenwood 1972:Table 44; also see Jones et al. 2008a, b).

South of Santa Barbara, early evidence of the use of maritime resources, such as shellfish, fish, and marine mammals, are known from a number of sites. Some of the most intriguing of these are located on the northern Channel Islands (as noted above), where access would require

FIGURE 7.2   The Cross Creek site (arrow) at the base of the hills above the Edna Valley, California (photo courtesy of Terry L. Jones; used with permission).

relatively sophisticated boat technology (e.g., Braje et al. 2004:24). The earliest occupation site known is Daisy Cave (Erlandson 1993, 1994:193–195; Erlandson et al. 1996; Rick et al. 2001; also see Rick et al. 2005). Daisy Cave is a multicomponent site, with a brief Paleoindian occupation at about 12,000 BP. A component dating between 9,700 and 8,000 BP contained evidence of intensive fishing (eighteen taxa from a variety of marine environments; Rick et al. 2001:609), implying the use of boats for fishing. Fragments of sandals and cordage made from sea grass discovered at the site are similar to those made by more recent coastal peoples and support the idea that the Chumash have been in the region since the Early Holocene (Connelly et al. 1995:316).

The Eel Point site (Fig. 7.3) on the southern channel island of San Clemente contains a large shell midden with a basal occupation dating to about 10,000 BP (Salls 1991:66, 68; Cassidy et al. 2004: Table 1; Raab and Cassidy 2009), although most of the deposit postdates 3,500 BP. San Clemente Island is located some fifty miles from the current mainland coast and would have required boats for access, even during the Pleistocene. Cassidy et al. (2004:109; also see Raab et al. 1994; Raab and Cassidy 2009) discovered evidence of boat manufacture at Eel Point, dating from about 8,000 BP, among the earliest such technology in North America.

Along the mainland coast of Southern California from Los Angeles south, the earliest coastal materials are called San Dieguito, part of the Western Stemmed Tradition materials from inland Southern California, first defined at the Harris site (Warren and True 1961; Warren 1966, 1967). In the coastal San Diego area, a number of sites dating to the latter portion of the San Dieguito Complex (ca. 8,500 to 8,000 BP) have been investigated, generally located on lagoons situated very close to the current coastline and seemingly representing a generalized economy that included marine resources.

In the interior of California (and of western North America), the Clovis Complex developed into the Western Stemmed Point Tradition or Western Pluvial Lakes Tradition (WPLT; Bedwell 1973), probably in response to the warming and drying climate of the early Holocene, and is

FIGURE 7.3 Excavations at the Eel Point site on San Clemente Island, California (photo by Jim Cassidy; used with permission).

characterized by crescents and large stemmed, shouldered, and lanceolate points (Willig and Aikens 1988:3) (see Fig. 3.3). The Western Stemmed Tradition generally dates between 10,000 and 9,000 BP, but perhaps as late as 8,000 BP. The Pleistocene-Holocene Transition marks the transformation from a Pleistocene Paleoindian adaptation to a more generalized Archaic adaptation.

WPLT sites are commonly found on the margins of one of the many lakes present in western North America at the end of the Pleistocene. By about 8,500 BP, however, the interior became drier and many of these lakes disappeared, although Lake Tulare in the San Joaquin Valley persisted. The WPLT is characterized by stemmed points (most commonly called Borax Lake in Northern California and Lake Mojave in central and Southern California), crescents, and an economy presumably based on the exploitation of marsh plants, fish, freshwater shellfish, and small game. There is very little evidence of the exploitation of large game during this time. There is little evidence of a San Dieguito (WPLT) presence in the Colorado Desert, probably just a few "small, mobile bands exploiting small and large game and collecting seasonally available wild plants" (Schaefer 1994:63; Schaefer and Laylander 2007).

Very few archaeological materials dating from Pleistocene/Holocene Transition times are known from the Sierra Nevada, a major exception being the Skyrocket site in the foothills of the Sierra Nevada forty miles east of Stockton (Bieling et al. 1996; La Jeunesse and Pryor 1998). Skyrocket contained eight components, the earliest of which dated between 9,400 and 7,000 BP and contained stemmed and side-notched points. Of note is the considerable number of ground stone tools (both metates and manos) present in the Skyrocket assemblage, among the earliest known for the region and seen as part of the transition from a Paleoindian to an Archaic economy (La Jeunesse et al. 2004).

In the San Joaquin Valley, WPLT materials are known from vandal collections taken from around Tulare Lake (Riddell and Olsen 1969; W. J. Wallace 1991). Further south, in the southern San Joaquin Valley, a deeply buried WPLT site was discovered at Buena Vista Lake (Fredrickson 1965; Fredrickson and Grossman 1977; Hartzell 1992). This site dated to about 8,000 BP (Fredrickson and Grossman 1977:174) and contained stemmed points, crescents, and freshwater shellfish remains. A better understanding of the WPLT in California continues to be an important research goal.

THE EARLY HOLOCENE (CA. 9,000 TO 7,000 BP)

Around 9,000 BP, the Early Holocene began, marked by a general warming trend that altered the biota of California and influenced changes in human adaptation. Millingstone technology, notably manos and metates, became widespread at this time and stemmed projectile points were replaced with side-notched forms. While millingstones have been found in some earlier sites, they have not been major elements of those artifact assemblages.

HIGHLIGHT 7.2

THE MILLINGSTONE PHENOMENON

Sites containing large numbers of manos and metates (Fig. 7.4), often along with scraper planes, choppers, core tools, and a paucity of projectile points and faunal remains, have been found all along coastal Southern California. These sites were first identified along the Santa Barbara coast by David B. Rogers (1929) and were named Oak Grove in that region. Similar materials have been found along the Southern California coast and are called La Jolla (M. J. Rogers 1939). William Wallace (1955) later designated these sites as part of a Southern California "Millingstone Horizon." Subsequently, a number of other millingstone entities have been identified in California, including manifestations in Northern California (True et al. 1979; True and Baumhoff 1985; Fitzgerald 1993; Fitzgerald and Jones 1999), the Central Valley (e.g., McGuire 1995), and the Central Coast (Fitzgerald 2000; Jones et al. 2002, 2008b; Jones 2008). Jones (2008) recently defined a "Millingstone Culture Area" across California that encompassed all of these regional expressions.

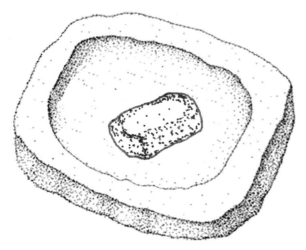

FIGURE 7.4   An example of a mano (handstone) and metate (the bottom grinding platform).

The "Millingstone Horizon" in Southern California was subsequently recast as the Encinitas Tradition (Warren 1968b; also see Sutton and Gardner 2010), in effect combining the various millingstone expressions of that region into a single cultural tradition. Warren (1968b:6) defined the ecological adaptation of the Encinitas Tradition as reflecting a well-developed collecting economy, with projectile points and faunal remains (i.e., evidence of hunting) being rare.

Inherent in the definition of the Encinitas Tradition is the premise that the use of manos and metates indicates the processing of small seeds, reflecting a fundamental shift from a reliance on marine resources (Paleocoastal) or hunting (WPLT) to one of dependence on gathered seeds, although shellfish remained important. The assumption that manos and metates equate to seed processing may be flawed, as it is known that Encinitas Tradition people also used manos and metates to process animals (Yohe et al. 1991; Sutton 1993a).

Northern California

The Early Holocene in Northern California is represented by the Borax Lake Pattern, named for the Early Holocene component identified at the Borax Lake site. The Borax Lake Pattern includes stemmed Borax Lake points, crescents, and coarse single-flake blades, as well as some manos and metates (Meighan 1955:26–27; also see Fredrickson 1974; Fredrickson and White 1988; Hildebrandt and Levulett 1997; Hildebrandt 2007). Borax Lake Pattern sites are located in upland settings in the North Coast ranges (Fredrickson 1984) and north-central California (Sundahl 1992; Sundahl and Henn 1993).

What little is known about the Borax Lake Pattern suggests a general hunting-and-gathering economy, with an emphasis on the collection of seeds (Fredrickson 1974:46), with shellfish and sea mammals being of lesser importance. Borax Lake Pattern people may have practiced a forager pattern (see Highlight 6.1; also see Hildebrandt and Hayes 1993:113; Hildebrandt 2007:89) with settlement characterized by frequent movements between high-quality resource patches, including some marine resources (T. L. Jones 1992:1).

The Northern Coast of California was not heavily occupied during the Early Holocene (Hildebrandt and Levulett 1997:143). Only one Borax Lake Pattern site is known on the coast, and the faunal data suggest that elk, rather than marine resources, were emphasized (Roscoe 1995). It is possible that the absence of Early Holocene sites along the coast may be due to inundation from sea level rises and/or erosion (see Hildebrandt and Levulett 1997:144). It is also possible that inland habitats were more stable and productive at that time (Hildebrandt and Levulett 1997:149). A second Early Holocene site, Duncans Point Cave, is situated north of San Francisco. This site has a deeply stratified shell midden dating between about 8,500 BP and Late Prehistoric times (Schwaderer 1992:57). The use of shellfish and sea mammals (seals and sea lions) suggests a long record of maritime adaptation in the region (Wake and Simmons 2002), although its relationship to the Borax Lake Pattern is unclear (Hildebrandt 2007:90–91).

The Central and Southern Coasts

Although the Millingstone is often associated with Southern California, it is also known along the Central Coast (Fitzgerald and Jones 1999). In fact, there is reason to suspect that the Millingstone could be older on the Central Coast, perhaps dating to the Late Pleistocene (Jones et al. 2002). Walter W. Taylor (1961:75; also see Moratto 1984:546–547) suggested that Hokan linguistic groups migrated to the Central Coast from the deserts sometime at the beginning of the Altithermal, possibly bringing the Millingstone culture with them. No such antecedent "Millingstone Culture" has yet been identified in the deserts.

TABLE 7.2 **Regional Manifestations of the Encinitas Tradition in Southern California (from Sutton and Gardner, 2010*)**

Age (BP)	LA/Orange County Coast	Northern Interior Southern California	San Diego Coast	Southern Interior Southern California
3,000 to 2,000	Topanga III	Greven Knoll III	La Jolla III	Pauma II
5,000 to 3,000	Topanga II	Greven Knoll II	La Jolla II	
8,500 to 5,000	Topanga I	Greven Knoll I	La Jolla I	Pauma I

*Used with permission from the Pacific Coast Archaeological Society.

In Southern California, the Early Holocene is dominated by the Encinitas Tradition (see Table 7.2), formerly called the "Millingstone Horizon." The Encinitas Tradition may have developed from a Paleocoastal/San Dieguito base, although it is not clear whether the "transitional phase" between San Dieguito and Encinitas in the Southern California region reflects a single group changing in place or the arrival of a new population into the region (e.g., B. F. Smith 1987). Moratto (1984:547) thought that the Encinitas Tradition developed in place, at least in the San Diego area. Whatever the case, the Encinitas Tradition incorporated (presumably) hard seed processing but included hunting, fowling, fishing, and the use of marine shellfish along the coast. Other Encinitas traits include side-notched projectile points, discoidals, cogged stones (Fig. 7.5), large numbers of millingstones, and the common occurrence of loosely flexed burials (Warren 1968b:2). In the interior, the Encinitas Tradition is known from only a few sites (see Sutton and Gardner 2010).

Along the Santa Barbara coast, a relatively large number of sites are known that date between 8,500 and 7,500 BP, suggesting a widespread Encinitas occupation (Glassow 1991, 1996:19; Glassow et al. 2007). These sites reflect a diverse diet that included seeds, shellfish, and a variety

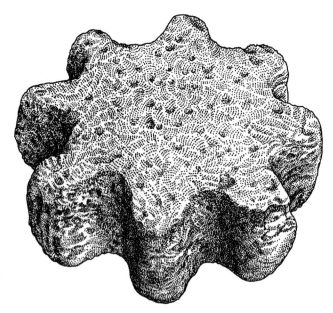

FIGURE 7.5 An example of a cogged stone from the Cogged Stone site in Southern California. The function of these artifacts is unknown (courtesy of Nancy Anastasia Desautels-Wiley; drawing by Joe Cramer; used with permission). The diameter of this specimen is 9.5 cm.

of terrestrial and marine mammals. Cemeteries appear as early as 7,000 BP, but there is little evidence of later Chumash-like social complexity (Erlandson 1997:91). In his study of the nutritional content of foods, Erlandson (1991) argued that the human diet during the time span of the Encinitas Tradition along coastal Santa Barbara must have consisted primarily of plants, although shellfish and other animal sources provided protein.

A relatively large number of Early Holocene sites are known along the mainland coast in the Santa Barbara area. The Browne site (Greenwood 1969), located just north of Ventura, contained a well-defined cemetery, a crescent, stemmed and side-notched points, scrapers, choppers, hammerstones, a large number of millingstones, and other artifacts.

On the northern Channel Islands from 8,000 to 6,500 BP, the situation was a bit different than on the mainland (see Rick et al. 2005). Few manos and metates are known, so there was probably little emphasis on seeds; however, apparent digging-stick weights have been found, suggesting a reliance on tubers. Marine resources were also important (Glassow 1996:20–21).

On San Clemente Island, a major occupation dating between 8,900 and 5,500 BP was documented at the Nursery site, where some eighteen large housepits built with whale bones were identified (see Salls et al. 1993), suggesting that sedentary groups of fishermen occupied the island (also see Byrd and Raab 2007). Interestingly, there is little evidence of any Encinitas Tradition influence on the southern Channel Islands.

The Sparsely Occupied Interior

The Early Holocene record in the interior of California is quite meager. Few sites or materials from this time period have been identified from the Cascade Range, the Sacramento Valley, or the southern San Joaquin Valley. In the Sierra Nevada, materials dating to the Early Holocene are known from the Skyrocket site (Bieling et al. 1996; La Jeunesse and Pryor 1998) and a few other sites (Hull 2007:189).

In the central San Joaquin Valley, however, there appears to have been a substantial Early Holocene occupation around Tulare Lake (see Rosenthal et al. 2007:151), as evidenced by the number of Pinto projectile points in vandal collections from the area (Riddell and Olsen 1969; Kaberline 1995). Unfortunately, very little else is known about this time, as no formal excavations have been undertaken at Early Holocene sites at Tulare Lake.

In the Colorado Desert, the Early Holocene is also poorly represented (Schaefer 1994:64; Schaefer and Laylander 2007). It has been suggested (Hayden 1976:288) that much of desert California, including the Colorado Desert, was abandoned during the Altithermal, but this is not yet clear (Schaefer 1994).

THE MIDDLE HOLOCENE (CA. 7,000 TO 3,000 BP)

By about 7,000 years ago, the climate generally improved and at about the same time, ocean temperatures appear to have cooled (Jones and Waugh 1997:117). During these more favorable times, it is thought that human population levels increased, presumably requiring additional food resources. The appearance of mortar and pestle technology across many regions of California during the Middle Holocene (between ca. 6,000 and 5,000 BP) is believed to represent the adoption of acorns into the diet on a relatively large scale. Acorns, along with the use of mortars and pestles to process them, are hallmarks of ethnographic California (e.g., Gifford 1936), and many California archaeologists equate the appearance of mortars and pestles with the adoption of acorns as a dietary staple (e.g., Moratto 1984; Basgall 1987). This premise is supported by the post-5,000 BP pattern of moderate to severe dental wear among many skeletal populations, presumably a result of people consuming acorns processed with stone mortars and pestles (e.g., Dickel et al. 1984). Thus, the Middle Holocene in California is seen as a time when conditions improved, populations expanded, acorns were adopted, and sociopolitical complexity increased.

In addition, sea levels generally stabilized about 5,000 years ago (Carbone 1991:12). This resulted in the establishment of sandy beaches, estuaries, mudflats, and marshes (e.g., Bickel 1978:11) that probably made the coast more attractive to people. As a result, after 5,000 BP, shore localities could be occupied without fear of inundation and were less subject to erosion. This also increased the likelihood of the survival and subsequent discovery of such sites.

Acorns and Salmon in Northern California

As in many other places in California, mortars and pestles appeared in Northern California about 5,000 BP, presumably reflecting the adoption of acorns on a large scale, identified as the inception of the Mendocino Pattern on the Northern Coast (see Hildebrandt 2007:91). Even with the addition of acorns, hunting seems to have increased and economies became more generalized, with shellfish collecting and sea mammal hunting becoming more common along the coast (Fredrickson 1974:46) and salmon fishing on inland rivers. It is thought that population growth resulted in the addition of resources (e.g., acorns) and the intensification of others (e.g., mammals). New artifact types also appeared in interior Northern California, and the number and size of sites increased (Sundhal 1992:102), suggesting a population movement—perhaps proto-Penutian people moving south into California from Oregon. In other places, such as along the upper Sacramento River, acorns seem to have been relatively unimportant at this time (e.g., Basgall and Hildebrandt 1989), perhaps reflecting other aspects of an overall adaptation.

The Northern Coast was not heavily occupied during the Middle Holocene (e.g., Hildebrandt and Levulett 1997:143; Hildebrandt 2007), as it was probably difficult to utilize marine resources along the rugged coastline. In addition, dense forests are not particularly productive places. As a result, it appears that people began to specialize in the exploitation of salmon and acorns (Hildebrandt and Hayes 1993:115).

Mortars and Shellmounds of the Central Coast

On the Central Coast, the Middle Holocene witnessed the beginning of "a more settled, intensified lifeway" (Jones and Waugh 1997:127; also see Jones et al. 2007). Mortars and pestles appeared and supplemented the existing mano and metate technology, and it may be that a relatively mobile pattern using coastal resources changed to a more sedentary pattern using terrestrial resources (e.g., acorns), coupled with an increase in hunting (T. L. Jones 1996). Employing data from a number of Central Coast sites, T. L. Jones (1996) maintained that the pattern of lineal descent organization and associated gender-specific task roles observed at contact appeared at this time (also see T. L. Jackson 1991).

At the beginning of the Middle Holocene, it is believed that the entire Central Coast was occupied by Hokan linguistic groups (e.g., Moratto 1984:547; Glassow 1997:152; also see Golla 2007:76). Sometime between 4,000 and 2,000 BP, Penutian (Costanoan) linguistic groups moved into the northern portion of the region, leaving the Hokan groups in the southern portion. This may be reflected in the archaeological record, as exemplified in a study of the development of sociopolitical organization on the San Francisco peninsula that posited the development of small, "multiple-village" entities after about 3,500 BP (Bocek 1991), perhaps corresponding to the ethnographic "tribelets" reported by Kroeber (1932).

Little is known about the Middle Holocene of the San Francisco Bay region until about 5,500 BP (see Milliken et al. 2007: Table 8.4), when the large shell middens that are characteristic of this region were first occupied (Lightfoot 1997:138). This is coincident with the slowing of sea level rise and the stabilization of the mudflats, marshes, and shellfish habitats of the bay (Bickel 1978:11). These sites generally contain a complex matrix of shell, ash, rock, soil, human inhumations and cremations, and other features but relatively few artifacts. Such sites have traditionally been viewed as the remains of large villages with substantial populations (see Lightfoot 1997:129–130). A relatively new interpretation has emerged, however, proposing that the shellmounds were purposeful constructions (Lightfoot 1997:131) that served as cemeteries and perhaps as territorial markers for villages (Lightfoot 1997:139). Some mounds apparently had small residences on top of them, perhaps serving as landmarks and "providing a cultural map of the communities along the bayshore" (Lightfoot 1997:139; also see Luby and Gruber 1999).

In the Santa Barbara area, the number of sites decreased dramatically between 6,500 and 5,500 BP (Glassow 1996:133; Glassow et al. 2007), suggesting that populations were suppressed during the Altithermal. After about 5,800 BP, estuarine shellfish species present in archaeological sites decreased significantly (Erlandson 1997:104), providing evidence that bays and estuaries were disappearing or declining in productivity after that time. Between about 5,200 and 4,800 BP, the percentage of shellfish species adapted to sandy beaches increased (Erlandson 1997:104), suggesting a shift from the exploitation of estuaries to the exploitation of sandy beaches, presumably due to geomorphic changes along the coast as a result of sea level rise (see Erlandson 1997:105). A similar pattern has been noted for the San Diego area after about 3,500 BP (e.g., Masters and Gallegos 1997:20; Byrd 1998:195). About 5,000 BP, conditions began to become cooler and wetter in California (Glassow 1996:133), and mortars and pestles began to appear. At this time, the Encinitas Tradition in the Santa Barbara area was replaced by the Campbell Tradition (see Harrison and Harrison 1966), which used mortars and pestles and had a greater emphasis on hunting.

During the Middle Holocene in the Santa Barbara area, the number of sites and the intensity of their occupation increased, suggesting an increase in population (Glassow 1996:21–22). At this time, acorns become more important, shellfish generally decreased in importance from Early Holocene levels, and marine mammals and fishing became more prominent (see R. H. Colten 1989; Colten and Arnold 1998; Rick and Glassow 1999; Vellanoweth and Erlandson 1999), indicating that people were exploiting open ocean resources. Ocean-going boats appeared by 5,000 BP (Gamble 2002) but may have been in use even earlier (Rick et al. 2001; Cassidy et al. 2004; Jones et al. 2008; Raab and Cassidy 2009). The northern Channel Islands were also heavily occupied during this time (Erlandson et al. 1992; Rick and Erlandson 2001; Rick et al. 2005).

Toward the end of the Middle Holocene at about 3,000 BP, populations along the Santa Barbara coast increased again and the specialization of labor for bead production may have triggered an elaboration of social complexity (C. D. King 1990), perhaps beginning the process that led to the development of chiefdoms during the Late Holocene. Other researchers (see below) believe that the beginning of chiefdoms occurred later in time.

More Millingstones in Southern California

The Encinitas Tradition persisted in mainland Southern California during the Middle Holocene. During this time, some diversification of subsistence took place, with the addition of mortars and pestles and an increased complexity in hunting and fishing technologies, which is evident by the faunal remains in archaeological assemblages.

On the coast south of Los Angeles, the Encinitas Tradition of the Middle Holocene may be part of "an expansion of settlement to take advantage of new habitats [kelp beds and estuaries] and resources [some shellfish and fish] that became available as sea levels stabilized between about five and six thousand years ago" (Mason et al. 1997:58). The expansion of Takic groups into Southern California at about 3,500 BP (Sutton 2009) ended the Encinitas Tradition along the coast, although it persisted in the interior until about 1,000 BP (see Table 7.2).

The longstanding marine adaptations along coastal San Diego County and the southern Channel Islands continued into the Middle Holocene, with economies characterized by shellfish collecting, fishing, and terrestrial hunting and gathering (see Byrd and Raab 2007). Ocean temperatures were cooler, kelp beds expanded, and fish from kelp habitats were commonly exploited (Masters and Gallegos 1997:20), probably with the aid of boats. Many small stone bowls and mortars have been found offshore along San Diego and may have been used to grind bait or poison (Hoover 1973).

The southern Channel Islands were intensively occupied during the Middle Holocene (see Rick et al. 2005). Major occupations are known at the Eel Point site on San Clemente Island (Raab et al. 1994; Raab and Cassidy 2009) and at the Little Harbor site on Santa Catalina Island (Meighan 1959b; Raab et al. 1995a). Both sites exhibited permanent occupations and maritime economies focused on the exploitation of seals, sea lions, and dolphins, with some fishing and shellfish collecting also taking place (Raab 1997:27; Raab 2009). Fishing was more important at Little Harbor, where large numbers of tuna were caught, and the co-occurrence of tuna and dolphins suggests that they may have been captured together in nets (see Raab 1997:28).

HIGHLIGHT 7.3

THE WESTERN NEXUS

In 1993, noting the distribution of Olivella *grooved rectangle beads in both Southern California and the northern Great Basin, Howard and Raab (1993; see Sutton and Koerper [2009] for the most recent discussion) proposed the existence of a socioeconomic interaction sphere linking the two regions that dated between about 5,100 and 4,500 BP. This interaction sphere, named the Western Nexus (Sutton and Koerper 2009), involved long-distance exchange of a number of artifact types and ideas relating to ritual–belief systems. Some Western Nexus artifacts have been found in caches, many in pairs or triads, and some have been found in mortuary contexts, all of which suggest that at least some ritual thoughts and behaviors were shared across 1,200 kilometers. It is possible that the Western Nexus involved interactions between Penutian and Hokan linguistic groups during a time of Penutian population movements that often occurred at the expense of Hokan groups. It seems likely that the Western Nexus was but one of the exchange systems operating in California during the Archaic (e.g., Chartkoff 1989).*

The Beginnings of Intensification: The Central Valley and Mountains

The Middle Holocene (or Middle Period) in the Sacramento Valley witnessed an intensification of the use of acorns and salmon and the introduction of corner and side-notched projectile points (see Rosenthal et al. 2007). Mortars and pestles appeared, or increased in number, after about 5,000 BP, indicating the adoption of the acorn. The adoption of acorns is seen as intensification of the economy, likely due to population increases.

At the beginning of the Middle Holocene, the Sacramento Valley was occupied by Hokan linguistic groups. Surrounding Penutian linguistic groups appear to have progressively expanded into the valley bottoms, establishing large villages (Fig. 7.6), and by about 2,500 BP, Hokan

FIGURE 7.6   A crew works at CA-KER-180, a large mound site in the San Joaquin Valley (photo by Lesile Hartzell, 1988; used with permission).

groups only retained possession of the foothills. In the rest of the Central Valley, the Middle Holocene is commonly called the Early Horizon, Early Period, or Windmiller Pattern, and it dates between about 5,000 and 3,500 BP. Windmiller was defined based on work at mound sites (such as the Windmiller site) in the delta region believed to have been villages with cemeteries (Heizer 1949; Ragir 1972). It is possible, however, that at least some of these mounds were purposefully constructed as cemeteries (Meighan 1987:28).

Mortars and pestles are common artifacts of the Windmiller Pattern, as are large numbers of baked clay balls presumably used as "cooking stones" for cooking acorn meal in basketry (Treganza 1946). Stemmed and lanceolate points, fishing gear, and numerous ornaments are also part of Windmiller assemblages. Windmiller people seem to have been adapted to "riverine and wetland environments" (Moratto 1984:207) and, while the presence of mortars implies the use of acorns (Ragir 1972:98), it is commonly held that Windmiller people were more dependent on hunting than on gathering (Moratto 1984:201, 203–204). Windmiller children suffered from numerous and recurrent nutritional deficiency events (McHenry 1968), and winter starvation was apparently a problem (Schulz 1970, 1981).

Extended burials are also an important Windmiller trait, and some 85 percent have contained associated artifacts. Men were often buried in separate areas, in deeper graves, and with more artifacts, suggesting greater status (see Ragir 1972:96–97). A small percentage of women and children had substantial grave goods, indicating some ascribed status (Ragir 1972:97). There is also evidence of violence in Windmiller burials, such as cranial and lower arm fractures, points embedded in bone, isolated skulls (perhaps as trophies), and the use of artifacts made from human bone, all suggestive of warfare (Ragir 1972:112).

The Middle Holocene is poorly known in the San Joaquin Valley but is presumably charac-terized by a more diversified and generalized subsistence pattern (Moratto 1984:183), with an increased emphasis on seed processing. The conventional view is that Penutian Yokuts groups moved into the San Joaquin Valley from the north about 3,500 BP (Moratto 1984:555), replacing Hokan groups, or perhaps Northern Uto-Aztecan (Takic?) linguistic groups (Moratto 1984:560; also see Golla 2007; Sutton 2009, 2010a).

One of the most interesting developments during the Middle Holocene in the Cascades and northern Sierra is the Martis Complex (see McGuire 2007:171–172; also see Heizer and Elsasser 1953; Elsasser 1960:66–73), dated between 5,000 and 1,500 BP (Elsasser and Gortner 1991:361). The Martis Complex is characterized by the use of basalt for flaked stone tools, includ-ing big, heavy, "crude" projectile points, scrapers, and manos and metates; an emphasis on hunt-ing and seed gathering (Heizer and Elsasser 1953:19); and an association with the Central Sierra Abstract style of rock art (Elsasser and Gortner 1991:370–371; also see Moratto 1984:294–303; Gortner 1990, 1994). Martis may represent the ancestral Maidu of the region (Moratto 1984:303). Early Martis (ca. 5,000 to 3,000 BP) is marked by dart points, Martis contracting stem points, and Martis split-stem points (see Rosenthal 2002:159).

The Middle Holocene record in the central and southern Sierra Nevada is poorly under-stood, as few sites dating from this time have been excavated. Nevertheless, it appears that foothill and upland environments were exploited, although few sites contain much in the way of subsis-tence evidence. Acorns appear to have been adopted but were not used intensively.

The Hot Colorado Desert

There is little evidence of occupation in the Colorado Desert during the Middle Holocene, con-tinuing the trend from the Early Holocene (Schaefer and Laylander 2007). The people living there were probably "diversified hunters and gatherers who adapted to drier and warmer Holocene conditions" (Schaefer 1994:64). The only well-documented Middle Holocene site in the region is Indian Hill Rockshelter (M. McDonald 1992), which was not occupied until about 4,000 BP, at the end of the Altithermal. Indian Hill contained a substantial deposit, diverse and numerous artifacts, and a series of rock-lined cache pits (Wilke and McDonald 1989) and may have served as a "home base" or "hunting camp" (M. McDonald 1992:155).

THE LATE HOLOCENE (CA. 3,000 TO 150 BP)

Beginning around 3,000 BP, much greater intensification of the use of acorns is believed to have commenced across California, strengthening a trend that began several thousand years earlier. Populations appear to have grown dramatically, sociopolitical organization became more com-plex, and many of the societies observed at contact appear to have been established. A number of groups developed quite complex sociopolitical organizations during the Late Holocene, with some polities viewed as chiefdoms. The role of resource intensification in this process is important.

Based on optimization (efficiency) theory, the general intensification model posits that growing populations placed too much pressure on higher ranked resources, such as large mam-mals and seeds, forcing the use of lower ranked (and so less efficient) resources, such as acorns, fish, and shellfish (see Basgall 1987; Bouey 1987; Beaton 1991a). This resulted in an increase in calories in exchange for more labor. Hunting would theoretically have declined in importance, although this may not have actually been the case (Hildebrandt and McGuire 2002).

An analysis of archaeobotanical materials from eleven central California sites found that Early Holocene peoples used relatively few acorns but did exploit a variety of small seeds, Middle Holocene people were more focused on acorns, and Late Holocene people used a great deal of both acorns and small seeds (Wohlgemuth 1996). Thus, it seems that Early Holocene people used small amounts of many things, Middle Holocene people began to focus on acorns at the expense of small seeds, and that Late Holocene people intensified the use of both acorns and small seeds, presumably in response to population increases.

Increasing Complexity: Northern California and the Central Coast

Across Northern California, the beginning of the Late Holocene is represented by a widespread but poorly known general hunting and gathering culture, called the Berkeley Pattern (ca. 2,500 to 1,500 BP; Fredrickson 1974; Hildebrandt 2007). This was a time of greatly increased political complexity and population growth as well as greater sophistication of exchange systems, and sedentary villages may have been established along rivers for the first time (Hildebrandt and Levulett 2002:303). Sometime around 1,500 BP, the bow and arrow was introduced, the use of shell bead money began (Farris 1992), and group boundaries became more important.

Along the far northwest coast of California, the Gunther Pattern (ca. 1,500 to 150 BP) is marked by Gunther barbed points and is believed to represent salmon fishers, presumably ancestors of the ethnographic Wiyot and Yurok. In the southern portion of the Northern Coast, where salmon were not as important, the widespread Augustine Pattern (M. E. White 2002; Hildebrandt 2007) is marked by small, triangular arrow points and is thought to represent the ethnographic Pomo. After about 1,500 BP, short-term-use shell middens appeared along the coast, and by 1,000 BP, large coastal residential sites became common (Hildebrandt and Levulett 2002). The development of marine-focused economies developed about 1,500 BP (Hildebrandt and Levulett 2002:318); this adaptation included "expensive" traits, such as large fish weir complexes, and facilitated the development of ranked societies.

Over the remainder of Northern California, essentially in the Coast and Cascade ranges and foothills surrounding the Sacramento Valley, the later Late Holocene is represented by the Tehama Complex. This complex (which has several phases) has been characterized by a generalized settlement/subsistence system, with relatively small sites, manos and metates, and small arrow points (see Sundahl 1992; also see Basgall and Hildebrandt 1989). The Tehama Complex is thought to represent the ancestors of the ethnographic Hokan groups not displaced by the migration of Penutian groups into California.

In the San Francisco Bay area, some of the major sites, such as the Emeryville Shellmound, were first occupied about 2,600 BP (see Broughton 1999; Lightfoot and Luby 2002; Milliken et al. 2007). The hunting of sea otters became a focus of the economy, perhaps due to habitat changes (Bickel 1978) or resource intensification (Broughton 1994a). The expansion and resource intensification believed to be reflected at Emeryville (Broughton 1997, 1999, 2002) might also be related to the introduction of the bow and arrow at ca. 1,500 BP (e.g., Wake 2003).

Along the Central Coast, a number of changes marked the beginning of the Late Holocene (Jones et al. 2007). Acorns, terrestrial hunting, and fishing became more prominent and shellfish and marine mammals became less important. Grooved net weights and fishhooks appeared about 2,600 BP, ushering in innovations in open-water fishing (Jones and Waugh 1997:127). As populations increased, health declined (Lambert 1993).

Money and Chiefdoms: The Santa Barbara Region

The Santa Barbara region was one of the most dynamic in California during the Late Holocene (Glassow et al. 2007). A fair amount of information is available on Late Holocene climatic conditions in the region, including changes in ocean temperature (called El Niño/Southern Oscillation [ENSO]) events (Pisias 1978), which would have disrupted the distribution of marine resources. In addition, the Medieval Climatic Anomaly (MCA; see Stine 1994) caused a drought between about 1,200 and 700 BP. As conditions changed, the MCA caused a ripple effect on resources and human adaptations (J. R. Johnson 2000).

Between 2,600 and 850 BP, there was a dramatic increase in the production of shell beads, significant population growth, and clear evidence of increasing social and political complexity. The single-piece fishhook (of shell or bone) was introduced about 2,500 BP (Glassow 1996:22), and at about the same time fish increased in importance (J. R. Johnson 2000:307). The Chumash plank canoe (*tomol*) may have appeared about 1,500 BP (Gamble 2002; J. E. Arnold 2007; also see Gamble 2008), with harpoons at about 1,000 BP, suggesting that the focus on sea mammals increased (but see Colten and Arnold 1998).

After about 1,500 BP, more sedentary villages developed, including both residential and communal structures (Gamble 1995), with these large villages becoming the dominant settlement type by 700 BP. It is also clear that there was intensification in the relationship between island and mainland peoples after 1,350 BP, with a concomitant increase in violence during this same time. Most of this violence was not lethal (Lambert 1993, 1997; Lambert and Walker 1991), indicating interpersonal fighting, perhaps over power or resources.

After about 850 BP, a number of important cultural changes are apparent in the archaeological record of the Santa Barbara region. The manufacture of shell beads increased, canoes became more important, populations grew and became more sedentary, and the dependence on fishing increased (J. E. Arnold 1991:955; Colten 2001:213). Full-time craft specialization (with other specializations, including those of third genders; see Hollimon 2000) also appears to have taken place at this time. Analyses of cemeteries from this time indicate that society was ranked (L. B. King 1969; Martz 1992; Gamble et al. 2002; also see Arnold and Green 2002).

THE DEVELOPMENT OF CHIEFDOMS   Much of the Santa Barbara coast and the northern Channel Islands were occupied by the Chumash at contact, and it is believed that they have lived in the region for at least the last 9,000 years (see Rick et al. 2005). At contact, the Chumash are believed to have been organized in a series of small but complex chiefdoms, with economies based on the use of shell bead money, large sedentary villages of more than one thousand people, extensive craft specialization, intervillage confederacies, and long-distance trade, with an overall population of about ten thousand (see Gamble 2008). Much of the research on Late Holocene times in the Santa Barbara region is focused on understanding the timing and conditions for the development of Chumash chiefdoms.

Four basic models for the development of Chumash chiefdoms have been put forth. First, based on his research on the mainland coast, Chester King (1990) argued that mortuary data suggested the presence of complex social organizations as early as 3,000 BP. King proposed that population growth and the specialization of labor needed for the massive increase in the production of shell beads resulted in the development of increasingly complex organizations in order to control and manage resources and labor.

A second model, proposed by Jeanne Arnold (e.g., 1992a, 1992b, 2001, 2007; also see Colten 1992, 1995, 2001; J. E. Arnold et al. 1997) for the northern Channel Islands, suggested that the stresses of environmental fluctuations (ENSO and MCA events) between about 850 and 700 BP created a shortage of resources and that complex social organizations evolved to manage these conditions. As plank canoes were the major carriers of commerce between the islands and mainland, control of these vessels by the elites was seen as a central factor (but see Spielmann 2002).

Based on their work on the southern Channel Islands, Raab et al. (1994:260; 1995b; also see Raab and Larson 1997) proposed a third model, suggesting that ENSO and MCA events did not greatly impact marine resources but that the MCA-related drought on the mainland created shortages that may have necessitated the development of social complexity. Raab (1996) also thought that the need to control warfare also may have been a factor in increasing social complexity. This model was supported by work on San Clemente Island (Yatsko and Raab 2009).

Finally, Kennett and Kennett (2000:391–392) suggested that ENSO events brought in cool (rather than warm) water and, coupled with the MCA, triggered an extended interval of high climatic instability that led to increasing social complexity. Interestingly, the Kennett and Kennett model would be applicable to both the northern and southern Channel Islands.

Trade during the Late Holocene in Southern California was dynamic (Jackson and Ericson 1994), with materials moving back and forth from the Southwest (Koerper and Hedges 1996) and the Mojave Desert. Obsidian was obtained from a number of sources, including the Obsidian Butte locality in the eastern Imperial Valley. When Lake Cahuilla was full, Obsidian Butte was underwater; thus, the availability of the obsidian fluctuated with the level of the lake.

Takic Expansion: Coastal Southern California

Less is known of the Late Holocene in coastal Southern California than in the Santa Barbara region. Although social complexity did increase, groups in coastal Southern California probably did not evolve chiefdoms. One of the major development during the Late Holocene in Southern California, including the northern portion of the Colorado Desert, was the arrival of Takic linguistic groups (Sutton 2009, 2010a) around 3,500 BP (signaling the beginning of the Del Rey Tradition [Sutton 2010b]). Probably originating in the region north of Los Angeles, Takic groups moved south and occupied coastal Southern California, including the southern Channel Islands, down to northern San Diego County. The Takic apparently moved eastward from the coast after about 1,500 BP (Sutton 2009).

Takic people brought with them a new burial pattern, settlement systems, and economy, a cultural pattern quite different from the preceding Encinitas Tradition. It is not clear why Takic groups moved south. Takic groups may have occupied the San Joaquin Valley during the Middle Holocene, and if they were pushed south by Penutians at the beginning of the Late Period, they may have continued south (Sutton 2010b).

The economic focus also changed during the Late Holocene in coastal Southern California (see Byrd and Raab 2007). The reliance on marine resources (sea mammals and shellfish) decreased, although fish became more important. Late Holocene economies had more of a terrestrial focus (Rosenthal et al. 2001), and it is possible that the ENSO/MCA events influenced that change. In the San Diego area south of the Takic region, however, coastal groups appear to have become more reliant on marine resources (Christenson 1992).

More Acorns in the Sierra Nevada

The Late Holocene was also a dynamic time in the Sierra Nevada. As elsewhere in California, acorn use greatly intensified, populations grew dramatically, corner-notched points were introduced, and large permanent villages were established along the major rivers. Trade greatly expanded, and obsidian from the eastern Sierra moved west while shell from the coast moved east.

In the northern Sierra Nevada, the Martis Complex continued from the Middle Holocene. Late Martis (ca. 3,000 to 1,500 BP) is characterized by Martis corner-notched points (see Rosenthal 2002:159) and an intensification of acorns. Martis was replaced by the Kings Beach Complex (1,500 to 150 BP), with the introduction of small side-notched points, the use of obsidian and silicates rather than basalts, and an economic emphasis on fishing and seed gathering (Heizer and Elsasser 1953:20). Kings Beach is thought to be the archaeological expression of the ethnographic Washo.

Over most of California, small corner-notched arrow points appeared about 1,500 BP. At about this same time, a warming-and-drying trend began (the MCA?) in the Sierra Nevada, populations likely declined, and the mountains were used on a temporary basis (Moratto 2002). Beginning about 700 BP, climatic conditions became cooler and wetter and people returned to the mountains as permanent residents to exploit acorns. Numerous large villages along major rivers dating to this time have been documented (e.g., F. Fenenga 1952; Pendergast and Meighan 1959; von Werlhof 1961; Moratto 2002). These large sites contain substantial middens, housepits (sometimes placed in two groups, suggesting a moiety organization), numerous bedrock mortar features (Fig. 7.7), burials and cremations, triangular arrow points, and a variety of other artifacts, including pottery and glass trade beads (after about 350 BP).

FIGURE 7.7   A bedrock mortar feature at the Long Canyon Village site in the southern Sierra Nevada (photo by the author, 1990).

Contact with Europeans and is marked by the appearance of trade goods and a massive population decline due to introduced diseases. It has been suggested that the "large and complex" groups observed just prior to contact actually formed as a result of an extensive trade network established with coastal groups who were trading with the newly arrived Spanish (Chartkoff 2001). The increase in sociopolitical complexity was a result of the need to administer the growing trade networks. The demise of cultures due to disease apparently halted this development.

Growth and Elaboration in the Central Valley

The Late Holocene prehistory of the Central Valley (Rosenthal et al. 2007) generally exhibits a pattern of population growth, establishment of large villages, resource intensification, and cultural elaboration. At the beginning of the Late Holocene, the Sacramento Valley (see Fig. 7.1) was occupied by groups (possibly Penutians) living in large villages on the valley bottom, with well-developed middens, housepits, and an economy focused on acorns and fish. The mountains and foothills surrounding the Sacramento Valley were occupied by people (possibly Hokan) living in small villages with a less specialized settlement and subsistence system, but still focused on acorns.

Intensification and pressure on resources is evident during this time, as the use of acorns and small animals increased and the exploitation of large mammals and large fish (e.g., salmon) decreased (Broughton 1994b:510), seemingly reflecting population growth and resource competition, declining mobility, and more intense usage of smaller tracts of land. A pattern of interpersonal violence has been noted in Late Holocene burials (J. S. Nelson 1997) that may reflect increasing resource stress, declining foraging efficiency, and/or increasing competition. Pottery is rare in California, but a pottery tradition, called Cosumnes Brown Ware, has been identified at several sites in the lower Sacramento Valley (see Moratto 1984:213).

At about 1,500 BP, small corner-notched arrow points were introduced into the Central Valley. At about this time, many large village sites were established throughout the valley, reflecting large and dense populations, elaborate ceremonialism, and a complex exchange system (Moratto 1984:211). It seems that by about 1,500 BP, the Penutian Yokuts had occupied the entire San Joaquin Valley. By about 700 BP, small side-notched and triangular points appeared, the number of settlements increased, trade intensified, shell bead money began to be used, and sociopolitical complexity increased. The contact period is characterized by widespread population losses and the introduction of European trade goods.

"Lake" Times in the Colorado Desert

Much of the Colorado Desert appears to have been sparsely occupied until about 1,500 BP (see Schaefer 1994; Schaefer and Laylander 2007). Beginning about 1,300 years ago, Yuman (Patayan I, see Chapter 9) agricultural groups along the Colorado River area began to influence Colorado Desert groups. After about 1,000 years ago, a number of cultural traits, including pottery, small triangular points, and cremations, appeared in the region, either through diffusion or perhaps carried by some migrating population (see Sutton 2009). Whatever the case, long-distance trade networks were established between the Imperial Valley and the Colorado River area.

Of great importance, however, was the presence of a huge lake. On numerous occasions during the last fifteen thousand years (and earlier; Weide 1976), the Colorado River broke its channel and flowed into the Imperial Valley, forming a large lake (184 km long, 54 km wide, and 96 m deep; Schaefer 1994:67). This lake, called Lake Cahuilla, eventually overflowed into the Gulf of California by a different route. When the Colorado River reestablished its original course, the lake evaporated and disappeared. In the last several thousand years, there have been three (Wilke 1978) or four (Waters 1983) such events. The most recent stand of Lake Cahuilla may have been brief, between about 800 and 500 BP (Laylander 1997a:68; Schaefer and Laylander 2007:250). The modern Salton Sea (created accidentally in 1906) is a small hint of what Lake Cahuilla would have been like.

Human adaptation to these cycles of "lake/no lake" is of great interest, and a model of changing settlement and subsistence was proposed by Wilke (1978:103–107), based primarily on ethnographic analogy and paleofecal data from several sites. When the lake was present, people would have had a stable economic base (fish, waterfowl, and marsh plants) capable of supporting a substantial population, permanent lakeshore villages, and seasonal camps to exploit terrestrial resources. After the lake disappeared, Wilke (1978) argued, the system would have become centered on permanent springs. The economic focus changed from aquatic to terrestrial resources, likely resulting in increasing utilization of the surrounding uplands and movement of populations to the west and east.

More recent excavations in the area (Sutton and Wilke 1988) and further reanalysis of the coprolite data (Sutton 1993b, 1998) revealed a pattern of seasonal resource use suggesting that the lakeshore sites were not occupied on a permanent basis. They may have been an aspect of a transition between lake and desert adaptations or part of a lake-adapted system that did not include large, permanent villages.

BAJA CALIFORNIA

Baja California is a long peninsula on the Pacific coast south of San Diego (Fig. 7.1). It is about one thousand miles long, averages some sixty miles wide, and is mostly arid, although the areas adjacent to the coasts contain many marine resources (L. G. Davis 2006b). Baja California is geographically isolated, and people moving into the region did so primarily from the north (some would argue that there were important movements into the peninsula from the east; others have even claimed they also arrived from the Southwest). Many of the same factors that kept Baja California isolated during prehistory are still in place, and as a result, the archaeology of Baja California is poorly known (but see Massey 1955, 1966; Ritter 1979; Laylander 1992, 2006; Moore 1999; Laylander and Moore 2006). Of interest is the fact that atlatls were still in use in southern Baja California as late as the 1600s (Massey 1961; Laylander 2007), so "dart points" are not the temporal markers they are elsewhere.

The Early Occupation of Baja California

Massey (1966:43–51, 57, Fig. 12; also see Willey 1966:356–361; Snow 1976:159–160) presented an outline of the prehistory of Baja California (see Table 7.3; also see Willey 1966: Fig. 6-19), known as the "layer cake" model. He suggested that the earliest people, perhaps "Lake Mojave" or "San Dieguito" populations, occupied the entire peninsula during a wetter time, possibly as early as 10,000 BP. As in other areas of the desert (see Chapter 8), the Pinto and Gypsum complexes followed the Lake Mojave Complex. Massey's model then posited that sometime before (perhaps well before) 1,500 BP, other groups from the north entered the peninsula and occupied the upper three-quarters of the region. Still later, about 1,000 BP, Yuman (Patayan II) groups from Alta California moved in and occupied the northern quarter of Baja California. This model may ultimately prove inadequate (Kowta 1984; Laylander 1997b), but it is a starting point.

TABLE 7.3 A Cultural Chronology for Baja California

Period	Southern Baja California	Central Baja California	Northern Baja California
Ethnohistoric Period	Guaycura, Pericú	Cochimí	Yuman
ca. 1,500 to 300 BP	Las Palmas	Comondú	Patayan
ca. 5,000 to 1,500 BP	Gypsum	La Jolla	
ca. 8,000 to 5,000 BP	Pinto		
ca. 10,000 to 8,000 BP	San Dieguito (Lake Mojave)		
to ca. 10,000 BP		Clovis	

There have been claims for a pre-Paleoindian presence in central Baja California (B. Arnold 1957:250), based on descriptions of "elongate-biface," scraper-plane," and "flake-core-chopper" assemblages, implying a pre-projectile point culture; some "weathered" tools suggesting antiquity; and associations with lakes thought to be Pleistocene in age. However, recent research has shown that the lakes date later in time (L. G. Davis 2003), a fact that does not support claims of pre-Paleoindian dates. A few Clovis points have been identified (at least four) from central Baja California (Hyland 2006; Des Lauriers 2008). In addition, several pre-10,000 BP radiocarbon dates have been reported from northern and central Baja California (Des Lauriers 2006a; Hyland 2006; Gruhn and Bryan 2009).

Southern Baja California

Following the layer cake model, the ethnographic peoples of the southern Baja California region may trace their local ancestry directly back to Paleoindian times. While there is still little direct archaeological evidence of such continuity, the languages at contact seem to be isolates, suggesting a long in situ development. In addition, the people exhibited extreme long-headedness (hyperdolichocrany), a physical type quite unusual for most Native Americans (Massey 1947) but is suggestive of a relic population, possibly related to Kennewick Man (González-José et al. 2003).

The best-documented complex in southern Baja California is the Las Palmas culture, found in the far southern cape region and dating between 1,800 and 350 BP (Molto et al. 1997: Table 1; Fujita 2006). Las Palmas is known for its distinctive secondary burials in caves, with defleshed bones painted with red ochre, wrapped, and covered with deer skins or palm fronds, a complex of traits unique in western North America (Massey 1966:49; also see Carmean and Molto 1991; Molto and Fujita 1995; Fujita 2006). Habitation sites are known along the coast (Fujita 1995).

A dental and isotopic analysis of some late Las Palmas burials (Molto and Kennedy 1991; also see Molto and Fujita 1995) suggested that marine resources and plants formed substantial constituents of the diet. It was further suggested that Las Palmas people exploited a wider range of resources than their neighbors to the north (Molto and Kennedy 1991:47). There is also evidence that dolphin hunting may have been a specialized adaptation during Las Palmas times (Porcasi and Fujita 2000).

Central Baja California

Sometime around 1,500 BP, a new migration of people from the north occupied the central half of the peninsula, replacing the earlier Lake Mojave/Pinto/Gypsum complexes (Massey 1966; Willey 1966). Archaeologically, this group is known as the Comondú culture. Snow (1976:160) argued that Comondú represented a society of hunters and gatherers that had changed little through time. Comondú is characterized by milling equipment, small (arrow) projectile points, perhaps a complex textile industry, and the absence of pottery. All of the ethnohistoric groups occupying the Comondú region speak the same basic language and seem to be a single cultural group.

Some investigations have been undertaken in central Baja California (e.g., Massey and Osborne 1961; E. L. Davis 1968; Ritter and Schulz 1975; Ritter 1979, 1981, 2006a, 2006b; Des Lauriers 2006b; Hyland 2006), but even the basic settlement and subsistence patterns of the region are still imperfectly understood. Of great interest is the spectacular great mural rock art (Fig. 7.8) known in the region (see Gutiérrez and Hyland 1994; Crosby 1997), some of which may be as old as 5,500 BP (Watchman et al. 2002).

Northern Baja California

The layer cake model suggests that Yuman groups occupied the northern quarter of Baja California sometime after 1,000 BP, replacing the Patayan in that area. It seems likely, however,

FIGURE 7.8 Mural of pictographs from San Borjitas Cave, Sierra Guadalupe, Baja California. The figures on the ceiling of the cave are each some ten feet in length (photo by Eric W. Ritter, 1969; used with permission).

that the Patayan were already Yuman. Horticulture probably diffused into the region and was practiced in the far northeastern corner of the region. Considerable archaeological research has now been accomplished in northern Baja California, but much of it is unpublished and has not been synthesized.

NATIVE CALIFORNIAN CULTURES AT CONTACT

At the time of European contact (ca. 400 BP), California was home to more than one hundred separate cultural groups (Heizer 1978), speaking over ninety languages belonging to twenty-three language families (e.g., Shipley 1978), a situation that suggests a complex series of population movements. There were perhaps between 500,000 and 700,000 people living in California at contact (S. F. Cook 1971, 1976, 1978; Stannard 1992:23–24), although this population level seems to have been reached only within the last 2,000 years or so (Glassow 1999:61). Today, there are perhaps some 80,000 California Indians, with individuals of many other tribes also currently residing in California. There are 112 federally recognized tribes in the state of California (including some Great Basin and Southwestern groups) that are living on reservations or *rancherías* (small reservations) totaling some 550,000 acres (as of 1960). Some forty other groups are not recognized by the federal government and are scattered throughout the state, although some members of the unrecognized groups also live on various reservations and rancherías.

Many California Indians are active in political issues that affect them, and there is a growing pride in their heritage. The state of California has established the Native American Heritage Commission to help native peoples deal with critical issues. A number of groups have developed business ventures on their reservations, such as casinos or tax-free tobacco stores, which form a source of considerable revenue.

Further Reading

There are now several major syntheses available for California. These include the various chapters on prehistory in the *Handbook of North American Indians* (Heizer 1978) but they are now out-of-date. The first real synthetic treatments were published in 1984, the first being *California Archaeology* (Moratto 1984), followed a few months later by *The Archaeology of California* (Chartkoff and Chartkoff 1984). In the last several years, a number of new treatments have appeared, including those by Brian Fagan (2003), Arnold et al. (2004), Jones and Klar (2007), and Arnold and Walsh (2010). A new synthesis on the Archaeology of Baja California is now available (Laylander and Moore 2006).

Several universities publish archaeological materials in the form of occasional papers (UC Berkeley and UCLA) and several important regional journals, including the *Journal of California and Great Basin Anthropology, California Archaeology*, and *Pacific Coast Archaeological Society Quarterly*, contain information on California prehistory. Also notable is the monograph series published by Coyote Press, called the Coyote Press Archives of California Prehistory.

Marshes and Deserts
The Great Basin

The Great Basin is the large interior basin lying between the Sierra Nevada to the west and the Rocky Mountains to the east and includes much of the western United States. Most of the native people in the Great Basin were hunters and gatherers, although a few groups, such as the Southern Paiute and perhaps the Owens Valley Paiute, practiced small-scale agriculture.

Although the Great Basin is generally arid, it has an unfair reputation as a sparsely vegetated and inhospitable place. Early anthropologists characterized Great Basin peoples as "poor hunter-gatherers" just getting by. It is important to understand, however, that the Indians of the Great Basin, past and present, were well adapted to their environment and that they were not the destitute people so commonly depicted in much of the literature. In addition, it should be noted that the Great Basin was not a monolithic "Desert West" but a place with highly variable environments and diverse cultural responses, through both space and time.

In general, the Great Basin consists of numerous mountain ranges and valleys in the center with extensive wetlands on the edges. Two major adaptations evolved from this ecological duality: relatively permanent systems that were centered around marshes and a more common, relatively mobile system that was centered on mountain and valley resources (D. B. Madsen 2002:387). A resource that defines a large part of the Great Basin is the pinyon nut, which formed the most important food item for many ethnographic groups. Pinyon is labor intensive, however, and may have not have been used extensively by people until fairly late in time (e.g., Simms 1985).

GEOGRAPHY AND ENVIRONMENT

The Great Basin can be defined in many ways (see Grayson 1993, 2008), including its physiographic and cultural aspects. The physiographic Great Basin is a large region of interior drainage that encompasses most of Nevada, southeastern Oregon, southern Idaho, western Utah, and portions of eastern California, including Owens Valley (see Fig. 8.1). Within this region are two major deserts: the Great Basin Desert in the north and the Mojave Desert in the south. The Great Basin Desert occupies most of the natural Great Basin and is generally wetter and cooler than the

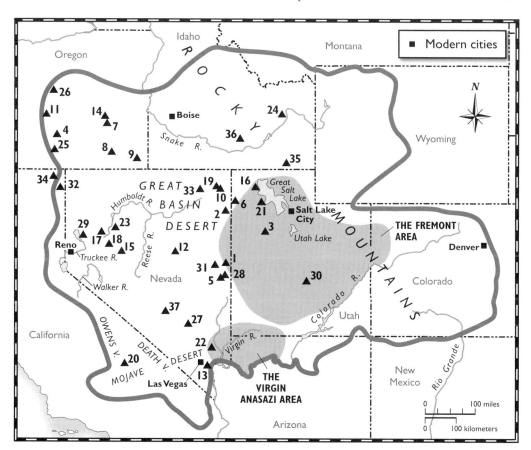

FIGURE 8.1 Map of the Great Basin showing the major subregions and the location of sites discussed in the text: 1) Baker Village; 2) Bonneville Estates Rockshelter; 3) Camels Back Cave; 4) Carlon Pithouse Village; 5) Council Hall Cave; 6) Danger Cave; 7) Diamond Swamp; 8) Dietz; 9) Dirty Shame Rockshelter; 10) Dry Susie; 11) Fort Rock Cave; 12) Gatecliff Shelter; 13) Gypsum Cave; 14) Headquarters; 15) Hidden Cave; 16) Hogup Cave; 17) Humboldt Lakebed; 18) Humboldt Cave; 19) James Creek Shelter; 20) Lake China; 21) Lakeside Cave; 22) Lost City; 23) Lovelock Cave; 24) Owl Cave; 25) Paisley Cave; 26) Paulina Lake; 27) Pintwater Cave; 28) Smith Creek Cave; 29) Spirit Cave; 30) Sudden Shelter; 31) Sunshine Locality; 32) Surprise Valley; 33) Tosawihi Quarries; 34) Tule Lake; 35) Weston Canyon Rockshelter; 36) Wilson Butte Cave; 37) Yucca Mountain.

Mojave Desert, although its northern regions are more arid (see Fowler and Koch 1982). The Great Basin Desert contains many rivers, lakes, and marsh systems, numerous pinyon-covered mountain ranges, and associated valleys. The Mojave Desert occupies much of southeastern California and portions of Arizona and Nevada (see Jaeger 1965; Rowlands et al. 1982). It is a dry desert characterized by hot summers and cold winters.

The Great Basin culture area is defined differently than the physiographic Great Basin, incorporating all of the territory inhabited by people speaking one of the Numic languages (with the exception of the Comanche on the southern Plains). The culture area covers approximately 400,000 square miles and comprises all of the natural Great Basin, in addition to large portions of Wyoming, Colorado, New Mexico, Arizona, and Idaho, including the Snake River Plain (see Fig. 8.1).

The environment of the Great Basin is highly varied and includes alpine zones, forests, rivers, marshes, and very arid deserts (see Harper 1986; Mehringer 1986). There are more than 150 small mountain ranges and an equivalent number of small valleys that lie within the Great Basin; hence, the term *Basin and Range Province* is commonly used to refer to the region. Elevations range from below sea level in Death Valley to over 12,000 feet in the Toquima Range in central Nevada. At one time, a number of the valleys contained rivers terminating in lakes or marshes, several of which were quite extensive.

The climate is generally arid with warm to very hot summers and cold winters. Precipitation is quite variable, with the southern Great Basin averaging four to six inches per year and the northern Great Basin receiving a few inches more. Many of the mountain ranges receive snowfall every year. The Sierra Nevada and Cascade Mountains create a rainshadow effect along the western edge of the Basin, although the runoff from these mountains produces a great deal of surface water in the region. The western edge of the Rocky Mountains has a similar effect on the eastern edge of the Great Basin.

The Great Basin contains many biotic communities, including alpine vegetation at high elevations. Many of the mountain ranges in the Great Basin are covered with extensive forests of pinyon and juniper, and pinyon nuts were a major staple food for people. Pinyon does not grow north of northern Nevada, and in the Mojave Desert to the south, pinyon and juniper only exist in the higher mountains. A sagebrush-grassland community dominates many of the valleys below the pinyon-juniper zone and extends to the north, past the boundaries of the pinyon. In the Mojave Desert, the creosote scrub community is dominant, with mesquite growing in the bottoms of valleys. In the marshlands, tule, cattail, sedge, and other marsh plants provided major sources of food and manufacturing materials.

Animals available in the Great Basin include deer, mountain sheep, and pronghorn antelope, along with a small population of bison in the north (Lupo and Schmitt 1997). Enormous numbers of rabbits, hares, rodents, reptiles, and insects (Sutton 1998) are also present. Beavers inhabited some of the rivers until they were trapped out by Europeans in the early 1800s. Waterfowl, particularly geese and ducks, are found in large numbers in the marsh habitats along the western and eastern edges of the Basin and were heavily utilized by the people in those areas. In addition, many dozens of species of fish are known throughout the Great Basin (see Hubbs et al. 1974), and freshwater shrimp were also used (Henrikson et al. 1998).

The environment of the Great Basin fluctuated through time, with extensive lake systems present at the end of the Pleistocene. Climate changed through time as well, and the typical Early, Middle, and Late Holocene periods are commonly recognized. Pinyon, a critical resource, originally moved north from the southern Basin, reaching its current distribution sometime in the mid-Holocene (see Zeanah 2002).

A BRIEF HISTORY OF RESEARCH

Great Basin peoples were first encountered by Euroamericans in 1776 but were largely unaffected by them until the 1850s, when Euroamerican settlements were established. Thus, by the time anthropologists began recording information on Great Basin groups in the early 1900s, there were still living people who had experienced a mostly "precontact" life, providing a rich ethnographic database (see D. D. Fowler 1986). This work, especially that of Julian Steward on ecology and ethnography (e.g., Steward 1938), provided the conceptual framework for much of the archaeology that has been conducted in the Great Basin since (see R. L. Kelly 1997; Bettinger 1998; C. M. Beck 1999). Steward worked mostly with people in the drier portions of the Great

Basin, and while other ethnographers worked with groups living in regions containing wetlands, much of that work was unpublished, resulting in a bias toward desert foragers (Fowler and Fowler 1990:10). This bias has perhaps held archaeological research "hostage" to a limited ethnographic perspective (a similar situation may be true in the Northwest Coast; see Chapter 5).

The first major excavation in the Great Basin was the 1912 work at Lovelock Cave, Nevada, an effort that yielded a huge quantity of materials. Partly due to the success of that work, much of the archaeology conducted in the Great Basin has focused on caves, and most of what is known about Great Basin prehistory has come from the excavation of caves and rockshelters (see Aikens 2008). This is less true in the eastern area, where considerable work has been done at open-air Fremont sites.

In the 1920s, the Smithsonian Institute and the Heye Foundation became active in Great Basin research and sponsored work at Lovelock Cave, Gypsum Cave, and Lost City, Nevada. By the 1930s, the University of Oregon began research in the northwestern Basin. The University of Utah began its statewide archaeological program under Jesse Jennings in 1948, the same year that UC Berkeley, under Robert Heizer, began its investigations in western Nevada. The universities of Nevada, Oregon, and Utah, joined by others including Brigham Young University and Hamilton College, continue their research programs in the Great Basin.

The excavation of Danger Cave (Fig. 8.2), located in the Great Salt Lake Desert, in the 1940s and 1950s resulted in Jesse Jennings (1957) proposing the "Desert Culture" concept, in which he argued that climate was essentially the same through time, that the material culture recovered from the site was basically the same for 10,000 years, and that there had been cultural continuity from ethnographic times back some 10,000 years (all based on the ethnographic model of Steward [1938]). This idea was challenged by Heizer and others (e.g., Heizer and Napton 1970),

FIGURE 8.2   Danger Cave, Utah (photo by the author, 1986).

who argued that climate had changed, and that adaptations had varied by region (e.g., the wetland-focused settlement system in western Nevada) and that there could not have been Basin-wide cultural continuity for 10,000 years. As a result, the "Desert Culture" idea was formally dropped (see Jennings 1973) in favor of a more general "Desert Archaic" model to allow for regional variation. Interestingly, this issue remains important, as many continue to use the Desert Culture concept.

In the 1970s, several major and innovative large-scale studies of settlement and subsistence systems were conducted, such as in the Reese River Valley of central Nevada (D. H. Thomas 1973) and in the Owens Valley of eastern California (Bettinger 1975). The Reese River project sought to test Steward's ethnographic data against the archaeological record, resulting in an archaeological model of cultural continuity for the last 5,500 years, at least in central Nevada (D. H. Thomas 1973). The American Museum of Natural History then undertook excavations at a number of sites in the central Basin, including Gatecliff Shelter (D. H. Thomas 1983b) and Hidden Cave (D. H. Thomas 1985). The unexpected discovery of sites in the alpine ecozones created new research opportunities (Bettinger 2008). Today, as in most places, CRM dominates the work being performed in the Great Basin, such as the fascinating study of the Tosawihi Quarries in north-central Nevada sponsored by the Bureau of Land Management (R. G. Elston 2006). In addition, the Utah State Antiquities Section has been a driving force behind much of the work in Utah in the last few decades.

MAJOR THEMES IN GREAT BASIN PREHISTORY

Early on, the Great Basin was seen as the definitive laboratory for developing and testing models of hunter-gatherer adaptations (recall Steward's work), and this research issue still dominates Great Basin archaeology. Integral to this line of inquiry are attempts to understand basic settlement and subsistence patterns, group mobility, sociopolitical organizations, and the collector-forager issue (refer to Highlight 6.1). Ultimately, the development of some sort of theoretical base will allow us to better understand the prehistory of the Great Basin (e.g., Bettinger 1993).

Partly in reaction to the Desert Culture concept, there has been a sustained effort to describe and understand the diversity of hunter-gatherer adaptations in the Great Basin, particularly within "desert" and "wetland" habitats (e.g., Janetski and Madsen 1990; R. L. Kelly 1995). Central to this effort is the application of models drawn from evolutionary ecology (e.g., Simms 1984; Bettinger 1987; R. L. Kelly 2001) in order to predict human behaviors in the past. This is usually accomplished through the use of optimal foraging models—essentially, the idea that humans will adopt "optimal" (least cost) behaviors to maximize their reproductive success, generally based on obtaining food (see discussion in Sutton and Anderson 2010:73–88). In essence, the researcher builds a model that ranks resources relative to each other based on net return and predicts which resources should be used in an optimal diet (along with other predictions, such as degrees of mobility) and then tests that model against archaeological data (also see Highlight 8.2). It should be noted, however, that optimal foraging models are difficult to apply given that the detailed data necessary to construct a model and then test it against the archaeological record are usually lacking (Beck and Jones 1992:29), but we are getting better at it!

The presence of farmer/foragers in the eastern Great Basin, collectively labeled the Fremont Tradition, has always been a puzzle. Who were they? Where did they come from? What happened to them? These questions are all still unanswered. Further, it is not clear what the relationship was between Great Basin foragers and the Fremont farmers. One possible answer is that what archaeologists see as two separate groups (foragers and farmers) were actually the same people with variable adaptations. It is also possible that some of the Fremont were Southwestern immigrants living among the foragers.

Another mystery in Great Basin prehistory is the distribution of the ethnographic peoples (the Numa), with just six basic Numic languages distributed across a considerable portion of western North America, even in areas that had been occupied by farmers in prehistory. How can this be explained? A number of ideas have been put forth, from a migration of people across the Basin to an in situ development, but the issue is far from settled (see below).

Several methodological issues are also important. For example, much of the archaeological record in the Great Basin before about 4,000 BP is confined to surface sites (with some prominent exceptions such as Danger Cave), making it difficult to date and understand such sites (Beck and Jones 1992:26). On the other hand, a surface record could imply a highly mobile and nonredundant settlement/subsistence pattern, although the presence of large and deep sites suggests that after 4,000 BP, people had settled into a recurring pattern of occupation (Beck and Jones 1992:26). Great Basin archaeologists are also trying to move in new directions, such as exploring the role of gender in the past (Leach 1999; also see Ardren 2008).

Projectile points are among the most commonly used artifacts for dating archaeological sites and components. Work in the Great Basin was instrumental in defining projectile point types and their dating for much of western North America (e.g., Heizer and Hester 1978; D. H. Thomas 1981), and these definitions are still widely used (see Fig. 8.3). Such classifications are not without their problems, however, as there is disagreement over the temporal sensitivity of certain atlatl dart point styles due to breakage and rejuvenation (Flenniken and Wilke 1989; but see Bettinger et al. 1991; Wilke and Flenniken 1991; O'Connell and Inoway 1994; Zeanah and Elston 2001). The classification of arrow points is also an issue (Bettinger and Eerkens 1999) in that the atlatl and dart system may have continued to be used after the introduction of the bow and arrow (Yohe 1998). A basic chronological sequence for the Great Basin is shown in Table 8.1.

THE PALEOINDIAN PERIOD (TO CA. 10,000 BP)

The Paleoindian Period in the Great Basin emerged at the end of the Pleistocene, when an extensive system of lakes was present in the Great Basin, the three largest being Lake Lahontan in Nevada, Lake Chewaucan in Oregon, and Lake Bonneville in Utah. Paleoindians lived on the margins of such lakes, as well as nearby upland habitats. A very early, perhaps even pre-Clovis, occupation may be present at Paisley Cave, along the shore of Pleistocene Lake Chewaucan (see Fig. 2.12). The site was initially excavated in 1938 (Cressman 1942), but additional work in the early 2000s resulted in the discovery of fourteen human coprolites (see Highlight 2.1), four of which were dated between about 13,000 and 13,800 years ago (Gilbert et al. 2008).

Clovis materials are present in the Great Basin (Warren and Phagan 1988; Basgall and Hall 1991; Beck and Jones 1997:188) but are mostly surface finds associated with fossil lakeshores (A. K. Taylor 2003). No Clovis sites with a clear association between extinct animals and humans have been found (Beck and Jones 1997:185), and very few artifacts of ground stone have been found in Clovis-age sites (Beck and Jones 1997:209). An exception to this pattern may be the Lake China site in the Mojave Desert (E. L. Davis 1978), where considerable Clovis material and extinct fauna have been found in general association. Another Clovis occupation may be represented at the Dietz site in Oregon (Willig 1990).

In the western Great Basin, early sites include Fort Rock Cave in Oregon, where sandals have been dated to about 11,000 BP (Cressman 1942; Bedwell and Cressman 1971; Bedwell 1973),

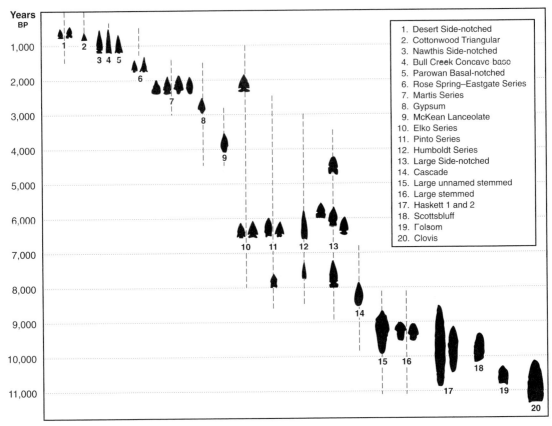

Great Basin Projectile Point Type Sequence

FIGURE 8.3 The projectile-point sequence for the Great Basin (adapted from *Handbook of North American Indian, Vol. 11, Great Basin*, Warren L. d'Azevedo 1986: Fig. 3; copyright © 1986 by the Smithsonian Institution. Reprinted with permission of the publisher).

Wilson Butte Cave in Idaho, with some material dated to about 11,000 BP (Gruhn 2006); and Owl Cave in southeastern Idaho, where mammoth bones were found in association with Folsom points and a piece of worked mammoth bone was dated to about 13,000 BP (S. J. Miller 1982:89). In northeastern California, a 13,400 BP date on a hearth was reported from a site near Tule Lake (Beaton 1991b). The remains of fish and waterfowl at the site suggested they were major resources.

In the central and eastern Great Basin, scant Paleoindian material has been discovered. A few fluted points have been found at the Sunshine Locality of east-central Nevada (G. T. Jones et al. 1996), and apparent early occupations were discovered at the bottom of Smith Creek and Council Hall caves in eastern Nevada (Bryan 1979a, 1979b). Danger Cave appears to have been first occupied about 11,000 BP (see Jennings 1957).

Only a few skeletal remains from this general time are known. A mummy found in Spirit Cave, Nevada, was dated to 10,600 BP (Dansie 1997; Touhy and Dansie 1997). It was wrapped in tule mats that were probably made on frames (see Nicholas 1998:724; also see Fowler and Hattori 2008). Two other early burials were found in the same general region (Touhy and Dansie 1997). All in all, virtually nothing is known of these early occupations.

TABLE 8.1 A Chronological Sequence for the Great Basin

Date (BP)	A Broad Outline	General Sequences by Region					General Climate
		Western Basin	Central Basin	Eastern Basin	Mojave Desert		
150	Late Archaic and Formative	Numic				Late Prehistoric	modern conditions
		Late Archaic	Underdown	Fremont		Virgin Anasazi	MCA; warmer than today
1,000					Rose Spring Complex		Medithermal; conditions similar to today
2,000	Middle Archaic	Middle Archaic	Reveille	Late Archaic	Gypsum Complex		
3,000			Devil's Gate				
4,000		Clipper Gap	Middle Archaic	Possible Hiatus		Altithermal; warmer than today
5,000		Early Archaic			Pinto/Deadman Lake Complexes		
6,000	Early Archaic		Early Archaic	Early Archaic			
7,000							Anathermal; cooler and moister than today but warming
8,000					Lake Mojave Complex		
9,000	Paleoar-chaic	Paleoarchaic					
to 10,000	Paleoindian	Paleoindian					colder and wetter than today

THE PALEOARCHAIC PERIOD (CA. 10,000 TO 9,000 BP)

Once the Pleistocene megafauna disappeared, the Paleoindian fluted-point traditions were replaced with stemmed points of the Great Basin Stemmed Tradition (called Lake Mojave in parts of the southern Basin and in the Mojave Desert), generally dated between 10,000 and 7,500 BP (Beck and Jones 1997:196). This transition between the Paleoindian and Archaic is generally called the Paleoarchaic Period (Willig 1988; Beck and Jones 1997; Jones and Beck 1999) and is associated with the Western Pluvial Lakes Tradition (e.g., Bedwell 1973). Paleoarchaic sites are much more numerous than Clovis sites and have been found in a larger number of habitats (Beck and Jones 1997:188, 189), suggesting both a larger population and a more generalized subsistence system in which a wider variety of resources was used, although large mammals were still targeted (Beck and Jones 1997). It may be that the foraging behavior of Paleoarchaic groups was quite different than that of later Great Basin foragers, with men and women using different strategies and exploiting a more narrow resource base, one oriented toward hunting (Elston and Zeanah 2002).

Paleoarchaic materials have been found across the Great Basin, most notably in the Alvord Basin, Oregon (Pettigrew 1984), the Paulina Lake site in Oregon (Connolly and Jenkins 1999), the Sunshine Locality of east-central Nevada (G. T. Jones et al. 1996), the Bonneville Estates Rockshelter in eastern Nevada (Goebel et al. 2003b), Yucca Mountain (Haynes 1996) and Pintwater Cave (Buck and DuBarton 1994) in southern Nevada, and at various locations in the Mojave Desert (see Sutton et al. 2007; also see below).

There are a relatively large number of Paleoarchaic sites located along the shore of ancient Lake Bonneville (Great Salt Lake is its remnant). It seems that the people using the wetlands along the shoreline (Fig. 8.4) were small groups visiting the area on a seasonal basis (Arkush and

FIGURE 8.4   Paleoarchaic site on the shore of Pleistocene Lake Bonneville (photo courtesy of Brooke S. Arkush; used with permission).

Pitblado 2000), although it is not clear where those people were during other times of the year. The focus on wetland resources in this area seems to have been abandoned ca. 9,500 BP (Duke et al. 2004).

An analysis of the location of lithic sources used by these early people suggested that the foraging territories in the central Great Basin Paleoindian and Paleoarchaic periods were large, some 400 kilometers north to south, and probably focused on wetland habitats (Jones et al. 2003). It was further argued that these territories shifted as wetland habitats began to diminish after about 9,500 BP.

THE ARCHAIC (CA. 9,000 TO 150 BP)

The Archaic began after the demise of the lake systems that had dominated human settlement since the late Pleistocene. The Archaic occupation of Danger Cave started at this time (ca. 9,000 BP) and set the stage for the idea of the Great Basin Archaic consisting of a monolithic, generalized hunting and gathering "Desert Culture" characterized by baskets and flat millingstones (e.g., Jennings 1957, 1964). The Desert Culture concept quickly gave way to the idea of a more variable Desert Archaic, and a variety of regional adaptations have since been recognized. Indeed, the Archaic of the Great Basin is much more dynamic than had been imagined even thirty years ago. The Archaic is herein divided into Early, Middle, and Late (generally following Simms 2008).

The Early Archaic (ca. 9,000 to 5,500 BP)

The Early Archaic is the time that people were required to adjust to the final desiccation of the various Pleistocene lakes on which they had relied for millennia. The environment became increasingly dry, and a generalized cultural adaptation developed. Stemmed points continued to be used (e.g., Beck and Jones 1997:196), but Pinto points were also introduced. The cultures of the Early Archaic are poorly known.

In southeastern Oregon, the Early Archaic equates to the Windust Phase on the Plateau (see Chapter 6). Of interest is the Paulina Lake site, dated between 9,500 and 7,700 BP and containing stemmed points, a light structure, several hearths, and the remains of large animals (Connolly and Jenkins 1999). This suggests a relatively mobile people with a focus on hunting large game. Small structures found in the lower levels of Dirty Shame Rockshelter in southeastern Oregon, dated between 9,500 and 5,900 BP (Aikens et al. 1977), were interpreted as winter houses, one part of a larger settlement system. Also of interest in that same region is the presence of early basketry and textiles from a number of sites (see Connolly et al. 1998; Fowler and Hattori 2008).

About 7,700 BP (Zdanowicz et al. 1999; Bacon and Lanphere 2006), Mt. Mazama in Oregon erupted, covering much of the northwestern Great Basin with ash (see Fig. 6.2). While the Mazama ash serves as an important stratigraphic and time marker in site deposits, some early sites might lie undiscovered under the ash, masking the archaeological record prior to that time.

Based on data from a number of Early Archaic sites in southeastern Nevada and northwestern Nevada, Layton (1985:193) suggested that at about 6,500 BP the northwestern Great Basin shifted cultural ties from the central Great Basin to the Columbia Plateau. Layton thought this might be related to the movement of Penutian groups from the Plateau into the Great Basin (also see Aikens 1994).

In the central Great Basin, Danger Cave (Jennings 1957) and Hogup Cave (Aikens 1970) produced the best records for the Early Archaic. Both sites contained a large number of artifacts, including textiles and detailed data on what people were eating. At Danger Cave, Jennings (1957) saw a similar adaptation throughout the Holocene (the origin of the Desert Culture concept), and a later reanalysis of the rabbit bones from Hogup Cave (Hockett 1994) generally supported this interpretation. Pinyon appears to have been used at Danger Cave as early as 7,500 BP (Rhode and Madsen 1998), and small seeds (e.g., pickelweed [*Allenrolfea occidentalis*]) appear not to have become part of the staple diet until about 8,700 BP, after populations of large mammal had begun to decline (Rhode et al. 2006).

In the eastern Great Basin, the Early Archaic (also called the Wendover Period; Aikens and Madsen 1986) is poorly represented. Sudden Shelter in south-central Utah (Jennings et al. 1980) was first occupied ca. 8,400 BP and served as a camp for hunters of deer and porcupine but was largely abandoned by about 6,300 BP (to be reoccupied later, see below). Weston Canyon Rockshelter (Fig. 8.5) in southeastern Idaho is another good example of a hunting camp. This shelter was used by people hunting large mammals (mostly sheep but including elk and bison) between 8,000 and 2,000 BP (S. J. Miller 1972; also see Arkush 1999; Plew 2000:43–46). Camels Back Cave (Schmitt and Madsen 2005) is a small hunting camp in central Utah and was occupied between about 7,500 and 400 BP, demonstrating a continued human presence in that region.

The use of upland areas increased over the earlier Paleoarchaic Period and may have been even more intensive than in later times (Curewitz 2001). These upland sites likely represent short-term visits from other (as yet unidentified) areas, as the uplands contain many discarded

FIGURE 8.5 Excavation of the Weston Canyon Rockshelter in southern Idaho (photo by Robert M. Yohe, II; used with permission).

tools but little evidence of tool manufacture or repair (implying such work was done else-where).

In general, Early Archaic groups in the Great Basin appear to have been highly mobile hunter-gatherers. Small seeds were apparently emphasized, and both large and small game was procured. While a number of special-use camps (e.g., hunting) are known, only a few base camps have been identified (e.g., Danger Cave). Very few human remains are known from the Early Archaic.

The Middle Archaic (ca. 5,500 to 2,000 BP)

The Altithermal, a period of very warm and dry environmental conditions, had dominated the Early Archaic, populations appear to have been much smaller across the Great Basin, and it is possible that some low-elevation areas were abandoned altogether. As the climate became cooler and wetter by about 5,500 BP, populations increased and sites became ubiquitous across the Great Basin. Although present earlier, Pinto points generally define the early Middle Archaic, while Elko points define the latter part of this period. Rockshelters became popular places to live after about 5,000 BP (R. L. Kelly 1997:9).

After about 5,500 BP, there is ample evidence that people were hunting pronghorn, sheep, and deer communally using large game traps (Raymond 1982; Pendleton and Thomas 1983; Delacorte 1985; Arkush 1986, 1995; McGuire and Hatoff 1991; Lubinski 1999). This tradition may well have emerged earlier than 5,500 years ago but has not yet been documented that early in the Great Basin. However, such techniques had been used on the Plains since Paleoindian times (see Chapter 10).

Although the lakes in the northwestern Great Basin had desiccated during the Altithermal, some of the lakes and associated wetlands became reestablished after about 5,000 BP. People exploited these lacustrine/marsh habitats, an adaptation sometimes called "Chewaucanian" (e.g., Aikens 1994; also see Upham 1994). There were major occupations of Harney, Alford, and Fort Rock basins in southeastern Oregon and of the Surprise Valley in northeastern California. In the Harney Basin (Harney and Malheur lakes), most sites reflect short-term use of marsh habitats, and few have deep deposits (Aikens and Greenspan 1988:32; Oetting 1992). An exception is the Headquarters site, a major camp occupied between about 7,000 and 200 years BP (Aikens and Greenspan 1988:45). Settlement at the nearby Diamond Swamp wetlands included pithouse villages after about 3,500 BP (Musil 1995). A similar pattern is evident in the Alvord Basin (Pettigrew 1984) and in the Fort Rock Basin (Jenkins et al. 2004), although several sites with sub-stantial domestic structures have been found, suggesting winter occupation.

Research in the Surprise Valley in northeastern California (O'Connell 1975) suggested that people were living in permanent pithouse villages near springs on the valley floor after about 6,000 BP, even during the height of the Altithermal. However, a reanalysis of the faunal remains from the Surprise Valley sites suggested that these "permanent villages" were actually winter camps and that the people were more mobile than had been thought (James 1983).

Lakes and wetlands also reappeared in the Carson Sink of western Nevada about 5,000 BP, and it appears that the small, mobile Early Archaic foragers of the area were replaced about 4,500 BP by semisedentary gatherers using marsh resources and perhaps hunting less. This suggests that the role of women and their labor changed over time (Zeanah 2004). On the other hand, there is evidence that the hunting of large mammals actually intensified in the western Great Basin after about 4,000 BP. To account for this, it has been argued that the increased use of seed resources indicates that women could provide most of the food and that men could hunt large animals as a prestige activity (Hildebrandt and McGuire 2002; McGuire and Hildebrandt 2005).

It is also possible that the increase in hunting may simply reflect larger game populations at the end of the Altithermal (Broughton and Bayham 2003; Byers and Broughton 2004:250). It may be that the need for meat protein, rather than just prestige, was the primary factor in hunting intensity (e.g., Zeanah 2004:27), although other readily available protein sources (e.g., insects; Sutton 1988) could have easily met those needs (see Highlight 8.2). Last, it is possible that a change in hunting tactics from the individual or family to communal hunting resulted in the capture of larger numbers of animals (Hockett 2005).

Exchange of obsidian and other materials between the western Great Basin and California has been documented during the Middle Archaic (Hughes 1994b). Of interest is the proposed connection of the northwestern Great Basin and Southern California in a trading network, called the Western Nexus (Sutton and Koerper 2009), that involved shell beads, obsidian bifaces, stone balls, other material items, and possibly ideology.

The central Great Basin was quite arid during the Middle Archaic, the Clipper Gap, Devil's Gate, and Reveille phases of the Gatecliff sequence (see D. H. Thomas 1983a) and there were no major lakes or wetlands present, although Danger and Hogup caves continued to be occupied. James Creek Shelter (Elston and Katzer 1990) in northern Nevada was first occupied ca. 3,200 BP by small groups using the site as a seasonal camp, and evidence of light structures was found at the Dry Susie site in northeastern Nevada (Smith and Reust 1995). The Dry Susie site dated to about 2,800 BP, and an infant burial was found there, suggesting that families were practicing a foraging strategy, moving entire groups from location to location.

Probably the most important study in the central Basin was the Reese River Valley project (D. H. Thomas 1973), which indicated that the valley (and likely other parts of the region) were not intensively occupied until about 5,500 BP. Excavations at nearby Gatecliff Shelter (Highlight 8.1) showed a similar occupational history.

HIGHLIGHT 8.1

GATECLIFF SHELTER

Gatecliff Shelter (D. H. Thomas 1983b), located in the Toquima Range in central Nevada, is one of the best known sites in the Great Basin. Based on a tip from a local geologist, the site was first discovered in 1970 and was described as a very small overhang (see Fig. 8.6) with a smoke-blackened ceiling, a few faded rock art elements on the back wall, but no artifacts visible on the surface. A small test excavation in that same year revealed a few artifacts, some burned bone, and a midden that was at least two meters deep.

The next year, a larger excavation was undertaken to determine the nature, extent, and age of the deposit, a task that took three years. Considerable cultural material was recovered, and it became clear that the site was both horizontally and vertically extensive, about twelve meters (forty feet) deep (perhaps the deepest rockshelter deposit in North America) with sixteen distinct cultural occupations (see Fig. 8.7) separated, isolated, and sealed by natural soil layers, a total of fifty-six strata in all (D. H. Thomas 1983b:172). In 1975, the excavation strategy changed from vertical excavation to horizontal in order to expose large areas, with the goal of revealing living surfaces that would contain information on specific activities at any given time. Artifacts recovered from the site included projectile points, basketry, cordage, shell beads, incised stone, millingstones, and bone tools. In addition, large quantities of food refuse bone from small to large animals were also recovered.

FIGURE 8.6 Gatecliff Shelter, Nevada, restored to its original condition after excavation (photo by the author, 1986).

Gatecliff Shelter was never a central occupation site (or base camp); rather, it functioned as a temporary camp for small groups of people exploiting resources in the vicinity of the site or as an overnight stop for travelers. When it was first occupied some 5,500 years ago (see D. H. Thomas 1983b:526–529), Gatecliff was used sporadically as a field camp by small groups of hunters, a pattern that lasted for about 2,000 years. Sometime about 3,500 BP, the site began to be used by larger groups of people, probably including women, and the variety and intensity of the activities being performed there increased. With more people living there over longer periods, the midden accumulated faster and the number of artifacts and other materials increased. About 700 years ago, a group of male hunters killed a herd of about a dozen bighorn sheep near the site and butchered the carcasses at the shelter.

Gatecliff Shelter is important for two major reasons. First, it contains a mostly continuous record of occupation from 5,400 years ago to about 700 years ago with radiocarbon-dated stratigraphy and many time-sensitive artifacts (e.g., projectile points). This well-dated occupational sequence now serves as the basis for the cultural chronologies employed for the central Great Basin. Second, the excavation itself was superb, a painstaking and meticulous field and laboratory effort that resulted in the recovery of an extremely detailed record of individual occupations through time that enabled David Hurst Thomas (1983b) to reconstruct specific behaviors, to show how and if these behaviors changed through time and then to test various models of settlement and subsistence to gain an understanding of occupation rarely achieved from the excavation of a single site.

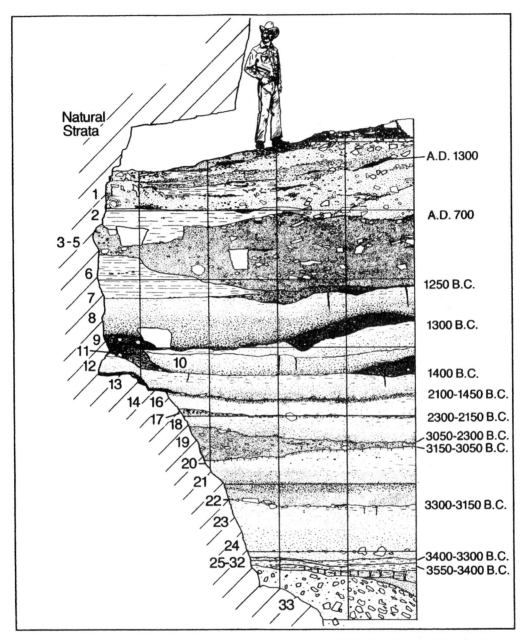

Natural Strata

A.D. 1300

A.D. 700

1
2
3-5
6
7
8
9
11
12
10
13
14 16
17 18
19
20
21
22
23
24
25-32
33

1250 B.C.

1300 B.C.

1400 B.C.
2100-1450 B.C.
2300-2150 B.C.
3050-2300 B.C.
3150-3050 B.C.

3300-3150 B.C.

3400-3300 B.C.
3550-3400 B.C.

FIGURE 8.7   Master stratigraphic profile of the deposits at Gatecliff Shelter, Nevada (drawing by Nick Amorosi; courtesy of the American Museum of Natural History).

The Middle Archaic record in the eastern Great Basin is similar to that of the central Basin, with a small population until the improvement of environmental conditions about 5,500 BP. The use of rockshelters and caves was common, and many have been investigated (see Jennings 1978). For example, Sudden Shelter (Jennings et al. 1980) in south-central Utah was first occupied ca. 8,400 BP, was abandoned by 6,300 BP, reoccupied about 4,600 BP, and abandoned again about

3,300 BP, all indicating a fluid settlement system. Sites near springs were occupied along the western edge of the Great Salt Lake Desert (Janetski 2006; also see Arkush 1998). Some sites were located along the margin of the Great Salt Lake, no doubt affording their inhabitants access to the resources offered by the lake habitat, including insects (see Highlight 8.2).

The relatively few Middle Archaic burials recovered from the eastern Basin (Janetski et al. 1992) show a pattern of interment in pits near residences and the use of grave goods. The skeletal data also indicate that these hunter-gatherers were relatively healthy, unlike the later Fremont farmers in the same region. One interesting burial found near Utah Lake contained a middle-aged male who died about 5,400 years ago and was buried with a number of items, including twined matting, coiled basketry, Northern Side–notched points, bone tools, and a dog (Janetski et al. 1992).

HIGHLIGHT 8.2

GRASSHOPPERS FOR DINNER AGAIN?

Research on diet in the prehistoric Great Basin has generally focused on the "big ticket" resources, such as seeds, pinyon nuts, rabbits, and pronghorn. While insects were known (Sutton 1988) to have been consumed by Great Basin peoples (and by all people for that matter), insect remains are difficult to recover, more difficult to identify, and even more difficult to positively link to human diet (Sutton 1995). Thus, they are easy for archaeologists to miss, so relatively little information on the dietary role of insects is available.

Lakeside Cave, Utah (Fig. 8.8) is located near the southwestern shore of Great Salt Lake and was first occupied about 5,000 years ago. Excavations were undertaken at the site in

FIGURE 8.8   Lakeside Cave in western Utah. The shoreline of the Great Salt Lake is a short distance to the left of the cave (photo by Monson Shaver; used with permission).

the 1980s to help gain an understanding of human adaptation to the lake environment. The work was conducted with standard procedures, and excavated soil was screened through 1/8-inch mesh. During that process, a small number of grasshopper femurs (legs) were found. Being curious, the investigators began to screen the soil with 1/16-inch mesh as a control sample, resulting in the recovery of a large number of grasshopper elements. Next, a large bulk sample of soil was collected and examined in the laboratory, at which time many thousands of grasshopper elements were recovered. Finally, human coprolites containing grasshopper remains were found at the cave (see Simms 2008: Fig. 4.7). It became obvious that the site was a major processing center for grasshoppers (Madsen and Kirkman 1988).

Where did these grasshoppers come from? It was discovered that swarms of grasshoppers would frequently fly out over the Great Salt Lake, become fatigued, fall into the lake, and drown. They would then wash up on the lakeshore and form windrows where they dried in the sun (a similar phenomenon occurred with brine fly larvae in the same region [Sutton 1988:45–49]). When this happened near the cave, the people would simply walk down to the lake and scoop them up by the basketload. This probably did not happen frequently, but when it did, people could obtain vast quantities of grasshoppers that were already dried, salted, and ready to eat or store. But first the legs were removed, as they are difficult to swallow—hence all of the grasshopper femurs in the midden.

The caloric return for collecting dried grasshoppers from the lakeshore was determined to be somewhere between 270,000 and 7 million calories per hour, far higher than any other resource (the next highest is deer, sheep, and antelope at about 30,000 calories [Simms 1984: Table 4]), making grasshoppers the highest ranked resource by far in the region. It was later determined that if the grasshoppers were transported to other localities (adding the caloric cost of carrying the grasshoppers from place to place), their return rate would be much lower, about 3,500 calories (Jones and Madsen 1989). However, the new calculations were based on the transportation of whole grasshoppers and did not account for the fact that at least some of the grasshoppers were eaten at the site and others may have been processed prior to transport, allowing individuals to carry many more grasshoppers at any one time and lowering transport costs.

We do not know the theoretical ranking of grasshoppers, or of other insects, among people in the Great Basin. The return on grasshoppers appears to have been very high, at least where they could be collected in abundance (e.g., Madsen and Schmitt 1998). A determination of whether the animals were processed prior to transport, if they were stored, and other factors must be made before the return rate—or rates, depending on conditions—can be calculated. In the meantime, models about prehistoric diets should include insect resources.

The Late Archaic (ca. 2,000 to 150 BP)

Beginning about 2,000 years ago, a series of dramatic changes occurred across the Great Basin (Bettinger 1999a). Pinyon, used sparingly for thousands of years, became a major resource after about 2,000 BP (see D. B. Madsen 1986a). Snares for trapping rodents appeared about 2,000 BP (see Janetski 1979), suggesting the addition of these animals as an important ingredient of the diet. Storage in built facilities (e.g., pits) increased, and pottery, ideal for storage anywhere, appeared in the eastern Basin after about 2,000 BP and after about 600 BP elsewhere (see Griset 1986). The bow and arrow diffused into the Basin after about 1,800 BP and may have resulted in a decrease in the importance of large game with an apparent increase in the importance of small game (R. L. Kelly 1997:28–29).

Later, alpine ecozones were settled and considerable evidence of substantial houses appeared, keeping in mind that evidence of earlier structures may be obscured due to poor preservation conditions. Specialized seed gathering and processing tools appeared within the last 1,000 years or so, and the "population [was] larger, more gregarious, and residentially tethered than at any time before" (Bettinger 1999a:69). This may be due to better environmental conditions after 2,000 BP, but there were droughts (e.g., the MCA) that were severe in some areas.

Another important development at this time seems to have been a shift from "public" goods to "private" goods—that is, from everyone owning and having access to everything to individuals or families controlling or owning things, such as hunting locations, pinyon groves, and equipment. It is possible that specialized small seed processing equipment developed concurrently with pottery (Eerkens 2004), as pottery could keep seeds "privately owned." Such developments could manifest in an increase in storage for private use, hunting for prestige, smaller trading areas, and the development of more complex social systems to deal with it all (see Simms 2008:177–180).

Perhaps related to the idea of "private goods" was the adoption of pinyon as a staple in many areas after about 1,500 BP. Ownership of pinyon groves and the use of "green cone" procurement may have allowed a focus on this resource (Bettinger 1976, 1989; Eerkens et al. 2004; Hildebrandt and Ruby 2006) which, coupled with population increases, a progressive shrinkage of group territories, and technological innovation (e.g., pottery), changed subsistence and settlement strategies from mobile foraging to sedentary collecting (Bettinger 1999b).

In the western Great Basin, some of the lakes and wetlands systems had reappeared by about 5,000 BP but were probably not extensive. In the Harney Basin in southeastern Oregon, people lived around Malheur Lake in substantial occupations after 2,000 BP (Oetting 1992:122), and these people probably did not travel far or trade much, as most of the obsidian they used was obtained locally (Lyons et al. 2001). In the nearby Fort Rock Basin, the large Carlon Pithouse Village was occupied in two major episodes, from 2,300 to 1,500 BP and from 700 to 500 BP (Wingard 2001), perhaps being abandoned during the MCA.

Occupation of the Carson Sink in western Nevada is of particular interest. Within the Carson Sink is Stillwater Marsh and Humboldt Lake (at the terminus of the Humboldt River). The modern Stillwater Marsh covers some 10,000 acres but was much larger (perhaps 25,000 acres) in the past. The Carson Sink wetlands were occupied about 5,000 BP but became more important beginning about 2,000 BP. The lacustrine/marsh adaptation in this region is sometimes called the "Lovelock Culture" (e.g., Aikens 1994; also see Upham 1994).

Although some sites had been known in the Carson Sink for decades, major flooding in the Stillwater Marsh between 1983 and 1986 exposed a large number of previously unknown sites, including major residential locations and a large number of burials (Raymond and Parks 1990). These sites generally dated between 3,000 and 500 BP, and while none of the sites appeared to be permanent year-round occupations, the marsh was a "hub of residential activity" between about 2,000 and 600 BP (R. L. Kelly 2001:290).

Considerable debate regarding the role of marsh resources in the settlement and subsistence systems of the region followed the discoveries at Stillwater Marsh, the results of which had implications for all wetland habitats across the Great Basin. Two models (Bettinger 1993:45–47) emerged from the debate: a "limogood" ("limo" referring to lakeshores) model stating that wetlands were oases supporting low-mobility, sedentary populations using highly ranked resources, and a "limobad" model stating that wetlands provided mostly low-ranked resources used by highly mobile groups who did not have permanent villages.

To address these issues (and others), the Stillwater mortuary population (dated between 2,000 and 700 BP) was examined for evidence of mobility patterns and subsistence practices (see Larsen and Kelly 1995). It was found that, in general, the people were healthy but that both males and females had high rates of osteoarthritis, indicative of heavy workloads (Larsen and Hutchinson 1999:201). Males had more problems with their legs and hips, likely due to long-distance travel in rough terrain (hunting trips?) (Larsen and Hutchinson 1999:196), which indicates that the people led a generally semisedentary lifestyle (Hemphill 1999). Isotopic and pathological data demonstrated a generalized subsistence strategy and periodic food shortages, with pinyon being relatively unimportant (Schoeninger 1999:165). Thus, the Stillwater people seem to have been "limoneutral," with a fair amount of mobility and a broad diet. Robert Kelly (1990) argued that after 1,500 BP, group mobility decreased in the Stillwater area, perhaps related to a decrease in moisture (the MCA?) that might have made marshes more attractive. In addition, some of the major sites (cache caves, see below) were not used after 1,500 BP, suggesting a change in settlement patterns (R. L. Kelly 2001:296).

Just to the north of Stillwater Marsh, a major "village" with many house features and burials was located along the shore of Humboldt Lake (Livingston 1986). The Humboldt Lakebed site dates between about 3,000 and 100 BP (Livingston 1986:111) and appears to have been a summer camp, as no hearth features have been found in the houses (fires for warmth would be needed in the winter). Considerable evidence of the use of marsh and lake resources was found, including the remains of waterfowl, aquatic plants, and small fish (see Raymond and Sobel 1990; Butler 1996). Lovelock Cave (see Highlight 8.3) lies on a hill just above the Humboldt Lakebed site and likely served as a storage facility for the people at that site. Thus, the evidence from these sites supports the idea that people were not living in the Carson Sink on a permanent basis (R. L. Kelly 1999:139, 2001:15). The locations of the winter sites are not yet known.

Another interesting aspect of the archaeology of the Carson Sink is the presence of "storage caves," used intensively to cache equipment and foods and as occasional shelter. At least three of these caves are known in the Carson Sink—Humboldt Cave (Heizer and Krieger 1956), Hidden Cave (D. H. Thomas 1985), and Lovelock Cave (see Highlight 8.3)—and were generally used between about 4,500 and 3,400 BP and then again between about 2,000 and 1,500 BP. Hidden Cave (D. H. Thomas 1985) appears to have been mostly used by women (Rhode 2003) who consumed a great deal of food derived from marsh resources (visit www.hearstmuseum.berkeley.edu/blm to see descriptions of Hidden Cave and photographs of some of the artifacts).

HIGHLIGHT 8.3

LOVELOCK CAVE

Lovelock Cave, the first major site excavated in Nevada, is located on a west-facing slope of the Humboldt Mountains, just above the eastern shore of Humboldt Lake in western Nevada northeast of Reno. It was used by people beginning about 4,500 BP and was the home of numerous bats for millennia. In fact, the site was first discovered by people removing bat guano from the cave for use as fertilizer. The guano had been deposited over the years and was mixed in with the archaeological materials. Guano miners removed many of the artifacts they found, and their activities damaged or destroyed many of the archaeological materials in the cave. An account of the site reached UC Berkeley in 1912, and one of the university staff, L. L. Loud, was sent to investigate. Loud found an incredibly rich cultural deposit and recovered some 10,000 artifacts. Additional excavations were undertaken in 1924 (Loud and Harrington 1929), and thousands more specimens were recovered. Further work was conducted at the site in the later 1960s (e.g., Heizer and Napton 1970).

The collection from Lovelock Cave included several thousand perishable artifacts, including basketry, matting, animal skin items, wood, cordage, rope, and duck decoys (real duck skins stretched over tule reed "bodies"). In addition, many artifacts of stone, bone, and shell were also recovered. Much of the material had been placed in caches and stored for future use. More than forty such caches were found that consisted of various items, such as one that was filled with dried fish, one that had eleven duck decoys in a basket (dated to 2,200 BP), and one that contained a basketmaker's kit. In addition, some five thousand human coprolites were recovered. The analysis of some of these coprolites (see Ambro 1967; R. A. Cowan 1967; Napton 1970) showed clear evidence that the users of the cave were eating lacustrine resources.

Interestingly, while Lovelock Cave contained a huge number of artifacts, there was no clear evidence that people had actually lived there. The Humboldt Lakebed site (Livingston 1986) is just below the cave, and it appears that the people from that site stored their material in Lovelock Cave, probably while they were elsewhere during other seasons of the year (R. L. Kelly 1999:139, 2001:15). The presence of coprolites in Lovelock Cave suggests that people stayed at the cave for short periods of time, perhaps using it as shelter from the summer heat or during inclement weather. More information on Lovelock Cave (including photographs of some of the artifacts) can be found at www.hearstmuseum.berkeley.edu/blm.

In the central Basin (the Underdown Phase of the Gatecliff sequence; see D. H. Thomas 1983a), the basic pattern of human adaptation first delineated at Danger Cave continued into the Late Archaic. Populations of large game increased dramatically as the climate became cooler and wetter, and hunting of these large animals intensified (Byers and Broughton 2004).

Of interest is a change in the use of alpine ecozones in the central and western Great Basin. Such localities were visited on a short-term basis, such as to hunt sheep, as early as 4,000 BP. After about 600 years ago, however, villages with houses and occupation debris appeared, suggesting that people were living at high altitudes for extended periods (Bettinger and Oglesby 1985; Bettinger 1991, 1993, 2008). These villages may have been related to population growth and perhaps the expansion of Numic groups across the Basin (Bettinger 1991:656; also see Scharf 2009) (see below). A similar pattern may have been found in Wyoming (Wingerson 2009).

By about 2,000 BP, much of the eastern Great Basin was occupied by the Fremont (discussed below). Fremont groups practiced a combined foraging and farming economy, so it is difficult to differentiate non-Fremont Archaic foragers (if there were any) in the archaeological record. By 2,000 BP, large wetlands along the eastern shore of the Great Salt Lake were heavily used (see below). Upland regions were also used, such as Weston Canyon in southeastern Idaho (see Arkush 1999, 2008; also see Plew 2000:43–46).

A NUMIC EXPANSION   Between about 1,000 BP in the southwestern Great Basin and 600 BP in the northeastern Great Basin, a number of distinct changes occurred. Material culture changed with the introduction of brownware pottery, small triangular Desert series projectile points, and new types of seed processing tools, as well as a replacement of earlier basketry styles with new ones. Mortuary patterns changed from cemeteries to isolated burials. The substantial pithouse architecture used for thousands of years was replaced with small wickiup-like structures. Settlement patterns changed in many areas: the housepit villages in the lake basins of southeastern Oregon disappeared, new villages were established in alpine zones, and a number of localities were either abandoned or only sporadically used. Last, the agricultural groups in the south and east apparently disappeared and were replaced by hunter-gatherers. The archaeological remains of these late peoples are meager and almost form a "veneer" over the earlier materials, and they are commonly assumed (following the direct historical approach) to belong to the ancestors of the ethnographic Numic groups (e.g., Janetski 1994; Janetski and Smith 2007:5).

What happened that could account for these changes? The diffusion of pottery and the appearance of new projectile point types are not particularly informative, but a replacement of basket types and changes in mortuary patterns, both sensitive "ethnic" markers, suggest the possibility of a population replacement late in time. What about other lines of evidence do we have to explain this phenomenon?

It was recognized early on that the entire Great Basin (and beyond) was occupied by ethnographic peoples that spoke very similar languages, generally referred to as "Shoshonean" and now classified as members of the Numic branch of the Northern Uto-Aztecan linguistic family. A number of ideas have been proposed to account for this language distribution, including a migration down from the north, a migration up from the Southwest, or an in situ development from existing populations (see Sutton and Rhode [1994] for a history of this issue). Using linguistic data, Lamb (1958) contended that the Numic had originated from a homeland somewhere in the southern Sierra Nevada/western Mojave Desert of California and that they had expanded north and east across the Great Basin beginning about 1,000 years ago. This expansion would have had a dramatic impact across much of western North America, with Numic groups moving into eastern California, the southern Plateau, a portion of the northern Plains (the Numic Comanche moved to the southern Plains), and the northwestern Southwest.

The Lamb model was accepted by some and challenged by others. The ideas about people coming from the north or south were revisited but generally rejected, since neither could explain the distribution of the Numic languages. The in situ model was also generally rejected for the same reasons, although some still champion that argument (e.g., Stoffle and Zedeño 2001). Others (e.g., Holmer 1994) argued that the expansion happened, but much earlier (e.g., 5,000 BP) than Lamb thought.

An alternative model (Aikens and Witherspoon 1986; Aikens 1994) proposed that the Numic homeland was in the central Great Basin (following the idea that there was cultural continuity in that area from the last 5,500 years [e.g., D. H. Thomas 1973]) and that the Numic had spread west and east from the central Basin at several times in the past. Although innovative, the Aikens and Witherspoon model did not explain the distribution of all the Numic languages and relied on the weak premise of cultural continuity in the central Great Basin. In addition, the linguistic and archaeological evidence pointed to a homeland in the southwest Great Basin.

After fifty years and a great deal of discussion and argument (see Madsen and Rhode 1994; R. L. Kelly 1997:31–35; Simms 2008:248–255), the general Lamb model of the Numic expansion is now generally accepted, and recent studies on DNA (Kaestle and Smith 2001) have provided additional support. Nevertheless, there is still much we do not know about this issue. A new idea is that the entire Uto-Aztecan language family developed in the Great Basin, perhaps as early as 8,900 BP (Merrill et al. 2009). If this is correct, it would necessitate a complete revision of early Great Basin (and Southwest) linguistic prehistory.

Why did the Numic expand? It is possible that population pressure was a factor; if there were too many people in the homeland, some may have been "forced" to move. A related factor may be a climatic change that took place about 1,000 years ago (the MCA), which may have lowered carrying capacity, creating population pressure. We still do not understand the possible relationship and mechanics of these factors.

How did the Numic expand against the various existing people throughout the west, generically called the "pre-Numic"? One idea is that the Numic employed their superior seed gathering technology (seed beaters and winnowing trays) and that they slowly outcompeted and replaced the pre-Numic (Bettinger and Baumhoff 1982). If the dating is correct, the Numic moved over a thousand miles in less than six hundred years, perhaps too rapid a movement if economic competition was the factor. In addition, the economic model would not apply to the Numic movement onto the Plains. Another idea is that warfare was an important factor (Sutton 1986), as the ethnohistoric record shows that the Numic were expanding violently against all of their neighbors at the time of historic contact. The warfare idea is not a popular one because many people cannot bring themselves to believe that hunter-gatherers had a violent side.

Last, it is possible that the Numic moved into areas that had already been abandoned by their previous inhabitants. If the MCA made life more difficult, people may have moved elsewhere, leaving areas uninhabited and "inviting" to the Numic. While this idea could have some explanatory power for areas occupied by agriculturalists, such as the Virgin Anasazi, it does not seem reasonable that much of western North America was abandoned by its hunter-gatherer occupants (who had stayed through the challenging climatic regimes of the Middle Holocene) and then occupied by other hunter-gatherers. The arguments continue.

THE FORMATIVE: AGRICULTURAL SOCIETIES OF THE GREAT BASIN

The Great Basin is typically viewed as having been occupied by hunting and gathering foragers, although several agricultural groups were also present. Corn agriculture diffused north from the Southwest, and several groups practiced agriculture—the Virgin Anasazi in southern Nevada and the Fremont in Utah. In addition, the Southern Paiute (who occupied the Virgin Anasazi area in ethnographic times) practiced small-scale farming, and some very late agriculture appears to have been practiced in the Owens Valley (Lawton et al. 1976; Bouey 1979).

The Virgin Anasazi (ca. 2,000 to 800 BP)

The Virgin Anasazi (see Shutler 1961; Lyneis 1995; Ahlstrom and Roberts 2008) are the westernmost branch of the Ancestral Puebloans (see Chapter 9). They occupied northwestern Arizona, southern Nevada (along the Virgin and Muddy rivers), and perhaps even a portion of the Mojave Desert (see Fig. 8.1). The Virgin Anasazi spanned Basketmaker II to early Pueblo III times (ca. 2,000 to 800 BP; see Chapter 9) and possessed the suite of Southwestern traits (pottery, masonry architecture, and agriculture).

The Virgin Anasazi practiced some farming, growing crops in the river floodplains; however, hunting and gathering were clearly important aspects of the economy. By about 800 BP, the Virgin Anasazi abandoned the southern Nevada area, apparently moving back to the east. The reason for this abandonment is unclear but may be related to the MCA. It is also possible that they were forced from the area by the Numic expanding from the west (see above).

The Fremont (ca. 2,100 to 700 BP)

Early archaeologists working in Utah observed numerous sites with mounds, pithouses, and pottery. These sites looked "Anasazi" and were described as constituting the "Northern Periphery" of the Puebloan Southwest (e.g., Kidder 1924). Further investigation determined that the remains represented something different from the Anasazi and the materials were then named "Fremont" (Morss 1931; also see Husted and Mallory 1967; Gunnerson 1969; Marwitt 1986; Madsen and Simms 1998; Talbot 2000; Madsen and Schmitt 2005; Janetski 2008); essentially farmers in the Great Basin.

The Fremont were mostly in Utah but extended into portions of Nevada and Idaho (see Fig. 8.1). This tradition dates between about 2,100 and 700 BP, but these dates vary by region. Their populations seem to have peaked about 900 BP (Simms 1999:42) with a much lower population density by 700 BP (Janetski 1994:159), although they may have persisted until about 500 BP in a few areas (Madsen and Simms 1998).

The Fremont have generally been defined by the presence of corn agriculture and distinctive grayware pottery (see D. B. Madsen 1986b). They appeared to have had a distinctive site structure and settlement pattern; unique pottery, clay figurines, basketry, footwear (Fig. 8.9); and rock art (see Schaafsma 1971). Farming was central in defining the Fremont, but it was always recognized that they also practiced some hunting and gathering. Thus, it was not clear to early researchers whether the Fremont were sedentary farmers who continued to hunt and gather, mobile hunters and gatherers who conducted some farming, or both (see Simms 1986).

In the last decade or so, a new view of the Fremont has emerged. It is now believed that hunting and gathering probably played a much larger role in their economy than previously thought. The Fremont is now defined by a matrix of adaptive variability that sometimes included agriculture (Madsen and Simms 1998:323), but some Fremont groups (such as in southern Idaho) may not have farmed at all. In addition, much of the "distinctive" Fremont material culture

FIGURE 8.9 Fremont moccasins recovered from the upper levels of Hogup Cave. (*Source:* Courtesy of Utah Museum of Natural History.)

is either rare or not widespread, making it problematic as "marker" traits of the Fremont (Madsen and Simms 1998:262).

The Fremont may not even have been a distinctive culture (e.g., one having a common language and religion) but a series of related groups with no single identity (D. B. Madsen 1979) and may well represent a series of separate genetic populations living in a similar manner (e.g., Parr et al. 1996; O'Rourke et al. 1999). Over time, it may be that various groups of "hunter-gatherers adopted, in a piecemeal fashion, many of the traits associated with the farming societies of the Southwest and Mexico" (Madsen and Schmitt 2005:9) to then "become" what archaeologists call the Fremont. Despite these issues, it is recognized that the Fremont, in some form, exist as an archaeological entity.

The Fremont have traditionally been classified into five variants, each based on the geographic distribution of pottery types (Uinta, San Rafael, Great Salt Lake, Sevier, and Parowan; see D. B. Madsen 1986b). However, defining variants of an entity that is itself not well understood is difficult (e.g., Madsen and Simms 1998). Complicating the "variant" issue further was the idea (Talbot and Wilde 1989) that the occupation of many Fremont sites fluctuated and that the Fremont occupation of various regions had expanded and contracted from a "core area" near the Colorado Plateau. A later study (Bright and Ugan 1999) did not show these patterns and suggested a much more "even" Fremont occupation.

FREMONT ORIGINS   Where did the Fremont come from? Early ideas included a migration of Southwestern people north, a migration of northern Athapaskan groups south (and eventually into the Southwest) (e.g., Aikens 1967; also see Loendorf and Conner 1993), or an in situ development. Genetic studies (e.g., Parr et al. 1996; O'Rourke et al. 1999) indicated that the Fremont were not closely related to Middle Archaic groups in the western Great Basin but had some affinity to some Southwestern groups. There is also some archaeological evidence, such as at the Steinaker Gap site in northeastern Utah, that small groups of Southwestern immigrants (e.g., Basketmaker II) migrated north when environmental conditions permitted (Talbot 2000:288; also see Simms 2008:208). Nevertheless, the prevailing view is that the Fremont, or at least most of the Fremont, developed in situ from local Archaic groups who adopted, in "piecemeal fashion," traits from the Southwest (Madsen and Simms 1998:260).

FREMONT ECONOMY AND ORGANIZATION   Corn appears to have diffused into southern Utah by 2,100 BP, into northern Utah by about 1,800 BP (Madsen and Simms 1998), and into southern Idaho by about 1,200 BP (Yohe 2000). Pottery may have come north with the corn and, as with corn, was probably adapted to local conditions by local groups. Farming was likely adopted slowly, while hunting and gathering remained dominant.

Simms (1986, 1999:39–41; also see Madsen and Simms 1998) outlined three basic, very flexible, Fremont adaptations: (1) primarily farming, (2) a mix of farming and foraging, and (3) primarily foraging, although corn agriculture would have played a role (Janetski 1994:162). Any given Fremont group, or individuals within a group, could have practiced any of these three adaptations at any given time depending on conditions (e.g., Barlow 2002, 2006), all of which would have resulted in demographic fluidity, variable settlement patterns, and shifting residential mobility. In addition, the use of wetland resources would have been important in each of these adaptations (Janetski 1990). These various factors complicate attempts to define the Fremont. One could conceptualize the Fremont as an array of groups using an assortment of tactics within an encompassing strategic inventory (e.g., Sutton 2000), somewhat like a set of tools within a toolbox. Each tactical action (e.g., farming or hunting) would result in a different archaeological signature, creating further difficulties in defining the overall group.

Many Fremont farming sites were located on alluvial fans near streams, and some irrigation of fields was practiced (Metcalfe and Larrabee 1985). Some of the sites in alluvial terrains were large pithouse villages (see Talbot 2000), but most settlements were small farmsteads located in a variety of settings and were probably occupied by a few families at any one time. Most sites contained a number of pithouses, surface structures (such as ramads), and storage facilities. The typical round pithouse changed to a square configuration about 900 BP (Simms 1999:35). Some Fremont sites were located away from farming areas, and these sites were presumably related to hunting-and-gathering activities.

During the MCA, agricultural production seems to have increased and villages became larger as people moved away from unproductive areas. Isotope analysis of burials from the Great Salt Lake area demonstrated such a pattern, with increased dependence on corn between 1,600 and 1,150 BP, marked economic diversity between 1,150 and 850 BP, then a return to a dependence on hunting and gathering after ca. 850 BP (Coltrain and Leavitt 2002).

Hunting was always important in the Fremont economy, and the populations of large game in the eastern Basin appear to have steadily declined during Fremont times. It is possible that this decline represents overhunting by growing Fremont populations over time (Janetski 1997) or decreasing populations of large animals due to drought (e.g., Ugan 2005). Smaller animals, such as rabbits, were also important. Bison were hunted in the northern part of the Fremont region (Arkush 2002).

Skeletal data from the Great Salt Lake region provides some interesting perspectives. The Fremont living in the Great Salt Lake wetlands appear to have been generally more healthy that the other Fremont populations (Bright and Loveland 1999:115), perhaps due to more reliable resources. Mobility patterns derived from the skeletal data are also informative (Brunson 2000) and suggest that, in general, the Great Salt Lake Wetlands Fremont were less mobile than western Great Basin foragers (e.g., Hemphill 1999) and that the males were more mobile than the females, all indicating a mixed economy.

Little is known about Fremont social or political organization, but it, too, was probably variable. Excavations at Baker Village in west-central Utah revealed five pithouses and seven aboveground storage structures arranged around a larger central structure, implying some sort of community planning (Hockett 1998). The distribution of faunal remains, mostly rabbits and deer, suggest that feasting took place in the central structure and may reflect some type of influence-based political power (Hockett 1998).

Fremont mortuary practices were highly varied, with inhumations in a variety of positions and orientations as the primary mode of interment. The dead were buried in pits under house floors or in the midden with no pits, and few had grave goods (Madsen and Lindsay 1977:76; Simms 1999; Talbot 2000:286). There is evidence (Novak and Kollmann 2000) to indicate that the Fremont sometimes processed human remains in the manner consistent with cannibalism in the Southwest (see Highlight 9.4), which provides some support for a linkage between the two regions.

Fremont exchange included trade in marine shell, turquoise, toolstone (e.g., obsidian), and pottery with groups in the Southwest (Janetski 2002) and groups to the north (Loosle 2000). A burial from central Utah dated to about 2,100 BP contained a bag with some two hundred corn cobs (Wilde and Tasa 1991), suggesting evidence of early trade rather than locally grown corn. Certainly, considerable trade between Fremont groups also took place, and it appears that these trade activities increased between 1,500 and 700 BP (see Janetski 2002).

WHAT HAPPENED TO THE FREMONT?   The Fremont "disappeared" about 700 BP, perhaps as late as 500 BP. They were replaced, it seems, by a new group of hunter-gatherers ancestral to the ethnographic Numa. What happened to cause the purported disappearance of the Fremont? The answer depends to some degree on who the Fremont were and how they originated (see discussion in Madsen and Simms 1998:313–314). By about 800 BP, the environment was particularly arid and perhaps unsuitable for agriculture and may have forced the abandonment of farming altogether (e.g., Coltrain and Leavett 2002).

If the Fremont were ancestral to the Numa, they would have simply stayed in place and become the ethnographic groups. If the Fremont were actually Southwestern peoples, they probably moved south as the environment became more arid about 800 BP and rejoined their relatives in the Southwest. If the Fremont were Athapaskan, they would have moved south about 800 BP to become the Apache and/or Navajo. Any movement of Southwestern or Athapaskan peoples out of the eastern Great Basin would have left the Basin "vacant," to be reoccupied by Numic groups moving east (see above). Finally, it is possible that incoming Numic groups "pushed" the Fremont out, killed them, and/or absorbed them. We are still not sure.

THE MOJAVE DESERT

The Mojave Desert (see Fig. 8.1) is essentially the southern quarter of the physiographic Great Basin, but most archaeologists consider it separately from the rest of the Basin. A general chronology for the Mojave Desert was presented in Table 8.1, and the various complexes are briefly discussed below (also see Sutton et al. 2007).

Materials dating to the **Paleoindian Period** (ca. 12,000 to 10,000 BP) in the Mojave Desert are confined to few isolated finds of fluted points and one presumed Clovis occupation site, located at Lake China (E. L. Davis 1978, 1982; Basgall 2003; Moore et al. 2003). Based on this limited evidence, Paleoindian groups were likely small bands of highly mobile people who lived in small temporary camps located near permanent water sources.

The first well-defined archaeological pattern in the Mojave Desert is the **Lake Mojave Complex** (ca. 10,000 to 8,000 BP), although not many sites are known. This complex is characterized by stemmed (Lake Mojave and Silver Lake) projectile points, abundant bifaces, unifaces, crescents, and some ground stone tools (e.g., Amsden 1937; Campbell et al. 1937). Lake Mojave sites include occupation sites, workshops, and small camps, some of which have been found along ancient lakeshores. Lake Mojave groups were probably small and highly mobile, practicing a generalized economy that focused on small game, the opportunistic hunting of large animals, and the exploitation of rich resource patches in a host of environmental situations, such as the shorelines of lakes.

The **Pinto Complex** (ca. 9,000 to 5,000 BP) overlaps and follows the Lake Mojave Complex, and it has been suggested that the two complexes formed a single cultural tradition (Warren 1991; but see Basgall 1995). The Pinto Complex is characterized by the appearance of indented-base Pinto series projectile points and a major increase in millingstones that were probably used for processing seeds. Small game remained the staple, and the hunting of large game appears to have declined from Lake Mojave times. The presence of *Olivella* beads indicates regular regional interaction with coastal groups.

Pinto sites are more numerous than Lake Mojave sites and are found across the Mojave Desert in a variety of environmental contexts (see Sutton et al. 2007:238). Pinto occupation sites oftentimes are associated with well-watered locations (e.g., springs) with access to plant resources. Such sites were probably occupied by multiple family groups on a consistent basis, inferring a collector-like strategy.

The **Deadman Lake Complex** (ca. 9,000 to 7,000 BP) appears to have been separate from, but contemporaneous with, the early Pinto Complex (Sutton et al. 2007). Deadman Lake materials are found in the southeastern Mojave Desert and might reflect some connection to Archaic groups in the Southwest. Artifacts of the Deadman Lake Complex include contracting-stem and lozenge-shaped points, abundant bifaces, and millingstones. Little else is yet known about this complex, although plant exploitation appears to have been more generalized than during Pinto times. It is also possible that the Deadman Lake Complex simply reflects a segment of the tactical inventory of the Pinto Complex, rather than a separate cultural entity.

For the years between about 5,000 and 4,000 BP (at the height of the dry and hot Altithermal), few sites have been identified in the Mojave Desert, suggesting that some areas were largely abandoned (although this is far from certain), perhaps for a thousand years. By about 4,000 BP, environmental conditions began to improve, and the desert appears to have been occupied once again. These new people, of the **Gypsum Complex** (ca. 4,000 to 1,800 BP) used a variety of corner-notched (cf. Elko series), concave-base (Humboldt series), and well-shouldered contracting-stem (Gypsum series) projectile point forms. Artifact assemblages also include evidence of ritual activities, such as quartz crystals, paint, and rock art (e.g., Davis and Smith 1981; Warren 1984; Warren and Crabtree 1986), as well as numerous bifaces and grinding implements. It seems that settlement and subsistence were centered on streams, and a variety of animals (including large game, rabbits, rodents, and tortoises) were utilized.

Sometime around 1,800 years ago, bow-and-arrow technology diffused into the Mojave Desert, and the large projectile points of the Gypsum Complex were replaced by smaller arrow points, marking the beginning of the **Rose Spring Complex** (ca. 1,800 to 900 BP). The environment appears to have been wetter and cooler during the early part of this complex, and there may have been some lakes present. Judging from the appearance of many sites with well-developed middens, there also appears to have been a major population increase. Common artifacts of the Rose Spring Complex consist of Eastgate and Rose Spring series projectile points, knives, drills, stone pipes, bone awls, various milling implements, marine shell ornaments, and a large quantity of obsidian (Warren and Crabtree 1986; Sutton 1996). A number of sites contain evidence of architecture, including wickiups and semisubterranean houses, suggesting intensive occupations. The use of obsidian for stone tools greatly increased, and a major trading network with California was established. Medium-sized to small animals, predominately rabbits and rodents, were the primary game. In addition, pinyon, juniper, and mesquite have all been recovered from Rose Spring sites.

The MCA began about 1,200 BP and intensified for several hundred years. As things became warmer and drier, Rose Spring settlement patterns apparently changed from being associated with permanent water sources to ephemeral ones (see J. K. Gardner 2007). The growing population and increased hunting efficiency of the bow and arrow may have impacted the availability of some resources, which became further stressed by the MCA, perhaps leading to the end of the Rose Spring Complex.

After 900 BP, the environment began to deteriorate, obsidian trade was disrupted, populations appear to have declined, and a number of separate **Late Prehistoric** cultural complexes, believed to represent the ancestors of the various ethnographic groups, emerged (Sutton 1989; but see Basgall and Hall 1992; Allen 1998; Eerkens 1999). Warren (1984:420) noted "strong regional developments" across the Mojave Desert during this time, including Anasazi interests in turquoise mining, Patayan influence from the Colorado River, and Numic groups that likely spread eastward (see above) after 1,000 years ago.

Late Prehistoric sites include a few major villages with associated cemeteries, as well as the occupation of rockshelters (Fig. 8.10), special-purpose sites, and seasonal sites. Artifact assemblages consist of Desert series (Desert Side–notched and Cottonwood Triangular) projectile points, buff and brownware pottery, shell and steatite beads, slate pendants, incised stones, and a variety of millingstones (Sutton 1990; Warren and Crabtree 1986). Faunal remains typically consist of lagomorphs, deer, rodents, reptiles, and tortoise.

FIGURE 8.10 The Rustler Rockshelter site in the eastern Mojave Desert (photo by the author, 1986).

Rock art is widely distributed across the Mojave Desert (and indeed across all of the Great Basin; see Woody and Quinlan [2008] and Schaafsma [1971, 2008]). It is dated to perhaps as early as the Late Pleistocene to very recent times. The art is primarily in the form of pecked petroglyphs (see Fig. 8.11) but includes some painted pictographs and geoglyphs (designs constructed on the ground; see von Werlhof 1987, 2004). Various styles of art have been identified, but little is known about the function of this art. Various interpretations have been suggested, including hunting and/or fertility rituals (e.g., Grant et al. 1968; Gilreath and Hildebrandt 2008) and rain magic (Whitley 1994). The Coso Rock Art District, located in the western Mojave Desert near Ridgecrest, is a World Heritage Site and is believed to contain more than 100,000 petroglyphs (visit http://www.nps.gov/archeology/rockart/index.htm).

NATIVE GREAT BASIN CULTURES AT CONTACT

More than 30,000 Great Basin native peoples still live in the region (Leland 1986:608), and that number continues to increase. Many Great Basin groups established formal tribal governments after the passage of the Indian Reorganization Act of 1934 (see Rusco and Rusco 1986:565–571), and there are some forty-five reservations. After 1964, the Bureau of Indian Affairs began to provide funds for housing, education, roads, community development, vocational training, and employment; as a result, Great Basin native peoples saw an increase in their standard of living and life expectancy. However, the economic situation for most Great Basin people remains substandard compared to non-Indians (see Knack 1986). Due to this situation, problems with alcohol, drugs, and domestic violence developed and continue to persist. Recently, casinos have been opened on several reservations, resulting in jobs and some tribal income.

FIGURE 8.11   Petroglyphs along the bank of the White River in southern Nevada. Note the apparent depictions of "sheep" and "humans" (photo by the author, 1986).

Many issues remain important and/or unresolved to Great Basin peoples (see Johnson 1986). The most crucial are issues of land rights, water rights, and the honoring of treaties and agreements. Another problem revolves around grazing. The government charges the Indians a fee to graze livestock on lands the Indians claim to own. Further, the government has decided that much of the Great Basin is only suitable for grazing, so they have destroyed large tracts of pine and juniper forests, replacing them with grassland. Other concerns include questions of jurisdiction on Indian lands, economic development, education, and tribal leadership. In addition, native people strive to have their voices heard and their viewpoints considered in the context of their cultures (see Alley 1986).

Further Reading

A number of older, but still useful, summaries of Great Basin prehistory by region and topic can be found in Madsen and O'Connell (1982) and in the fourteen prehistory chapters in the *Handbook of North American Indians, Vol. 11, Great Basin* (d'Azevedo 1986). A number of topical monographs have been published since 1986, and some more recent general treatments were provided by Grayson (1993), Beck and Jones (1997), Kelly (1997), Fowler and Fowler (2008), and Simms (2008).

The most recent general treatment of Mojave Desert prehistory was provided by Sutton et al. (2007).

Several universities publish archaeological materials in the form of occasional papers and monographs, most notably the University of Oregon, the University of Utah, and Brigham Young University. Several important regional journals, including the *Journal of California and Great Basin Anthropology, Utah Archaeology*, and *Tebiwa*, contain information on Great Basin prehistory.

Pithouses and Pueblos
The Southwest

The Southwest (Fig. 9.1) is primarily a desert region that encompasses most of Arizona and New Mexico, southern Colorado, southern Utah, and the states of Sonora and Chihuahua in northern Mexico. The *Handbook of North American Indians* includes Baja California within the Southwest, but for the purposes of this book, it is discussed with California (see Chapter 7). Most archaeological work in the Southwest has been conducted within the United States portion, often called the "American Southwest." The term "Greater Southwest" is sometimes used to ensure the inclusion of northern Mexico. Recall that in the Southwest (and in this chapter) researchers commonly use the BC/AD dating system instead of the Before Present (BP) system.

Some of the most spectacular prehistoric ruins in North America are large pueblos, many seemingly hanging off the sides of cliffs. These ruins, and similar towns still occupied by Pueblo peoples, form a romantic impression of the past connecting to the present. Largely for that reason, many generations of archaeologists have been drawn to the Southwest, and American archaeology in general has been greatly influenced by this work (D. D. Fowler 2000). The Southwest has become the most studied archaeological region in North America and continues to be the focus of much research.

Archaeological cultures in the Southwest are popularly known for several major traits. The first is agricultural economies, with corn, beans, squash, and cotton being the major crops. The second is the large number of sites with standing architecture, mostly pueblos in the northern Southwest, but including the platform mounds, ball courts, and irrigation systems in the Phoenix and Tucson areas of Arizona. Last, the Southwest is known for its ubiquitous pottery of enormous variety and design. Since most Southwestern archaeologists seem to focus on groups with standing architecture and pottery, few have worked on materials older than about 2,000 years (when these traits became common), and as a result, our knowledge of earlier Southwestern prehistory is substantially less, although it has expanded greatly in the last decade.

The other major factor that sets Southwestern archaeology apart from the remainder of North America is chronology. As pottery is so varied and abundant, chronologies based on sequences of changing pottery styles in the Southwest are well developed and useful, at least for

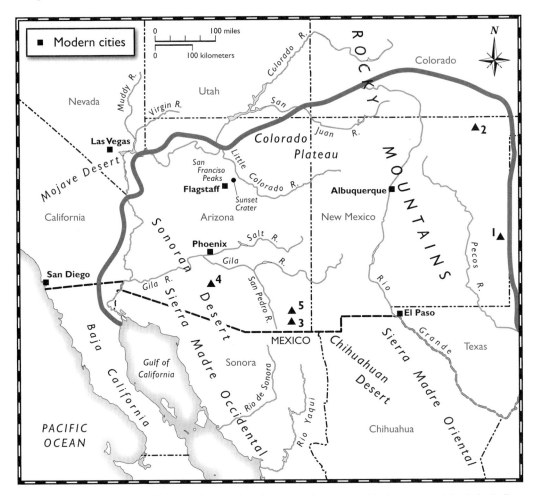

FIGURE 9.1 General map of the Southwest, showing the major geographic features and the Paleoindian sites discussed in the text: 1) Blackwater Draw; 2) Folsom; 3) San Pedro Valley sites; 4) Ventana Cave; and 5) Whitewater Draw.

the last 2,000 years. In addition, many of the ancient pueblos were constructed using wooden beams that have preserved well over the millennia, and the year that the beams were cut (and presumably used) can be precisely calculated through the use of dendrochronology (Nash 1999). Of course, radiocarbon dating is also widely employed. Most Southwest archaeologists report time using the AD/BC system, and that custom is followed in this chapter.

GEOGRAPHY AND ENVIRONMENT

Three major geographic and environmental regions are commonly recognized for the Southwest: the Colorado Plateau, the Sonoran and Chihuahua deserts, and the mountains. The Colorado Plateau lies in the northern Southwest, at elevations above 4,500 feet. The plateau contains many flat-topped mesas and deep canyons, such as the Grand Canyon. Some mountain ranges are present within the plateau, and several rise to an elevation of 13,000 feet with forests of pine, oak, and juniper. The plateau is generally cool and has more precipitation than the deserts to the south, although much of the area is relatively arid.

The Sonoran and Chihuahua deserts lie to the south of the plateau and extend into northern Mexico. Elevations are generally below 3,000 feet, and there are occasional low mountain ranges. The region is quite arid and has very hot summers, often exceeding 100°F. The large saguaro cactus (in the Sonoran desert) is the most conspicuous plant, but mesquite, prickly pear, and agave are also common. Animals include mountain sheep, deer, rabbits, tortoises, and many rodents.

Several major mountain ranges stretch along the eastern and southern portions of the Southwest. The southern Rocky Mountains run along the northeastern edge, while the Sierra Madre Oriental and Sierra Madre Occidental span most of northern Mexico. All of these mountain ranges are relatively well watered and contain forests as well as a wide diversity of animals.

Many rivers drain the Southwest, the major permanent ones being the Rio Grande, Colorado, Little Colorado, Salt, Gila, Pecos, Rio Yaqui, and Rio de Sonora. Agriculture is quite practical in these river valleys, and many of the major farming cultures were centered on them. In addition, the rivers provided reliable water and other resources, such as fish.

The climate throughout the Southwest consists of hot summers and fairly cold winters. Rainfall is variable, depending on the region. In the far western Southwest, most rain falls in the winter and derives from Pacific storms. In the rest of the Southwest, rainfall comes in the summertime in the form of thunderstorms from moist air originating in the Gulf of Mexico.

A VERY BRIEF HISTORY OF RESEARCH

Although living native peoples were "discovered" by the Spanish in the 1500s and some ruins were noted at that time, it was not until the late 1800s that any real attention was paid to the archaeological record of the Southwest. Early ranchers discovered many of the famous Pueblo sites while chasing cattle. For example, the spectacular sites at Mesa Verde, such as Cliff Palace (Fig. 9.2), were discovered in 1888 by rancher Richard Wetherill. He contacted the Bureau of American Ethnology (BAE, later to become part of the Smithsonian Institution) and the Peabody Museum, both of which largely ignored him. Wetherill and his family then proceeded to remove and sell many artifacts until the government realized the scale and importance of what he had found and banned his antiquities activities. The BAE and other museums then sent research teams into the region. Research programs were begun by various universities (e.g., the University of Arizona and University of New Mexico), and some new institutions were founded, such as the School of American Research in Santa Fe (1907) and the Museum of Northern Arizona (1928), both of which are still in operation. Another major research institution, Crow Canyon Archaeological Center, was founded in the early 1980s.

A great deal of pioneering archaeological research was conducted in the early twentieth century, and the first synthesis of Southwestern prehistory was published in 1924 (A. V. Kidder 1924). Soon after, the Pecos Classification for the Ancestral Puebloans (Anasazi) was formulated (A. V. Kidder 1927), and it is still used today. Other work defined the Hohokam (e.g., Gladwin et al. 1938) and Mogollon (e.g., Haury 1936). After 1929, tree rings could be used for dating and to explore past climate. During this same general time, a number of major archaeological areas were designated as national parks or monuments.

In the 1950s and 1960s, much research was conducted by various universities. For example, the University of Arizona conducted a major field project in the Point of Pines area of eastern

FIGURE 9.2 The Ancestral Puebloan site of Cliff Palace at Mesa Verde. (*Source:* Rough Guides Dorling Kindersley.)

Arizona from 1948 to 1960, investigating more than two hundred Mogollon sites. They later worked at nearby Grasshopper Pueblo for another twenty years. After the 1970s, most work was related to federally mandated environmental studies. These studies, such as the work on the coal leases in northeastern Arizona and northwestern New Mexico (e.g., Plog and Powell 1984; Powell and Smiley 2002), dam construction at Cochiti Reservoir in New Mexico (Biella and Chapman 1979) and in Glen Canyon in southeastern Utah (Jennings 1998), Army Corps of Engineers work on the Verde Valley in central Arizona (Whittlesey et al. 1997), and military activities in southwestern Arizona and southern New Mexico (e.g., Altschul and Rankin 2008) have all made significant contributions to our knowledge of the Southwest.

Many of the federal parks also have research programs conducted by archaeologists employed at the parks, such as Mesa Verde, Chaco Canyon, and Bandelier National Monument. For example, a fire in 2000 in Mesa Verde resulted in the clearing of brush from large areas and an opportunity for archaeologists to examine that burned area. As a result, several hundred new sites were discovered.

Unfortunately, relatively little work has been done in the southern portion of the Southwest that lies in northern Mexico. A major exception is the work conducted at the large site of Paquimé (Casas Grandes; see Highlight 9.7) in the 1950s. More recently, however, additional research has been carried out in northern Mexico (e.g., Whalen and Minnis 2001a; Newell and Gallaga 2004; Carpenter et al. 2005).

MAJOR THEMES IN SOUTHWESTERN PREHISTORY

The Southwest, with its relatively well-dated and documented archaeological past and its direct historic connections with ethnographic peoples, provides amazing opportunities for the research of interesting anthropological questions. Some of the first scientific studies on past sociopolitical systems were conducted in the Southwest (e.g., J. N. Hill 1970; Longacre 1970). The study of tree rings, originally undertaken by astronomer A. E. Douglas, has provided not only a method of precise dating but also a very detailed record of climate. Thus, a great deal of research has been conducted on paleoclimate and the impact of climatic change on both agricultural and hunter-gatherer societies.

The transition between hunter-gatherer and farming subsistence systems is another major research issue. It is not clear why successful hunter-gatherers would have adopted agriculture. A number of possibilities have been advanced (see Doleman 2005; Hard and Roney 2005; Mabry 2005; Phillips 2009), including an improving climate that made farming possible, population growth that pressured increased food production, changing strategies and conditions that made agriculture more productive than hunting and gathering, and changes in mobility patterns that favored farming.

Associated with the transition to farming issue is how and why small groups of people with relatively simple social and political systems developed into larger societies, such as those of the Pueblos. At least two basic models of this process have been proposed: the network model and the corporate model, combined in the Southwest as the "Dual-Processual Theory" (Feinman 2000). In the network model, certain individuals came to control surpluses and their distribution within a limited area. As their power and prestige increased, their networks grew and incorporated other centers into a growing polity. Elites developed and a ranked society evolved, with powerful individuals in control of a network of smaller, dependent centers. Control extended to both goods and labor, and the construction of public architecture served to reinforce the power and prestige of the ruling elites. In the corporate model, the focus would have been on group decision making, which would have minimized the need for prestige items to symbolize individual status. Similar models have been proposed in the Southeast (see Chapter 12).

Given that farming was adopted and that many of these groups developed relatively complex societies, what ultimately happened to them? Each of the major Southwestern "cultures"—the Puebloans, Hohokam, and Mogollon—"collapsed" at about the same time, with only the Pueblos surviving relatively intact into historic times. Why did this happen? It seems clear that environmental change was a factor, but other factors, such as warfare, were likely also involved. Warfare, in varying intensities, was present all across the Southwest throughout space and time (Haas and Creamer 1996; S. A. LeBlanc 1999; also see Rice and LeBlanc 2001; Kuckelman 2002) and was an important factor in culture and adaptation, with shifting enemies and allies and changing political and environmental landscapes. While warfare could be solely political in nature, it could also be related to resource competition (Lekson 2002a). A basic chronological sequence for the Southwest is provided in Table 9.1.

THE PALEOINDIAN PERIOD

The Paleoindian Period in the Southwest covers the time between about 11,500 and 8,500 BC. Both the Clovis and Folsom complexes were first identified in New Mexico, and considerable research on Paleoindian sites and issues has been conducted in the Southwest (see Chapters 2 and 3).

TABLE 9.1 A Basic Chronological Sequence for the Southwest

Date	Northwest Arizona, Colorado River	Colorado Plateau	Mogollon Region	Sonoran Desert	General Climate
AD 1850	Ethnographic Yuman groups	Historic Pueblos / Navajo	Apache	O'odham	current conditions
	Patayan	Ancestral Puebloans (Anasazi) — Pueblo V, Pueblo IV, Pueblo III, Pueblo II, Pueblo I, Basketmaker III	Mogollon — Late, Aggregation, Postclassic, Classic, Late Pithouse, Early Pithouse	Hohokam — Postclassic, Classic, Sedentary, Colonial, Pioneer	MCA; the "Great Drought"
AD 1000		Basketmaker II			conditions similar to today
AD 1	Western Archaic	Northern Archaic / En Medio	Southern Archaic / Cienega		
1,000 BC	Gypsum	Armijo	San Pedro		
2,000 BC		San José			warmer, summer rain
3,000 BC	Pinto	Bajada	Chiricahua		
4,000 BC					increase in effective moisture, change to summer rain
5,000 BC		Jay	Sulphur Spring		
6,000 BC	Lake Mojave				
to 8,500 BC	Paleoindian				cool and wet, winter rain

The Clovis Complex, dated between about 11,500 and 10,900 BC, was first identified at the Blackwater Draw site near Clovis, New Mexico (Howard 1935; Hester 1972), where Clovis points were found in association with mammoth remains. A number of other Clovis sites, mostly kill and butchering localities, have since been discovered in the Southwest, including a group in the San Pedro Valley of south-central Arizona. In this valley, several famous Clovis sites have been found, including Lehner, Naco, and Murray Springs. In addition to a kill site, a small camp near a spring was found at Murray Springs (Haynes and Huckell 2007), one of the few Clovis camps known (also see Huckell 2004).

The subsequent Folsom Complex, dated between 10,900 and 10,200 BC, was also first identified in the Southwest. The discovery of fluted points in direct association with extinct bison at a site near Folsom, New Mexico (Fig. 9.1; also see Fig. 3.3) in 1926 (Figgins 1927; also see Meltzer 2006) finally convinced most archaeologists that people were present in North America during the terminal Pleistocene. Clovis has generally been associated with mammoths and Folsom with bison, indicating that there was a major environmental change and/or a shift in adaptation sometime around 10,900 BC.

Understanding the Paleoindian Period, a time when people generally focused on bison hunting, gets more complex after Folsom. In the western half of the Southwest, the Western Stemmed Tradition appeared, with changes in subsistence (no bison) and technology (stemmed points replaced fluted points). The Western Stemmed Tradition, dating between 8,500 and 6,500 BC, is linked to the Great Basin and California and is usually viewed as Archaic (e.g., Huckell 1996).

In the eastern Southwest, however, new Paleoindian complexes appeared and persisted until later in time. These complexes, such as Plainview and Cody, were focused on bison, which persisted in the eastern Southwest longer than in the west. The Western Stemmed Tradition also appeared in the eastern Southwest, but later than in the west. Thus, the division between the Paleoindian and the Archaic in the Southwest is unclear at best.

THE ARCHAIC

The Archaic of the Southwest (ca. 8,500 BC to ca. AD 1 and later) is a poorly known time period that has attracted relatively little interest by archaeologists and is generally characterized by hunter-gatherers and not farmers. The Archaic is generally viewed as commencing after the Paleoindian Period (ca. 8,500 BC) in the western part of the Southwest but began later, about 6,500 BC, in the eastern part (e.g., Huckell 1996). Corn entered the Southwest as early as 2,000 BC and was adopted by Archaic groups but did not become the primary staple until much later. The Archaic lasted until pottery was adopted and farming became the dominant subsistence system, after which the groups in question would be considered Formative. In some areas, this occurred as early as AD 1, while in other areas it took place much later. With a few groups, agriculture never became the primary subsistence system, and those groups remained "Archaic" until contact.

The Archaic record in the Southwest has much less archaeological visibility than the more obtrusive Formative record and tends to get less attention (e.g., Upham 1988, 1994; Huckell 1996:306). Archaic groups were generally mobile hunters and gatherers who did not possess pottery. They undoubtedly practiced a seasonal round, moving between various ecozones (e.g., valleys and mountains) and subsisted on grasses, pine nuts, mesquite, cacti, rabbits, and the occasional deer or mountain sheep. Manos and metates for processing plant foods appeared during the Archaic, and flaked stone tools tended to be large and rudimentary.

Several different ways of dividing the Archaic have been proposed, including a single general "Desert Culture" concept (see Huckell 1996:322; also see Upham 1994), an early-middle-late model (Berry and Berry 1986; Matson 1991; Huckell 1996), and by geographic region. The latter approach is adopted here and three major divisions of the Archaic are discussed below (following Cordell 1997:107–114; see Table 9.2). A fourth division of the Archaic, the Eastern (or Southeastern) has been proposed (see discussion in Cordell 1997:110–111) but is not included here.

HIGHLIGHT 9.1

MESOAMERICAN INFLUENCES IN THE SOUTHWEST

The Southwest formed part of a larger system of interaction (for example, with the Southeast; see Chapter 12) that included considerable influences from Mesoamerican groups to the south (Riley 2005), particularly after about AD 1,200. One of the major traits, corn, was domesticated in Mesoamerica some 5,000 BC and diffused north into the Southwest by about 2,200 BC (Mabry 2008:36). Beans, squash, and cotton followed the same basic route but later in time, although squash may have come in with corn (Mabry 2008:36).

There was considerable trade between Mesoamerica and the Southwest (see Ericson and Baugh 1993). Exotic birds from Mesoamerica, such as macaws, were traded live in large numbers, carried north in wooden cages. Copper bells, shell from the Gulf of California (see Mitchell and Foster 2000), and turquoise from Mexico also came north. Architectural traits with roots in Mesoamerica were also felt, with ball courts and platform mounds being the most prominent. Religious influences, such as katsinas and other deities, may have been important, and some ceremonial architecture (e.g., the sipapu in kivas) may have had a Mesoamerican origin. Cannibalism (see Highlight 9.4) might also be linked to Mesoamerica. It is also possible that Mesoamerican people came to the Southwest, either as immigrants or traders (e.g., pochteca).

The Western Archaic

The Western Archaic (see Table 9.2) is found in western Arizona and the Colorado River region, beginning about 8,500 BC and lasting until about AD 1, when agriculture became the dominant subsistence system along the Colorado River. The Western Archaic has been called San Dieguito (Cordell 1997:93), although this term should only be applied to specific early Archaic materials from Southern California (e.g., Sutton et al. 2007). The basic early to middle Archaic chronology employed for portions of California and much of the Great Basin (Warren 1984; Sutton et al. 2007; also see Chapters 7 and 8; Table 8.1) is used here, divided into three complexes: Lake Mojave, Pinto, and Gypsum.

None of the three complexes of the Western Archaic are well represented in the Southwest. The Lake Mojave Complex is associated with Late Pleistocene/early Holocene lakeshores (presumably a lacustrine adaptation) and is best known in the Mojave Desert of eastern California. The Pinto Complex seems to have developed from, and with, Lake Mojave, but it appears to have had a different subsistence focus, perhaps on large game (e.g., mountain sheep) rather than lake resources. There may be an occupational hiatus between Pinto and Gypsum, between ca. 3,000 and 2,000 BC, when conditions became hotter and drier in the

TABLE 9.2 A Summary of the Archaic in the Southwest

Tradition/Dates	Divisions/Dates	Characteristics
Western Archaic (ca. 8,000 BC to AD 1)	Gypsum (ca. 2,000 BC to AD 1)	change in settlement patterns, increasing social complexity, split-twig figurines (see Highlight 9.2), Gypsum and Elko points
	Pinto (ca. 7,000 to 3,000 BC)	associated with springs, change in adaptation away from lakes, small mobile populations, Pinto points
	Lake Mojave (8,000 to 6,000 BC)	associated with lacustrine environments, little subsistence evidence, stemmed (Lake Mojave and Silver Lake) points
Northern Archaic (ca. 7,000 BC to AD 400)	En Medio (ca. 800 BC to AD 400)	part-time agriculturalists, overlapping with Basket-maker II, separate adaptations in the same area for a time, apparently the ancestors of the Puebloans
	Armijo (ca. 1,800 to 800 BC)	corn diffused in and groups adopted some agriculture, population increased, and mobility decreased
	San José (ca. 3,200 to 1,800 BC)	mobile hunter-gatherers, Gypsum points
	Bajada (ca. 4,800 to 3,200 BC)	mobile hunter-gatherers, concave-based points
	Jay (ca. 7,000 to 4,800 BC)	mobile hunter-gatherers, stemmed points, perhaps related to late Paleoindians
Southern Archaic (ca. 8,500 to 200 BC)	Cienega (ca. 800 BC to AD 150)	perhaps ancestors of both the Hohokam and Mogollon, appearance of pottery ca. AD 1, corn agriculture began to dominate
	San Pedro (ca. 1,200 to 800 BC)	pithouses appear, indication of some irrigation and terracing of fields, agriculture more important but hunting and gathering remained primary, Elko points
	Chiricahua (ca. 4,000 to 1,200 BC)	first appearance of corn, but hunting and gathering still primary, change in technology, a variety of projectile points
	Sulphur Spring (ca. 8,500 to 4,000 BC)	small groups of generalized hunter-gatherers, early manifestations may be associated with lacustrine adaptations (e.g., Lake Mojave), stemmed points

region (Sutton et al. 2007). The Pinto Complex is poorly known in the Southwest, as it is elsewhere in the West.

After about 2,000 BC, environmental conditions improved and the Gypsum Complex emerged. A new settlement system (sites near streams) and new point types (Gypsum and Elko) appeared. Subsistence included the exploitation of deer and mountain sheep, rabbits, and rodents, and there is evidence of increases in trade and social complexity (see Highlight 9.2). The Gypsum Complex was replaced by the Patayan as agriculture became the dominant subsistence activity.

HIGHLIGHT 9.2

SPLIT-TWIG FIGURINES

In 1930, small wooden figurines (Fig. 9.3) began to be discovered in the Grand Canyon area. These small (ca. 10 to 15 cm long) effigies are depictions of animals, assumed by most researchers to represent large game, such as mountain sheep. Some specimens even have horns. The figurines were made by splitting twigs of willow or skunkbush and folding the twig sections into a depiction of an animal. Currently, there are some four hundred split-twig figurines from at least thirty sites in the northwestern Southwest, mostly in the Grand Canyon area, and are dated between 2,900 and 1,250 BC (Schroedl 1976; Huckell 1996:342; Coulam and Schroedl 2004:41).

The figurines were usually found in caches in generally inaccessible places, usually in pairs, suggesting that they were related to ceremonialism of some sort. Their function is unknown, but some have suggested fetishes for hunting magic (some have been found pierced by a stick, perhaps representing a spear) or for use by shamans as magical items.

Two types of figurines have been identified: Green River and Grand Canyon (S. Schroedl 1976) and are thought to represent change over time. Coulam and Schroedl (2004:43), however, have suggested that the two types actually represent symbols for different social groups (e.g., clans) and that they were placed across the landscape as part of a ceremonial system to mark group territories.

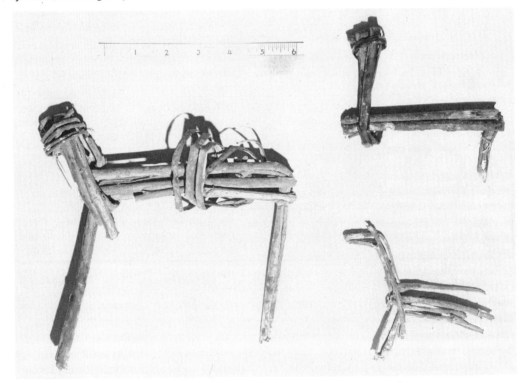

FIGURE 9.3 Examples of split-twig figurines from Newberry Cave, California (image courtesy of the San Bernardino County Museum Association; used with permission).

The Northern Archaic

The Northern Archaic is that of the Colorado Plateau, including the upper Rio Grande (Irwin-Williams 1973; Cordell 1997:108–109). The Northern Archaic was originally called the Oshara Tradition by Irwin-Williams (1973), who noted that it eventually developed into the Puebloan groups. Five subdivisions of the Northern Archaic have been defined (see Table 9.2), based mostly on changes in projectile point types. The Rio Grande Valley served as a north/south corridor between the Rocky Mountains and the Chihuahua Desert in northern Mexico throughout prehistory from Paleoindian times, and groups moved in and out of the Southwest along that route. This ease of movement by many groups over time has resulted in a very complex Archaic record, one that is still not well understood.

The earliest Northern Archaic groups (the Jay Phase; Table 9.2) used Jay points, stemmed forms of the Western Stemmed Tradition. Jay sites have contained milling tools, indicating an Archaic lifestyle. However, some feel Jay points are related to Cody (Paleoindian) forms, suggesting that Jay may have been Paleoindian rather than Archaic. Thus, it is not clear whether Archaic groups developed from Paleoindian or were a new population that replaced them. About 4,800 BC, concave-based Bajada points appear (Bajada Phase) and San Jose Points (San José Phase) are present after about 3,000 BC. The groups during each of these three phases were likely small and highly mobile.

By about 2,000 BC, corn entered the area from the south and represents the beginning of the transition to agriculture, called the Armijo Phase. It is possible that this represents a migration of farmers who brought corn with them (e.g., Turner 1993:45), but this is not yet clear (see Matson 2005). If there was a migration, it is not clear what happened to the preceding groups. As corn was adopted, even part-time, it seems likely that populations increased and mobility decreased. After about 800 BC, southern Archaic groups had become more dependent on corn (the En Medio Phase) and it is possible that the En Medio groups were the Basketmaker II groups. The adoption of domesticated plants was generally rapid but occurred late in some regions, leading to different interactions between later foragers and incipient farmers (e.g., Vierra and Ford 2007).

The Southern Archaic

Across much of the southern Southwest, the Southern Archaic was defined but was sometimes called the Cochise Tradition. There has been so little research conducted in northern Mexico that it is unclear whether the Southern Archaic should be used for that region. In the Sonoran Desert (e.g., Arizona), the Southern Archaic eventually developed into the Hohokam, while in the mountains to the east (e.g., New Mexico), it developed into the Mogollon. Four broad subdivisions of the Southern Archaic have been defined (see Table 9.2) and are discussed below.

The earliest phase of the Southern Archaic is Sulphur Spring, dating between ca. 8,500 and 4,000 BC. Originally believed to have begun about 6,500 BC, it now seems clear that Sulphur Spring began earlier (Waters 1986b). A marker of Sulphur Spring is Western Stemmed points (similar to Lake Mojave in the Western Archaic), and there is some suggestion that it was associated with Pleistocene lakes, but not all scholars agree (e.g., Woosley and Waters 1990). Manos and metates also began to appear at this time. Sulphur Spring materials have been found at Ventana Cave west of Tucson (Haury 1950; Huckell and Haynes 2003), and several burials from that time were found at Whitewater Draw, Arizona (Waters 1986a; Steele 1989:307). The available evidence suggests that Sulphur Spring groups were small, highly mobile, generalized hunter-gatherers.

By about 4,000 BC, the technology of the Southern Archaic changed and the Chiricahua Phase (ca. 4,000 to 1,200 BC) emerged. Mortars and pestles, plus Elko and Pinto points (Cordell 1997:110) became more common, although manos and metates remained important as well. Corn diffused into the region from the south; the earliest corn has been dated between about 2,200 and 1,700 BC (Mabry 2005:53, 2008:36), and it is possible that other cultigens, (e.g., beans, squash, cotton, and tobacco) also date this early (Mabry 2005:55). While cultigens were present, hunting and gathering remained the dominant subsistence system, and populations remained small and mobile. Some archaeologists are now using the term "Early Agricultural Period" to refer to any Archaic sites containing the remains of domesticated plants, even if they were minor components of the subsistence system (e.g., Mabry 2008).

Sometime during the subsequent San Pedro Phase (ca. 1,200 to 800 BC), pithouses began to be constructed, demonstrating that settlements, perhaps the first villages, were becoming more permanent. In addition, there is evidence that terraced fields were built and that some irrigation was practiced (Mabry 2005:55–56). While it seems clear that agriculture was increasing in importance, hunting and gathering still dominated and populations remained small.

By Cienega times (ca. 800 BC to AD 150), agriculture had become a central element of the subsistence system, on its way to replacing hunting and gathering as the primary subsistence system. Pottery began to appear in various areas after about AD 200. Some of the earliest irrigation canals known in the Tucson Basin of southern Arizona have been dated to this time (e.g., Bellwood 2005:151), the beginning of a pattern that would culminate in the development of the Hohokam.

The Advent of Agriculture

When domesticated crops, such as corn, diffused into the Southwest, many of the Archaic groups ultimately developed into full-time farmers and fairly complex societies, the major cultural marker of the Southwest. How and why this happened remain intriguing questions. Hunting and gathering had long been a successful adaptation across the planet and was used for millennia in the Southwest. Why did this change? Agriculture is more work, less nutritious, and carries great potential for disease (larger populations in tighter quarters) and conflict over land and water. It seems that the adoption of agriculture was often a gradual process whose eventual ramifications were unknown by the people of the Southwest.

There are at least two competing models for the initial adoption of agriculture in the Southwest. The first is that small groups of farmers from Mesoamerica, possessing corn and other Mesoamerican traits, migrated into Arizona some 2,000 BC (Berry 1985:304; also see Berry and Berry 1986; Matson 2002:349–350).

As it became clear that corn was earlier than once believed, a second model of gradual diffusion of corn into the Southwest from Mesoamerica became dominant (e.g., Wills 1995). The late Cienega record of the Southern Archaic (see above) shows that corn (and perhaps beans and squash) had diffused into Arizona between about 2,100 and 1,700 BC (Mabry 2005:53; also see Bellwood 2005:151). Thus, corn is now known to have been present well before other Mesoamerican traits, suggesting that no migration of Mesoamerican people had taken place and that agriculture was adopted at varying times in different places.

The migration model has recently resurfaced. Based on linguistic data, it has been argued that groups speaking Uto-Aztecan languages migrated into the Southwest from Mexico about 1,000 BC, bringing corn with them (J. H. Hill 2001, 2002a, 2002b). When first proposed, this date seemed too early, but now corn is dated to that same basic time frame (e.g., Kohler et al. 2008), and the model appears to have some merit. However, Mabry et al. (2008; also see LeBlanc

2008) argued that a simple migration of Uto-Aztecan people from Mexico carrying corn does not fit the archaeological data well and suggested that the arrival of Uto-Aztecans and corn from the south was more complex and intermittent.

Most recently, it has been argued (Merrill et al. 2009) that Uto-Aztecan languages developed in the Great Basin to the north, perhaps as early as 8,900 BP, split into northern and southern subfamilies, with the southern Uto-Aztecan groups migrating into the Southwest from the north very early. In this model, corn would have diffused north into the Southwest through existing southern Uto-Aztecan groups rather than by migrating farmers (Merrill et al. 2009).

It is possible that groups with agriculture first migrated into the western Southwest with agriculture perhaps diffusing east. Hard et al. (1995) suggested that the adoption of agriculture followed one of three patterns: (1) substantial early use and increasing dependence, (2) substantial early use with little subsequent change, and (3) minor early use followed by increasing dependence. Planting fields of corn, leaving them unattended, and returning to collect them as one would wild plant seeds may have been more productive than seed collecting and may have been an important strategy to early "farmers" (e.g., Barlow 2002).

How did agriculture impact hunting-and-gathering societies? Kohler et al. (2008) argued that corn came in a bit before 2,000 BC but was a minor component of the subsistence system (also see Diehl and Waters 2006). Once major milestones were met, such as the perfection of necessary farming techniques, the development of efficient exchange systems, the addition of beans and squash, and the adoption of pottery, population expanded and sedentary village life evolved. Kohler et al. (2008) suggested that these conditions were met between about AD 1 and 500. The adoption of agriculture would have entailed major cultural changes, as Archaic hunter-gatherers would have altered their subsistence seasonal movements to include agricultural fields, land use would have changed to possess and improve fields, mobility would have decreased to remain near crops, and social systems would have changed to include some sort of landholding organization.

Jeffrey Dean (2000a:97) noted that over the last 2,000 years, most of the Southwest was occupied by small groups of subsistence farmers living in environments marginal for agriculture. He argued that in times and places where conditions were more favorable, agricultural production could have increased and some groups may have developed larger and more complex societies. Even small environmental fluctuations "had major effects on the population of the entire region" (J. S. Dean 2000a:97) and required constant behavioral adjustments. Such constant cultural adjustments have created a diverse archaeological record across space and time.

This regional cultural diversity, coupled with variety in the natural geography of the Southwest, resulted in a number of cultural adaptations in the Southwest. In broad terms, four major areas of cultural development have been identified (Fig. 9.4): (1) the Ancestral Puebloans (Anasazi), (2) the Mogollon, (3) the Hohokam, and (4) the Patayan. Each of these developments had clear differences in architecture, settlement and subsistence, and pottery styles, but there is still some debate about whether these developments represent different cultures, different ethnic groups, or simply adaptations (Bayman 2001:260). Indeed, a number of "other" cultural developments do not neatly fit into one of these categories, making a complex situation even more difficult. Each of these four major cultural developments (and several others) is discussed below.

THE ANCESTRAL PUEBLOANS (ANASAZI)

The ancient pueblos are the most recognizable of Southwestern archaeological sites, and the Puebloan people have long been the subject of intense interest, partly because they have been viewed as the direct ancestors of the contemporary Pueblo groups. The peoples who built and

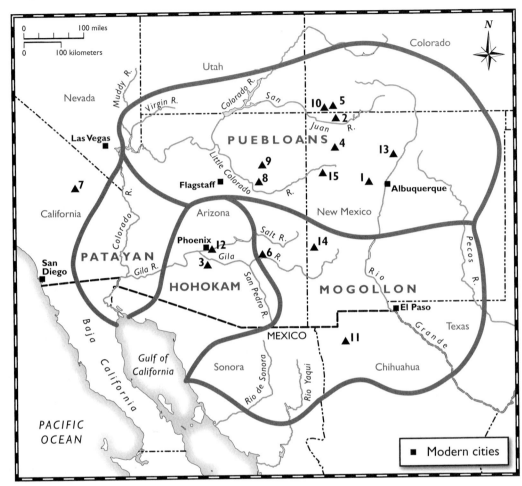

FIGURE 9.4 Map showing the Formative cultural regions and locations of sites discussed in the text: 1) Acoma; 2) Aztec; 3) Casa Grande; 4) Chaco Canyon (including Pueblo Bonito); 5) Cowboy Wash; 6) Grasshopper Pueblo; 7) Halloran Springs; 8) Homol'ovi; 9) Hopi; 10) Mesa Verde; 11) Paquimé; 12) Snaketown; 13) Taos; 14) Tularosa Cave; 15) Zuni. (Adapted from F. Plog "Prehistory of the Western Anasazi," Fig. 1; G. J. Gumerman and E. W. Haury "Prehistory: Hohokam," Fig. 1; A. H. Schroeder: Fig. 1; and P. S. Martin "Prehistory: Mogollon," Fig. 1 in *Handbook of North American Indians, Vol. 9, Southwest*, A. Ortiz, ed.; copyright © 1979 by the Smithsonian Institution. Reprinted with permission of the publisher.)

occupied the ancient pueblos were originally called the Anasazi, a term used widely in the literature until about ten years ago. However, the term *Anasazi* is a Navajo word roughly translated as "ancient enemy," and the contemporary Puebloan peoples do not care for the term, partly because it is not in any Puebloan language. Thus, many anthropologists now use the phrase *Ancestral Puebloans* to refer to the Anasazi, and that practice is generally followed herein.

    The Ancestral Puebloans are the best known of the major Southwestern cultures, having been the subject of investigation for over 130 years. They occupied the Colorado Plateau of the northern Southwest, all around the Four Corners area (where Arizona, New Mexico, Utah, and

Colorado meet) (see Fig. 9.4). Their territory was very diverse and included plateaus, desert, and major forested mountain ranges. Several major rivers (e.g., the Colorado, Little Colorado, and San Juan) cross the region.

The Ancestral Puebloans, known for their spectacular ruins at places such as Chaco Canyon and Mesa Verde, are generally viewed as having evolved in place from the Basketmaker people that occupied the same region beginning several thousand years ago (see below). A number of branches of Ancestral Puebloans have been identified in different geographic regions (e.g., the Virgin Branch), and several major "centers" of cultural development (e.g., Chaco Canyon) have also been identified. In 1927, a classification of Ancestral Puebloan prehistory was proposed (the Pecos Classification; Kidder 1927), and that general classification (the Pueblo Sequence, see Table 9.3) continues to be employed today. In sum, the sequence proposes that the Ancestral Puebloans were originally Archaic hunters and gatherers (Basketmaker I) who adopted agriculture (Basketmaker II), added pottery and bow/arrow (Basketmaker III), evolved into the ancient Pueblo groups (Pueblo I–IV), and are still present today (Pueblo V).

The Basketmakers

The term *Basketmaker* (coined by Richard Wetherill) originated when sites were discovered in the northern Southwest that contained the remains of corn but not pottery; thus, the people must have been "Basketmakers." The sites were not pueblos, but the people clearly practiced some agriculture, and it seemed that they were the ancestors of the later Puebloan cultures in the same region. It was reasoned that they must have lived in the region as hunter-gatherers prior to obtaining corn, and these earlier groups were classified as "pre-Basketmaker" or Basketmaker I. The designation Basketmaker I is not used, as it is really the Middle Archaic (the Armijo and En Medio phases; see above), so the Basketmaker sequence actually begins with Basketmaker II. Basketmaker II groups, hunter-gatherers who did practice some agriculture, could be classified as Late Archaic, and many researchers use that designation.

BASKETMAKER II (CA. 400 BC TO AD 400)   Perhaps as early as 2,000 BC, corn entered the northern Southwest, perhaps carried by migrants from Mexico. Hunting and gathering remained primary and pottery was rare. At some point, agriculture diffused north and became the principal economic pursuit, with those groups then becoming Basketmaker II. The timing of this transition is unclear but is often dated at about 400 BC, although some believe it was as early as 1,000 BC (Reed 2000:6) or even 1,500 BC (Huckell 1996:347).

Basketmaker II groups commonly lived in caves and rockshelters, and by about AD 100 they were also living in small villages with one to three pithouses. They manufactured well-made basketry, used the atlatl, and stored corn in underground rock-lined storage pits. By AD 300, they were manufacturing plain pottery. The dead were buried (inhumation), sometimes in old storage pits. In some instances, and for reasons unknown, skulls and long bones were removed from burials and burned.

Although Basketmaker II people were farmers (growing corn and squash but not beans), they relied heavily on hunting and gathering, with deer and pine nuts as major resources. The role of wild resources in Basketmaker II times is a matter of some debate. Using coprolite constituent data and carbon isotope data from human bone, Matson and Chisholm (1991) argued that Basketmaker II groups in southeastern Utah were fully dependent on corn by ca. AD 1 and that this dependence was probably widespread during Basketmaker II (also see Matson 2002:344; Schollmeyer and Turner 2004). Based on isotopic studies on human bone, Coltrain et al. (2007)

TABLE 9.3 The Ancestral Puebloan (Anasazi) Sequence on the Colorado Plateau

Period	Dates	Settlements	Architecture	Subsistence	Other Traits
Pueblo V	AD 1540 to present	relatively few large towns	aboveground structures for living and storage, underground kivas	agriculture dominant, some herding, some hunting and gathering	contact with Europeans
Pueblo IV	AD 1300 to 1540	far fewer settlements, contraction of territories	aboveground structures for living and storage, underground kivas, smaller multi-storied room complexes	agriculture dominant, some hunting and gathering	reduction in population, warfare
Pueblo III	AD 1150 to 1300	many towns of varying sizes, some very large	aboveground structures for living and storage, underground kivas, large multistory room complexes	agriculture dominant, some hunting and gathering	consolidation of settlements and population, evidence of warfare and violence
Pueblo II	AD 900 to 1150	larger villages (up to 10 rooms), largest geographic extent of Puebloan people	aboveground structures for living and storage, underground kivas, increased town planning	agriculture dominant, some hunting and gathering	favorable climate, some apparent cannibalism
Pueblo I	AD 750 to 900	villages (3–5 rooms)	aboveground structures for living and storage, underground kivas	agriculture becoming dominant	expansion of population and territory
Basketmaker III	AD 400 to 750	larger villages (3–5 pithouses)	pithouses for living, aboveground storage, some underground kivas	hunting and gathering, increasing agriculture, addition of beans	decorated pottery, bow and arrow
Basketmaker II	400 BC to AD 400	small villages (1–3 pithouses), increasing sedentism	pithouses for living, belowground storage, no kivas	mostly hunting and gathering, but agriculture increasing in importance	atlatl and dart, some pottery (late)

suggested that at least some Basketmaker II groups were heavily dependent on corn as early as 400 BC. Nevertheless, wild resources continued to be important in Basketmaker and even later Pueblo times (e.g., Sutton and Reinhard 1995).

BASKETMAKER III (CA. AD 400 TO 750)   Beginning about AD 400, the Basketmaker "pattern" had expanded across most of the northern Southwest. It is possible that the Basketmaker II groups in the western part of the northern Southwest were descendants of the earlier immigrants from Mexico and that the Basketmaker pattern diffused east into populations biologically unrelated to the western Basketmakers, setting the stage for the east/west distinctions seen in the later Pueblos (e.g., Matson 2005:281). Agriculture diffused north into the Great Basin and was adopted by groups collectively known as the Fremont (discussed in Chapter 8).

Basketmaker III groups began to live in larger and more elaborate villages. Caves and rockshelters were still used, but most village sites were moved to be close to agricultural fields located near watercourses. The primary dwelling was still the pithouse, but they began to build aboveground structures for storage. Some of the pithouses were quite large and may have evolved into the "Great Kivas" of the later Pueblo periods (see below). Also about this time, the bow and arrow was introduced and the earlier plain pottery was replaced by gray, white, and red forms (Reed 2000:7–8), although basketry remained important.

Agriculture increased in importance during Basketmaker III, and beans were added to the crops. The production of pottery appears to have greatly increased at this same time (e.g., Kohler et al. 2008). While it is clear that agriculture was important and that Basketmaker III peoples lived in villages near their fields, many view Basketmaker III populations as mobile hunter-gatherers who were also dependent on corn agriculture. It is possible that the villages were not occupied year-round, and they may have lived in several different villages at different times of the year, following a seasonal round to obtain both wild and cultivated resources (e.g., Wills and Windes 1989).

There is some evidence of conflict in some areas during Basketmaker III times. Some Basketmaker villages had stockades and some had burned structures (Vivian 2000:253–254). It is not clear whether this represents general warfare, small-scale raiding, or some other competition (there was a drought in the AD 700s, perhaps increasing pressure on crop production). Obviously, more research is needed to address this issue.

The Puebloans

The adoption of aboveground structures for houses, replacing the subterranean pithouse, is the major marker change from Basketmaker to Pueblo, although some Pueblo groups continued to use pithouses. In essence, the sequence of architecture from Basketmaker to Pueblo was the movement from living below ground to above ground, with the ceremonial structure (the kiva) remaining below ground (see Table 9.3). Even by Basketmaker II times, a general division between the western and eastern groups could be seen based on a variety of traits, including pottery, architecture, settlement patterns, and social organization (e.g., J. S. Dean 1996:29). This may be the antecedent of the western and eastern divisions later seen in the Pueblos (Matson 2002:349) and might even reflect a biological difference between western and eastern Basketmakers (e.g., Turner 1993; Matson 2005:281). Of interest is the Puebloan habit of using flat stones in their masonry, a trait that allowed for the construction of large, stable, multistory structures. Kantner (2004) provided a summary of the Puebloan Southwest, from which much of the following was taken.

PUEBLO I (CA. AD 750 TO 900)   The Pueblo I period marked the change to people living in aboveground houses. Villages were not much larger than in Basketmaker III times (three to five structures) and probably reflected the presence of small kin groups (e.g., extended families). Although the transition from the "old" pithouse dwelling to a kiva had begun in Basketmaker times, it became much more important during Pueblo I, and this initiated the beginning of a rich ceremonial life that would afterward typify Southwestern groups. Agriculture increased in importance, and black-on-white pottery appeared during Pueblo I.

The shift from Basketmaker to Pueblo may have involved population growth, increasing agricultural efficiency, and a breakdown of "large" Basketmaker groups into smaller dispersed settlements that were later reorganization into Pueblo groups. Some areas saw the development of relatively large communities, some of which included Great Kivas. These groups rapidly declined, however, and were, perhaps, part of some short-lived ritual system (Schachner 2001).

HIGHLIGHT 9.3

THE VIRGIN ANASAZI

The Virgin Anasazi (see Lyneis 1995) are the westernmost branch of the Ancestral Puebloans. They occupied northwestern Arizona, southern Nevada (along the Virgin and Muddy rivers), and perhaps even a portion of the Mojave Desert of California, an area generally outside the "traditional" Puebloan region. The Virgin Anasazi spanned Basketmaker II to early Pueblo III times (ca. AD 1 to 1200) and possessed the suite of Southwestern traits (pottery, architecture, and agriculture). They are unusual in that they moved into a region occupied by "non-Southwestern" groups, maintained contact with other Puebloan groups to the east, and then abandoned the area for reasons unknown, apparently moving back east to rejoin their Puebloan relatives.

The earliest Virgin Anasazi sites date to Basketmaker II times, when pithouse villages were built along the rivers. By early Pueblo II times, the Virgin Anasazi were building aboveground dwellings, but the construction was different from those to the east. Wood and tabular stone were difficult to find, so most of the construction was of adobe. Habitation sites were generally small and located on ridges, terraces, and/or knolls along the rivers. Turquoise from the Halloran Springs turquoise mines in the eastern Mojave Desert has been identified across the Southwest, and it has been suggested that the Virgin Anasazi were present at the mines (Leonard and Drover 1980; Warren 1984).

While the Virgin Anasazi did practice farming, it is not clear to what degree. Fields were located in the floodplains of the rivers, and corn, beans, and squash (and perhaps cotton) were grown. Hunting-and-gathering was clearly an important aspect of the economy, and it may be that the Virgin Anasazi practiced a mixed economy, moving around the landscape with farming just one aspect of the overall economy.

By about AD 1200, the Virgin Anasazi abandoned the Nevada area, apparently moving back to the east. The reason for the abandonment is unclear. It occurred before the "Great Drought" of AD 1275, but there were other periods of decreased rainfall that could have impacted water availability in the Virgin River, perhaps forcing the farmers out. However, if the Virgin Anasazi practiced a mixed economy, it would seem less likely that they would be affected by drought. It is also possible that they were pushed out by Numic groups moving eastward from California at about that same time (see Ambler and Sutton 1989 and Chapter 8).

PUEBLO II (AD 900 TO 1150)   The steady increase in the dependence on agriculture between about 400 BC and AD 900 occurred during a time that was not particularly favorable for agriculture. Beginning about AD 900, however, rainfall increased and farming became more productive. In addition, areas not previously suitable for farming due to lack of water became more desirable. Thus, during the Pueblo II period, Puebloan peoples expanded into new areas and achieved the greatest geographical extent of Puebloan peoples.

Population likely increased, as did the size of villages, from three to five rooms in Pueblo I times to as many as ten structures per village (about half of which were for storage). This increase in the number of dwellings suggests that kin groups at the sites were larger than in Pueblo I times, from extended families to small groups of families, perhaps even social units that controlled agricultural fields. As one might expect, agriculture became more important, even dominant.

The Chaco Phenomenon   Chaco Canyon is located in the San Juan Basin of northwestern New Mexico, and nine major pueblos are known within the canyon itself. The sites were observed by Mexican explorers as early as 1823 and by American settlers in 1849, with formal investigations beginning there in 1895. The canyon is now a National Historic Park and has been intensively investigated by several archaeologists (e.g., Vivian 1990; Lekson 2006a; Van Dyke 2007a). A good summary of Chaco was presented by Brian Fagan (2005b).

Chaco Canyon is a unique and remarkable place. It was first occupied during Basketmaker II times, and farming was probably marginal (Sebastian 1992), supporting only small populations. By Pueblo I times, conditions had improved and agriculture became more productive. Chacoan farmers probably expanded into new territories, a pattern typical for Pueblo I groups. However, while the rest of the Pueblo world changed slowly, Chaco Canyon diverged from that path to develop an unprecedented culture, unique for Pueblo II times.

Beginning in the late AD 800s, construction within Chaco Canyon exploded and a number of large "Great Houses," a hallmark of Chacoan culture, were built. Great Houses are large, multi-story pueblos with hundreds of rooms (see Mahoney and Kantner 2000; Vivian and Hilpert 2002; Windes 2007), often D-shaped in outline. After AD 1040, "Great Kivas" were added to many of the Great House pueblos (Van Dyke 2007b; Mahoney and Kantner 2000:8).

Within Chaco Canyon itself are a variety of planned settlements, from small to very large, including four Great House communities (Penasco Blanco, Kin Bineola, Una Vida, and Pueblo Bonito). The largest and most famous is Pueblo Bonito (see J. E. Neitzel 2003, 2007), consisting of perhaps eight hundred rooms (see Fig. 9.5) on at least four stories (and it may still have an unexcavated buried story). It may be that Pueblo Bonito was the center of the Center Place (Neitzel 2003). The space immediately east of Pueblo Bonito occupies a natural amphitheater that may have functioned as an outdoor performance area (Stein et al. 2007).

It has been estimated that some 200,000 construction beams were needed to build the pueblos in the canyon (Dean and Warren 1983:202–207). If so, it is possible that the nearby area may have been stripped of pine (e.g., Samuels and Betancourt 1982), affecting the ecology of the region. However, recent calculations of timber resources suggest that this was not the case, and isotopic analysis of the timbers indicates that some timber came from places at least seventy-five kilometers away (Betancourt et al. 1986; English et al. 2001; Reynolds et al. 2005). In addition, while farming was certainly practiced within the canyon, chemical analyses of corn from the Chacoan Great Houses suggests that much of it was grown elsewhere and imported (Benson et al. 2003; Cordell et al. 2008). Other items, such as macaws, copper bells, and turquoise, were also imported.

FIGURE 9.5 Pueblo Bonito, the largest of the pueblo sites in Chaco Canyon. (*Source:* Robert Harding World Imagery.)

The scale of the construction and organization within Chaco Canyon is remarkable. Even more remarkable was the development of what has been called the Chacoan Regional System (see Lekson 2006b; Van Dyke 2007a), which at its height dominated some 40,000 square miles of the northern Southwest (Fig. 9.6). Perhaps as many as two hundred other Chacoan Great House communities (called outliers) have been discovered outside the canyon, some as far as eighty kilometers away. A number of high towers are present in the canyon, each visible by the next, and are thought to be a communication system (e.g., fire towers). Some irrigation facilities are present in the canyon bottom, and there are water control systems (dams and small reservoirs) on the tops of the surrounding mesas.

Some of the outliers are apparently connected to Chaco Canyon and to each other by an extensive network of "roads" (see Fig. 9.6). These roads are not casual foot trails but ran straight for considerable distances and were mostly constructed to a standard of about nine meters in width (Vivian 1997a). Between 130 and 1,500 miles of roads (depending on one's definition of "road") are known. The roads may have been multifunctional and used to integrate the participants in the Chacoan system (Vivian 1997b). They do not appear to have been used for the transportation of people or goods (Mahoney and Kantner 2000:10) but, based on their orientation, may be associated with astronomical phenomena such as solstice alignments (e.g., Sofaer 2007). Thus, Chaco Canyon is not merely a place but a "Center Place" from which spread a cultural phenomenon that is still not fully understood (Van Dyke 2007a).

What was the nature of the "Chacoan Regional System"? Unfortunately, we do not yet know. It is possible that Chaco Canyon, and perhaps even Pueblo Bonito itself, was the center of a large centralized economic and/or religious authority (such as a chiefdom) that controlled

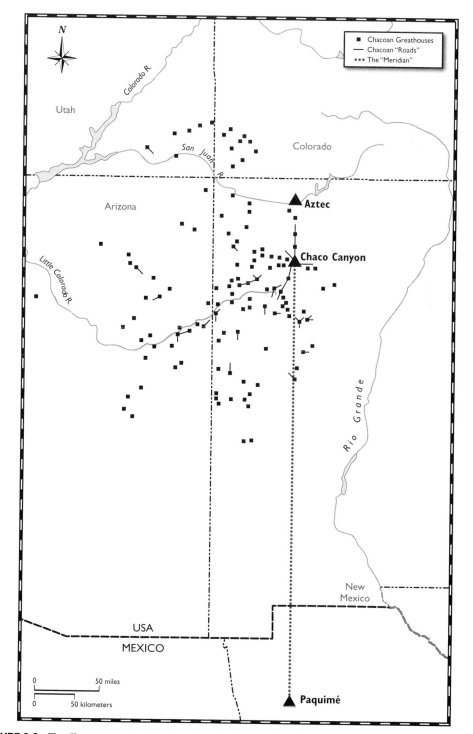

FIGURE 9.6 The Chacoan Regional System, showing the location of Great House Communities and known segments of Chacoan roads. Note the "Chaco Meridian" linking Aztec, Chaco, and Paquimé. (Adapted from Great House Communities Across the Chacoan Landscape by John Kantner and N. M. Mahoney. © 2000 The Arizona Board of Regents. Reprinted by permission of the University of Arizona Press.)

the outliers and their resources. It may have been led by political leaders (e.g., Kantner 1996) or perhaps by "priests" who controlled labor and resources by holding elaborate rituals, both secret (in Great Kivas) and in public (in town squares) to validate their power. Another view (e.g., Wills 2000) is that Great Houses were built by corporate, landholding entities with the goal of validating their claims. In either case, the mortuary patterns (Akins 2001) provide evidence of ranking, differential access to resources (some people were healthier than others), and settlement hierarchy.

The transport of goods (e.g., timber and corn) from the periphery to the center argues that Chaco controlled the system. However, it could be that the outliers were independent "imitations" of Chaco and that the various Chacoan communities were linked together as a "macroregional peer-polity system" of competing polities (Wilcox 1996:245). The diversity in architectural styles among the outliers suggests that they may not have been tightly integrated into the Chacoan system (Van Dyke 1999).

By the early AD 1100s, the system began to collapse and Pueblo III groups, perhaps from Mesa Verde to the north, moved into the region. The reason for the collapse is unclear, but there are various possibilities, including drought or stresses from overexploitation of resources, farmland, forests, and/or game (Stuart 2000:197). Another possibility was a lack of public confidence in the system (e.g., Van Dyke 2004).

An intriguing possibility is that while Chaco Canyon itself may have diminished, the Chacoan system may not have. Lekson and Cameron (1995) and Lekson (1999, 2005) suggested that as Chaco Canyon declined, the center of the system was moved north to the major center of Aztec. As Aztec declined, the center of the system was moved south to Paquimé in northern Mexico. Interestingly, each of these three sites (Chaco, Aztec, and Paquimé) is situated on a precise north/south line, suggesting a planned succession of centers (see Fig. 9.6).

It is also possible that Chaco may have been a decadent and malevolent place (see Highlight 9.4) and perhaps its people rebelled. Lekson (2006a:29; also see Cameron and Duff 2008) analyzed the historical trajectories of Chacoan localities outside Chaco Canyon itself and argued that Chaco was both a "wonderful and awful" place where "people got power over people." After about AD 1300, the modern Pueblos developed as a reaction against Chaco so that the "bad" Chacoan experience would not be repeated (Lekson 2006a:29; Cameron and Duff 2008).

HIGHLIGHT 9.4

CANNIBALISM!

Since the early 1900s, archaeologists have noticed the presence of cut and burned human bone at a number of Ancestral Pueblo sites, suggesting that portions of these individuals had been butchered, cooked, and perhaps even eaten. The evidence pointed toward cannibalism, but this was too terrible to contemplate, so the idea was generally ignored and considered too sensitive to research. Beginning in the 1970s, however, studies on human bone (e.g., Turner and Morris 1970; Turner 1983; T. D. White 1992; Turner and Turner 1999) provided a convincing argument that cannibalism had indeed occurred. At least 286 individuals from 38 Puebloan sites dating between AD 900 and 1200 were documented (Turner and Turner 1999), each exhibiting evidence of butchering and cooking and mostly mixed in with other food bones in trash middens. The skeletal remains of these men, women, and children possessed the same cut marks, breakage patterns, and burn patterns as the associated food animal remains.

Opponents of cannibalism argued that butchering and cooking did not demonstrate actual consumption and suggested that other activities, such as the execution of witches (Darling 1999) or violent competition between rival priesthoods (J. Miller 2001:507), could explain the patterns seen in the bones. The case for actual cannibalism was strengthened when muscle proteins (myoglobin) from one human individual were discovered in the fecal material of another human individual at the Cowboy Wash site in Utah (Marlar et al. 2000; also see Dongoske et al. 2000).

It seems that cannibalism first appeared about AD 1000 in Chaco society (White 1992; Turner and Turner 1999) but was also present at the same time in the Mesa Verde area (White 1992; Billman et al. 2000) to the north of Chaco. Turner and Turner (1999:483–484) suggested that the practice could have been related to influences from Mesoamerica. A sharp increase in cannibalism was noted in Mesa Verde about AD 1150, about the same time as the drought and the collapse of Chaco (Billman et al. 2000:173), and it was thought that it could be related to warfare and raiding (Lambert et al. 2000; also see Hurlbut 2000; Kuckleman et al. 2002). Cannibalism was apparently widespread in the Chaco and Mesa Verde worlds (and perhaps with the Fremont in the Great Basin as well; Novak and Kollmann 2000) but was not common and was not employed as a regular part of the economic system. Clearly, it was part of some ritual or religious system or some effort to intimidate enemies.

Still, not all are convinced that cannibalism was practiced (e.g., Reinhard 2006) and even if it was, its meaning is unclear (e.g., Rautman and Fenton 2005). It has been argued that even the suggestion that some Ancestral Puebloan peoples practiced cannibalism "condemns" all Ancestral Puebloans as cannibals and is insulting to contemporary native peoples. Ritual cannibalism is actually fairly common around the world (e.g., Askenasy 1994; but see Arens 1979), however, and forms an aspect of the variety of human behavior.

HIGHLIGHT 9.5

THE SINAGUA

In the fall of AD 1064, Sunset Crater, located on the southern Colorado Plateau near Flagstaff, Arizona (see Fig. 9.1), erupted and spewed ash (tephra) over some eight hundred square miles of northern Arizona. The initial eruption must have been a spectacular event, and smaller eruptions continued for the next fifty years. Many sites were buried under the ash, and many were subsequently constructed on top of the ash. The prehistoric people of this region were called the "Sinagua" (a Spanish term for "without water"; H. S. Colton 1960), and their culture spanned most of the Pueblo sequence (ca. AD 700 to 1450; F. Plog 1989:267; also see Pilles 1979:460). Both northern and southern aspects of the Sinagua have been identified, but it is still not clear who the Sinagua actually were (F. Plog 1989:264).

Prior to the eruption of Sunset Crater, the Sinagua were Pueblo I and II farmers living on the western Colorado Plateau, with Mogollon-looking pithouses and Hohokam-looking pottery. The Sinagua population grew after ca. AD 825, and their villages became larger. Agriculture expanded into new areas and food production generally increased. People in the area of Sunset Crater had some warning of the eruption and moved out of the area, sometimes even taking their wooden house beams with them.

After the eruptions subsided, people moved back into the region and constructed new villages on top of the ash, apparently many more sites than before the eruption, and a few were even large "pueblos" (Fig. 9.7). This suggested that population had increased dramat-

FIGURE 9.7 The Sinagua site of Montezuma's Castle, south of Flagstaff. (*Source:* Charles Kogod/ National Geographic Image Collection.)

ically, and it was argued (e.g., H. S. Colton 1960) that the ash formed a "mulch" that enriched the soil, conserved water, and created new farmland. Thus, the argument went, people came from everywhere to take advantage of the new farming opportunities, leading to the development of the post-eruption Sinagua. It seems likely that at least some Hohokam entered the area, as seen by the presence of Hohokam houses, ball courts, and pottery (Pilles 1979:470), but there is little evidence that other groups, such as the Mogollon, came in (Pilles 1979:477; also see Pilles 1996).

More recent research has questioned the agricultural advantage of the ash. The ash did not contain many nutrients and did not make, by itself, good farmland. However, rainfall did increase between AD 1050 and 1130, which would have made the area more attractive to farmers even without the ash. In addition, the ash buried many earlier sites, suggesting that the population expansion (based on the number of rooms at some sites) after the eruption was more apparent than real, especially given that there was a population increase all across the Southwest at that time (Pilles 1979:480). Kamp and Whittaker (1999) argued that the Sinagua were successful because they lived in small, self-sufficient villages dispersed across the landscape.

A new model (see Reid and Whittlesey 1997:217) suggested that it was not the ash and agricultural opportunities that drew people into the region after the eruption but the eruption itself. It may be that the eruption was viewed as a supernatural event and religious pilgrims from various places may have come to the region to take advantage of the opportunity to commune with the supernatural. Indeed, the Hopi deities are believed to reside in the nearby San Francisco Peaks. By about AD 1220, the model goes, many Sinagua sites were abandoned and others had smaller populations, perhaps due to the loss of the "magic" after the eruptions ceased (Reid and Whittlesey 1997:220). As in other places in the Colorado Plateau, many of the Sinagua consolidated into several large villages by AD 1300, but even those were abandoned after AD 1450.

The identity of the Sinagua is still unclear. Some (e.g., Pilles 1979) believe that they were not Ancestral Puebloans, but others think they were. They may have been Mogollon or Hohokam or some combination thereof. Still others see the Sinagua as an independent entity (see F. Plog 1989) having "pueblo" villages, "Hohokam" ball courts, and unique pottery. After about AD 1400, some of the northern Sinagua may have joined the Hopi, while the southern Sinagua may have moved south to the Hohokam (or even the Salado; see Highlight 9.8) area.

PUEBLO III (AD 1150 TO 1300)   Beginning about AD 1150, the Puebloan world began to change dramatically. The many relatively small, dispersed communities of Pueblo II times were abandoned in favor of fewer, but much larger, pueblos. This aggregation resulted in the construction of many of the famous large pueblos in the ancient Southwest, and Pueblo III represents the "stereotypic" Ancestral Puebloans known to most people, and some call it the "Great Pueblo" period (see Adler 1996a). As part of this consolidation, many Ancestral Puebloan communities moved from the edges of the Pueblo world toward the center, and the overall geographic extent of the Puebloans became smaller than during Pueblo II times.

Perhaps following the lead of Chaco, large pueblos, many with Great Kivas and hundreds of rooms, were constructed across the northern Southwest. Some were D-shaped, like the earlier Chaco Great Houses. Many pueblos (especially in the east) were constructed in "halves," apparently reflecting some sort of dual social organization, such as moieties. Considerable labor must have been mobilized to build these towns, which included both private and public architecture, indicating a relatively high degree of social control and powerful political institutions (e.g., Lipe 2002:230). There is, however, little evidence of powerful individuals, suggesting that corporate social organizations, such as moieties, were in control (as they are in contemporary Pueblo towns).

After ca. AD 1225, community architecture increased in scale and variety (Lipe 2002:221). Community architecture included some defensive structures, perhaps some roads, Tower Kivas, and Great Kivas. While small kivas were present in many Pueblo I and II sites, the addition of Great Kivas suggests that larger social units had gained importance, arguing that a major shift in the scale of organization, community ritual, and control had taken place. This change from small ritual spaces to larger ones implies that the control of ritual may have been as important as performance of ritual (Feinman 2000). Indeed, it was suggested that aggregated villages incorporated their village and surrounding spaces into a complex representation of social order and of the cosmos (Fowles 2009).

Subsistence systems also changed. In Pueblo II times, people, communities, and farms were "spread out" across the landscape. With the condensation of many small communities into fewer larger ones, agricultural lands were also consolidated. Thus, agriculture became more "intensive" and less "extensive," and land tenure patterns appear to have changed from a system in which individuals or families controlled land to one where the land was controlled by villages or other larger social (corporate) units (Adler 1996b). The establishment of large settlements across the Southwest may have been due to a decrease in rainfall, a reduction in farmland, and the necessity of pooling more labor to maintain agricultural production (Leonard and Reed 1993:648; also see Cordell 1997:365–428).

Corn, beans, and squash remained the major crops, and cotton was also grown. Domesticated turkeys were raised for food and feathers; turkey feather blankets were important trade items. The use of wild foods remained important, but it appears that fewer game animals were captured, perhaps due to overhunting (Muir and Driver 2002). In some areas, however, the use of large game increased, perhaps due to ritual behaviors related to community integration (e.g., R. M. Dean 2001).

After about AD 1275, a number of pueblos were constructed on and in cliffs (the famous "cliff dwellings" of the Southwest). It is commonly assumed that the placement of these settlements was for defensive purposes (e.g., Lipe 2002:212), but it is also possible that they were so placed to avoid using good agricultural land. In many cases, the sites were placed where the sun exposure was the best (Reid and Whittlesey 1997:196), perhaps to get out of the cold canyon bottoms or to avoid the windy canyon tops. This pattern can especially be seen in the Mesa Verde area of northwestern New Mexico (now a national park) where many of the cliff dwellings are located. In general, construction of pueblos in the northern Southwest stopped about AD 1280 (Lipe 2002:215). A video on Mesa Verde is available at www.archaeologychannel.org, "Mesa Verde: Legacy of Stone."

By AD 1300, the northern Southwest had been virtually abandoned. Many of its people moved south, into the northern Rio Grande, Mogollon, and Hohokam areas (Lipe 1995). However, as people moved south, it seems that many of their cultural traits (e.g., small kivas, D-shaped pueblos, and bilateral layout of villages) did not move with them (Lipe 2002:232), indicating major cultural changes at that time (recall the idea of erasing the memories of Chaco; see above).

Why did this happen? It has been known for a long time that a major drought began about AD 1276 and lasted until about AD 1299 (as measured in tree rings), almost precisely matching the end of the construction of pueblos and the abandonment of the region. This "Great Drought" of the Southwest was one part of a worldwide climatic anomaly (the MCA; e.g., Larson and Michaelsen 1990; J. S. Dean 1994; Jones et al. 1999) but seems to have been particularly felt in the northern Southwest. This drought, so the thinking went, decreased agricultural production and forced the people to move south; a flow of Puebloan refugees that subsequently impacted the Mogollon and Hohokam and perhaps hastened their demise as well.

Why did this drought force everyone to leave? There had been other droughts in the Southwest that were as bad or worse (Van West and Dean 2000). Some have argued that even during the Great Drought, rainfall was still sufficient to keep the agricultural system viable (Van West 1996:223; Van West and Dean 2000; Varien et al. 2007), although perhaps at a decreased level of productivity. If the population was too high for a decreased productivity, the movement of some of the people from the area would have improved the situation for remaining people (Lipe 1995).

Van West and Kohler (1996) suggested that food-sharing (cooperative) systems allowed the Pueblo populations to grow and that a breakdown in food-sharing (perhaps due to shortages from the drought) may have been a factor in the collapse (also see Cordell et al. 2007). It is possible that environmental circumstances other than drought could also have been involved. There may have been a loss of soil fertility, a reduction in the water table due to arroyo cutting, and/or a reduction in actual farmland acreage due to erosion (Van West and Dean 2000). Such things could have magnified the impact of a drought. It has also been suggested (Benson and Berry 2009) that an overdependence on corn and the cultivation of marginal areas during good times led to catastrophic declines in food availability in bad times, forcing people to starve or move, and that many Puebloans either "died in place or in transit" (Benson and Berry 2009:110).

Still other factors may have been involved. Warfare, almost certainly coupled with poor environmental conditions, may have "pushed" people out. It seems clear that some sort of warfare was taking place (Kuckelman 2002), and it is possible that drought weakened Pueblo III groups to the point that they began fighting among themselves for resources, eventually leading to abandonment. It has also been proposed that outside groups moved in and pushed out the weakened Pueblo III groups, perhaps Numic groups from the Great Basin (e.g., Ambler and Sutton 1989) or Athapaskan groups from the north (Matson 2002:350–351).

There may also have been factors that served to "pull" people to the south (e.g., Lipe 1995; also see Ahlstrom et al. 1995). These may have included new religious developments, such as the appearance of the Katsina cult (e.g., Adams 2001) or a pan-Southwest earth and fertility cult (Crown 1994).

Whatever the reason (or reasons), the Ancestral Puebloans abandoned much of the northern Southwest and those regions were occupied by other groups (the Numic and Athapaskan). But one could also view the contraction from the north as an expansion to the south, an expansion of Puebloan people and traits that had considerable impact on the southern groups.

PUEBLO IV (AD 1300 TO 1540)   By AD 1300, most of the northern Southwest had been abandoned by Puebloan groups, and as they relocated and coalesced they formed into the two major groupings of pueblos (western along the Little Colorado River and the eastern along Rio Grande) seen in historic times (recall that this pattern may date from Basketmaker III times). There was a major population decrease in the west, an increase in the east, and settlement consolidation into a just few large towns (or clusters of towns). Community spaces (e.g., kivas) became even more important.

The new pattern, called Pueblo IV (see Adams and Duff 2004), showed a high level of social conflict and the appearance of new ritual systems. The Katsina system developed (or was imported) about AD 1350 (Adams 1991; Adams and LaMotta 2006) and resulted in the formation of new social arrangements. It is possible that this development was related to the new stresses of the Pueblo IV world, and as conditions changed, a new ritual system developed to control them.

While a number of large pueblos and pueblo site complexes existed during Pueblo IV times, they were under constant pressure. These stresses included continued environmental degradation and resource depletion, such as loss of soil fertility, the overuse of forests for construction and fuel (e.g., Minnis 1979; Kohler and Matthews 1988), and an overexploitation of local large animal populations that forced a shift to the use of smaller species (see Fish and Fish 1994:92). In addition, internal warfare (LeBlanc 1999) and external warfare (e.g., Ambler and Sutton 1989) remained important issues.

Some of the pueblo site complexes were quite extensive, such as the one at Homol'ovi (Adams 2002). Homol'ovi consisted of a cluster of seven major pueblos along the Little Colorado River with some 3,300 rooms and perhaps some 2,300 people (Adams 2002: Table 1.1). The various pueblos at Homol'ovi began to be built about AD 1260, but not all were occupied at the same time. By AD 1400, the sites had been abandoned and some were purposefully burned. By AD 1540, only a few pueblos remained occupied in the west, with a larger number surviving along the Rio Grande in the east. A video on Homol'ovi is available at www.archaeologychannel.org, "Hopi Fires."

PUEBLO V (HISTORIC PUEBLOS, AFTER AD 1540)   By the time the Spanish arrived in the Southwest in AD 1540, the Pueblos had already realigned themselves into their familiar western and eastern groupings that reflected their distinct linguistic and architectural differences. Most of the Pueblos that were occupied in AD 1540 are still occupied today, although some were abandoned due to pressure from the Spanish (see Liebmann and Preucel 2007).

Beginning in the late 1800s, a great deal of information was obtained on extant Pueblo groups (and other Southwestern groups; refer to volumes 9 and 10 of the *Handbook of North American Indians* [Ortiz 1979, 1983]). The archaeology, coupled with ethnographic data, made it clear that there was significant cultural continuity between the contemporary and Ancestral Puebloans. Some of the ethnographic data were developed into innovative models to test against archaeological data (Hill 1970; Longacre 1970), and those types of efforts continue.

THE MOGOLLON

The Mogollon, first described in detail by Haury (1936; also see Wheat 1955), lived in the mountains of southern Arizona, New Mexico, and well into northern Mexico (see Fig. 9.4). The Mogollon originated about AD 1, when Archaic groups in the region adopted agriculture. A good record of continuity from the Archaic to the Mogollon is present at Tularosa Cave, New Mexico (see Martin et al. 1952). The Mogollon can be divided into a number of regional branches (see Cordell 1997: Table 7.4), one of which, the Mimbres, is famous for its pottery (see Highlight 9.6), but they are often divided into five basic developmental periods, as is done here (Table 9.4).

TABLE 9.4 The Mogollon Sequence in the Southwest (compiled from Reid and Whitney 1997; Diehl and LeBlanc 2001)

Period	Dates	Settlements/Architecture	Subsistence	Other Traits
Late	AD 1400 to 1700	small scattered settlements, mostly in northern Mexico	total dependence on agriculture	
Aggregation	AD 1300 to 1400	founding of large pueblos, population aggregation	total dependence on agriculture	artificial skull deformation
Postclassic	AD 1150 to 1300	depopulation of larger villages and shift to dispersed settlements, may have adopted a seasonal round	hunting and gathering reassume a prominent role	
Classic	AD 1000 to 1150	shift from pithouses to above-ground masonry in same site locations, field houses in field locations	dependence on corn	some new pottery styles, cotton, possible presence of katsina cult
Late Pithouse	AD 550 to 1000	pithouses, villages on floodplains, increasing sedentism, pithouse groups organized around "courtyards"	increasing dependence on corn	black-on-white pottery, change in pithouse architecture from roundish to rectangular
Early Pithouse	AD 200 to 550	pithouses, villages on hilltops	relatively low dependence on corn	mobile populations, first systematic use of pottery

The Pithouse Period (AD 200 to 1000)

About AD 200, Southern Archaic groups in the mountains of western New Mexico began to adopt agriculture. They lived in small pithouse villages of one or two families, often with a large "communal" pithouse, on the tops of hills (Early Pithouse) (Diehl and LeBlanc 2001). They adopted plain brown pottery but retained their mobile hunter-gatherer system and farmed a little along the valley bottom, although they relied very little on corn (Lekson 1992). The locations of villages on hilltops could suggest that they were placed for defensive purposes, but this remains debated.

After about AD 550 (Late Pithouse), people had increased their dependence on farming and the population increased dramatically. The hilltop villages were abandoned, and new, larger villages of pithouses (Fig. 9.8) were constructed near good farmland along the river terraces in the valleys. Some of the larger villages contained larger communal structures, while some of the smaller villages did not, suggesting that some smaller villages relied on larger villages for ceremonies (Cordell 1997:206). It also seems that there was group-level control in the villages (Lightfoot and Feinman 1982:78). Hunting and gathering remained the primary economic focus until about AD 800, when agriculture became dominant. Pottery became decorated, and there is evidence of increased contact with the Ancestral Puebloans and Hohokam. These contacts, along with the intensification of agriculture after about AD 800, led to rapid and significant changes in Mogollon society, leading to the development of the Classic Period (Creel and Anyon 2003).

FIGURE 9.8 Pithouse No. 36 at the Harris site, a Mogollon site in New Mexico (photo by Barbara Roth; used with permission).

The Classic Period (AD 1000 to 1150)

Starting about AD 1000, the Mogollon adopted aboveground masonry and began to build "pueblos" (although this varied from area to area, with some Mogollon not building pueblos until the AD 1200s). This trait seems to be a clear indication of influence from the Ancestral Puebloans to the north, who had undergone a similar transition some 250 years earlier (Pueblo I times; see above). However, instead of using a stable masonry of flat stones, the Mogollon used rounded cobbles and adobe, a technique not well suited to the construction of large multistory buildings. The early Mogollon pueblos were generally small and constructed in the same valley floor locations as their pithouse villages had been. It is possible that the change from pithouse to pueblo architecture involved the development of corporate groups (e.g., clans). At this same time, pottery decoration changed to black-on-white, another Ancestral Puebloan trait. These influences have led some to suggest that after AD 1000 a "mixed" Ancestral Puebloan/Mogollon "culture" developed, called Mimbres (see Lekson 1993; Hegmon 2002; Highlight 9.6).

Although the Mogollon continued to hunt and gather wild foods (especially deer), agriculture increased in importance and formed a major aspect of the subsistence system. The agricultural techniques of the Mogollon were not identical to either the Ancestral Puebloan or the Hohokam, but they did use some irrigation. Domesticated turkeys were also important. Although the Mogollon generally "consolidated" their populations into pueblos, they grew corn at distant locations, where they maintained small "field houses" (single family farm houses) to stay in while they farmed.

The Postclassic Period (AD 1150 to 1300)

The time after about AD 1150 was difficult for most everyone in the Southwest. Drought, warfare, crop failures, too many mouths to feed, and other pressures impacted virtually everyone, and the Mogollon were no exception. Environmental conditions appear to have begun to deteriorate such that by about AD 1200 many Mogollon sites were abandoned. It is not yet clear what actually happened, but it seems that large mammals (e.g., deer) may have been overexploited, forcing an increased dependence on agriculture (M. D. Cannon 2000:340–341). Growing populations, including groups of Ancestral Puebloan people from the north, may have overtaxed the system and forced it to break down.

Although the term *collapse* has been used, it is clear that the Mogollon actually reorganized themselves and continued to live under a new system (Hegmon 2002:322, 327–329; Nelson et al. 2006). The Mogollon adopted the earlier (e.g., Late Pithouse) system of small, dispersed villages with smaller populations and increased their dependence on wild foods. It is possible that they even adopted a seasonal round, living in different places at different times of the year to exploit local resources.

A few new "pueblos" appear to have been founded during this time. By the late 1200s (the Great Drought), tensions rose and conflict ensued (Reid and Whittlesey 1997:147). Some Mogollon people may have moved into northern Mexico, founding the major center of Paquimé (Highlight 9.7). After AD 1300, larger numbers of people migrated into the Mogollon region, changing the system again.

The Aggregation Period (AD 1300 to 1400)

The drought of the late 1200s and other issues (see discussion above) seem to have caused a large number of Puebloan peoples in the northern Southwest to migrate to other areas. Many Puebloan people apparently moved into the Mogollon region (e.g., Ezzo and Price 2002; Riggs 2007), perhaps establishing a few separate Ancestral Puebloan communities. Some of the migrants may have been war refugees with a larger proportion of females than males (Lowell

2007), and burial data from some sites (e.g., Grasshopper Pueblo) suggest that many Ancestral Puebloan women married into Mogollon families.

With the population increase, and following the pattern seen in Pueblo IV to the north, the Mogollon appear to have aggregated into a number of larger settlements, constructing large pueblos with more than one hundred rooms. Grasshopper Pueblo (Fig. 9.9), located in the mountains of east-central Arizona (see Fig. 9.4), was one of the latest and largest, with about five hundred rooms (see Reid and Whittlesey 1999, 2005). Grasshopper Pueblo was founded in about AD 1276, reaching its maximum size about AD 1350. Other large pueblos were also constructed in the same general area, and it is evident that a fairly large population was present.

In the early 1300s, times were good at Grasshopper Pueblo, with agriculture supplementing hunting and gathering. However, a drought in the mid-1300s apparently forced people to abandon hunting and gathering altogether in favor of farming, and people eventually had to move out of the mountains to find better farmland (Reid and Whittlesey 1997:155). Studies of burial populations (e.g., Ezzo 1993) show that the general health at Grasshopper Pueblo was poor, with very poor dental health (due to grinding their corn on stone) and chronic nutrient shortages that caused anemia and other health problems. Child mortality was greater than 50 percent, and few people lived into their fifties (Reid and Whittlesey 1997:157). Men generally had better diets than women or children (Ezzo 1993:83), perhaps reflecting power relationships within the community. A similar pattern is present in other Mogollon communities.

Ceremonial life revolved around kiva rituals, and at least four kiva societies have been identified at Grasshopper Pueblo (Reid and Whittlesey 1997:159). Further, it seems that landholding kinship groups developed, perhaps as farmland became a critical resource.

FIGURE 9.9 Grasshopper Pueblo in east-central Arizona, prior to excavation. Note the two major room blocks, with the left one having a large central plaza (photo by J. Jefferson Reid; used with permission).

The Late Period (AD 1400 to 1700)

Like much of the Southwest, the Mogollon region was abandoned by about AD 1400. The Puebloans consolidated and are still in place in the northern Southwest, but it is not at all clear what happened to the Mogollon or the Hohokam (see below). Perhaps the two most plausible scenarios are that (1) they were absorbed by the Ancestral Puebloans and incorporated into their Pueblo V communities, or (2) they moved south to Paquimé, where they persisted until about AD 1700. There is evidence for both of these scenarios, and it is possible that they are both correct for different parts of the Mogollon region.

HIGHLIGHT 9.6

MIMBRES

Mimbres (see Powell-Marti and Gilman 2006) is a distinctive regional development, or branch, of the Mogollon, centered in the Mimbres Valley in south-central New Mexico. Mimbres, like much of the Mogollon, possessed a number of Ancestral Puebloan traits, and their development generally followed the broad outline of Mogollon prehistory (see Table 9.4). What sets the Mimbres apart is their unique pottery tradition, lasting from about AD 1000 to 1200.

Mimbres pottery included mundane, undecorated ware for everyday use and a decorated ware unique in its quality of artistic expression (Brody 2004). This latter ware, called Mimbres Black-on-White, usually consisted of bowls (Fig. 9.10) that contained "complex geometric, representational, and narrative paintings" (Brody 2004:xxiii), many of which were closely tied to the natural world, primarily plants and animals. In addition it its artistic beauty, Mimbres

FIGURE 9.10 Mimbres pot decorated with a scene of childbirth. The hole in the bottom represents the "killing" of the bowl for burial with the dead. (*Source:* © Werner/Forman/Art Resource, NY.)

pottery decoration conveyed considerable ideology and information about Mimbres cere-mony, gender, and economics, with some of the elements being linked to both Mesoamerican and Ancestral Puebloan symbolism. Mortuary practices appear to have been very important to the Mimbres, and the function of public structures changed from ceremonial to mortuary complexes (Creel and Anyon 2003:87), perhaps coupled with the development of a "corpo-rately organized feasting complex based on ancestor veneration." The decorated pottery is generally found with burials and seems to have been specifically produced as mortuary offer-ings. Unfortunately, Mimbres mortuary pottery is highly prized on the antiquities market, resulting in a great deal of looting and destruction of Mimbres sites and cemeteries.

HIGHLIGHT 9.7

PAQUIMÉ AND THE CASAS GRANDES WORLD

One of the most impressive sites in the Southwest is Paquimé (also known as Casas Grandes), located on the floodplain of the Río Casas Grandes in northern Mexico (see Fig. 9.4). The site was first investigated in the 1930s and extensively excavated in the 1950s (Di Peso et al. 1974). Additional work has been undertaken at the site and its surroundings since. The site covers more than one square kilometer and had a planned layout, with perhaps as many as 1,500 rooms, ball courts, platform and effigy mounds, and a water system (including canals and reservoirs), and was constructed with a mud and gravel "concrete." Paquimé is probably "the most complex prehistoric site in the Greater Southwest" (Wilcox 1995:287).

Paquimé was built on top of earlier pithouse and pueblo villages. The primary occupation of the site occurred between about AD 1200 and 1450 (the Medio Period; see Table 9.5), but small numbers of people lived at the site until contact. Beginning about AD 1275, there was a massive building program that included the construction of many public spaces, such as plazas, ball courts, and platform mounds. The architecture and pottery were suggestive of a Mogollon derivation, but it also contained many Mesoamerican traits, such as unique I-shaped ball courts (see Harmon 2006). The ball-court game may have been integrated into an exchange system dominated by Paquimé (Wilcox 1995) or perhaps tied to religious and political activities used as control mechanisms (Harmon 2006).

Di Peso et al. (1974) discovered large quantities of materials from distant sources at the site, such as copper bells, macaws, Salado pottery (see Highlight 9.8), and more than 4 million shell ornaments. Much of this material, it was suggested, had been manufactured at the site by craft specialists and warehoused for export to other places, perhaps with Mesoamerican merchants (pochteca) being involved (Di Peso 1974). Information regarding gender roles, cosmology, ritual, and social hierarchies at the site may be present in ceramic figurines (VanPool and VanPool 2006; also see Munson 2000). Hundreds of ritualized burials of macaws and turkeys have also been found at the site, suggestive of religious behaviors. It may be that Mesoamerican religious cults were imported and that priests and shamans con-trolled the site (see VanPool and VanPool 2007).

A number of other sites have since discovered in the region that appear to be linked, at least by architecture and some trade materials, to Paquimé. This suggests that Paquimé was the center of a regional exchange system, much like the earlier Chacoan system (see above), but much larger. The system may have been mostly in northern Mexico but included parts of southern Arizona and New Mexico (see Schaafsma and Riley 1999). The exact nature of this

TABLE 9.5 A General Chronology of the Paquimé Region (following VanPool and VanPool 2007:Table 1.1)

Period	Dates	Traits
Espanoles	AD 1660 to 1821	Spanish entrada
Tardío	AD 1450 to 1660	major decrease in population, return to hunting and gathering
Medio	AD 1200 to 1450	1. initial construction of Paquimé about AD 1200 on top of a Viejo Period village, some 350 rooms 2. massive construction program between AD 1275 and 1350 at Paquimé (to about 1,500) with many public facilities, such as ball courts and platform mounds 3. between AD 1350 and 1450 large aggregate towns (Paquimé being the largest) surrounded by smaller communities, greater reliance on corn, more complex pottery decoration
Viejo	AD 600 to 1200	1. small, scattered pithouse settlements between AD 600 and 800, similar to the Mogollon to the north 2. increasing village size after AD 800 3. switch to aboveground structures after AD 975, increasing village size to small pueblos, some copper and considerable shell from the south, increasing complexity of mortuary practices
Plainware	AD 1 to 600	small pithouse settlement, plain pottery, inception of corn agriculture
Late Archaic (prepottery)	800 BC to AD 1	no pottery, generalized hunting and gathering

regional system, if it is real, is unclear, but it may have been religious in nature and not political (see Skibo et al. 2002).

Not all researchers view Paquimé as the center of a large regional system. It has been argued (see Whalen and Minnis 2000, 2001a, 2001b, 2001c) that the role of the site was less than first thought and that no huge regional center exerting political power across the Southwest existed. Instead, Whalen and Minnis (2001b) proposed that a series of smaller centers, each with elites controlling public architecture, controlled a prestige goods network system, forming a peer-polity system, as had been suggested for the Chacoan system (see above). Minnis et al. (2006) argued that no evidence of a large center with small satellite centers, such as seen in the Mississippian chiefdoms (see Chapter 12), has been found. Thus, Paquimé was seen as an "intermediate" society, with leaders of limited authority using prestige goods to form alliances and so gain power (Whalen and Minnis 2000:177–179). All the stockpiled materials, first thought to be warehoused for trade, were reinterpreted as prestige goods stockpiled for distribution by elites at the site (Whalen and Minnis 2001a:206). Further, Paquimé was seen as having developed from local antecedents, rather than the result of foreign intrusion (Whalen and Minnis 2003).

Others (see VanPool and VanPool 2007:17–18) have argued that there is no evidence of the existence of these other small centers and that Paquimé was indeed a major center controlling, at least to some extent, a system of wide-ranging trade across the Southwest. VanPool and Leonard (2002) argued that the stockpiles of shell beads, pottery, and other items, as well as the presence of standardized artifacts (such as metates) did support the idea of large-scale production and trade across the Southwest. The debate continues.

Lekson (1999) suggested that Paquimé was the latest of three centers of power in the Southwest. The first was Chaco, then Aztec (a center north of Chaco), with Paquimé being the latest and last. Most interestingly, each of these three "centers," hundreds of miles apart, align on a north-south axis (refer to Fig. 9.6). If this alignment is more than a coincidence, the nature of such a large, complex, and long-lasting system (perhaps over five hundred years) is largely unknown.

Paquimé was mostly abandoned by about AD 1450, but the reasons for this are unknown (perhaps disease). It has been speculated that the site was sacked by invaders, but there is little to suggest that a battle took place. Walker (2002) suggested that the site was not raided but ritually abandoned as the result of warfare elsewhere; that is, the houses of warriors killed in battle were ritually abandoned one by one and not reoccupied, eventually leading to the abandonment of so many rooms that the site itself became abandoned.

THE HOHOKAM

The Hohokam were farmers that occupied the Sonoran Desert in south-central Arizona (Fig. 9.4). Many of their settlements are known along the valleys of the Salt, Gila, and San Pedro rivers, although they also occupied some upland regions away from the rivers, including habitation sites and special-purpose sites, such as for hunting and gathering (e.g., Wells et al. 2004). The Hohokam are defined by large-scale canal irrigation agriculture, red-on-buff pottery, and monumental buildings, such as ball courts (Fig. 9.11) and platform mounds (Bayman 2001:257). The Hohokam were probably a multi-ethnic group that included a number of linguistic groups (e.g., Shaul and Hill 1998) and an amalgamation of nearby related groups that had adopted Hohokam traits, particularly agriculture, pottery, and presumably ritual.

FIGURE 9.11   The excavated west half of Ballcourt 1 at the Hohokam village of Snaketown (Plate VIII from Excavations at Snaketown, by Harold Gladwin, et al. 1938, © 1965 by The Arizona Board of Regents. Reprinted by permission of the University of Arizona Press).

TABLE 9.6 The Hohokam Sequence in the Sonoran Desert

Period	Dates	Settlements/Architecture	Subsistence	Other Traits
Postclassic	AD 1450 to 1540	small villages along rivers	agriculture	continued use of irrigation systems
Classic	AD 1150 to 1450	appearance of aboveground adobe structures, often in walled compounds	agriculture	major changes, possible Puebloan immigrants
Sedentary	AD 975 to 1150	more and larger settlements, increase in public spaces (plazas, ball courts, mounds)	expansion of agriculture	extensive use of etched shell, decorated slate palettes
Colonial	AD 750 to 975	major expansion of settlements across southern Arizona, increase in village size	major expansion of irrigation systems	ball courts and platform mounds, cotton becoming more important, macaws, craft specialization
Pioneer	AD 1 to 750	relatively small but permanent villages, pithouses	corn, addition of squash and beans, some irrigation	red-slipped pottery now common
Early Agricultural (Cienega Phase)	800 BC to AD 1	pithouses	some corn agriculture, some irrigation	some early pottery

The Hohokam are mostly known from excavations at relatively few major centers in the Salt and Gila valleys, although this is rapidly changing. The most famous Hohokam site, Snaketown, is on the Gila River near the modern city of Phoenix (the latter so named since it "rose from the ashes" of Snaketown). The Hohokam were first explored in detail in the 1930s (Gladwin et al. 1938) and later in the 1960s (Haury 1976), primarily by excavations at Snaketown. Since that time, considerable work on the Hohokam has been undertaken, largely due to development projects (e.g., Whittlesey et al. 1997; H. D. Wallace 2003). Important recent summaries of the Hohokam are available in Crown (1990), Bayman (2001), and Fish and Fish (2008).

The basic Hohokam chronology was developed from the work at Snaketown (Haury 1976) and is still widely used (see Table 9.6), although some (e.g., Bayman 2001) use a more general "Formative, Preclassic, Classic, and Postclassic" sequence. Haury believed that Mesoamerican groups had migrated into southern Arizona about AD 1 and "founded" the Hohokam; thus, the initial two periods of the Hohokam chronology were called "Pioneer" and "Colonial." A Mesoamerican origin is no longer generally accepted, as it is now known that the earliest (Pioneer) Hohokam were established before most of the Mesoamerican traits appeared. Early agricultural communities developed in northern Mexico (called Trincheras; see Fish et al. [2007] for a recent review) by about 1,200 BC (Gallaga and Newell 2004:7) with villages located on hilltops and evidence of warfare (Roney and Hard 2004). Early agricultural communities were also present in the Sonoran Desert by about 1,000 BC (Bayman 2001:265), and the Hohokam appear to have developed from this base. It is not yet clear precisely where in southern Arizona the "first" Hohokam lived, but it may have been the Tucson area (Bayman 2001:267; H. D. Wallace 2003).

The Hohokam had many settlements, some of which were large towns along the flood-plains of the major rivers in the region. These rivers generally flowed year-round and were rela-tively stable, allowing irrigation and sustained agricultural production. In some cases, such as along the Salt River near Phoenix, the Hohokam built large and extensive irrigation systems that resulted in considerable alteration of river habitats (Fish 2000). Some Hohokam settlements were at higher elevations close to conifer forests, where they obtained timber (Fish 2000:252).

As elsewhere in the Southwest, the Hohokam grew corn, beans, and cotton. With irriga-tion, the system was probably very productive. Crops were supplemented by a variety of wild foods, and most meat was from wild animals, including deer, mountain sheep, rabbits, rodents, and fish. The Hohokam also used the three-quarter grooved axe, a stereotypical "Southwestern" artifact.

A number of Mesoamerican traits were adopted by the Hohokam, including, ball courts, trough metates, platform mounds, macaws, acid-etched shells, turquoise mosaics, pyrite mirrors, and copper bells. This demonstrates an extensive trade in distant materials, but they appear to have been dispersed throughout the population rather than hoarded by elites. More than one hundred platform mounds are known, and it has been suggested that the mounds were elite resi-dences. A different view (Elson 1998) is that the mounds were not residential but were con-structed by competing descent groups for ceremonies revolving around the management of resources (e.g., water), ancestor worship, and the integration of immigrant groups.

Hohokam leadership appears to have been made up of hierarchically ranked groups, and the Hohokam could be viewed as a chiefdom-level society. There was considerable variability in sociopolitical forms from place to place, however, making classification difficult (Fish and Fish 2000:154). In fact, Hohokam leaders are difficult to detect in the archaeological record as there are few indications of individuals with extravagant wealth. It may be that the Hohokam developed under the Dual-Processual Theory (Feinman 2000), with both corporate entities and kinship net-works being important (Fish and Fish 2000:156).

Several models of Hohokam settlement and influence have been proposed (see discussion in Whittlesey 1997). The first was that the Hohokam migrated into the Phoenix area (the Pioneer Period), developed their distinctive culture, and then expanded from their core area to colonize similar locales (the Colonial Period), only to withdraw later to their core area (the Sedentary Period). The second, called the core-periphery model, suggested that Hohokam influences expanded from the core to other cultures on the Hohokam periphery (rather than a uniform Hohokam culture as envisioned by the first model). Dissatisfaction of both of these models resulted in the formation of a third, that of a Hohokam Interaction Sphere, or regional system. This latter model focused less on trying to identify Hohokam ethnicity and more on Hohokam interac-tion. In reality, each of these approaches (models) is useful in any exploration of the development and operation of Hohokam society. It is clear that there is no "single 'Hohokam culture' represented by a unified and coherent set of . . . traits" (Whittlesey 1997:619) and that what we know as "Hohokam" is highly variable throughout space and time. Still, while Hohokam exhibits consider-able internal diversity, it remains distinct from other cultural adaptations in the Southwest.

The Early Agricultural Hohokam (Cienega Phase) (ca. 800 BC to AD 1)

Archaic hunters and gatherers in the Tucson basin appear to have begun adopting corn agricul-ture by about 1500 BC (Whittlesey and Ciolek-Torrello 1996). At this time, agriculture was not very important, so that any crop failure would not have been a disaster. Dependence on agricul-ture appears to have increased gradually, and by AD 200 corn was the dominant resource (Diehl 2005). People lived in small villages, often in floodplains, and there is evidence for increasing sedentism, although this may have been relatively minor until after about AD 750 (R. M. Dean 2005). This time, called Early Agricultural (following Bayman 2001), is the transition from the Archaic to the Formative. The discovery of some irrigation facilities from this period links the Cienega Period groups in the Tucson area to the Hohokam.

The Pioneer Period (AD 1 to 750)

By about AD 1, the Hohokam had become fairly dependent on farming and had occupied many of the "good" agricultural localities along the Salt and Gila rivers. Most Hohokam towns were relatively small but were occupied year-round. Beans and squash were added as crops. The Hohokam "core" areas were near modern Phoenix and Tucson, and Snaketown was founded during this time. Most of the agricultural fields were located in the river floodplains, and floodwater irrigation was generally employed.

Complex canal irrigation appears to date from about AD 450 (see Fish and Fish 1994:88; H. D. Wallace 2003). The presence of a complex and permanent irrigation system with facilities that required maintenance suggests that the sociopolitical system was sufficiently complex to permit the mobilization and control of substantial labor.

The Colonial Period (AD 750 to 975)

The success and productivity of irrigated agriculture likely led to an increase in Hohokam population, an increase in village size, and the establishment of new villages or towns. The Hohokam expanded into new areas, including areas away from rivers, and nearby groups appear to have been incorporated into the Hohokam tradition. A possible road system emanating from Snaketown has also been discovered (Motsinger 1998).

By the beginning of the Colonial Period (ca. AD 750), the Hohokam had adopted a number of Mesoamerican traits, including ball courts; trash mounds; cremation rituals including the use of palettes and figurines; and the use of macaws. Hohokam material culture also changed, and a number of items appear to have been manufactured in large numbers, such as jewelry of marine shells and turquoise and highly decorated slate palettes, suggestive of craft specialization. In addition, pottery improved and the designs became more complex. The apparent sudden adoption of this trait complex led Wallace et al. (1995) to suggest that it marked the beginning of a new religious movement or cult.

After about AD 800, irrigation projects expanded in both size and scope, and an extensive canal system was constructed along the Salt River near Phoenix (Fig. 9.12). These canals began upriver from the fields, and water was moved by gravity through a system of large canals to smaller canals to individual fields. The larger canals were perhaps sixty feet in diameter. Gates were constructed at strategic points along the canals so that water could be moved in different directions as needed. Many of the canals were clay lined to reduce seepage. This extensive canal system required enormous labor to construct, a great deal of labor to maintain, and managers to decide how much water went where. It has been estimated that the Hohokam eventually constructed some six hundred miles of canals, one of the largest construction projects in ancient North America.

The Sedentary Period (AD 975 to 1150)

The time after about AD 975 was one of above average rainfall in the mountains that fed the major rivers in the Hohokam region, increasing average river flow and water available for irrigation. The population grew and the number and size of settlements increased to their greatest extent. Many of the towns were permanently occupied, and the people were "sedentary" (hence

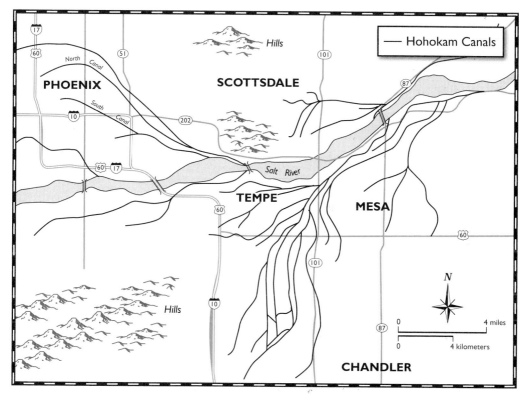

FIGURE 9.12 Hohokam irrigation canals along the Salt River just east of the city of Phoenix (adapted from Cordell 1997: Fig. 9.4; used with permission of Left Coast Press).

the period name). Small settlements located in upland settings provided agricultural products to larger villages on the floodplains (Roth 2000).

Platform mounds were formalized and purposefully constructed for the first time. They were generally circular with flat tops, and some were surrounded by wooden palisades, perhaps to isolate them from the general population. There was also a dramatic increase in the number of ball courts in the core Hohokam area, to as many as 225, and it has been suggested that ball-court games served as focal points for large markets (Abbott et al. 2007). In outlying Hohokam areas, ball courts were abandoned. Some towns had central plazas, and the amount of public/religious space (like plazas and platform mounds) increased. Pottery was mass produced, including large jars for the storage of agricultural surpluses, by specialists, perhaps part of a marketplace system (Abbott 2009). Copper bells were imported after AD 1000.

The Classic Period (AD 1150 to 1450)

After the Sedentary Period, a number of changes occurred. Some view the Hohokam as "broken down" at the end of the Sedentary Period and reorganizing during the Classic Period, but it is not clear to what extent this happened. A system of large central towns and smaller peripheral villages was established, and major changes in pottery types and designs occurred. Rainfall patterns changed, perhaps becoming more erratic and unpredictable (Nials et al. 1989), and it seems clear that at least some western Pueblo traits were adopted by the Hohokam. In some places, aboveground adobe structures appeared, often in walled compounds, and some large, pueblo-like, multistory Great

Houses (such as the Casa Grande site near Phoenix) were constructed. After AD 1300, Puebloan people from the north moved into the Hohokam area, undoubtedly straining an already stressed system.

Most ball-court construction ceased, and platform mounds became more important, changing from round to rectangular and surrounded by adobe walls rather than wooden ones. There is some evidence to suggest that people (elites?) began to live on top of the mounds. The dead were either buried or cremated (Mitchell and Brunson-Hadley 2001), suggesting that there was a cultural difference between groups (poor and rich?), and distinct cemeteries have been associated with specific settlement compounds. Little evidence of "chiefs" has been found, and it seems that the political system was controlled by "powerful religious leaders and wealthy lineages" (Mitchell and Brunson-Hadley 2001:63).

The Hohokam virtually disappeared by AD 1450. What happened to them? The influx of Puebloan people after AD 1300 may have stressed the economy to the point of collapse. Indeed, Rebecca Dean (2007) argued that demographic and resource stresses (loss of game animals) can be seen in the major centers along the Salt and Gila rivers prior to the "collapse." However, Hill et al. (2004) argued that the Hohokam suffered from a general population decline beginning in the late AD 1200s and that there was not a sudden collapse. Perhaps the collapse was a social, and not population, issue.

The current prevailing view of the Hohokam demise is environmental. Changes in rainfall may have caused a variety of major problems with the irrigation system (Nials et al. 1989), causing the agricultural system to fail. Major floods, such as those documented for the AD 1380s, could have overwhelmed and destroyed canals, and downcutting of the riverbed could have left the canals above the water (Graybill 1989; Nials et al. 1989; Graybill et al. 2006). There is evidence that many canals were damaged and repaired repeatedly and that the canal entrances at the rivers were moved upstream as downcutting occurred. Alternatively, Ingram (2008) argued that Hohokam populations actually increased during the periods of flooding and streamflow variation, suggesting that these events may have actually been beneficial. It is also possible that a buildup of salt from the irrigation water may have contaminated the soil to the point that agricultural productivity dropped dramatically (Reid and Whittlesey 1997:108). Whatever the specifics, it appears that there were too many people and too few resources to sustain the system.

The Postclassic Period (AD 1450 to 1540) and Beyond

By AD 1450, the Hohokam essentially disappeared from the archaeological record, although it appears that a few people endured, as evidenced by the presence of a few fortified sites. However, when the Spanish arrived in the region in AD 1540, it was occupied by the O'odham (the Papago and Upper Pima). The O'odham still live in the region today and continue to use the irrigation system built by the Hohokam centuries earlier (Ravesloot 2008). It is commonly believed that the O'odham are the descendants of the Hohokam, although this is not fully demonstrated.

HIGHLIGHT 9.8

THE SALADO ENIGMA

In 1930, a new archaeological entity was identified along the Salt River east of Phoenix. This entity, known as the Salado, was defined as possessing a unique combination of traits, including distinctive black-and-white-on-red polychrome pottery (Gladwin and Gladwin 1930). Confusing matters is the fact that many Salado traits have also been traced to other surrounding groups, such as Pueblo domestic architecture (but no kivas), Hohokam platform mounds and irrigation (but no ball courts), and other influences attributed to the Mogollon (e.g., J. S. Dean 2000b:4). Salado is now known to extend over an area of central Arizona to western New Mexico and is thought to date between about AD 1250 and 1450.

Researchers have postulated that the Salado may have been Puebloan refugees from the north who moved south into the eastern Hohokam area (e.g., J. S. Dean 2000b). Others have argued that the Salado were a branch of Hohokam, while others have considered the Salado as an assortment of Ancestral Puebloans, Mogollon, and Hohokam that somehow combined and formed a new culture.

Beginning about AD 1250, people all across the Southwest were moving, some to escape the drought in the Colorado Plateau, some to avoid the refugees escaping the drought, and some to exploit new opportunities. It is at about this time that the Salado "appeared." Thus, the idea that the Salado constituted a new and distinctive culture developing from a multi-ethnic base seems reasonable. Following the same general pattern seen across much of the Southwest, the Salado abandoned many of their towns after about AD 1350, occupying just a few very large pueblos. In addition, some evidence of raiding and violence has been observed at some sites. For reasons still unknown, the region was abandoned after about AD 1450, but the abandonment occurred immediately after a period of disastrous floods and more drought.

So, who were the Salado? The short answer is that, even after decades of work, we still do not know (J. S. Dean 2000b:8). It is possible that they may be a specific culture, or an enclave of an ethnic unit within a larger culture. It may also be that Salado is just a pottery style and not an actual "culture" (Lekson 2002b:68). Given that much of the Salado-style pottery is found in mortuary contexts, it may merely be a reflection of a religious ideology (e.g., Crown 1994), perhaps the Southwestern Cult, characterized by redware pottery that rapidly spread across the Southwest (see Kantner 2004:228–229). People bearing Salado pottery moved into areas unoccupied by others, however, suggesting that at least some migrations took place. Interestingly, a great deal of Salado pottery has been found at Paquimé in northern Mexico (see Highlight 9.7), but instead of being in mortuary contexts, this pottery appears to have been warehoused for shipment elsewhere, to places and peoples unknown.

THE PATAYAN

Patayan is a name that encompasses the agricultural groups living along the Colorado and Gila rivers of the far western Southwest. They also occupied, or at least visited regularly, much of western Arizona and portions of the eastern Mojave Desert in California. These groups developed out of the Western Archaic (see above) and belonged to the Yuman linguistic grouping. The name Yuman was originally proposed (Rogers 1945) for this pattern, later changed to Hakataya (see A. H. Schroeder 1957, 1979), and then to Patayan.

Both upland and lowland expressions of Patayan have been designated, but very little is known about the Upland Patayan. The Lowland Patayan pattern (see Table 9.7) is better known, where agriculture and well-made pottery, known as Lower Colorado River Buff ware, was present. It seems possible that the Upland Patayan was the hunting-and-gathering aspect of the Patayan, with the Lowland Patayan being the agricultural expression.

Lowland Patayan includes a prepottery phase (Rogers 1945:170; also see Waters 1982) and three pottery (Patayan I, II, and III) phases (Rogers 1945:Table 1. The prepottery Patayan could easily be classified as late Western Archaic, as no agriculture was present until after about AD 700.

TABLE 9.7 The Lowland Patayan Sequence in the Western Southwest

Periods	Dates	Subsistence	Other Traits	Comments
III	AD 1500 to 1900	primarily agriculture and fishing, with gathering and some hunting	large settled groups along the Colorado River	historic groups after contact
II	AD 1000 to 1500	primarily agriculture and fishing, with gathering and some hunting	new pottery forms, including stucco ware	archaeological expressions of the historic groups
I	AD 700 to 1000	beginnings of agriculture, fishing and some hunting and gathering	appearance of redware pottery, settlements along the rivers	archaeological cultures
prepottery	before AD 700	hunting and gathering	no pottery	archaeological cultures

By the beginning of Patayan I (ca. AD 700 to 1000), however, corn and pottery diffused from the east and some farming of the river floodplains began. Hunting and gathering remained important, and fishing became important (there are many large fish in the Colorado River; see McGinnis 1984). Populations and settlements were small and moved around to exploit various resources, mostly along the rivers but including the uplands (e.g., for pine nuts) as well.

By AD 1000 (Patayan II, ca. AD 1000 to 1500), farming had become central, although hunting, gathering, and fishing remained important. Populations were larger, and large permanent villages were established along the rivers. When Lake Cahuilla formed in the Imperial Valley of California to the west about AD 1200 (see Chapter 7), groups of Patayan II people likely moved west, perhaps returning when the lake dried up about AD 1500. Patayan II peoples were great traders, well known for their travels from the California coast in the west to Hohokam territory in the east, and it seems likely that they interacted with the Hohokam in the Gila Bend region (Doyel 2008:241).

Patayan III (AD 1500 to 1900) is the time after contact. When first contacted by Europeans, the various ethnographic Yuman groups living along the Colorado and Gila rivers had large populations, large settlements, extensive trade networks, and fairly complex sociopolitical organizations and were involved in considerable warfare. The antiquity of this latter trait is unknown.

NATIVE SOUTHWESTERN CULTURES AT CONTACT

About AD 1,500, dramatic changes occurred all across the Southwest. New peoples (the Numic, see Chapter 8) pushed south from the Great Basin and occupied areas abandoned by the Ancestral Puebloans. At the same time, Athapaskan groups (the Navajo and Apache) moved into the eastern Southwest and occupied large regions that had been abandoned by the Puebloans and the Mogollon. Finally, the Spanish moved into the Southwest from the south and subjugated the Pueblos along the Rio Grande. Groups in the western Southwest were not impacted in any major way by these developments. The result of these migrations and incursions was a very different Southwest at contact than was seen just a century before.

By the time the Spanish arrived in AD 1540, Puebloan peoples had coalesced into a relatively few Pueblos, generally divided into western (desert) and eastern (along the Rio Grande) groups. They suffered greatly at the hands of the Spanish, Mexicans, and Americans (see Spicer

1962) but have been remarkably resilient in the face of Western culture and pressures to assimilate. The Pueblo population has increased in the last one hundred years, and in 1990 there were some 55,000 Pueblo people (Reddy 1995:Table 120). Economic development, health services, and education have improved over the last few decades but still lag behind those available to their white neighbors.

Virtually all of the Pueblos have reservations, with those for the Western Pueblos being established fairly early. The federal government did not recognize most of the Eastern Pueblos as formal tribes until the 1920s, meaning that many Pueblo lands were taken by whites before they were protected. As a result, the reservations of the eastern groups are generally smaller. Taos Pueblo did not settle their claims until 1970, when they obtained a 48,000-acre reservation.

Most Pueblo people continue to work as farmers, but increasing numbers have sought their living from wage labor, often away from the reservation. The production of arts and crafts for the tourist and collector markets is big business, and many individual Indians are engaged in this endeavor. Tourism is considerable, and many of the Pueblos receive large numbers of visitors each year. Since the Indians are still living in the places being visited, access is restricted in some areas, and some pueblos are closed to the public for certain ceremonies. Nevertheless, visitors are welcome if they respect the Indians and their beliefs. Some of the major tourist destinations include Taos, Acoma, Hopi, and Zuni. Several groups in the Rio Grande Valley have built casinos to take advantage of the tourist trade.

The majority of non-Pueblo groups has survived into contemporary times, although several were largely destroyed by disease and conquest. In the United States, most groups were placed on reservations, with the Navajo reservation eventually becoming the largest in the country. Most of the Apache groups received reservations. The Havasupai still live on the Colorado River at the bottom of the Grand Canyon. Many of the groups along the Lower Colorado River were placed on a single reservation on the river and organized themselves into a single entity, the Colorado River Indian Tribes (CRIT). Virtually all of these groups continue to suffer from poverty and lack of opportunity, although conditions on the various reservations are improving. Most of the groups are becoming more self-sufficient, and management of their own affairs is increasing.

The O'odham (the Pima and Papago) live in the southern Sonoran Desert and may be the descendants of the Hohokam. The Akimel O'odham, "River People" (Upper Pima), live along the western Gila River and practice agriculture, while the Lower Pima live in northern Mexico. The Tóhono O'odham, "Desert People" (Papago), rely more on hunting and gathering.

In northern Mexico, most native groups still live in their traditional homelands but not on reservations. Thus, they are largely unprotected against encroaching non-Indians, and much of their native culture is gradually being assimilated into the larger Mexican culture. The vast majority of these people lives as subsistence farmers, with few opportunities, little education, and poor health care.

Further Reading

There is a vast literature on the archaeology of the Southwest, much of which is relatively technical. Several good recent general summaries of Southwestern prehistory are available, including Cordell (1994, 1997), S. Plog (1997), Reid and Whittlesey (1997), and Kantner (2004). A summary of the prehistory of the southern portion of the Southwest was provided by Phillips (1989). Given the popularity of archaeology in the Southwest, monographs and site reports are published by many outlets, with the University of Arizona producing regular contributions. Most journals publish the results of Southwestern research, but *Kiva* and *Southwestern Lore* specialize in the Southwest.

CHAPTER 10

Following Bison
The Great Plains

People have been hunting large animals on the Plains for at least 12,000 years. It is the place of gigantic herds of bison, of some of the earliest Paleoindian sites, and of the majestic Indian mounted on his horse, so well known around the world. While most people view the Plains as the place where highly mobile people hunted bison from horseback, that specific adaptation is very recent: for most of prehistory, people hunted bison on foot. After 2,000 years ago, some Plains groups adopted corn agriculture.

GEOGRAPHY AND ENVIRONMENT

The Great Plains consists of immense grassland spread across the heartland of North America, extending from southern Canada for about 1,500 miles to southern Texas, and from the eastern slope of the Rocky Mountains for about 1,000 miles east to the Mississippi River Valley (Fig. 10.1). Due to the rainshadow effect of the Rocky Mountains, there is relatively little water on the Plains; water and trees are found only in the river valleys that run east from the Rockies to eventually join with the Mississippi River. These rivers dissect the Plains into a myriad of separate longitudinal geographic entities, each bounded by rivers to the north and south.

The western portion of the Plains is a vast, generally flat area of grassland (short grasses with shallow roots) with little surface water and few trees, often called the High Plains (it was called the "Great American Desert" by American settlers in the early 1800s). It has been estimated that some 60 million bison lived on the High Plains in 1800, plus large numbers of pronghorn antelope. This region was inhabited by mobile hunter-gatherers.

The eastern part of the Plains consists of a number of widely spaced, broad valleys of the eastern-flowing rivers. This region, generally called the Prairies, is relatively well-watered and wooded and contains tall grasses with deep roots. Fewer bison lived on the Prairies, and after about 2,000 BP, it was inhabited by settled agriculturalists who also hunted bison. Some researchers have defined the Prairies as a separate culture area from the Plains, but the people of

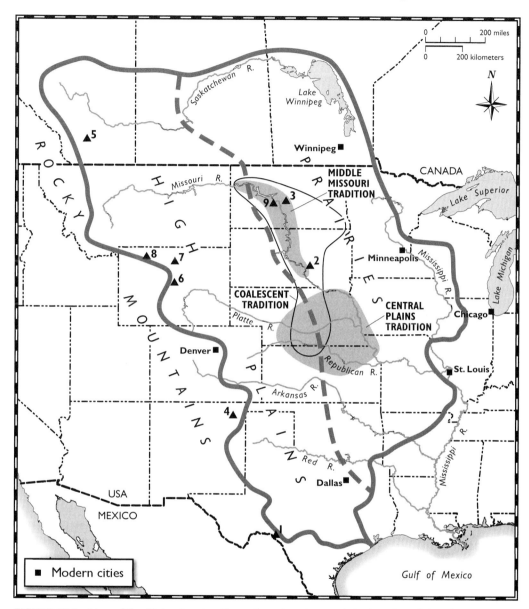

FIGURE 10.1 Map of the Plains showing the major subregions and the location of sites discussed in the text: 1) Bonfire Shelter; 2) Crow Creek; 3) Double Ditch; 4) Folsom; 5) Head-Smashed-In; 6) Helen Lookingbill; 7) Medicine Lodge Creek; 8) Mummy Cave; 9) Sakakawea.

both regions shared a common tradition of bison hunting, horse utilization, and warfare (see Bamforth 1994).

The climate of the Plains is quite variable, with much colder winters in the north and hotter summers in the south. Rainfall is also variable, ranging from less than eight to twenty inches a year, and it is very windy at times. There is considerable snow on the High Plains, especially in the north. Native agriculture was dependent on two critical environmental variables: at least eight inches of rain and a minimum of one hundred frost-free days. Corn could not be grown unless these two conditions were met.

A BRIEF HISTORY OF RESEARCH

Although antiquities had been noted on the Plains for centuries, professional investigations began in about 1900 with work sponsored by museums and similar institutions (Wedel and Krause 2001; also see Krause 1998). Excavations were undertaken at a variety of sites all across the Plains, and a number of state historical societies and professional organizations were formed during this time. By the 1930s, several initial syntheses of Plains prehistory had been produced (e.g., Strong 1935; Wedel 1936), setting the stage for future investigations. One of the important results of the work on the Plains was the development of a method for classifying archaeological remains, called the Midwestern Taxonomic System (McKern 1939; also see Wedel 1940). This system was developed and adopted by scholars conducting research on the Plains and later over much of North America. Further, the direct connection between living native peoples and their archaeological remains on the Plains led to the development of the direct historical approach (e.g., Wedel 1938), a method widely employed throughout archaeology.

The origin of people in North America has always been an important research topic, but the discovery of Paleoindian materials at Folsom, New Mexico, in 1928 (see Chapter 3) opened the door for Paleoindian research on the Plains. In the last eighty years, large numbers of Paleoindian sites have been discovered on the Plains.

Between the 1930s and 1960s, the federal government became involved in Plains archaeology in several ways. First, funding made available through the Works Progress Administration (WPA) resulted in a great deal of work being done. Second, the government constructed a series of large dams along the eastern-flowing rivers on the Plains after World War II. The archaeological work associated with the construction of these dams, called the River Basin Surveys, was primarily conducted by the Smithsonian Institution. As a result of this and other projects, the Midwestern Taxonomic System classification for the northern Plains was replaced with three major traditions—Central Plains, Middle Missouri, and Coalescent (Lehmer 1954, 1971)—a system that is still in use, although it has been expanded and modified over the years. The cultural classifications for the central and southern Plains are less developed (e.g., Wedel and Krause 2001:18).

With the advent of "processual archaeology" in the 1960s, archaeologists became less interested in culture history and more interested in how people and cultures adapted to the changing Plains environments, particularly during the Pleistocene/Holocene transition and the Altithermal. However, culture history and classificatory issues continue to dominate Plains research, perhaps to the detriment of other research approaches (e.g., Mitchell 2006).

MAJOR THEMES IN PLAINS PREHISTORY

Many of the Paleoindian sites known in North America are located on the Plains, signifying the beginnings of a hunting tradition that has lasted more than 12,000 years. This provides a natural laboratory for the investigation of hunting adaptations, which can change due to environmental fluctuations, differences in game animals (e.g., hunting mammoths versus bison), the technology associated with game procurement (see Frison 1991; Kornfeld et al. 2009), and the other aspects of cultural systems that are focused on hunting.

After about 2,000 years ago, agriculture was adopted by some groups on the Plains. It is not clear why or how this happened, but it did have profound impacts on the cultures in the region. Understanding the development of larger scale societies whose economies were based on a combination of farming and hunting is an important issue that has ramifications well beyond the Plains. An understanding of the development of the various traditions within the Plains village pattern is also of great interest.

While indigenous developments on the Plains are of great interest, a number of outside influences have also attracted considerable research attention. Eastern Woodland groups influenced the eastern Plains, and it is possible that some migrations into the Plains did occur, possibly even by Hopewell groups (see Chapter 11). Later, Athapaskan groups entered the western Plains from the north and moved south (e.g., Ives 2003), with some of these groups staying on the Plains (e.g., the Plains Apache) while others entered the Southwest. Great Basin Shoshoneans (the Numic; see Chapter 8) also came onto the Plains late in time. In addition, the adoption of the horse enhanced bison hunting to such a degree that settled agricultural peoples from a number of areas entered the Plains to become bison hunters, eventually becoming some of the most famous Plains groups known in history. The processes of such major cultural changes are of vital research interest. Finally, Plains archaeology has always been at the forefront of archaeological theory regarding the taxonomy of archaeological units. This remains an issue on the Plains, perhaps too much so.

The division of the Plains culture area into the High Plains and Prairies slightly confuses a presentation of its basic prehistory (see Wedel 1961; Frison 1991; Kornfeld et al. 2009). The discussion of the Paleoindian and Archaic periods includes the entire Plains, while the treatment of the Formative, after about 2,000 BP when corn agriculture was adopted, is limited to the Prairies. A very basic chronological sequence for the Plains is provided in Table 10.1.

THE PALEOINDIAN PERIOD

A substantial Paleoindian record is contained within the Plains, as was discussed in Chapter 3. Clovis and Folsom materials are known at various locations, and evidence of many regionally specific Paleoindian complexes has been documented across the Plains, primarily the High Plains, where bison were more numerous. The Paleoindian Period on the southern High Plains was discussed by Holliday (1997) and the northern High Plains was reported by Frison (1991; also see Hofman and Graham 1998; Kornfeld et al. 2009).

Clovis hunters focused on mammoths, while later Paleoindians exploited bison. Grassland became established on the Plains by at least 12,000 years ago, habitat ideal for the bison. By about 8,500 BP, the grasslands were fully developed and bison had reached their modern geographic distribution. The earliest bison species on the Plains was *Bison antiquus*, a relatively large animal. Sometime between 6,000 and 5,000 BP, *B. antiquus* was replaced by the smaller (and current species) *B. bison bison* (McDonald 1981:92–93), perhaps in response to the Altithermal.

Post-Clovis Paleoindians focused on the exploitation of bison and other large game, including horses (which then became extinct in North America only to be reintroduced by the Spanish), camelids, peccaries, deer, pronghorn antelope, and a variety of small mammals (see Hofman and Graham 1998:118–119). Most Paleoindian bison kills involved a relatively small number of animals, perhaps due to the comparatively small size of bison herds at the time. Nevertheless, pedestrian bison hunting became the primary economic focus of all post-Clovis Paleoindians. Other aspects of Paleoindian subsistence are poorly known.

A variety of methods was employed to obtain bison (see Frison 1991; Kornfeld et al. 2009). These included driving the animals into "pounds," confined places such as an arroyo or corral,

TABLE 10.1 A General Chronological Sequence for the Plains

Date (BP)	Central and Southern High Plains	Northern High Plains	Prairies	General Climate
100	Protohistoric		Plains Historic	conditions similar to today
	Late Prehistoric	Late Prehistoric	Late Plains Village	
			Early Plains Village	
1,000	Middle Prehistoric		Plains Woodland	cooler and wetter
2,000	A R C H A I C		Late Archaic	warmer and drier
3,000			Middle Archaic	conditions similar to today
4,000				
5,000	Late Mobile Foraging			very warm and dry
6,000		Early Archaic		becoming warmer and drier than today
7,000				
8,000	Early Mobile Foraging			
9,000		Paleoindian		glacial conditions
to 10,000	Paleoindian			

where the bison would become trapped and could be killed and butchered (refer to Fig. 3.5). Bison could also be stampeded off a cliff (called a "jump"), where they were killed by the fall or by hunters at the base of the cliff and then butchered (Fig. 10.2). Bison may have been driven into pounds and jumps using drive lines, fire, and/or dogs. Finally, bison could be taken by individual hunters by ambush or by using disguises of juvenile bison.

THE ARCHAIC

There are few data regarding the Archaic on the Plains, sometimes called the Plains Hunting and Gathering Tradition. This tradition is characterized by small, mobile populations, people who were focused on bison hunting but who also used a variety of other resources. It seems likely that these groups split into smaller groups and came back together into larger groups (fission/fusion) as hunting dictated (Bamforth 1988). Housepits are known throughout the Archaic, often containing storage pits and fire hearths suggestive of winter habitation. This implies that Archaic groups occupied the Plains on a permanent basis.

FIGURE 10.2 Artist conception of hunters driving bison off a cliff. (*Source:* Denver Museum of Nature and Science.)

Archaic groups also had dogs, important animals that served as labor by (presumably) pulling small travois, or sled (Fig. 10.3), and helping to drive game. Dogs were also an emergency food resource, camp protection (they bark at intruding people or animals), and camp cleaners who would eat the garbage. However, dogs needed to be fed, and since they generally ate what people ate, they were "expensive" to keep.

FIGURE 10.3 Indians on the Plains using a horse-drawn travois in the late 1800s. A smaller version of the travois would have been pulled by dogs before 1700 (courtesy of the Library of Congress).

The Northern High Plains

The northern High Plains lie north of Nebraska and include the Canadian Plains (see Wright 1995). The Archaic record of this region is better known than the central or southern High Plains. Two important sites in Wyoming, Mummy Cave and Medicine Lodge Creek, were occupied throughout the entire Holocene and provide an excellent background to understand the prehistory of the region. Mummy Cave (Wedel et al. 1968; Husted and Edgar 2002), excavated between 1963 and 1966, contained thirty-eight cultural levels, was well dated from 9,000 to 400 BP, and demonstrated a complete sequence of projectile-point types through time. Several other sites also contained complete Archaic records, including the Medicine Lodge Creek site in Wyoming with sixty cultural levels, dating from 10,000 years ago (see Frison 1991:69–70, 1998; Frison and Walker 2007), and the Helen Lookingbill site in Montana, dating from 10,400 BP (Kornfeld et al. 2001). A number of cultural complexes have been identified for the northern Plains Archaic but can generally be divided into early, middle, late, and prehistoric periods. A simplified culture history for the northern High Plains Archaic is presented in Table 10.2.

EARLY ARCHAIC (CA. 9,000 TO 6,000 BP)   After about 10,000 years ago, the Plains began to become warmer and drier, at the beginning of the Altithermal (sometimes called the Atlantic on the Plains). It became hot and dry, with periods of severe drought (Frison 1998:160). As it became increasingly warmer and drier, there were fewer bison in constricted areas, and the people who were so heavily dependent on bison must have had a difficult time. Due to these stresses, it seems possible that portions of the Plains may have been largely abandoned between about 6,000 and

TABLE 10.2 A Highly Simplified Culture History* for the Northern High Plains Archaic

Period	Complex	Approximate Dates	Characteristics
Late Prehistoric	various	1,200 to 300	archaeological expressions of ethnographic groups
	Avonlea	1,800 to 1,000	bow and arrow, small side-notched point, pottery, protohistoric groups late in time
Late Archaic	Besant	2,000 to 1,500	large side-notched points, pottery, burial mounds, Woodland influences but no agriculture
	Pelican Lake	3,500 to 1,650	corner-notched points, secondary bundle burials
Middle Archaic	McKean	4,700 to 2,700	indented base and shouldered points, burials in house floors with no ochre and occasional cremations, greater use of plants, tepee foundations
	Oxbow	5,000 to 3,000	different large side-notched points, cemeteries with the use of red ochre, evidence for long-distance trade
Early Archaic	Mummy Cave	9,000 to 6,000	large side-notched points, small mobile populations with large territories, pithouses appear late

*Although listed sequentially here, some of these complexes overlap in both space and time, and there is not necessarily a "neat" progression from one to another.

5,000 BP (e.g., Wedel 1986:72). Nevertheless, bison hunting remained the primary focus, and bison jumps (see Highlight 10.1) were commonly used. Interestingly, there are relatively few faunal remains found at early Archaic sites, with most being bison, although many other animals have been identified. The presence of manos and metates during this time indicate some plant usage.

HIGHLIGHT 10.1

HEAD-SMASHED-IN BISON JUMP SITE

While a number of bison jumps are known across the Plains, none are as well preserved or as well documented as the jump at Head-Smashed-In in Alberta, Canada. This site, used over the last 5,800 years (and possibly earlier), consists of a number of facilities for gathering, driving, dispatching, and processing bison, as well as areas where people lived and distributed themselves over a landscape covering many square miles (see Reeves 1978; Brink 2008). The Head-Smashed-In site represents the best example of a bison jump in North America and has been designated as a UNESCO World Heritage site. A museum at the site tells the story (visit the Web site at www.Head-Smashed-In.com).

The heart of the site is a sheer cliff that runs some one thousand feet and is today some thirty feet high (Fig. 10.4). At the bottom of the cliff are processing areas with archaeological deposits containing bison remains and butchering tools more than thirty feet thick. At the

FIGURE 10.4 The cliff at the Head-Smashed-In bison jump site in Alberta, Canada. Bison would be driven off the cliff, then killed and butchered at the base of the cliff. (*Source:* © Walter Bibikow/ DanitaDelimont.com.)

beginning of a hunt, bison would be slowly, gently, and loosely gathered up in a natural basin west and out of sight of the cliff. Once a sufficient number of bison were assembled, they would be driven toward the cliff, guided by drive lines constructed along strategic places to ensure that the bison went where the hunters wanted them to go (Brink and Rollans 1990). Finally, the bison would crest a small ridge just short of the cliff, where they were then stampeded downhill to, and over, the cliff. Many of the bison were killed by the fall, but some survived, only to be killed by waiting hunters. Some undoubtedly escaped, but in some cases as many as one hundred animals were killed at one time.

Along the base of the cliff were several large work areas, where the bison would be skinned and dismembered, with the flesh and bones being removed for processing. Some of the meat would be cooked for immediate consumption, but most was probably dried for storage. The bones would be smashed; the skulls to obtain the brains used in tanning skins and the leg bones to obtain the marrow (called "grease"). Pemmican was also produced. Interestingly, many of the skulls seem to be missing from the site, suggesting that they were taken for use in ceremonies and decoration, as was done in ethnographic times (Brink 2008:213–214).

Many other bison jumps and pounds are known on the Plains (see Speth 1983; Frison 1991). Another excellent example is Bonfire Shelter in Texas. This is the southernmost bison jump and is the earliest known, dating from 11,700 BP (see Dibble and Lorain 1968; Byerly et al. 2005).

The Mummy Lake Complex is perhaps the earliest Archaic complex in the region. It is defined by a change from lanceolate and stemmed points to side-notched forms (Dyck and Morlan 2001:115). Mummy Cave groups were bison hunters with small populations occupying large territories. Little else is known about these people. However, the processing of bison bone for the production of bone grease, commonly used in the production of pemmican, appears to date from this time, as evidenced from the presence of boiling pits, fire-cracked rock, and smashed bison bone. This indicates the storage of food, a trait that would permit more stable economic and social systems and increased population levels (Dyck and Morlan 2001:118; also see Reeves 1990:170).

The earliest pithouses may date from the later part of the Early Plains Archaic (Frison 1991:83–86; 2001:135; C. S. Smith 2003) but have not been found on the Canadian Plains. Some of these structures contain associated storage features, suggesting that they may have been occupied during the winter, although it is unclear whether they represent year-round occupation. In addition, the procurement and transport of tool stone was a major effort, requiring the movement of people across large distances, and is poorly understood for this period of time (Frison 1998:165).

THE MIDDLE ARCHAIC (CA. 5,000 TO 2,700 BP)   About 5,000 years ago, the climate abruptly became cooler and wetter. Grasslands expanded and the population and range of bison increased. Areas abandoned by people during the early Archaic were reoccupied, human populations increased, and there was an expansion in the use of foothill and mountain regions.

The Oxbow Complex (ca. 5,000 to 3,000 BP; also see Frison 1991:86; D. C. Green 2005) is poorly known but appears to be related to the earlier Mummy Cave Complex (a related type of side-notched projectile point), and bison was the primary resource. Camps are larger, suggesting an increase in the size of the social units. Oxbow is noteworthy for its mortuary practices, with primary interments covered in red ocher placed in cemeteries away from camps (Dyck and Morlan 2001:119). The presence of Gulf and Pacific coast shells is evidence of long-distance trade (Vehik and Baugh 1994).

The McKean Complex (ca. 4,700 to 2,700 BP) is slightly later than Oxbow and is a "hunting and gathering manifestation . . . distinguished by several projectile-point styles" (Frison

1998:163). McKean first appeared in the Yellowstone area and spread across the northern Plains (see Dyck and Morlan 2001:120). While some pithouses have been documented (Frison 1991:97–100), McKean groups also used rockshelters and caves, and large stone rings (perhaps tepee foundations) first appear. Bison remains are much more common than in earlier sites, and there is evidence of a diversified economy, including increased plant usage (millingstones and charred seeds from some sites) and the use of insects (e.g., Mormon crickets) as food (Frison 2001:138). McKean mortuary patterns included burials under house floors and occasional cremations (Walker 1984).

The origin of McKean is unclear. Some believe it is intrusive from the Great Basin, similar to the "Desert Culture" (see Chapter 8), but most scholars now think that it is a development from Early Archaic complexes in the northern Plains (e.g., Keyser 1986). As such, it is possible that McKean is a variant of the Oxbow Complex, with different mortuary patterns and no use of red ochre as was used in Oxbow burials (Dyck and Morlan 2001:120). McKean generally occupied the same area at the same basic time as Oxbow, but their relationship is unclear. While it is possible that McKean and Oxbow represent different aspects of the same cultural entity (e.g., summer and winter camps), the major difference in mortuary patterns suggests that the two complexes were separate cultural groups that lived "together" in the same region. Such a situation would be unusual and has interesting anthropological implications.

Stone circles appear in large numbers during the Middle Archaic. They range from three to seven meters in diameter and have been most often interpreted as tepee foundations (L. B. Davis 1983; also see Frison 1991:93–97). Medicine wheels, enigmatic stone structures that typically display a central cairn and concentric circles of stones, also appear (Fig. 10.5). The function of these

FIGURE 10.5 Oblique aerial of the Big Horn Medicine Wheel in northern Wyoming (courtesy of Roger M. Williams, U. S. Forest Service).

features is unknown, but some have suggested that they are related to memorials (see Mirau 1995), astronomical associations, or shamanistic activities.

THE LATE ARCHAIC (CA. 3,500 TO 1,500 BP)   Beginning about 3,500 years ago, the climate became warmer and drier once again, and portions of the Plains may have been abandoned during the early part of the Late Archaic (e.g., Wedel 1986:72). Projectile-point forms changed from side notched to corner notched. Conditions improved after about 2,000 BP, bison populations increased, and communal pedestrian bison hunting reached its peak about 1,500 BP.

The earliest known Late Archaic complex is Pelican Lake (ca. 3,500 to 1,650 BP), characterized by corner-notched points and intensive bison exploitation, including mass bison kills at jumps and the use of sophisticated log corral traps. While there was an overwhelming focus on bison, some other animals were taken as well, including shellfish and fish at some sites. Pelican Lake groups were small and highly mobile, used hide tepees, traded with Pacific and Gulf coast groups, and had variable mortuary patterns. These included some secondary bundle burials (suggestive of the technique of scaffold burials known late in time) with ochre and some primary interments.

The origin of the Pelican Lake Complex is a mystery, as it seems to have appeared "suddenly" across much of the northern Plains (Dyck and Morlan 2001:122). This suggests that Pelican Lake evolved from the Oxbow and McKean complexes of the Middle Archaic. Alternatively, it may represent a migration of peoples from the west. The fate of the Pelican Lake Complex remains unknown.

After about 2,000 BP, once environmental conditions on the Plains had improved, a new cultural complex, Besant, appeared along the eastern portion of the northern Plains (see Wright 1995:781–847). The Besant Complex (ca. 2,000 to 1,500) is defined by the appearance of a new projectile-point type (a large, side-notched form) and the appearance of pottery and burial mounds, illustrating considerable influence from the Woodland complexes in the east. Besant people were committed bison hunters with no evidence of agriculture and little suggestion of plant use. The mortuary pattern of burials in mounds, called the Sonota Burial Complex (see Johnson and Johnson 1998:220–221; Dyck and Morlan 2001:124–125), is very unusual. Tombs were constructed, and secondary burials covered with red ochre were placed in a pit within the tomb. The burials were accompanied by numerous grave goods that included marine shells, copper from the east, pottery, many utilitarian items, and the bones of various animals. Most interesting is the incorporation of complete bison skeletons and arrangements of bison skulls within the tomb. Some of the grave offerings are clearly Hopewell in character, although this pattern is limited to a relatively small portion of Besant territory. The mortuary pattern for the remainder of Besant is unknown, as is the fate of Besant.

THE LATE PREHISTORIC (CA. 1,800 TO 300 BP)   Bow-and-arrow technology first appeared on the far northern Plains about 1,800 BP and rapidly diffused south. The Avonlea Complex (ca. 1,800 to 1,000 BP) is the result of the incorporation of bow-and-arrow technology to bison hunting, and the adoption of small side-notched points for arrows is a major marker trait (Schlesier 1994; Johnson and Johnson 1998:221–222; Dyck and Morlan 2001:125–127). Communal bison hunting remained the focus, but there was an increased emphasis on plant gathering as seen in the presence of millingstones. Avonlea groups used pottery, some with Woodland influences, but a new form, the distinctive Intermountain Tradition pottery, was also present in some areas. The pottery of this time is often linked with Great Basin groups. Avonlea groups were mobile and used tepees. Their fate is uncertain, but it is generally suspected that some developed into the subsequent Old Woman Complex (Dyck and Morlan 2001:125).

Communal bison hunting reached its peak about 1,500 BP, and bison populations declined until about 800 BP. A number of regional variants of bison-hunting complexes developed under these circumstances, such as the Pehonan Complex (see Johnson and Johnson 1998:223–224). Of interest is the Old Woman Complex (ca. 1,000 to 300 BP), a bison-hunting group that incorporated small-scale agriculture into their economic system as a supplement (Dyck and Morlan 2001:127).

In the western portion of the northern Plains, Athapaskan groups from Canada began moving south (e.g., Ives 2003), ultimately entering the Southwest about 500 years ago. A bit later, about 400 years ago, the Northern Shoshone entered the northwestern Plains and expanded against the Blackfoot, who in turn pushed them back into the Great Basin (see Chapter 8). Beginning about 300 BP, the Comanche (a group of Northern Shoshone) moved onto the Plains, traveled south, and eventually settled in Texas.

The Central and Southern High Plains

The central and southern High Plains are not as well understood as the northern High Plains, and a different cultural chronology applies (Kay 1998; Vehik 2001; T. R. Hester 2005), but there was not a uniform cultural development (Kay 1998:193; Vehik 2001). Prior to about 5,000 BP, times were very difficult on the Plains, and some areas may have been abandoned for periods of time.

Kay (1998:194) identified five major subsistence strategies for the Archaic on the central and southern High Plains: (1) communal bison hunting, (2) use of hunting facilities (e.g., traps), (3) use of specialized cooking facilities for plants and animals, (4) a "mixed" economy focused on seasonally available resources, and (5) small-scale horticulture late in time.

EARLY MOBILE FORAGING (CA. 10,000 TO 7,000 BP)   As in the northern High Plains, the environment became warmer and drier after 10,000 BP on the central and southern High Plains. During this time, small groups of highly mobile bison hunters traversed the central and southern Plains, as well as the uplands in the eastern Rocky Mountains (Kay 1998:185). The diet was relatively broad and incorporated deer, fish, fowl, and numerous plant species. Little else is known about these people.

LATE MOBILE FORAGING (CA. 7,000 TO 5,000 BP)   During the later part of the Altithermal, the Plains were very dry, particularly on the southern Plains. The dry conditions affected grass growth, which would have impacted bison populations and influenced how many bison hunters there could be, and people would have had to spend more of their time locating animals.

Few sites of this time period are known, and some areas may have been abandoned, but it is also possible that some sites were destroyed by erosion due to the dry climate (see Meltzer 1999). Populations were probably very small and likely tethered to base camps (Vehik 2001:150). Some hand-dug wells dating from this period have been documented (Meltzer and Collins 1987), and it seems likely that, in addition to bison, smaller animals and plants were exploited.

MIDDLE PREHISTORIC (CA. 5,000 TO 1,100 BP)   As in the north, conditions improved after about 5,000 years ago, resulting in the expansion of grasslands and an increase in bison populations. McKean Complex materials from the north are present in the central Plains, and a number of temporally and regionally specific bison-hunting complexes developed across the region (see Vehik 2001).

Bison was the primary game animal, but other animals, such as deer and turtles, were also hunted. The presence of millingstones and rock-lined hearths indicate the processing of plant resources (e.g., acorns, walnuts, and hickory nuts), but plant use seems to have declined in some places after about 4,500 BP, perhaps reflecting the increasing reliance on bison. After about 3,000 BP, small quantities of corn seem to have been traded in from the Southwest, reflecting influences from the eastern Plains and some experimentation with agriculture.

The primary weapon was the atlatl, used with side- and corner-notched points, until bow-and-arrow technology was introduced about 1,500 BP, after which small side-notched points were used. Relatively little evidence of long-distance trade has been found (Vehik and Baugh 1994), but there was some exchange of marine shells and obsidian (from the north). Some pottery has been documented after about 2,000 BP, reflecting influences from the east and the Southwest.

Social groups appear to have been small and highly mobile, reflecting a lifestyle focus on bison. Beginning about 3,000 BP, however, small pithouse villages appeared in some areas, perhaps indicating the presence of quantities of predictable resources (Vehik 2001:154). A variety of mortuary customs are known, including primary and secondary inhumations and cremations. The presence of cemeteries suggests that some groups were tied to specific territories (Vehik 2001:153).

Groups on the central and southern Plains, particularly the latter, may have been related to intrusive Southwestern groups occupying the same broad region. The sparse evidence of conflict (Vehik 2001:154) appears to indicate that the Plains and Southwestern traditions may not have been particularly congenial.

LATE PREHISTORIC (CA. 1,100 TO 300 BP) By Late Prehistoric times (Schlesier 1994; Vehik 2001), the early experiments with agriculture resulted in the adoption of farming by some of the eastern groups, although agriculture became less important through time. Corn, and probably other cultigens, had reached the far northern Plains (Boyd et al. 2006) and were used on a small scale. Bison populations increased on the southern Plains after about 800 BP, and the hunting of bison became more important, as did the use of wild plants. Bison were supplemented by deer and pronghorn, the latter two being hunted exclusively in some places.

The decline in the importance of agriculture may be related to the increased availability of game, with people being too busy hunting to properly tend to fields. There was an increase in violence, as seen in fortifications and skeletal injuries (Vehik 2001:155), suggesting the possibility that this new mobility brought hostile people into contact with each other more often. On the other hand, trade increased, indicating more cordial relationships.

As populations of bison continued to increase, their importance intensified and many groups dropped the exploitation of other resources to pursue bison. Human populations increased and villages became larger and more numerous, leading to greater competition. By about 400 years ago, the Plains Apache (Athapaskans from the north; see above), Caddo (from the Southeast; see Chapter 12), and Oneota (from the Northeast; see Highlight 11.4) had also entered the Plains, further escalating competition. Thus, there was an increase in both trade and warfare.

The Protohistoric Period on the High Plains (300 to 100 BP)

The introduction of the horse onto the southern Plains by the Spanish after 360 BP and onto the northern Plains by the Northern Shoshone by about 300 BP profoundly changed High Plains cultures (Highlight 10.2). There was a major population movement onto Plains by groups who abandoned farming in favor of mounted hunting, such as the Cheyenne and many Sioux groups (Dakota, Lakota, Nakota, and Oglala). Thus, after 300 BP, the emblematic Plains Indians on horseback became the face of the Plains.

HIGHLIGHT 10.2

HORSES!

Plains Indians on horseback, the iconic image of North American Indians, is a very recent phenomenon, as horses were only acquired from Europeans after about 360 years ago. Ironically, horses first evolved in North America during the Pleistocene. They migrated into Asia across the Bering Land Bridge and subsequently became extinct in North America. Horses were eventually domesticated in the Old World and then reintroduced into North America by the Spanish, who brought them to the Southwest. There, horses were stolen from the Spanish by a number of native groups, including the Apache and Ute. The Apache began to spread horses onto the southern Plains by the mid-1600s. The Ute traded horses north to the Northern Shoshone, who introduced them onto the northern Plains beginning about 1690 (see Haines 1938; Secoy 1953; Ewers 1955; Holder 1970). First viewed as a pack and/or food animal (they were initially called "big dogs" or "spirit dogs"), the potential of the horse was rapidly recognized, and they soon became very highly desired. Although horses could be obtained through breeding and trade, they were most frequently acquired by raiding.

Horses brought about several major changes to general Plains culture, the most important being mobility. Prior to the horse, all travel was on foot, limiting the distance one could cover in a day. With horses, people could travel farther and faster, making both water and bison much more accessible. Thus, many more people could support themselves on the Plains as bison hunters. Before horses, essential materials (e.g., tepee poles and covers) were transported on travois pulled by dogs, which had to be fed meat. Horses ate grass and could pull larger travois (see Fig. 10.3) with considerably more goods, including food and larger tepees. Life as a bison hunter on the Plains became much easier.

Horses also radically changed the nature of Plains warfare. Horses had rapidly become a central aspect of Plains culture and were so important that they essentially became "currency," and the major goal of most warfare became the acquisition of horses. Raiding for horses rapidly evolved into a major activity, with great prestige awarded to those men who were successful. The more horses a man owned, the more prestige he had. The various pressures from groups moving onto the Plains and competing with each other for hunting territories and horses also increased Plains warfare.

With increased mobility and ease of hunting, the Plains suddenly became a very attractive region. Prairie groups adopted horses and expanded their territories to include the High Plains. Other groups that had been agriculturalists prior to the horse moved onto the High Plains and adopted a mobile hunting culture, partly to hunt bison and partly due to pressure from expanding American settlements to the east.

The Formative

Although corn was traded onto the Plains from the Southwest as early as 3,000 BP, active agriculture was not adopted on the Plains until about 2,000 years ago, influenced by developments in the Eastern Woodlands. Agriculture was mostly limited to the better watered portions of the eastern Plains, known as the Prairies. A basic chronology of the Plains Formative is presented in Table 10.3.

TABLE 10.3 The Formative on the Plains

Period	Dates (BP)	Characteristics
Plains Historic	300 to 100	addition of horses, bison and warfare more important
Late	700 to 300	fewer but larger villages, mostly unfortified, bison more important, warfare less important
Early	1,000 to 700	small to medium-sized fortified villages, diversified subsistence, but bison not primary
Plains Village	1,000 to 300	generally along eastern margins of Plains, permanent villages, subterranean earth lodges, both agriculture and hunting/gathering important
Plains Woodland	2,500 to 1,000	appearance of pottery and agriculture, diffusion of Eastern Woodland mortuary customs and some Hopewell populations, bow and arrow after ca. 1,500

Plains Woodland (2,500 to 1,000 BP)

To the east of the Plains, groups had begun to experiment with agriculture and produce pottery (see Chapters 11 and 12). By about 2,500 BP, influences from these Woodland cultures had started to spread west onto the Prairies (which were suitable for agriculture), and the bison hunters of that region adopted some of the eastern traits. Thus, the Plains Woodland developed, first by adopting pottery and later by adopting some agriculture while maintaining a hunting-and-gathering economy. Other influences included some architecture and burial mounds (A. E. Johnson 2001:159). Besant groups on the northern Plains (see above) had pottery and mounds but no agriculture.

The Plains Woodland can be divided into early, middle, and late periods (Johnson 2001:159; Logan 2006). **Early Plains Woodland** (ca. 2,500 to 2,000 BP) witnessed the adoption of pottery, and a number of regional cultural variants are recognized, primarily defined on pottery styles. **Middle Plains Woodland** (ca. 2,000 to 1,500 BP) is defined by the emergence of corn and bean agriculture from east. **Late Plains Woodland** (ca. 1,500 to 1,000 BP) is defined by the adoption of the bow and arrow from the north. In the far western Prairies, the Plains Woodland looks much like the Plains Archaic but with pottery, and a few of these groups persisted until contact, having never adopted a Plains Village way of life (see below).

In general, Plains Woodland groups focused on bison hunting, although deer, elk, pronghorn, mountain sheep, and many small animals were also taken, and the presence of milling-stones suggests that wild plants were important as well. The overall importance of corn and beans is unclear but was probably not great until after about 1,000 years ago. Groups remained small and highly mobile. The exchange of high-quality Knife River flint from North Dakota for stone tools between Plains Woodland groups was important and remained so until historic times. The presence of large villages/trading centers in that area, such as the Sakakawea site (Fig. 10.6) through time attests to the importance of the toolstone resources.

Of great interest during this time is the burial ceremonialism that derived from the east. This ceremonial complex apparently diffused in from the east and included dry masonry tombs covered with earth to make mounds, although some mounds did not contain burials. Burials in mounds included primary inhumations, defleshed bundle burials, and some cremations. Some

FIGURE 10.6 Aerial view of a portion of the Sakakawea village site on the Knife River, North Dakota. This is the Hidatsa village where Sacagawea (or Sakakawea) is believed to have lived. (*Source:* Knife River Indian Villages National Historic Site, National Park Service. Photo by Fred Armstrong.)

ossuaries have also been reported (Johnson 2001:172). Analyses of these remains suggest that many people were in poor health and suffered from malnutrition and arthritis. Such a mound-building complex is similar to the Eastern Woodland Hopewell to the east (see Chapter 11), although Plains groups practiced much more hunting and gathering than did the eastern Hopewell.

On the other hand, a "Hopewell" Plains Woodland variant (e.g., Kansas City Hopewell) has been identified on the far eastern edge of the Plains (Wedel 1986:81; Johnson and Johnson 1998:203). This variant included mounds and materials linked to the Hopewell to the east (see Chapter 11), but the economy was much more focused on hunting and gathering than any Hopewell groups in the east. Wedel (1986:85) suggested that there may have been a biological relatedness to eastern Hopewellians, so it is possible that some actual Hopewell populations may have migrated onto the Prairies (Key 1994).

Plains Village (1,000 to 300 BP)

Beginning about 1,000 years ago, agriculture greatly increased in importance and agricultural settlements were established along the higher terraces of the major rivers (Missouri, Platte, Republican, Arkansas, Red), with farming being undertaken in the floodplains of the valleys. Bison hunting remained important, and Plains Village groups continued to venture out onto the High Plains to hunt. Prairie groups became "Bison-hunting Farmers" (Ahler and Kay 2007).

All Plains Village groups can be characterized by (1) an economy of corn agriculture, hunting (primarily bison), gathering, and fishing; (2) semipermanent to permanent villages, often fortified with stockades and moats; (3) large, square to rectangular multifamily earthlodges (see Roper and Pauls 2005), often semisubterranean; (4) the use of bison scapula hoes; (5) small triangular arrow points, some with side notches; and (6) round-bottomed pottery (e.g., Wedel 2001:Table 1; also see Henning 2001, 2005). For the following discussion, the Plains Village period is divided into Early and Late (also see Table 10.3).

EARLY PLAINS VILLAGE (1,000 TO 700 BP)   As agriculture became more important, the bison hunters of the Prairies began to consolidate their settlements into small to medium villages of perhaps three hundred people living in six to twenty large (ca. 900 square foot) rectangular, semisubterranean earthlodges with sloping entrances (see Fig. 10.7). These structure were not pithouses but were constructed with heavy wood superstructures that were covered with soil and sod, providing excellent insulation against the cold winters. Although corn and bison were the primary foods, other resources included deer, pronghorn antelope, fowl, fish, freshwater shellfish (there are some sites with shell middens), dog, beaver, turtle, beans, squash, sunflowers, and many wild plants. Bison were hunted on an individual basis year-round or communally during the summer, sometimes in association with other villages. Burials were often secondary, but some primary burials under the floors of earthlodges are also known. The bow and arrow was used.

In the northern Plains during this period of time, the Middle Missouri Tradition (MMT), originally defined by Lehmer (1954, 1971; Lehmer and Caldwell 1966; also see Winham and

FIGURE 10.7   A large Pawnees earthlodge of the Plains Village style in the late 1800s. Note the people on top of the lodge and the tipi poles (for summer houses) stored across the entrance tunnel (photo by William Henry Jackson, courtesy of the National Anthropological Archives).

Calabrese 1998; Wood 2001; C. M. Johnson 2007), developed along the Middle Missouri River in North and South Dakota. The people of the MMT are believed to be the ancestors of the ethnographic Mandan, Arikara, and Hidatsa tribes. The origins of the MMT are unclear (Wood 2001:190), but it likely developed from Late Woodland groups (Ahler 2007; Tiffany 2007) who took advantage of a northern expansion of corn agriculture due to warming climate (Wood 2001:190). Wood (1974) suggested that MMT villages were located to partition resources, were politically autonomous, and were economically self-sufficient, although they did trade with hunter-gatherers in the area. Alternatively, Krause (1999) argued that the MMT settlement pattern was considerably influenced by the desire to be close to relatives and not solely on economic factors.

The Initial Middle Missouri (1,000 to 700 BP) marked the first occupation of the Middle Missouri River by village agriculturalists, who transformed from people living in "dispersed, unfortified farming hamlets [of the Plains Woodland] to nucleated, fortified farming villages" (Tiffany 2007:3). During the Initial MMT, a number of semipermanent, large villages were constructed along the lower Missouri River. Many of these villages were fortified, perhaps due to conflict with mobile hunter-gatherers in the area. By 800 BP, MMT groups were beginning to move farther north along the Missouri River. This period of time, called the Extended Middle Missouri (800 to 600 BP), saw the establishment of relatively small and unfortified villages, particularly in the northern part of MMT territory.

Sometime after about 600 BP, MMT groups within the Terminal Middle Missouri (600 to 450 BP) moved still farther north along the Missouri River, reaching their northernmost extent. During this time, it may be that Central Plains Tradition (CPT) groups (see below) from the Nebraska area moved north into the southern portion of MMT territory, creating conflict and initiating a merger of the MMT and CPT into a new tradition, the Coalescent Tradition (see below). The smaller unfortified villages of the Extended MMT contracted into a smaller number of larger fortified villages, perhaps reflecting conflict with CPT groups. The sociopolitical organization of MMT groups is presumed to be tribal in nature. In one interesting study of MMT social structure, Prine (2000) sought to identify domestic space occupied by people of third or fourth genders, commonly called berdaches.

In the central Plains (e.g., Nebraska), the CPT developed (Steinacher and Carlson 1998; Wedel 2001; Roper 2006, 2007). These groups consisted of small social units, sometimes single families or a few families, in small villages with earthlodges. They practiced small-scale corn agriculture but continued hunting and gathering. Rockshelters and caves with CPT materials are known on the High Plains and may have been bison hunting camps. In addition, some related groups may have lived in the central High Plains (Lindsey and Krause 2007). The CPT incorporated a new adaptive system of "low-level food production" (Roper 2007:55), new technologies such as pottery for cooking corn, a new settlement pattern to accommodate residence near fields, and different social organizations to deal with new social needs, such as landholding (Roper 2007:55).

The early CPT is perhaps best characterized by materials from the Upper Republican River (Wedel 1986, 2001). These people were small-scale farmers who lived in small unfortified villages along tributaries with better soils and more trees than on the main river. Upper Republican people used some forty species of mammals (Wedel 2001:175), as well as birds, fish, and shellfish. There are few data on the use of plants. Some shell from the Gulf Coast is present at early CPT sites, as well as copper artifacts, suggesting trade contacts to the north. Burials were secondary.

The origins of the CPT are not well understood (e.g., Roper 2007) but like the MMT is likely a development from the Plains Woodland. By 700 BP, CPT groups had begun moving north into the Missouri River region, contacting MMT groups and perhaps combining with them to form the Coalescent Tradition (see below).

In the southern Plains (e.g., Oklahoma and Texas), the Plains Village pattern was established along the major rivers by about 1,200 BP and lasted until contact, about 500 BP (Bell and Brooks 2001). The developments in the southern Plains during this time appear to have been generally independent of those of the central and northern Plains Village, and some southern Plains Village people may have even lived in the High Plains (Gunnerson 2001). The Plains Village pattern does not appear to have been present in central and southern Texas, which continued to be occupied by mobile Plains Archaic hunter-gatherers (Bell and Brooks 2001:207).

As elsewhere during Plains Village times, various Early Plains Village groups existed on the southern Plains and likely evolved from earlier Plains Woodland groups in the same area (Drass 1998:446). People generally lived in small, unfortified villages, suggesting that warfare was not an important activity. Unlike the other Plains Village groups, however, house types varied greatly in the southern Plains and included earthlodges, masonry buildings, and multiroom structures reminiscent of small pueblos in the Southwest. This reflects influences from the Southwest in the development of the southern Plains.

The Dismal River Aspect on the southern Plains during this time is associated with the Plains Apache (Wedel 1986:148; Gunnerson 2001; Scheiber 2006:141–148), Athapaskans who may have arrived in the area about 475 BP as "dog-nomads," hunter-gatherers using dogs as labor animals. They adopted some horticulture and later acquired horses and lived in small, round houses very unlike Plains earthlodges. Other Apachean groups moved into the Southwest at this time, and there is evidence of contact with Rio Grande Puebloan groups, and some Puebloan refugees may have even joined the Plains Apache after the failed Pueblo revolt of 1680.

Southern Plains Village cultures appear to have been disrupted due to desiccating climatic conditions ca. 700 BP, and the distribution of water may have forced the relocation and consolidation of agricultural fields to major river valleys. However, it may be that settlement patterns changed due to the focus on agriculture, rather than climate change (Blakeslee 1993). Some Plains Village groups were replaced by hunter-gatherers about 600 BP, perhaps pushed out by Athabaskan (Apachean) groups moving into the region from the north.

LATE PLAINS VILLAGE (700 TO 300 BP)   The Late Plains Village is characterized by the Coalescent Tradition on the central and northern Prairies. The Coalescent Tradition did not occur in the southern Plains during this time. This tradition is commonly divided into Initial (ca. 700 to 500 BP), Extended (ca. 600 to 300 BP), and Post-Contact (ca. 300 to 150 BP) periods. Villages of the Coalescent Tradition were generally located on the upper terraces of rivers and consisted of many earthlodges packed into heavily fortified villages. Corn, beans, and squash were grown, but many wild plants were also used. Bison constitutes as much as 90 percent of the faunal remains, but many other animals were also exploited.

The Coalescent Tradition was originally conceptualized as a combination of the CPT and MMT into a new entity (Lehmer 1971; also see C. M. Johnson 1998; Krause 2001). In this model (Model A; see Table 10.4), CPT populations would have moved north and "coalesced" with MMT people into the Coalescent Tradition to become the ancestors of the Mandan and Hidatsa (Siouan linguistic groups) and the Arikara and Pawnees (Caddoan linguistic groups). However, this model has been rejected by some researchers (e.g., Steinacher and Carlson 1998:258), and recent findings suggest that the Coalescent Tradition developed largely from the CPT and then incorporated the MMT (Lehmer and Caldwell 1966:Fig. 2; A. E. Johnson 1998:308) (Model B; see Table 10.4). The issue remains unresolved.

TABLE 10.4 Two Models of the Development of the Coalescent Tradition on the Plains

Model A		Model B		
Post-Contact Coalescent		Post-Contact Coalescent		
Extended Coalescent		Terminal	Extended	Coalescent
		Middle	Missouri	
Initial Coalescent				Initial Coalescent
Terminal Middle Missouri	Late Central Plains	Extended Middle Missouri		Late Central Plains
Extended Middle Missouri	Middle Central Plains			Middle Central Plains
Initial Middle Missouri	Early Central Plains	Initial Middle Missouri		Early Central Plains

Krause (2001:196) summarized the current thinking about the development of the Coalescent Tradition. About 1,000 BP, CPT people with small villages and a mixed agricultural and hunting-gathering economy settled in the eastern and central Plains; at the same time, MMT groups with fortified villages and a mixed economy settled in the Missouri River Valley. About 750 years ago, a warming and drying trend initiated a movement of both Central Plains and Middle Missouri groups northward to wetter and cooler regions, which resulted in closer contact with each other (Initial Coalescent). This eventually led to warfare, such as the massacre at Crow Creek (see Highlight 10.3). As environmental conditions improved after about 600 years ago, each of these groups began to compete for space and resources (Extended Coalescent), but conflict appears to have declined. Ultimately, the two groups generally combined (Post-Contact Coalescent) and became the ancestors of the Missouri River villagers encountered by Lewis and Clark in 1804.

HIGHLIGHT 10.3

THE CROW CREEK MASSACRE

Crow Creek is a fortified Initial Coalescent village dating to about 675 BP (it also contains an earlier Initial Middle Missouri component), located on the Missouri River in south-central South Dakota. The site covers some eighteen acres on a triangular protrusion on the river terrace and has steep drops to the river on two sides. The land approach was fortified by a series of ditches, walls, and bastions. Crow Creek was first excavated between 1954 and 1955 (Kivett and Jensen 1976).

In 1978, a mass burial was discovered eroding out of the edge of the site. The mass grave was excavated and the remains were studied and reburied (see P. Willey 1990). The results of that excavation showed that on a day some 675 years ago, the people of Crow Creek were attacked by an unknown group. The attackers penetrated the defenses, burned the village (the earlier excavations had detected burned earthlodges but did not determine why they had burned), and massacred nearly five hundred people (men, women, and children)— perhaps 60 percent of the village population. Their bodies were then dumped in the fortification ditch of the site (Willey and Emerson 1993). The fate of the surviving inhabitants, if any, is unknown.

Most of the people had been scalped, decapitated, and/or mutilated. Scavenger gnaw marks on the bones show that they were not buried, but left exposed on the surface, to be buried later by natural processes. Other analyses demonstrated that many of the people suffered from malnutrition, perhaps due to warfare and competition over resources (Zimmerman and Bradley 1993). It is believed that the occupants of the site were probably ancestral Arikara.

The mere presence of large fortified villages had long been seen as an indication of hostilities among the various Plains Village groups. The discovery of a mass grave of massacred people clearly supports the warfare model, and the remains from Crow Creek constitute the largest recovered skeletal population from a massacre in the world. At first, Crow Creek was viewed as unique, perhaps an isolated incident, but it is now apparent that warfare and interpersonal violence was relatively common during this time (P. Willey 1990:xxiii–xxiv). More information on Crow Creek can be obtained by visiting www.mnsu.edu/emuseum/archaeology/sites/northamerica/crowcreekmassacre.html.

By the Extended Coalescent, after about 600 BP, conflict appears to have declined, as seen by the decrease in fortified villages. The presence of some fortified villages, however, suggests that they served to harbor refugees from surrounding villages in times of conflict (A. E. Johnson 1998:318). Extended Coalescent villages tended to be permanent, larger (up to forty-two houses), and with more substantial houses (ten to fifteen meters in diameter). Bison remained the primary game animal, and agriculture was dominant. Many trade goods have been found in Extended Coalescent sites, including shell from the Pacific, Atlantic, and Gulf coasts and Euroamerican trade goods (e.g., glass beads and metal tools) after about 400 BP.

The Double Ditch site along the Missouri River in North Dakota is an extraordinarily large (containing one hundred earthlodges), fortified, ancestral Mandan Extended Coalescent site. It was first investigated in 1905 and thought to have been initially occupied about 400 BP (Will and Spinden 1906). However, a recent remote sensing study demonstrated that the site was actually much larger than first thought and revealed many more earthlodges, features, and additional fortifications (Kvamme and Ahler 2007). Excavations showed that the site dated from 700 BP, had a population of about two thousand, and was abandoned after a smallpox outbreak in AD 1785.

Plains Historic (300 to 100 BP)

After the introduction of horses onto the Plains about 300 years ago, cultures all across the Plains changed dramatically (see Highlight 10.2). In the south, Plains Historic is the same as Late Plains Village but with horses, while in the central and northern Plains, the Post-Contact Coalescent has been defined. Major changes included an increase in warfare and raiding (mostly for horses), changes in bison hunting tactics (mounted bison hunters who were more productive than hunters on foot), and the expansion in size of the traditional earthlodge so that horses could be stabled indoors for protection against raiders and weather.

Disease impacted post-contact Plains Village groups very early and very severely, and many of these groups were destroyed before they could be documented. The major surviving post-contact Plains Village ethnographic groups (from north to south) include Hidatsa, Mandan, Arikara, Pawnees, and Wichita (Lehmer 2001).

NATIVE PLAINS CULTURES AT CONTACT

Most Plains peoples encountered horses long before they saw any Europeans. Once obtained, horses became the most important aspect of Plains culture, and many agricultural groups abandoned farming and moved out onto the High Plains to pursue bison hunting, quickly leading to the complex patchwork of ethnographic groups reported by early European travelers (see Hanson 1998).

The first contact by Plains groups with Europeans was with the Spanish on the southern Plains in the late 1500s. De Soto crossed the southern Plains in 1540, almost certainly spreading disease and decimating the populations to near zero by the time other Europeans visited the Plains. The groups on the northern Plains (e.g., the Blackfoot) were first contacted by Hudson's Bay Company traders in 1690, at which time a major trade in furs was established, continuing for about 175 years.

Americans first contacted Plains groups in 1804, when the expedition led by Lewis and Clark encountered the Mandan, Hidatsa, and Arikara groups on the Missouri River. Native peoples with horses were just beginning to enter the High Plains at that time. American contact had relatively little impact until the late 1840s, however, when settlers began to cross the Plains to get to California and Oregon. Many Plains groups signed the famous Fort Laramie Treaty of 1851, in which some tribes in the central and southern Plains agreed that the United States could build roads and military posts, and that settlers could move through their territory, in exchange for guarantees of land rights.

In the 1860s, increasing numbers of settlers began to move through Sioux territory on the northern Plains. Under their great leader, Red Cloud, the Sioux resisted, fought, and defeated the U.S. Army and in 1868 signed the Fort Laramie Treaty ending the war and creating a large Sioux reservation that included the sacred Black Hills. Other Sioux leaders, including Sitting Bull and Crazy Horse, refused to sell their lands and did not sign the treaty. That same year, gold was discovered in the Black Hills and white miners illegally flooded the area. The Sioux defended their territory and with the Cheyenne fought a major war with the United States. Although the Indians won several important victories, such as the famous Battle of the Little Big Horn, they were finally defeated in 1877 and the great Sioux reservation was broken up. Once large steel plows became available after the Civil War, the Plains were increasingly colonized by white farmers, referred to as "sodbusters." Cattle ranching also became an important aspect of American colonization of the Plains.

Most Plains cultures have survived, and like many other Native American groups, their populations are growing and they are gaining political power in recent times (see Iverson [1985] for a series of articles on Plains people in the twentieth century). Many Plains groups have reservations and reserves in either the United States or Canada. Most of these reservations are isolated from population and transportation centers, however, making it difficult to attract industry, thus inhibiting economic development. The major reservation enterprises continue to be wheat farming and cattle ranching, and there has been some reintroduction of bison to their former range.

Some attempts have been made to bring modern development to Plains reservations. For example, a large dam project was built on the Missouri River to provide water and power for Indian agriculture. However, all it really accomplished was to flood the best farmland, thus decreasing farm productivity. Tourism has generally increased in recent times and has provided some employment. People are attracted to the region to view the natural beauty of the Plains and to attend a variety of cultural events, including powwows, ceremonies, and reenactments (e.g., the Little Big Horn battle). A statue of Crazy Horse, a famous Lakota (Sioux) leader, is currently being carved into a mountain near Mount Rushmore and should also be a tourist attraction.

Huge problems still remain for Plains peoples. While the decline in mortality and improvement in birth rates have greatly increased the populations of Plains groups, the lack of economic opportunities has forced many individuals to move to the cities to seek employment. Discrimination, unemployment, alcoholism, suicide, and family violence remain at epidemic levels.

Further Reading

Much of the literature about the archaeology of the Plains is contained in government publications, such as the River Basin Surveys published by the Bureau of American Ethnology. Several syntheses are available (see Wood 1998), as are reviews of the archaeology of specific states, such as South Dakota (Zimmerman 1985), Missouri (O'Brien and Wood 1998), Iowa (Alex 2000), and Kansas (Hoard and Banks 2006). Finally, the most recent general treatments of Plains prehistory (and ethnography) were published in the Plains volume of the *Handbook of North American Indians* (DeMallie 2001) and by Kornfeld et al. (2009). Several journals publish materials on the Plains, including the *Midcontinental Journal of Archaeology*, *Plains Anthropologist,* and the *Canadian Journal of Archaeology.*

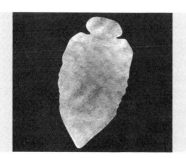

Corn and Villages
The Northeast

The Northeast is a broad region of lakes and forests that was home to many tribes of farmer/hunters, including some very complex societies. The primary agricultural crops were corn, beans, and squash (the "Three Sisters") along with sunflowers. Groups living in the northern part of the Northeast and around the Great Lakes depended less on agriculture and more on hunting, fishing, and gathering, and groups living in the far Northeast never adopted farming at all.

European contact (including disease and warfare) seriously impacted most groups, and many had disappeared before any record of them could be made. Warfare, a trait commonly seen as a hallmark of the native Northeast, was important but not "universal" and varied in intensity (Milner 2007). It seems that conflict, cooperation, and diplomacy "coevolved" over the millennia in eastern North America (Dye 2009).

Northeastern groups spoke languages from three principal language families: Algonquian, Northern Iroquoian, and Siouan. Groups speaking Algonquian languages lived along the Atlantic coast and in the Great Lakes region, while most of the groups speaking Northern Iroquoian languages lived inland and in the northern portion of the Northeast culture area. A few groups speaking Siouan languages lived in the far western portion of the Northeast.

GEOGRAPHY AND ENVIRONMENT

The Northeast culture area consists essentially of the northeastern United States and southeastern Canada. It lies east of the Mississippi River, south of the Subarctic, and generally north of the 35th parallel. The Northeast is divided into four major regions (see Fig. 11.1) the Great Lakes and St. Lawrence, the Ohio River Valley, the Middle Atlantic coast, and the Maritimes. The Great Lakes/St. Lawrence region is dominated by a long depression running from the Great Lakes northeast to the Gulf of St. Lawrence. The Great Lakes include Superior, Michigan, and Huron in the east and Erie and Ontario in the west, with the St. Lawrence River flowing from the lakes east

FIGURE 11.1   The Northeast showing the major subregions and the location of sites discussed in the text: 1) Adena; 2) Big Bone Lick; 3) Bull Brook; 4) Caradoc; 5) Chillicothe; 6) Debert; 7) Fort Ancient; 8) Great Serpent Mound; 9) Hopewell; 10) Koster; 11) L'Anse Amour; 12) Lamb; 13) Moatfield; 14) Newark; 15) Norris Farms No. 36; 16) Peace Bridge; 17) Port au Choix; 18) Seip Earthworks; 19) Shawnee Minisink; 20) Sheriden Cave; 21) Vail; 22) Varney Farm.

to the Atlantic Ocean. This is a region of thick forests, many rivers and streams, and numerous lakes. Severe weather is not uncommon on the Great Lakes.

The Ohio River and its tributaries traverse through much of the interior Northeast, flowing west to join the Mississippi River. The central Appalachians, including some very rugged areas, run along the southern portion of the Ohio Valley, while the northern portion consists of a relatively flat, heavily forested area. The Middle Atlantic region extends along the Atlantic coast from Virginia north to New England. A broad alluvial plain dominates the coast south of New York. The Appalachian Mountains run along the western side of the coast and extend into southern Canada. In their northern reaches, the Appalachians are well-eroded, low mountains that are much less rugged. Several rivers flow from the mountains east to the sea. The Maritimes lie along the coast, from Maine to Newfoundland, and are characterized by a cold climate and thick forests.

A vast, deciduous forest of maple, birch, oak, hickory, elm, and willow extends across much of the Northeast, slowing grading into a coniferous boreal (e.g., pine, fir, spruce) forest on the northern margins and into oak parkland in the far west. The most important game animal in the Northeast is deer, but the region also supports bears, rabbits, squirrels, beavers, many varieties of fish, shellfish, crawfish, snakes, turtles, waterfowl, and numerous other birds (e.g., turkeys). A wide variety of plants was used by prehistoric peoples of the region, including a number of nuts, grasses, berries, and roots (see C. M. Scarry 2003).

The Northeast has a generally temperate climate, with abundant precipitation. The winters are usually quite cold, with considerable snowfall. Depending on location, there are between 140 and 210 frost-free days, and agriculture could be practiced in all areas except in the Maritimes. Summer temperatures are warm to hot, often reaching a humid 100°F along the coast and 90°F in the interior.

A BRIEF HISTORY OF RESEARCH

Thomas Jefferson conducted the first problem-oriented archaeological investigation in the Northeast, indeed in all of North America, when he excavated a mound on his own property in Virginia in 1784 and published a report on the results (Jefferson 1797). Other serious work began early with the mound explorations of the early to middle 1800s, much of it conducted in the Ohio River Valley. Of note are the mound explorations of Squier and Davis (1848) conducted to address the moundbuilder question (see below). One of the earliest archaeological societies in North America was formed in Wisconsin in the late 1800s, and their journal, *Wisconsin Archaeologist,* is the longest continually published archaeological journal in North America.

Much of the archaeological work done in the Northeast prior to World War II was conducted by avocational organizations. In New England, the R. S. Peabody Foundation actively funded several projects undertaken by universities. In the 1920s, a fairly large number of cemeteries were excavated and a variety of speculative interpretations were made (e.g., the Red Paint People of Maine; see Highlight 11.1). During the 1930s, federal funding of the Works Progress Administration (WPA) and the Civilian Conservation Corps (CCC) was used to investigate many of the mounds in the Ohio River Valley. Such excavations resulted in a great deal of general information, but the level of recordation in the field was not very detailed, making the interpretation of this work by scholars today difficult.

As data accumulated, syntheses of regional prehistories began to appear (e.g., W. A. Ritchie 1938), and after the development of radiocarbon dating, these syntheses (e.g., Griffin 1952; Caldwell 1958) benefitted from a more reliable dating method. For example, the Center for American Archaeology in Kampsville, Illinois (see www.caa-archaeology.org) was founded in 1953 and became involved in the excavation of the Koster site in Illinois, one of the most important sites in the Northeast (Struever and Holton 1979).

The presence of large, and apparently complex, societies that constructed mounds in the Ohio River Valley, such as the Hopewell, is the focus of much attention for research in the Northeast. The abundant rock art in both open sites and caves, as well as dendroglyphs (carvings in tree trunks), are also research issues (Diaz-Granadon and Duncan 2004). As is the case across North America, most archeological research is now associated with CRM projects.

MAJOR THEMES IN NORTHEAST PREHISTORY

Archaeological research in the Northeast is dominated by the investigation of complex Woodland societies. Inquiries into how these societies developed, from what economic base, how environmental change may have affected them, how they were organized (socially, politically, and ritually), and what happened to them dominate this work. The relatively recent research conducted on Woodland sites through CRM projects has greatly expanded our understanding of that tradition.

Integral to these latter questions is research into the development of domesticated plants and the spread of farming across the region. What plants were domesticated and when did this happen? When did farming become dominant in the Northeast, and how did that affect the development of the various societies?

Research into the Paleoindian presence in the Northeast has always been a major topic. Some of North America's best known Paleoindian sites (e.g., Vail and Debert) are present in the Northeast, and while the Paleoindian occupation does not appear to have been substantial, several newly discovered sites have shed light on Paleoindian rituals and settlement patterns. The idea of a Solutrean connection (see Chapter 2) has increased interest in locating earlier sites.

The migrations of people across the Northeast continue to be an important issue, especially the movement of the Iroquoian groups. Certainly, populations did migrate in the past, but it can be difficult to detect those movements in the archaeological record. A basic chronological sequence for the Northeast is shown in Table 11.1.

THE PALEOINDIAN PERIOD (TO 9,500 BP)

At the height of the last glacial episode, ice sheets extended well south into what is now the United States, encompassing the northern portion of the Northeast and forming the basins of the Great Lakes. A tundra-like spruce parkland environment existed just to the south of the ice sheets, with a band of boreal forest to the south of the tundra and a band of deciduous forest further south. As the ice retreated at the end of the Pleistocene, the tundra and forests moved north and formed the major environments present during Paleoindian times. Mammoths apparently did not live in the east in large numbers, but mastodons were relatively common.

Some researchers have argued that Paleoindians in the tundra focused on caribou, while those in the boreal forest had a more generalized adaptation (e.g., Meltzer 1988; Lepper and Meltzer 1991; Spiess et al. 1998). This generalized boreal forest adaptation would have resulted in reduced residential mobility and fewer sites (Lepper and Meltzer 1991), although if game animals were scarce in the boreal forest (e.g., W. A. Ritchie 1980) it would have made occupation difficult. It may be that Paleoindians were in the northern regions but focused on lowland, post-glacial wetland resources (Smith and Laub 2000). Given two apparent adaptations (tundra and boreal forest), there may have been several migrations into the region during Paleoindian times (Spiess et al. 1998). In any case, Paleoindian populations were generally small and mobile.

The Early Paleoindian Period (ca. 11,500 to 10,900 BP)

The earliest known archaeological site in the Northeast is Meadowcroft Rockshelter, located in Pennsylvania. It has been argued (e.g., Adovasio and Pedler 2005) that this site has a continuous occupation dating back to at least 19,000 BP, but there is considerable controversy regarding the accuracy of this early date, and most researchers will accept only the more accurately dated initial occupation beginning about 14,000 BP. Other materials dating from the Early Paleoindian Period are very rare. A Clovis occupation dated to about 10,600 BP was identified at the Shawnee

TABLE 11.1 A Chronological Sequence for the Northeast

Date (BP)	A Broad Outline	General Sequences by Region				General Climate
		Great Lakes/ St. Lawrence	Ohio River	Middle Atlantic	Maritimes	
150	Late Woodland	Late Woodland			Late Archaic	similar to today
1000						cooler than today
2000	Middle Woodland	Middle Woodland	Hopewell	Middle Woodland	Dorset (see Chapter 4)	similar to today
			Late Adena			
	Early Woodland	Early Woodland	Middle Adena	Early Woodland	Late Maritime Archaic	
			Early Adena			
3000	Late Archaic	Lake Forest Archaic	Narrow Point Archaic			
4000						becoming cooler and wetter
5000	Middle Archaic	Middle Archaic				
6000					Early Maritime Archaic	warmer and drier than today
7000						
8000	Early Archaic	Early Archaic				
9000						cooler and wetter than today but warming
Paleoindian	Paleoindian	Paleoindian Middle Paleoindian (e.g., non-Clovis fluted) Early Paleoindian (e.g., Clovis)				
to 10,000						colder and wetter than today

Minisink site in Pennsylvania (McNett 1986), where prehistoric people camped in the summer to fish, collect plants, and repair their equipment. Other Clovis materials have been found at Big Bone Lick, Kentucky (Tankersley et al. 2009), and at Sheriden Cave in Ohio (Waters et al. 2009). All, in all, however, there is very little evidence of an Early Paleoindian presence in the Northeast.

The Middle Paleoindian Period (ca. 10,900 to 10,200 BP)

The Middle Paleoindian Period is better represented, and a number of well-documented Paleoindian sites have been found. One of the better known is the Debert site in Nova Scotia (MacDonald 1968; Tuck 1984:7–10), a hunting camp dating to about 10,000 BP. People at the Debert site exploited caribou and perhaps sea mammals and used fluted points (generally called Bull Brook and Vail/Debert points). The discovery of eleven discrete areas with hearths and artifacts suggested that they lived in small wood or skin-covered structures. Other Paleoindian sites dating to about the same time as Debert include the Vail site in Maine (Gramly 1982), the Lamb site in New York (Gramly 1999), and the Bull Brook site in Massachusetts (D. A. Byers 1954). Bull Brook appears to have been a large "aggregation" of Paleoindians who left some thirty-six discrete concentrations of artifacts arranged in a large circle, perhaps associated with communal caribou hunting (Robinson et al. 2009).

A variety of Middle Paleoindian site types are known in the Northeast, including quarries, habitation sites, kill sites, and caches (Gramly and Funk 1990). Kill sites are rare, but several are large enough to suggest that they may have also been used for habitation (Curran 1999:4). Based on this, Dincauze (1993:45) proposed that such "big residential" sites served as centers for early colonization of the region. Encampments such as Debert, Vail, Bull Brook, and Lamb may be examples of such centers.

Middle Paleoindian subsistence in eastern North America was highly variable, and there is little to suggest that these people were specialized hunters (Lepper 1999:378). In fact, it is clear that subsistence was broad spectrum, including the hunting of caribou (in the north), deer, hare, fox, fish, and many other species (see Ellis et al. 1998:157–158; Lepper 1999:376). This economic variability may reflect the flexibility of pioneers who took advantage of the many opportunities that were available (Tankersley 1998; Curran 1999:21). The distribution of fluted points in eastern North America, generally in discrete sites in the Northeast and as isolated finds in the Southeast, may be indicative of environmental variability and regional adaptations (Lepper 1999:362) as well as lithic procurement activities (Tankersley 1995). Other Paleoindian sites have been found in southern Ontario and also exhibit a range of variability and adaptations (Ellis and Deller 1997).

The Late Paleoindian Period (ca. 10,200 to 9,500 BP)

The Late Paleoindian Period (also called Plano) spans the transition between Pleistocene and modern environments throughout North America (Goodyear 1982:392; also see J. V. Wright 1995), and the bands of tundra and forests expanded north at this time. This period is characterized by various nonfluted lanceolate and stemmed point forms, commonly called Dalton (Tuck 1974; Morse et al. 1996:328) or "Hi-Lo" in the Great Lakes region (Stothers and Abel 1991:206; also see C. Ellis 2006; L. J. Jackson 2006b). Dalton materials are present in much of the Northeast, including some earlier Paleoindian sites, such as Vail, Debert, and Bull Brook. A single component Late Paleoindian site was found at Varney Farm, Maine (Petersen et al. 2000), where thin, nonfluted points were found.

It appears that fluted and Dalton points have a disparate distribution in the Northeast, suggesting the use of fluted points for caribou in boreal forests and Dalton points for deer in deciduous forest (Morse 1997a:138). As the boreal forests moved northward, both fluted and Dalton forms were replaced by side- and corner-notched points of the Archaic, perhaps as the result of increased populations and new hunting techniques (such as the atlatl).

While large game (e.g., caribou and deer) were hunted, Late Paleoindian groups appear to have practiced a generalized foraging strategy, at least in the Great Lakes region (Kuehn 1998). Along the coast of the Maritimes, however, Late Paleoindians may have been more marine adapted (fish and sea mammals) and appear to have contributed to the later development of the Maritime Archaic (Keenlyside 1985:84).

It is believed that Late Paleoindian groups had larger populations, more regular and formalized intergroup contacts, and smaller but bounded territories than Early Paleoindian groups (D. A. Anderson 1995a:21). An analysis of the distribution of artifact forms and lithic sources suggested the existence of band territories in the Great Lakes region (Stothers 1996). All of this indicates a rapid and substantial change in organization and behavior from earlier Paleoindian times. Little is known of ritual behaviors at this time, but the discovery of "killed" tools at the Caradoc site in southwestern Ontario provides some insight (see Deller and Ellis 2001).

THE ARCHAIC (CA. 9,500 TO 150 BP)

In the Northeast, the Archaic is generally defined as a time of primarily hunting-and-gathering economies, an absence of pottery, no artificial burial mounds, and various diagnostic projectile points (Stoltman 1997:112; also see W. A. Ritchie 1938; Lovis 2008). Climate regimes had changed, and it was becoming warmer. The Archaic is divided into Early, Middle, and Late. While the Archaic ended in most areas with the advent of pottery about 3,000 years ago, some groups in the far north and northeast never adopted pottery or farming and so remained "Archaic" until contact.

The Early Archaic (ca. 9,500 to 8,000 BP)

The climate was warming after the Pleistocene, and by about 8,500 BP the boreal forests (which are not very productive for humans) expanded, which combined with increasing temperature, lower precipitation, and lower lake levels may have resulted in the general abandonment of large parts of the east (Morse et al. 1996:332; also see McWeeney and Kellogg 2001). Indeed, there is relatively little Early Archaic material in the Northeast (e.g., Tuck 1984:14; J. V. Wright 1995:64; Stoltman 1997:116), suggesting a low population density.

Nevertheless, there are a number of Early Archaic projectile point types, arranged in a chronological sequence from side-notched, to corner-notched, to split-stemmed, to stemmed forms. It is possible that the appearance of side-notched points marked the introduction of the atlatl, or at least a major design change in existing atlatl technology (Morse et al. 1996:331).

Within the Early Archaic is a span of time known as the Kirk Horizon, which is marked by corner-notched points (Tuck 1974:76; Morse et al. 1996:330), is known throughout eastern North America, and dates from about 10,200 to 7,800 BP (Sherwood et al. 2004). Materials from this time have been found as far north as southern Ontario (Ellis et al. 1991) and along the Atlantic coast (Lowery and Custer 1990). In addition to diagnostic point forms, the Kirk Horizon also includes large triangulate bifacial knives, celts, ovate chopper/scrapers, and small-end scrapers (Ellis et al. 1998:162). The Kirk Horizon, with the same basic toolkit, is found a bit earlier in the Southeast (see Chapter 12), suggesting the possibility that there was a population migration northward from the Southeast in early Archaic times (Stothers and Abel 1991:223).

A number of important Early Archaic sites have been investigated. One of the better known is the Koster site (Fig. 11.2) in Illinois (Struever and Holton 1979; also see Table 11.2). Here, several Early Archaic components were found. The first (Level 14) was dated to about 9,500 BP but contained few materials. The second (Level 11) was dated to about 8,500 BP. This second component represented a small camp and had evidence of a generalized diet. Importantly, Level 11 contained a small cemetery, one of the earliest known in North America.

The Middle Archaic (ca. 8,000 to ca. 5,000 BP)

The Middle Archaic in the Northeast was perhaps even less hospitable than the Early Archaic. The climate was warm and major drought persisted until about 6,000 BP, perhaps even later in the far Northeast (Joyce 1988:204; Sanger et al. 2007), after which conditions began to improve. There are relatively few Middle Archaic sites in the Northeast (J. V. Wright 1995:80; Robinson 2006:344–346; Sanger 2006:235), suggesting low population density, perhaps due to the low productivity of the pine forests (e.g., Fitting 1968; also see Funk 1991). It is also possible that Middle Archaic sites are present but unrecognized, perhaps because they are deeply buried, are undated, lack diagnostic artifacts, or have become inundated by rising sea levels (see Cross 1999:58, 60).

FIGURE 11.2 Excavations at the Koster site. (Photo by Del Baston and courtesy of the Center for American Archaeology).

TABLE 11.2 A Cultural Sequence from the Koster Site (from Struever and Holton 1979)

Level	Dates BP	General Description
1	1,600 to 800	Late Woodland/Mississippian, site then abandoned
2	2,200 to 2,100	Early Woodland, first pottery, substantial population increase
3	3,500 to 3,200	Late Archaic, small camp
4	4000	Late Archaic, camp for deer processing
6	ca. 5,900 to 4,800	Middle Archaic, permanent village, shift from river to marsh species of fish, hickory and acorn, waterfowl, copper items
8	ca. 7,500	Middle Archaic, substantial settlement with houses, perhaps year-round, dog burials
10	ca. 8,000 to 7,800	Early Archaic, stone tool manufacturing
11	ca. 8,500	Early Archaic, small camp, generalized diet, small cemetery
14	ca. 9,500	Paleoindian, small camp

Indeed, many Archaic artifacts have been found in fishing nets as far as 24 km. off the coast (see Deal et al. 2006:257). In general, the Middle Archaic is marked by the appearance of polished stone tools (e.g., axes), copper artifacts, specialized fishing gear, and evidence of the use of shell-fish (Stoltman 1997:126).

In the Great Lakes/St. Lawrence region, large side-notched points appeared at this time (Stoltman 1997:121) and the number of sites increased, suggesting larger populations. Lake levels appear to have been higher (due to isostatic rebound) so fishing may have been better. Groups appear to have lived in relatively permanent settlements following a collector strategy (see Highlight 6.1) (Lovis et al. 2005).

The Middle Archaic in the Ohio River region also apparently witnessed a population growth after about 6,000 BP. The appearance of cemeteries in some areas after 6,000 BP suggests some form of sedentism, with fixed territories and "corporate" behavior. In Level 8 at the Koster site, three dog burials were found and dated to about 8,500 BP, among the earliest in North America (Morey and Wiant 1992). A substantial Middle Archaic settlement with house structures was dated to about 7,500 BP. It is possible that this settlement was year-round (see Struever and Holton 1979).

Very little is known of the Middle Archaic along the Middle Atlantic coast. Stemmed points were part of the toolkit, and there are similarities in lithic technology seen all along the Atlantic Coast, suggesting a common cultural tradition (see Dincauze 1971).

An important regional variant of the Middle Archaic, known as the Maritime Archaic, was identified in the Maritimes region, dating between about 8,000 and 3,200 BP (see Fitzhugh 1978, 2006; Spiess 1993; J. V. Wright 1995; Renouf and Bell 2006). The Early Maritime Archaic (ca. 8,000 to 5,500 BP) extended from Maine to Newfoundland, into the Gulf of St. Lawrence area, and north into coastal Quebec and Labrador. Most sites have been found along the coast and it is clear that the Early Maritime Archaic was an adaptation that emphasized fishing and sea mammal hunting with little evidence of the use of interior resources. Ground slate was used for some tools (e.g., points and ulus), with quartz and Ramah Chert also being important toolstones. Initially, people lived in circular pithouses, but by 6,000 BP the pithouses had become rectangular, and some had several rooms. Some exchange can be seen across this region even this early (J. V. Wright 1994), as Ramah Chert toolstone from Labrador was highly valued and widely traded.

Of note is the L'Anse Amour burial mound in Labrador (Tuck and McGhee 1976). This burial, dated to about 7,500 BP, contained the remains of a twelve-year-old child. The body was placed in a large pit that was then covered with rocks. Numerous artifacts and other materials (e.g., foods) had been interred with the body. It is clear that this burial represents an important ceremonial tradition, and the age of the individual suggests that he/she was imbued with some sort of special status.

The Late Archaic (ca. 5,000 to 3,000 BP)

In sites dated after about 5,000 BP, there is a substantial increase in both the quantity and complexity of archaeological manifestations in the Northeast, including an elaboration of mortuary patterns (Fitting 1978:14), marking the beginning of the Late Archaic. Three major patterns for the Late Archaic have been proposed (Tuck 1978; also see Snow 1980): the Lake Forest Archaic of the Great Lakes/St. Lawrence region, the Narrow Point Archaic of the Ohio River and Middle Atlantic regions, and the Late Maritime Archaic of the Maritime region, each of which incorporates a number of traditions and complexes. Although quite general, this scheme is still followed today, recognizing that the Late Archaic reflects a "seemingly endless variation, not only in the range of artifact traits present but also in technology, regional land use, functional site types, and cultural complexity" (Versaggi et al. 2001:123).

Even as early about 7,000 BP, people in the eastern United States had begun to experiment and manipulate native plants, and by about 3,500 BP, perhaps a bit earlier, several were being cultivated and domesticated (e.g., Smith and Cowan 2003). These plants did not form a major part of any of the Archaic economies but would become more important in the subsequent Woodland Tradition (see below).

THE LAKE FOREST ARCHAIC   The Late Archaic in the Great Lakes/St. Lawrence region has been broadly designated the Lake Forest Archaic (e.g., Tuck 1978), named for the lakes and mixed conifer and hardwood forests that dominate the region. The Lake Forest Archaic is marked by the appearance of small stemmed and corner-notched points (Stoltman 1997:134). Trade was likely facilitated by the ease of water travel, and copper artifacts from the western Great Lakes were popular trade items.

HIGHLIGHT 11.1

THE OLD COPPER COMPLEX

The discovery of copper artifacts in ancient sites in the western Great Lakes region (see Fig. 11.1) in the 1800s led some scholars to speculate that these metal artifacts represented some sort of European presence, such as the Norse, Egyptians, or one of the Lost Tribes (R. J. Mason 1981:181). It was later realized that this material was manufactured by ancient Indians of the region and was called the "Old Copper Culture" or "Old Copper Complex." It is now known that the Old Copper Complex dates to the Late Archaic, between about 5,000 and 3,000 BP (see Binford 1962; Pleger 2000). The complex is known for its copper artifacts and several cemeteries, but virtually nothing is known about other aspects of their culture, such as residential sites or subsistence economy.

Raw copper was cold-hammered into a variety of artifacts. Some of these artifacts were utilitarian—including awls, projectile points, fishhooks, adzes, and axes—and have been found in a variety of settings. Others, such as beads, bracelets, rings, and crescent-shaped objects, were apparently used as adornments and have been found within burials (e.g., Stoltman 1997:127–131; also see Binford 1962), although copper artifacts as mortuary goods are actually rather rare.

Artifacts of the Old Copper Complex have been found across much of the Northeast, suggesting a considerable trade network during the Late Archaic (see J. V. Wright 1994). Most of the copper came from mines (see Vernon 1990) around western Lake Superior, but numerous other sources are also known (Levine 1999, 2007). Interestingly, once the Old Copper Complex ended, copper artifacts, particularly beads, continued to be manufactured and traded widely.

By the Late Archaic in the Great Lakes region, the Middle Archaic pattern of relatively permanent settlements and collector strategy changed. The rising levels of Lake Huron apparently created a land shortage, an overpopulation of existing territories, and a resultant shift to a more mobile settlement pattern (Lovis et al. 2005). The economy was based primarily on fishing and the hunting of deer, rabbits, and beaver. There is evidence for the early domestication of some local plants, and squash appears to have been grown in the Great Lakes region by 3,800 BP and was fully domesticated by about 3,000 BP (Monaghan et al. 2006). The use of cultigens in the upper Great Lakes region could be related to the productivity of regional wetlands (Lovis et al. 2001).

The Lake Forest Archaic in the interior of the eastern Northeast is called the Laurentian Tradition (W. A. Ritchie 1980; Tuck 1984:20–26; Funk 1988; see J. V. Wright 1995:221; Sanger 2006:237–239). The Laurentian Tradition is viewed as a number of regional groups sharing some elements of technology and ideology (Chapdelaine and Clermont 2006:203–204), including large notched points, ground slate tools, copper goods from the west (awls, fishhooks, needles, and projectile points), and Onondaga chert from the New York area. Several Laurentian phases have been defined (see Funk 1988; J. V. Wright 1995), including the Vergennes Phase in northern New England (see Cox 1991; J. V. Wright 1995:224–229), identified by large notched points (often called "Otter Creek" points) and possibly reflecting a movement of interior peoples to the coast (e.g., Bourque 1995). The Laurentian Tradition has many traits in common with the coastal Maritime Archaic, confusing the distinction between the two (see Deal et al. 2006:263–265).

THE NARROW POINT ARCHAIC   To the south of the Great Lakes/St. Lawrence region are the Ohio River and Middle Atlantic regions, most of which are covered by a large deciduous forest with many nut-bearing species (e.g., acorns, hickory nuts, and chestnuts). The Late Archaic of this region is called the Narrow Point Archaic (Tuck 1978), although the term "Mast Forest Tradition" is also employed ("mast" refers to tree nuts). Extensive exchange networks continued to develop, with trade of copper, marine shell, and stone from distant sources (R. M. Stewart 1994a; Theler and Boszhardt 2003:89–90).

Narrow Point groups were generalized hunter-gatherers that emphasized the hunting of deer. The use of fish generally increased over the Early and Middle Archaic (Spiess and Mosher 2006:386). A large fish weir complex was discovered in central Maine that was first used about 5,000 years ago. This facility not only demonstrates the substantial use of fish but also a major investment in labor for communal fishing (Petersen et al. 1994). Several native species of plants, including squash gourds (cf. *Cucurbita* sp.), goosefoot (*Chenopodium* sp.), sunflowers (*Helianthus* sp.), and marshelder (*Iva* sp.), were cultivated and domesticated (Crites 1993; Gremillion 1996a, 2006; Peterson and Sidell 1996; Fritz 2000:230; Smith and Cowan 2003) but did not form a major element of Archaic diets.

A number of relatively large base camps in lowland settings along river valleys and lake shores have been excavated, revealing a pattern of major use of lowland areas. Upland habitats, often considered marginal, were also used (Levine 2004) and emphasized the procurement and processing of nut resources. At Koster (Level 6), a permanent village was present that dated between 5,900 and 4,800 BP and showed a shift from the use of river fish to marsh fish, along with the use of acorns, hickory nuts, and waterfowl (see Struever and Holton 1979).

In the Middle Atlantic region, the Narrow Point Archaic is called the Small Stemmed Archaic (see Sanger 2006:239). The Susquehanna Tradition is generally representative of the Small Stemmed Archaic across the Middle Atlantic coastal region and is sometimes called "transitional" between Archaic and Woodland. Susquehanna is marked by broad-bladed points and the use of steatite bowls. Having such containers may have made it easy to adopt pottery when it arrived on the coast by about 3,000 BP. Susquehanna mortuary practices included cremations in pits lined with red ochre and containing grave goods. The development of estuarine and riverine adaptations along the coast resulted in the formation of relatively large communities, with some groups exhibiting mortuary complexity, at least in the Delaware region (Custer 1984:77).

The early portion of the Late Archaic in coastal New England is generally called the Moorehead Phase, also part of the Small Stemmed Archaic (see Bourque 1995:231; Sanger 2006). The Moorehead Phase appeared about 4,500 BP (Bourque 1995:243) and consisted of coastal settlements whose occupants exploited cod and swordfish from the Gulf of Maine, some deer and elk from the coastal forests, and perhaps oysters from the shore (Spiess and Mosher 2006). The diet was skewed toward marine resources, as shown by the analysis of human remains from burials at the Nevin site in Maine, which also demonstrated that the population there was in generally good health (Bourque 1995:243). By about 3,800 BP, the ocean became colder, the swordfish populations declined, and the Moorehead Phase ended (Bourque 1995:244).

Susquehanna groups from the south apparently moved north into Maine about 3,800 BP and replaced Moorehead Phase groups (Dincauze 1975; Tuck 1982:208; also see Bourque 1995:247, 252–253), bringing with them their distinctive material culture (e.g., broad blades and steatite bowls) and mortuary customs (cremations in pits). Susquehanna groups relied more heavily on land mammals than Moorehead Phase groups did, although they also exploited marine fish (but not swordfish), freshwater fish, shellfish, and waterfowl (Spiess and Mosher 2006:397). Susquehanna groups disappeared from the record in New England by about 3,500 BP, and it is not known what happened to them, but one theory proposed that they developed into the later groups in the region (Bourque 2001).

HIGHLIGHT 11.2

THE RED OCHRE BURIALS

A number of regional mortuary traditions, all characterized by the use of red ocher, were present across the Northeast during the Late Archaic. These include the Red Ochre Complex of the Upper Great Lakes (e.g., Theler and Boszhardt 2003:90–92), the Glacial Kame people of the Ohio area (e.g., O'Donnell 2004), and the Red Paint People of Maine (Robinson 1996, 2006, 2008). The origin and meaning of these traditions are poorly understood, but there must have been some sort of region-wide ritual system involved, perhaps linked to trade and travel. Indeed, many of the burials contained exotic (from distant sources) materials such as copper ornaments and large flaked bifaces, many of which were found with women and children (Pleger 2000).

One of the first of these burial traditions to be identified was in the far Northeast, named the "Red Paint People" due to the presence of cemeteries containing graves covered in red ochre (e.g., Moorehead 1913). And since bone did not preserve in the acidic soils of the region, many of the burials were just discolored areas of soil, called "shadow burials." Many of these cemeteries were dug up by amateurs before they could be fully investigated, and so the Red Paint People remained an enigma for a long time, until research in the region and across the Northeast revealed the presence of other mortuary traditions that also used red ochre and dated about the same time. The Red Paint People, now included in the Moorehead Burial Tradition (Belcher et al. 1994; Bourque 1995; Robinson 1996, 2006, 2008), is only one of the red ochre mortuary complexes known in the Northeast.

The Moorehead Burial Tradition of the Late Archaic (not to be confused with the later Moorehead Phase) is generally dated between 5,000 and 3,800 BP, although several cemeteries dated as early as 8,500 BP are known (see Robinson 2006). The poorly preserved, ochre-covered burials have contained a variety of grave goods, including gouges, whetstones, adzes, celts, ground slate points (often called "bayonets"), woodworking implements, and distinctive flaked stone stemmed points. None of the cemeteries so far identified have been found along the coast, but all are in locations suitable for freshwater fishing.

A large "Red Paint" Maritime Archaic cemetery was discovered at the Port au Choix-3 site on northwestern coast of Newfoundland (see Tuck 1976). The cemetery contained around one hundred well-preserved burials and dated between about 5,100 and 3,400 BP (Jelsma 2006:87). The preserved skeletons allowed the identification of sex and age of most of the individuals, permitting linkage of those data with the grave goods. Analyses of the grave goods, DNA, and isotopic values suggested the presence of three groups of different social status (Jelsma 2006). One was of young and relatively inexperienced hunters who had a diet of mostly marine mammals, the second was of older and/or less capable hunters who ate mostly fish, and the third had the most elaborate graves with the most skilled hunters who had a varied diet of marine mammals and fish. This reconstruction provided a glimpse at what must have been a fairly complex society.

THE LATE MARITIME ARCHAIC   In the Maritimes of the far Northeast, the Late Maritime Archaic (5,500 to 3,200 BP) developed from the Early Maritime Archaic (see Tuck 1984:26–30; Spiess 1993; J. V. Wright 1995; Fitzhugh 2006; Renouf and Bell 2006) but occupied a smaller region, having been replaced by Laurentian groups along the coasts of Quebec and Labrador. In Newfoundland, Maritime Archaic groups were present between about 4,500 and 3,200 BP (Renouf 1999) and were replaced by Dorset groups between 2,800 and 1,200 BP (see Chapter 4), who were themselves replaced by Subarctic Late Shield Archaic groups (see Chapter 13).

As did its predecessor, the Late Maritime Archaic shared many traits with the Laurentian Archaic, masking the distinction between the two (see Deal et al. 2006:263–265). In addition, it is believed that many Maritime Archaic sites are now underwater (Bell and Renouf 2003), making it very difficult to develop an understanding of the group.

Late Maritime groups had a greater focus on large land mammals than Early Maritime groups did, but fish, intertidal resources, and perhaps some sea mammals remained important (J. V. Wright 1995:589). Large stemmed points, scrapers, and ground slate tools were used, and semisubterranean "longhouses" were adopted.

HIGHLIGHT 11.3

THE DEVELOPMENT OF INDIGENOUS AGRICULTURE IN EASTERN NORTH AMERICA

The domestication of various plants and the adoption of farming as the major economic pursuit in eastern North America were very important developments. While corn and beans were first domesticated in Mesoamerica and diffused into North America from there, several other plants were independently domesticated in eastern North America. By about 7,000 BP, people began experimenting with squash gourds (cf. Cucurbita sp.). In the eastern United States, and by 6,000 BP, gourds were used as containers in central Maine (Peterson and Sidell 1996) and northern Pennsylvania (see Fritz 2000:230). The first solid evidence of actual domestication of gourds is at about 4,300 BP, and they were eventually used for food perhaps as early as 3,000 BP in New York (Hart et al. 2007). By about 3,500 BP (perhaps a bit earlier), a number of other native plants, including goosefoot (Chenopodium sp.), sunflowers (Helianthus sp.), and marshelder (or sumpweed, Iva sp.), were also being cultivated and domesticated (Crites 1993; Gremillion 1996a, 2006; Fritz 2000:230; Smith and Cowan 2003). The adoption of farming, even as an adjunct to hunting and gathering, marked the inception of the Woodland Tradition (see below).

Why did people begin the process of plant domestication? One model (e.g., B. D. Smith 1987, 1989, 1992, 1993) proposed that people occupied floodplain habitats during the drier Middle Archaic and found a number of plants (chenopods, sunflowers, and sumpweed) that produced a relatively large number of seeds. They may have eventually come to depend on these plants and began to intensively manage them, which eventually led to their domestication. Evidence of this is seen in the appearance and number of occurrences of these plant remains in archaeological sites and in the increasing evidence of sedentism (e.g., substantial structures and cemeteries) in sites.

Watson and Kennedy (1991:268) suggested that the first gardens were developed by women, who are presumed to have developed the techniques for "tilling, harvesting, and processing the new domesticates." Plants with small seeds, which have low return rates, may have been adopted as early as 3,500 BP if they were processed during the winter when there was little else to do (Gremillion 2004a). It was further suggested (Watson and Kennedy 1991:268) that the techniques and technology later utilized for corn agriculture were adapted from the preexisting systems developed for the indigenous domesticates.

Sometime before 2,300 BP, corn had diffused into the east and joined other crops in the agricultural system. This new corn was adapted to more southerly environments and was not immediately suited to the colder eastern environment, although several new varieties (e.g., Northern and Eastern Flints) adapted to these colder regions were developed (Watson and Kennedy 1991:265–266; Scarry 1993a:78). Corn was grown by groups as far north as New York by about 2,300 BP (Hart et al. 2003, 2007) and southern Ontario by about 1,600 BP (Katzenberg et al. 1995; Boyd and Surette 2010). As further research is conducted and better methods for detecting corn are used, it may be shown that corn was being cultivated even earlier (e.g., Hart 1999).

Certainly by 1,200 BP, corn had become very important, and corn, beans, and squash, collectively known as the "Three Sisters," along with sunflowers, formed the backbone of agricultural production (Fritz 2000:225). By 1,000 years ago, farming had become the pillar of subsistence economies all across eastern North America, as far north as the climate would permit.

THE WOODLAND TRADITION (CA. 3,000 BP TO CONTACT)

The Woodland Tradition in the Northeast (see Yerkes 1988) is characterized by the convergence of three innovative processes: (1) the adoption of farming as an important economic pursuit, (2) the widespread use of pottery, and (3) the construction of burial mounds. Although each of these traits predated the Woodland Tradition, they were either not very important or had different uses. Plants had been domesticated rather early, but they were economically peripheral. Pottery may be as old as 4,500 BP in some places but was not widespread. Mounds were constructed during the Archaic but were apparently used for ritual rather than burials. When farming began to increase in importance, pottery was adopted, settled village life became common, and the use of mounds for burials began.

A complete understanding of the function of burial mounds is elusive. Although they were clearly used to bury the dead, burial mounds may have also been places where (1) elites were buried, with others being cremated; (2) bodies were processed in ritual space and not just buried; and/or (3) they may have been territorial markers that also served as cemeteries (see Fenton 2001:143–144).

The Woodland Tradition can also be generally viewed as tribal-level farming societies that occupied the forests of eastern North America (also see Chapter 12), although Early Woodland groups relied little on farming. The Woodland is marked by a considerable diversity of adaptations that included large-scale public works (e.g., mound complexes), a variable reliance on farming, multiple levels of sedentism, considerable warfare, a variety of mortuary customs, and a diversity of pottery types. The Woodland also marks the evolution and development of complex social systems and institutionalized inequality.

There are a number of models to explain the development of Woodland complexity (see Seeman 1992:5–11; McElrath et al. 2000:6–11). One model is that increasing population density "forced" people to intensify their use of resources (e.g., domestication) and then move into productive river valleys, leading to control of resource bases. Second, it may be that a general increase in the desire for status, independent of other factors such as population growth or climatic variation, led to greater and greater inequality. Third, networks of prestige goods may have developed in conjunction with the establishment of tribal-level social networks as a response to stress; that is, risk was shared through the establishment of formalized exchange networks that linked polities (see R. B. Stewart 1994a; also see Braun and Plog 1982). Fourth, a corporate model suggests that the focus would have been on the group, with a lack of prestige items to symbolize individual status and lack of aggrandizement of individuals. Fifth, it is possible that powerful individuals (or families) gained control of a society, with their power and wealth being highly visible. Finally, a dual-processual model was proposed where the corporate and individuals models compete back and forth in place and time, resulting in considerable variation (see Coon 2009).

The Early Woodland (ca. 3,000 to 1,900 BP)

The Early Woodland marks the beginning of farming societies, although corn was not yet present. Hunting and gathering continued to form the cornerstone of Early Woodland economies. Pottery was also adopted. Smoking pipes at least as old as 2,300 BP have been found in a number of Woodland sites (Rafferty 2006), indicating the use of tobacco.

An apparent decline in the number of sites from the preceding Late Archaic suggests a population decline, possibly due to a cooling climate (see Fiedel 2001:118) or disease. It is also possible that people were consolidating into fewer sites located in good farming areas. A number of regional Early Woodland complexes has been identified, the most notable being Adena.

A notable Early Woodland site is the Peace Bridge site (Fig. 11.3), located in Fort Erie, Ontario, on the Niagara River across from Buffalo, New York. This site was first occupied in the Late Archaic and used throughout the Woodland until about 500 years ago. Excavations revealed a very large village and toolstone quarry/workshop and considerable information on lifeways (Williamson et al. 2006). Of note was the cooperation between the Native American community and archaeologists in the interpretation of the site. A short video on the site, "Legacy of Stone," can be found at www.archaeologychannel.org.

THE ADENA COMPLEX   Beginning about 2,500 BP, a number of groups in the central Ohio Valley began to construct mound complexes, so named after the Adena site in Ohio. Most of the mounds were used for burials, but others were built within enclosures that contained ritual space of unknown function (see Milner 2004:80). Collectively, these Early Woodland groups are called the Adena Complex. Adena is not a single "culture" but refers to early moundbuilding groups in the same general region that share similar traits (see Milner 2004).

The construction of mounds and the development of elaborate mortuary practices are believed to indicate an increase in sociocultural complexity (cf. Lindauer and Blitz 1997). It requires labor to build mounds, power to control labor, economic surpluses to feed and reward labor, and a sophisticated organization to accomplish it all. Adena must have been more socially and politically complex than anything before. However, most archaeological research has been conducted

FIGURE 11.3   Excavations at the Peace Bridge site, Fort Erie, Ontario. Note the use of a mechanical scraper to expose the various storage features (the round patches of dark soil) (photo courtesy of Archaeological Services, Inc.).

on Adena mound complexes, meaning that more is known about Adena mortuary behavior than anything else. Adena has been divided into Early, Middle, and Late.

Most known Early and Middle Adena (ca. 3,000 to 2,200 BP) sites are burial mounds; few habitation sites have been identified. Those that are known tend to be small, and only a few contain domestic structures. It appears that Adena populations were widely dispersed, perhaps in small farmsteads. People would presumably have gathered together at mound sites for special purposes, such as to bury the dead, conduct ceremonies, or build mounds.

The dead were buried (within primary interments) in small, log-lined tombs, each of which would contain a few individuals buried with functional "personal" grave goods with red ochre (or other pigments) on them. The tomb and grave goods were burned and covered with earth, creating a mound over the burned structure. As tombs accumulated, the mound grew, the largest reaching sixty-seven feet high (Bense 1994:121). Some mounds had small occupation sites on top but is it not known who lived in them.

The grave goods include copper artifacts, marine shell ornaments, mica sheets cut into shapes (e.g., heads and hands), obsidian toolstone, and other material from distant sources. This demonstrated the existence of an extensive long-distance trade network between the various Adena groups (see R. B. Stewart 1994a). By 2,700 BP, Adena mortuary traits had diffused to the north and east, influencing other Woodland groups in those areas (e.g., the Middlesex Complex; see below).

Late Adena (ca. 2,200 to 1,900 BP) is marked by the development of a new mortuary pattern and much more elaborate mounds. Burials changed from primary inhumations to secondary burials with ochre-painted bones, although cremation was also practiced. Burial mounds were still used, but geometric and representational mounds were added (see Milner 2004:73–82). The function and meaning of the new mound types are not clear. A video on the Adena is available at www.archaeologychannel.org, "The Adena People: Moundbuilders of Kentucky."

OTHER EARLY WOODLAND DEVELOPMENTS   The Early Woodland witnessed a variety of other developments throughout the Northeast as pottery diffused into new areas and farming gradually increased in importance. A representative example is the Meadowood Complex (ca. 2,700 to 2,300 BP; see R. J. Mason 1981; J. V. Wright 1995:619–629), located primarily in the eastern Great Lakes region but extending as far east as New England. Meadowood is identified by the appearance of pottery and the presence of distinctive Meadowood points, manufactured from specialized preform blades. It is possible that these points could be related to the introduction of the bow and arrow into the region (J. V. Wright 1995:620).

The Meadowood mortuary pattern was one of primary and secondary inhumations, as well as some cremation, with grave goods and occasional red ochre, a mortuary tradition perhaps related to the Adena complex to the south (see J. V. Wright 1995:660–664). However, Meadowood people were buried in natural mounds, rather than purposefully constructed mounds. Caches of Meadowood blades were sometimes placed within burials, and one example from the Meadowood site contained a cache of 243 blades (see R. J. Mason 1981:213).

Adena influenced materials have been found in various places along the Middle Atlantic coast, including Delaware, New Jersey, and New England (Ritchie and Dragoo 1959; Dragoo 1976). In northern New England and the Maritimes, the Middlesex and Boucher burial complexes (ca. 2,700 to 2,000 BP) appear to be related to Adena. These complexes included small burial mounds (with primary and secondary burials) and some similarities in artifacts. A good example is the Augustine Mound in New Brunswick (Turnbull 1976), an artificially constructed burial mound that contained primary and secondary inhumations and cremations. Many grave goods were recovered, including large bifaces and copper beads, but most of the material was of local origin, making it clear that local people were responsible.

The similarities between Middlesex/Boucher and Adena are striking, and it has been suggested that some Adena groups migrated east into the greater Maine region sometime before 2,000 BP (Ritchie and Dragoo 1959). It was later argued that there was not a migration of Adena people but that Adena mortuary traits had diffused into the region (Rutherford 1990; also see R. B. Stewart 1994a), perhaps as part of a larger ceremonial complex (see Bourque 1994).

The Middle Woodland (ca. 2,200 to ca. 1,600 BP)

The Middle Woodland marks the appearance of corn into much of eastern North America, although corn did not become a critical resource until 1,200 BP (Scarry 1993a:78). The Middle Woodland also refers to the time when the Early Woodland Adena evolved into the more complex Hopewell (see below), an assortment of groups practicing a general mortuary pattern in the Ohio River Valley and beyond (e.g., Theler and Boszhardt 2003:109).

The diversity of Middle Woodland groups suggests that there may have been significant social and political instability, with considerable population redistribution (Charles 1992). Trade was substantial and widespread, particularly as it involved the Hopewell (see below). Hopewell influences do not appear to have penetrated the coastal Middle Atlantic (R. B. Stewart 1994a) or

New England regions. Nevertheless, new pottery styles and the adoption of corn farming mark the Middle Woodland in those regions. The northern Maritimes were occupied by the Dorset at this time (see Chapter 4).

Of note is the Point Peninsula Complex in the northeastern Great Lakes region. This Middle Woodland culture appears to have been related to the Hopewell, both by trade items and the use of burial mounds. One such mound is the "Serpent Mounds" site in southern Ontario (see J. V. Wright 1995:675). Point Peninsula may have been ancestral to the Iroquoian groups.

THE HOPEWELL   The Hopewell are the "Moundbuilders" of early archaeology (see Chapter 1), originally thought to represent non-Indians but later clearly shown to be Indian in origin (e.g., Thomas 1894). Hopewell, much like Adena before it, is actually a number of related groups spanning the Middle Woodland who practiced a similar mortuary pattern that included mound construction. Hopewell is a considerable elaboration of Adena, with much larger mounds and sites, but is quite variable, with different groups occupying different areas throughout different periods of time. All "Hopewellian" groups "shared three basic features: mound building, Hopewelllian pottery, and a suite of personal ornaments and raw materials" (Bense 1994:141). The most recent general reviews of Hopewell were provided by Dancey (2005), Carr and Case (2006), and Charles and Buikstra (2006). A different and innovative way of looking at Hopewell through symbolism was presented by A. M. Byers (2004; also see J. A. Brown 1998).

The Hopewell pattern extended across much of the interior Northeast and even into the Southeast (see Chapter 12). Hopewell can be divided into a number of regional entities, such as "Havana" along the upper Mississippi and lower Illinois rivers; "Mann" (formerly Crab Orchard) along the lower Ohio River near its confluences with the Wabash River; "Miami" along the Ohio, Great Miami, and Little Miami rivers in western Ohio; "Scioto" in central Ohio along the Scioto River; and "Southern Appalachian" along the middle Tennessee River (actually in the Southeast, see Chapter 12). The Hopewell, subject of more than a century of work, is "one of the best-known but least-understood prehistoric cultures in the world" (Yerkes 2006:50).

Considerable research has been conducted on interpreting Hopewell social organization from mortuary data, but little work has been done on nonmortuary ritual or organization, gender, religion, or other aspects of society (Carr and Case 2006:19). Differences in mound size, population estimates, and implied social/political organizations have been noted between various groups, but an understanding of Hopewell settlement patterns is only now beginning to emerge (e.g., Pacheco and Dancey 2006).

The range and variation of Hopewell mortuary practices are reasonably well known but poorly understood. A combination of primary and secondary inhumations and cremations was practiced. Most people were buried, but the bones of some people (perhaps elites) were disinterred, stored in charnel houses, then reinterred in a mass log tomb covered by a mound. Other people (commoners?) were cremated, a process that entailed the bodies being left to decompose above ground in a special structure, which was then burned and a mound built over it. The different mortuary treatments, coupled with the analysis of grave goods, suggest a significant level of social differentiation. Some burials have been interpreted as "sacrificial," individuals killed as part of the burial ceremony of high-status people. However, it is possible that these "victims" had died earlier and their remains placed in high-status graves as offerings and had not actually been sacrificed (e.g., A. M. Byers 2004:185–190).

The burial mounds were purposefully constructed, and large mounds were often formed by an accumulation of smaller mounds covering previous burials. Eventually, a mound would be "full" and a new one started. These burial mounds were not just piles of dirt over burials but were carefully constructed with "layers of selected earths, clays, stones, and gravels" placed over the tombs and covered with "an extremely durable mixed sand and clay surface" (A. M. Byers 2004:3), a construction that might be related to symbolism associated with "newly created earth" from floods (Van Nest 2006:426). This construction proved quite durable to the natural elements until they were destroyed by plowing in the last hundred years. A variation of the generally round burial mound was the platform mound, a rectangular mound less than ten feet high and fifty to seventy-five feet long.

In addition to burial mounds, Hopewell groups constructed a variety of other types of mounds, including linear mounds, geometric mounds, and embankments. Some linear mounds were constructed to enclose specific areas (Mainfort and Sullivan 1998), including groups of circular mounds on the tops of hills (recall Fig. 1.1). These hilltop enclosures, such as the Fort Ancient site in Ohio (see R. P. Connolly 1998; Drooker and Cowan 2001), were called "forts" by early Europeans. The Hopewell site (for which the Hopewell groups were named) consists of many mounds within several enclosures of ditches and embankments, the largest of which encompassed approximately one hundred acres (see Greber and Ruhl 1989). A number of other Hopewell mound complexes are known that include circular and rectangular embankment mounds, often hundreds of feet in diameter (Fig. 11.4), although their function is unclear. These mound complexes do not appear to be villages or towns, and most Hopewell settlements appear to be small, dispersed communities associated with mound complexes (Pacheco and Dancey 2006:25). Thus, it seems that the mound complexes were constructed by people from these different settlements within a shared ritual environment (Bernardini 2004). The question of whether Hopewell groups lived in sedentary or mobile communities has yet to be resolved (Cowan 2006).

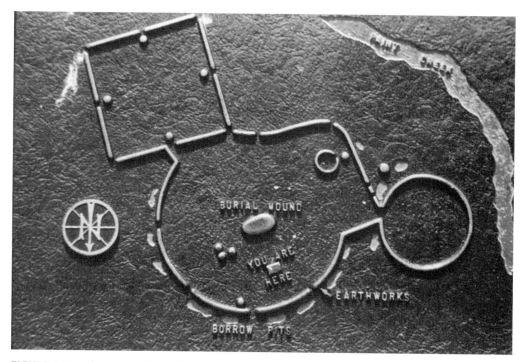

FIGURE 11.4   Plan map of the Seip Earthworks, a Hopewell site in Ohio.

Other mound complexes were long, parallel embankments called "roads," only a few of which are known (and some scholars discount). These embankment features were wide (ca. 150 ft.) lanes created by high (8 to 10 ft.), parallel earthen walls and may have connected mound complexes. For example, the "Great Hopewell Road" in Ohio (first discovered in 1862 and rediscovered with modern aerial photos; see Lepper [1995, 2006]) consists of a parallel embankment lane extending several miles from the Newark mound complex in Ohio toward the nearly identical Chillicothe mound complex some fifty-five miles away. Despite several hundred years of plowing, traces of this feature can still be seen today, although it is not clear whether the "road" actually connected the two centers. If these "road" features are real, their function is quite unclear (compare to the Chacoan roads from Chapter 9) but may be related to world renewal rituals (see A. M. Byers 2004) or pilgrimages of people to special places (Lepper 2006).

Although poorly known, Hopewellian groups appear to have had a variety of "leaders," including shamans, political figures, and war leaders (Carr 2006a), some of which were women (Field et al. 2006). Other data indicate the presence of a clan social organization (Thomas et al. 2006). The apparent social and political variability of Hopewell groups suggests that a dual-processual model may explain Hopewell development (Coon 2009). The persistence of Hopewellian traits over hundreds of years and across a large area suggests that the general sociopolitical structure was relatively stable (Dancey 2005:128).

Relatively little is known about Hopewell subsistence. Based on assumptions about complexity and size of populations, it was initially thought that the Hopewellian subsistence economies were based on corn agriculture. However, relatively few Hopewell sites have produced corn remains, and more recent work has shown that subsistence was based on intensive exploitation of goosefoot (*Chenopodium* sp.) and knotweed (*Polygonum erectum*), plants that had been domesticated locally (see Yerkes 2006). The use of tree nuts seems to have been important, as nut debris is common in the botanical remains from Hopewell sites (Ford 1979:238). Finally, it is clear that hunting, gathering, and fishing were important.

One of the intriguing aspects of the Hopewell is their material culture. Classic Hopewellian materials, commonly found in mortuary contexts, include copper panpipes, shell bowls, sheets of carved mica (Fig. 11.5), earspools, large obsidian blades, pipes and axes of polished stone, elaborate pottery, and ornaments of copper (Fig. 11.6), silver, shell, and stone. The pottery was manufactured in a variety of forms, but one of the most characteristic was small bowls decorated with bird or geometric motifs. Much of the material used to manufacture these items was imported, attesting to the reach of Hopewellian trade.

This far-flung exchange system, originally called the "Hopewell Interaction Sphere" (Struever and Houart 1972; Seeman 1979) included the trade of raw materials, finished artifacts, and ideology across the much of the interior Northeast during Hopewell times. Streuver and Houart (1972) argued that Hopewell was a series of separate but highly organized and interrelated polities adapted to localized environmental conditions and that they interacted within the trading system, although not all groups were participants. This proposed interaction sphere may have linked communities together to share the risk of resource shortages. On the other hand, some sort of competition or conflict is suggested by the presence of human skulls as possible trophies (Seeman 1988).

But perhaps the concept of an interaction sphere suggesting any singular identity or organizational entity is actually misleading (Carr 2006b). Hopewell trade may not have been the result of any single organization but was the cumulative result of individuals from different groups pursuing a variety of goals that were local in origin (rather than trans-Hopewellian), including trade, political power, spiritual power, and marriage (see Fie 2006). Yet, Hopewell

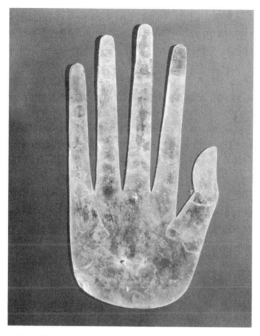

FIGURE 11.5   A Hopewell "hand" made from mica. (*Source:* Art Resource, N.Y.)

FIGURE 11.6   Copper implements from an Ohio Hopewell site (courtesy of the Field Museum, Chicago).

groups did share a common worldview, as can be seen, for instance, in their mortuary practices, which linked trade and interaction to some degree. Interestingly, there seems to have been little trade between the northern and southern Hopewell groups (e.g., Bense 1994:143).

Hopewellian groups began to decline beginning about 1,700 BP. Various ideas have been offered to explain this, including overpopulation, changes in climate (although conditions appear to have actually improved), and the introduction of the bow and arrow, the latter resulting in an increase in hunting efficiency and the decimation of game and/or an increase in warfare. However, since Hopewell is defined by its ritual system (mortuary and mound patterns), the disappearance of those features suggests a collapse of the ritual system. It has also been argued that these proposed possible causes are misleading and that the real issue was the effort expended in cultural elaboration (e.g., earthworks), which may have reduced reproductive capacity, resulting in an eventual abandonment of such elaborations (Dunnell and Greenlee 1999). In some areas, however (e.g., the Illinois Valley), there is little evidence of decline, and all indications point to a smooth transition to Late Woodland (Charles 1992). It may be that Hopewell did not collapse (Dancey 2005:131); rather, it evolved into the Late Woodland groups (some of which built mounds) and into the ethnographic groups in the region.

The Late Woodland (ca. 1,600 to 150 BP)

The Late Woodland is generally marked by the disappearance of the ceremonial complexes and earthworks that marked Hopewell, although the practice of moundbuilding persisted with a few groups (e.g., Fort Ancient, see below). The disappearance of the mounds and artistic traditions, as well as a decline in interregional trade, suggests a decrease in social and political complexity, a pattern that lasted until ethnographic times. Farming diffused north as far as Manitoba (Nicholson 1990), but some groups in the far Northeast (too far north for farming) remained Archaic hunter-gatherers until contact.

Farming became more important during the Late Woodland, and by about 1,200 BP corn had become a staple crop across the Northeast, perhaps earlier in the western Northeast (Rose 2008), although in some Late Woodland communities, other crops were more important than corn. As corn assumed a dominant role in most late Woodland economies, squash also increased in importance, and beans were introduced about 700 BP (Hart and Scarry 1999; Hart et al. 2002). Hunting and gathering, especially the hunting of deer, remained important.

Settlement patterns also changed. The numerous small, dispersed settlements that marked the Middle Woodland were gradually replaced by fewer and larger nucleated settlements. Early Late Woodland settlements were hamlets or villages, but after about 700 BP, most settlements were relatively large villages with large populations (R. B. Stewart 1994b:201; also see Hasenstab 1996). Many of these villages were fortified, attesting to the practice of warfare.

A number of these Late Woodland groups, such as the Powhatan and Iroquois, developed very complex sociopolitical organizations. It is possible that this increase in social complexity was related to the adoption of corn as a staple (Schurr and Schoeninger 1995). The larger village sizes and the necessity to control fields may have led to this increased complexity.

FORT ANCIENT (CA. 1,600 TO 600 BP)   Fort Ancient (named after the famous site first occupied by the Hopewell) consisted of a number of related Late Woodland groups that derived from local Hopewell groups in the Ohio River Valley (see Connolly and Lepper 2004). Fort Ancient groups (see Fig. 11.1) were farmers who lived in fortified villages. Like their Hopewellian ancestors, Fort Ancient people continued to construct mounds, but there was a change from conical to

FIGURE 11.7   The Great Serpent Mound in Ohio. (*Source:* The Ohio Historical Society.)

linear and effigy mounds. Many of the linear mounds were small with burials in the effigy "heads," while the effigy mounds were shaped like animals (e.g., birds, bears, and turtles) or "spirits" (see Milner 2004:106–109). One of the prime examples of a Fort Ancient effigy mound is the Great Serpent Mound in Ohio (Fig. 11.7). It measures 1,200 feet long, 20 feet high, and 5 feet wide and was constructed about 1,000 years ago. The head of the "serpent" points to the summer solstice.

Fort Ancient groups may have been influenced by Middle Mississippian groups to the south (see Chapter 12). Trade items appear to be Mississippian, as were village organization (houses around a central plaza) and some mortuary practices (pottery in burials). This is not to say that Fort Ancient was Mississippian, only that there were Mississippian influences (Pollack and Henderson 1992:289–293). Robert Cook (2008) argued that Fort Ancient societies interacted with, and were more influenced by, Middle Mississippian groups than was earlier thought and suggested that they were essentially a small-scale version of Middle Mississippian, just lacking ceremonial mound complexes. Fort Ancient groups, or at least some of them, may have eventually evolved into the ethnographic Shawnee.

THE IROQUOIAN LATE WOODLAND   The prehistory of Iroquoian groups (a linguistic grouping that includes the ethnographic Iroquois, Huron, and Neutral) is a major research issue in the Northeast (see Warrick 2000; Chilton 2005b). The Iroquoian Period in the New York/southern Ontario region is often divided into Early (1,100 to 700 BP), Middle (700 to 600 BP), and Late

(600 to 350 BP). Iroquoian is generally considered to have developed in situ from a Middle Woodland (Point Peninsula) base some 1,500 BP (Warrick 2000). However, there are others (e.g., Snow 1995) that believe Iroquoian groups migrated into the region after about 1,100 BP, marking the beginning of the Late Woodland in that region. Still others continue to support the in situ model, arguing that the adoption of corn agriculture was the impetus behind the development of matrilocality, a hallmark of the Iroquoian (Hart 2001; also see S. W. J. Martin 2008).

Iroquoian populations were relatively large (Chilton 2005b:145) and generally resided in permanent villages. These villages were paired, separated by a few kilometers from each other and twenty to thirty kilometers from the next group (Warrick 2000:434, 438). Each village contained some four or five longhouses, each of which was divided into family compartments. Each village contained between seventy-five and two hundred people. Iroquoian groups had complex sociopolitical organizations and depended on farming (see Bamann et al. 1992). The dead were buried in ossuaries (e.g., Mullen and Hoppa 1992; see Highlight 11.3).

The earliest Iroquoian longhouses date to about 1,100 BP and were relatively small (Warrick 1996; also see Kapches 1990). The longhouses gradually became larger until about 500 BP and probably supported matrilineal extended families. They then became smaller, perhaps due to political power moving from the lineages to clans (Warrick 1996:20). Populations appear to have grown after about 700 BP, perhaps due to lower infant mortality resulting from a greater reliance on corn (Warrick 2000:444).

HIGHLIGHT 11.4

THE MOATFIELD OSSUARY

In 1997, human burials were discovered on the edge of a soccer field in Moatfield, near Toronto, Canada. Subsequent investigation (Williams and Pfeiffer 2003) revealed the presence of an ossuary, later found to have been located on the periphery of an Iroquoian village dated to about 700 BP (Williamson et al. 2003). Some eighty-seven individuals were discovered, some as single interments and some as multiple burials. As was typical of the time, all were secondary burials, the bones wrapped in bundles and buried.

Men, women, and children were represented, and many of the adults were older than fifty, suggesting an overall healthy population. However, many individuals suffered from a variety of ailments, including sinusitis probably brought on by constant exposure to smoke from fires (Merrett 2003). Nutritional deficiencies were also noted among the children (Pfeiffer 2003). Isotopic data suggested that fish was an important food but that corn was also critical (also see Van der Merwe et al. 2003).

Information on social organization was also derived from the site. An analysis of the cranial morphology suggested that the females were more genetically diverse than the males. This led to the hypothesis that the females came from other populations, married Moatfield men, and moved to Moatfield to live with their husbands (DeLaurier and Spence 2003).

OTHER LATE WOODLAND GROUPS   A variety of sociopolitical organizations developed in the Northeast, although most Late Woodland groups developed tribal-level societies. In some areas, chiefdom-level societies developed, the best examples being the Iroquois and the Powhatan Confederacy in Virginia (see Gallivan 2003). Hantman and Gold (2002) argued that there was a cyclical pattern of the rise and fall of various chiefdoms across the Middle Atlantic region and that after about 800 BP the chiefdoms became larger and more powerful, the Powhatan being an example.

In Ohio and Pennsylvania, the Monongahela (ca. 950 to 365 BP) were a dominant Late Woodland group. They had disappeared just prior to contact (see W. C. Johnson 2001), perhaps destroyed by the Iroquoian Seneca over trade issues (W. C. Johnson 2001:82). It is also possible that a severe drought disrupted their farming (Richardson et al. 2003), decreased corn yields, and forced them to "disband" as a group.

A large variety of groups existed in the Middle Atlantic region, including bands, tribes, and chiefdoms (Custer 1984). Some lived in small hamlets and others in large fortified villages (R. B. Stewart 1993), and there was a marked decline in trade of everything except shell, which increased (R. B. Stewart 1994a). In some areas, such as New England, there is no evidence that horticulture was intensive before contact (Chilton 2005b:142).

The prehistory of the Algonquians (a linguistic grouping, like the Iroquoians), located across much of the northern Northeast, may have been less complex than the Iroquoians. It has generally been assumed that the Algonquians developed in place from a population movement into the area during Paleoindian times, suggesting a cultural continuity for some 10,000 years. Others (e.g., Fiedel 1987) argued that the Algonquians migrated from the north some 3,000 years ago, meaning that there was not a general cultural continuity from Paleoindian to contact.

Algonquian groups, while growing some crops, lacked large, sedentary villages, suggesting that they may have focused more on fishing than farming (Hasenstab 1999:152). In fact, some interior Algonquian groups may have been mostly hunter-gatherers with seasonal rounds (Chilton 2005b:150).

HIGHLIGHT 11.5

THE ONEOTA TRADITION

About 1,200 BP, a number of Late Woodland groups in the upper Midwest appear to have adopted Mississippian traits, collectively forming the Oneota Tradition (see Fig. 11.1). This tradition first appeared in the upper Mississippi Valley and then spread across much of the region (primarily Wisconsin but as far south as Missouri), even out onto the Plains (see Henning 1998, 2001, 2005:169–178; Berres 2001; Theler and Boszhardt 2003). The Oneota seem to represent a "marriage between Late Woodland people and Mississippian ideas" (Theler and Boszhardt 2003:157), perhaps originating as a result of the movement of some groups out of the region, with the remaining groups reforming into a "new" Oneota culture (Theler and Boszhardt 2003, 2006). The Oneota are often divided into Emergent, Developmental, and Classic horizons (see Berres 2001:Table 1), each with a variety of regional phases usually identified by pottery types and distributions. The Oneota occupied portions of the Plains, Mississippi Valley, and eastern forests, so they do not "neatly fit" into any single culture area.

Oneota groups were primarily corn farmers, but hunting and gathering remained important, with bison, elk, and deer being the primary game. Oneota groups were organized into tribes with semipermanent settlements and a seasonal round (farming and hunting). Early Oneota villages were small and unfortified, and some had burial mounds and enclosures. Later in time, Oneota villages were fortified and became much larger (Berres 2001:3), and mortuary practices changed to include cemeteries, all of which attest to complex settlement, subsistence, ritual, and political systems (see S. Schroeder 2004). Warfare was prevalent among Oneota groups (Milner et al. 1991b; Milner 1999), as seen by the skeletal evidence from the Norris Farms No. 36 site, dating to about 700 BP. At this site, a mound containing 264 burials included at least 43 men, women, and children that had met violent deaths, likely due to chronic warfare (Milner et al. 1991a).

The Oneota disappeared before contact, but it is not clear why. It may be that corn farming became less productive after the onset of a warmer climatic period ca. 800 BP. Agriculture would have become less important, hunting may have become more important, and as a result, groups became more mobile (F. B. King 1993:233), so they were no longer "Oneota." Some Oneota groups may have moved out onto the central Plains (Ritterbush 2006). It is also possible that warfare and perhaps even European diseases that arrived before actual Europeans impacted the Oneota (see Henning 2005:174).

NATIVE NORTHEAST CULTURES AT CONTACT

Many Northeastern Indian groups, particularly those along the Atlantic coast, did not survive into the twentieth century. Other coastal groups fled to the west and/or were forced to move onto reservations in Oklahoma. Only a few groups managed to retain some of their original lands, and a number of small reservations, some federal and some state, were established. Some tribes are reorganizing, seeking to recover members who had lost their identity and petitioning the government for formal recognition. The biggest issue is the reestablishment of tribal land bases.

Some groups, such as the Iroquois, have reservations and are doing reasonably well. Many other groups lack formal federal recognition and cannot get assistance. However, this situation is improving. For example, in 1980, Congress passed the Maine Indian Settlement Act, which allowed the federal government to purchase 300,000 acres for several Maine tribes and provided $27,000,000 for economic development. Other groups are helping themselves. Several tribes have opened casinos and are using the profits to establish health, police, fire, and educational services, as well as to purchase land within their traditional boundaries. One of these casinos is the Foxwoods Casino in eastern Connecticut, owned and operated by the Mashantucket Pequot tribe, and it is one of the largest casinos in the world.

The future for most Northeastern groups seems good. They are beginning the long process of regaining lands, revitalizing their cultures, and developing their economic bases. It will not be an easy task, but progress is being made.

Further Reading

A considerable body of literature is available on the prehistory of the Northeast. The various prehistory chapters in the *Handbook of North American Indians* (Trigger 1978) are generally out-of-date but remain a good place to begin research. Several more recent general treatments of the Northeast have been published (Muller 1986; Dent 1995; and Milner 2004), and more specific regional treatments are available for New England (Snow 1980), the Great Lakes region (R. J. Mason 1981), Delaware (Custer 1984), Vermont (Haviland and Power 1994), Maine (Bourque 2001), and Ohio (Lepper 2005).

In addition, a number of monograph series are currently being published, such as *Occasional Publications in Northeastern Anthropology*. Some of the journals that deal with Northeastern prehistory are *Archaeology of Eastern North America, Canadian Journal of Archaeology, Ontario Archaeology, Journal of Middle Atlantic Archaeology, Man in the Northeast, Midcontinental Journal of Archaeology, Northeast Anthropology, Wisconsin Archaeologist* (published since the late 1800s), *Illinois Archaeology, Pennsylvania Archaeologist*, and *Ohio Archaeologist*.

CHAPTER 12

Mounds and Towns
The Southeast

The Southeast (Fig. 12.1) is a region containing a substantial Paleoindian record and has recently become the focus of ideas regarding where the earliest people in North America originated and how they adapted (see Chapter 2). The Southeast is also well known for its very complex prehistoric groups, many of which were at their peak at the time of European contact about 450 BP. The evolution of these complex societies, whether chiefdoms or states, provides an exciting laboratory for discovering the conditions and processes that led to their development. In addition, the northern Southeast appears to have been an independent center of early domestication in North America, making it a region of great importance to the study of early agriculture. Thus, an understanding of the prehistory of the Southeast is essential for addressing a number of issues that transcend simple chronology.

GEOGRAPHY AND ENVIRONMENT

The Southeast is divided into three basic environmental zones (see Hudson 1976; Fig. 12.1; also see Gremillion 2004b): the Coastal Plain, the Piedmont, and the southern Appalachian Mountains. The Coastal Plain extends the entire length of the coast of the Southeast and is dominated by an extensive pine forest along with slow-moving rivers, bayous, and swamps, particularly along the coasts and in southern Florida. The Mississippi River, the largest river in North America, flows south through the western part of the plain, creating extensive alluvial terrain ideal for flood-irrigated agriculture.

The Piedmont encompasses the rolling hills below the Appalachian Mountains and contains a broad hardwood forest dominated by oak and hickory but includes pine, poplar, and sycamore trees. The Piedmont is transected by many rivers flowing south and east, creating many valleys surrounded by forested hills. This combination of environmental factors presented an extensive array of resources and highly productive fishing areas. The southern Appalachian Mountains are situated within the northeastern Southeast and contain a vast forest of poplar, chestnut, hickory, walnut, and pine. The mountains also contain a variety of stone for toolmaking, which was lacking on the coastal plains.

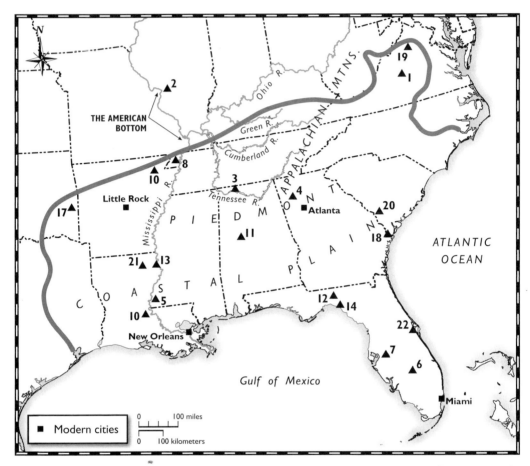

FIGURE 12.1 Map of the Southeast showing the major subregions and the location of sites discussed in the text: 1) Cactus Hill; 2) Cahokia; 3) Dust Cave; 4) Etowah; 5) Fatherland; 6) Fort Center; 7) Harney Flats; 8) Helena Mound; 9) Icehouse Bottom; 10) Marksville; 11) Moundville; 12) Page-Ladson; 13) Poverty Point; 14) Ryan/Harley; 15) Salts-Mammoth caves; 16) Sloan; 17) Spiro; 18) Stallings Island; 19) Thunderbird; 20) Topper; 21) Watson Brake; 22) Windover.

Many plants (see Gremillion 2004b: Table 1) were utilized by ancient populations of the Southeast, including nuts (e.g., walnuts, hazelnuts, chestnuts, beechnuts, acorns, hickory), various berries, grapes, gourds, chenopods, sunflowers, and sumpweed. Among the many animals (see Gremillion 2004b:63–66) exploited by these people were deer (the most important game animal in the Southeast), bears, opossums, rabbits, raccoons, squirrels, otters, beavers, waterfowl, turkeys, turtles, fish, shellfish, crawfish, shrimp, and crabs.

Like the rest of North America, the climate of the Southeast has varied over time (see Tables 1.1 and 12.1). As the climate changed, the distribution of the forest zones also changed, with the boreal forest moving north during the early Holocene and being replaced by a more temperate forest. These changing ecozones played a significant role in human adaptation through time. Today, the Southeast has a generally mild climate with abundant rainfall. There are between 210 and 270 frost-free days, ideal for agriculture.

TABLE 12.1 A Chronological Sequence for the Southeast

Date (BP)	A Broad Outline	General Sequences by Region				General Climate
		Mississippi Valley	Central Region	Southeastern Region	Atlantic Coast	
450	Mississippian	Late Mississippian		Late	Woodland	similar to today
		Middle Mississippian				
		Emergent Mississippian				
1,000	Middle Woodland	Hopewell		Middle Woodland		similar to today
2,000	Early Woodland	Adena	Poverty Point	Early Woodland		
3,000	Late Archaic			Late Archaic		
4,000						
5,000	Middle Archaic		Middle Archaic			becoming cooler and wetter
6,000						warmer and drier than today
7,000						
8,000	Early Archaic		Early Archaic (Kirk Horizon)			
9,000						cooler and wetter than today but warming
10,000			Early Archaic (Big Sandy Horizon)			
to 11,000	Paleoindian		Late Paleoindian (e.g., Dalton)			cooler and wetter than today
			Middle Paleoindian (e.g., non-Clovis fluted)			
			Early Paleoindian (e.g., Clovis)			

A BRIEF HISTORY OF RESEARCH

The first archaeological work in the Southeast was conducted by Thomas Jefferson in the late 1700s with his investigations of earthen mounds in Virginia (Jefferson 1797). In the nineteenth century, the moundbuilder issue dominated early research in the Southeast, and numerous mound sites were investigated, many of which have subsequently been destroyed by agriculture and development. During the Great Depression of the early twentieth century, the U.S. government sponsored a great deal of work, the results of which were used to form the basic outline of Southeastern prehistory (e.g., Griffin 1952). After about 1970, government-mandated environmental work resulted in a considerable expansion of archaeological research, and much additional knowledge was obtained. Enough is now known to begin investigating the formation of complex societies, the development of indigenous agriculture, and the impact of European contact on native groups. More detailed histories of Southeastern archaeology were provided by Bense (1994:25–36), Tushingham et al. (2002), and Stoltman (2004), and the results of an intensive study of the late prehistory and ethnohistory of St. Catherine's Island, Georgia, are now available (D. H. Thomas 2008).

MAJOR THEMES IN SOUTHEASTERN PREHISTORY

A variety of important research issues continue to dominate Southeastern archaeology. The recent discovery of several possible pre-Clovis sites (e.g., Cactus Hill, see Chapter 2) suggest the possibility of a pre-Clovis occupation, and the large number of Clovis points known from the region have led some to suggest the Southeast as the origin point for Clovis. Work continues on these questions.

Another important research focus is on the origin of agriculture and the timing of the domestication of native plants. It is clear that some domestication occurred in the Southeast prior to the introduction of corn from Mesoamerica, making southeastern North American one of the centers of independent agriculture in the world. The discoveries of the types of plants that were domesticated and the circumstances under which that happened remain significant topics.

An understanding of the nature and complexity of the Mississippian societies is still evolving and remains an important issue, with some arguing that some Mississippian polities were states and others refusing to budge from the traditional chiefdom interpretation. Considerable research continues to be conducted on Mississippian politics, ecology, and ideology, but the origin of these systems in the preceding Woodland Tradition is not well understood. Research on Mississippian questions continues to dominate archaeological research in the Southeast. A basic chronological sequence of the Southeast is shown in Table 12.1.

THE PALEOINDIAN PERIOD (TO CA. 11,000 BP)

A considerable Paleoindian record (see Chapter 3) has been documented in the Southeast (see Lane and Anderson 2001). Two sites, Cactus Hill in Virginia and Topper in South Carolina, may contain pre-Clovis components, but Topper does not appear promising and Cactus Hill has not been confirmed. A few sites with Western Clovis (Early Paleoindian) materials are known, such as the Thunderbird site in Virginia (W. M. Gardner 1974:5, 37; also see Goodyear 1999:435) and the Page-Ladson site in Florida (Milanich 1994:47; Webb 2005), but Western Clovis is uncommon in the Southeast.

Of great interest is the large number of Paleoindian projectile points discovered in the Southeast (see Fig. 2.7), forming the greatest concentration in North America (Anderson et al. 2010). The large number of fluted points has suggested to some that Clovis first developed in the Southeast and then moved west. The inconsistent use of point typologies confuses the argument, as does the fact that most of these artifacts are isolated surface finds and few actual habitation sites are known. Most of the Paleoindian record from the Southeast appears to postdate Clovis

(Early Paleoindian), falling into the Middle and Late Paleoindian Periods (ca. 11,900 to 11,000 BP; Goodyear 1999:439; also see D. G. Anderson 2004a:Table 1).

While the Middle Paleoindian Period (ca. 11,900 to 11,500 BP) in the Southeast is not well understood, it is typically characterized by the presence of large fluted points (refer to Fig. 2.2), generally called Cumberland, Ross County, Suwannee, and Redstone. What little is known about Middle Paleoindian subsistence systems suggests a general broad-spectrum pattern, rather than one of specialized hunting (Lepper 1999:378). In Florida, Paleoindian settlement may have centered on "oases" during a drought that occurred during the Late Pleistocene (Neill 1964:17; also see Milanich 1994:40–44; Goodyear 1999:444). Excavations at the Harney Flats Paleoindian site near Tampa, Florida, revealed a tool rejuvenation locality (Daniel and Weisenbaker 1987), and an occupation locality was found at the Ryan/Harley site in north Florida (Dunbar et al. 2005).

The Late Paleoindian Period (ca. 11,500 to 11,000 BP) was a time of transition from the Pleistocene to the Holocene, marked by a change in projectile-point forms from fluted to unfluted lanceolate and stemmed-point forms. These points are known by a variety of names, including Dalton, Holcombe, and Quad (Ellis et al. 1998; Goodyear 1999). Some side-notched point forms appear at the terminus of the Late Paleoindian Period (Lane and Anderson 2001:95).

The Late Paleoindian Period in the Southeast is also referred to as the Dalton Period (e.g., McNutt 1996:189). Dalton points are generally lanceolate and stemmed, often with basal indentations. Overall, Dalton technology is similar to earlier Paleoindian toolkits, with the addition of a chipped stone adze (Goodyear 1982:384). Some Dalton points are fluted, suggesting continuity from earlier forms (McNutt 1996:190). The fluted forms occur mostly in the northern boreal forest environments and may be associated with caribou procurement (see Morse 1997a:138). In the Southeast, most Dalton points are unfluted and are "most evident in the central oak-hickory vegetation zone" (Morse et al. 1996:329), suggesting an adaptation to deer hunting in that biotic community.

A variety of Dalton sites has been documented, including habitation sites, cemeteries, and butchering sites, both as open sites and in caves. It is believed that Dalton (and other Late Paleoindian groups) had larger populations, more regular and formalized intergroup contacts, and smaller, more bounded territories than Early Paleoindian groups, reflecting considerable cultural change in a relatively short time (D. G. Anderson 1995a:21). In addition, the first systematic use of rockshelters occurred during Dalton times (Walthall 1998), suggesting a fundamental reorganization of subsistence strategies during this time, including the establishment of seasonal rounds. This use of rockshelters has provided an excellent record of Southeastern culture during the Late Paleoindian Period (Walthall 1998:234). It is not yet clear whether Dalton groups moved around the landscape strictly on a seasonal basis (cf. Schiffer 1975) or had at least some permanent settlements (cf. Morse 1997a:128).

One of the more spectacular Dalton sites is the Sloan site, located in Arkansas. Sloan is a Dalton cemetery containing one or two dozen burials (Condon and Rose 1997) and about 500 artifacts, including 146 Dalton points (Morse 1997b: Table 3.1). All of the points were in pristine condition, apparently unused, and some were made of chert from a source about two hundred miles to the north. The presence of Dalton Period cemeteries suggests that at least some long-term settlements were part of the Dalton settlement pattern.

The subsistence pattern of Dalton is poorly known but undoubtedly involved the exploitation of a broad spectrum of resources. Deer seems to have been a staple (McNutt 1996:189), and there is little doubt that a number of small animal species, as well as a variety of plants, were also exploited.

THE ARCHAIC (CA. 11,000 TO 2,700 BP)

At the end of the Pleistocene, the climate became warmer and drier, and as a consequence the forest communities began to move northward. People adopted more generalized hunting and gathering economies. During the Middle Archaic, the climate became even drier, greatly impacting biotic communities' human adaptations. As the climate became wetter and cooler in the Late Archaic, human populations expanded, and the first domesticated species appeared. A few Late Archaic groups began to develop increased political complexity that foreshadowed later periods. Recent reviews of the Southeastern archaic were provided by Anderson and Sassaman (2004) and Sassaman and Anderson (2004).

The Early Archaic (ca. 11,000 to 8,000 BP)

The Early Archaic roughly equates to the Early Holocene, a time when the cooler and wetter times of the Late Pleistocene began to give way to warmer conditions. Much of the Southeast was covered by an oak-hickory forest during the Early Archaic, and the large animals characteristic of the Pleistocene disappeared. Sea levels were lower, and the Early Archaic sites on the ancient coastline are now underwater (see Faught 2002, 2004).

As conditions began to change, Paleoindian groups "became" Archaic over the course of 500 years or so, although this transition is difficult to ascertain with any clarity (Milanich 1994:63). By about 11,000 BP, the cultural and technological changes were distinct enough to classify groups as Early Archaic. The Early Archaic is characterized by a succession of projectile-point types from side notched, to corner notched, to split stemmed, to stemmed forms. The Early Archaic can be divided into two horizons, Big Sandy (Early Side–notched) and Kirk, although these terms are not employed all across the Southeast (Morse et al. 1996:330). The Big Sandy Horizon, beginning perhaps as early as 11,200 BP in some places (see Morse et al. 1996:330) is characterized by side-notched points (Tuck 1974:75; Morse et al. 1996:330), completely replacing the earlier Late Paleoindian lanceolate and stemmed forms (Ellis et al. 1998:161; also see Driskell 1994; Faught et al. 2003), perhaps due to changing technological requirements for hunting. The Dust Cave site in Alabama has a good radiocarbon-dated stratigraphic record (Driskell 1994:17; Sherwood et al. 2004), with a Late Paleoindian component (10,500 to 10,000 BP) followed by a Big Sandy Horizon component (10,000 to 9,000 BP), as well as a Kirk Horizon component (ca. 8,500 to 7,000 BP).

Another important Early Archaic site is Icehouse Bottom in Tennessee, first occupied at about 9,500 BP (see Chapman 1994). The early components at the site contained many hearths, considerable diversity in botanical specimens (e.g., hickory nuts), and faunal remains (mammals, fish, and shellfish), indicating a diverse diet at that time. Icehouse Bottom continued to be occupied until the Late Woodland (see Fig. 12.2).

The Kirk Horizon, characterized by corner-notched points (Tuck 1974:76; Morse et al. 1996:330), generally follows Big Sandy and dates between about 10,200 to 7,800 BP (Sherwood et al. 2004). Kirk Horizon technology includes large triangulate bifacial knives, celts, ovate chopper/scrapers, and small end scrapers (Ellis et al. 1998:162). Kirk Horizon materials are widely distributed throughout eastern North America, although they occur somewhat later in the Northeast, suggesting the possibility that there was a population migration northward from the Southeast during Early Archaic times (Stothers and Abel 1991:223), perhaps following the northward migration of forest ecozones.

Early Archaic groups exploited a variety of food resources, including mammals, fish, shellfish, and many plants, and some lived in relatively large villages. The Early Archaic adaptation can

FIGURE 12.2   The stratigraphy at the Icehouse Bottom site, with the sequence of Archaic projectile point styles illustrated. (*Source:* Courtesy of Frank H. McClung Museum, The University of Tennessee, Knoxville.)

be viewed as a bridge between a Paleoindian lifestyle and that of the "more settled coastal- and riverine-associated" patterns of the Middle Archaic (Milanich 1994:64).

Along the south Atlantic coast, a model was developed that proposed that each of the major watersheds along the coast was occupied by a relatively large group that practiced a mobile mixed forager/collector strategy (Anderson and Hanson 1988). These groups would then have traded materials and possibly marriage partners with the other groups that occupied the watersheds on either side of them. However, it has been suggested (Daniel 2001) that groups were not restricted to particular watersheds but that group territories cross-cut watersheds, with high-quality toolstone being a major resource.

A very interesting Early Archaic locality is the Windover site in Florida. Windover is a cemetery in a peat bog, with the result that the preservation of bodies and perishable artifacts is very good. Some 168 burials were discovered, 91 of which contained preserved brain tissue. Few lithic artifacts were recovered, but numerous preserved pieces of wood (Adovasio et al. 2002), bone (Penders 2002), and textiles (Andrews et al. 2002) were found. A series of radiocarbon dates on human bone, artifacts, and associated peat placed the use of this cemetery at about 8,200 BP (Doran 2002: Fig. 3.1; also see Doran et al. 1986; Doran and Dickel 1988; Milanich 1994:70–75). The bodies represented all ages and sexes (Dickel 2002) and the demographics and pathologies suggest a difficult life: 20 percent infant mortality, only 20 percent living into their forties, many with broken arms and legs, arthritis, and some evidence of malnutrition (Bense 1994:80). Analysis of dental traits showed greater variability among females, suggesting the possibility of a patrilocal postmarital pattern (Tomczak and Powell 2003). Of great interest was the analysis of mtDNA (Smith et al. 2002) that suggested that the Windover population was the remnant of a group that has no living relatives in the New World, perhaps a surviving group from one of the initial migrations into the New World.

The Middle Archaic (ca. 8,000 to 5,750 BP)

The Middle Archaic generally coincides with the Middle Holocene, a time when the climate became much warmer and drier (called the Altithermal or Hypsithermal; see Anderson et al. 2007). Reduced rainfall resulted in lower water tables and less water flow in the rivers. Much of the hardwood forest in the southern half of the Southeast burned off, perhaps due to lightning strikes, and was replaced by pine forests that generally contain fewer resources of value to humans.

It appears that some portions of the Southeast were more sparsely occupied during the Middle Archaic (e.g., McNutt 1996:196), and some scholars think it is possible that entire regions, such as the lowlands in the Mississippi Valley, were unoccupied (e.g., Morse and Morse 1996:124). Other major river valleys (e.g., the Tennessee and Cumberland) were occupied during the Middle Holocene, presumably to utilize aquatic resources, including shellfish (see Sassaman 2001:109). It may be that the continuing desiccation of the highlands "forced" people down into some of the river valleys at this time (McNutt 1996:197). In Florida, people lived mainly along the coast (perhaps using the easily available fish and shellfish) with little occupation of the interior forests.

During the Middle Archaic, use of the coastal plain increased dramatically (Anderson et al. 2007:457), and there is evidence that the variety of foods eaten increased, with riverine resources, particularly shellfish (see Highlight 12.1), becoming more important. The botanical record of the Middle Archaic reflects a "long-term continuity" in plant use (Gremillion 1996b:99), providing evidence of some stability even during a time of resource stress. Important plants included walnuts, hazelnuts, chestnuts, beechnuts, and acorns, with either hickory nuts (Gremillion 1996b:104) or acorns (Yarnell and Black 1985) being predominant. The use of deer appears to have increased (Styles and Klippel 1996:115).

HIGHLIGHT 12.1

THE SHELL MOUND ARCHAIC

One of the most interesting manifestations of the Middle Archaic was the "Shell Mound Archaic" of the north-central Southeast, characterized by the extensive use of shellfish from rivers and the development of large mounds of shell debris. The Shell Mound Archaic first appeared about 7,000 BP along portions of the Green River in Kentucky and the Tennessee River of Tennessee and Alabama, later spreading to other river basins in the northern Southeast, lasting until about 2,500 BP (see Claassen 1996; Marquardt and Watson 2005). Shell Mound Archaic peoples developed an extensive trade in shell beads and copper and began the construction of burial mounds, a hallmark of the Southeast, by 5,500 BP. Not all mounds were for burial purposes; others must have been used for some sociopolitical or religious purpose, possibly the construction of a sacred landscape connecting the living and their ancestors (Buikstra and Charles 1999). Warfare was apparently a common feature of the Shell Mound Archaic (e.g., Marquardt and Watson 2005:634–635), and infant mortality was very high.

The Shell Mound Archaic ended when shellfishing ceased along these rivers, perhaps due to overexploitation of shellfish, some environmental change, emigration, or a combination of all three (see Claassen 1991:290). Claassen (1991) hypothesized that shell itself (rather than just the meat inside the shell) was an important ceremonial material, presumably gathered by women to build burial mounds, and that the shift to horticulture resulted in a change in ceremonialism that no longer emphasized shell. Thus, the Shell Mound Archaic ended.

Some technological changes also mark the Middle Archaic. Early Archaic point types were replaced by basally notched and stemmed forms, and ground grooved axes and distinctive atlatl weights began to be used. In addition, there was an increase in the use of shell, stone, and bone for ornaments.

By the end of the Middle Archaic (ca. 5,750 BP), cemeteries were common, suggesting the beginning of some form of sedentism, fixed territories, and more complex political and social organizations. Moreover, some long-distance trade networks were established (Jefferies 1996), and a number of interaction spheres seem to have developed. These regional entities may have developed in conjunction with the establishment of tribal-level social networks as a response to resource stress; that is, risk sharing through exchange (also see Braun and Plog 1982; Anderson et al. 2007).

The Late Archaic (ca. 5,750 to 2,700 BP)

After about 6,000 BP, the climate began to cool and rainfall increased, and by 5,000 BP, climatic conditions similar to those of today were established. More rainfall meant greater water flow in rivers, and the Mississippi River enlarged, entrenched, and became a very attractive place again. Occupation of the interior valleys and mountains continued from the Middle Archaic. By about 5,000 BP, occupation of the coastal regions is evident, but as sea levels stabilized at about that same time, it is likely that the coast was occupied much earlier, with those sites now being under-water (e.g., Blanton 1996; Russo 1996a; Faught 2002, 2004). The coast may not have been a very attractive place until sea level stabilized and estuaries formed.

The Late Archaic is sometimes called the Archaic Resurgence (cf. McNutt 1996:199). This was a time of significant population expansion, an increase in sedentism, the intensification of roots and aquatic resources, the expansion of regional exchange networks, and the amplification of burial ceremonialism.

Sometime before about 4,000 BP, people began to experiment with the cultivation and do-mestication of native plants, such as squash/gourds, chenopods, sunflowers, and sumpweed (see Smith and Cowan 2003). Despite this early agriculture, the primary subsistence system remained focused on hunting and gathering, and a major investment in agriculture did not occur in the east-ern Southeast until corn became important after ca. 1,200 BP (Gremillion 1996b:108; see below).

A major hallmark of the Late Archaic is the development of pottery (see Sassaman 2002). Perhaps the earliest (ca. 4,500 BP) undecorated pottery known in the Southeast has been found along the Atlantic Coastal Plain (e.g., the Stallings Island Culture near Savannah, Georgia; see Sassaman et al. 2006) and was present in Florida by about 4,000 BP. Decorated pottery appeared by about 3,650 BP. By about 3,000 BP, pottery was widespread across the Southeast, and by 2,500 BP, virtually all groups used pottery (Sassaman 2002:416).

By about 4,000 BP, several distinctive regional cultures were present. A few of these, most notably the Poverty Point culture, included the construction of mounds. Until recently, it was thought that people began to purposefully construct mounds only after about 3,000 BP (during the Woodland; see below). While mounds dating to the Archaic had long been recognized, they were generally considered to be incidental and/or just cemeteries, seen as a step in the evolution to the larger, more purposeful mounds of the later Woodland Tradition. More recently, there is a growing appreciation that the tradition of mound construction, with all of its sociopolitical background, originated in the Archaic (F. E. Hamilton 1999; Anderson 2004b; Gibson 2004), and there seems now to be "wide agreement that these features [mounds] arose in direct response to the regionalism brought about by increasing populations, which resulted in the need for sym-bolic markers of territory, lineage, and status" (Russo 1996b:259).

It may also be that the building of mounds, particularly burial mounds, could be the result of the construction of a ritual landscape connecting the living and the dead, reflecting "a deeply-rooted ancient cosmology which lodged the ancestors [the dead] in places where the ancient worlds [of the living and the dead] conjoined" (Buikstra and Charles 1999:222). Some sixty known mound complexes thought to date to the Middle and Late Archaic, including the Poverty Point complex, are located mostly in Louisiana (Russo 1996b:281). Some archaic shell mounds are also known along the coasts of South Carolina, Georgia, and Florida (Randall 2008; Russo 2008).

The earliest mound complex currently recognized is at Watson Brake, located in northeast Louisiana (Saunders et al. 2005). The site consists of a series of eleven mounds, the largest of which is 7.5 meters high, connected by ridges to form an oval structure some 280 meters in diameter. Excavations (see Saunders et al. 2005) at several of the mounds produced materials radiocarbon dated to about 5,400 BP, indicating that the mounds were constructed in the very early Late Archaic (or late Middle Archaic). Fish and seeds were identified as the primary subsistence resources (Saunders et al. 2005).

The clear presence of Archaic mounds indicates that sedentary populations and the complex social structures needed to construct such mounds were in place prior to agriculture and that not all Archaic groups were seasonally mobile hunter-gatherers (Russo 1996b:282). While the hunter-gatherer sociopolitical systems that created mounds are very poorly understood, it seems clear that they were different than those of the later agriculturalists that also created mounds. It was suggested (Hamilton 1999) that the mounds were constructed as ritual to mitigate a fluctuating environment. Unfortunately, there have been few investigations of Archaic sites without mounds, and the overall Archaic settlement patterns and trade networks are not well understood, although mound sites are generally located near aquatic ecozones, indicating that aquatic resources were important. Understanding these systems is a major research goal.

POVERTY POINT (CA. 3,600 TO 3,100 BP)   Probably the most elaborate of the Late Archaic entities was that of Poverty Point, which extended over much of the lower Mississippi River Valley. Poverty Point manifests an abrupt increase in scale and complexity of the longstanding, but poorly understood, Archaic mound tradition. Poverty Point also contains a diversity of trade items, clay cooking balls (called Poverty Point objects), microblade technology, and a lapidary industry. It has been speculated that the Poverty Point people may have adopted some Mesoamerican traits (e.g., mounds and ball courts), but this remains an open question.

It was originally assumed that the Poverty Point culture had an agricultural base in order to support a complex system capable of creating mounds, but the evidence suggests that the cultivation of native plants (e.g., gourds, chenopods, sunflower, sumpweed) was minor. Generally speaking, the Poverty Point people were fisher-hunter-gatherers. While the details of the sociopolitical organization remain unclear, it seems evident that labor was directed and controlled, although it is difficult to fit such complexity into existing models of Poverty Point (Gibson 1996:289).

The growth of long-distance exchange appears to have been an important in the development of Poverty Point factor (Gibson 1996:292, 2006), with trade in argillite, copper, fluorite, galena, hematite, jasper, magnetite, marine shell, quartzite, slate, and steatite. These materials were utilized by the majority of the population and not just by the elite (as seen in the later Hopewell pattern). Perhaps one of the most important traded materials was stone, a basic necessity for cooking and food processing but unavailable in the alluvial valleys of the lower Mississippi region (Gibson 2001:214–215). Obtaining stone may have been the focus of the economy, and the trade for stone may have encouraged the exchange of other materials as well. In lieu of stone, baked clay balls, probably produced by the millions at Poverty Point, also had been manufactured for trade. Perhaps Poverty Point centers formed around "trade fairs" (e.g., H. E. Jackson 1991). It is unclear why the Poverty Point culture declined, but it may be related to the adoption of horticulture and a decline in the control of trade, or to climate change (T. R. Kidder 2006).

The Poverty Point site itself is located in northern Louisiana on a bluff on the western edge of the Mississippi River Valley. The site (Figs. 12.3 and 12.4) consists of an open plaza area on the edge of the bluff surrounded by a complex of six semicircular ring mounds in six groupings (Gibson 2001:83) with a maximum diameter of 1,200 meters (about three-quarters of a mile) and a combined total length of about 18 kilometers. It is possible that the current semicircular configuration of the complex is the result of erosion, with an eastern half being lost to the river, meaning that the original configuration of the site may have been circular, or even octagonal. Of great interest is that the major breaks (aisles) in the ring mounds point toward the summer and winter solstice points (Haag 1993:107). A number of other mounds lie outside the semicircular complex, including a structure thought to have been a ball court (a Mesoamerican trait). The site was constructed mostly between 3,600 and 3,300 BP, although some outlying mounds may have been built earlier and then incorporated into the larger complex at a later date, suggesting a continuation of existing traditions (Gibson 2001:99).

The largest mound (Mound A; Fig. 12.3) at Poverty Point measures some 600 by 650 feet and 70 feet high, containing some 230,000 cubic yards of earth (Gibson 2001:83). As much as 1 million cubic yards of earth was employed in the construction of the site (Gibson 2001:109), built by people dumping basket loads of soil into piles and making it the second largest site in North America (behind Cahokia). Wooden buildings were erected at various places on the mounds and a variety of associated materials, including pigments (ochre, kaolinite, and galena), suggest the use of body painting and ritual activities on the larger mounds. Gibson (2001:101) suspected that houses were built on the ring mounds, indicating that the site was probably a town rather than a largely uninhabited ceremonial center. This argument is supported by the great quantities of midden and trash found at the site. It appears Poverty Point supported a sedentary population (Gibson 2006). It was proposed that the population at Poverty Point consisted of a large multi-ethnic community (Sassaman 2005), but it was later argued (Gibson 2007) that the population consisted of local people.

A number of smaller Poverty Point habitation sites have been found around the main Poverty Point site, some nearby and many at some distance. It seems that Poverty Point itself was a major center, surrounded by smaller, satellite sites. This organization, coupled with the ubiquity of common trade items, suggests a networking strategy, where individuals networked and traded with distant groups (see Gibson 2001:209). Such an economy would have been relatively simple and not driven by elites. No cemeteries are known in the region, so the method of disposal of the dead is unknown, although some charred human bone has been found at the site, suggesting at least some cremation. Pottery is present but uncommon at Poverty Point and is probably the earliest in the region.

The structure and complexity of the Poverty Point site has been variously explained as representing (1) a large village with houses on platforms, (2) an accidental accumulation of assorted occupations, (3) a ceremonial center with a small permanent and large seasonal population, and (4) a trade center (see Gibson 1996:291), all of which are unique to the Late Archaic. But why did Poverty Point develop when other Late Archaic centers did not? Gibson (1996:292) believed that it was the unique combination of its strategic location on the Mississippi River, the need to import useable stone, a productive environment, and the large-scale moundbuilding expertise that set Poverty Point apart from other Late Archaic localities. A video on the Poverty Point site is

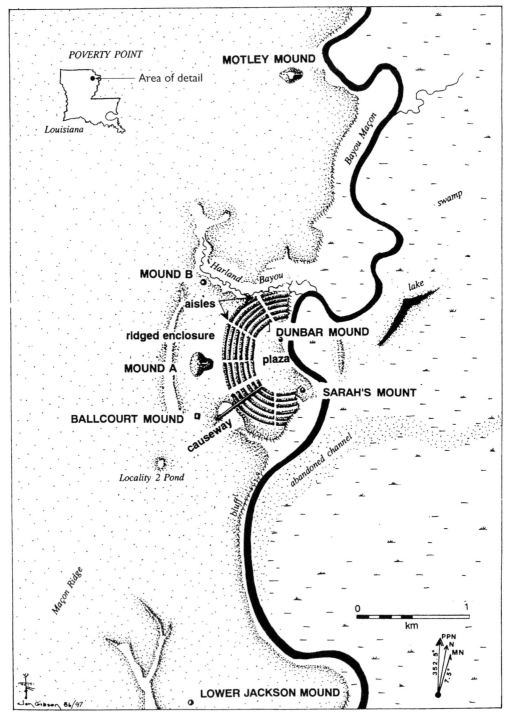

FIGURE 12.3 Map of the Poverty Point site (from Gibson 2001: Fig. 5.2; reprinted with permission of the University Press of Florida).

FIGURE 12.4 Artist's depiction of the Poverty Point site. (*Source:* Jon L. Gibson.)

available at www.archaeologychannel.org, "Poverty Point Earthworks: Evolutionary Milestones of the Americas."

The transition from the Archaic to the Woodland is generally thought of as having been gradual, that Archaic groups increasingly adopted agriculture and then became Woodland. There is evidence to suggest, however, that a major climatic change occurred about 3,000 years ago that resulted in severe flooding in the Mississippi watershed system, making river bottoms high-risk places to live (T. R. Kidder 2006). Thus, it is possible that the shift from Archaic to Woodland was an abrupt change in response to climate change.

THE WOODLAND TRADITION (CA. 2,700 BP TO CONTACT)

The Woodland Tradition in the Southeast (see Yerkes 1988; Anderson and Mainfort 2002; Jefferies 2004) marks the beginnings of widespread village life and the development of agriculture, which became increasingly important through time, although its economic role varied from region to region (Gremillion 2002:483). In addition, mortuary patterns became more elaborate in some places. Another important Woodland trait is pottery, which spread across the Southeast after 3,000 BP. By the beginning of the Woodland, the climate was similar to that of today. In many areas of the Southeast, the Woodland lasted until about AD 1,000 but persisted in a few areas until contact.

In the Southeast, the Woodland is really just "more" than the Archaic; more people, more pottery, more mounds, more trade, more elaborate burials, and more domesticated plants (Bense 1994:110; also see Anderson and Mainfort 2002:2–4). Woodland groups were generally tribal-level horticultural societies with a variety of adaptations depending on location, including varying degrees of farming, sedentism, hunting and gathering, fishing, and shellfishing. A number of Woodland societies had complex mortuary customs and built large-scale public works (mounds), but only about 1 percent of Woodland sites have an associated mound (Bense 1994:114).

The Early Woodland (ca. 2,700 to 2,100 BP)

The marker characteristic for the Early Woodland in the Southeast is the spread of pottery from the Atlantic Coastal Plain westward. Different pottery regional traditions developed, with variations in decoration and temper. Long-distance trade continued, although local, rather than imported, materials were used for the production of most flaked stone tools.

The Early Woodland witnessed a substantial increase in the cultivation of domesticated native plants (see discussion of early agriculture in Chapter 11). Corn appears to have diffused into the Southeast from the west after about 2,000 BP (at the beginning of the Middle Woodland), but there is some pollen evidence of corn in southern Florida as early as 2,500 BP (at the Fort Center site; see Sears 1982; Milanich 1994:287). Even if it was present during the Early Woodland, corn was not an important crop until after about 1,200 BP (see below). Hunting and gathering remained very important.

In most Early Woodland cultures, sociopolitical organizations were tribal with relatively little stratification. Little is known about sex and gender roles during this time, although there is some suggestion that the first gardens were developed by women (Watson and Kennedy 1991:268). In contrast, it has been suggested that caves, such as the Salts-Mammoth cave system in Kentucky, may have been "male places," as only mummified bodies and coprolites from males (the latter sexed by hormone analysis; see Sobolik et al. 1996) have been recovered from them (Claassen 2001:23). The purpose of these "underground" activities is unknown.

A few Southeastern groups were influenced by the Adena Complex that developed during the Early Woodland to the north in the Ohio River Valley (see Chapter 11). Adena represented a dramatic increase in social complexity, with elaborate burial mounds and extensive trade in materials from distant sources, such as copper, marine shells, and mica. Adena appears to have been a precursor for the later, more elaborate Hopewell and Mississippian developments.

A variety of Early Woodland groups developed in other parts of the Southeast. In the lower Mississippi Valley, the Poverty Point culture persisted for a time into the Early Woodland but was gone by 2,500 BP. Along the Atlantic Coast, where horticulture was less important, a number of complex groups developed based on hunting and gathering (see Thompson and Turck 2009). Among these was the St. Johns group of cultures on the northeastern Florida coast, where hunter-gatherers emphasizing shellfish, fish, and probably some agriculture had large populations, pottery, and burial mounds (see Milanich 1994:247, 2004:191–193).

The Middle Woodland (ca. 2,000 to 1,200 BP)

The major development of the Middle Woodland in the Southeast was the spread of Hopewellian practices and goods across much of the region. Trade, particularly of materials from distant sources, became more important as Hopewell influence expanded. The climate was relatively stable during this time, and agriculture was becoming more important, although corn was not yet a major crop. Pottery became more important, and small triangular projectile points became common. Although Hopewell influences extended across much of the Southeast, some groups followed a different path. Bow-and-arrow technology diffused into the Southeast after about 1,400 BP (Nassaney and Pyle 1999).

THE HOPEWELL IN THE SOUTHEAST   The cultural phenomenon known as Hopewell first developed in the southern Northeast (see Chapter 11) and diffused south, although it was never as complex in the Southeast as it was to the north (Bense 1994:141). Hopewell was an elaboration of the Adena Complex, which was also present in the Southeast during the Early Woodland (ca. after about 2,500 BP). Some groups in the Mississippi River Valley, having developed from a Poverty Point base, were already practicing the moundbuilding that was so typical of Adena and Hopewell.

The spread of Hopewell brought with it a significant increase in sociocultural complexity, with much larger sites and mound complexes. As in the Northeast, the Hopewell pattern in the Southeast is known mostly from mortuary practices. People were buried, but the bones of presumably important people would sometimes be exhumed, stored in charnel houses, and then reinterred in a mass grave during a special event, such as the death of a leader. This clear differential treatment of the dead implies status differentiation and considerable social complexity. Classic Hopewellian materials, such as panpipes, ornaments of shell and stone, shell bowls, sheets of mica cut into shapes (e.g., heads and hands), earspools, and pottery, would be buried with the dead. Much of this material was imported, attesting to the reach of Hopewell trade. The considerable trade seen in Hopewell groups in the Northeast (see Chapter 11) was also present among the Hopewell of the Southeast, but there seems to have been little trade between the two regions (Bense 1994:143). Hopewellian subsistence in the Southeast appears to have been based on agriculture, but corn was still a minor crop. Hunting and gathering remained important, as did fishing.

About one thousand Hopewell mound sites are known in the Southeast, but only about fifty are major centers containing more than one mound. Most Hopewellian sites in the Southeast are in the Mississippi Valley region and along the middle Tennessee River. Further east, less Hopewellian influence is evident, but some is known along the Gulf Coast as far east as Florida, while there is very little along the Atlantic Coast. Some Southeastern Hopewellian sites are quite impressive. For example, the Marksville site in Louisiana contains many mounds and was the "center of the classic Hopewellian culture of the lower Mississippi Valley" (Bense 1994:143). The Helena Mound site, located in northern Arkansas, is another major Hopewellian center and is very similar to Ohio Hopewell sites, suggesting a close connection between those two areas.

By ca. 1,700 BP, the Hopewell complex in the Southeast began to decline. A number of hypotheses has been proposed to explain this decline, including overpopulation, climate change, an increase in warfare, and/or a decrease in game populations due to increased hunting efficiency, perhaps due to the introduction of the bow and arrow. At this point, the cause of the Hopewell decline is unclear, but by 1,500 BP, it was gone.

OTHER MIDDLE WOODLAND CULTURES   Not all Southeastern Woodland groups participated in the Hopewell system. Along the Atlantic coast, the cultures of the Early Woodland continued a hunting and gathering lifestyle, but with an increasing dependence on horticulture.

A group of related cultures, collectively known as Weeden Island (ca. 1,800 to 1,100 BP), existed in southern Georgia and Alabama, as well as northern Florida (see Fewkes 1924; Willey 1945, 1949; Milanich et al. 1997; Milanich 2002, 2004:195–196). Weeden Island appears to have been influenced by developments to the north and west, such as the construction of relatively small, low mounds for burials (including some mass secondary burials) and distinctive pottery effigy vessels with depictions of animals (such as birds and dogs). Settlements were organized as clusters of villages associated with one or more burial mounds, perhaps a group of related villages that shared a common identity and used a communal burial mound (see Milanich 1994:168–169). These features imply the presence of complex social structures similar to, and contemporaneous with, Hopewell to the north and can be viewed as a "Middle Woodland" manifestation, although that term is not generally used in Florida (see Kohler 1991:106).

Weeden Island was not based on agriculture but rather a specialized hunting and gathering highly dependent on either marine or riverine resources, depending on location. After about 1,400 BP, some groups began to adopt horticulture, although corn was not present in Florida until after about 1,000 BP (but it may have been at Fort Center in southern Florida at 2,500 BP). Weeden Island was replaced by the less complex "Late Woodland" Alachua Tradition about 1,100 BP.

The Late Woodland (ca. 1,200 to Contact)

The beginning of the Late Woodland is the time of the Hopewell decline, as the construction of major mound complexes virtually ceased. The cultural diversity evident during the Middle Woodland increased, and the variable nature of Southeastern groups became a marker of the Late Woodland (Bense 1994:162). Agriculture expanded across the region, and corn became important after about 1,200 BP (e.g., C. M. Scarry 1993a). Although mound construction slowed, social systems remained complex and settlements grew larger, a pattern that would "foreshadow the later development of the Mississippian" (Dunnell and Feathers 1991:42).

Beginning about 1,200 BP, many Southeastern groups, primarily in the western part of the region, developed new social, political, and subsistence systems generally known as Mississippian (cf. Muller 1997:140). Most of the groups along the Atlantic coast, from Virginia to Florida, did not adopt the Mississippian cultural system and "remained" Late Woodland until contact (Milanich 1994:331–412; Ward and Davis 1999). These groups included a large number of diverse societies with less complex social and political systems, smaller populations and settlements, and an economic system that emphasized horticulture. Nevertheless, burial mounds and ossuaries continued to be used. Some of the ethnographically known groups become archaeologically recognizable during the Late Woodland.

THE MISSISSIPPIAN TRADITION (CA. 1,200 TO 400 BP)

Sometime about 1,200 BP, highly complex, ranked societies began to develop in the American Bottom, an eighty-mile-long floodplain at the confluence of the Mississippi and Missouri rivers (see Fig. 12.1), an area outside of the "Southeast" but included here due to the relationship between the region and the cultures to the south. The relatively simple chiefdoms of the preceding Hopewell Tradition were reconstituted into larger and more complex chiefdoms with centralized political authority over more than one town (Pauketat 1994:52). The Mississippian pattern did not represent a single society or even one time period but consisted instead of numerous complex chiefdoms, waxing and waning in power and influence. During this time, people were impacted by population growth and decline, variable agricultural productivity, warfare, and other factors. The term *Mississippian* was originally used to define a pottery complex but now applies to aspects of economy, ideology, and political structure (J. F. Scarry 1996a:13; Muller and Stephens 2000:297), although the term "Pan-Southern" is sometimes used instead, resulting in some confusion (see Muller 1997:118, Table 3.1; Nassaney 2000:714).

The Mississippian sociopolitical pattern first took root in the American Bottom and spread south through the various groups occupying the major river valleys (see J. F. Scarry 1996a). By 1,000 BP, groups along the Gulf Coast had adopted the Mississippian pattern, which then spread east into Georgia and perhaps into western Florida (Milanich 1994:371; J. F. Scarry 1996b) but not as far as the Atlantic coast. The Mississippian pattern also influenced some groups to the north, even as far as north as southern Wisconsin (the Aztalan site; Goldstein 2002). As the Mississippian cultural tradition spread to the south and east, local groups adapted it to their own circumstances, resulting in a variety of unique societies (e.g., Cobb and Garrow 1996). Thus, Mississippian was a "many-faceted phenomenon that exhibited myriad vibrant expressions during the last millennium of prehistory" (Brain and Phillips 1996:2) across much of the Southeast until shattered by Euroamerican contact. The Mississippian pattern gave rise to the most complex groups in native North America, and some believe that at least one, Cahokia, developed into a state (see Highlight 12.2).

The Structure of Mississippian Societies

Mississippian groups all shared a common basic structure. Each had complex and hierarchical political and social organizations (chiefdom level or even state level, depending on one's perspective), had organized labor, practiced large-scale agriculture that focused on corn, and shared a common ideological system, including mortuary ritual (Peebles and Kus 1977; J. F. Scarry 1996a:13; Cobb 2003).

MISSISSIPPIAN SOCIOPOLITICAL ORGANIZATION Mississippian polities comprised major centers that exercised control over a larger region. Mississippian settlement organization, at least in the American Bottom (e.g., M. L. Fowler 1978; also see Milner 1996:35–36), probably consisted of a number of levels or tiers, beginning with small, dispersed farmsteads and small settlements without mounds. In this model, each of these small settlements would have owed allegiance to a small regional center with a small number of mounds. These centers would, in turn, have owed allegiance to a larger regional center with a larger number of mounds. Each of the larger centers would have been associated with one of the monumental centers, such as Cahokia (see below).

Whichever the number of tiers, major Mississippian polities probably consisted of a paramount chiefdom controlling a number of smaller communities. Each of these communities, perhaps simple chiefdoms, were still complex, probably with ranked elites of a particular kinship group exercising power over the remainder of the population (the commoners) and controlling agricultural surpluses, labor, and prestige items. The major towns of each of the chiefdoms contained massive public works (mounds), with the paramount chiefdoms having the largest and most impressive architecture. The territorial size of individual Mississippian chiefdoms is an open question, although Hally (1993:143) argued that data from northern Georgia indicated that they were generally small, no larger than forty kilometers in maximum dimension. In the center of these territories would have been heavily occupied core areas with more sparsely occupied buffer zones (Hally 1999:112).

Other ideas regarding the development and operation of Mississippian polities have been proposed. Blitz (1999) suggested that a fission fusion mechanism for the development of large centers in which the aggregation of basic political units would result in the formation of a center and the resulting conflict within that amalgamation of those groups would ultimately cause the dispersal of the groups into new centers. R. A. Beck (2003) suggested that power shifted back and forth between regional and local centers, depending on the administrative requirements at the time.

HIGHLIGHT 12.2

THE STATE OF THE STATE

Mississippian polities were very complex, but how complex were they? In general, archaeologists around the world employ a four-part hierarchy of increasing complexity (band, tribe, chiefdom, and state [or civilization]) to classify political systems. How is this measured? The difference between band, tribe, and chiefdom is usually based on population, and the levels of power invested in the political leaders and the classification of a group into one of these categories does not generally generate much controversy. Admission of a group into the exclusive "state club," however, is usually a contested event. Typically, the requirements for being classified as a state include writing (or some complex record system), cities, large populations, and monumental architecture (usually of stone, so archaeologists can easily find it), all of which demonstrate that the group had a very complex political system.

Of the many thousands of polities that have existed around the world through time, very few have been judged complex enough to be classified as a state. The Mississippian polities, at least some of them, are close enough to generate a debate.

Most archaeologists believe that Mississippian systems, even the most complex ones, were chiefdoms. At least one Mississippian polity, Cahokia (see below), may have been the capital of a state-level polity, sometimes called the "Ramey State" (named after a former landowner). This argument was based on estimates of a very large population and extensive trade network, both of which must have required a remarkably complex government, more complex than a chiefdom (e.g., O'Brien 1989; also see Cobb 2003; Pauketat 2004, 2007).

It has been countered (Milner 1998:13; Milner and Oliver 1999), however, that the interpretation of Cahokia as highly centralized "state" is misleading and that Cahokia society was much smaller and more similar to the large chiefdoms known from the Late Woodland. This interpretation was based on two factors. First, Milner and Oliver (1999:90–92) argued that the high population estimates (such as those of Gregg [1975]) were based on double and triple counting of architectural features, liberal estimates of people per structure, and other similar factors, all of which contributed to an overestimate of the number of people at the site. Second, Milner and Oliver (1999) evaluated the settlement data from around Cahokia and concluded that the surrounding population was smaller than previously thought. Therefore, it was argued that while many people lived in the region around Cahokia, the population of the site itself was "no more than several thousand people, certainly not tens of thousands of them" (Milner and Oliver 1999:90).

This argument remains unresolved and awaits further archaeological data. There are, however, several other aspects to consider. The categories of chiefdom and state and the criteria formulated to measure complexity were created by archaeologists, who place groups in one category or another. Thus, the categories are just tools used to describe and analyze but not to judge. On the other hand, no group in North America is universally accepted as a state, unlike Mesoamerica, where numerous states are recognized, and, as a result, native groups in North America are generally seen as less complex than their Mesoamerican neighbors. If we were to accept the presence of states in North America, we might be forced to reconsider this view.

THE MISSISSIPPIAN ECONOMY The economies of most Mississippian societies were based on agriculture. Corn had been farmed since about 2,000 BP but became an essential crop after about 1,200 BP (cf. C. M. Scarry 1993a), the same time that Mississippian polities emerged. In fact, corn may have played a major role in Mississippian development. It has been suggested (see Schroedl and Boyd 1991:86; C. M. Scarry 1993a:89) that the adoption of the more productive Eastern Flint corn variety ca. 1,200 BP created major surpluses whose control and distribution may have served as an impetus for the rapid development of cultural complexity. While it is clear that crop production and reliance on corn increased, it is also possible that this was the result, rather than the cause, of increasing populations and political complexity. This cause-and-effect relationship between corn and sociopolitical complexity remains an important research topic.

Mississippian subsistence included fewer resources than its predecessors, and protein was derived less from hunting and more from fishing (see Styles and Klippel 1996: Figs. 7.17 and 7.18). Beans diffused into the region after ca. 1,000 BP and became prominent after 800 BP. The reliance on corn may have resulted in dietary stress, manifested in poor dental health, anemia, and arthritis (Goodman and Armelagos 1985:17; Armelagos and Hill 1990). Other aspects of the Mississippian economy included extensive trade networks, with copper coming from the north, shells from the coast, and stone from the mountains.

Two major subsistence systems were practiced by Mississippian groups, depending on location (Bense 1994:184–191). The first, the riverine system, involved farming along floodplains using natural irrigation. Major crops included corn, sunflower, gourds, squash, and beans. The hunting of deer, raccoon, turkey, waterfowl, turtles, and other small animals; the collection of shellfish; and the gathering of nuts, fruits, and berries remained important. The second, the coastal system, was practiced along the coasts. In these areas, farming was less important, as the soils were poor and not flood irrigated. Instead, shifting cultivation, probably using slash-and-burn technique, was used. Fishing in bays and estuaries was very productive, as were hunting and gathering.

MISSISSIPPIAN IDEOLOGY   One of the most interesting aspects of the Mississippian system was its ideology. A primary component of this ideology was mound construction, greatly elaborated from the Poverty Point, Adena, and Hopewellian traditions. Unlike the earlier conical mounds of the Woodland used for burials, the Mississippian mounds were of the platform type, constructed to provide lofty places for ceremonial use by high-status elites and perhaps as a public demonstration of power. Some believe that Mississippian elites manipulated the cosmos through ceremony to stabilize and enhance their positions within the sociopolitical hierarchy (e.g., Emerson 1997a:190). Such a cosmos may have been four-sided, represented in Mississippian architecture by the manner in which platform mounds were placed around plazas and by circular wooden structures, and by evidence of celestial alignments at a number of Mississippian sites in the Southeast (Haag 1993).

Other indications of Mississippian ideology can be gleaned from mortuary customs and materials. The treatment of the dead varied by rank, with elites often being buried in mounds around the major plazas, sometimes in log-lined tombs and sometimes with what appear to have been sacrificial victims. Burial goods for the elite were frequently elaborate and included copper artifacts, beads, and special pottery. Commoners were buried in separate cemeteries with utilitarian items or no goods at all. In addition to learning about ideology, the abundance of mortuary materials at Mississippian sites has the potential to make the study of gender easier than in other systems (see Claassen 2001; also see Ardren 2008).

Fertility cults, probably for agricultural production, may be represented in the symbolism of some Mississippian figurines and pottery designs (Emerson 1997b:228). The Southeastern Ceremonial Complex (SECC), sometimes called the "Southern Cult" (see Highlight 12.3), was first thought to date from early Mississippian times and to reflect the cognitive side of the Mississippian. This ceremonial complex is now known to date much later, to the end of the Mississippian.

The Rise of Mississippian Polities

Why did some Middle Woodland societies become much more elaborate and complex during the Late Woodland while others did not? The adoption of corn as a major crop at about the same time as the development of the Mississippian system may be more than just a coincidence, perhaps even a central factor. Corn is very productive, but corn crops were likely susceptible to failure, and if growing populations encouraged the intensification of corn farming, hunting and gathering may have been unable to mitigate a major crop failure. To deal with this risk, so the model goes, powerful chiefs may have arisen to store surpluses and redistribute them in time of need (see C. M. Scarry 1993b:157–158).

Two other related models of how Mississippian political systems developed have been proposed: the network model and the corporate model (see A. King 2003). In the network model, certain individuals would have controlled surpluses and their distribution within a limited area. As their power and prestige increased, their networks would have grown and incorporated other centers into a growing polity. Elites developed and a ranked society evolved with powerful individuals in control of a network of smaller, dependent centers. Control extended to both goods and labor, and the construction of public architecture served to reinforce the power and prestige of the ruling elites. In the corporate model, the focus would have been on group decision making, a lack of prestige items to symbolize individual status, and less aggrandizement of individuals.

In both cases, large and complex polities would have developed, although chiefdoms that developed under the corporate model would probably be smaller and exhibit less evidence of high status. Many of the Mississippian chiefdoms east of the Mississippi Valley have demonstrated these traits and may have evolved following the corporate model (e.g., A. King 2003:291). Thus, it seems that several trajectories toward social complexity were followed in the Southeast. Interestingly, despite their success, none of the Mississippian polities lasted more than a few hundred years (Pauketat 1998:56).

EMERGENT MISSISSIPPIAN (CA. 1,200 TO 1,000 BP)   The first groups referred to as Mississippian emerged in the American Bottom, in the central Mississippi River Valley (see J. E. Kelly 1990; Morse and Morse 1990). The earlier Hopewellian pattern had disappeared, replaced by smaller communities of farmers. Sometime about 1,200 BP, these farming communities began to coalesce into larger sociopolitical units, commencing their development into Mississippian polities. This early time is called the Emergent Mississippian, or sometimes the Early or Developmental Mississippian (McNutt 1996:225; also see Kelly et al. 1984; B. D. Smith 1990; Pauketat 1994:51–65).

Emergent Mississippian is marked by an abrupt increase in the production of corn and a movement of farms onto floodplains. Hunting and gathering remained important but secondary, and the wetlands of the floodplains were a vital source of wild foods. Although it is clear that corn increased in importance, it is still not known whether corn production was intensified to accommodate growing populations or whether populations grew because they had more corn. Either way, populations expanded, agriculture intensified, settlements proliferated, and social complexity increased. Another common trait of the Emergent Mississippian is the introduction of shell-tempered pottery.

Emergent Mississippian towns were generally small, with some of the larger towns possibly containing earthen platform mounds arranged around plazas, although it is not clear how early this trait appeared (Milner and Oliver 1999:86). Houses were larger and organized in rows rather than in circular patterns. Numerous farmsteads were located away from the towns, and farmers expanded into previously unoccupied river valleys. Flooding was a constant risk (as it is today), adding uncertainty to crop production.

There is clear evidence of ranked social organization and specialization of labor, and political organization appears to have been at the chiefdom level as deduced from architecture, site size, the nature and quantity of prestige goods, and evidence of storage facilities for surpluses, the latter being perhaps a key to the development of the system (Wesson 1999). A system of warfare (e.g., Dye and King 2007; Emerson 2007), ancestor worship, and fertility developed at this time. The regalia, particularly copper and shell artifacts, worn by Mississippian chiefs and other prominent officials reflected their power and connection with the supernatural (see J. A. Brown 1985:108–123). The few burial data available from Emergent Mississippian times indicate a pattern of commoners being buried in houses or cemeteries with either utilitarian items or no burial items at all, while elites were buried in or near mounds with elaborate burial goods. In some cases, important people appear to have been buried with sacrificial victims.

MIDDLE MISSISSIPPIAN (CA. 1,000 TO 850 BP)   Emergent Mississippian was the time of the development of Mississippian ideology and organization in the American Bottom and its spread across much of the Southeast. Although not all scholars recognize a "middle" period, the Middle Mississippian was a time when the groups that adopted the Mississippian pattern adapted it to their own conditions, resulting in a great variety of individualized Mississippian polities. During this time, many of the simple chiefdoms of Emergent times became more complex chiefdoms, and the ceremonialism of Emergent Mississippian began to be replaced by more secular political institutions. Warfare increased, moundbuilding and mortuary complexity peaked, and the basic Mississippian pattern "settled in" in most places.

LATE MISSISSIPPIAN (CA. 850 TO 450 BP)   Late Mississippian was characterized by localized political instability and change. As the power of leaders evolved, agricultural production varied, military success fluctuated, and chiefdoms rose and fell with regularity. This made the overall Mississippian sociopolitical landscape highly variable, with shifting centers of power and influence. Established centers declined, new powers emerged, and the "hubs" of the Mississippian world moved around from place to place as individual polities expanded and contracted.

The population continued to increase, as did the expansion of farming into new river valleys and floodplains. Warfare also increased, and many Late Mississippian settlements were fortified (see Dye and King 2007). Social complexity remained high, and the basic subsistence system remained unchanged but intensified.

It is commonly believed that the Mississippian pattern began to decline prior to contact. Ceremonial centers in some areas of river floodplain seem to have been abandoned around 650 BP or a bit later, particularly in the area of the American Bottom (called the "Vacant Quarter"; Williams 1990, 2001; B. D. Smith 1996:316), perhaps part of a larger contraction of settlements across eastern North America in response of environmental conditions (cf. Cobb and Butler 2002). A number of other groups became less complex. In other regions, however, Mississippian groups were at their height of power and complexity at contact (e.g., in northern Georgia; see Hally 2008), only to be decimated by warfare and European diseases. The most complex group encountered by Europeans in North America was the Natchez, a Late Mississippian group in Louisiana (see below).

HIGHLIGHT 12.3

THE SOUTHEASTERN CEREMONIAL COMPLEX

The Southeastern Ceremonial Complex (SECC; see Brain and Phillips 1996; J. A. Brown 1998; A. King 2007), sometimes called the "Southern Cult," is known across much of the Southeast. It consists of a distinctive group of artifacts, generally found with burials of high-ranking individuals and is presumed to be ceremonial. The SECC is marked by distinctive shell gorgets, copper earspools, stone axes, smoking pipes, and iconography on pottery thought to represent the "zenith of southeastern artistic and technical sophistication" (Brain and Phillips 1996:2). The SECC was first believed to date from about 1,000 BP and to reflect the cognitive side of the Mississippian. It is now known that the SECC dates much later in time, beginning around 750 BP and ending about 450 BP, about the time of European contact. The SECC may have originated in the Caddoan area (Arkansas), perhaps even at the Spiro site (La Vere 1998:26), where a very large quantity of SECC goods has been recovered.

The SECC was probably not a cult as such, nor even tied specifically to religion, but it may be reflective of a trading system devoted to reinforcing status, the "ceremonial side of a concomitant trade in useful goods and other interactions" (Brain and Phillips 1996:400), perhaps something similar to the Pochtecha of Mesoamerica. The specific styles of these artifacts were different from area to area (Brain and Phillips 1996:398), although the striking similarities between some of the shell gorgets suggest that they were manufactured in workshops (Brain and Phillips 1996:390). Clearly, the SECC materials represent a complex set of beliefs and trade relationships all across the Southeast.

SOME MISSISSIPPIAN POLITIES   A fairly large number of Mississippian polities developed and flourished in different regions at different times. Some were quite large and powerful, while others were smaller and less complex. Brief histories of four such polities are provided below.

Cahokia   Perhaps one of the best known Mississippian centers from any time period is Cahokia, which became the dominant political entity in the American Bottom for hundreds of years. With more than 120 mounds (Milner and Oliver 1999:90), Cahokia contains the largest mound complex in North America (Fig. 12.5). Archaeological work has been conducted at Cahokia since the 1920s (see Young and Fowler 2000), and as a result, a great deal has been learned about Cahokian society. Much of the site now is incorporated into a state park.

The Cahokia site is very large, covering some five square miles. At its center lies Mound 38, called Monks Mound after a colony of Trappist monks who farmed the area in the early 1800s. This structure is a large, rectangular platform mound some 100 feet high and covering sixteen acres at its base. It contains some 731,000 cubic meters of soil (Muller 1997: Table 6.6) and probably took about 3 million man hours to build, making it the single largest mound in North America. Monks and several other mounds were once within a two-hundred-acre walled enclosure containing a large forty-acre plaza. To the east of the plaza was a 410-foot diameter circle of wooden posts, called "Woodhenge," thought to be related to astronomical ceremonies. In fact, many of the mounds align in significant celestial directions (see Haag 1993:106).

In addition to the public buildings, many residential structures are known at the site, spread out over thousands of acres. The population of Cahokia at its height is unknown, but early estimates have been as high as fifty thousand people. Most scholars now believe that the population

FIGURE 12.5 Artist's depiction of Cahokia during its occupation. (*Source:* © Richard Schlecht/National Geographic Image Collection).

was somewhere between ten thousand (Pauketat and Lopinot 1997:121) and fifteen thousand (Young and Fowler 2000:316).

Cemeteries and burial mounds are also present at Cahokia, many of them very elaborate. For example, excavations at Mound 72 revealed 272 burials. Included was the burial of a forty-year-old male laid on a bird-shaped platform and accompanied by some twenty thousand shell beads. In the same mound, four mass burials of some 120 women, aged fifteen to twenty-five years, with poor skeletal health indicative of low status were found, suggesting human sacrifice (see Iseminger 1996:35). Other individuals had been buried after their hands and heads had been removed. Dietary analysis showed that the lower status people had diets primarily of corn while high status individuals ate much more protein (Ambrose et al. 2003). Fish and deer were major protein staples, with elites apparently having greater access to such foods (Yerkes 2005).

It is widely considered that Cahokia was the center of a vast trading sphere where goods flowed over hundreds of miles to support the huge population responsible for the construction of the many mounds. Given its location, Cahokia may have been a "gateway" to the resources from the north flowing south (J. E. Kelly 2000). Interestingly, little is known about what was manufactured at, or exported from, Cahokia. Most of what is known of the Cahokia trade system "comes from things found *at* Cahokia [rather than things] *from* Cahokia" (McNutt 1996:230; italics in original), suggesting that Cahokia was a place where items were simply exchanged and not manufactured for trade. Thus, there is little evidence of full-time craft specialists at Cahokia (Milner 1996:38) and no real evidence of a Cahokia-dominated trade system (Milner 1996:46), although Cahokia-style figurines are common elements in cemeteries in the Caddoan region to the south and west (Emerson et al. 2003).

Cahokia was first established during the Middle Woodland (Table 12.2) and was just one of many settlements on the valley floor. By the beginning of Emergent times, Cahokia gradually became larger and more complex, and the elites began to control the surrounding smaller settlements. Cahokia eventually developed into a simple chiefdom by about 1,000 BP (Emerson 1997b: Table 9.1), and there is evidence that floodplain farmers were resettled to upland habitats, perhaps

TABLE 12.2 A Cultural Chronology for Cahokia

Date (BP)	Period	Phase	Description and Comments
750 to 600	Mississippian	Sand Prairie	continued population decline, abandonment of many outlying centers, decline in social stratification, shift from multiple community to individual community cemeteries, final abandonment of Cahokia
800 to 750		Moorehead	populations begin to decline, defensive architecture appears, trade still extensive and important, social stratification still evident
900 to 800	Middle Mississippian	Stirling	height of population size, power, and extent of influence and trade
950 to 900		Lohmann	coalescence of populations into large and well-organized towns, appearance of an elite social stratum marked by separate cemeteries, construction of many mounds and other facilities, human sacrifice at major events
1,200 to 950	Emergent Mississippian	various	abrupt increase in corn agriculture, development of large settlements, beginnings of well-developed and ranked political and social structures, initiation of platform mound construction
2,000 to 1,200	Middle Woodland	various	a small farming community

as part of the social construction of a Cahokian identity (Pauketat 2003:55). By about 900 BP, Cahokia had rapidly transformed into a significant regional center, exerting control over a large area, particularly Mississippian groups to the south (Hall 2000:33). The surrounding smaller towns began to disappear, their people moved to Cahokia, and the countryside was dominated by small farms allied to Cahokia. By 800 BP, Cahokia had expanded its size and power, evolving into a paramount chiefdom, or perhaps even a state (see Highlight 12.2). Cahokia eventually developed its own distinctive "Cahokia Mississippian tradition" (Hall 2000:33) and gained influence over large areas to the east and west. Mississippian groups to the south eventually exerted control over Cahokia once again, and, coupled with resource overexploitation and the developing Oneota influence from the north (Lopinot and Woods 1993), these events may have led to the decline of the Cahokia polity after about 750 BP. The rise of Cahokia appears to have occurred during a climate very favorable to farming (Benson et al. 2009), and its decline seems to correspond with a time of severe drought (Benson et al. 2007, 2009).

The sheer size of Cahokia has suggested to some (e.g., O'Brien 1989; Pauketat 2004, 2007) that it was a state rather than a chiefdom. Others (Milner 1998:13; Milner and Oliver 1999) have maintained that Cahokia was more similar to the major chiefdoms known from the Late Woodland, arguing that the population estimates were too high. It is also possible that Cahokia was the center of a cult system focused on the yearly renewal of the agricultural cycle, such as ensuring that the sun rose and the rains fell (Byers 2006). A fourth view, perhaps related to the cult system model, is that Cahokia may have been a "theater state," one that relied on its ceremonial lure, rather than on political power per se (Holt 2009). Whatever the case, Cahokia was a large and complex polity that had great influence over much of eastern North America. The Emergent developments at Cahokia "acted as a trigger, sparking evolutionary change in the societies around it, which in turn had a ripple effect over a much larger area" (D. G. Anderson 1997:261). The Mississippian pattern spread south and east from Cahokia, into societies that already had chiefdoms and corn agriculture, rather than to the north, where societies were less complex (D. G. Anderson 1997:268).

The Caddo   Caddo groups lived along the western portion of the southern Mississippi Valley, in what is now Arkansas and eastern Texas. A variety of independent groups made up the Caddo, which is a language rather than a single political group. Caddo populations were among the earliest to adopt the Mississippian pattern (see Perttula 1991, 1992, 1996; La Vere 1998). The Caddo chiefdoms first appeared during the Emergent Mississippian, ca. 1,200 BP, and lasted until the early nineteenth century.

The Caddo were organized as complex chiefdoms, and many sites with mound complexes are known. These chiefdoms were organized at several levels, beginning with many small, dispersed villages with no mounds, where people lived in large communal houses. These villages were associated with larger towns containing ceremonial complexes with temple mounds, some of which, in turn, were associated with still larger centers. These larger centers were independent chiefdoms that exercised social, economic, and political control over their regions. While the various chiefdoms were generally affiliated and allied, their control and influence waxed and waned through time, and no single overall Caddo political center has been recognized.

The early historical records suggest that Caddo political authority was based on kinship, with the ruling class claiming to be related to the Sun, forming, in essence, a theocracy. The actual ruler would have been a "God-King" with great power. The archaeological evidence of complex mortuary customs, including shaft burials (Feit 2003:13) and probable human sacrifice, support this interpretation.

The Caddo were involved in extensive long-distance trade, obtaining copper from the Great Lakes region, marine shells from the Gulf Coast and Florida, and turquoise from the Southwest. They also participated in the SECC during Late Mississippian times. Trade goods were probably controlled by elites, with prestige and religious items eventually ending up in the graves of chiefs (La Vere 1998:25), a typical Mississippian pattern.

The Caddo primarily utilized the riverine subsistence system (see above). Corn, beans, squash, and melons were the primary crops, and the small villages were generally situated in favorable agricultural locations along rivers or on terraces. Hunting and gathering remained important, with men hunting, women gathering, and both sexes contributing to agricultural labor. Some of the western Caddo groups hunted bison on the Plains.

The Caddo were encountered by the Spanish in 1542 (see Swanton 1942; Perttula 1993; Carter 1995; F. T. Smith 1995; La Vere 1998; Swagerty 2001:256), who noted large and complex groups. Europeans who traversed the same region several generations later observed that it was devoid of people; many of the Caddo groups had been destroyed by introduced diseases. The survivors formed a number of new chiefdoms that persisted relatively intact until the mid-nineteenth century (see La Vere 1998:8).

One of the major Caddo chiefdoms was apparently centered at the Spiro site in eastern Oklahoma, occupied between 1,200 and 650 BP. Six major mounds around a plaza are present at Spiro, and most of the site seems to date from the Middle Mississippian, although it may have had its origins as early as the Late Woodland (Schambach 1993:187, 189). One of the many interesting aspects of this site was the discovery of a large quantity of Mississippian materials (Fig. 12.6) associated with burials in the Craig Mound, a group of four connected burial mounds called the "Great Mortuary" (see B. D. Smith 1996:308–316). These and other materials were used to infer that Spiro was a full-fledged Mississippian center with a hierarchical relationship to nearby sites (J. D. Rogers 1996: Figs. 4.2 and Fig. 4.3), perhaps similar to Cahokia. It has been suggested that

FIGURE 12.6   Male profile in copper from the Spiro Mound. (*Source:* The Ohio Historical Society).

Spiro was not Mississippian per se but may have been a major trading center, with bison hides being traded to the east for high-status Mississippian materials (e.g., Schambach 1988:8) and perhaps shell beads from the Gulf of California (Kozuch 2002). It has also been suggested that the SECC originated at Spiro (La Vere 1998:26) and spread to the Mississippian societies to the east. Spiro appears to have been abandoned about 700 BP, at about the same time as a major drought occurred. People may have lost confidence in a chief who could not guarantee harvests and moved to the south (La Vere 1998:3–4).

Moundville   The Moundville site in west-central Alabama is the largest known mound complex in the Southeast outside of the Mississippi River Valley. The site covers some 370 acres and had a palisade that enclosed at least twenty-nine large pyramidal mounds (and there may still be others) oriented around a central plaza (Fig. 12.7). The site has been investigated since the 1840s, with major work being done in the early 1900s and 1930s (see Peebles and Black 1987; Knight and Steponaitis 1998; Blitz 2008; Wilson 2008, 2010).

Moundville was established about 1,100 BP as a small village along the Black Warrior River above the large floodplain of the Black Warrior Valley. The region appears to have been heavily populated during Late Woodland times and suffered from endemic warfare and resource stress (Knight and Steponaitis 1998:10). At the beginning of Middle Mississippian times (ca. 950 BP), the Mississippian pattern diffused into the region, and a number of existing Late Woodland sites along the river contain single mounds. Moundville began its rise to prominence about this time (Knight and Steponaitis 1998:12), and a mound was built at the site. During this period (Moundville I), agriculture intensified, corn became more important, and the site settlement was unstructured, with dwellings scattered about the site area (Knight and Steponaitis 1998:15).

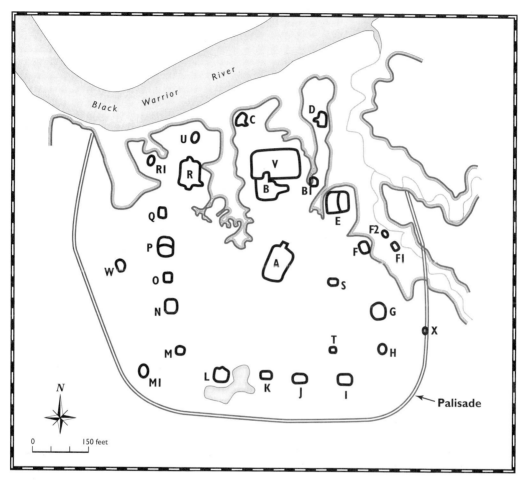

FIGURE 12.7   Map of the Moundville site. The various mounds are identified by letters and a palisade surrounded the site (courtesy of John Blitz; used with permission of the University of Alabama Press).

The size, character, and complexity of the Moundville changed after about 800 BP (Moundville II). The palisade and the other mounds were constructed, the nearby population moved into the protected area, and many houses were constructed in an organized manner within the town walls. Nearby, many small, outlying sites were abandoned while several new second-tier mound sites were constructed, perhaps as secondary administrative centers to Moundville (Knight and Steponaitis 1998:16). By 700 BP, Moundville had become the largest Mississippian polity in west-central Alabama (Fig. 12.8).

Just after 700 BP, Moundville appears to have radically changed again (Moundville III), from a major town with a large number of people to a locality occupied only by a relatively few elite (Knight and Steponaitis 1998:19). The majority of the population, consisting of commoners, appears to have moved back into small farms in the countryside, and the palisade was no longer maintained. Three possible explanations have been proposed for the depopulation of Moundville (Knight and Steponaitis 1998:18–19): (1) the elite wanted the people to move so as to make the mound center more sacred, (2) local resources (e.g., farmland or firewood) had been exhausted,

FIGURE 12.8   A portion of the Moundville site as it appears today. (*Source:* National Geographic Image Collection).

and/or (3) the need to keep people within a walled town no longer existed. The continued burial of high-status individuals within the site complex attests to its enduring ritual importance and its involvement in the SECC (see Fig. 12.9).

By about 600 BP, some of the mounds at Moundville appear to have been abandoned (Moundville IV), although smaller mound sites were built in the vicinity, probably to administer a growing rural population (Knight and Steponaitis 1998:20). Most of Moundville appears to have fallen into disuse by 550 BP, but the importance of the outlying mound centers seems to have increased, and small nucleated settlements appeared in the region for the first time since the ascent of Moundville. The influence of Moundville declined rapidly, and it was abandoned by about 350 BP (see Welch 1996; Knight and Steponaitis 1998:8, 22).

As in other Mississippian polities, it is believed that a small elite class at Moundville ruled the remaining population, a pattern that can be seen in the archaeology of the site. Considerable evidence of residential occupation by the common class is present along the margins of the site, with relatively little activity in the center. Some of the mounds appear to have been used as residences for the elite (as witnessed by house foundations and debris), others as craft centers (as evidenced by the presence of manufacturing debris; see Knight 2004), some as burial mounds (as demonstrated by tombs found in them), and others for display of the disinterred remains of important people (as seen from pigments and other ritual materials, as at Poverty Point). It has been suggested that the organization of space, mounds, and dwellings at the site reflected the rank ordering of kinship organizations within the site (Knight 1998:60). The food consumed by the

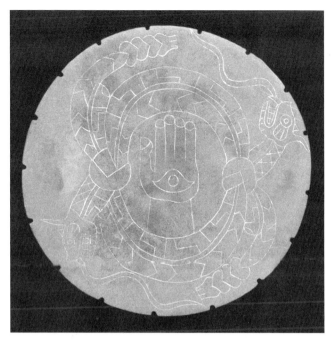

FIGURE 12.9 Rattlesnake disk made from stone found at the Moundville site. (*Source:* University of Alabama/Museum of Natural History).

elites was likely provided by commoners, as little evidence of food processing has been found in elite dwellings (Knight and Steponaitis 1998:16). In addition, analysis of the food remains from several elite households reflects the control of food resources and the status held by those households (Jackson and Scott 2003).

In an analysis of the grave goods recovered from 2,053 of the more than 3,000 burials excavated from Moundville, Peebles and Black (1987) offered a glimpse of the social structure at the site ca. 600 BP (Table 12.3). Only seven burials were found with copper axes, all of which were apparently adult males, interred at mounds in the center of the site. These seven individuals (classified as IA) were most likely the highest status individuals, perhaps the primary chiefs. The next highest ranking individuals (IB, $n = 43$), were all adult males and children (perhaps also males) and were buried in mounds (and other places) with copper earspools and other materials. The next highest status group (II, $n = 67$) consisted of individuals buried away from mounds with a variety of objects, including copper gorgets. These individuals were of both sexes and of all ages, probably the nobility. The remainder of the burials show a descending order of rank, as deduced from grave goods. The majority of the burials ($n = 1,256$, 61%) had no grave goods and likely represent the commoners. This pattern appears to reflect a patrilineal, hierarchical society with ascribed status. A video on the Moundville site is available at www.archaeologychannel.org, "Moundville: Journey Through Time."

Etowah Another major Mississippian center was Etowah, located in northwestern Georgia. This site (Fig. 12.10) had six major mounds and a central plaza within a palisade. One of the Etowah mounds, Mound A, is the second largest after Monks Mound at Cahokia, containing

TABLE 12.3 Social Structure at Moundville from an Analysis of Burial Location and Grave Goods (after Peebles and Kus 1977; Peebles and Black 1987)

Burial Location	Grave Goods	Number	Age/Sex	Inferred Social Rank (highest to lowest)
in central mounds	copper axes	7	adults, probably males	IA
mostly in mounds	copper earspools, bear teeth, and stone discs	43	adult males, children	IB
near mounds	copper gorgets, shell beads, and galena	67	all ages and both sexes	II
near mounds	pottery effigy vessels, animal bone, and shell gorgets	221	all ages and both sexes but many children	III
near mounds	discoidals, bone awls, projectile points	50	all ages and both sexes	IV
away from mounds	pottery bowls	55	all ages and both sexes, mostly adults but many children	V
away from mounds	water bottles	45	mostly adults of both sexes	VI
away from mounds	water bottles	55	mostly adults of both sexes	VII
away from mounds	pottery bowls	70	all ages and both sexes, mostly adults but many children	VIII
away from mounds	water bottles	46	mostly adults of both sexes	IX
away from mounds	pottery sherds	70	mostly adults of both sexes	X
away from mounds	none	1256	all ages and both sexes but many children	XI

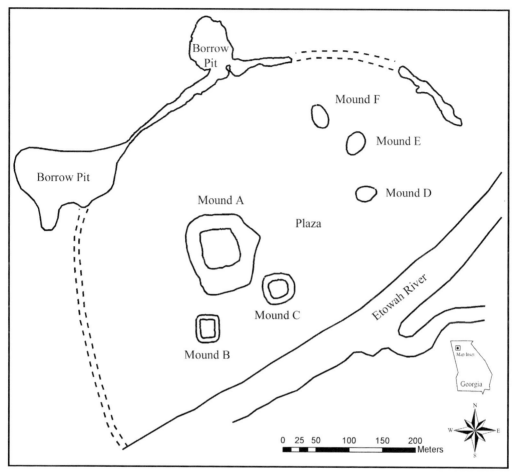

FIGURE 12.10 Map of the Etowah site. (*Source:* Drawing by Christopher Thornock. Courtesy of Adam King.)

some 114,000 cubic meters of fill (Muller 1997: Table 6.6; also see A. King 2003). Etowah was apparently the center of several chiefdoms at different times, each perhaps formed through different combinations of social factors.

Etowah was first occupied about 1,000 BP and developed as a relatively small chiefdom. It emerged as the dominant center of the various Late Woodland cultures in that region. Some (e.g., A. King 2003:285, 290) believe that Etowah developed under the corporate model, through the accommodation and cooperation of smaller centers. It has further been suggested that many of the chiefdoms of the Southeast may have been on the same developmental trajectory (A. King 2003:291). Others (e.g., Little 1999) favor the network model and the use of force, with ranked elites. For unknown reasons, the system collapsed and the site was abandoned about 800 BP.

Some hundred years later, the site was reoccupied and developed into the center of a large and complex chiefdom. At this time, Mound A was expanded and a new burial mound, Mound C, was constructed. Many SECC materials were found in the Mound C burials, suggesting that Etowah was reenergized during the advent of the SECC. If so, the SECC may have been the impetus for the formation of a new social organization, one based on a network strategy that led to the development of a new class of elites (A. King 2003:293). The new inhabitants of the site constructed a palisade, and there is evidence that the site was destroyed by unknown invaders ca. 625 BP. The site was reoccupied again about 550 BP, and a new chiefdom dominated by an elite class was reestablished. By the time Europeans entered the region in AD 1540, Etowah was a minor settlement within a much larger chiefdom (the Coosa; see M. T. Smith 2000, 2001), which later became part of the Creek confederacy.

NATIVE SOUTHEASTERN CULTURES AT CONTACT

In ethnographic times, the Southeast is defined primarily by the large and extraordinarily complex cultures that inhabited the woodlands that run in an arc from Virginia south and west to Texas (see Fig. 12.1). Spanish explorers called the entire Southeast La Florida. Most Southeastern cultures are characterized by agriculture, complex political and social organizations—several of the cultures in the Southeast are the most complex in North America—and large, sedentary populations; there were as many as 1,250,000 people in the Southeast in AD 1500. Not all Southeast groups practiced agriculture, however. The Calusa in southern Florida, for example, were largely hunters and gatherers (with some small gardens), mostly gathering fish and shellfish. Nevertheless, their culture was quite large and complex, and like many groups in the Southeast, they appear to have had a hierarchical organization (see Marquardt 2001).

In spite of the size and complexity of many ethnographic Southeast groups, they remain poorly known. By the time Europeans took an interest in recording information about these groups, many had ceased to exist and others had changed significantly. The Spanish entered the Southeast in the early 1500s, at which time European diseases began to wreak havoc on the large, sedentary populations of the region. As a result, many groups were utterly destroyed before anything was known about them. By 1750, some of the surviving groups absorbed the remnants of destroyed tribes and merged into larger but very different-looking confederacies. Thus, many of the southeastern groups known today did not exist prior to about three hundred years ago, a very interesting and dynamic situation.

It is generally agreed that the Mississippian chiefdoms of the Southeast were in decline prior to the Spanish *entrada* into the region in AD 1540 and that European diseases were not the cause of their decline (see Knight and Steponaitis 1998:23). There is no doubt that European contact severely impacted the extant societies through warfare and disease, resulting in the deaths of many and the severe disruption of social and political systems (see Powell 1992; Thornton et al. 1992; Hudson 1994, 1997). By the time Europeans again entered the region more than one hundred years later, the survivors had reconstituted themselves into societies, such as the Creek, Choctaw, and Cherokee, structurally different than their Mississippian ancestors.

There were a few groups that managed to retain their Mississippian organization well into historic times. Perhaps the best known were the Natchez (see Du Pratz 1758; Hudson 1976). The Natchez, who called themselves Thelöel, lived along the lower Mississippi River in what is now Louisiana and Mississippi. They were encountered by the French in 1682 and were subsequently destroyed by them in 1731. The historical records of Natchez society provide a glimpse of the complexity and grandeur of Late Mississippian times and an analog for understanding those societies.

The leader of the Natchez was the Great Sun, a man who held the dual offices of "king" and "high priest." The Great Sun was a theocratic ruler who traced his ancestry back to the sun itself. The Great Sun had total power over his people but was assisted in his rule by a council of advisers consisting of men of the Sun class (see below). People bowed in the presence of the Great

Sun, and he and his close relatives were carried on litters. When a Great Sun died, his sister's son became the next Great Sun.

The Great Sun resided at the Natchez capital, now known as the Fatherland site, located just a few miles southeast of the current city of Natchez, Mississippi. The Fatherland site is believed to have served as the Natchez capital for at least 500 years prior to French intrusion. The site contains a number of mounds organized around a large central plaza used for public ceremonies (see Neitzel 1965). The Great Sun and other important officials lived in houses built on platform mounds around the plaza. Directly across from the Great Sun's residence was the large main temple mound. The primary religious activities were carried out at this temple, and an eternal flame was kept there. Ordinary citizens lived in houses away from the plaza. The Natchez also resided in a number of smaller towns, each organized in a manner similar to the capital (mounds around a plaza). Each town was protected from attack with a palisade.

The social organization of the Natchez was quite complex, consisting of four major classes of people: Sun, Noble, Honored, and Common. The Sun class was at the top of the social pyramid and had few members. There were more Nobles and still more Honored, but the vast majority of the Natchez people were Commoners. Human sacrifice was conducted at major ceremonial events (e.g., the burial of a Great Sun).

Many of the specific practices seen in the historical records of Natchez society can also be detected in the archaeological record of Mississippian societies. The Fatherland site had an architectural organization and mound function much like that proposed for Moundville (Knight 2004), and the Natchez had a class system similar to that of Moundville (Peebles and Black 1987). Human sacrifice appears to have been practiced, as was likely the case in a number of Mississippian polities. The hierarchical political organization of a paramount chief proposed for many Mississippian polities is quite similar to the position of Great Sun and his kin group among the Natchez.

Further Reading

The most recent summary of Southeastern prehistory can be found in the chapters of the Southeastern volume of the *Handbook of North American Indians* (Fogelson 2004). Other synthetic treatments include B. D. Smith (1986), Bense (1994), and M. E. White (2002). Papers on the history of research are present in Tushingham et al. (2002), and many works are available on a variety of topics, including Sassman and Anderson (1996) on the Mid-Holocene, Anderson and Mainfort (2002) on the Woodland, and a wide range of materials on the Mississippian (e.g., B. D. Smith 1990; J. F. Scarry 1996a; Muller 1997; Pauketat 1994, 2007). Important monograph series include those published by the University of Florida and the University of Alabama Press. Important regional journals include *Archaeology of Eastern North America*, *Southeastern Archaeology*, and *Journal of Alabama Archaeology*.

CHAPTER 13

Moose and Fish
The Subarctic

The Subarctic culture area is the largest in North America, encompassing most of the northern portion of the continent, much of it covered with an extensive pine forest. The Subarctic was almost completely covered by ice at the end of the Pleistocene and was settled by people only after the ice had retreated and the land had been colonized by plants and animals (the eastern Subarctic was colonized even later as the ice retreated north; see Chapter 4). As the Subarctic became habitable, Athapaskan peoples from the west moved east and Algonquian peoples from the south moved north, culturally dividing the region into two halves. Thus, to understand the origins of Subarctic cultures, it is necessary to have some understanding of the Northwest Coast, Plains, and Northeast; this is the reason the Subarctic is discussed last.

GEOGRAPHY AND ENVIRONMENT

The Subarctic (Fig. 13.1) is the largest natural region in North America, consisting of some 3 million square miles (4.5 million km²) stretching from central Alaska across Canada to the Atlantic Ocean (see J. S. Gardner 1981). Three major physiographic regions are herein defined for the Subarctic: the Alaska Plateau, the Western Subarctic, and the Canadian Shield. A large number of lakes and regions of muskeg (swamp) are found throughout the Subarctic. The Labrador and Newfoundland regions along the Atlantic coast, sometimes considered a part of the Subarctic, are included in the Northeast culture area (see Chapter 11).

The Alaska Plateau (see Hosley 1981) consists of a large region of interior highlands in eastern Alaska and the western Yukon Territory of Canada dominated by the Yukon and Kuskokwim rivers. The Western Subarctic is dominated by the northern Rocky Mountains (called the Cordillera; see McClellan and Denniston 1981) and is roughly bordered on the east by the Mackenzie River. The Canadian Shield consists of the eastern two-thirds of the Subarctic (see Rogers and Smith 1981) and includes the Canadian Shield proper, an area of mostly exposed granite bedrock, many lakes, and few hills or mountains. The Mackenzie Borderlands, essentially

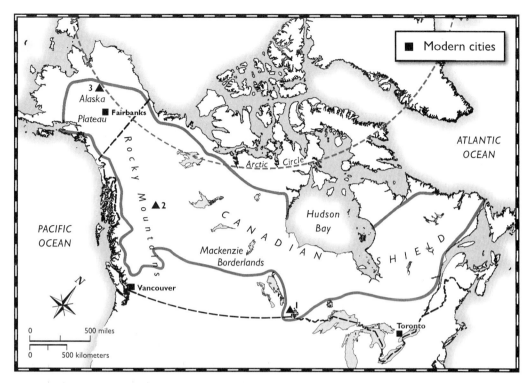

FIGURE 13.1 Map of the Subarctic showing major subregions and the location of sites discussed in the text: 1) Ballynacree; 2) Charlie Lake Cave; 3) Onion Portage.

the northern physical extension of the Plains, constitutes the western portion of the Shield, but the area is too cold to support grasslands and bison.

The climate of the Subarctic consists of long, cold winters (e.g., −20 F) and short, warm summers (Bone 1992:19–21). Precipitation is limited but evaporation rates are low, so there is no shortage of water. Most precipitation falls as snow, which covers the ground for more than six months each year. The deep and unpacked snow, coupled with the rivers and streams that are frozen between about November and May, restricted the movements of prehistoric people and limited their ability to obtain food. As a result, storage of food was always an important task.

Three major biotic communities characterize the Subarctic from north to south. In the north, a zone of tundra with permafrost and low vegetation of lichen and mosses is punctuated with woodland areas containing pine trees and shrubs. To the south of the tundra zone is the boreal forest that dominates most of the Subarctic. This large forest consists primarily of conifers, including spruce, pine, and birch trees. A small region of deciduous forest lies to the south of the boreal forest.

The boreal forest, covering the bulk of the Subarctic, contains relatively little biodiversity and has a limited number of resources. Important animals included caribou, moose, deer, bears, hares, waterfowl (in the summer), and a number of fish species. Relatively few plants were available.

A BRIEF HISTORY OF RESEARCH

Although ethnographic research has been conducted since the late 1800s, relatively little archaeological work was done in the Subarctic until fairly recently, mostly after World War II. Much of the earliest research was conducted in Alaska and focused on Paleoindians (D. W. Clark 1991b:5).

Research in the interior of the Subarctic began in the late 1940s, but most has been done since the 1960s. One of the many early contributors was Richard S. MacNeish, who formulated the first summaries of regional chronologies and set the standard for future work (see D. W. Clark 1981; Clark and Morlan 1982).

Since World War II, the Subarctic has seen considerable development of oil, gas, timber, and minerals and the construction of a number of large hydroelectric projects, all of which has spurred a great deal of compliance archaeology. However, the scale of the development is so vast that the compliance work has not been able to keep pace, creating a problem in resource management (e.g., S. Hamilton 2000). Several other factors also hamper research in the Subarctic, including low visibility of sites in the forests due to thick layers of duff, the tendency of sites to have thin deposits, soil acidity that causes poor preservation, and the difficult logistics of research.

Another important issue in understanding Subarctic prehistory is the way in which it is visualized (e.g., Holly 2002). There is a tendency to see the Subarctic as "marginal" to the important areas of cultural change, such as the Northwest Coast or Northeast, or to see it as a region whose environment is excessively constraining to cultural development. Either view, sometimes held concurrently, results in an archaeological perspective that prehistory was virtually static, with little change through time. This most certainly is not true.

MAJOR THEMES IN SUBARCTIC PREHISTORY

Several major research issues pervade Subarctic research. The first is the search for the first Paleoindians. If they initially took a coastal route into North America, they would not have passed through the Subarctic. Alternatively, the route south could lie in the western Subarctic, perhaps along the putative "ice-free corridor" that would have extended from eastern Alaska to the northern Plains (see Chapter 2). Moving forward a bit in time, the role of Paleoindian and Paleoarctic groups in the prehistory of the western Subarctic is of considerable interest.

Associated with this later question is the proposed Northern Archaic Tradition (NAT) in the western Subarctic. There is considerable debate regarding the reality of the NAT and, if real, its relationship with Paleoarctic microblade complexes. The characteristics of the NAT are also unclear, and it is not known what its fate was.

Related to the question of the relationship of NAT with other Archaic groups is the connection between these archaeological traditions and the ethnographic groups of the region. Is it correct to presume that, throughout prehistory, all of the western groups were Athapaskan ancestors and all of the eastern groups were Algonquian ancestors? Probably not, although there are reasons to believe that the two are connected at some level.

The Apache and Navajo peoples of the Southwest are speakers of southern Athapaskan languages, related to the northern Athapaskan groups in the western Subarctic. It is clear that the southern Athapaskans migrated south from the western Subarctic, across the Plains, and into the Southwest. Some Athapaskan groups even found their way into California (e.g., Ives 2003). The whys and hows of these population movements are of considerable interest.

Finally, many researchers presume that caribou was the game animal of primary importance through time, hunted on the tundra during the short summers (Gordon 1996). While this is a reasonable premise, a great deal more work on prehistoric subsistence systems will be required to understand the types of resources that were used by different groups at different points in time.

A basic chronological sequence for the Subarctic is shown in Table 13.1.

TABLE 13.1 A Chronological Sequence for the Subarctic

Date (BP)	Alaska Plateau/Western Subarctic		Canadian Shield	General Climate
200	Ethnographic Athapaskans		Ethnographic Algonkians	as today
1,000	Ancestral Athapaskans	Taltheilei Tradition	Shield Woodland (Laurel)	generally warmer than today
2,000				
			Pre-Dorset	very cold
3,000	Northern Archaic		Shield Archaic	colder than today
4,000	Arctic Small Tool Tradition			
5,000				
6,000	Paleoarctic	UNOCCUPIED		warmer than today
7,000			Northern Plano	
8,000			Late Paleoindian (far south)	colder but warming
9,000				
to 10,000	Paleoindian			very cold

THE PALEOINDIAN PERIOD (TO 10,000 BP)

The majority of the Subarctic was glaciated during Paleoindian times (see Fig. 2.3), thus, the Paleoindian record is limited. Several regions were not glaciated, however, including much of interior Alaska, which contains a good record of Paleoindian occupation (see Chapter 2). In addition, as the glaciers retreated north, Paleoindian groups in the eastern United States migrated north into what is now the Subarctic.

It remains possible that the ancestor of the Clovis Complex (see Chapter 2) is to be found in Alaska, and research on that issue is ongoing. The northern entrance of the ice-free corridor would be in the Alaska region as well. Whether Paleoindians moved south along the coast or through an ice-free corridor is still unknown, but at least some Paleoindians seem to have stayed in the region to evolve into the subsequent Paleoarctic groups.

Charlie Lake Cave in northeastern British Columbia (Fladmark 1996) contains a record beginning in Paleoindian times. The lowest level of the site, Component 1 dated to about 10,500 BP, contained a fluted point, a scraper, a bead, flakes, and bison bone, the remains of animals apparently hunted by the occupants of the site (Driver 1996). Two raven skeletons were also found at the site, apparently purposefully buried more than 10,000 years ago (Driver 1999).

As the glaciers began to retreat about 10,000 years ago, late Paleoindians with stemmed points began to move north into the Subarctic, following the forest and tundra zones as they progressed north. By about 8,000 BP, these groups began to occupy the northern reaches of the Subarctic with a technology similar to the earlier Plano Complex of the Plains (see Chapter 3). These "Northern Plano" groups (J. V. Wright 1981:87, 1995; Gordon 1996:219) focused on caribou rather than the bison of the Plains, but little else is known about them. Some have likened these groups with the Old Cordilleran culture of the Northwest Coast.

THE PALEOARCTIC (CA. 10,000 TO 6,000 BP)

Paleoarctic groups (see Chapter 4) in the Subarctic were generally limited to the Alaska Plateau and may reflect the Na-Dene linguistic group that migrated from Asia into Alaska as early as 12,000 BP. These new people apparently brought with them the microblade Dyuktai Complex from Asia (e.g., Goebel et al. 1991:74) and occupied central and northern Alaska. A number of regional groups later developed from these Paleoarctic groups, including the Arctic Small Tool Tradition (ASTt), the Pre-Dorset, and possibly even the Northern Archaic Tradition (see below).

The Arctic Small Tool Tradition

The Arctic Small Tool Tradition (ASTt, discussed in Chapter 4), a technology based on small cores and microblades, appeared in interior Alaska from the Arctic coast as early as about 6,000 BP (or perhaps a bit earlier; e.g., Greer 1993). The ASTt appears to have been related to the earlier Paleoarctic groups that may have come into contact with Archaic groups in the interior. The ASTt was distinctive for a time but then appears to have mixed with, or was perhaps absorbed by, Northern Archaic groups. This "mixture" is often included within the Northern Archaic Tradition (see D. W. Clark 1991b:53–55) but is sometimes called the Northwest Microblade Tradition (D. W. Clark 2001).

Pre-Dorset (ca. 3,000 to 2,300 BP)

About 3,000 years ago, the climate cooled and the tundra and forest ecozones moved south, expanding the geographic Arctic into what is now the Subarctic. When this happened, some Arctic Pre-Dorset groups (see Chapter 4) also moved south, apparently to exploit caribou (see Gordon 1996). When the climate warmed again, the Arctic ecozones moved north again, and the Pre-Dorset people went with them. Thus a few Pre-Dorset sites are known in what is now the Subarctic but do not represent Subarctic peoples.

THE NORTHERN ARCHAIC (CA. 6,000 TO 3,000 BP)

The Northern Archaic Tradition (NAT) was an Indian (rather than Eskimo) tradition of hunters and gatherers who occupied the mountains and interior river valleys of the northwestern

Subarctic west of the Mackenzie River. These people, living in small, highly mobile groups, generally occupied forest habitats, although there was some use of the coastal plain in northern Alaska (Lobdell 1986). The beginning of the NAT is usually viewed as dating to about 6,000 BP (Esdale 2008), although there is some evidence of it being earlier, perhaps 7,000 BP (Greer 1993).

The origin of NAT is unclear. It was originally defined at the Onion Portage site (D. D. Anderson 1968, 1988) and was characterized by large side-notched points, along with the use of bone and antler tools and points. There are similarities between these points and some southern types (see D. W. Clark 1991b:49), leading to the idea that NAT groups migrated into the region from the south (e.g., D. D. Anderson 1968). Others (e.g., Morrison 1987:66) argued against a migration but supported the idea of a diffusion of traits from the south, such as the Mummy Cave Complex on the Plains. More recent analyses suggest a northern origin (Esdale 2008:11), perhaps related to earlier Paleoarctic and ASTt groups. It seems possible that the NAT groups are the ancestors of the Athapaskan groups living in the region in ethnographic times.

The NAT is now divided into a series of phases, identified by a progression of projectile point forms, from side-notched to stemmed to lanceolate (Morrison 1987; D. D. Anderson 1988; Ackerman 2004:153). Microblades, the hallmark of the ASTt, were not originally a characteristic of the NAT, although microblades are occasionally found at NAT sites. This suggested to some (e.g., Schoenberg 1995; Esdale 2008) that there was some relationship between the ASTt and NAT: either (1) the coexistence of the two groups in the region for a time, (2) a direct development of ASTt into NAT, or (3) some sort of mixture of ASTt and NAT technologies within what is called NAT. Indeed, it has recently been suggested that the projectile-point sequence that defined the NAT phases may not be chronological but functional, with lanceolate points being used on spears, side-notched points on darts, and microliths on arrows (Rasic and Slobodina 2008). Clearly, NAT is not well understood.

Northern Archaic groups could be characterized as "people of the forest," and there is a general feeling that such groups followed the expansion of forests during the Middle Holocene. It may not be quite that simple. It is possible (e.g., Mason and Bigelow 2008) that as the technology to exploit forest resources developed, NAT groups moved into existing forests, rather than simply following the forests as they expanded.

The primary economy of the NAT was based on caribou hunting, primarily in forest habitats, although there is evidence of caribou hunting on the north coastal Plain of Alaska during the summer as early as 6,000 BP (e.g., Lobdell 1986). Caribou were hunted in a number of ways, including the use of spears as they crossed rivers and with the aid of traps and corrals (D. W. Clark 1991b:77), the earliest of which are dated to 4,100 BP (Ackerman 2004:161). Other animals, including musk-ox, elk, small mammals, and waterfowl, may also have been important. Moose is often viewed as having been an important resource from early times, but the use of moose may actually be a very late, even historic, pattern (Yesner 1989).

Northern Archaic groups participated in a great deal of trade with others. Items traded included perishable foodstuffs, obsidian and other stone, and *Dentalium* shell from the coast. Copper nuggets were obtained and cold hammered into beads, awls, knives, and the occasional projectile point.

The Northern Archaic is commonly presumed to represent the ancestors of the Athapaskans, and some researchers have suggested that the NAT lasted until contact. However, the Proto-Athapaskan linguistic grouping likely did not differentiate until sometime about 3,500 BP (e.g., Krauss and Golla 1981:68), making any linguistic association prior to that time quite tenuous. Thus, the end of the NAT is now considered to have been about 3,000 BP (Esdale 2008;

also see D. D. Anderson 2008). At about 3,000 BP, the western NAT became the Athapaskan Tradition, cultures that led to the ethnographic Athapaskan groups in the western Subarctic. At about that same time, some Northern Archaic groups moved east onto the northern Canadian Shield to become the Taltheilei Tradition (see below), also ancestral to ethnographic Athapaskan groups in that region.

THE SHIELD ARCHAIC (CA. 6,500 BP TO CONTACT)

On the Canadian Shield in the eastern Subarctic, the Archaic is often called the Shield Archaic, sometimes divided into Early, Middle, and Late (Wright 1995). The concept of the Shield Archaic was developed as an organizational device (e.g., Wright 1981:88, 1995; D. W. Clark 1991b:98) but has not been adopted by some archaeologists, believing it to be too restrictive (see McCaffrey 2006:178). Shield Archaic groups were primarily forest dwellers and had the same basic adaptation as their Northern Archaic neighbors to the west, fishing and using side-notched points to hunt caribou and other game. The storage of food was an important aspect of the economy (Stopp 2002), and caribou meat would be dried and processed into a pemmican-like material or stored as carcasses in rock or log-covered caches. The Shield Archaic adaptation was very successful.

The Shield Archaic is generally viewed as being the ancestors, or ancestors of the ancestors, of the ethnographic Algonquian groups, the people who occupied the eastern Subarctic at contact. On the other hand, the Taltheilei Tradition, located in the northwestern Shield, was ancestral to Athapaskan groups, having moved east onto the Shield fairly late in time (see above).

Beginning about 2,200 years ago, many Shield Archaic groups adopted pottery and became Woodland groups, ending the Shield Archaic in those areas. However, a few Shield Archaic groups did not adopt pottery and so remained Shield Archaic until contact.

The Taltheilei Tradition (ca. 2,600 to Contact)

Sometime about 3,000 BP, ancestral Athapaskans from the NAT moved east into the northwestern Canadian Shield, apparently following an expansion of the forest north as the climate warmed. These groups, called the Taltheilei Tradition, are also known as the Taltheilei Shale Tradition due to their considerable use of gray shale for tools.

The Taltheilei Tradition can be divided into early, middle, and late periods (following Gordon 1996; also see Wright 1995:1000–1009). Early Taltheilei (ca. 2,600 to 1,800 BP) is characterized by stemmed points. Middle Taltheilei (ca. 1,800 to 1,300 BP) is characterized by fewer stemmed and more lanceolate points. Interestingly, Middle Taltheilei tools tend to be worn to a greater degree than during other times, perhaps due to the difficulty in obtaining the necessary raw materials for new tools due to the cold (Gordon 1996:113). Late Taltheilei (ca. 1,300 BP to contact), also called the Diné, is characterized by side-notched and corner-notched points that were used on arrows. In addition, a few points were made from native copper.

The economy of the Taltheilei Tradition was based on caribou hunting on the tundra during the summer. The animals would be taken, their hides prepared, and their meat processed for storage through the winter. The winters would have been spent in small, sedentary villages located in the forest, with relatively little activity beyond tool maintenance. This pattern was quite successful and apparently lasted several millennia.

THE SHIELD WOODLAND (CA. 2,200 TO 800 BP)

The Shield Woodland in the Subarctic is defined by the diffusion of pottery from the south after about 2,200 BP. These first Shield Woodland groups were initially called "Middle Woodland," since they derived from Middle Woodland groups to the south. Subarctic Woodland groups are now generally called the Laurel Complex or Laurel Culture (Wright 1981:90, 1995; also see R. J. Mason 1981:284–292). The bow and arrow diffused into the region at about the same time.

The Laurel Complex is poorly known (although Wright [1995:725–780] provided an extensive discussion), as few sites associated with the complex have been excavated. Based on changes in pottery styles, perhaps four different phases of the Laurel Complex can be identified (Reid and Rajnovik 1991:206), but they can be more simply divided into Initial (Early Laurel) Woodland and Terminal (Late Laurel) Woodland (Dawson 1981). It is possible that Laurel simply represents the diffusion of pottery from the south, although it may represent an actual movement of people who came from the south and combined with the Shield Archaic groups (Dawson 1981). It has recently been discovered that corn formed an important aspect of Laurel diets by about 1,500 BP (see Boyd and Surette 2010), this being the northernmost extent of its cultivation.

A complete Late Laurel village was discovered at the Ballynacree site along the Winnipeg River in southern Ontario (Reid and Rajnovik 1991). The site contained three houses with hearths, exterior activity areas, and storage pits (Fig. 13.2). When compared to other Laurel sites, the size and structure of the Ballynacree site led Reid and Rajnovik (1991:219) to suggest that there had been little change in social structure over the span of Laurel (Reid and Rajnovik 1991:220).

Laurel mortuary patterns include the use of large burial mounds containing secondary burials. This mortuary pattern is characteristic of the Woodland groups to the south and supports the idea of at least some population movement. In some cases, bones were perforated, perhaps to "release spirits" (Torbenson et al. 1992).

After 800 BP, regional variants of Laurel may have evolved into the Blackduck and Selkirk cultures (defined by pottery types), ancestors of the Northern Ojibwa and Cree, respectively (see Dawson 1981). Late in time, some of the Cree moved out onto the Plains (see Chapter 10).

NATIVE SUBARCTIC CULTURES AT CONTACT

By the time Europeans began to enter the Subarctic, it was mostly controlled by France (and later England), powers that wanted to exploit the Indians but were not bent on colonizing the region (as was the case in the United States to the south), although this had changed by the 1800s. Thus, while native Subarctic people did not have to fight for their land (at least not at first), they were faced with two major issues: trade and disease. European trading companies (e.g., the Hudson's Bay Company) partnered with Indian groups to provide furs for the European market. This fur trade dramatically altered the settlement and subsistence systems of the native groups (see Ray 1974; Krech 1984; Ives 1990), as men hunted animals for their furs instead of their meat. Eventually, native settlements coalesced around trading posts, and by 1800 the depletion of fur and game resources due to overhunting in more constricted hunting grounds had forced most groups into a dependent relationship with the trading posts.

Disease devastated native populations, although the small size and relative isolation of many groups protected them from some of the major diseases. Nevertheless, major smallpox epidemics swept through the eastern Subarctic in 1737 and 1781, and a large number of Indians died. In addition, in the 1930s, tuberculosis became a major problem.

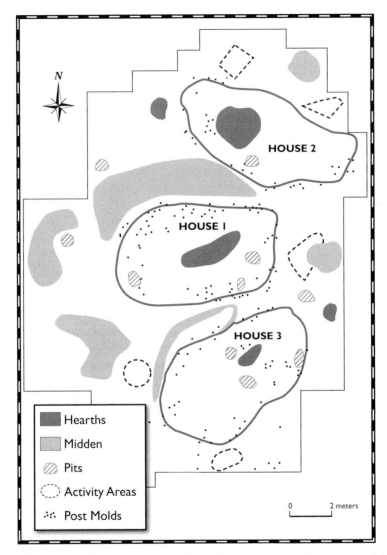

FIGURE 13.2   Map of the Ballynacree site in southern Ontario, showing the houses and features believed to represent a complete Laurel village (reproduced and modified from Reid and Rajnovich 1991:Fig. 3, with permission of the Canadian Archaeological Association).

In 1991, there were about 600,000 native people living in Canada (Reddy 1995: Table 924), including Indians and Métis (of mixed Indian and European heritage) people. They are organized into some 570 recognized native groups, often called First Nations, living on 2,240 reserves (roughly equivalent to reservations in the United States). Subarctic peoples today have generally managed to maintain their cultural identities and much of their traditional culture while adapting to and using much of Western technology (see Honigmann 1981). Until fairly recently, many groups still subsisted by hunting and trading; however, this is changing rapidly as development projects become more common in the region. The construction of all-weather roads and the use of aircraft have greatly increased the human population in the region.

There have been some land claim settlements in the Subarctic. The western Diné were involved in the Alaska Native Claims Settlement Act (ANCSA) in 1971, and the Cree signed the James Bay Settlement in 1975 (see McCutcheon 1991). Also in 1975, a few groups banded together and declared a "Diné Nation," with the goal of forming a province within the national Canadian government, as the Inuit have done.

Further Reading

The literature on Subarctic prehistory is rather limited. General treatments on the prehistory of the Subarctic can be found in D. W. Clark (1981, 1991b), Noble (1981), and J. V. Wright (1981). More recently, brief general summaries of Subarctic prehistory can be found in Dumond (1987a:47–54), J. V. Wright (1995), B. M. Fagan (2005a:187–189), and Neusius and Gross (2007:149–155, 173–174).

The Canadian Museum of Civilization publishes monographs that deal with the Subarctic. In addition, the journals *Arctic Anthropology, Canadian Journal of Archaeology*, and *Ontario Archaeology* carry papers on the subject.

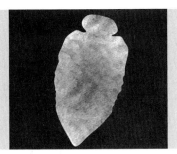

Epilogue
After Prehistory

In 1492, North America was a lively place with many hundreds of separate cultures. The Thule had moved east into Greenland, California was home to perhaps 500,000 people, some Mississippian polities had faltered while others prospered, agriculture had spread across much of the continent, and the Southwest was in turmoil. Native populations may have peaked at about 850 BP and may have begun to decline, perhaps due to increased sedentism (Peros et al. 2010). In the far north, the Norse had apparently contacted native groups some 500 years before but to little effect. The impact of the arrival of Columbus would be far different.

Once they were contacted by Europeans, the prehistory of a particular native group technically ended and the ethnohistoric period, a time when the native peoples were interacting with Europeans but were still independent, began. This occurred at different times in different places—the 1490s in the Caribbean and as late as the 1840s with some groups in the Great Basin. In some cases, knowledge of the European presence, some of their trade goods, and even perhaps their diseases moved ahead of the Europeans themselves.

While not the subject of this book, the archaeology of the Ethnohistoric Period explores the impact of European contact and the native responses to that trauma. Eventually, and sometime very quickly, native peoples were subjugated by the Europeans and adopted some European traits (e.g., housing, employment, and some material culture), at which time their history became intertwined with that of the Euroamericans.

Historical archaeology is generally seen as the archaeology of intrusive, nonindigenous cultures (Orser and Fagan 1995:5), such as the Norse, Chinese, Dutch, English, French, Portuguese, Russian, Spanish, and later the Anglo-Americans. Native people also have a historical archaeology, but there has been little attention given it (see Rubertone 2000). One of the major goals of historical archaeology is to elucidate the lives of those who are under represented in written history, particularly the poor or minorities, including most Native Americans. For native peoples, this work includes research into understanding the actual impact of contact (which may not be reflected in the written record) and into understanding the acculturation and cultural survival process. In some cases, European contact was short-term (e.g., trade relationships) and had a very different impact that one of long-term colonialism (Sillman 2005).

OUTSIDE CONTACTS WITH NATIVE AMERICANS

The earliest documented contact between Europeans and native peoples of the New World was that of the Vikings from Scandinavia, known as the Norse, about 1,000 years ago (McGovern 1980, 1990). Beginning in AD 982, the Norse established several colonies in Greenland. In AD 986, a lost Norse ship apparently observed some unknown land west of Greenland, and ten years later, Lief Erikson sailed west to explore this newfound land (hence the place name, Newfoundland) and established a small, short-lived colony in AD 1004. This small settlement was apparently discovered in 1960 at L'Anse aux Meadows (Fig. 14.1), on the northeastern tip of Newfoundland (see McGhee 1984; Fitzhugh 1985; A. Ingstad 1985; H. Ingstad 1985). Foundations for eight turf buildings, including a blacksmith shop, were found, along with a number of iron artifacts. There are indications that this site was probably not intended as a permanent settlement, as it is located in an area unprotected from the weather. There is no evidence that this colony had any lasting impact on the native groups in the area.

FIGURE 14.1   The L'Anse aux Meadows site in Newfoundland (see Fig. 4.1 for location), with reconstructed Norse houses (photo courtesy of Virginia Osborne).

To the north, the Norse had also contacted the Inuit (Thule) as they moved east into Greenland (see Highlight 4.3). The relationship seems to have been based on trading (e.g., McGhee 2009) and was probably not very intense or sustained for very long. It is also possible that the Dorset (see Chapter 4) had contact with the Norse (Sutherland 2009), which may have resulted in the Dorset being substantially impacted by European diseases (Agger and Maschner 2009), although direct evidence for this is lacking.

There may have been other visits to North America prior to 1492. There is reason to believe that Basque fishermen briefly visited the New England region in the mid-1400s (Quinn 1974). In addition, it is possible that the Chinese and Japanese had some very limited contact with groups along the Pacific coast (G. Menzies 2003). None of these possible contacts appears to have had any lasting impact on native populations or culture.

Columbus, an Italian working for Spain, landed on a small island in the Caribbean in October of 1492. He thought that he was in the Indies of Southeast Asia and that the people he encountered were "Indians." Columbus is generally credited with the discovery of North America, but when he set out on his voyage, he thought he was going somewhere else; when he got there, he did not know where he was; and when he returned, he did not know where he had been (Brace and Montagu 1977:6). Columbus later returned to the Caribbean, and soon after the Spanish came in force. The Spanish began their conquest of Central and South America (plus Florida and the Southwest) while other Europeans rushed to exploit the resources of eastern North America. By 1497, the English were fishing off Newfoundland, and by 1536, French Basque whalers were operating off the shores of eastern North America. These very early contacts were relatively minor and had an unknown impact on the native peoples. The first colony in North America was established by the Spanish in South Carolina in 1526. Things went south from there.

THE IMPACT OF EUROPEAN CONTACT

When Europeans contacted native peoples, their goals varied. The Spanish were interested in obtaining wealth (e.g., gold), labor to obtain more wealth, and in converting the native population to Christianity, but they were not interested in colonization with large numbers of Spanish people. As a result, the Spanish took over political power in the regions under their control, looted, and established missions, including systems in California, the Southwest, and Southeast. The French were mostly interested in trade and in countering the English but never were much interested in colonization. The English, on the other hand, were very interested in colonization, and hundreds of thousands of people immigrated from England (and later other European countries) in search of land. Thus, the Indians were in the way and were displaced and/or eliminated.

The impact on native cultures was varied. Disease was an immediate and obvious impact, but in the absence of other factors, such as genocide, most populations eventually recovered. In fact, most people now living in Central and South America are biologically Native American, but this is not the case in North America. As a group was contacted, impacted, and conquered, their belief systems would have been shattered (how does one explain the new white people, and why would the gods allow this to happen?). In the face of disease, social and political institutions would have broken down, often replaced by European ones. Some groups would have allied themselves with the Europeans against old enemies, only to meet the same fate later. In addition to the loss of land, many aspects of the culture would have been ravaged, including livelihoods, culture, and language. Added to this were the biological impacts.

The Spanish Mission System

One of the major aspirations of the Spanish in the New World was to convert the native peoples to Christianity. Religion was intertwined with colonialism and conquest and was often seen as the moral force behind "civilizing" native populations (this is still the case all over the world). Convinced of the superiority of their culture and religion, missionaries imposed their beliefs and values on native peoples, by force if necessary (this is also still occurring). The intentions of most of the missionaries may have been good, but their methods were often brutal, and the long-term impacts on native cultures were often disastrous, resulting in cultural genocide (see Tinker 1993).

In the late 1500s, the Spanish granted exclusive rights to missionize specific regions to both the Jesuit and Franciscan orders, with the Jesuit territories subsequently being given to the Franciscans after 1767. The Spanish established mission systems in four major centers of North America: California, the Southwest, the Southeast, and northern Mexico.

In California, mission organizations were established in both Alta and Baja California (see Costello and Hornbeck 1989; Mathes 1989; Crosby 1994), with the Jesuits building a series of 17 missions in Baja California and the Franciscans building 21 additional missions in Alta California. In the Southwest, another series of missions was established in the Rio Grande Valley (see Kubler 1940; Spicer 1962; Kessell 1979; R. H. Jackson 2000). An extensive mission system was established in La Florida in the southeastern United States (see D. H. Thomas 1990; Milanich 1994), where as many as 130 mission localities were founded, although not all of them were occupied at the same time. The most extensive system of missions was established in northern Mexico (the southern portion of the Southwest), with hundreds of churches being built (Dunne 1948; Roca 1979; Polzer et al. 1991; Sheridan et al. 1991; R. H. Jackson 1994).

In general, popular beliefs regarding missions and missionaries in the New World are highly romanticized and mythical versions of what people wish they had been. People want to believe that missions were wonderful places where the natives could escape their primitive lives and to discover and embrace the superior ways of the Europeans (see D. H. Thomas [1991] for a perspective on how this myth developed). This version continues to be widely taught in schools and remains the "party line" for tourists at many of the surviving missions, some of which are now parks.

In truth, many of the missions were little more than concentration camps, where the natives were imprisoned, forced to abandon their culture, and enslaved as labor, although one must remember that these judgments are based on today's standards (see Guest 1979, 1983). Entire cultures were wiped out, dying from overwork, disease, and loss of the ability to reproduce. Native peoples were viewed as "children," who required stern treatment and discipline if they were to be elevated from their savage or barbarian roots. This attitude is vividly conveyed in the term "Great White Father," often applied to the president of the United States.

European Diseases and Population Decline

The impact of Europeans, particularly that of their diseases, on native groups has been investigated at some length, particularly in the last twenty-five years or so (see Cockburn 1971; Fitzhugh 1985; Ramenofsky 1987; Stannard 1992; Dobyns 1993; Larsen and Milner 1994; Settipane 1995; Baker and Kealhoffer 1996; Thornton 1997, 2000; N. D. Cook 1998; Mancall and Merrell 2000; Axtell 2001; Larsen et al. 2001). Populations declined by perhaps as much as 95 percent in some areas (Stannard 1992:268). Thus, of the estimated 8 to 12 million people in North America 500 years ago (other estimates are lower, e.g., Peros et al. 2010), only about 300,000 survived into the twentieth century (see Stannard 1992).

Most of these population losses were due to the many diseases inadvertently brought to the New World by Europeans, including smallpox, measles, influenza, malaria, typhus, bubonic plague, whooping cough, tuberculosis, diphtheria, yellow fever, cholera, and typhoid fever (see Diamond 1992). Population decline was due to a number of factors beyond direct disease mortality, including greatly increased infant mortality and a decline in birth rates. Other stressors, such as military conquest, forced conversion, and starvation, added to the mayhem. Thus, many of the vibrant societies present in North America 500 years ago rapidly disappeared. Some are only known today through archaeology.

A FEW EXAMPLES OF CONTACT STUDIES

The historical archaeology of native people is conducted to illuminate the lives and conditions of those not represented in the historical record. It may also serve to develop analogies for the investigation of native systems in the prehistoric past. Although not the subject of this book, two examples of Native American historical archaeology are briefly discussed below—one study of gender and one of contact and adjustment—to illustrate what can be learned through Native American historical archaeology.

Gender and the Dakota

The study of gender in the archaeological record is difficult and only in its infancy. One of the problems in gender study is that the effects of gender systems are most visible in the archaeological record at the scale of the household. Most archaeology, with an emphasis on large-scale processes of development, simply was not looking where gender relations would be most evident (Conkey and Spector 1984:22–23). To pursue the goal of elucidating gender, there would need to be a focus on daily life at the local scale.

Such a study was undertaken by Janet Spector at the village of Little Rapids, Minnesota, a Native American site occupied by members of the Wahpeton culture in the 1800s (Spector 1991, 1993). Spector first looked at the ethnographic record to determine what gender-specific tasks, behaviors, and beliefs were and how those could seen in the archaeological record through material regularities or patterns about different types of task systems.

Spector involved local descendants of the Wahpeton in her project and discovered that her Native American collaborators had different types of research questions, different ways of looking at the archaeological record, and different interpretations. She found that the involvement of members of another culture had fundamentally altered archaeological questions and conclusions.

Among the artifacts recovered by Spector in her excavation was the decorated handle of an awl. At Little Rapids after European contact, many awls were made with a metal tip set in an antler handle. Although most archaeological descriptions of awls emphasize the "working end" of the awl and its functional utility, Spector found ethnohistoric accounts that described the importance of the handles to their female owners, who sometimes painstakingly carved designs into them. Through the use of ethnohistoric sources, Spector discovered that the symbols carved on the handles recorded specific accomplishments, such as the completion of a hide robe (1991:395).

This particular awl handle provided the basis of a narrative about the awl and its owner—fictional, but grounded in the archaeology and ethnohistory. This approach illustrates the role of changing the scale of archaeological research and how that changes the questions that can be asked and answered about the past.

Cultures in Contact: Colony Ross, California

In 1812, the Russians established a small trading colony along the California coast at Colony Ross (now Fort Ross State Historic Park), some sixty miles north of San Francisco. Additional facilities, such as a port and several cattle ranches, were established nearby. The primary reason for the colony was to hunt seals and sea otters for their furs, but attempts were made to grow wheat and manufacture other goods, such as timber and bricks, for other Russian colonies in the North Pacific. Local Indians were hired to accomplish a variety of tasks. Of great interest is the fact that the Russians brought native Alaskans (Aleut and Eskimo) with them to Colony Ross to hunt seals and sea otters. The merging and mixing of Russian, Aleut, Eskimo, Pomo, and Miwok people and cultures is unique.

The Colony Ross region was inhabited by the Pomo and Coast Miwok Indians. These groups were already aware of Europeans, as Spanish and other explorers had visited the area, but contact had been brief. Things changed in 1812.

Kent Lightfoot of the University of California, Berkeley, instituted a multidisciplinary, multi-agency, and multi-ethnic investigation of the colony and its effect on its various actors. Lightfoot involved the university, state parks, and Pomo elders in the project and expanded the breadth of the approaches and interpretations from that of traditional archaeology (see Lightfoot 2005, Lightfoot et al. 1991a, 1991b; Lightfoot and Simmons 1998). One of the goals of the study was to compare the experiences of the Pomo in a mercantile setting with the Russians with those of other native Californians in mission, rancho, pueblo, and presidio settings with the Spanish, Mexicans, and Americans.

The written evidence (Russian records and journals) were very detailed about what the Russians were doing but contained little information about the Aleut, Eskimo, Pomo, or Coast Miwok. Thus, a major research goal was to illuminate the lives of these other groups. Unlike the Spanish to the south, the Russians did not initially attempt to suppress native lifeways or beliefs, and so Colony Ross was a vibrant multi-ethnic community. As time went on, however, this changed. Seal and sea otter populations declined and demand for agricultural labor increased such that the Russians began to force the Pomo to work, even raiding villages for labor (much like the Spanish).

Lightfoot and his colleagues were able to discover a great deal about ethnic interactions at Colony Ross, providing a basis for similar work in many other regions. In addition, his collaboration with living Pomo elders provided for a more in-depth understanding of the record. Finally, a significant effort for public outreach and education was made with state parks, enabling the work at Colony Ross to filter past just academia and into the mainstream of public awareness.

GLOSSARY

absolute dating   a class of dating techniques that provides information on the actual age of a sample in years

accelerator mass spectrometry (AMS)—a technique of radiocarbon dating in which the ^{14}C atoms are directly counted

acculturation—an exchange of cultural features between two groups or societies in which parts of both cultures change but each group remains distinct

achieved status—status that one obtains through his or her own actions

activity areas—a location within a site where specific activities were conducted, such as where cooking was done, where tools were manufactured, or where ceremonies were conducted

AD—years "after death" of Christ, computed to be after about 2,000 years ago, so AD 1500 is 500 years ago

aDNA—Ancient DNA, see DNA

adze—a tool used to shape wood, such as in making planks

agriculture—the cultivation and/or raising and use of domesticated plants and animals

alluvium—soils deposited through the action of water

Altithermal—the warm period in the Middle Holocene

Amerind—the predominant human genetic type throughout the New World; also the largest of the three major linguistic groupings in the New World

AMS—see accelerator mass spectrometry

anadromous fish—species of fish, such as salmon, that are born in freshwater, migrate to the ocean to mature, and return to freshwater to spawn

analogy—using a known to infer an unknown

Anasazi—one of the major prehistoric agricultural cultures that occupied the Southwest between 2,000 and 500 years ago. The Anasazi are the ancestors of the contemporary Pueblo groups living in the region today. Many contemporary Pueblo people prefer the use of "Puebloans" rather than Anasazi.

Anathermal—the warming, but still generally cool, climate in the Early Holocene

Ancestral Puebloans—one of the major prehistoric agricultural cultures that occupied the Southwest between 2,000 and 500 years ago. They are the ancestors of the contemporary Pueblo groups living in the region today and have been called the Anasazi.

antemortem—changes in organic material that took place before death; generally used to refer to human remains

anthropogenic—human-caused changes in the environment; often used to refer to midden soils

anthropological linguistics—the study of human languages, including the historical relationships between languages, syntax, meaning, cognition, and other aspects of communication

anthropology—the study of humans, including their biology, culture, and language, both past and present

antiquarians—people interested in archaeology prior to the development of the formal discipline; primarily hobbyists

archaeoastronomy—the study of ancient astronomical knowledge, practices, oral tradition, and cosmology

archaeological record—the record of past human behavior; the material remains of past human activities distributed in patterns across the landscape and in varying degrees of condition

archaeological cultures—an archaeological entity defined by a pattern of common traits; thought to possibly represent a past cultural group

archaeology—the scientific study of the human past

Archaic—the cultural stage that is generally marked by a dependence on hunting and gathering

architecture—the design and building of structures, primarily those in which people lived or worked; also used to describe a particular style or method of construction

art—a form of expression—symbolic, abstract, and representational. Art may be performance based, such as dance and theater, or representational, such as painting or sculpture.

artifact—a portable object made, modified, or used by humans. Artifacts are the basic "unit" of archaeological analysis.

ascribed status—status assigned to an individual based on some association with people of some existing status (e.g., the son of a king is automatically of high status)

asphaltum—natural tar used as a mastic and sealant

assemblage—all of the materials, artifacts, and ecofacts collected from a site representing all of the evidence of the activities at a site

assimilation—the absorption of one group by another where cultural differences disappear

atlatl and dart—a weapons system where a dart (essentially a large arrow) is thrown with the aid of a "spear thrower" (the atlatl)

attribute—a descriptive aspect of an artifact or site, such as its size, content, material, or shape

ball court—a large, open structure used as a "stadium" for the playing of a ball game involving two teams; generally confined to Mesoamerica and the Southwest

band—a small-scale society without formal leaders in which the family is the primary sociopolitical and economic unit

baseline data—the basic discovery, description, and classification of artifacts and sites

BC—years before Christ, computed to be before about 2,000 years ago; thus, 1,000 BC is about 3,000 years ago

BCE—before the common era, computed to be before about 2,000 years ago; thus, 1,000 BCE is about 3,000 years ago; used instead of BC to avoid the religious connotation

beardache—a person of a third or fourth gender, such as a transvestite, often considered to be an important and powerful individual

Beringia—the land mass formed by the connection of eastern Siberia and western Alaska when the sea level dropped and exposed the Bearing Straight Land Bridge

biface—a flaked stone tool flaked on both sides, such as most projectile points and knives

bifacial—an artifact flaked on both its dorsal and ventral sides

bioarchaeology—the analysis of past people and their individual lives by studying and interpreting their mortal remains

biological anthropology—the study of human biology through time, focusing specifically on biological evolution and human variation

biostratigraphy—a dating technique that uses the known ages of certain index fossils from one region to estimate the age of those same fossils in another region

bioturbation—any disturbance or movement of deposited materials by biological means

blade—flakes manufactured in particular shapes and sizes (generally at least twice as long as wide); often for use in specialized composite tools, such as a sickle

block excavations—a large excavation unit (two to ten meters square or larger) designed to expose a large area in a site

botanical remains—the remains of plants, from logs to pollen, found in archaeological sites

BP—years before present (technically before AD 1950); essentially "years ago"

burin—a specialized flaked stone tool used for engraving

cache—a group of objects placed and stored together

carrying capacity—a measure of the maximum number of individuals of a particular species that can be supported within a specific place for a specific time

casual tools—objects used as a tool once or twice for a specific purpose and discarded with no purposeful modification

catalog—a list and record of archaeological materials, including their provenance, classification, and attributes

catchment analysis—the study of where the materials found in a site were obtained, how much of an effort was necessary to procure those resources, and how that procurement affected settlement patterns

ceramics—artifacts made from clay and other organic and inorganic materials (temper) that are fired at relatively high temperatures. Containers or vessels made from clay are generally called pottery.

charmstone—a groundstone object, generally round and elongate in shape

chiefdom—a society with a relatively large population, permanent settlements, some central authority, and a stratified social structure

chronology—a description and dated sequence of material

classification—the placement of materials into categories that can be used for identification and comparison

cogged stone—a groundstone artifact shaped somewhat like a gear; generally found only in Southern California

collector—a category of hunter-gatherers who tend to collect resources for transport back to their camp rather than moving their camps to resource localities (also see **foragers**)

colonization—the movement of a cultural group into a region where they establish a permanent occupation

complex—a classification of associated archaeological materials

component—that portion of a site or site deposit representing occupation by an identified archaeological culture over a specific time

composite tool— a tool made from more than one part, such as a knife with a stone blade and wooden handle (see **simple tool**)

coprolites—paleofecal specimens that are individually distinct

Cordilleran ice sheet—the large ice sheet in the mountains of northwestern North America; combined with the Laurentide ice sheet, they covered most of northern North America at the end of the Pleistocene

core—an artifact used as a source of material to manufacture flaked stone tools. Some cores were also used as tools, such as choppers or hammerstones.

cosmology—the explanation of the origin of the universe and those things contained in it

cremation—mortuary practice of burning the dead

crescent—a flaked stone tool in the shape of a small crescent, generally associated with Late Pleistocene or Early Holocene cultures

cross-dating—the use of materials dated at one site to infer the age of similar materials at another

cultural anthropology—the study of the multifaceted aspects of human culture, generally of extant cultures

cultural chronology—the description and sequences of cultures through space and time

cultural conflict—conflict of some sort between two cultures, often due to competition for territory or access to other resources

cultural contact—the constant interplay between groups, involving the diffusion of technology and ideas, immigration, emigration, exchange of mates, and the like

cultural resource management (CRM)—work related to the preservation and management of cultural resources, including archaeological resources

culture—learned and shared behavior in humans passed from generation to generation

culture area—a large geographic region containing a relatively homogeneous environments and cultures of a similar adaptation

cultural ecology—the interaction between people and their environment, including aspects of technology, economy, and social organization

culture history—a description of past events and when and where they occurred

curation—the process of preparing archaeological materials for permanent storage and the storage of that material

debitage—the waste debris resulting from the manufacture or maintenance of flaked stone tools

dendrochronology—an absolute dating technique in which the tree rings of certain archaeological specimens are matched to a master ring plot to determine the age of the specimen

diachronic—data, hypotheses, or models that deal with a single time

diet—the long-term patterns and trends of foods that are and are not eaten, how and when foods are obtained and processed, their nutritional value, their overall role in the diet, and how those patterns change over time

diet-breadth—an optimization model that predicts the order in which resources (foods) will be added to the diet

diffusion—the movement of ideas or technologies from one culture to another without the movement of people

direct historical approach—the idea that the latest archaeological group in an area has continuity with the earliest ethnographic group in that same area

discoidal—a round groundstone artifact generally flat on both surfaces

DNA analysis—the recovery of deoxyribonucleic acid (DNA) from archaeological specimens, replicated by polymerase chain reaction (PCR). The sequence of genes can be read to determine hereditary relationships between populations and even between individuals.

domestication—a process by which organisms and/or landscapes are "controlled." In agriculture, domestication means that the genetic makeup of an organism is purposefully altered by humans to their advantage.

earspool—a decorative object, generally made of stone, worn in a pierced earlobe

ecofact—the unmodified remains of biological materials used by, or related to the activities of, people, such as discarded animal bone, charcoal from hearth fires, or natural pollen in an archaeological site

ecology—the study of the relationships between an organism(s) and its (their) environment

ecosystem—an area where the abiotic and biotic components are tied together in a system

ecotone—the intersection of, and transition between, two ecozones; usually a more productive place than in either of the ecozones

ecozone—an area defined by biotic communities and/or geographic criteria (short for *environmental zone*)

egalitarian—where social status within a culture is rather informal, mostly achieved, and with no formalized statuses or ranks

El Niño-Southern Oscillation (ENSO)—a pattern of warmer water moving north of the tropics, disrupting the normal patterns of rainfall in southwestern North America

element—a term used in faunal analysis to describe a particular specimen, such as a femur or rib

empirical—objects and patterns that physically exist and can be observed, measured, and tested

environment—living (biotic) and nonliving (abiotic) systems interacting within a bounded geographic unit

environmental manipulation—large-scale alteration of the environment by people to effect changes to the advantage of the culture

estuary—a partly closed body of water with a stream or river flowing into it and with it emptying into a lake or ocean

ethnoarchaeology—the study of how living traditional people do things and how archaeologists might apply that information to the past

ethnocentrism—the view that one's group is superior to another group

ethnographic analogy—the use of information about living cultures to help construct models of past cultures

ethnographic data—information on a particular living group at a particular time

ethnography—a comprehensive study of a particular living group at a particular time

evolutionary ecology—the application of the principles of biological selection to the understanding of how organisms adapt; used by archaeologists to study past cultural adaptation

faunal remains—the remains of animals found in archaeological sites, including bone, flesh, hair, skin, hide, and chitin

feature—nonportable thing constructed by humans for some task, such as hearths, roads, or dams

fission-fusion pattern—the seasonal and routine splitting (fission) of a group into several smaller groups and the recombination (fusion) of those groups later in time

flake—a small piece of stone removed from a larger artifact during the process of manufacture

flaked stone—a general class of artifacts made from breaking fine-grained stones to form sharp edges used for piercing, cutting, and scraping

flintnapping—the process of making flaked stone tools

fluted—projectile points with large flakes removed from the base up into the body of the point, creating a channel along a portion of the length of the point

forager—a category of hunter-gatherers who tend to move their camps to resource localities rather than collecting resources for transport back to their camp (also see **collectors**)

Formative—the cultural stage that is marked by food production, generally agriculture

fraud—the purposefully faking of data in an attempt to fool both scientists and laypersons

gender—a culturally constructed category used to group people and defined by the role behavior that a person is expected to have in the culture, regardless of sex

geoarchaeology—the study of the relationship between geology and geological processes and archaeological interpretation

geochemical sourcing—determining the chemical composition of an artifact and comparing that with known sources of the material to determine where the artifact material originated

geoglyph—large-scale images or designs made by removing soil or by piling rocks to create lines or designs

geomorphology—the study of landforms and how they change through time

gorget—a small bipointed tool, often used to catch fish

great house—a large, generally round communal structure found in the Southwest

groundstone—a general class of artifacts used for grinding, crushing, or pounding materials, commonly food materials

habitat—the place an organism lives, where its niche is located geographically in the environment

haft—the attachment of an artifact, such as an arrowhead, to its shaft or handle

half-life—the time it takes for one-half of the total amount of radioactive carbon in a given sample to decay; about 5,700 years

handstone—see **mano**

haplogroup—a group of specific mutations that can be traced in populations

historical archaeology—the archaeology of literate societies, primarily those of the recent past, often referring to the remains of European cultures outside of Europe

Holocene—the most recent geologic period, after the Pleistocene; from about 10,000 years ago to the present

hopper mortar—a generally flat stone with a basket glued to it to act as the sides of a mortar

horizon—a generally short temporal period marked by the appearance and rapid spread of some specific trait, such as a technology

horticulture—low-intensity agriculture involving relatively small-scale fields, plots, and gardens; food raised primarily for personal consumption rather than for trade or a central authority

household—the smallest economic unit in archaeological analysis

housepit—the remains of a subterranean or semisubterranean structure; generally not made from masonry

human remains—the physical remains of humans found in sites, including bone and soft tissues

hunter-gatherers—groups that make their primary living from the exploitation of wild foods

hypothesis—a proposal to explain some relationship between two or more variables (data) that must be testable and refutable

Hypsithermal—the term used for the Altithermal in the Southeast

iconography—the use of artistic images to represent information and aspects of belief systems

in situ—a Latin term meaning "found in place"; commonly applied to items discovered in place during an excavation

inhumation—mortuary practice of burying the dead

isostatic rebound—the rising of land that had been depressed once the ice (e.g., glacier) that covered it was gone

kinship—the way people figure their relationships with, and responsibilities to, other people

kiva—a structure, often round and subterranean, in which religious activities took place

labret—a decorative object, generally made of stone, worn in a pierced lip

lanceolate—long and narrow in form

Laurentian ice sheet—the large ice sheet that covered most of northeastern North America; combined with the Cordilleran ice sheet, they covered most of northern North America at the end of the Pleistocene

locus—a distinct place defined within a site, such as a cemetery, public square, or ceramic manufacturing area

longhouse—a large, long, and narrow house containing a number of families (an apartment)

mano—(also called a handstone) the upper portion of a milling tool set for grinding; used in conjunction with a metate

manuport—materials, such as an unusual stone from a distant source, clearly transported by humans but showing no evidence of use or modification

medicine wheel—a large circular arrangement of stones, often with "spokes," and believed to have been used for ritual purposes; generally confined to the Plains

Medieval Climatic Anomaly (MCA)—a warming trend between about 1,200 and 700 BP; often resulted in drought

Medithermal—the climate in the Late Holocene, as it is today

megafauna—the large animals (e.g., mammoths) that lived in North America during the Pleistocene

mesic—generally wet conditions

metate—the bottom portion of a milling tool set for grinding; used in conjunction with a mano (or handstone)

microblade—a very small blade, generally used in composite tools

midden—site soil deposits containing broken and used-up artifacts plus decayed organic materials such as shell, plants, bones, grease, charcoal and ash from fires, and general household trash

migration—the actual movement of a population of people, such as an ethnic group, from one locality to another

model—a proposed construct of some entity, generally consisting of a series of interrelated hypotheses

moiety—a dual social organization where kinship is divided into "halves," each half being one moiety

mortar—the bottom portion of the milling tool set for pulverizing; used in conjunction with a pestle

mortuary analysis—the study of burial data to determine patterns of demography, status, and politics

mound—a pile of soil, often purposefully constructed

mtDNA—mitochondrial DNA; found outside the nucleus of the cell, passed on by the female to her children, and so useful for tracing relatedness between people

mummification—the process of drying out of a body such that it is preserved, sometimes occurring naturally and sometimes a purposeful procedure

Na-Dene—a grouping of related languages; also called Athapaskan; also the name given to a number of specific cultures, such as the Navajo

Native American Graves Protection and Repatriation Act of 1990 (NAGPRA)—a federal law requiring that Native American skeletal remains be identified if possible and returned to their descendants

niche—the role an organism plays in the environment; what it eats and how it reproduces

nonstratified societies—societies in which no one is significantly wealthier, more powerful, or higher status than others

normative view—the idea that culture is patterned, consists of certain behaviors (norms) passed from generation to generation, and generates a material record that can be discovered, recovered, and interpreted

obsidian—natural volcanic glass; very easy to manufacture into tools and very sharp but fragile

obsidian hydration—a relative dating technique that measures the amount of water penetration into the surface of a break to estimate how long ago the piece was broken

ochre—a soft, iron-based mineral that can be used as a pigment; comes in several colors but is generally red

optimization—the idea that people will attempt to maximize their net efficiency and minimize their risk; a basic premise in optimization models

oral tradition—an oral record of the beliefs, values, morals, and history of a group, transmitted from generation to generation through the narration of stories

ossuary—a location where the bones of individuals would be interred together, having been removed from temporary graves where the bodies had been put to decompose

osteobiography—information about an individual's appearance, health, age at death, cause of death, and other characteristics derived from an analysis of the skeleton

paddle-and-anvil—a ceramic manufacturing technique in which a mass of clay is pounded into shape with the aid of small tools

paleoclimate—past climate; the long-term average of weather, including temperature and precipitation

paleodemography—the study of prehistoric populations, including their number, distribution, density, sex and age structure, mortality, and fertility

paleoecology—the relationship of past peoples to their environments

paleoenvironment—the study of the environment of the prehistoric past

Paleoindian—the time period of the earliest occupation of the New World; individuals who lived during that time are called Paleoindians.

palynology—the study and analysis of pollen

paradigm—a philosophical framework within which a discipline operates

pathologies—indications of ancient disease or trauma in human remains

pemmican—a mixture of dried meat, berries, fat, and bone grease packaged as a long-lasting stored food

percussion flaking—flaking stone by striking it, either directly with a hammer or indirectly through the use of a punch

perishables—a class of artifacts made of organic material, such as wood, fiber, and bark, that decompose rapidly and are not ordinarily recovered from the archaeological record

pestle—the upper portion of the milling tool set for pulverizing; used in conjunction with a mortar

petroglyph—depictions pecked into the surface of stone

phase—a time span defined by the presence of specific traits, such as artifact types

phytolith—small calcium carbonate structures within plant cells, often diagnostic of the genus of plant

pictograph—depictions painted onto the surface of stone

Pleistocene—the geologic period lasting from about 1.9 million years to about 10,000 years ago; essentially the "ice ages"

polity—an organized political entity, of whatever size or scale

Pochtecha—Mesoamerican merchants and traders

postulate—fundamental assertions upon which theories are grounded

pottery—vessels (e.g., bowls and jars) made from ceramic materials

Pre-Columbian—the time in Mesoamerica prior to the arrival of Columbus in A.D. 1492

prehistoric archaeology—the archaeology before written records from anytime and anywhere

prehistory—the time before written records, constituting some 99 percent of the time humans have been on Earth

preservation—the state of decomposition of materials in archaeological sites. If things are well preserved, they are more likely to be recognized and recovered.

pressure flaking—flaking stone by using a small tool to apply pressure to the edges of the stone until it breaks

primary context—when the location of an item is its original location; when something has not been moved

primary inhumation—a burial in its original place and position

processual archaeology—the theoretical paradigm in archaeology in which the past is believed to be objective and knowable

projectile points—a type of biface used on the tips of many spears, darts, and arrows

protein residue analysis—the chemical recovery and identification of plant and/or animal proteins surviving on tools, in paleofeces, or in soils

radiocarbon dating—an absolute dating method in which the amount of radiocarbon (^{14}C) within an organic sample is measured and used to determine how long ago the specimen died

radiocarbon years—the unit of measurement reflected in a radiocarbon date. To equate to calendar years, the radiocarbon date has to be calibrated.

research design—a plan for an archaeological investigation, stating the question(s) or problem(s) to be addressed, the theoretical approach used, the biases of the investigators, the kinds of data sought to address the question, and the methods to be used to recover the data

residue—preserved foreign material, generally on an artifact such as pottery or basketry

resource—something used by an organism

scientific method—the method employed in Western science in which data are combined to form a hypothesis, which is tested against new data, rejected or accepted, with either a new hypothesis being formed or the old one being retested

scraper—a tool used for scraping, such as in the removal of flesh from hide

seasonal transhumance—a seasonal round in which only one segment of the population, such as the herders, move with their animals seasonally while the rest of the population stays in one place

seasonal round—the system of the timing and movement of groups across the landscape

secondary context—when the location of an item is not its original location; when something has been moved

secondary inhumations—a burial that had occurred in an original location and was exhumed and reburied elsewhere, such as in an ossuary

sedentary—living in one place all the time

settlement pattern—the manner in which a particular group organized its settlements and occupied its geographic space

shell midden—an accumulation of cultural debris containing large quantities of shell

sherd—a broken piece of a pottery vessel; also called shard

simple tool—a tool with only one part, such as a throwing stick (see **composite tool**)

site—a geographic locality where there is some evidence of past human activity, such as artifacts and/or features

stable isotope analysis—the measurements of stable isotopes in bone, primarily carbon and nitrogen, to analyze aspects of past behavior, such as diet

state—a society with a large population, complex social and political structures, central authority, complex record keeping, urban centers (cities), and monumental architecture

steatite—a soft, easy-to-carve stone used to manufacture various implements and ornaments; sometimes called soapstone

stratified societies—societies in which social roles and statuses are many and diverse, formally defined, inherited, and often institutionalized through the creation of castes or classes

stratigraphy—the layers of soil within a site, usually defined by color, soil type, obvious artifact content (e.g., a layer of pottery), or some other measure

surface collection—a collection of materials lying on the surface of the site

survey—the process of actually going out into the landscape and looking for sites

synchronic—data, hypotheses, or models that deal with conditions from the same basic time period

taphonomy—the study of what happens to biological materials after they enter the archaeological record

temporal types—artifacts of known age that can be used to date associated materials or activities

tephra—volcanic ash

theory—a systematic explanation for observations that relate to a particular aspect of the empirical world

toggle harpoon head—a harpoon head that detaches from the shaft of the harpoon and lodges "sideways" in the body of an animal, making the harpoon more effective

tool kits—groups of tools used in conjunction for a specific task. Sometimes this term is used to include all of the tools of a particular complex.

toolstone—any stone, such as chert or obsidian, used to manufacture flaked stone tools

trade—the exchange of ideas or materials between individuals and groups

tradition—a trait tradition is the persistence of a particular trait, such as a type of artifact or art style, across time. A whole culture tradition is the persistence of a group of traits that define a whole culture, such as language, religion, and economy.

travois—a construct of poles containing cargo pulled by an animal (dog or horse)

tribe—a society with a relatively large population, formal leaders, and some social segmentation based on criteria other than kinship

tribelet—a very small tribe

trinomial system—the site-numbering system used throughout the United States that uses the state, county, and consecutive number to identify sites

typology—the classification of materials into categories based on morphology

ulu—a "half-moon"–shaped knife, often made of slate

uniface—a flaked stone tool flaked on only one side, such as some knives, burins (a tool used for engraving), some scrapers, and many utilized flakes

use wear analysis—examining the wear patterns, microscopic striations, and polish on the surface of tools to determine what the tools were used on

use-life—the functional life of a tool, from its manufacture, to rejuvenation, to discard

utilized flake—a flake used as a casual tool, not specifically made as a tool

vacant quarter—the Mississippi River Valley south of St. Louis, which was apparently abandoned about 650 BP

warfare—the organized and sanctioned conflict between two groups

worldview—a shared framework of assumptions held by a culture on how the world works

Younger Dryas—the brief return to glacial conditions about 12,000 BP

zooarchaeology—the study of archaeological faunal remains

REFERENCES

Abbott, David R. 2009 "Extensive and Long-Term Specialization: Hohokam Ceramic Production in the Phoenix Basin." *American Antiquity* 74(3):531–557.

Abbott, David R., Alexa M. Smith, and Emiliano Gallaga 2007 "Ballcourts and Ceramics: The Case for Hohokam Marketplaces in the Arizona Desert." *American Antiquity* 72(3):461–484.

Ackerman, Robert E. 1984 Prehistory: "The Asian Eskimo Zone." In: *Handbook of North American Indians, Vol. 5, Arctic,* David Damas, ed., pp. 106–118. Washington, D.C.: Smithsonian Institution.

1992 "Earliest Stone Industries on the North Pacific Coast of North America." *Arctic Anthropology* 29(2):18–27.

1996a "Bluefish Caves." In: *American Beginnings: The Prehistory and Paleoecology of Beringia,* Frederick Hadleigh West, ed., pp. 511–513. Chicago: University of Chicago Press.

1996b "Cave 1, Lime Hills." In: *American Beginnings: The Prehistory and Paleoecology of Beringia,* Frederick Hadleigh West, ed., pp. 470–477. Chicago: University of Chicago Press.

1996c "Ground Hog Bay, Site 2." In: *American Beginnings: The Prehistory and Palaeoecology of Beringa,* Frederick Hadleigh West, ed., pp. 424–430. Chicago: University of Chicago Press.

1998 "Early Maritime Traditions in the Bering, Chukchi, and East Siberian Seas." *Arctic Anthropology* 35(1):247–262.

2001 "Spein Mountain: A Mesa Complex Site in Southwestern Alaska." *Arctic Anthropology* 38(2):81–97.

2004 "The Northern Archaic Tradition in Southwest Alaska." *Arctic Anthropology* 41(2):153–162.

2008 "Continental Shelves, Sea Levels and Early Maritime Adaptations in the North Pacific." *North Pacific Prehistory* 2:51–92.

Adams, E. Charles 2001 *Origin and Development of the Pueblo Katsina Cult.* Tucson: University of Arizona Press.

2002 *Homol'ovi: An Ancient Hopi Settlement Cluster.* Tucson: University of Arizona Press.

Adams, E. Charles, and Andrew I. Duff (eds.) 2004 *The Protohistoric Pueblo World, A.D. 1275–1600.* Tucson: University of Arizona Press.

Adams, E. Charles, and Vincent M. LaMotta 2006 "New Perspectives on an Ancient Religion: Katsina Ritual and the Archaeological Record." In: *Religion in the Prehispanic Southwest,* Christine S. VanPool, Todd L. VanPool, and David A. Phillips, eds., pp. 53–66. Lanham, MD: AltaMira Press.

Adams, J. M., G. R. Foote, and M. Otte 2001 "Could Pre-Last Glacial Maximum Humans Have Existed in North America Undetected? An Interregional Approach to the Question." *Current Anthropology* 42(4):563–566.

Adler, Michael A. 1996a (ed.) *The Prehistoric Pueblo World, A.D. 1150–1350.* Tucson: University of Arizona Press.

1996b "Land Tenure, Archaeology, and the Ancestral Pueblo Social Landscape." *Journal of Anthropological Archaeology* 15(4):337–371.

Adovasio, James M. 1993 "The Ones That Will Not Go Away: A Biased View of Pre-Clovis Populations in the New World." In: *From Kostenki to Clovis: Upper Paleolithic—Paleo-Indian Adaptations,* Olga Soffer and N. D. Praslov, eds., pp. 199–218. New York: Plenum Press.

Adovasio, James M., and Ronald C. Carlisle 1988 "The Meadowcroft Rockshelter." *Science* 239:713–714.

Adovasio, James M., J. Donahue, and R. Stuckenrath 1990 "The Meadowcroft Rockshelter Radiocarbon Chronology 1975–1990." *American Antiquity* 55(2):348–354.

Adovasio, James M., J. Donahue, J. E. Guilday, R. Stuckenrath, J. D. Gunn, and W. C. Johnson 1983 "Meadowcroft Rockshelter and the Peopling of the New World." In: *Quaternary Coastlines and Marine Archaeology: Towards the Prehistory of Land Bridges and Continental Shelves,* P. M. Masters and N. C. Flemming, eds., pp. 413–439. London: Academic Press.

Adovasio, James M., J. D. Gunn, J. Donahue, and R. Stuckenrath 1978 "Meadowcroft Rockshelter, 1977: An Overview." *American Antiquity* 43(4):632–651.

Adovasio, James M., J. D. Gunn, J. Donahue, R. Stuckenrath, J. E. Guilday, and K. Volman 1980 "Yes Virginia, It Really Is That Old: A Reply to Haynes and Mead." *American Antiquity* 45(3):588–595.

Adovasio, James M., D. C. Hyland, R. L. Andrews, and J. S. Illingsworth 2002 "Wooden Artifacts." In: *Windover: Multidisciplinary Investigations of an Early Archaic Florida Cemetery,* Glen H. Doran, ed., pp. 166–190. Gainesville: University Press of Florida.

1982 "Meadowcroft Rockshelter, 1973–1977: A Synopsis." In: *Peopling of the New World,* Jonathon E. Ericson, R. E. Taylor, and Rainer Berger, eds., pp. 97–132. Los Altos, CA: Ballena Press Anthropological Papers No. 23.

Adovasio, James M., and Jake Page 2002 *The First Americans: In Pursuit of Archaeology's Greatest Mystery.* New York: Random House.

Adovasio, James M., and David R. Pedler 2004 "Pre-Clovis Sites and Their Implications for Human Occupation before the Last Glacial Maximum." In: *Entering America: Northeast Asia and Beringia Before the Last Glacial Maximum,* David B. Madsen, ed., pp. 139–158. Salt Lake City: University of Utah Press.

2005 "A Long View of Deep Time at Meadowcroft Rockshelter." In: *Paleoamerican Origins: Beyond Clovis,* Robson Bonnichsen, Bradley T. Lepper, Dennis Stanford, and Michael R. Waters, eds., pp. 23–28. Texas A&M University: Center for the Study of the First Americans.

Adovasio, James M., D. Pedler, J. Donahue, and R. Stuckenrath 1999 "No Vestige of a Beginning nor Prospect for an End: Two Decades of Debate on Meadowcroft Rockshelter." In: *Ice Age Peoples of North America: Environments, Origins, and*

Adaptations of the First Americans, Robson Bonnichsen and Karen L. Turnmire, eds., pp. 416–431. Oregon State University: Center for the Study of the First Americans.

Agenbroad, Larry D. 1984 "New World Mammoth Distribution." In: *Quaternary Extinctions: A Prehistoric Revolution*, Paul S. Martin and Richard G. Klein, eds., pp. 90–108. Tucson: University of Arizona Press.

Agenbroad, Larry D., Jim I. Mead, and Lisa W. Nelson (eds.) 1990 *Megafauna & Man: Discovery of America's Heartland*. Flagstaff: Northern Arizona University Press.

Agger, William A., and Herbert D. G. Maschner 2009 "Medieval Norse and the Bidirectional Spread of Epidemic Disease Between Europe and Northeastern America: A New Hypothesis." In: *The Northern World: AD 900–1400*, Herbert D. G. Maschner, Owen Mason, and Robert McGhee, eds., pp. 321–337. Salt Lake City: University of Utah Press.

Ahler, Stanley A. 2007 "Origins of the Northern Expression of the Middle Missouri Tradition." In: *Plains Village Archaeology: Bison-hunting Farmers in the Central and Northern Plains*, Stanley A. Ahler and Marvin Kay, eds., pp. 15–31. Salt Lake City: University of Utah Press.

Ahler, Stanley A., and Marvin Kay (eds.) 2007 *Plains Village Archaeology: Bison-hunting Farmers in the Central and Northern Plains*. Salt Lake City: University of Utah Press.

Ahlstrom, Richard V. N., and Heidi Roberts 2008 "Who Lived on the Southern Edge of the Great Basin?" In: *The Great Basin: People and Place in Ancient Times*, Catherine S. Fowler and Don D. Fowler, eds., pp. 128–135. Santa Fe: School of American Research.

Ahlstrom, Richard V. N., Carla R. Van West, and Jeffrey S. Dean 1995 "Environmental and Chronological Factors in the Mesa Verde–Northern Rio Grande Migration." *Journal of Anthropological Archaeology* 14(2):125–142.

Aikens, C. Melvin 1967 "Plains Relationships of the Fremont Culture: A Hypothesis." *American Antiquity* 32(2):198–209.

 1970 "Hogup Cave." University of Utah Anthropological Papers No. 93.

 1994 "Adaptive Strategies and Environmental Change in the Great Basin and Its Peripheries as Determinants in the Migrations of Numic-speaking Peoples." In: *Across the West: Human Population Movement and the Expansion of the Numa*, David B. Madsen and David Rhode, eds., pp. 36–43. Salt Lake City: University of Utah Press.

 2008 "Great Basin Cave Archaeology and Archaeologists." In: *The Great Basin: People and Place in Ancient Times*, Catherine S. Fowler and Don D. Fowler, eds., pp. 26–33. Santa Fe: School of American Research.

Aikens, C. Melvin, David L. Cole, and Robert Stuckenrath 1977 *Excavations at Dirty Shame Rockshelter, Southeastern Oregon*. Tebiwa: Miscellaneous Papers of the Idaho State University Museum of Natural History No. 4.

Aikens, C. Melvin, and Ruth L. Greenspan 1988 "Ancient Lakeside Culture in the Northern Great Basin: Malheur Lake, Oregon." *Journal of California and Great Basin Anthropology* 10(1):32–61.

Aikens, C. Melvin, and David B. Madsen 1986 "Prehistory of the Eastern Area." In: *Handbook of North American Indians, Vol. 11, Great Basin*, Warren L. d'Azevedo, ed., pp. 149–160. Washington, D.C.: Smithsonian Institution.

Aikens, C. Melvin, and Younger T. Witherspoon 1986 "Great Basin Prehistory: Linguistics, Archaeology, and Environment." In: *Anthropology of the Desert West: Papers in Honor of Jesse D. Jennings*, Carol Condie and Don D. Fowler, eds., pp. 7–20. University of Utah Anthropological Papers No. 110.

Akins, Nancy J. 2001 "Chaco Canyon Mortuary Practices: Archaeological Correlates of Complexity." In: *Ancient Burial Practices in the American Southwest: Archaeology, Physical Anthropology, and Native American Perspectives*, Douglas R. Mitchell and Judy L. Brunson-Hadley, eds., pp. 167–190. Albuquerque: University of New Mexico Press.

Alex, Lynn M. 2000 *Iowa's Archaeological Past*. Iowa City: University of Iowa Press.

Allen, Mark W. 1998 "Fort Irwin Archaeology: A Preserved Past for the Mojave Desert." *San Bernardino County Museum Association Quarterly* 45:71–75.

Alley, John R., Jr. 1986 "Tribal Historical Projects." In: *Handbook of North American Indians, Vol. 11, Great Basin*, Warren L. d'Azevedo, ed., pp. 601–607. Washington, D.C.: Smithsonian Institution.

Alroy, John 2001 "A Multispecies Overkill Simulation of the End-Pleistocene Megafaunal Mass Extinction." *Science* 292:1893–1896.

Alt, David D. 2001 *Glacial Lake Missoula and Its Humongous Floods*. Missoula, Montana: Mountain Press Publishing Company.

Altschul Jeffrey H., and Adrianne G. Rankin (eds.) 2008 *Fragile Patterns: The Archaeology of the Western Papagueria*. Tucson: SRI Press.

Ambler, J. Richard, and Mark Q. Sutton 1989 "The Anasazi Abandonment of the San Juan Drainage and the Numic Expansion." *North American Archaeologist* 10(1):39–54.

Ambro, R. D. 1967 "Dietary-technological-ecological Aspects of Lovelock Cave Coprolitea." *University of California Archaeological Survey Reports* 70:37–47.

Ambrose, Stanley H., Jane E. Buikstra, and Harold W. Krueger 2003 "Status and Gender Differences in Diet at Mound 72, Cahokia, Revealed by Isotopic Analysis of Bone." *Journal of Anthropological Archaeology* 22(3):217–226.

Ames, Kenneth M. 1988 "Early Holocene Forager Mobility Strategies on the Southern Columbia Plateau." In: *Early Human Occupation in Far Western North America: The Clovis-Archaic Interface*, Judith A. Willig, C. Melvin Aikens, and John L. Fagan, eds., pp. 325–360. Nevada State Museum Anthropological Papers No. 21.

 1994 "The Northwest Coast: Complex Hunter-Gatherers, Ecology, and Social Evolution." *Annual Review of Anthropology* 23:209–229.

 1998 "Economic Prehistory of the Northern British Columbia Coast." *Arctic Anthropology* 35(1):69–87.

 2001 "Slaves, Chiefs and Labour on the Northern Northwest Coast." *World Archaeology* 33(1):1–17.

2003 "The Northwest Coast." *Evolutionary Anthropology* 12:19–33.

2005 *The North Coast Prehistory Project Excavations in Price Rupert Harbour, British Columbia: The Artifacts.* Oxford: British Archaeological Reports International Series 1342.

2006 "Thinking about Household Archaeology on the Northwest Coast." In: *Household Archaeology on the Northwest Coast*, Elizabeth A. Sobel, D. Ann Trieu Gahr, and Kenneth M. Ames, eds., pp. 16–36. Ann Arbor: International Monographs in Prehistory, Archaeological Series 16.

Ames, Kenneth M., Don E. Dumond, Jerry R. Galm, and Rick Minor 1998 "Prehistory of the Southern Plateau." In: *Handbook of North American Indians, Vol. 12, Plateau*, Deward E. Walker, Jr., ed., pp. 103–119. Washington, D.C.: Smithsonian Institution.

Ames, Kenneth M., Kristen A. Fuld, and Sara Davis 2010 "Dart and Arrow Points on the Columbia Plateau of Western North America." *American Antiquity* 75(2):287–325.

Ames, Kenneth M., and Herbert D. G. Maschner 1999 *Peoples of the Northwest Coast: Their Archaeology and Prehistory.* London: Thames and Hudson.

Ames, Kenneth M., Dora F. Raetz, Stephen Hamilton, and Christine McAfee 1992 "Household Archaeology of a Southern Northwest Coast Plank House." *Journal of Field Archaeology* 19(3):275–290.

Amick, Daniel S. 1996 "Regional Patterns of Folsom Mobility and Land Use in the American Southwest." *World Archaeology* 27(3):411–426.

1999a (ed.) *Folsom Lithic Technology.* Ann Arbor, MI: International Monographs in Prehistory, Archaeological Series 12.

1999b "Raw Material Variation on Folsom Stone Tool Assemblages and the Division of Labor in Hunter-Gatherer Societies." In: *Folsom Lithic Technology*, Daniel S. Amick, ed., pp. 169–187. Ann Arbor, MI: International Monographs in Prehistory, Archaeological Series 12.

Amsden, Charles Avery 1937 "The Lake Mojave Artifacts." In: *The Archeology of Pleistocene Lake Mojave: A Symposium*, by Elizabeth W. Crozer Campbell, William H. Campbell, Ernst Antevs, Charles A. Amsden, Joseph A. Barbier, and Francis D. Bode, pp. 51–98. Southwest Museum Papers No. 11.

Anderson, Elaine 1984 "Who's Who in the Pleistocene: A Mammalian Bestiary." In: *Quaternary Extinctions: A Prehistoric Revolution*, Paul S. Martin and Richard G. Klein, eds., pp. 40–89. Tucson: University of Arizona Press.

Anderson, David G. 1995a "Paleoindian Interaction Networks in the Eastern Woodlands." In: *Native American Interaction: Multiscalar Analyses and Interpretations in the Eastern Woodlands*, Michael S. Nassaney and Kenneth E. Sassaman, eds., pp. 3–26. Knoxville: University of Tennessee Press.

1995b "Recent Paleoindian and Archaic Period Research in the Southeastern United States." *Archaeology of Eastern North America* 23:145–176.

1997 "The Role of Cahokia in the Evolution of Mississippian Society." In: *Cahokia: Domination and Ideology in the Mississippian World*, Timothy R. Pauketat and Thomas E.

Emerson, eds., pp. 248–268. Lincoln: University of Nebraska Press.

2004a "Paleoindian Occupations in the Southeastern United States." In: *New Perspectives on the First Americans*, Bradley T. Lepper and Robson Bonnichsen, eds., pp. 119–128. Texas A&M University: Center for the Study of the First Americans.

2004b "Archaic Mounds and the Archaeology of Southeastern Tribal Societies." In: *Signs of Power: The Rise of Cultural Complexity in the Southeast*, Jon L. Gibson and Philip J. Carr, eds., pp. 270–299. Tuscaloosa: University of Alabama Press.

Anderson, David G., and Michael K. Faught 2000 "Palaeoindian Artefact Distributions: Evidence and Implications." *Antiquity* 74(285):507–513.

Anderson, David G., and J. Christopher Gillam 2000 "Paleoindian Colonization of the Americas: Implications from an Examination of Physiography, Demography, and Artifact Distribution." *American Antiquity* 65(1):43–66.

Anderson, David G., and Glen T. Hanson 1988 "Early Archaic Settlement in the Southeastern United States: A Case Study from the Savannah River Valley." *American Antiquity* 53(2):262–286.

Anderson, David G., and Robert C. Mainfort, Jr. 2002 "Introduction to the Woodland Archaeology in the Southeast." In: *The Woodland Southeast*, David G. Anderson and Robert C. Mainfort, Jr., eds., pp. 1–19. Tuscaloosa: University of Alabama Press.

Anderson, David G., D. Shane Miller, Stephen J. Yerka, J. Christopher Gillam, Erik N. Johanson, Derek T. Anderson, Albert C. Goodyear, and Ashley M. Smallwood 2010 "PIDBA (Paleoindian Database of the Americas) 2010: Current Status and Findings." *Archaeology of Eastern North America* 38 (in press).

Anderson, David J., Michael Russo, and Kenneth E. Sassaman 2007 "Mid-Holocene Cultural Dynamics in Southeastern North America." In: *Climate Change and Cultural Dynamics: A Global Perspective on Mid-Holocene Transitions*, David G. Anderson, Kirk A. Maasch, and Daniel H. Sandweiss, eds., pp. 457–489. New York: Elsevier Press.

Anderson, David G., and Kenneth E. Sassaman 2004 "Early and Middle Holocene Periods, 9500 to 3750 B.C." In: *Handbook of North American Indians, Vol. 14, Southeast*, Raymond D. Fogelson, ed., pp. 87–100. Washington, D.C.: Smithsonian Institution.

Anderson, Douglas D. 1968 "A Stone Age Campsite at the Gateway to America." *Scientific American* 218(6)24–33.

1984 "Prehistory of North Alaska." In: *Handbook of North American Indians, Vol. 5, Arctic*, David Damas, ed., pp. 80–93. Washington, D.C.: Smithsonian Institution.

1988 "Onion Portage: The Archaeology of a Stratified Site from the Kobuk River, Northwestern Alaska." *Anthropological Papers of the University of Alaska* 22(1–2).

2008 "Northern Archaic Tradition Forty Years Later: Comments." *Arctic Anthropology* 45(2):169–178.

Andrefsky, William, Jr. 2004 "Materials and Contexts for a Culture History of the Columbia Plateau." In: *Complex Hunter-Gatherers: Evolution and Organization of Prehistoric*

Communities on the Plateau of Northwestern North America, William C. Prentiss and Ian Kuijt, eds., pp. 23–35. Salt Lake City: University of Utah Press.

Andrews, R. L., James M. Adovasio, B. Humphery, D. C. Hyland, J. S. Gardner, and D. G. Harding 2002 "Conservation and Analysis of Textile and Related Perishable Artifacts." In: *Windover: Multidisciplinary Investigations of an Early Archaic Florida Cemetery*, Glen H. Doran, ed., pp. 121–165. Gainesville: University Press of Florida.

Antevs, Ernst 1948 "Climate Changes and Pre-White Man." In: *The Great Basin with Emphasis of Glacial and Post-Glacial Times*, pp. 168–191. Salt Lake City: University of Utah Bulletin 38(2), Biological Series 10(7).

Aoki, Kenichi 1993 "Modeling the Dispersal of the First Americans through an Inhospitable Ice-Free Corridor." *Anthropological Science* 101(1):79–89.

Appelt, Martin, and Hans Christian Gulløv 2009 "Tunit, Norsemen, and Inuit in Thirteenth-Century Northwest Greenland-Dorset Between the Devil and the Deep Sea." In: *The Northern World: AD 900–1400*, Herbert D. G. Maschner, Owen Mason, and Robert McGhee, eds., pp. 300–320. Salt Lake City: University of Utah Press.

Archer, David J. W. 2001 "Village Patterns and the Emergence of Ranked Society in the Prince Rupert Area." In: *Perspectives on Northwest Coast Prehistory*, Jerome S. Cybulski, ed., pp. 203–222. Canadian Museum of Civilization, Mercury Series, Archaeological Survey of Canada, Paper 160.

Ardren, Traci 2008 "Studies of Gender in the Prehispanic Americas." *Journal of Archaeological Research* 16(1):1–35.

Arens, William 1979 *The Man-Eating Myth: Anthropology and Anthropophagy*. New York: Oxford University Press.

Arkush, Brooke S. 1986 "Aboriginal Exploitation of Pronghorn in the Great Basin." *Journal of Ethnobiology* 6(2):239–255.

1995 "The Archaeology of CA-MNO-2122: A Study of Pre-Contact and Post-Contact Lifeways Among the Mono Basin Paiute." University of California Anthropological Records Vol. 31.

1998 *Archaeological Investigations at Mosquito Willie Rockshelter and Lower Lead Mine Hills Cave, Great Salt Lake Desert, Utah*. Salinas: Coyote Press Archives of Great Basin Prehistory No. 2.

1999 "Recent Small-Scale Excavations at Weston Canyon Rockshelter in Southeastern Idaho." *Tebiwa* 27(1):1–64.

2002 *Archaeology of the Rock Springs Site: A Multi-Component Bison Kill and Processing Camp in Curlew Valley, Southeastern Idaho*. Boise: Boise State University Monographs in Archaeology No. 1.

2008 *The Archaeology of Standing Rock Overhang: A Long-term Record of Bighorn Sheep Hunting and Processing in Southeastern Idaho*. Ogden, UT: United States Forest Service Heritage Report 3-06/2008.

Arkush, Brooke S., and Bonnie L. Pitblado 2000 "Paleoarchaic Surface Assemblages in the Great Salt Lake Desert, Northwestern Utah." *Journal of California and Great Basin Anthropology* 22(1):12–42.

Armelagos, George J., and M. Cassandra Hill 1990 "An Evaluation of the Biocultural Consequences of the Mississippian Transformation." In: *Towns and Temples Along the Mississippi*, David H. Dye and Cheryl Anne Cox, eds, pp. 16–37. Tuscaloosa: University of Alabama Press.

Arnold, Brigham A. 1957 "Late Pleistocene and Recent Changes in Land Forms, Climate, and Archaeology in Central Baja California." *University of California Publications in Geography* 10(4).

Arnold, Jeanne E. 1991 "Transformation of a Regional Economy: Sociopolitical Evolution and the Production of Valuables in Southern California." *Antiquity* 65(249):953–962.

1992a "Complex Hunter-Gatherer-Fishers of Prehistoric California: Chiefs, Specialists, and Maritime Adaptations of the Channel Islands." *American Antiquity* 57(1):60–84.

1992b "Cultural Disruption and the Political Economy in Channel Islands Prehistory." In: *Essays on the Prehistory of Maritime California*, Terry L. Jones, ed., pp. 129–144. Center for Archaeological Research at Davis, Publication No. 10.

2001 "The Chumash in World and Regional Perspective." In: *The Origin of a Pacific Coast Chiefdom: The Chumash of the Channel Islands*, Jeanne E. Arnold, ed., pp. 1–19. Salt Lake City: University of Utah Press.

2007 "Credit Where Credit is Due: The History of the Chumash Oceangoing Plank Canoe." *American Antiquity* 72(2):196–209.

Arnold, Jeanne E., Roger H. Colten, and Scott Pletka 1997 "Contexts of Cultural Change in Insular California." *American Antiquity* 62(2):300–318.

Arnold, Jeanne E., and Terisa M. Green 2002 "Mortuary Ambiguity: The Ventureño Chumash Case." *American Antiquity* 67(4):760–771.

Arnold, Jeanne E., and Michael R. Walsh 2010 *California's Ancient Past: From the Pacific to the Range of Light*. Washington, D.C.: Society for American Archeeology.

Arnold, Jeanne E., Michael R. Walsh and Sandra E. Hollimon 2004 "The Archaeology of California." *Journal of Anthropological Research* 12(1):1–73.

Askenasy, Hans 1994 *Cannibalism: From Sacrifice to Survival*. Amherst, NY: Prometheus Books.

Axtell, James 2001 *Natives and Newcomers: The Cultural Origins of North America*. Oxford, UK: Oxford University Press.

Bacon, Charles R., and Marvin A. Lanphere 2006 "Eruptive History and Geochronology of Mount Mazama and the Crater Lake Region, Oregon." *Geological Society of American Bulletin* 118(11–12):1331–1359.

Baker, Brenda J., and Lisa Kealhoffer (eds.) 1996 *Bioarchaeology of Native American Adaptation in the Spanish Borderlands*. Gainesville: University Press of Florida.

Baldwin, John D. 1871 *Ancient America, in Notes on American Archaeology*. New York: Harper & Brothers.

Bamann, Susan, Robert Kuhn, James Molnar, and Dean Snow 1992 "Iroquoian Archaeology." *Annual Review of Anthropology* 21:435–460.

Bamforth, Douglas B. 1988 *Ecology and Human Organization on the Great Plains.* New York: Plenum Press.

1994 "Indigenous People, Indigenous Violence: Precontact Warfare on the North American Great Plains." *Man* 29(1):95–115.

2002 "High-Tech Foragers? Folsom and Later Paleoindian Technology on the Great Plains." *Journal of World Prehistory* 16(1):55–98.

Bard, E., M. Arnold, R. G. Fairbanks, and B. Hamelin 1993 "²³⁰Th-²³⁴U and ¹⁴C Ages Obtained by Mass Spectrometry on Corals." *Radiocarbon* 35(1):191–199.

Barlow, K. Renne 2002 "Predicting Maize Agriculture among the Fremont: An Economic Comparison of Farming and Foraging in the American Southwest." *American Antiquity* 67(1):65–88.

2006 "A Formal Model for Predicting Agriculture among the Fremont." In: *Behavioral Ecology and the Transition to Agriculture*, Douglas J. Kennett and Bruce Winterhalder, eds., pp. 87–102. Berkeley: University of California Press.

Basgall, Mark E. 1987 "Resource Intensification Among Hunter-Gatherers: Acorn Economies in Prehistoric California." In: *Research in Economic Anthropology 9*, Barry L. Issac, ed., pp. 21–52. Greenwich, CT: JAI Press.

1995 "Obsidian Hydration Dating of Early Holocene Assemblages in the Mojave Desert." *Current Research in the Pleistocene* 12:57–60.

2003 "Revisiting the Late-Pleistocene/Early Holocene Archaeology of Pleistocene Lake China and the CRBR Locality." *Current Research in the Pleistocene* 20:3–5.

Basgall, Mark E., and M. C. Hall 1991 "Relationships Between Fluted and Stemmed Points in the Mojave Desert." *Current Research in the Pleistocene* 8:61–64.

1992 "Fort Irwin Archaeology: Emerging Perspectives on Mojave Desert Prehistory." *Society for California Archaeology Newsletter* 26(5):1–7.

Basgall, Mark E., and William R. Hildebrandt 1989 "Prehistory of the Sacramento River Canyon, Shasta County, California." Center for Archaeological Research at Davis, Publication No. 9.

Bayman, James M. 2001 "The Hohokam of Southwest North America." *Journal of World Prehistory* 15(3):257–311.

Beardsley, Richard K. 1954a *Temporal and Areal Relationships in Central California Archaeology, Part One.* Berkeley: Reports of the University of California Archaeological Survey No. 24.

1954b *Temporal and Areal Relationships in Central California Archaeology, Part Two.* Berkeley: Reports of the University of California Archaeological Survey No. 25.

Beaton, John M. 1991a "Extensification and Intensification in Central California Prehistory." *Antiquity* 65(249):946–952.

1991b "Paleoindian Occupation Greater than 11,000 y B.P. at Tule Lake, Northern California." *Current Research in the Pleistocene* 8:5–7.

Beattie, Owen, Brian Apland, Erik W. Blake, James A. Cosgrove, Sarah Gaunt, Sheila Greer, Alexander P. Mackie, Kjerstin E. Mackie, Dan Straathof, Valerie Thorp, and Peter M. Troffee

2000 "The Kwäddy Dän Ts'inchi Discovery from a Glacier in British Columbia." *Canadian Journal of Archaeology* 24(1&2):129–147.

Beck, Charlotte, and George T. Jones 1990 "The Late Pleistocene/Early Holocene Archaeology of Butte Valley, Nevada: Three Seasons' Work." *Journal of California and Great Basin Anthropology* 12(1):231–261.

1992 "New Directions? Great Basin Archaeology in the 1990s." *Journal of California and Great Basin Anthropology* 14(1):22–36.

1997 "The Terminal Pleistocene/Early Holocene Archaeology of the Great Basin." *Journal of World Prehistory* 11(2):161–236.

2010 "Clovis and Western Stemmed: Population Migration and the Meeting of Two Technologies in the Intermountain West." *American Antiquity* 75(1):81–116.

Beck, Colleen M. 1999 "Ethnography and Archaeology in the Great Basin." In: *Models for the Millennium: Great Basin Anthropology Today*, Charlotte Beck, ed., pp. 13–28. Salt Lake City: University of Utah Press.

Beck, Robin A., Jr. 2003 "Consolidation and Hierarchy Chiefdom Variability in the Mississippian Southeast." *American Antiquity* 68(4):641–661.

Bednarik, R. G. 1989 "On the Pleistocene Settlement of South America." *Antiquity* 63(238):101–111.

Bedwell, Stephen F. 1973 *Fort Rock Basin: Prehistory and Environment.* Eugene: University of Oregon Books.

Bedwell, Stephen F., and Luther S. Cressman 1971 "Fort Rock Report: Prehistory and Environment of the Pluvial Fort Rock Lake Area of South-Central Oregon." In: *Great Basin Anthropological Conference 1970: Selected Papers*, C. Melvin Aikens, ed., pp. 1–25. University of Oregon Anthropological Papers No. 1.

Belcher, William R., David Sanger, and Bruce J. Bourque 1994 "The Bradley Cemetery: A Moorehead Burial Tradition Site in Maine." *Canadian Journal of Archaeology* 18:3–28.

Bell, Robert E., and Robert L. Brooks 2001 "Plains Village Tradition: Southern." In: *Handbook of North American Indians, Vol. 13, Plains*, Raymond J. DeMallie, ed., pp. 207–221. Washington, D.C.: Smithsonian Institution.

Bell, Trevor, and M. A. P. Renouf 2003 "Prehistoric Cultures, Reconstructed Coasts: Maritime Archaic Indian Site Distribution in Newfoundland." *World Archaeology* 35(3):350–370.

Bellwood, Peter 2005 *First Farmers: The Origin of Agricultural Societies.* Oxford, UK: Blackwell Publishers.

Bense, Judith A. 1994 *Archaeology of the Southeastern United States: Paleoindian to World War I.* San Diego: Academic Press.

1996 "Overview of the Mississippian Stage in the Southeastern United States." *Journal of American Archaeology* 10:53–71.

Benson, Larry V., and Michael S. Berry 2009 "Climate Change and Cultural Response in the Prehistoric American Southwest." *Kiva* 75(1):89–117.

Benson, Larry V., Timothy R. Pauketat, and Edward R. Cook 2009 "Cahokia's Boom and Bust in the Context of Climate Change." *American Antiquity* 74(3):467–483.

Benson, Larry V., Michael S. Berry, Edward A. Jolie, Jerry D. Spangler, David W. Stahle, and Eugene M. Hattori 2007 "Possible Impacts of Early-11th-, Middle-12th-, and Late-13th-Century Droughts on Western Native Americans and the Mississippian Cahokians." *Quaternary Science Reviews* 26(3–4):336–350.

Benson, Larry V., Linda S. Cordell, Kirk Vincent, Howard Taylor, John Stein, G. Lang Farmer, and Kiyoto Futa 2003 "Ancient Maize from Chacoan Great Houses: Where Was It Grown?" *Proceedings of the National Academy of Sciences* 100(23):13111–13115.

Bernardini, Wesley 2004 "Hopewell Geometric Earthworks: A Case Study in the Referential and Experimental Meaning of Monuments." *Journal of Anthropological Archaeology* 23(3):331–356.

Berres, Thomas Edward 2001 *Power and Gender in Oneota Culture: A Study of a Late Prehistoric People.* DeKalb: Northern Illinois University Press.

Berry, Claudia, and Michael S. Berry 1986 "Chronological and Conceptual Models of the Southwestern Archaic." In: *Anthropology of the Desert West: Papers in Honor of Jesse D. Jennings,* Carol Condie and Don D. Fowler, eds., pp. 253–327. University of Utah Anthropological Papers No. 110.

Berry, Michael S. 1985 "The Age of Maize in the Greater Southwest: A Critical Review." In: *Prehistoric Food Production in North America,* Richard I. Ford, ed., pp. 279–307. University of Michigan, Museum of Anthropology, Anthropological Papers No. 75.

Betancourt, Julio L., Jeffrey S. Dean, and Herbert M. Hull 1986 "Prehistoric Long-distance Transport of Construction Beams, Chaco Canyon, New Mexico." *American Antiquity* 51(2):370–375.

Bettinger, Robert L. 1975 "The Surface Archaeology of Owens Valley, Eastern California: Prehistoric Man-Land Relationships in the Great Basin." Ph.D. dissertation, University of California, Riverside.

1976 "The Development of Pinyon Exploitation in Central Eastern California." *Journal of California Anthropology* 3(1):81–95.

1987 "Archaeological Approaches to Hunter-Gatherers." *Annual Review of Anthropology* 16:121–142.

1989 "The Archaeology of Pinyon House, Two Eagles, and Crater Middens: Three Residential Sites in Owens Valley, Eastern California." Anthropological Papers of the American Museum of Natural History 67.

1991 "Aboriginal Occupation at High Altitude: Alpine Villages in the White Mountains of Eastern California." *American Anthropologist* 93(3):656–679.

1993 "Doing Great Basin Archaeology Recently: Coping with Variability." *Journal of Archaeological Research* 1(1):43–66.

1998 "Cultural, Human, and Historical Ecology in the Great Basin: Fifty Years of Ideas About Ten Thousand Years of Prehistory." In: *Advances in Historical Ecology,* William Balée, ed., pp. 169–189. New York: Columbia University Press.

1999a "What Happened in the Medithermal?" In: *Models for the Millennium: Great Basin Anthropology Today,* Charlotte Beck, ed., pp. 62–74. Salt Lake City: University of Utah Press.

1999b "From Traveler to Processor: Regional Trajectories of Hunter-Gatherer Sedentism in the Inyo-Mono Region, California." In: *Settlement Pattern Studies in the Americas: Fifty Years Since Virú,* Brian R. Billman and Gary M. Feinman, eds., pp. 39–55. Washington, D.C.: Smithsonian Institution Press.

2008 "High Altitude Sites in the Great Basin." In: *The Great Basin: People and Place in Ancient Times,* Catherine S. Fowler and Don D. Fowler, eds., pp. 86–93. Santa Fe: School of American Research.

Bettinger, Robert L., and Martin A. Baumhoff 1982 "The Numic Spread: Great Basin Cultures in Competition." *American Antiquity* 47(3):485–503.

Bettinger, Robert L., and Jelmer W. Eerkens 1999 "Point Typologies, Cultural Transmission, and the Spread of Bow-and-Arrow Technology in the Prehistoric Great Basin." *American Antiquity* 64(2):231–242.

Bettinger, Robert L., James F. O'Connell, and David Hurst Thomas 1991 "Projectile Points as Time Markers in the Great Basin." *American Anthropologist* 93(1):166–172.

Bettinger, Robert L., and Robert Oglesby 1985 "Lichen Dating of Alpine Villages in the White Mountains, California." *Journal of California and Great Basin Anthropology* 7(2):202–224.

Bever, Michael R. 2001a "Stone Tool Technology and the Mesa Complex: Developing a Framework of Alaskan Paleoindian Prehistory." *Arctic Anthropology* 38(2):98–118.

2001b "An Overview of Alaskan Late Pleistocene Archaeology: Historical Themes and Current Perspectives." *Journal of World Prehistory* 15(2):125–191.

2006 "Too Little, Too Late? The Radiocarbon Chronology of Alaska and the Peopling of the New World." *American Antiquity* 71(4):595–620.

Bickel, Polly McW. 1978 "Changing Sea Levels Along the California Coast: Anthropological Considerations." *Journal of California Anthropology* 5(1):6–20.

Bielawski, E. 1988 "Paleoeskimo Variability: The Early Arctic Small-Tool Tradition in the Central Canadian Arctic." *American Antiquity* 53(1):52–74.

Bieling, David G., Roger M. La Jeunesse, and John H. Pryor 1996 "Skyrocket, A Central Sierran Paleoindian Archaic Transition Site." *Current Research in the Pleistocene* 13:4–6.

Biella, Jan, and Richard Chapman (eds.) 1979 *Archeological Investigations in Cochiti Reservoir, New Mexico.* Albuquerque: University of New Mexico, Office of Contract Archeology.

Billman, Brian R., Patricia M. Lambert, and Banks L. Leonard 2000 "Cannibalism, Warfare, and Drought in the Mesa Verde Region during the Twelfth Century A.D." *American Antiquity* 65(1):145–178.

Binford, Lewis R. 1962 "Archaeology as Anthropology." *American Antiquity* 28(2):217–225.

1964 "A Consideration of Archaeological Research Design." *American Antiquity* 29(4):425–441.

1980 "Willow Smoke and Dog's Tails: Hunter-Gatherer Settlement Systems and Archaeological Site Formation." *American Antiquity* 45(1):4–20.

Binford, Sally, and Lewis R. Binford (eds.) 1968 *New Perspectives in Archaeology.* Chicago: Aldine.

Black, Lydia T. 1988 "The Story of Russian America." In: *Crossroads of Continents: Cultures of Siberia and Alaska,* William W. Fitzhugh and Aron Crowell, eds., pp. 70–82. Washington, D.C.: Smithsonian Institution Press

Blakeslee, Donald J. 1993 "Modeling the Abandonment of the Central Plains: Radiocarbon Dates and the Origin of the Initial Coalescent." In: "Prehistory and Human Ecology of the Western Prairies and Northern Plains," Joseph A. Tiffany, ed., pp. 199–214. *Plains Anthropologist Memoir* 27, *Plains Anthropologist* 38(145).

Blanton, Dennis B. 1996 "Accounting for Submerged Mid-Holocene Archaeological Sites in the Southeast: A Case Study from the Chesapeake Bay Estuary, Virginia." In: *Archaeology of the Mid-Holocene Southeast*, Kenneth E. Sassaman and David G. Anderson, eds., pp. 200–217. Gainesville: University Press of Florida.

Blitz, John H. 1988 "Adoption of the Bow in Prehistoric North America." *North American Archaeologist* 9(2):123–145.

1999 "Mississippian Chiefdoms and the Fission-Fusion Process." *American Antiquity* 64(4):577–592.

2008 *Moundville.* Tuscaloosa: University of Alabama Press.

Boas, Franz 1888 "The Central Eskimo." In: *Sixth Annual Report of the Bureau of American Ethnology*, pp. 409–669. Washington, D.C.: Government Printing Office.

Bocek, Barbara 1991 "Prehistoric Settlement Pattern and Social Organization on the San Francisco Peninsula, California." In: *Between Bands and States*, Susan A. Gregg, ed., pp. 68–86. Southern Illinois University, Carbondale, Center for Archaeological Investigations, Occasional Paper No. 9.

Boldurian, Anthony T., and John L. Cotter 1999 *Clovis Revisited: New Perspectives on Paleoindian Adaptations from Blackwater Draw, New Mexico.* University of Pennsylvania, University Museum Monograph 103.

Bonatto, Sandro L., and Francisco M. Salzano 1997a "A Single and Early Migration for the Peopling of the Americas Supported by Mitochondrial DNA Sequence Data." *Proceedings of the National Academy of Sciences* 94(5):1866–1871.

1997b "Diversity and Age of the Four Major Haplogroups, and Their Implications for the Peopling of the New World." *American Journal of Human Genetics* 61(6):1413–1423.

Bone, Robert M. 1992 *The Geography of the Canadian North: Issues and Challenges.* Toronto: Oxford University Press.

Bonnichsen, Robson (ed.) 1999 *Who Were the First Americans?* Oregon State University: Center for the Study of the First Americans.

Bonnichsen, Robson, and Alan L. Schneider 1999 "Breaking the Impasse on the Peopling of the Americas." In: *Ice Age Peoples of North America: Environments, Origins, and Adaptations of*

the First Americans, Robson Bonnichsen and Karen L. Turnmire, eds., pp. 497–519. Oregon State University: Center for the Study of the First Americans.

Bonnichsen, Robson, and D. Gentry Steele (eds.) 1994 *Method and Theory for Investigating the Peopling of the Americas.* Oregon State University: Center for the Study of the First Americans.

Bonnichsen, Robson, and Karen L. Turnmire (eds.) 1991 *Clovis: Origins and Adaptations.* Oregon State University: Center for the Study of the First Americans.

1999 *Ice Age Peoples of North America: Environments, Origins, and Adaptations of the First Americans.* Oregon State University: Center for the Study of the First Americans.

Bonnichsen, Robson, Bradley T. Lepper, Dennis Stanford, and Michael R. Waters (eds.) 2005 *Paleoamerican Origins: Beyond Clovis.* Texas A&M University: Center for the Study of the First Americans.

Borden, Charles E. 1975 "Origins and Development of Early Northwest Coast Culture to About 3000 B.C." Canadian Museum of Civilization, Mercury Series, Archaeological Survey of Canada, Paper 45.

Borrero, Luis Alberto 2006 "Paleoindians without Mammoths and Archaeologists without Projectile Points?" In: *Paleoindian Archaeology: A Hemispheric Perspective*, Juliet E. Morrow and Cristóbal Gnecco, eds., pp. 9–20. Gainesville: University Press of Florida.

Bouey, Paul D. 1979 "Population Pressure and Agriculture in Owens Valley." *Journal of California and Great Basin Anthropology* 1(1):162–170

1987 "The Intensification of Hunter-Gatherer Economics in the Southern North Coast Ranges of California." In: *Research in Economic Anthropology 9*, Barry L. Issac, ed., pp. 53–101. Greenwich, CT: JAI Press.

Bourque, Bruce J. 1994 "Evidence for Prehistoric Exchange on the Maritime Peninsula." In: *Prehistoric Exchange Systems in North America*, Timothy G. Baugh and Jonathon E. Ericson, eds., pp. 23–46. New York: Plenum Press.

1995 *Diversity and Complexity in Prehistoric Maritime Societies: A Gulf of Maine Perspective.* New York: Plenum Press.

2001 *Twelve Thousand Years: American Indians in Maine.* Lincoln: University of Nebraska Press.

Boyd, Matthew, and Clarence Surette 2010 "Northernmost Precontact Maize in North America." *American Antiquity* 75(1):117–133.

Boyd, Matthew, Clarence Surette, and B. A. Nicholson 2006 "Archaeobotanical Evidence of Prehistoric Maize (*Zea maize*) Consumption at the Northern Edge of the Great Plains." *Journal of Archaeological Science* 33(8)1129–1140.

Brace, C. L., and Ashly Montagu 1977 *Human Evolution.* New York: Macmillan Publishing Company.

Bradley, Bruce, and Dennis J. Stanford 2004 "The North Atlantic Ice-Edge Corridor: A Possible Palaeolithic Route to the New World." *World Archaeology* 36(4):459–478.

2006 "The Solutrean-Clovis Connection: Rely to Straus, Meltzer and Goebel." *World Archaeology* 38(4):704–714.

Brain, Jeffrey P., and Phillip Phillips 1996 *Shell Gorgets: Styles of the Late Prehistoric and Protohistoric Southeast.* Cambridge, MA: Harvard University, Peabody Museum Press.

Braje, Todd J., Jon M. Erlandson, and Torben C. Rick 2004 "An 8700 CALYBP Shell Midden from the South Coast of San Miguel Island, California." *Current Research in the Pleistocene* 21:24–26.

Braun, David P., and Stephen Plog 1982 "Evolution of 'Tribal' Social Networks: Theory and Prehistoric North American Evidence." *American Antiquity* 47(3):504–525.

Breschini, Gary S., and Trudy Haversat 1991 "Early Holocene Occupation of the Central California Coast." In: *Hunter-Gatherers of Early Holocene Coastal California*, Jon M. Erlandson and Roger H. Colten, eds., pp. 125–132. University of California Los Angeles, Institute of Archaeology, Perspectives in California Archaeology, Vol. 1.

Breternitz, David A., Alan C. Swedlund, and Duane C. Anderson 1971 "An Early Burial from Gordon Creek, Colorado." *American Antiquity* 36(2):170–182.

Brigham-Grette, Julie, Anatoly V. Lozhkin, Patricia M. Anderson, and Olga Y. Glushkova 2004 "Paleoenvironmental Conditions in Western Beringia before and during the Last Glacial Maximum." In: *Entering America: Northeast Asia and Beringia before the Last Glacial Maximum*, David B. Madsen, ed., pp. 29–61. Salt Lake City: University of Utah Press.

Bright, Jason R., and Carol J. Loveland 1999 "A Biological Perspective on Prehistoric Human Adaptation in the Great Salt Lake Wetlands." In: *Prehistoric Lifeways in the Great Basin Wetlands: Bioarchaeological Reconstruction and Interpretations*, Brian E. Hemphill and Clark Spencer Larsen, eds., pp. 103–116. Salt Lake City: University of Utah Press.

Bright, Jason R., and Andrew Ugan 1999 "Ceramics and Mobility: Assessing the Role of Foraging Behavior and Its Implications for Culture-History." *Utah Archaeology* 12:17–29.

Brink, Jack W. 2008 *Imagining Head-Smashed-In: Aboriginal Buffalo Hunting on the Northern Plains.* Edmonton, Alberta, Canada: Athabasca University Press.

Brink, John W., and Maureen Rollans 1990 "Thoughts on the Structure and Function of Drive Lane Systems at Communal Buffalo Jumps." In: *Hunters of the Recent Past*, Leslie B. Davis and Brian O. K. Reeves, eds., pp. 152–167. London: Unwin Hyman.

Brodie, Neil, Jennifer Doole, and Colin Renfrew (eds.) 2001 *Trade in Illicit Antiquities: The Destruction of the World's Archaeological Heritage.* Cambridge, UK: McDonald Institute for Archaeological Research.

Brody, J. J. 2004 *Mimbres Painted Pottery.* Santa Fe, NM: School of American Research Press.

Broughton, Jack M. 1994a "Declines in Mammalian Foraging Efficiency During the Late Holocene, San Francisco Bay, California." *Journal of Anthropological Archaeology* 13(4):371–401.

1994b "Late Holocene Resource Intensification in the Sacramento Valley, California: The Vertebrate Evidence." *Journal of Archaeological Science* 21(4):501–514.

1997 "Widening Diet Breadth, Declining Foraging Efficiency, and Prehistoric Harvest Pressure: Ichthyofaunal Evidence from the Emeryville Shellmound, California." *Antiquity* 71(274):845–862.

1999 "Resource Depression and Intensification During the late Holocene, San Francisco Bay: Evidence from the Emeryville Shellmound Vertebrate Fauna." *University of California Anthropological Records* 32.

2002 "Pre-Columbian Human Impact on California Vertebrates: Evidence from Old Bones and Implications for Wilderness Policy." In: *Wilderness and Political Ecology: Aboriginal Influences and the Original State of Nature*, Charles E. Kay and Randy T. Simmons, eds., pp. 44–71. Salt Lake City: University of Utah Press.

Broughton, Jack M., and Frank E. Bayham 2003 "Showing Off, Foraging Models, and the Ascendance of Large Game Hunting in the California Middle Archaic." *American Antiquity* 68(4):783–789.

Brown, Douglas 2003 "Shell Middens and Midden Burials in Southern Strait of Georgia Prehistory." In: *Archaeology of Coastal British Columbia: Essays in Honour of Professor Philip M. Hobler*, Roy L. Carlson, ed., pp. 153–164. Burnaby, B.C.: Simon Fraser University, Archaeology Press, Publication No. 30.

Brown, James A. 1985 "The Mississippian Period." In: *Ancient Art of the American Woodland Indians*, David S. Brose, James A. Brown, and David W. Penny, pp. 93–145. New York: Harry N. Abrams, Inc.

1996 *The Spiro Ceremonial Center: The Archaeology of Arkansas Valley Caddoan Culture in Eastern Oklahoma.* University of Michigan, Museum of Anthropology, Memoirs No. 29 (2 vols.).

1998 "The Archaeology of Ancient Religion in the Eastern Woodlands." *Annual Review of Anthropology* 26:465–485.

Brown, Michael D., Seyed H. Hosseini, Antonio Torroni, Hans-Jürgen Bandelt, Jon C. Allen, Theodore G. Schurr, Rosaria Scozzari, Fulvio Cruciani, and Douglas C. Wallace 1998 "mtDNA Haplogroup X: An Ancient Link Between Europe/Western Asia and North America?" *American Journal of Human Genetics* 63(6):1852–1861.

Bruhns, Karen Olsen, and Karen E. Stothert 1999 *Women in Ancient America.* Norman: University of Oklahoma Press.

Brunson, Emily 2000 "Osteoarthritis, Mobility and Adaptive Diversity among the Great Salt Lake Fremont." *Utah Archaeology* 13(1):1–14.

Brunswig, Robert H., and Bonnie L. Pitblado (eds.) 2007 *Frontiers in Colorado Paleoindian Archaeology: From the Dent Site to the Rocky Mountains.* Boulder: University Press of Colorado.

Bryan, Alan L. 1979a "Smith Creek Cave." In: "The Archaeology of Smith Creek Canyon, Eastern Nevada," Donald R. Tuohy and Doris L. Rendall, eds., pp. 162–253. Special issue. *Nevada State Museum Anthropological Papers* No. 17.

1979b "Council Hall Cave." In: "The Archaeology of Smith Creek Canyon, Eastern Nevada," Donald R. Tuohy and Doris L. Rendall, eds., pp. 254–271. Special issue, *Nevada State Museum Anthropological Papers* No. 17.

1986 (ed.) *New Evidence of the Pleistocene Peopling of the Americas.* University of Maine, Orono: Center for the Study of the First Americans.

1988 "The Relationship of the Stemmed Point and Fluted Point Traditions in the Great Basin." In: "Early Human Occupation in Far Western North America: The Clovis-Archaic Interface," Judith A. Willig, C. Melvin Aikens, and John L. Fagan, eds., pp. 53–74. Special issue, *Nevada State Museum Anthropological Papers* No. 21.

Buchanan, Briggs, and Mark Collard 2007 Investigating the Peopling of North America Through Cladistic Analyses of Early Paleoindian Projectile Points. *Journal of Anthropological Archaeology* 26(3):366–393.

Buchanan, Briggs, Mark Collard, and Kevan Edingorough 2008 "Paleoindian Demography and the Extraterrestrial Impact Hypothesis." *Proceedings of the National Academy of Sciences* 105(33):11651–11654.

Buck, Paul E., and Anne DuBarton 1994 "Archaeological Investigations at Pintwater Cave, Nevada, During the 1963–64 Field Season." *Journal of California and Great Basin Anthropology* 16(2):221–242.

Buikstra, Jane E., and Douglas K. Charles 1999 "Centering the Ancestors: Cemeteries, Mounds, and Sacred Landscapes of the Ancient North American Midcontinent." In: *Archaeologies of Landscape: Contemporary Perspectives*, Wendy Ashmore and A. Bernard Knapp, eds., pp. 201–228. Oxford, UK: Blackwell Publishers.

Burchell, Meghan 2006 "Gender, Grave Goods and Status in British Columbia Burials." *Canadian Journal of Archaeology* 30(2):251–271.

Burke, Heather, Claire Smith, Dorothy Lippert, Joe Watkins, and Larry Zimmerman (eds.) 2008 *Kennewick Man: Perspectives on the Ancient One.* Walnut Creek, CA: Left Coast Press.

Burley, David V. 1980 *Marpole: Anthropological Reconstructions of a Prehistoric Northwest Coast Culture Type.* Burnaby, B.C.: Simon Fraser University, Department of Archaeology, Publication 8.

Burns, James A. 1990 "Paleontological Perspectives on the Ice-Free Corridor." In: *Megafauna & Man: Discovery of America's Heartland*, Larry D. Agenbroad, Jim I. Mead, and Lisa W. Nelson, eds., pp. 61–66. Flagstaff: Northern Arizona University Press.

Butler, B. Robert 1961 *The Old Cordilleran Culture in the Pacific Northwest.* Pocatello: Occasional Papers of the Idaho Museum of Natural History, No. 5.

1963 "An Early Man Site at Big Camas Prairie, South-Central Idaho." *Tebiwa* 6(1):22–33.

Butler, Virginia L. 1993 "Natural Versus Cultural Salmonid Remains: Origin of the Dalles Roadcut Bones, Columbia River, Oregon, U.S.A." *Journal of Archaeological Science* 20(1):1–24.

1996 "Tui Chub Taphonomy and the Importance of Marsh Resources in the Western Great Basin of North America." *American Antiquity* 61(4):699–717.

Butler, Virginia L., and Sarah K. Campbell 2004 "Resource Intensification and Resource Depression in the Pacific Northwest of North America: A Zooarchaeological Review." *Journal of World Prehistory* 18(4):327–405.

Butzer, Karl W. 1991 "An Old World Perspective on Potential Mid-Wisconsin Settlement of the Americas." In: *The First Americans: Search and Research*, Thomas D. Dillehay and David J. Meltzer, eds., pp. 137–156. Boca Raton, FL: CRC Press.

Byers, A. Martin 2004 *The Ohio Hopewell Episode: Paradigm Lost and Paradigm Gained.* Akron, OH: University of Akron Press.

2006 *Cahokia: A World Renewal Cult Heterarchy.* Gainesville: University Press of Florida.

Byers, David A., and Jack M. Broughton 2004 "Holocene Environmental Change, Artiodactyl Abundances, and Human Hunting Strategies in the Great Basin." *American Antiquity* 69(2):235–255.

Byers, David A., and Andrew Ugan 2005 "Should We Expect Large Game Specialization in the Late Pleistocene? An Optimal Foraging Perspective on Early Paleoindian Prey Choice." *Journal of Archaeological Science* 32(11):1624–1640.

Byers, Douglas A. 1954 "Bull Brook—A Fluted Point Site in Ipswich, Massachusetts." *American Antiquity* 19(4):343–351.

Byrd, Brian F. 1998 "Harvesting the Littoral Landscape During the Late Holocene: New Perspectives from Northern San Diego County." *Journal of California and Great Basin Anthropology* 20(2):195–218.

Byrd, Brian F., and L. Mark Raab 2007 "Prehistory of the Southern Bight: Models for a New Millennium." In: *California Prehistory: Colonization, Culture, and Complexity*, Terry L. Jones and Kathryn A. Klar, eds., pp. 215–227. Lanham, MD: AltaMira Press.

Byerly, Ryan M., Judith R. Cooper, David J. Meltzer, Matthew E. Hill, and Jason M. LaBelle 2005 "On Bonfire Shelter (Texas) as a Paleoindian Bison Jump: An Assessment Using GIS and Zooarchaeology." *American Antiquity* 70(4):595–629.

Caldwell, Joseph R. 1958 "Trend and Tradition in the Prehistory of the Eastern United States." *Memoirs of the American Anthropological Association* No. 88.

Cameron, Catherine M., and Andrew I. Duff 2008 "History and Processes in Village Formation: Context and Contrasts from the Northern Southwest." *American Antiquity* 73(1):29–57.

Campos, Paula F., Eske Willerslev, Andrei Sher, Ludovic Orlando, Erik Axelsson, Alexei Tikhonov, Kim Aaris-Sørensen, Alex D. Greenwood, Ralf-Dietrich Kahlke, Pavel Kosintsev, Tatiana Krakhmalnaya, Tatyana Kuznetsova, Philippe Lemey, Ross MacPhee, Christopher A. Norris, Kieran Shepherd, Marc A. Suchard, Grant D. Zazula, Beth Shapiro, and M. Thomas P. Gilbert 2010 "Ancient DNA Analyses Exclude Humans as the Driving Force Behind Late Pleistocene Musk Ox (*Ovibos moschatus*) Population Dynamics." *Proceedings of the National Academy of Sciences* 107(12):5675–5680.

Cannon, Aubrey 1996 "The Early Namu Archaeofauna." In: *Early Human Occupation in British Columbia*, Roy L. Carlson and Luke Dalla Bona, eds., pp. 103–110. Vancouver: University of British Columbia Press.

2002 "Sacred Power and Seasonal Settlement on the Central Northwest Coast." In: *Beyond Foraging and Collecting: Evolutionary Change in Hunter-Gatherer Settlement Systems*, Ben Fitzhugh and Junko Habu, eds., pp. 311–338. New York: Kluwer Academic/Plenum Publishers.

2003 "Long-term Continuity in Central Northwest Coast Settlement Patterns." In: *Archaeology of Coastal British Columbia: Essays in Honour of Professor Philip M. Hobler*, Roy L. Carlson, ed., pp. 1–12. Burnaby, B.C.: Simon Fraser University, Archaeology Press, Publication No. 30.

Cannon, Aubrey, and Dongya Y. Yang 2006 "Early Storage and Sedentism on the Pacific Northwest Coast: Ancient DNA Analysis of Salmon Remains from Namu, British Columbia." *American Antiquity* 71(1):123–140.

Cannon, Aubrey, Henry P. Schwartz, and Martin Knyf 1999 "Marine-Based Subsistence Trends and the Stable Isotope Analysis of Dog Bones from Namu, British Columbia." *Journal of Archaeological Science* 26(4):399–407.

Cannon, Michael D. 2000 "Large Mammal Relative Abundance in Pithouse and Pueblo Period Archaeofaunas from Southwestern New Mexico: Resource Depression Among the Mimbres-Mogollon?" *Journal of Anthropological Archaeology* 19(3):317–347.

Cannon, Michael D., and David J. Meltzer 2004 "Early Paleoindian Foraging: Examining the Faunal Evidence for Large Mammal Specialization and Regional Variability in Prey Choice." *Quaternary Science Review* 23(18–19):1955–1987.

Campbell, Elizabeth W. Crozer, William H. Campbell, Ernst Antevs, Charles A. Amsden, Joseph A. Barbier, and Francis D. Bode 1937 "The Archeology of Pleistocene Lake Mojave: A Symposium." *Southwest Museum Papers* No. 11.

Carbone, Larry A. 1991 "Early Holocene Environments and Paleoecological Contexts on the Central and Southern California Coast." In: *Hunter-Gatherers of Early Holocene Coastal California*, Jon M. Erlandson and Roger H. Colten, eds., pp. 11–17. University of California Los Angeles, Institute of Archaeology, Perspectives in California Archaeology, Vol. 1.

Carlisle, Ronald C. (ed.) 1988 "Americans before Columbus: Ice-Age Origins." *University of Pittsburgh, Department of Anthropology, Ethnology Monographs* No. 12.

Carlson, Roy L. 1982 (ed.) *Indian Art Traditions of the Northwest Coast*. Burnaby, B.C., Canada: Simon Fraser University, Archaeology Press.

1983 "The Far West." In: *Early Man in the New World*, Richard Shutler, Jr., ed., pp. 73–96. Beverly Hills: Sage Publications.

1990 "History of Research in Archaeology." In: *Handbook of North American Indians, Vol. 7, Northwest Coast*, Wayne Suttles, ed., pp. 107–115. Washington, D.C.: Smithsonian Institution.

1994 "Trade and Exchange in Prehistoric British Columbia." In: *Prehistoric Exchange Systems in North America*, Timothy G. Baugh and Jonathon E. Ericson, eds., pp. 307–361. New York: Plenum Press.

1996a "Introduction to the Early Human Occupation in British Columbia." In: *Early Human Occupation in British Columbia*, Roy L. Carlson and Luke Dalla Bona, eds., pp. 3–10. Vancouver: University of British Columbia Press.

1996b "Early Namu." In: *Early Human Occupation in British Columbia*, Roy L. Carlson and Luke Dalla Bona, eds., pp. 83–102. Vancouver: University of British Columbia Press.

1998 "Coastal British Columbia in the Light of North Pacific Maritime Adaptations." *Arctic Anthropology* 35(1):23–35.

2008 "The Rise and Fall of Native Northwest Coast Cultures." *North Pacific Prehistory* 2:93–121.

Carmean, Kelli, and J. Eldon Molto 1991 "The Las Palmas Burial Tradition of the Cape Region, Baja California Sur, Some Research Questions." *Pacific Coast Archaeological Society Quarterly* 27(4):23–38.

Carpenter, John P., Guadalupe Sánchez, and María Elisa Villalpando C. 2005 "The Late Archaic/Early Agricultural Period in Sonora, Mexico." In: *The Late Archaic Across the Borderlands: From Foraging to Farming*, Bradley J. Vierra, ed., pp. 13–40. Austin: University of Texas Press.

Carr, Christopher 2006a "The Nature of Leadership in Ohio Hopewellian Studies: Role Segregation and the Transformation from Shamanism." In: *Gathering Hopewell: Society, Ritual, and Ritual Interaction*, Christopher Carr and D. Troy Case, eds., pp. 177–237. New York: Springer.

2006b "Rethinking Interregional Hopewellian 'Interaction.'" In: *Gathering Hopewell: Society, Ritual, and Ritual Interaction*, Christopher Carr and D. Troy Case, eds., pp. 575–623. New York: Springer.

Carr, Christopher, and D. Troy Case 2006 "The Gathering of Hopewell." In: *Gathering Hopewell: Society, Ritual, and Ritual Interaction*, Christopher Carr and D. Troy Case, eds., pp. 19–50. New York: Springer.

Carr, Kurt W., James M. Adovasio, and David R. Pedler 2001 "Paleoindian Populations in Trans-Appalachia." In: *Archaeology of the Appalachian Highlands*, Lynne P. Sullivan and Susan C. Prezzano, eds., pp. 67–87. Knoxville, University of Tennessee Press.

Carter, Cecile Elkins 1995 *Caddo Indians: Where We Come From*. Norman: University of Oklahoma Press.

Cartier, Robert (ed.) 1993 *The Scotts Valley Site: CA-SCr-177*. Santa Cruz, CA: Santa Cruz Archaeological Society.

Cassidy, Jim 2008 "What if by Sea? An Assessment of the Colonization of Coastal and Insular North America by Maritime Societies During the Early Holocene." *North Pacific Archaeology* 2:17–49.

Cassidy, Jim, L. Mark Raab, and Nina A. Kononenko 2004 "Boats, Bones, and Biface Bias: The Early Holocene Mariners of Eel Point, San Clemente Island, California." *American Antiquity* 69(1):109–130.

Catto, Norm, and Carole A. Mandryk 1990 "Geology of the Postulated Ice-Free Corridor." In: *Megafauna & Man: Discovery of America's Heartland*, Larry D. Agenbroad, Jim L. Mead, and Lisa W. Nelson, eds., pp. 80–85. Flagstaff: Northern Arizona University Press.

Cavalli-Sforza, Luigi Luca 2000 *Genes, Peoples, and Languages*. New York: North Point Press.

Cavalli-Sforza, Luigi Luca, A. Piazza, P. Menozzi, and J. Mountain 1988 "Reconstruction of Human Evolution: Bringing Together Genetic, Archaeological, and Linguistic Data." *Proceedings of the National Academy of Sciences* 85(16):6002–6006.

Chapdelaine, Claude, and Norman Clermont 2006 "Adaptation, Continuity and Change in the Middle Ottawa Valley: A View from the Morrison and Allumettes Islands Late Archaic Sites." In: *The Archaic of the Far Northeast*, David Sanger and M. A. P. Renouf, eds., pp. 191–219. Orono: University of Maine Press.

Chapman, Jefferson 1994 *Tellico Archaeology: 12,000 Years of Native American History*. Knoxville: University of Tennessee Press.

Charles, Douglas K. 1992 "Woodland Demographic and Social Dynamics in the American Midwest: Analysis of a Burial Mound Survey." *World Archaeology* 24(2):175–197.

Charles, Douglas K., and Jane E. Buikstra (eds.) 2006 *Recreating Hopewell*. Gainesville: University Press of Florida.

Chartkoff, Joseph L. 1989 "Exchange Systems in the Archaic of Coastal Southern California." In: *Proceedings of the Society for California Archaeology* 2:167–186. San Diego: Society for California Archaeology.

2001 "Exchange Systems and Sociopolitical Complexity in the Central Sierra Nevada: Perspectives on the Impact of Coastal Colonization on Inland Communities." *Journal of California and Great Basin Anthropology* 23(1):125–138.

Chartkoff, Joseph L., and Kerry Kona Chartkoff 1984 *The Archaeology of California*. Stanford, CA: Stanford University Press.

Chatters, James C. 1995 "Population Growth, Climatic Cooling, and the Development of Collector Strategies on the Southern Plateau, Western North America." *Journal of World Prehistory* 9(3):341–400.

1997 "Encounter with an Ancestor." *Anthropology Newsletter* 38(1):9–10.

1998 "Environment." In: *Handbook of North American Indians, Vol. 12, Plateau*, Deward E. Walker, Jr., ed., pp. 29–48. Washington, D.C.: Smithsonian Institution.

2000 "The Recovery and First Analysis of an Early Holocene Human Skeleton from Kennewick, Washington." *American Antiquity* 65(2):291–316.

2001 *Ancient Encounters: Kennewick Man and the First Americans*. New York: Simon and Schuster.

2004 "Safety in Numbers: The Influence of the Bow and Arrow on Village Formation on the Columbia Plateau." In: *Complex Hunter-Gatherers: Evolution and Organization of Prehistoric Communities on the Plateau of Northwestern North America*, William C. Prentiss and Ian Kuijt, eds., pp. 67–83. Salt Lake City: University of Utah Press.

Chatters, James C., Sarah K. Campbell, Grant D. Smith, and Phillip E. Minthorn, Jr. 1995 "Bison Procurement in the Far West: A 2,100-Year-Old Kill Site on the Columbia Plateau." *American Antiquity* 60(4):751–763.

Chatters, James C., Walter A. Neves, and Max Blum 1999 "The Kennewick Man: A First Multivariate Analysis." *Current Research in the Pleistocene* 16:87–90.

Chatters, James C., and David L. Pokotylo 1998 "Prehistory: Introduction." In: *Handbook of North American Indians, Vol. 12, Plateau*, Deward E. Walker, Jr., ed., pp. 73–80. Washington, D.C.: Smithsonian Institution.

Chatters, James C., and William C. Prentiss 2005 "A Darwinian Macro-Evolutionary Perspective on the Development of Hunter-Gatherer Systems in Northwestern North America." *World Archaeology* 37(1):46–65.

Chester, Sharon, and James Oetzel 1998 *The Arctic Guide*. San Mateo, CA: Wandering Albatross.

Chilton, Elizabeth S. 2005a "Beyond 'Big': Gender, Age, and Subsistence Diversity in Paleoindian Societies." In: *The Settlement of the American Continents*, C. Michael Barton, Geoffrey A. Clark, David R. Yesner, and George A. Pearson, eds, pp. 162–172. Tucson: University of Arizona Press.

2005b "Farming and Social Complexity in the Northeast." In: *North American Archaeology*, Timothy R. Pauketat and Diana DiPaolo Loren, eds., pp. 138–160. Malden, MA: Blackwell Publishing.

Chisholm, Brian S., and D. Erle Nelson 1983 "An Early Human Skeleton from South-Central British Columbia: Dietary Inferences from Carbon Isotopic Evidence." *Canadian Journal of Archaeology* 7(1):85–86.

Christenson, Lynne E. 1992 "The Late Prehistoric Yuman Settlement and Subsistence System: Coastal Adaptation." In: *Essays on the Prehistory of Maritime California*, Terry L. Jones, ed., pp. 217–230. Center for Archaeological Research at Davis, Publication No. 10.

Cinq-Mars, Jacques, and Richard E. Morlan 1999 "Bluefish Caves and Old Crow Basin: A New Rapport." In: *Ice Age Peoples of North America: Environments, Origins, and Adaptations of the First Americans*, Robson Bonnichsen and Karen L. Turnmire, eds., pp. 200–212. Oregon State University: Center for the Study of the First Americans.

Claassen, Cheryl P. 1991 "Gender, Shellfishing, and the Shell Mound Archaic." In: *Engendering Archaeology: Women and Prehistory*, Joan M. Gero and Margaret W. Conkey, eds., pp. 276–300. Oxford, UK: Blackwell Publishers.

1996 "A Consideration of the Social Organization of the Shell Mound Archaic." In: *Archaeology of the Mid-Holocene Southeast*, Kenneth E. Sassaman and David G. Anderson, eds., pp. 235–258. Gainesville: University Press of Florida.

2001 "Challenges for Regendering Southeastern Prehistory." In: *Archaeological Studies of Gender in the Southeastern United States*, Jane M. Eastman and Christopher B. Rodning, eds., pp. 10–26. Gainesville: University Press of Florida.

Clark, Donald W. 1966 "Perspectives in the Prehistory of Kodiak Island, Alaska." *American Antiquity* 31(3):358–371.

1979 "Ocean Bay: An Early North Pacific Maritime Culture." *Canadian Museum of Civilization, Mercury Series, Archaeological Survey of Canada*, Paper 86.

1981 "Prehistory of the Western Subarctic." In: *Handbook of North American Indians, Vol. 6, Subarctic*, June Helm, ed., pp. 107–129. Washington, D.C.: Smithsonian Institution.

1984 "Prehistory of the Pacific Eskimo Region." In: *Handbook of North American Indians, Vol. 5, Arctic*, David Damas, ed., pp. 136–148. Washington, D.C.: Smithsonian Institution.

1991a "The Northern (Alaska-Yukon) Fluted Points." In: Clovis: Origins and Adaptations, Robson Bonnichsen and Karen L. Turnmire, eds., pp. 35–48. Oregon State University: Center for the Study of the First Americans.

1991b *Western Subarctic Prehistory.* Hull, Quebec: Canadian Museum of Civilization.

1997 "The Early Kachemak Phase on Kodiak Island at Old Kiavak." *Canadian Museum of Civilization, Mercury Series, Archaeological Survey of Canada*, Paper 155.

1998 "Kodiak Island: The Later Cultures." *Arctic Anthropology* 35(1):172–186.

2001 "Microblade-Culture Systematics in the Far Interior Northwest." *Arctic Anthropology* 38(2):64–80.

Clark, Donald W., and A. McFadyen Clark 1983 "Paleo-Indians and Fluted Points: Subarctic Alternatives." *Plains Anthropologist* 28(102, pt. 1):283–292.

Clark, Donald W., and Richard E. Morlan 1982 "Western Subarctic Prehistory: Twenty Years Later." *Canadian Journal of Archaeology* 6:79–93.

Clark, Geoffrey A. 1988 "The Upper Paleolithic of Northeast Asia and Its Relevance to the First Americans: A Personal View." *Current Research in the Pleistocene* 5:3–7.

2005 "Deconstructing the North Atlantic Connection." In: *The Settlement of the American Continents*, C. Michael Barton, Geoffrey A. Clark, David R. Yesner, and George A. Pearson, eds, pp. 103–112. Tucson: University of Arizona Press.

Clarke, David L. 1968 *Analytical Archaeology.* London: Methuen & Co.

Cobb, Charles R. 2003 "Mississippian Chiefdoms: How Complex?" *Annual Review of Anthropology* 32:63–84.

Cobb, Charles R., and Brian M. Butler 2002 "The Vacant Quarter Revisited: Late Mississippian Abandonment of the Lower Ohio Valley." *American Antiquity* 67(4):625–641.

Cobb, Charles R., and Patrick H. Garrow 1996 "Woodstock Culture and the Question of Mississippian Emergence." *American Antiquity* 61(1):21–37.

Cockburn, T. Aidan 1971 "Infectious Diseases in Ancient Populations." *Current Anthropology* 12(1):45–62.

Codere, Helen 1950 *Fighting with Property: A Study of Kwakiutl Potlatching and Warfare, 1792–1930.* Glückstadt, Germany: J. J. Agstin.

Cohen, Fay G. 1986 *Treaties on Trial: The Continuing Controversy over Northwest Indian Fishing Rights.* Seattle: University of Washington Press.

Collins, Henry B. 1984 "History of Research Before 1945." In: Handbook of North American Indians, Vol. 5, Arctic, David Damas, ed., pp. 8–16. Washington, D.C.: Smithsonian Institution.

Collins, Michael B. 1999a "Reply to Fiedel, Part II." *Discovering Archaeology, Special Report* (November/December):14–15.

1999b *Clovis Blade Technology: A Comparative Study of the Keven Davis Cache, Texas.* Austin: University of Texas Press.

2002 "The Gault Site, Texas, and Clovis Research." *Athena Review* 3(2):31–41, 100–102.

2005 "Comparing Clovis and the Western European Upper Paleolithic: What are the Rules of Evidence?" In: *Paleoamerican Origins: Beyond Clovis*, Robson Bonnichsen, Bradley T. Lepper, Dennis Stanford, and Michael R. Waters, eds., pp. 43–50. Texas A&M University: Center for the Study of the First Americans.

Colton, Harold S. 1960 *Black Sand: Prehistory in Northern Arizona.* Albuquerque: University of New Mexico Press.

Colten, Roger H. 1989 "Prehistoric Shellfish Exploitation Around the Goleta Lagoon, California." *Journal of California and Great Basin Anthropology* 11(2):203–214.

1992 "Preliminary Analysis of Faunal Remains from Four Sites on Santa Cruz Island." In: *Proceedings of the Society for California Archaeology, Vol. 5*, Martin D. Rosen, Lynne E. Christenson, and Don Laylander, eds., pp. 247–267. San Diego: Society for California Archaeology.

1995 "Faunal Exploitation During the Middle to Late Period Transition on Santa Cruz Island, California." *Journal of California and Great Basin Anthropology* 17(1):93–120.

2001 "Ecological and Economic Analysis of Faunal Remains from Santa Cruz Island." In: *The Origins of a Pacific Coast Chiefdom: The Chumash of the Channel Islands*, Jeanne E. Arnold, ed., pp. 199–219. Salt Lake City: University of Utah Press.

Colten, Roger H., and Jeanne E. Arnold 1998 "Prehistoric Marine Mammal Hunting on California's Northern Channel Islands." *American Antiquity* 63(4):679–701.

Coltrain, Joan Brenner, Joel C. Janetski, and Shawn W. Carlyle 2007 "The Stable- and Radio-Isotope Chemistry of Western Basketmaker Burials: Implications for Early Puebloan Diets and Origins." *American Antiquity* 72(2):301–321.

Coltrain, Joan Brenner, and Steven W. Leavitt 2002 "Climate and Diet in Fremont Prehistory: Economic Variability and Abandonment of Maize Agriculture in the Great Salt Lake Basin." *American Antiquity* 67(3):453–485.

Condon, Keith W., and Jerome C. Rose 1997 "Bioarchaeology of the Sloan Site." In: *Sloan: A Paleoindian Dalton Cemetery in Arkansas*, Dan F. Morse, ed., pp. 8–13. Washington, D.C.: Smithsonian Institution Press.

Conkey, Margaret W., and Janet D. Spector 1984 "Archaeology and the Study of Gender." In: *Advances in Archaeological Method, Vol. 7*, Michael J. Schiffer, ed., pp. 1–38. New York: Academic Press.

Connolly, Robert P. 1998 "Architectural Grammar Rules at the Fort Ancient Hilltop Enclosure." In: *Ancient Earthen Enclosures of the Eastern Woodland*, Robert C. Mainfort, Jr. and Lynne P. Sullivan, eds., pp. 85–113. Gainesville: University Press of Florida.

Connolly, Robert P., and Bradley T. Lepper (eds.) 2004 *The Fort Ancient Earthworks: Prehistoric Lifeways of the Hopewell Culture in Southwestern Ohio.* Columbus: Ohio Historical Society.

Connolly, Thomas J. 1992 "Human Response to Change in Coastal Geomorphology and Fauna on the Southern Northwest Coast:

Archaeological Investigations at Seaside, Oregon." *University of Oregon Anthropological Papers* No. 45.

Connolly, Thomas J., Catherine S. Fowler, and William J. Cannon 1998 "Radiocarbon Evidence Relating to Northern Great Basin Basketry Chronology." *Journal of California and Great Basin Anthropology* 20(1):88–100.

Connolly, Thomas J., and Dennis L. Jenkins 1999 "The Paulina Lake Site (35DS34)." In: "Newberry Crater: A Ten-Thousand-Year Record of Human Occupation and Environmental Change in the Basin-Plateau Borderlands," by Thomas J. Connolly, pp. 86–127. Special issue, *University of Utah Anthropological Papers* No. 121.

Connolly, Thomas J., Jon M. Erlandson, and Susan E. Norris 1995 "Early Holocene Basketry and Cordage from Daisy Cave, San Miguel Island, California." *American Antiquity* 60(2):309–318.

Cook, Noble David 1998 *Born to Die: Disease and New World Conquest, 1492–1650.* Cambridge, UK: Cambridge University Press.

Cook, Robert A. 2008 *SunWatch: Fort Ancient Development in the Mississippian World.* Tuscaloosa: University of Alabama Press.

Cook, Sherburne F. 1971 "The Aboriginal Population of Upper California." In: *The California Indians: A Source Book*, Robert F. Heizer and M. A. Whipple, eds., pp. 66–72. Berkeley: University of California Press.

1976 *The Population of California Indians 1769–1970.* Berkeley: University of California Press.

1978 "Historical Demography." In: *Handbook of North American Indians, Vol. 8, California*, Robert F. Heizer, ed., pp. 91–98. Washington, D.C.: Smithsonian Institution.

Coon, Matthew S. 2009 "Variation in Ohio Hopewell Political Economies." *American Antiquity* 74(1):49–76.

Corbett, Debra G., Christine Lefevre, and Douglass Siegel-Causey 1997 "The Western Aleutians: Cultural Isolation and Environmental Change." *Human Ecology* 25(3):459–479.

Cordell, Linda S. 1994 *Ancient Pueblo Peoples.* Washington, D.C.: Smithsonian Books.

1997 *Archaeology of the Southwest* (2nd ed.). San Diego: Academic Press.

Cordell, Linda S., H. Wolcott Toll, Mollie S. Toll, and Thomas C. Windes 2008 "Archaeological Corn from Pueblo Bonito, Chaco Canyon, New Mexico: Dates, Contexts, Sources." *American Antiquity* 73(3):491–511.

Cordell, Linda S., Carla R. Van West, Jeffrey S. Dean, and Deborah A. Muenchrath 2007 "Mesa Verde Settlement History and Relocation: Climate Change, Social Networks, and Ancestral Pueblo Migration." *Kiva* 72(4):391–417.

Costello, Julia G., and David Hornbeck 1989 "Alta California: An Overview." In: *Columbian Consequences, Vol. 1, Archaeological and Historical Perspectives on the Spanish Borderlands West*, David Hurst Thomas, ed., pp. 303–331. Washington: Smithsonian Institution Press.

Coulam, Nancy J., and Alan R. Schroedl 2004 "Late Archaic Totemism in the Greater Southwest." *American Antiquity* 69(1):41–62.

Coupland, Gary 1985 "Household Variability and Status Differentiation at Kitselas Canyon." *Canadian Journal of Archaeology* 9(1):39–56.

1988 "Prehistoric Cultural Change at Kitselas Canyon." *Canadian Museum of Civilization, Mercury Series, Archaeological Survey of Canada*, Paper 138.

1996 "The Evolution of Multi-Family Households on the Northwest Coast of North America." In: *People Who Lived in Big Houses*, Gary Coupland and E. B. Banning, eds., pp. 121–130. Madison, WI: Prehistory Press, Monographs in World Archaeology No. 27.

1998 "Maritime Adaptation and Evolution of the Developed Northwest Coast Pattern on the Central Northwest Coast." *Arctic Anthropology* 35(1):36–56.

2006 "A Chief's House Speaks: Communicating Power on the Northern Northwest Coast." In: *Household Archaeology on the Northwest Coast*, Elizabeth A. Sobel, D. Ann Trieu Gahr, and Kenneth M. Ames, eds., pp. 80–96. Ann Arbor, MI: International Monographs in Prehistory, Archaeological Series 16.

Coupland, Gary, Craig Bissell, and Sarah King 1993 "Prehistoric Subsistence and Seasonality at Prince Rupert Harbour: Evidence from the McNichol Creek Site." *Canadian Journal of Archaeology* 17:59–73.

Coupland, Gary, Roger H. Colton, and Rebecca Case 2003 "Preliminary Analysis of Socioeconomic Organization at the McNichol Creek Site, British Columbia." In: *Emerging from the Mist: Studies in Northwest Coast Culture History*, R. G. Matson, Gary Coupland, and Quentin Mackie, eds., pp. 152–169. Vancouver: University of British Columbia Press.

Cowan, Frank L. 2006 "A Mobile Hopewell? Questioning Assumptions of Ohio Hopewell Sedentism." In: *Recreating Hopewell*, Douglas K. Charles and Jane E. Buikstra, eds., pp. 26–49. Gainesville: University Press of Florida.

Cowan, R. A. 1967 "Lake Margin Ecological Exploitation in the Great Basin as Demonstrated by an Analysis of Coprolites from Lovelock Cave, Nevada." *University of California Archaeological Survey Reports* 70:21–36.

Cox, Steven L. 1991 "Site 95.20 and the Vergennes Phase in Maine." *Archaeology of Eastern North America* 19:135–161.

Craven, Sloan L. 2004 "New Dates for the Lind Coulee Site (45GR97)." *Current Research in the Pleistocene* 21:28–30.

Crawford, Michael H. 1998 *The Origins of Native Americans: Evidence from Anthropological Genetics.* Cambridge: Cambridge University Press.

Creel, Darrell, and Roger Anyon 2003 "New Interpretations of Mimbres Public Architecture and Space: Implications for Culture Change." *American Antiquity* 68(1):67–92.

Cressman, Luther S. 1942 *Archaeological Researches in the Northern Great Basin.* Washington, D.C.: Carnegie Institution of Washington Publication No. 538.

Cressman, Luther S., David L. Cole, Wilbur A. Davis, Thomas M. Newman, and Daniel J. Scheans 1960 "Cultural Sequences at the Dalles, Oregon a Contribution to Pacific Northwest Prehistory." *Transactions of the American Philosophical Society* 50(10).

Crites, Gary D. 1993 "Domesticated Sunflower in Fifth Millennium B.P. Temporal Context: New Evidence from Middle Tennessee." *American Antiquity* 58(1):146–148.

Croes, Dale R. 1995 *The Hoko River Archaeological Site Complex: The Wet/Dry Site (45CA213), 3,000–1,700 B.P.* Pullman: Washington State University Press.

2003 "Northwest Coast Wet-Site Artifacts: A Key to Understanding Resource Procurement, Storage, Management, and Exchange." In: *Emerging from the Mist: Studies in Northwest Coast Culture History*, R. G. Matson, Gary Coupland, and Quentin Mackie, eds., pp. 51–75. Vancouver: University of British Columbia Press.

2005 *The Hoko River Archaeological Site Complex: The Rockshelter (45CA21), 1,000–100 B.P., Olympic Peninsula, Washington.* Pullman: Washington State University Press.

Croes, Dale R., and Steven Hackenberger 1988 "Hoko River Archaeological Complex: Modeling Prehistoric Northwest Coast Economic Evolution." In: *Research in Economic Anthropology, Supplement 3, Prehistoric Economies of the Pacific Northwest Coast*, Barry L. Isaac, ed., pp. 19–85. Greenwich, CT: JAI Press.

Crosby, Harry W. 1994 *Antigua California: Mission and Colony on the Peninsular Frontier, 1697–1768.* Albuquerque: University of New Mexico Press.

1997 *The Cave Paintings of Baja California: Discovering the Great Murals of an Unknown People.* San Diego: Sunbelt Publications.

Cross, John R. 1999 "'By Any Other Name . . .': A Reconsideration of Middle Archaic Lithic Technology and Typology in the Northeast." In: *The Archaeological Northeast*, Mary Ann Levine, Kenneth E. Sassaman, and Michael S. Nassaney, eds., pp. 57–73. Westport: Bergin & Garvey.

Crowe, Keith J. 1991 *A History of the Original Peoples of Northern Canada.* Montreal: McGill-Queen's University Press.

Crown, Patricia L. 1990 "The Hohokam of the American Southwest." *Journal of World Prehistory* 4(2):223–255.

1994 *Ceramics and Ideology: Salado Polychrome Pottery.* Albuquerque: University of New Mexico Press.

Curewitz, Diane C. 2001 "High Elevation Land-use on the Northern Wasatch Plateau, Manti-La Sal National Forest, Utah." *Journal of California and Great Basin Anthropology* 23(2):249–272.

Curran, Mary Lou 1996 "Paleoindians in the Northeast: The Problem of Dating Fluted Point Sites." *Review of Archaeology* 17(1):2–11.

1999 "Exploration, Colonization, and Settling." In: The Bull Brook Phase, Antecedents, and Descendants. In: *The Archaeological Northeast*, Mary Ann Levine, Kenneth E. Sassaman, and Michael S. Nassaney, eds., pp. 3–24. Westport: Bergin & Garvey.

Custer, Jay F. 1984 *Delaware Prehistoric Archaeology: An Ecological Approach.* Newark: University of Delaware Press.

Cybulski, Jerome S. 1978 "Modified Human Bones and Skulls from Price Rupert Harbour, British Columbia." *Canadian Journal of Archaeology* 2:15–32.

1992 "A Greenville Burial Ground: Human Remains and Mortuary Elements in British Columbia Coast Prehistory." *Canadian Museum of Civilization, Mercury Series, Archaeological Survey of Canada*, Paper 146.

Cybulski, Jerome S., Donald E. Howes, James C. Haggarty, and Morley Eldridge 1981 "An Early Human Skeleton from South-Central British Columbia: Dating and Bioarchaeological Inference." *Canadian Journal of Archaeology* 5:49–59.

Cybulski, Jerome S., Alan D. McMillan, Ripan S. Malhi, Brian M. Kemp, Harold Harry, and Scott Cousins 2007 "The Big Bar Lake Burial: Middle Period Human Remains on the Canadian Plateau." *Canadian Journal of Archaeology* 31(1):55–78.

d'Azevedo, Warren L. (ed.) 1986 *Handbook of North American Indians, Vol. 11, Great Basin.* Washington, D.C.: Smithsonian Institution.

Daly, Patricia 1969 "Approaches to Faunal Analysis in Archaeology." *American Antiquity* 34(2):146–153.

Damkjar, Eric 2005 "Late Dorset Longhouses: A Look Inside." In: *Contributions to the Study of the Dorset Paleoindians*, Patricia D. Sutherland, ed., pp. 147–165. *Canadian Museum of Civilization, Mercury Series, Archaeological Survey of Canada*, Paper 167.

Dancey, William S. 2005 "The Enigmatic Hopewell of the Eastern Woodlands." In: *North American Archaeology*, Timothy R. Pauketat and Diana DiPaolo Loren, eds., pp. 108–137. Malden, MA: Blackwell Publishing.

Daniel, I. Randolf, Jr. 2001 "Stone Raw Material Availability and Early Archaic Settlement in the Southeastern United States." *American Antiquity* 66(2):237–265.

Daniel, I. Randolf, Jr., and Michael Weisenbaker 1987 *Harney Flats: A Florida Paleo-Indian Site.* Farmingdale, NY: Baywood Publishing.

Dansie, Amy J. 1997 "Early Holocene Burials in Nevada: Overview of Localities, Research and Legal Issues." *Nevada Historical Society Quarterly* 40(1):4–14.

Darling J. Andrew 1999 "Mass Inhumation and the Execution of Witches in the American Southwest." *American Anthropologist* 100(3):732–752.

Daugherty, Richard, and Janet Friedman 1982 "An Introduction to Ozette Art." In: *Indian Art Traditions of the Northwest Coast*, Roy L. Carlson, ed., pp. 183–195. Burnaby, B.C.: Simon Fraser University, Archaeology Press.

Davis, C. Alan, and Gerald A. Smith 1981 *Newberry Cave.* Redlands, CA: San Bernardino County Museum Association.

Davis, Emma Lou 1968 *An Archaeological Reconnaissance in the Central Desert of Baja California.* University of California, Los Angeles, Archaeological Survey Annual Report 10:176–208.

1978 (ed.) *The Ancient Californians: Rancholabrean Hunters of the Mojave Lakes Country.* Natural History Museum of Los Angeles County Science Series 29.

1982 "The Geoarchaeology and History of China Lake, California." In: *Peopling of the New World*, Jonathan E. Ericson, R. E. Taylor, and Rainer Berger, eds., pp. 203–228. Los Altos, CA: Ballena Press Anthropological Papers No. 23.

Davis, Leslie B. 1983 "From Microcosm to Macrocosm: Advances in Tipi Ring Investigation and Interpretation." *Plains Anthropologist Memoir* 19.

Davis, Loren G. 2003 "Geoarchaeology and Geochronology of Pluvial Lake Chapala, Baja California, Mexico." *Geoarchaeology* 18(2):205–224.

2006a "Geoarchaeological Insights from Indian Sands, a Late Pleistocene Site on the Southern Northwest Coast, USA. *Geoloarchaeology* 21(4):351–361.

2006b "Baja California's Paleoenvironmental Context." In: *Advances in the Archaeology of the Forgotten Peninsula*, Don Laylander and Jerry D. Moore, eds., pp. 14–23. Gainesville: University Press of Florida.

Davis, Loren G., Michele L. Punke, Roberta L. Hall, Matthew Fillmore, and Samuel C. Willis 2002 "A Late Pleistocene Occupation on the Southern Oregon Coast." *Journal of Field Archaeology* 29(1/2):7–16.

Davis, Loren G., and David A. Sisson 1998 "An Early Stemmed Point Cache from the Lower Salmon River Canyon of West-Central Idaho." *Current Research in the Pleistocene* 15:12–14.

Davis, Stanley D. 1990 "Prehistory of Southeastern Alaska." In: *Handbook of North American Indians, Vol. 7, Northwest Coast*, Wayne Suttles, ed., pp. 197–202. Washington, D.C.: Smithsonian Institution.

Dawson, K. C. A. 1981 "The Wabinosh River Site and the Laurel Tradition in Northwestern Ontario." *Ontario Archaeology* 36:3–46.

Deal, Michael, Douglas Rutherford, Brent Murphy, and Scott Buchanan 2006 "Rethinking the Archaic Sequence for the Maritime Provinces." In: *The Archaic of the Far Northeast*, David Sanger and M. A. P. Renouf, eds., pp. 253–283. Orono: University of Maine Press.

De la Luz Gutiérrez, Maria, and Justin Hyland 1994 "Arte Rupestre de Baja California Sur." *Arqueología Mexicana* 2(10):84–89.

Dean, Jeffrey S. 1994 "The Medieval Warm Period on the Southern Colorado Plateau." *Climate Change* 26:225–242.

1996 "Kayenta Anasazi Settlement Transformations in Northeastern Arizona, A.D. 1150 to 1350." In: *The Prehistoric Pueblo World, A.D. 1150–1350*, Michael A. Adler, ed., pp. 29–47. Tucson: University of Arizona Press.

2000a "Complexity Theory and Sociocultural Change in the American Southwest." In: *The Way the Wind Blows: Climate, History, and Human Action*, Roderick J. McIntosh, Joseph A. Tainter, and Susan Keech McIntosh, eds., pp. 89–118. New York: Columbia University Press.

2000b "Introduction: The Salado Phenomenon." In: *Salado*, Jeffrey S. Dean, ed., pp. 3–16. Albuquerque: University of New Mexico Press.

Dean, Jeffrey S., and Richard L. Warren 1983 "Dendrochronology." In: *The Architecture and Dendrochronology of Chetro Ketl, Chaco Canyon, New Mexico*, Stephen H. Lekson, ed., pp. 105–240. National Park Service, Division of Cultural Research, Reports of the Chaco Center No. 6.

Dean, Rebecca M. 2001 "Social Change and Hunting during the Pueblo III to Pueblo IV Transition, East-Central Arizona." *Journal of Field Archaeology* 28(3/4):271–285.

2005 "Site-Use Intensity, Cultural Modification of the Environment, and the Development of Agricultural Communities in Southern Arizona." *American Antiquity* 70(3):403–431.

2007 "Hunting Intensification and the Hohokam 'Collapse.'" *Journal of Anthropological Archaeology* 26(1):109–132.

Dekin, Albert A., Jr. 1976 "The Arctic Small Tool Horizon: A Behavioral Model of Human Population into an Unoccupied Niche." In: "Eastern Arctic Prehistory: Paleoeskimo Problems," Moreau S. Maxwell, ed., pp. 156–163. Special issue, *Memoirs of the Society for American Archaeology* No. 31.

1978 *Arctic Archaeology: A Bibliography and History*. New York: Garland Publishing, Inc.

Delacorte, Michael G. 1985 "The George T. Hunting Complex, Deep Springs Valley, California." *Journal of California and Great Basin Anthropology* 7(2):225–239.

DeLaurier, April, and Michael W. Spence 2003 "Cranial Genetic Markers: Implications for Postmarital Residence Patterns." In: *Bones of the Ancestors: The Archaeology and Osteobiography of the Moatfield Ossuary*, Ronald E. Williamson and Susan Pfeiffer, eds., pp. 263–294. Canadian Museum of Civilization, Mercury Series, Archaeological Survey of Canada, Paper 163.

Deller, D. Brian, and Christopher J. Ellis 2001 "Evidence for a Late Paleoindian Ritual from the Caradoc Site (AfHj-104), Southwestern Ontario, Canada." *American Antiquity* 66(2):267–284.

Deller, D. Brian, Christopher J. Ellis, and James R. Keron 2009 "Understanding Cache Variability: A Deliberately Burned Early Paleoindian Tool Assemblage from the Crowfield Site, Southwestern Ontario, Canada." *American Antiquity* 74(2):371–397.

DeMallie, Raymond J. (ed.) 2001 "Plains." In: *Handbook of North American Indians, Vol. 13* (2 parts). Washington, D.C.: Smithsonian Institution.

Dent, Richard J. 1995 *Chesapeake Prehistory: Old Traditions, New Directions*. New York: Plenum Press.

Des Lauriers, Matthew R. 2006a "Terminal Pleistocene and Early Holocene Occupations of Isla de Cedros, Baja California, Mexico." *Journal of Island and Coastal Archaeology* 1(2):255–270.

2006b "Isla Cedros." In: *The Prehistory of Baja California: Advances in the Archaeology of the Forgotten Peninsula*, Don Laylander and Jerry D. Moore, eds., pp. 153–166. Gainesville: University Press of Florida.

2008 "A Paleoindian Fluted Point from Isla Cedros, Baja California." *Journal of Island and Coastal Archaeology* 3(2):271–276.

Di Peso, Charles C. 1974 *Casas Grandes: A Fallen Trading Center of the Gran Chichimeca* (3 vols.). Dragoon, AZ: Amerind Foundation Series 9.

Diamond, Jared 1992 "The Arrow of Disease." *Discover* 13(10):64–73.

2005 *Collapse: How Societies Choose to Fail or Succeed*. New York: Viking.

Diaz-Granados, Carol, and James R. Duncan (eds.) 2004 *The Rock-Art of Eastern North America*. Tuscaloosa: University of Alabama Press.

Dibble, David S., and Dessamae Lorrain 1968 *Bonfire Shelter: A Stratified Bison Kill Site, Val Verde County, Texas*. Austin: University of Texas, Texas Memorial Museum, Miscellaneous Papers No. 1 (2 vols.).

Dickel, David N. 2002 "Analysis of Mortuary Patterns." In: *Windover: Multidisciplinary Investigations of an Early Archaic Florida Cemetery*, Glen H. Doran, ed., pp. 73–96. Gainesville: University Press of Florida.

Dickel, David N., Peter D. Schulz, and Henry M. McHenry 1984 "Central California: Prehistoric Subsistence Changes and Health." In: *Paleopathology at the Origins of Agriculture*, Mark N. Cohen and George J. Armelagos, eds., pp. 439–461. New York: Academic Press.

Diehl, Michael W., and Steven A. LeBlanc 2001 "Early Pithouse Villages of the Mimbres Valley and Beyond: The McNally and Thompson Sites in their Cultural and Ecological Contexts." *Papers of the Peabody Museum of Archaeology and Ethnology* 83.

Diehl, Michael W., and Jennifer A. Waters 2006 "Aspects of Organization and Risk During the Early Agricultural Period in Southeastern Arizona." In: *Behavioral Ecology and the Transition to Agriculture*, Douglas J. Kennett and Bruce Winterhalder, eds., pp. 63–86. Berkeley: University of California Press.

Dikov, Nikolai N. 1996 "The Ushki Sites, Kamchatka Peninsula." In: *American Beginnings: The Prehistory and Paleoecology of Beringia*, Frederick Hadleigh West, ed., pp. 244–250. Chicago: University of Chicago Press.

Dikov, Nikolai N., and E. E. Titov 1984 "Problems of the Stratification and Periodization of the Ushki Sites." *Arctic Anthropology* 21(2):69–80.

Dillehay, Thomas D. 1989 (ed.) *Monte Verde: A Late Pleistocene Settlement in Chile: Palaeoenvironment and Site Context, Vol. I*. Washington, D.C.: Smithsonian Institution Press.

1997 (ed.) *Monte Verde: A Late Pleistocene Settlement in Chile: The Archaeological Context and Interpretation, Vol. II*. Washington, D.C.: Smithsonian Institution Press.

2000 *The Settlement of the Americas: A New Prehistory*. New York: Basic Books.

Dillehay, Thomas D., and Michael B. Collins 1988 "Early Cultural Evidence from Monte Verde in Chile." *Nature* 332:150–152.

1991 "Monte Verde, Chile: A Comment on Lynch." *American Antiquity* 56(2):333–341.

Dillehay, Thomas D., and David J. Meltzer (eds.) 1991 *The First Americans: Search and Research*. Boca Raton, FL: CRC Press.

Dillehay, Thomas D., Mario Pino, Jack Rossen, Carlos Ocampo, Pilar Rivas, David Pollack, and Gwynn Henderson 1999 "Reply to Fiedel, Part I." *Discovering Archaeology, Special Report* (November/December):12–14.

Dillehay, Tom D., C. Ramírez, Mario Pino, Michael B. Collins, Jack Rossen, and J. D. Pino-Navarro 2008 "Monte Verde: Seaweed, Food, Medicine, and the Peopling of South America." *Science* 320:784–786.

Dillehay, Thomas D., and Jack Rossen 2002 "Plant Food and Its Implications for the Peopling of the New World: A View from South America." In: "The First Americans: The Pleistocene Colonization of the New World," Nina G. Jablonski, ed., pp. 237–253. Special issue, *Memoirs of the California Academy of Sciences* No. 27.

Dincauze, Dena F. 1971 "An Archaic Sequence for Southern New England." *American Antiquity* 36(2):194–198.

1975 "The Late Archaic Period in Southern New England." *Arctic Anthropology* 12(2):23–34.

1981 "The Meadowcroft Papers." *Quarterly Review of Anthropology* 2:3–4.

1984 "An Archaeo-Logical Evaluation of the Case for Pre-Clovis Occupations." *Advances in World Archaeology* 3:275–323.

1993 "Pioneering in the Pleistocene: Large Paleoindian Sites in the Northeast." In: *Archaeology of Eastern North America: Papers in Honor of Stephen Williams*, James B. Stoltman, ed., pp. 43–60. Jackson: Mississippi Department of Archives and History, Archaeological Report No. 25.

2000 *Environmental Archaeology: Principles and Practice*. Cambridge: Cambridge University Press.

Dixon, E. James 1985 "The Origins of the First Americans." *Archaeology* 38(2):22–27.

1999 *Bones Boats & Bison: Archaeology and the First Colonization of Western North America*. Albuquerque: University of New Mexico Press.

2001 "Human Colonization of the Americas: Timing, Technology, and Process." *Quaternary Science Reviews* 20(1–3):277–299.

2002 "How and When Did People First Come to North America?" *Athena Review* 3(2):23–27, 99.

Dixon, E. James, William F. Manley, and Craig M. Lee 2005 "The Emerging Archaeology of Glaciers and Ice Patches: Examples from Alaska's Wrangell-St. Elias National Park and Preserve." *American Antiquity* 70(1):129–143.

Dobyns, Henry F. 1993 "Disease Transfer at Contact." *Annual Review of Anthropology* 22:273–291.

Doleman, William H. 2005 "Environmental Constraints on Forager Mobility and the Use of Cultigens in Southeastern Arizona and Southern New Mexico." In: *The Late Archaic Across the Borderlands: From Foraging to Farming*, Bradley J. Vierra, ed., pp. 113–140. Austin: University of Texas Press.

Dongoske, Kurt E., Debra L. Martin, and T. J. Ferguson 2000 "Critique of the Claim of Cannibalism at Cowboy Wash." *American Antiquity* 65(1):179–190.

Doran, Glen H. 2002 "The Windover Radiocarbon Chronology." In: *Windover: Multidisciplinary Investigations of an Early Archaic Florida Cemetery*, Glen H. Doran, ed., pp. 59–72. Gainesville: University Press of Florida.

Doran, Glen H., and David N. Dickel 1988 "Multidisciplinary Investigations at the Windover Site." In: *Wet Site Archaeology*, Barbara Purdy, ed., pp. 263–289. Caldwell, NJ: Telford Press.

Doran, Glen H., David N. Dickel, William E. Ballinger, Jr., O. Frank Agee, Philip J. Laipis, and William W. Hauswirth 1986

"Anatomical, Cellular, and Molecular Analysis of 8,000-yr-old Human Brain Tissue from the Windover Archaeological Site." *Nature* 323:803–806.

Dove, Carla J., P. Gregory Hare, and Marcy Heacker 2005 "Identification of Ancient Feather Fragments Found in Melting Alpine Ice Patches in Southern Yukon." *Arctic* 58(1):38–43.

Doyel, David E. 2008 "Edge Work: The Late Prehistory of the Gila Bend Frontier." In: *Fragile Patterns: The Archaeology of the Western Papagueria*, Jeffrey H. Altschul and Adrianne G. Rankin, eds., pp. 233–251. Tucson: SRI Press.

Dragoo, Don W. 1976 "Adena and the Eastern Burial Cult." *Archaeology of Eastern North America* 4:1–9.

Drass, Richard R. 1998 "The Southern Plains Villagers." In: *Archaeology on the Great Plains*, W. Raymond Wood, ed., pp. 415–455. Lawrence: University of Kansas Press.

Driskell, Boyce N. 1994 "Stratigraphy and Chronology at Dust Cave." In: *Preliminary Archaeological Papers on Dust Cave, Northwest Alabama*, Nurit S. Goldman-Finn and Boyce N. Driskell, eds., pp. 17–34. *Journal of Alabama Archaeology* 40(1&2).

Driver, Jonathan C. 1996 "The Significance of the Fauna from the Charlie Lake Cave Site." In: *Early Human Occupation in British Columbia*, Roy L. Carlson and Luke Dalla Bona, eds., pp. 21–28. Vancouver: University of British Columbia Press.

1998 "Human Adaptation at the Pleistocene/Holocene Boundary in Western Canada, 11,000 to 9,000 BP." *Quaternary International* 49/50:141–150.

1999 "Raven Skeletons from Paleoindian Contexts, Charlie Lake Cave, British Columbia." *American Antiquity* 64(2):289–298.

Drooker, Penelope B., and C. Wesley Cowan 2001 "Transformation of the Fort Ancient Cultures of the Central Ohio Valley." In: *Societies in Eclipse: Archaeology of the Eastern Woodlands Indians, A.D. 1400–1700*, David S. Brose, C. Wesley Cowan, and Robert C. Mainfort, Jr., eds., pp. 83–106. Washington, D.C.: Smithsonian Institution Press.

Drucker, Philip, and Robert F. Heizer 1967 *To Make My Name Good.* Berkeley: University of California Press.

Du Pratz, M. Le Page 1758 *Histoire de la Louisiane* (3 vols.). Paris (translated into English and published in London in 1776, and reprinted in 1975 by the Louisiana State University Press).

Dugmore, Andrew J., Christian Keller, and Thomas H. McGovern 2007 "Norse Greenland Settlement: Reflections on Climate Change, Trade, and the Contrasting Fates of Human Settlements in the North Atlantic Islands." *Arctic Anthropology* 44(1):12–36.

Duke, Daron G., Craig Young, and James A. Carter 2004 "A Unique Example of Early Technology and Land Use in the Eastern Great Basin." *Current Research in the Pleistocene* 21:32–34.

Dumond, Don E. 1980 "The Archaeology of Alaska and the Peopling of America." *Science* 209:984–991.

1984 "Prehistory: Summary." In: *Handbook of North American Indians, Vol. 5, Arctic*, David Damas, ed., pp. 72–79. Washington, D.C.: Smithsonian Institution.

1987a *The Eskimos and Aleuts* (2nd ed.). Boulder, CO: Westview Press.

1987b "A Reexamination of Eskimo-Aleut Prehistory." *American Anthropologist* 89(1):32–56.

1998 "Maritime Adaptation on the Northern Alaska Peninsula." *Arctic Anthropology* 35(1):187–203.

2000 "The Norton Tradition." *Arctic Anthropology* 37(2):1–22.

2001 "The Archaeology of Eastern Beringia: Some Connections and Contrasts." *Arctic Anthropology* 38(2):196–205.

2009 "The 'Arctic Maritime' Expansion: A View from the South." In: *The Northern World: AD 900–1400*, Herbert D. G. Maschner, Owen Mason, and Robert McGhee, eds., pp. 58–75. Salt Lake City: University of Utah Press.

Dumond, Don E., and Richard L. Bland 1995 "Holocene Prehistory of Northernmost North Pacific." *Journal of World Prehistory* 9(4):401–451.

Dunbar, James S., and Ben I. Waller 1983 "A Distributional Analysis of Clovis/Suwannee Paleo-Indian Sites of Florida — A Geographic Approach." *Florida Anthropologist* 36(1–2):18–30.

Dunbar, James S., C. Andrew Hemmings, Pamela K. Vojnovski, S. David Webb, and William M. Stanton 2005 "The Ryan/Harley Site 8Je1004: A Suwannee Point Site in the Wacissa River, North Flordia." In: *Paleoamerican Origins: Beyond Clovis*, Robson Bonnichsen, Bradley T. Lepper, Dennis Stanford, and Michael R. Waters, eds., pp. 81–96. Texas A&M University: Center for the Study of the First Americans.

Dunbar, Robert B. 2000 "Climate Variability during the Holocene: An Update." In: *The Way the Wind Blows: Climate, History, and Human Action*, Roderick J. McIntosh, Joseph A. Tainter, and Susan Keech McIntosh, eds., pp. 45–88. New York: Columbia University Press.

Dunne, Peter M. 1948 *Early Jesuit Missions in Tarahumara*. Berkeley: University of California Press.

Dunnell, Robert C., and James K. Feathers 1991 "Late Woodland Manifestations of the Malden Plain, Southeast Missouri." In: *Stability, Transformation, and Variation: The Late Woodland Southeast*, Michael S. Nassaney and Charles R. Cobb, eds., pp. 21–45. New York: Plenum Press.

Dunnell, Robert C., and Diana M. Greenlee 1999 "Late Woodland Period 'Waste' Reduction in the Ohio River Valley." *Journal of Anthropological Archaeology* 18(3):376–395.

Dyck, Ian, and Richard E. Morlan 2001 "Hunting and Gathering Tradition: Canadian Plains." In: *Handbook of North American Indians, Vol. 13, Plains*, Raymond J. DeMallie, ed., pp. 115–130. Washington, D.C.: Smithsonian Institution.

Dye, David H. 2009 *War Paths: Peace Paths: An Archaeology of Cooperation and Conflict in Native Eastern North America.* Lanham, MD: AltaMira Press.

Dye, David H., and Adam King 2007 "Desecrating the Sacred Ancestor Temples: Chiefly Conflict and Violence in the American Southeast." In: *North American Indigenous Warfare and Ritual Violence*, Richard J. Chacon and Rubén G. Mendoza, eds., pp. 160–181. Tucson: University of Arizona Press.

Echo-Hawk, Roger C. 2000 "Ancient History in the New World: Integrating Oral Traditions and the Archaeological Record in Deep Time." *American Antiquity* 65(2):267–290.

Eerkens, Jelmer W. 1999 "Common Pool Resources, Buffer Zones, and Jointly Owned Territories: Hunter-Gatherer Land and Resource Tenure in Fort Irwin, Southeastern California." *Human Ecology* 27:297–318.

2004 "Privatization, Small-Seed Intensification, and the Origins of Pottery in the Western Great Basin." *American Antiquity* 69(4):653–670.

Eerkens, Jelmer W., Jerome King, and Eric Wohlgemuth 2004 "The Prehistoric Development of Intensive Green-Cone Piñon Processing in Eastern California." *Journal of Field Archaeology* 29(1/2):17–27.

Elias, Scott A. 2002 "Setting the Stage: Environmental conditions in Beringia as People Entered the New World." In: "The First Americans: The Pleistocene Colonization of the New World," Nina G. Jablonski, ed., pp. 9–25. Special issue, *Memoirs of the California Academy of Sciences* No. 27.

Elias, Scott A., Susan K. Short, C. Hans Nelson, and Hillary H. Birks 1996 "Life and Times of the Bering Land Bridge." *Nature* 382(6586):60–63.

Ellis, Christopher 2006 "Hi-Lo: An Early Lithic Complex in the Great Lakes Region." In: *The Late Palaeo-Indian Great Lakes: Geological and Archaeological Investigations of Late Pleistocene and Early Holocene Environments*, Lawrence J. Jackson and Andrew Hinshelwood, eds., pp. 57–83. Canadian Museum of Civilization, Mercury Series, Archaeological Survey of Canada, Paper 165.

2008 "The Fluted Point Tradition and the Arctic Small Tool Tradition: What's the Connection?" *Journal of Anthropological Archaeology* 27(3):298–314.

Ellis, Christopher, and D. Brian Deller 1997 "Variability in the Archaeological record of Northeastern Early Paleoindians: A View from Southern Ontario." *Archaeology of Eastern North America* 25:1–30.

Ellis, Christopher, Stanley Wortner, and William A. Fox 1991 "Nettling: An Overview of an Archaic 'Kirk Corner-notched Cluster' Site in Southwestern Ontario." *Canadian Journal of Archaeology* 15:1–34.

Ellis, Christopher, Albert C. Goodyear, Dan F. Morse, and Kenneth B. Tankersley 1998 "Archaeology of the Pleistocene-Holocene Transition in Eastern North America." *Quaternary International* 49/50:151–166.

Ellis, David V. 2006 "Of a More Temporary Cast: Household Production at the Broken Tops Site." In: *Household Archaeology on the Northwest Coast*, Elizabeth A. Sobel, D. Ann Trieu Gahr, and Kenneth M. Ames, eds., pp. 120–139. Ann Arbor, MI: International Monographs in Prehistory, Archaeological Series 16.

Elmendorf, William W. 1965 "Linguistic and Geographic Relations in the Northwest Plateau Area." *Southwest Journal of Anthropology* 21(1):63–78.

Elsasser, Albert B. 1960 *The Archaeology of the Sierra Nevada in California and Nevada.* Berkeley: University of California Archaeological Survey Reports No. 51.

Elsasser, Albert B., and Willis A. Gortner 1991 "The Martis Complex Revisited." *North American Archaeologist* 12(4):361–376.

Elson, Mark D. 1998 "Expanding the View of Hohokam Platform Mounds: An Ethnographic Perspective." *Anthropological Papers of the University of Arizona* No. 63.

Elston, Robert G. 2006 *Tosawihi Quarries: Archaeological Investigations and Ethnographic Studies in Nevada.* Reno: Nevada Bureau of Land Management Cultural Resource Series No. 16.

Elston, Robert G., and Keith L. Katzer 1990 "Conclusions." In: "The Archaeology of James Creek Shelter," Robert G. Elston and Elizabeth E. Budy, eds., pp. 257–274. Special issue, *University of Utah Anthropological Papers* No. 115.

Elston, Robert G., and David W. Zeanah 2002 "Thinking outside the Box: A New Perspective on Diet Breadth and Sexual Division of Labor in the Prearchaic Great Basin." *World Archaeology* 34(1):103–130.

Emerson, Thomas E. 1997a "Cahokian Elite Ideology and the Mississippian Cosmos." In: *Cahokia: Domination and Ideology in the Mississippian World*, Timothy R. Pauketat and Thomas E. Emerson, eds., pp. 190–228. Lincoln: University of Nebraska Press.

1997b *Cahokia and the Archaeology of Power.* Tuscaloosa: University of Alabama Press.

2007 "Cahokia and the Evidence for Late Pre-Columbian War in the North American Mid-Continent." In: *North American Indigenous Warfare and Ritual Violence*, Richard J. Chacon and Rubén G. Mendoza, eds., pp. 129–148. Tucson: University of Arizona Press.

Emerson, Thomas E., Randall E. Hughes, Mary R. Hynes, and Sarah U. Wisseman 2003 "The Sourcing and Interpretation of Cahokia-Style Figurines in the Trans-Mississippi South and Southeast." *American Antiquity* 68(2):287–313.

English, Nathan B., Julio L. Betancourt, Jeffrey S. Dean, and Jay Quade 2001 "Strontium Isotopes Reveal Distant Sources of Architectural Timber in Chaco Canyon, New Mexico." *Proceedings of the National Academy of Sciences* 98(21):11891–11898.

Ericson, Jonathon E., and Timothy G. Baugh (eds.) 1993 *The American Southwest and Mesoamerica: Systems of Prehistoric Exchange.* New York: Plenum Press.

Ericson, Jonathon E., R. E. Taylor, and Rainer Berger (eds.) 1982 *Peopling of the New World.* Los Altos, CA: Ballena Press Anthropological Papers No. 23.

Erlandson, Jon M. 1991 "Shellfish and Seeds as Optimal Resources: Early Holocene Subsistence on the Santa Barbara Coast." In: *Hunter-Gatherers of Early Holocene Coastal California*, Jon M. Erlandson and Roger H. Colten, eds., pp. 89–100. University of California Los Angeles, Institute of Archaeology, Perspectives in California Archaeology, Vol. 1.

1993 "Evidence for a Terminal Pleistocene Human Occupation at Daisy Cave, San Miguel Island, California." *Current Research in the Pleistocene* 10:17–21.

1994 *Early Hunter-Gatherers of the California Coast.* New York: Plenum.

1997 "The Middle Holocene on the Western Santa Barbara Coast." In: *Archaeology of the California Coast During the Middle Holocene*, Jon M. Erlandson and Michael A. Glassow, eds., pp. 91–109. University of California Los Angeles, Institute of Archaeology, Perspectives in California Archaeology, Vol. 4.

2001 "The Archaeology of Aquatic Adaptations: Paradigms for a New Millennium." *Journal of Archaeological Research* 9(4):287–350.

2002 "Anatomically Modern Humans, Maritime Voyaging, and the Pleistocene Colonization of the Americas." In: "The First Americans: The Pleistocene Colonization of the New World," Nina G. Jablonski, ed., pp. 59–92. Special issue, *Memoirs of the California Academy of Sciences* No. 27.

Erlandson, Jon M., Michael A. Glassow, Charles Rozaire, and Don Morris 1992 "4,000 Years of Human Occupation on Santa Barbara Island, California." *Journal of California and Great Basin Anthropology* 14(1):85–93.

Erlandson, Jon M., Michael H. Graham, Bruce J. Bourque, Debra Corbett, James A. Estes, and Robert S. Steneck 2007a "The Kelp Highway Hypothesis: Marine Ecology, the Coastal Migration Theory and the Peopling of the Americas." *Journal of Island & Coastal Archaeology* 2(2):161–174.

Erlandson, Jon M., Douglas J. Kennett, B. Lynn Ingram, Daniel A. Guthrie, Don P. Morris, Mark A. Tveskov, G. James West, and Philip L. Walker 1996 "An Archaeological and Paleontological Chronology for Daisy Cave (CA-SMI-261), San Miguel Island, California." *Radiocarbon* 38(2):355–373.

Erlandson, Jon M., and Madonna L. Moss 1996 "The Pleistocene-Holocene Transition along the Pacific Coast of North America." In: *Humans at the End of the Ice Age: The Archaeology of the Pleistocene-Holocene Transition*, Lawrence Guy Straus, Berit Valentin Eriksen, Jon M. Erlandson, and David R. Yesner, eds., pp. 277–301. New York: Plenum Press.

Erlandson, Jon M., Torben C. Rick, Terry L. Jones, and Judith F. Porcasi 2007b "One if by Land, Two if by Sea: Who Were the First Californians?" In: *California Prehistory: Colonization, Culture, and Complexity*, Terry L. Jones and Kathryn A. Klar, eds., pp. 53–62. Lanham, MD: AltaMira Press.

Erlandson, Jon M., Torben C. Rick, René L. Vallenoweth, and Douglas J. Kennett 1999 "Maritime Subsistence at a 9300 Year Old Shell Midden on Santa Rosa Island, California." *Journal of Field Archaeology* 26(3):255–265.

Erlandson, Jon M., Mark A. Tveskov, and R. Scott Byram 1998 "The Development of Maritime Adaptations on the Southern Northwestern Coast of North America." *Arctic Anthropology* 35(1):6–22.

Erlandson, Jon M., Mark A. Tveskov, and Madonna L. Moss 1997 "Return to Chetlessenten: The Antiquity and Architecture of an Athapaskan Village on the Southern Northwest Coast." *Journal of California and Great Basin Anthropology* 19(2):226–240.

Erwin, John C., Donald H. Holly, Jr., Stephen H. Hull, and Timothy L. Rust 2005 "Form and Function of Projectile Points and the Trajectory of Newfoundland Prehistory." *Canadian Journal of Archaeology* 29(1):46–67.

Esdale, Julie A. 2008 "A Current Synthesis of the Northern Archaic." *Arctic Anthropology* 45(2):3–38.

Eshleman, Jason A., Ripan S. Malhi, John R. Johnson, Frederika A. Kastle, Joseph Lorenz, and David G. Smith 2004 "Mitochondrial DNA and Prehistoric Settlements: Native Migrations on the Western Edge of North America." *Human Biology* 76(1):55–75.

Ewers, John C. 1955 "The Horse in Blackfoot Indian Culture." *Bureau of American Ethnology Bulletin* 159.

Ezzo, Joseph A. 1993 *Human Adaptation at Grasshopper Pueblo, Arizona: Social and Ecological Perspectives.* Ann Arbor: International Monographs in Prehistory, Archaeological Series 4.

Ezzo, Joseph A., and T. Douglas Price 2002 "Migration, Regional Reorganization, and Spatial Group Composition at Grasshopper Pueblo, Arizona." *Journal of Archaeological Science* 29(5):499–520.

Fagan, Brian M. 1999 *Floods, Famines and Emperors: El Niño and the Fate of Civilizations.* New York: Basic Books.

2000 *The Little Ice Age: How Climate Made History 1300–1850.* New York: Basic Books.

2003 *Before California: An Archaeologist Looks at Our Earliest Inhabitants.* Walnut Creek, CA: AltaMira Press.

2005a *Ancient North America: The Archaeology of a Continent* (4th ed.). New York: Thames and Hudson.

2005b *Chaco Canyon: Archaeologists Explore the Lives of an Ancient Society.* Oxford, UK: Oxford University Press.

Fagan, John L. 1984 "The Dietz Site: A Clovis Base Camp in South-Central Oregon." Paper presented at the annual meetings of the Society for American Archaeology, Portland.

Farris, Glenn J. 1992 "'Women's Money': Types and Distributions of Pine Nut Beads in Northern California, Southern Oregon, and Northwestern Nevada." *Journal of California and Great Basin Anthropology* 14(1):55–71.

Faught, Michael K. 2002 "Submerged Paleoindian and Archaic Sites of the Big Bend, Florida." *Journal of Field Archaeology* 29(3/4):273–290.

2004 "The Underwater Archaeology of Paleolandscapes, Apalachee Bay, Florida." *American Antiquity* 69(2):275–289.

2008 "Archaeological Roots of Human Diversity in the New World: A Compilation of Accurate and Precise Radiocarbon Ages from Earliest Sites." *American Antiquity* 73(4):670–686.

Faught, Michael K., Michael B. Hornum, R. Christopher Goodwin, Brinnen Carter, and S. David Webb 2003 "Earliest-Holocene Tool Assemblages from Northern Florida with Stratigraphically Controlled Radiocarbon Estimates (Sites 8LE2105 and 8JE591)." *Current Research in the Pleistocene* 20:16–18.

Fedje, Daryl W. 2002 "The Early Post-Glacial History of the Northern Northwest Coast: A View From Haida Gwaii and Hecate Strait." *Athena Review* 3(2):28–30, 100.

Fedje, Daryl W., and Tina Christensen 1999 "Modeling Paleoshorelines and Locating Early Holocene Coastal Sites in Haida Gwaii." *American Antiquity* 64(4):635–652.

Fedje, Daryl W., and Heiner Josenhans 2000 "Drowned Forests and Archaeology on the Continental Shelf of British Columbia, Canada." *Geology* 28(2):99–102.

Fedje, Daryl W., and Quentin Mackie 2005 "Overview of Culture History." In: *Haida Gwaii: Human History and Environment from the Time of Loon to the Time of the Iron People*, Daryl W. Fedje and Rolf W. Mathewes, eds., pp. 154–162. Vancouver: University of British Columbia Press.

Fedje, Daryl W., Quentin Mackie, E. James Dixon, and Timothy H. Heaton 2004 "Late Wisconsin Environmental and Archaeological Visibility on the Northern Northwest Coast." In: *Northeast Asia and Beringia Before the Last Glacial Maximum*, David B. Madsen, ed., pp. 97–138. Salt Lake City: University of Utah Press.

Fedje, Daryl W., Martin P. R. Magne, and Tina Christensen 2005 "Test Excavations at Raised Beach Sites in Southern Haida Gwaii and Their Significance to Northwest Coast Archaeology." In: *Haida Gwaii: Human History and Environment from the Time of Loon to the Time of the Iron People*, Daryl W. Fedje and Rolf W. Mathewes, eds., pp. 205–244. Vancouver: University of British Columbia Press.

Feinman, Gary M. 2000 "Dual-Processual Theory and Social Formations in the Southwest." In: *Alternative Leadership Strategies in the Prehispanic Southwest*, Barbara J. Mills, ed., pp. 207–224. Tucson: University of Arizona Press.

Feit, Rachel 2003 "Defining the Caddoan Culture." *American Archaeology* 7(1):12–19.

Fenenga, Frank F. 1952 "The Archaeology of the Slick Rock Village, Tulare County, California." *American Antiquity* 17(4):339–347.

Fenenga, Gerrit L. 1991 "A Preliminary Examination of the Faunal Remains from Early Sites in the Tulare Lake Basin." In: *Background to a Study of Tulare Lake's Archaeological Past*, William J. Wallace and Francis A. Riddell, eds., pp. 11–22. Redondo Beach, CA: The Tulare Lake Archaeological Research Group, Contributions to Tulare Lake Archaeology I.

1993 "Test Excavations at the Witt Site (CA-KIN-32)." In: *Finding the Evidence: The Quest for Tulare Lake's Archaeological Past*, William J. Wallace and Francis A. Riddell, eds., pp. 25–38. Redondo Beach: Tulare Lake Archaeological Research Group, Contributions to Tulare Lake Archaeology II.

Fenton, James P. 2001 "Early Woodland Burial Mounds of Kentucky." In: *Archaeology of the Appalachian Highlands*, Lynne P. Sullivan and Susan C. Prezzano, eds., pp. 137–148. Knoxville, University of Tennessee Press.

Fewkes, Jesse W. 1924 "Preliminary Archaeological Investigations at Weeden Island, Florida." *Smithsonian Miscellaneous Collections* 76(13):1–26.

Fie, Shannon M. 2006 "Visiting in the Interaction Sphere: Ceramic Exchange and Interaction in the Lower Illinois Valley." In: *Recreating Hopewell*, Douglas K. Charles and Jane E. Buikstra, eds., pp. 427–445. Gainesville: University Press of Florida.

Fiedel, Stuart J. 1987 "Algonquian Origins: A Problem in Archaeological-Linguistic Correlation." *Archaeology of Eastern North America* 15:1–11.

1992 *Prehistory of the Americas* (2nd ed.). Cambridge, UK: Cambridge University Press.

1999a "Older Than We Thought: Implications of Corrected Dates for Paleoindians." *American Antiquity* 64(1):95–115.

1999b "Artifact Provenience at Monte Verde, Chile: Confusion and Contradictions. *Discovering Archaeology, Special Report* (November/December):1–12.

2000 "The Peopling of the New World: Present Evidence, New Theories, and Future Directions." *Journal of Archaeological Research* 8(1):39–103.

2001 "What Happened in the Early Woodland?" *Archaeology of Eastern North America* 29:101–142.

2005a "Rapid Clovis Colonization of the Americas: Chronological Evidence and Archaeological Analogues." In: *Paleoamerican Origins: Beyond Clovis*, Robson Bonnichsen, Bradley T. Lepper, Dennis Stanford, and Michael R. Waters, eds., pp. 97–102. Texas A&M University: Center for the Study of the First Americans.

2005b "Man's Beat Friend—Mammoth's Worst Enemy? A Speculative Essay on the Role of Dogs in Paleoindian Colonization and Megafaunal Extinction." *World Archaeology* 37(1):11–25.

2006 "Points in Time: Establishing a Precise Hemispheric Chronology for Paleoindian Migration." In: *Paleoindian Archaeology: A Hemispheric Perspective*, Juliet E. Morrow and Cristóbal Gnecco, eds., pp. 21–43. Gainesville: University Press of Florida.

Fiedel, Stuart J., and Gary Haynes 2004 "A Premature Burial: Comments on Grayson and Meltzer's 'Requiem for Overkill.'" *Journal of Archaeological Science* 31(1):121–131.

Field, Stephanie, Anne J. Goldberg, and Tina Lee 2006 "Gender, Status, and Ethnicity in the Scioto, Miami, and Northeastern Ohio Hopewellian Regions as Evidenced by Mortuary Practices." In: *Gathering Hopewell: Society, Ritual, and Ritual Interaction*, Christopher Carr and D. Troy Case, eds., pp. 386–404. New York: Springer.

Figgins, Jesse D. 1927 "The Antiquity of Man in America." *Natural History* 27(3):229–239.

1933 *A Further Contribution to the Antiquity of Man in America.* Denver: Colorado Museum of Natural History Proceedings No. 12.

Fine-Dare, Kathleen S. 2002 *Grave Injustice: The American Indian Repatriation Movement and NAGPRA.* Lincoln: University of Nebraska Press.

Finney, Bruce P., Irene Gregory-Eaves, Marianne S. V. Douglas, and John P. Smol 2002 "Fisheries Productivity in the Northeastern Pacific Ocean Over the Past 2,200 Years." *Nature* 416:729–733.

Firestone, R. B., A. West, J. P. Kennett, L. Becker, T. E. Bunch, Z. S. Revay, P. H. Schultz, T. Belgya, D. J. Kennett, J. M. Erlandson, O. J. Dickenson, A. C. Goodyear, R. S. Harris, G. A. Howard, J. B. Kloosterman, P. Lechler, P. A. Mayewski, J. Montgomery, R. Poreda, T. Darrah, S. S. Que Hee, A. R. Smith, A. Stich, W. Topping, J. H. Wittke, and W. S. Wolbach 2007 "Evidence for an Extraterrestrial Impact 12,900 Years Ago That Contributed to the Megafaunal Extinctions and the

Younger Dryas Cooling." *Proceedings of the National Academy of Sciences* 104(41):16016–16021.

Fish, Suzanne K. 2000 "Hohokam Impacts on Sonoran Desert Environments." In: *Imperfect Balance: Landscape Transformations in the Precolumbian Americas*, David L. Lentz, ed., pp. 251–280. New York: Columbia University Press.

Fish, Suzanne K., and Paul R. Fish 1994 "Prehistoric Desert Farmers of the Southwest." *Annual Review of Anthropology* 23:83–108.

2000 "The Institutional Contexts of Hohokam Complexity and Inequality." In: *Alternative Leadership Strategies in the Prehispanic Southwest*, Barbara J. Mills, ed., pp. 154–167. Tucson: University of Arizona Press.

Fish, Suzanne K., and Paul R. Fish (eds.) 2008 *The Hohokam Millennium*. Santa Fe: School for Advanced Research Press.

Fish, Suzanne K., Paul R. Fish, and M. Elsa Villalpando (eds.) 2007 *Trincheras Sites in Time, Space, and Society*. Tucson: University of Arizona Press.

Fitting, James E. 1968 "Environmental Potential and the Postglacial Readaptation in Eastern North America." *American Antiquity* 33(4):441–445.

1978 "Prehistory: Introduction." In: *Handbook of North American Indians, Vol. 15, Northeast*, Bruce Trigger, ed., pp. 14–15. Washington, D.C.: Smithsonian Institution.

Fitzgerald, Richard T. 1993 *Archaic Milling Cultures of the Southern San Francisco Bay Region*. Coyote Press Archives of California Prehistory No. 35. Salinas: Coyote Press.

2000 *Cross Creek: An Early Holocene/Millingstone Site*. California State Water Project, Coastal Branch Series Paper No. 12. San Luis Obispo County Archaeological Society.

Fitzgerald, Richard T., and Terry L. Jones 1999 "The Milling Stone Horizon Revisited: New Perspectives from Northern and Central California." *Journal of California and Great Basin Anthropology* 21(1):67–93.

2003 "On the Weight of the Evidence from Cross Creek: A Reply to Turner." *American Antiquity* 68(2):396–399.

Fitzgerald, Richard, Terry L. Jones, and Adella B. Schroth 2005 "Ancient Long-Distance Trade in Western North America: New AMS Radiocarbon Dates from Southern California." *Journal of Archaeological Science* 32(5):423–434.

Fitzhugh, Ben 2002 "Residential and Logistical Strategies in the Evolution of Complex Hunter-Gatherers on the Kodiak Archipelago." In: *Beyond Foraging and Collecting: Evolutionary Change in Hunter-Gatherer Settlement Systems*, Ben Fitzhugh and Junko Habu, eds., pp. 257–304. New York: Kluwer Academic/Plenum Publishers.

Fitzhugh, William W. 1978 "Maritime Archaic Cultures of the Central and Northern Labrador Coast." *Arctic Anthropology* 15(2):61–95.

1985 "Early Contacts North of Newfoundland Before A.D. 1600: A Review." In: *Cultures in Contact: The Impact of European Contacts on Native American Cultural Institutions A.D. 1000–1800*, William W. Fitzhugh, ed., pp. 23–43. Washington, D.C.: Smithsonian Institution Press.

1988 "Comparative Art on the North Pacific Rim." In: *Crossroads of Continents: Cultures of Siberia and Alaska*, William W.

Fitzhugh and Aron Crowell, eds., pp. 294–312. Washington, D.C.: Smithsonian Institution Press.

1997 "Biogeographical Archaeology in the Eastern North American Arctic." *Human Ecology* 25(3):385–418.

2006 "Settlement, Social and Ceremonial Change in the Labrador Maritime Archaic." In: *The Archaic of the Far Northeast*, David Sanger and M. A. P. Renouf, eds., pp. 47–81. Orono: University of Maine Press.

1985 (ed.) *Cultures in Contact: The Impact of European Contacts on Native American Cultural Institutions A.D. 1000–1800*. Washington, D.C.: Smithsonian Institution Press.

Fladmark, Knut R. 1975 "A Paleoecological Model for Northwest Coast Prehistory." Canadian Museum of Civilization, Mercury Series, Archaeological Survey of Canada, Paper 43.

1979 "Routes: Alternative Migration Corridors for Early Man in North America." *American Antiquity* 44(1):55–69.

1982 An Introduction to the Prehistory of British Columbia. *Canadian Journal of Archaeology* 6:95–156.

1983 "Times and Places: Environmental Correlates to Mid-to-Late Wisconsin Human Population Expansion in North America." In: *Early Man in the New World*, Richard Shutler, Jr., ed., pp. 13–42. Beverly Hills: Sage Publications.

1996 "The Prehistory of Charlie Lake Cave." In: *Early Human Occupation in British Columbia*, Roy L. Carlson and Luke Dalla Bona, eds., pp. 11–20. Vancouver: University of British Columbia Press.

Fladmark, Knut R., Kenneth M. Ames, and Patricia D. Sutherland 1990 "Prehistory of the Northern Coast of British Columbia." In: *Handbook of North American Indians, Vol. 7, Northwest Coast*, Wayne Suttles, ed., pp. 229–239. Washington, D.C.: Smithsonian Institution.

Flenniken, J. Jeffrey, and Philip J. Wilke 1989 "Typology, Technology, and Chronology of Great Basin Dart Points." *American Anthropologist* 91(1):149–158.

Fogelson, Raymond D. (ed.) 2004 *Handbook of North American Indians, Vol. 14, Southeast*. Washington, D.C.: Smithsonian Institution.

Ford, Richard I. 1979 "Gardening and Gathering: Trends and Consequences of Hopewell Subsistence Strategies." In: *Hopewell Archaeology: The Chillicothe Conference*, David S. Brose and N'omi B. Greber, eds., pp. 234–238. *Mid-Continental Journal of Archaeology Special Paper 3*.

Forster, Peter, Rosalind Harding, Antonio Torroni, and Hans-Jürgen Bandelt 1996 "Origin and Evolution of Native American mtDNA Variation: A Reappraisal." *American Journal of Human Genetics* 59(4):935–945.

Fowler, Catherine S., and Don D. Fowler 1990 "A History of Wetlands Anthropology in the Great Basin." In: *Wetlands Adaptation in the Great Basin*, Joel C. Janetski and David B. Madsen, eds., pp 5–16. Provo, UT: Brigham Young University, Museum of Peoples and Cultures, Occasional Paper No. 1.

2008 (eds.) *The Great Basin: People and Place in Ancient Times*. Santa Fe, NM: School of American Research.

Fowler, Catherine S., and Eugene M. Hattori 2008 "The Great Basin's Oldest Textiles." In: *The Great Basin: People and Place* *in Ancient Times*, Catherine S. Fowler and Don D. Fowler, eds., pp. 60–67. Santa Fe, NM: School of American Research.

Fowler, Don D. 1986 "History of Research." In: *Handbook of North American Indians, Vol. 11, Great Basin*, Warren L. d'Azevedo, ed., pp. 15–30. Washington, DC: Smithsonian Institution.

2000 *A Laboratory for Anthropology: Science and Romanticism in the American Southwest, 1846–1930*. Albuquerque: University of New Mexico Press.

Fowler, Don D., and David Koch 1982 "The Great Basin." In: *Reference Handbook on the Deserts of North America*, Gordon L. Bender, ed., pp. 7–63. Westport, CT: Greenwood Press.

Fowler, Melvin L. 1978 "Cahokia and the American Bottom: Settlement Archaeology." In: *Mississippian Settlement Patterns*, Bruce D. Smith, ed., pp. 455–478. New York: Academic Press.

Fowles, Severin M. 2009 "The Enshrined Pueblo: Villagescape and Cosmos in the Northern Rio Grande." *American Antiquity* 74(3):448–466.

Fredrickson, David A. 1965 "Buena Vista Lake: Thirty Years After Wedel." Paper presented at the annual meetings of the Southwestern Anthropological Association, University of California, Los Angeles.

1974 "Cultural Diversity in Early Central California: A View from the North Coast Ranges." *Journal of California Anthropology* 1(1):41–54.

1984 "The North Coastal Region." In: *California Archaeology*, Michael J. Moratto, pp. 471–527. Orlando: Academic Press.

Fredrickson, David A., and Joel W. Grossman 1977 "A San Dieguito Component at Buena Vista Lake, California." *Journal of California Anthropology* 4(2):173–190.

Fredrickson, David A., and Gregory G. White 1988 "The Clear Lake Basin and Early Complexes in California's North Coast Ranges." In: "Early Human Occupation in Far Western North America: The Clovis-Archaic Interface," Judith A. Willig, C. Melvin Aikens, and John L. Fagan, eds., pp. 75–86. Special issue, *Nevada State Museum Anthropological Papers* No. 21.

Friesen, T. Max 2004 "Contemporaneity of Dorset and Thule Cultures in the North American Arctic: New Radiocarbon Dates from Victoria Island, Nunavut." *Current Anthropology* 45(5):685–691.

2007 "Hearth Rows, Hierarchies and Arctic Hunter-Gatherers: The Construction of Equality in the Late Dorset Period." *World Archaeology* 39(2):194–214.

Friesen, T. Max, and Charles D. Arnold 2008 "The Timing of the Thule Migration: New Dates from the Western Canadian Arctic." *American Antiquity* 73(3):527–538.

Friesen, T. Max, and Andrew M. Stewart 2004 "Variation in Subsistence among Inland Inuit: Zooarchaeology of Two Sites on the Kazan River, Nunavut." *Canadian Journal of Archaeology* 28(1):32–50.

Frink, Lisa, and Karen G. Harry 2008 "The Beauty of 'Ugly' Eskimo Cooking Pots." *American Antiquity* 73(1):103–118.

Frison, George C. 1991 *Prehistoric Hunters of the High Plains* (2nd ed.). San Diego: Academic Press.

1998 "The Northwestern and Northern Plains Archaic." In: *Archaeology on the Great Plains*, W. Raymond Wood, ed., pp. 140–172. Lawrence: University of Kansas Press.

1999 "The Late Pleistocene Prehistory of the Northwestern Plains, the Adjacent Mountains, and Intermontane Basin." In: *Ice Age Peoples of North America: Environments, Origins, and Adaptations of the First Americans*, Robson Bonnichsen and Karen L. Turnmire, eds., pp. 264–280. Oregon State University: Center for the Study of the First Americans.

2001 "Hunting and Gathering Tradition: Northwestern and Central Plains." In: *Handbook of North American Indians, Vol. 13, Plains*, Raymond J. DeMallie, ed., pp. 131–145. Washington, D.C.: Smithsonian Institution.

Frison, George C., and Robson Bonnichsen 1996 "The Pleistocene-Holocene Transition on the Plains and Rocky Mountains of North America." In: *Humans at the End of the Ice Age: The Archaeology of the Pleistocene-Holocene Transition*, Lawrence Guy Straus, Berit Valentin Eriksen, Jon M. Erlandson, and David R. Yesner, eds., pp. 303–318. New York: Plenum Press.

Frison, George C., and Bruce Bradley 1999 *The Fenn Cache: Clovis Weapons and Tools*. Santa Fe: One Horse Land and Cattle Company.

Frison, George C., and Dennis J. Stanford 1982 *The Agate Basin Site: A Record of the Paleoindian Occupation of the Northwestern High Plains*. New York: Academic Press.

Frison, George C., and Danny N. Walker (eds.) 2007 *Medicine Lodge Creek: Holocene Archaeology of the Eastern Big Horn Basin, Wyoming, Volume 1*. Phoenix: Clovis Press.

Frison, George C., R. L. Andrews, James M. Adovasio, Ronald C. Carlisle, and Robert Edgar 1986 "A Late Paleoindian Animal Trapping Net from Northern Wyoming." *American Antiquity* 51(2):352–361.

Fritz, Gayle J. 2000 "Native Farming Systems and Ecosystems in the Mississippi River Valley." In: *Imperfect Balance: Landscape Transformations in the Precolumbian Americas*, David L. Lentz, ed., pp. 225–249. New York: Columbia University Press.

Fujita, Harumi 1995 "Prehistoric Coastal Adaptations in the Cape Region, Baja California." *Pacific Coast Archaeological Society Quarterly* 31(1–2):4–19.

2006 "The Cape Region." In: *Advances in the Archaeology of the Forgotten Peninsula*, Don Laylander and Jerry D. Moore, eds., pp. 82–98. Gainesville: University Press of Florida.

Funk, Robert E. 1988 "The Laurentian Concept: A Review." *Archaeology of Eastern North America* 16:1–42.

1991 "The Middle Archaic in New York." *Journal of Middle Atlantic Archaeology* 7:7–18.

Gallaga, Emiliano, and Gillian E. Newell 2004 "Introduction." In: *Surveying the Archaeology of Northwest Mexico*, Gillian E. Newell and Emiliano Gallaga, eds., pp. 1–23. Salt Lake City: University of Utah Press.

Gallivan, Martin D. 2003 *James River Chiefdoms: The Rise of Social Inequality in the Chesapeake*. Lincoln: University of Nebraska Press.

Galm, Jerry R. 1994 "Prehistoric Trade and Exchange in the Interior Plateau of Northwestern North America." In: *Prehistoric Exchange Systems in North America*, Timothy G. Baugh and Jonathon E. Ericson, eds., pp. 275–305. New York: Plenum Press.

Galm, Jerry R., and Stan Gough 2000 "Site 45KT1362, a c. 10,000 yr B.P. Occupation in Central Washington." *Current Research in the Pleistocene* 17:29–31.

Gamble, Lynn H. 1995 "Chumash Architecture: Sweatlodges and Houses." *Journal of California and Great Basin Anthropology* 17(1):54–92.

2002 "Archaeological Evidence for the Origin of the Plank Canoe in North America." *American Antiquity* 67(2):301–315.

2008 *The Chumash World at European Contact.* Berkeley: University of California Press.

Gamble, Lynn H., Phillip L. Walker, and Glenn S. Russell 2001 "An Integrative Approach to Mortuary Analysis: Social and Symbolic Dimensions of Chumash Burial Practices." *American Antiquity* 66(2):185–212.

2002 "Further Considerations on the Emergence of Chumash Chiefdoms." *American Antiquity* 67(4):772–777.

Gardner, James S. 1981 "General Environment." In: *Handbook of North American Indians, Vol. 6, Subarctic,* June Helm, ed., pp. 5–14. Washington, D.C.: Smithsonian Institution.

Gardner, Jill K. 2007 *The Potential Impact of the Medieval Climatic Anomaly on Human Populations in the Western Mojave Desert.* Salinas: Coyote Press Archives of Great Basin Prehistory No. 7.

Gardner, William M. 1974 "The Flint Run Complex: Pattern and Process During the Paleo-Indian to Early Archaic." In: *The Flint Run Paleo-Indian Complex: A Preliminary Report 1971–73 Seasons,* William M. Gardner, ed., pp. 5–47. Washington, D.C.: Catholic University of America, Archaeology Laboratory, Occasional Paper No. 1.

Gerlach, Craig, and Owen K. Mason 1992 "Calibrated Radiocarbon Dates and Cultural Interaction in the Western Arctic." *Arctic Anthropology* 29(1):54–81.

Gibbon, Guy (ed.) 1998 *Archaeology of Prehistoric Native America: An Encyclopedia.* New York: Garland Publishing, Inc.

Gibson, Jon L. 1996 "Poverty Point and Greater Southeastern Prehistory." In: *Archaeology of the Mid-Holocene Southeast,* Kenneth E. Sassaman and David G. Anderson, eds., pp. 288–305. Gainesville: University Press of Florida.

2001 *The Ancient Mounds of Poverty Point: Place of Rings.* Gainesville: University Press of Florida.

2004 "The Power of Beneficent Obligation in First Mound-Building Societies." In: *Signs of Power: The Rise of Cultural Complexity in the Southeast,* Jon L. Gibson and Philip J. Carr, eds., pp. 254–269. Tuscaloosa: University of Alabama Press.

2006 "Navels of the Earth: Sedentism in Early Mound-Building Cultures in the Lower Mississippi Valley." *World Archaeology* 38(2):311–329.

2007 "'Formed from the Earth at that Place': The Material Side of Community at Poverty Point." *American Antiquity* 72(3):509–523.

Giddings, James L., Jr. 1951 "The Denbigh Flint Complex." *American Antiquity* 16(3):193–203.

1964 *The Archaeology of Cape Dinbigh.* Providence, RI: Brown University Press.

Giddings, James L., and Douglas D. Anderson 1986 *Beach Ridge Archeology of Cape Krusenstern: Eskimo and Pre-Eskimo Settlements Around Kotzebue Sound, Alaska.* Washington, DC: National Park Service, Publications in Archeology 20.

Gifford, Edward W. 1947 "Californian Shell Artifacts." *University of California Anthropological Records* 9(1).

Gilbert, M. Thomas P., Dennis L. Jenkins, Anders Götherstrom, Nuria Naveran, Juan J. Sanchez, Michael Hofreiter, Philip Francis Thomsen, Jonas Binladen, Thomas F. G. Higham, Robert M. Yohe II, Robert Parr, Linda Scott Cummings, and Eske Willerslev 2008 "DNA from Pre-Clovis Human Coprolites in Oregon, North America." *Science* 320:786–789.

Gill, George W. 2005 "Appearance of the 'Mongoloid Skeletal Trait Complex' in the Northwestern Great Plains: Migration, Selection, or Both?" In: *Paleoamerican Origins: Beyond Clovis,* Robson Bonnichsen, Bradley T. Lepper, Dennis Stanford, and Michael R. Waters, eds., pp. 257–266. Texas A&M University: Center for the Study of the First Americans.

Gill, Jacquelyn L., John W. Williams, Stephen T. Jackson, Katherine B. Lininger, and Guy S. Robinson 2009 "Pleistocene Megafaunal Collapse, Novel Plant Communities, and Enhanced Fire Regimes in North America." *Science* 326:1100–1103.

Gillespie, Jason D. 2007 "Enculturing an Unknown World: Caches and Clovis Landscape Ideology. *Canadian Journal of Archaeology* 31(2):171–189.

Gilreath, Amy J., and William R. Hildebrandt 2008 "Coso Rock Art within Its Archaeological Context." *Journal of California and Great Basin Anthropology* 28(1):1–22.

Gladwin, Winifred, and Harold S. Gladwin 1930 *Some Southwestern Pottery Types: Series I.* Globe, NM: Medallion Papers No. 8.

Gladwin, Harold S., Emil W. Haury, Edwin B. Sayles, and Nora Gladwin 1938 *Excavations at Snaketown I: Material Culture.* Globe, NM: Medallion Papers No. 25.

Glassow, Michael A. 1991 "Early Holocene Adaptations on Vandenberg Air Force Base, Santa Barbara County." In: *Hunter-Gatherers of Early Holocene Coastal California,* Jon M. Erlandson and Roger H. Colten, eds., pp. 113–124. University of California Los Angeles, Institute of Archaeology, Perspectives in California Archaeology, Vol. 1.

1996 *Purisimeño Chumash Prehistory: Maritime Adaptations Along the Southern California Coast.* Fort Worth: Harcourt Brace.

1997 "Research Issues of Importance to Coastal California Archaeology of the Middle Holocene." In: *Archaeology of the California Coast During the Middle Holocene,* Jon M. Erlandson and Michael A. Glassow, eds., pp. 151–161. University of California Los Angeles, Institute of Archaeology, Perspectives in California Archaeology, Vol. 4.

1999 "Measurement of Population Growth and Decline During California Prehistory." *Journal of California and Great Basin Anthropology* 21(1):45–66.

Glassow, Michael A., Lynn H. Gamble, Jennifer E. Perry, and Glenn S. Russell 2007 "Prehistory of the Northern California Bight and the Adjacent Transverse Ranges." In: *California*

Prehistory: Colonization, Culture, and Complexity, Terry L. Jones and Kathryn A. Klar, eds., pp. 191–213. Lanham, MD: AltaMira Press.

Goddard, Ives, and Lyle Campbell 1994 "The History and Classification of American Indian Languages: What Are the Implications for the Peopling of the New World?" In: *Method and Theory for Investigating the Peopling of the Americas*, Robson Bonnichsen, and D. Gentry Steele, eds., pp. 189–207. Oregon State University: Center for the Study of the First Americans.

Goebel, Ted 1999 "Pleistocene Human Colonization of Siberia and Peopling of the Americas: An Ecological Approach." *Evolutionary Anthropology* 8(6):208–227.

2002 "The 'Microblade Adaptation' and Recolonization of Siberia during the Late Upper Pleistocene." In: "Thinking Small: Global Perspectives on Microlithization," Robert G. Elston and Steven L. Kuhn, eds., pp. 117–131. Special issue, *Archeological Papers of the American Anthropological Association*, No. 12.

2004 "The Search for a Clovis Progenitor in Sub-Arctic Siberia." In: *Entering America: Northeast Asia and Beringia Before the Last Glacial Maximum*, David B. Madsen, ed., pp. 311–356. Salt Lake City: University of Utah Press.

Goebel, Ted, and Nancy H. Bigelow 1992 "The Denali Complex at Panguingue Creek, Central Alaska." *Current Research in the Pleistocene* 9:15–18.

Goebel, Ted, Kelly E. Graf, Bryan Scott Hockett, and David Rhode 2003b "Late-Pleistocene Humans at Bonneville Estates Rockshelter, Eastern Nevada." *Current Research in the Pleistocene* 20:20–23.

Goebel, Ted, W., Roger Powers, and Nancy H. Bigelow 1991 "The Nenana Complex of Alaska and Clovis Origins." In: *Clovis: Origins and Adaptations*, Robson Bonnichsen and Karen L. Turnmire, eds., pp. 49–79. Oregon State University: Center for the Study of the First Americans.

Goebel, Ted, W., Roger Powers, Nancy H. Bigelow, and Andrew S. Higgs 1996 "Walker Road." In: *American Beginnings: The Prehistory and Paleoecology of Beringia*, Frederick Hadleigh West, ed., pp. 356–363. Chicago: University of Chicago Press.

Goebel, Ted, and Sergei B. Slobodin 1999 "The Colonization of Western Beringia: Technology, Ecology, and Adaptations." In: *Ice Age Peoples of North America: Environments, Origins, and Adaptations of the First Americans*, Robson Bonnichsen and Karen L. Turnmire, eds., pp. 104–155. Oregon State University: Center for the Study of the First Americans.

Goebel, Ted, Michael R. Waters, and Margarita A. Dikova 2003a "The Archaeology of Ushki Lake, Kamchatka, and the Pleistocene Peopling of the Americas." *Science* 301:501–505.

Goebel, Ted, Michael R. Waters, and Dennis H. O'Rourke 2008 "The Late Pleistocene Dispersal of Modern Humans in the Americas." *Science* 319:1497–1502.

Goldberg, Paul, and Trina L. Arpin 1999 "Micromorphological Analysis of Sediments from Meadowcroft Rockshelter, Pennsylvania: Implications for Radiocarbon Dating." *Journal of Field Archaeology* 26(3):325–342.

Goldstein, Lynne 2002 "Exploring Aztalan and Its Role in Mississippian Societies." In: *Archaeology: Original Readings in*

Method and Practice, Peter N. Peregrine, Carol R. Ember, and Melvin Ember, eds., pp. 337–359. Upper Saddle River, NJ: Prentice Hall.

Golla, Victor 2007 "Linguistic Prehistory." In: *California Prehistory: Colonization, Culture, and Complexity*, Terry L. Jones and Kathryn A. Klar, eds., pp. 71–82. Lanham, MD: AltaMira Press.

González, Arturo H., and Carmen A. Sandoval 2005 "Early Humans South of the Border: New Finds from the Yucatán Peninsula." *Mammoth Trumpet* 20(3):8–11.

González-José, Rolondo, Antonio González-Martin, Miquel Hernández, Héctor M. Pucciarelli, Marina L. Sardi, Alfonso Rosales, and Silvina Van der Molen 2003 "Craniometric Evidence for Palaeoamerican Survival in Baja California." *Nature* 425:62–65.

Goodman, Alan H., and George J. Armelagos 1985 "Disease and Death at Dr. Dickson's Mounds." *Natural History* 94(9):12–18.

Goodyear, Albert C. 1982 "The Chronological Position of the Dalton Horizon in the Southeastern United States." *American Antiquity* 47(2):382–395.

1999 "The Early Holocene Occupation of the Southeastern United States: A Geoarchaeological Summary." In: *Ice Age Peoples of North America: Environments, Origins, and Adaptations of the First Americans*, Robson Bonnichsen and Karen L. Turnmire, eds., pp. 432–481. Oregon State University: Center for the Study of the First Americans.

2003 "Backhoes, BBQs, and B Horizons: The 2002 Allendale Paleoindian Expedition." South Carolina Institute of Archaeology and Anthropology, *Legacy* 8(1):22–29.

2005 "Evidence for Pre-Clovis Sites in the Eastern United States." In: *Paleoamerican Origins: Beyond Clovis*, Robson Bonnichsen, Bradley T. Lepper, Dennis Stanford, and Michael R. Waters, eds., pp. 103–112. Texas A&M University: Center for the Study of the First Americans.

Goodyear, Albert C., and Kenn Steffy 2003 "Evidence of a Clovis Occupation at the Topper Site, 38AL23, Allendale County, South Carolina." *Current Research in the Pleistocene* 20:23–25.

Gordon, Bryan C. 1996 "People of Sunlight, People of Starlight: Barrenland Archaeology in the Northwest Territories of Canada." Canadian Museum of Civilization, Mercury Series, Archaeological Survey of Canada, Paper 154.

Gortner, Willis A. 1990 "Evidence for a Prehistoric Trail Map in the Sierra Nevada III: A Fourth 'Glyph Map' and a Composite of the Trails." *North American Archaeologist* 11(2):99–106.

1994 "Bear Paw Petroglyphs and the Prehistoric Martis Complex." *North American Archaeologist* 15(1):69–76.

Gould, Richard A. 1966 "Archaeology of the Point St. George Site, and Tolowa Prehistory." *University of California Publications in Anthropology* No. 4.

Graburn, Nelson H. H. 1976 "Eskimo Art: The Eastern Canadian Arctic." In: *Ethnic and Tourist Arts: Cultural Expressions from the Fourth World*, Nelson H. H. Graburn, ed., pp. 39–55. Berkeley: University of California Press.

Gramly, Richard M. 1982 "The Vail Site: A Palaeo-Indian Encampment in Maine." *Bulletin of the Buffalo Society of Natural Science* 30.

1991 "Blood Residues upon Tools from the East Wenatchee Clovis Site, Douglas County, Washington." *Ohio Archaeologist* 41(4):4–9.

1993 *The Richey Clovis Cache: Earliest Americans along the Columbia River*. Buffalo, NY: Persimmon Press.

1999 *The Lamb Site: A Pioneering Clovis Encampment*. Buffalo, NY: Persimmon Press.

Gramly, Richard M., and Robert E. Funk 1990 "What Is Known and Not Known about the Human Occupation of the Northeastern Untied States until 10,000 B.P." *Archaeology of Eastern North America* 18:5–31.

Grant, Campbell, James W. Baird, and J. Kenneth Pringle 1968 *Rock Drawings of the Coso Range, Inyo County, California*. Maturango Museum Publication No. 4.

Graumlich, Lisa J. 1993 A 1000-Year Record of Temperature and Precipitation in the Sierra Nevada. *Quaternary Research* 39(2):249–255.

Graybill, Donald A. 1989 "The Reconstruction of the Prehistoric Salt River Streamflow." In: *The 1982–1984 Excavations at Las Colinas: Environment and Subsistence*, Lynn S. Teague and William L. Deaver, eds., pp. 25–38. Tucson: Arizona State Museum, Archaeological Series No. 162, Vol. 5.

Graybill, Donald A., David A. Gregory, Gary S. Funkhouser, and Fred L. Nials 2006 "Long-Term Streamflow Reconstructions, River Channel Morphology, and Aboriginal Irrigation Systems along the Salt and Gila Rivers." In: *Environmental Change and Human Adaptation in the Ancient American Southwest*, David E. Doyel and Jeffrey S. Dean, eds., pp. 69–123. Salt Lake City: University of Utah Press.

Grayson, Donald K. 1991 "Late Pleistocene Mammalian Extinctions in North America: Taxonomy, Chronology, and Explanations." *Journal of World Prehistory* 5(3):193–231.

1993 *The Desert's Past*. Washington, D.C.: Smithsonian Institution Press.

2001 "The Archaeological Record of Human Impacts on Animal Populations." *Journal of World Prehistory* 15(1):1–68.

2008 "Great Basin Natural History." In: *The Great Basin: People and Place in Ancient Times*, Catherine S. Fowler and Don D. Fowler, eds., pp. 6–17. Santa Fe, NM: School of American Research.

Grayson, Donald K., and David J. Meltzer 2002 "Clovis Hunting and Large Mammal Extinction: A Critical Review of the Evidence." *Journal of World Prehistory* 16(4):313–359.

2003 "A Requiem for North American Overkill." *Journal of Archaeological Science* 30(5):585–593.

Greber, N'omi B., and Katharine C. Ruhl 1989 *The Hopewell Site: A Contemporary Analysis Based on the Work of Charles C. Willoughby*. Boulder: Westview Press Investigations in American Archaeology.

Green, D'Arcy Clarke 2005 "A Re-Evaluation of the Oxbow Dam Site (DhMn-1): Middle Holocene Cultural Continuity on the Northern Plains." *Occasional Papers of the Archaeological Society of Alberta* No. 5.

Green, Thomas J. 1993 "Aboriginal Residential Structures in Southern Idaho." *Journal of California and Great Basin Anthropology* 15(1):58–72.

Green, Thomas J., Max G. Pavesic, James C. Woods, and Gene L. Titmus 1986 "The DeMoss Burial Locality: Preliminary Observations." *Idaho Archaeologist* 9(2):31–40.

Green, Thomas J., Bruce Cochran, Todd W. Fenton, James C. Woods, Gene L. Titmus, Larry Tieszen, Mary Anne Davis, and Susanne J. Miller 1998 "The Buhl Burial: A Paleoindian Woman from Southern Idaho." *American Antiquity* 63(3):437–456.

Greenberg, Joseph H. 1987 *Language in the Americas*. Stanford: Stanford University Press.

Greenberg, Joseph H., Christy G. Turner II, and Stephen L. Zegura 1986 "The Settlement of the Americas: A Comparison of the Linguistic, Dental, and Genetic Evidence." *Current Anthropology* 27(5):477–497.

Greenwood, Roberta S. 1969 "The Browne Site: Early Milling Stone Horizon in Southern California." *Society for American Archaeology Memoir* No. 23.

1972 "9000 Years of Prehistory at Diablo Canyon, San Luis Obispo County, California." *San Luis Obispo County Archaeological Society Occasional Paper* No. 7.

Greer, Sheila C. 1993 "Annie Lake: A Southern Yukon Mid-Holocene Cultural Complex." *Canadian Journal of Archaeology* 17:26–42.

Gregg, Michael L. 1975 "A Population Estimate for Cahokia." In: *Perspectives in Cahokia Archaeology*, James A. Brown, ed., pp. 126–136. Urbana: Illinois Archaeological Survey, Bulletin 10.

Gremillion, Kristen J. 1996a "Early Agricultural Diet in Eastern North America: Evidence from Two Kentucky Rockshelters." *American Antiquity* 61(3):520–536.

1996b "The Paleoethnobotanical Record for the Mid-Holocene Southeast." In: *Archaeology of the Mid-Holocene Southeast*, Kenneth E. Sassaman and David G. Anderson, eds., pp. 99–114. Gainesville: University Press of Florida.

2002 "The Development and Dispersal of Agricultural Systems in the Woodland Period Southeast." In: *The Woodland Southeast*, David G. Anderson and Robert C. Mainfort, Jr., eds., pp. 483–501. Tuscaloosa: University of Alabama Press.

2004a "Seed Processing and the Origins of Food Production in Eastern North America." *American Antiquity* 69(2):215–233.

2004b "Environment." In: *Handbook of North American Indians, Vol. 14, Southeast*, Raymond D. Fogelson, ed., pp. 53–67. Washington, D.C.: Smithsonian Institution.

2006 "Central Place Foraging and Food Production on the Cumberland Plateau, Eastern Kentucky." In: *Behavioral Ecology and the Transition to Agriculture*, Douglas J. Kennett and Bruce Winterhalder, eds., pp. 41–62. Berkeley: University of California Press.

Grier, Colin 2003 "Dimensions of Regional Interaction in the Prehistoric Gulf of Georgia." In: *Emerging from the Mist: Studies in Northwest Coast Culture History*, R. G. Matson, G. Coupland, and Q. Mackie, eds., pp. 170–187. Vancouver: University of British Columbia Press.

Griffin, James B. 1952 *Archeology of the Eastern United States.* Chicago: University of Chicago Press.

Griset, Suzanne (ed.) 1986 "Pottery of the Great Basin and Adjacent Areas." *University of Utah Anthropological Papers* No. 111.

Grønnow, Bjarne 1994 "Qeqertasussuk: The Archaeology of a Frozen Saqqaq Site in Disko Bugt, West Greenland." In: *Threads of Arctic Prehistory, Papers in Honor of William E. Taylor, Jr.*, David Morrison and Jean-Luc Pilon, eds., pp. 197–238. Canadian Museum of Civilization, Mercury Series, Archaeological Survey of Canada, Paper 149.

Gruhn, Ruth 1988 "Linguistic Evidence in Support of a Coastal Route of Earliest Entry into the New World." *Man* 23(1):77–100.

1994 "The Pacific Coast Route of Initial Entry: An Overview." In: *Method and Theory for Investigating the Peopling of the Americas*, Robson Bonnichsen, and D. Gentry Steele, eds., pp. 249–256. Oregon State University: Center for the Study of the First Americans.

1997 "The South American Context of the Pedra Pintada Site in Brazil." *Current Research in the Pleistocene* 14:29–32.

2004 "Current Archaeological Evidence of Late-Pleistocene Settlement of South America." In: *New Perspectives on the First Americans*, Bradley T. Lepper and Robson Bonnichsen, eds., pp. 27–34. Texas A&M University: Center for the Study of the First Americans.

2005 "The Ignored Continent: South America in Models of Earliest American Prehistory." In: *Paleoamerican Origins: Beyond Clovis*, Robson Bonnichsen, Bradley T. Lepper, Dennis Stanford, and Michael R. Waters, eds., pp. 199–208. Texas A&M University: Center for the Study of the First Americans.

2006 "New Excavations at Wilson Butte Cave, South-Central Idaho. Pocatello." *Occasional Papers of the Idaho Museum of Natural History* 38.

Gruhn, Ruth, and Alan R. Bryan 1991 "A Review of Lynch's Descriptions of South American Pleistocene Sites." *American Antiquity* 56(2):342–348.

2009 "An Interim Report on Two Rockshelter Sites with Early Holocene Occupation in the Northern Baja California Peninsula." *Pacific Coast Archaeological Society Quarterly* 42(2&3):1–16.

Guest, Francis F., O.F.M. 1979 "An Examination of the Thesis of S. F. Cook on the Forced Conversion of Indians in the California Missions." *Southern California Quarterly* 61(1):1–77.

1983 "Cultural Perspectives on California Mission Life." *Southern California Quarterly* 65(1):1–65.

Guidon, Nìede, and B. Arnaud 1991 "The Chronology of the New World: Two Faces of One Reality." *World Archaeology* 23(2):167–168.

Guidon, Nìede, and G. Delibrias 1986 "Carbon-14 Dates Point to Man in the Americas 32,000 Years Ago." *Nature* 321:769–771.

Guidon, Nìede, A. M. Pessis, Fabio Parenti, Michel Fontugue, and Claude Guérin 1996 "Nature and Age of the Deposits in Pedra Furada, Brazil: Reply to Meltzer, Adovasio, and Dillehay." *Antiquity* 70(268):408–421.

Gumerman, George J., and Emil W. Haury 1979 "Prehistory: Hohokam." In: *Handbook of North American Indians, Vol. 9, Southwest*, Alfonzo Ortiz, ed., pp. 75–90. Washington, D. C.: Smithsonian Institution.

Gunnerson, James H. 1969 "The Fremont Culture." *Papers of the Peabody Museum of Archaeology and Ethnology* 59(2).

2001 "Plains Village Tradition: Western Periphery." In: *Handbook of North American Indians, Vol. 13, Plains*, Raymond J. DeMallie, ed., pp. 234–244. Washington, D.C.: Smithsonian Institution.

Gusev, Sergey V., Andrey V. Zagoroulko, and Aleksey V. Porotov 1999 "Sea Mammal Hunters of Chukotka, Bering Strait: Recent Archaeological Results and Problems." *World Archaeology* 30(3):354–369.

Guthrie, R. Dale 2003 "Rapid Body Size Decline in Alaskan Pleistocene Horses before Extinction." *Nature* 426:169–171.

Haag, William G. 1993 "Archaeoastronomy in the Southeast." In: *Archaeology of Eastern North America: Papers in Honor of Stephen Williams*, James B. Stoltman, ed., pp. 103–110. Jackson: Mississippi Department of Archives and History, Archaeological Report No. 25.

Haas, Jonathan, and Winifred Creamer 1996 "The Role of Warfare in the Pueblo III Period." In: *The Prehistoric Pueblo World, A.D. 1150–1350*, Michael A. Adler, ed., pp. 205–213. Tucson: University of Arizona Press.

Haines, Francis 1938 "The Northward Spread of Horses among the Plains Indians." *American Anthropologist* 40(3):429–437.

Hall, Robert L. 2000 "Cahokia Identity and Interaction Models of Cahokia Mississippian." In: *Cahokia and the Hinterlands: Middle Mississippian Cultures of the Midwest*, Thomas E. Emerson and R. Barry Lewis, eds., pp. 3–34. Chicago: University of Illinois Press.

Hall, Roberta, Diana Roy, and David Boling 2004 "Pleistocene Migration Routes into the Americas: Human Biological Adaptations and Environmental Constraints." *Evolutionary Anthropology* 13:132–144.

Hallett, D. J., L. V. Hills, and J. J. Clague 1997 "New Accelerator Mass Spectrometry Radiocarbon Ages for the Mazama Tephra Layer from Kootenay National Park, British Columbia, Canada." *Canadian Journal of Earth Sciences* 34(9):1202–1209.

Hally, David J. 1993 "The Territorial Size of Mississippian Chiefdoms." In: *Archaeology of Eastern North America: Papers in Honor of Stephen Williams*, James B. Stoltman, ed., pp. 143–168. Jackson: Mississippi Department of Archives and History, Archaeological Report No. 25.

1999 "The Settlement Pattern of Mississippian Chiefdoms in Northern Georgia." In: *Settlement Pattern Studies in the Americas: Fifty Years Since Virú*, Brian R. Billman and Gary M. Feinman, eds., pp. 96–115. Washington, D.C.: Smithsonian Institution Press.

2008 *King: The Social Archaeology of a Late Mississippian Town in Northwestern Georgia.* Tuscaloosa: University of Alabama Press.

Ham, Leonard C. 1990 "The Cohoe Creek Site: A Late Moresby Tradition Shell Midden." *Canadian Journal of Archaeology* 14:199–121.

Hamilton, Fran E. 1999 "Southeastern Archaic Mounds: Examples of Elaboration in a Temporally Fluctuating Environment?" *Journal of Anthropological Archaeology* 18(3):344–355.

Hamilton, Scott 2000 "Archaeological Predictive Modelling in the Boreal Forest: No Easy Answers." *Canadian Journal of Archaeology* 24:41–76.

Hamilton, Thomas D., and Ted Goebel 1999 "Late Pleistocene Peopling of Alaska." In: *Ice Age Peoples of North America: Environments, Origins, and Adaptations of the First Americans*, Robson Bonnichsen and Karen L. Turnmire, eds., pp. 156–199. Oregon State University: Center for the Study of the First Americans.

Hanson, Diane K. 2008 "Salmon and Models of Social Complexity on the Northwest Coast." *North Pacific Prehistory* 2:123–152.

Hanson, Jeffrey R. 1998 "The Late High Plains Hunters." In: *Archaeology on the Great Plains*, W. Raymond Wood, ed., pp. 456–480. Lawrence: University of Kansas Press.

Hansen, Jens Peder Hart, Jørgen Meldgaard, and Jørgen Nordqvist (eds.) 1991 *The Greenland Mummies*. Washington, D.C.: Smithsonian Institution Press.

Hantman, Jeffrey L., and Debra Gold 2002 "The Woodland in the Middle Atlantic: Ranking and Dynamic Political Stability." In: *The Woodland Southeast*, David G. Anderson and Robert C. Mainfort, Jr., eds., pp. 270–291. Tuscaloosa: University of Alabama Press.

Hard, Robert J., Raymond P. Mauldin, and Gerry R. Raymond 1966 "Mano Size, Stable Carbon Isotope Ratios, and Macrobotanical Remains as Multiple Lines of Evidence of Maize Dependence in the American Southwest." *Journal of Archaeological Method and Theory* 3(4):253–318.

Hard, Robert J., and John R. Roney 2005 "The Transition to Farming on the Río Casas Grandes and in the Southern Jornada Mogollon Region." In: *The Late Archaic Across the Borderlands: From Foraging to Farming*, Bradley J. Vierra, ed., pp. 141–186. Austin: University of Texas Press.

Hare, P. Gregory, Sheila Greer, Ruth Gotthardt, Richard Farnell, Vandy Bowyer, Charles Schweger, and Diane Strand 2004 "Ethnographic and Archaeological Investigations of Alpine Ice Patches of Southwest Yukon, Canada." *Arctic* 57(3):260–272.

Harmon, Marcel J. 2006 "Religion and the Mesoamerican Ball Game in the Casas Grandes Region of Northern Mexico." In: *Religion in the Prehispanic Southwest*, Christine S. VanPool, Todd L. VanPool, and David A. Phillips, eds., pp. 185–217. Lanham, MD: AltaMira Press.

Harp, Elmer, Jr. 1976 "Dorset Settlement Patterns in Newfoundland and Southeastern Hudson Bay." In: "Eastern Arctic Prehistory: Paleoeskimo Problems," Moreau S. Maxwell, ed., pp. 119–138. Special issue, *Memoirs of the Society for American Archaeology* No. 31.

1984 "History of Archaeology After 1945." In: *Handbook of North American Indians, Vol. 5, Arctic*, David Damas, ed., pp. 17–22. Washington, D.C.: Smithsonian Institution.

Harper, Kimball T. 1986 "Historical Environments." In: *Handbook of North American Indians, Vol. 11, Great Basin*, Warren L. d'Azevedo, ed., pp. 51–63. Washington, D.C.: Smithsonian Institution.

Harrington, Mark R. 1938 "Early Man at Borax Lake." *Carnegie Institution of Washington News Service Bulletin, School Edition* 4:259–261.

1948 "An Ancient Site at Borax Lake, California." *Southwest Museum Papers* No. 16.

Harrison, W. M., and E. S. Harrison 1966 *An Archaeological Sequence for the Hunting People of the Santa Barbara, California*. Los Angeles: University of California Archaeological Survey Annual Report, 1964–1965:91–178.

Hart, John P. 1999 "Maize Agriculture Evolution in the Eastern Woodlands of North America: A Darwinian Perspective." *Journal of Archaeological Method and Theory* 6(2):137–180.

2001 "Maize, Matrilocality, Migration, and Northern Iroquoian Evolution." *Journal of Archaeological Method and Theory* 8(2):151–182.

Hart, John P., and C. Margaret Scarry 1999 "The Age of Common Beans (*Phaseolus vulgaris*) in the Northeastern United States." *American Antiquity* 64(4):653–658.

Hart, John P., Hetty Jo Brumbach, and Robert Lusteck 2007 "Extending the Phytolith Evidence for Early Maize (*Zea mays ssp. mays*) and Squash (*Cucurbita sp.*) in Central New York." *American Antiquity* 72(3):563–583.

Hart, John P., Robert G. Thompson, and Hetty Jo Brumbach 2003 "Phytolith Evidence for Early Maize (*Zea mays*) in the Northern Finger Lakes Region of New York." *American Antiquity* 68(4):619–640.

Hart, John P., David L. Asch, C. Margaret Scarry, and Gary W. Crawford 2002 "The Age of the Common Bean (*Phaseolus vulgaris*) in the Northern Eastern Woodlands of North America." *Antiquity* 76(292):377–385.

Hartzell, Leslie Louise 1992 Hunter-Gatherer Adaptive Strategies and Lacustrine Environments in the Buena Vista Lake Basin, Kern County, California. Ph.D. dissertation, University of California, Davis.

Hasenstab, Robert J. 1996 "Aboriginal Settlement Patterns in Late Woodland Upper New York State." *Journal of Middle Atlantic Archaeology* 12:17–26.

1999 "Fishing, Farming, and Finding the Village Sites: Centering Late Woodland New England Algonquians." In: *The Archaeological Northeast*, Mary Ann Levine, Kenneth E. Sassaman, and Michael S. Nassaney, eds., pp. 139–153. Westport, CT: Bergin & Garvey.

Hassan, Fekri A. 1981 *Demographic Archaeology*. New York: Academic Press.

Haury, Emil W. 1936 *The Mogollon Culture of Southwestern New Mexico*. Globe, NM: Medallion Papers No. 20.

1976 *The Hohokam: Desert Farmers and Craftsmen: Excavations at Snaketown 1964-1965*. Tucson: University of Arizona Press.

Haviland, William A., and Marjory W. Power 1994 *The Original Vermonters: Native Inhabitants, Past and Present*. Hanover, NH: University Press of New England.

Haven, Samuel F. 1856 *Archaeology of the United States or Sketches, Historical and Bibliographical, of the Progress of Information and Opinion Regarding Vestiges of Antiquity in the United States*. Washington, D.C.: Smithsonian Contributions to Knowledge 8(2).

Hayden, Brian 1997a "Observations on the Prehistoric Social and Economic Structure of the North American Plateau." *World Archaeology* 29(2):242–261.

1997b *The Pithouses of Keatley Creek.* Fort Worth, TX: Harcourt Brace.

2005 "The Emergence of Large Villages and Large Residential Cooperate Group Structures Among Complex Hunter-Gatherers at Keatley Creek." *American Antiquity* 70(1):169–174.

Hayden, Brian, and Ron Adams 2004 "Ritual Structures in Transegalitarian Communities." In: *Complex Hunter-Gatherers: Evolution and Organization of Prehistoric Communities on the Plateau of Northwestern North America,* William C. Prentiss and Ian Kuijt, eds., pp. 84–102. Salt Lake City: University of Utah Press.

Hayden, Brian, and June M. Ryder 1991 "Prehistoric Cultural Collapse in the Lillooet Area." *American Antiquity* 56(1):50–65.

Hayden, Brian, and Rick Schulting 1997 "The Plateau Interaction Sphere and Late Prehistoric Cultural Complexity." *American Antiquity* 62(1):51–85.

Hayden, Brian, Edward Bakewell, and Rob Gargett 1996 "The World's Longest-Lived Corporate Group: Lithic Analysis Reveals Prehistoric Social Organization Near Lillooet, British Columbia." *American Antiquity* 61(2):341–356.

Hayden, Brian, Morley Eldridge, Anne Eldridge, and Aubrey Cannon 1985 "Complex Hunter-Gatherers in Interior British Columbia." In: *Prehistoric Hunter-Gatherers: The Emergence of Cultural Complexity*, T. Douglas Price and James A. Brown, eds., pp. 181–199. Orlando: Academic Press.

Hayden, Julian D. 1976 "Pre-Altithermal Archaeology of the Sierra Pinacate, Sonora, Mexico." *American Antiquity* 41(3):274–289.

Hayes, Geoffrey, Joan Brenner Coltrain, and Dennis O'Rourke 2005 "Molecular Archaeology of the Dorset, Thule, and Sadlermiut: Ancestor-Descent Relationships in Eastern North American Arctic Prehistory." In: *Contributions to the Study of the Dorset Paleoindians*, Patricia D. Sutherland, ed., pp. 11–32. Canadian Museum of Civilization, Mercury Series, Archaeological Survey of Canada, Paper 167.

Haynes, C. Vance, Jr. 1964 "Fluted Projectile Points: Their Age and Dispersion." *Science* 145:1408–1413.

1966 "Elephant Hunting in North America." *Scientific American* 214:104–112.

1980 "Paleoindian Charcoal from Meadowcroft Rockshelter: Is Contamination a Problem?" *American Antiquity* 45(3):582–587.

1991 "Geoarchaeological and Paleohydrological Evidence for a Clovis-Age Drought in North America and its Bering on Extinction." *Quaternary Research* 35(3):438–450.

1992 "Contributions of Radiocarbon Dating to the Geochronology of the Peopling of the New World." In: *Radiocarbon Dating after Four Decades: An Interdisciplinary Perspective*, R. E. Taylor, A. Long, and R. S. Kra, eds., pp. 355–374. New York: Springer-Verlag.

1993 "Clovis-Folsom Geochronology and Climate Change." In: *From Kostenki to Clovis: Upper Paleolithic—Paleo-Indian Adaptations*, Olga Soffer and N. D. Praslov, eds., pp. 219–236. New York: Plenum Press.

1995 "Geochronology of Paleoenvironmental Change, Clovis Type Site, Blackwater Draw, New Mexico." *Geoarchaeology* 19(5):317–388.

1999a "Clovis, Climate Change, and Extinction." Paper presented at the Clovis and Beyond Conference, Santa Fe.

1999b "Monte Verde and the Pre-Clovis Situation in America." *Discovering Archaeology, Special Report* (November/December):17–19.

2005 "Clovis, Pre-Clovis, Climate Change, and Extinction." In: *Paleoamerican Origins: Beyond Clovis*, Robson Bonnichsen, Bradley T. Lepper, Dennis Stanford, and Michael R. Waters, eds., pp. 113–132. Texas A&M University: Center for the Study of the First Americans.

2006 "The Rancholabrean Termination: Sudden Extinction in the Sand Pedro Valley, Arizona, 11,000 BC." In: *Paleoindian Archaeology: A Hemispheric Perspective*, Juliet E. Morrow and Cristóbal Gnecco, eds., pp. 139–163. Gainesville: University Press of Florida.

2008 "Younger Dryas 'Black Mats' and the Rancholabrean Termination in North America." *Proceedings of the National Academy of Sciences* 105(18):6520–6525.

Haynes, C. Vance, Jr., and George A. Agogino 1986 *Geochronology of Sandia Cave.* Oregon State University: Center for the Study of the First Americans.

Haynes, C. Vance, Jr., and Bruce B. Huckell (eds.) 2007 "Murray Springs: A Clovis Site with Multiple Activity Areas in the San Pedro Valley, Arizona." *Anthropological Papers of the University of Arizona* No. 71.

Haynes, C. Vance, Jr., D. J. Donahue, A. J. T. Jull, and T. H. Zabel 1984 "Application of Accelerator Dating to Fluted Point Paleoindian Sites." *Archaeology of Eastern North America* 12:184–191.

Haynes, Gary 1991 *Mammoths, Matadonts, and Elephants: Biology, Behavior, and the Fossil Record.* Cambridge, UK: Cambridge University Press.

2002a *The Early Settlement of North America: The Clovis Era.* Cambridge: Cambridge University Press.

2002b The Catastrophic Extinction of North American Mammoths and Mastodonts. *World Archaeology* 33(3):391–416.

2009 (ed.) *American Megafaunal Extinctions at the End of the Pleistocene.* New York: Springer.

Haynes, Gary, David G. Anderson, C. Reid Ferring, Stuart J. Fiedel, Donald K. Grayson, C. Vance Haynes, Jr., Vance T. Holliday, Bruce B. Huckell, Marcel Kornfeld, David J. Meltzer, Julie Morrow, Todd A. Surovell, Nicole M. Waguespack, Peter Wigand, and Robert M. Yohe, II 2007 "Comment on 'Redefining the Age of Clovis: Implications for the Peopling of the Americas.'" *Science* 317:320b.

Haynes, Gregory M. 1996 "Evaluating Flake Assemblages and Stone Tool Distributions at a Large Western Stemmed Tradition Site Near Yucca Mountain, Nevada." *Journal of California and Great Basin Anthropology* 18(1):104–130.

Hegmon, Michelle 2002 "Recent Issues in the Archaeology of the Mimbres Region of the North American Southwest." *Journal of Archaeological Research* 10(4):307–357.

Heizer, Robert F. 1949 "The Archaeology of Central California I: The Early Horizon." *University of California Anthropological Records* 12(1).

1951 "Preliminary Report on the Leonard Rockshelter Site, Pershing County, Nevada." *American Antiquity* 17(2):89–98.

1971 "Village Shifts and Tribal Spreads in California Prehistory." In: *The California Indians, A Source Book*, Robert F. Heizer and M. A. Whipple, eds., pp. 480–484. Berkeley: University of California Press.

1978 (ed.) *Handbook of North American Indians, Vol. 8, California.* Washington, D.C.: Smithsonian Institution.

Heizer, Robert F., and Albert B. Elsasser 1953 *Some Archaeological Sites and Cultures of the Central Sierra Nevada.* Berkeley: Reports of the University of California Archaeological Survey No. 21.

Heizer, Robert F., and Franklin F. Fenenga 1939 "Archaeological Horizons in Central California." *American Anthropologist* 41(3):378–399.

Heizer, Robert F., and Thomas R. Hester 1978 *Great Basin Projectile Points: Forms and Chronology.* Socorro, NM: Ballena Press Publications in Archaeology, Ethnology and History No. 10.

Heizer, Robert F., and Alex D. Krieger 1956 "The Archaeology of Humboldt Cave, Churchill County, Nevada." *University of California Publications in American Archaeology and Ethnology* 47(1).

Heizer, Robert F., and L. K. Napton 1970 *Archaeology and the Prehistoric Great Basin Lacustrine Subsistence Regime as Seen from Lovelock Cave, Nevada.* Berkeley: Contributions of the University of California Archaeological Research Facility No. 10.

Heizer Robert F., and M. A. Whipple (eds.) 1971 *The California Indians: A Source Book.* Berkeley: University of California Press.

Helgason, Agnar, Gísli Pálsson, Henning Sloth Pedersen, Emily Angulalik, Ellen Dröfn, Gunnarsdóttir, Bryndis Yngvadóttir, and Kári Stefánsson 2005 "mtDNA Variation in Inuit Populations of Greenland and Canada: Migration History and Population Structure." *American Journal of Physical Anthropology* 130(1):123–134.

Helm, June (ed.) 1981 *Handbook of North American Indians, Vol. 6, Subarctic.* Washington, D.C.: Smithsonian Institution.

Helmer, James W. 1986 "A Face from the Past: An Early Pre-Dorset Ivory Maskette from North Devon Island, N. W. T." *Etudes/Inuit Studies* 10(1–2):179–202.

1991 "The Palaeo-Eskimo Prehistory of the North Devon Lowlands." *Arctic* 44(4):301–317.

Helwig, Kate, Valery Monahan, and Jennifer Poulin 2008 "The Identification of Hafting Adhesive on a Slotted Antler Point from a Southwest Yukon Ice Patch." *American Antiquity* 73(2):279–288.

Hemphill, Brian E. 1999 "Wear and Tear: Osteoarthritis as an Indicator of Mobility among Great Basin Hunter-Gatherers." In: *Prehistoric Lifeways in the Great Basin Wetlands: Bioarchaeological Reconstruction and Interpretations*, Brian E. Hemphill and Clark Spencer Larsen, eds., pp. 241–289. Salt Lake City: University of Utah Press.

Henning, Dale R. 1998 "The Oneota Tradition." In: *Archaeology on the Great Plains*, W. Raymond Wood, ed., pp. 345–414. Lawrence: University of Kansas Press.

2001 "Plains Village Tradition: Eastern Periphery and Oneota Tradition." In: *Handbook of North American Indians, Vol. 13, Plains*, Raymond J. DeMallie, ed., pp. 222–233. Washington, D.C.: Smithsonian Institution.

2005 "The Evolution of the Plains Village Tradition." In: *North American Archaeology*, Timothy R. Pauketat and Diana DiPaolo Loren, eds., pp. 161–186. Malden, MA: Blackwell Publishing.

Henrikson, Lael Suzann 2003 "Bison Freezers and Hunter-Gatherer Mobility: Archaeological Analysis of Cold Lava Tube Caves on Idaho's Snake River Plain." *Plains Anthropologist* 48(187):263–285.

Henrikson, Lael Suzann, Robert M. Yohe, II, Margaret E. Newman, and Mark Druss 1998 "Freshwater Crustaceans as an Aboriginal Food Resource in the Northern Great Basin." *Journal of California and Great Basin Anthropology* 20(1):72–87.

Hester, James J. 1972 *Blackwater Draw Locality No. 1: A Stratified, Early Man Site in Eastern New Mexico.* Rancho de Taos, NM: Fort Burgwin Research Center Publication No. 8.

Hester, James J., and Sarah M. Nelson (eds.) 1978 *Studies in Bella Bella Prehistory.* Burnaby, BC: Simon Fraser University, Department of Archaeology, Publication No. 5.

Hester, Thomas R. 1973 *Chronological Ordering of Great Basin Prehistory.* Berkeley: Contributions of the University of California Archaeological Research Facility No. 17.

1982 "Robert Fleming Heizer, 1915–1979." *American Antiquity* 47(1):99–107.

2005 "An Overview of the Late Archaic in Southern Texas." In: *The Late Archaic across the Borderlands: From Foraging to Farming*, Bradley J. Vierra, ed., pp. 259–278. Austin: University of Texas Press.

Hewes, Gordon W. 1941 "Reconnaissance of the Central San Joaquin Valley." *American Antiquity* 7(2):123–133.

Hildebrandt, William R. 2007 "Northwest California: Ancient Lifeways among Forested Mountains, Flowing Rivers, and Rocky Ocean Shores." In: *California Prehistory: Colonization, Culture, and Complexity*, Terry L. Jones and Kathryn A. Klar, eds., pp. 83–97. Lanham, MD: AltaMira Press.

Hildebrandt, William R., and Terry L. Jones 1992 "Evolution of Marine Mammal Hunting: A View from the California and Oregon Coasts." *Journal of Anthropological Archaeology* 11(4):360–401.

2002 "Depletion of Prehistoric Pinniped Populations Along the California and Oregon Coasts: Were Humans the Cause?" In: *Wilderness and Political Ecology: Aboriginal Influences and the Original State of Nature*, Charles E. Kay and Randy T. Simmons, eds., pp. 72–110. Salt Lake City: University of Utah Press.

Hildebrandt, William R., and John F. Hayes 1993 "Settlement Pattern Change in the Mountains of Northwest California: A View from Pilot Ridge." In: "There Grows a Green Tree: Papers in Honor of David A. Fredrickson," Greg White, Pat

Mikkelsen, William R. Hildebrandt, and Mark E. Basgall, eds., pp. 107–120. Special issue, *Center for Archaeological Research at Davis, Publication* No. 11.

Hildebrandt, William R., and Valerie A. Levulett 1997 "Middle Holocene Adaptations on the Northern California Coast." In: *Archaeology of the California Coast During the Middle Holocene*, Jon M. Erlandson and Michael A. Glassow, eds., pp. 143–150. University of California Los Angeles, Institute of Archaeology, Perspectives in California Archaeology, Vol. 4.

2002 "Late Holocene Emergence of Marine-focused Economies in Northwest California." In: *Catalysts to Complexity: Late Holocene Societies of the California Coast*, Jon M. Erlandson and Terry L. Jones, eds., pp. 303–319. University of California Los Angeles, Institute of Archaeology, Perspectives in California Archaeology, Vol. 6.

Hildebrandt, William R., and Kelly R. McGuire 2002 "The Ascendance of Hunting During the California Middle Archaic: An Evolutionary Perspective." *American Antiquity* 67(2):231–256.

Hildebrandt, William R., and Allika Ruby 2006 "Prehistoric Pinyon Exploitation in the Southwestern Great Basin: A View from the Coso Range." *Journal of California and Great Basin Anthropology* 26(1):11–31.

Hill, J. Brent, Jeffrey J. Clark, William H. Doelle, and Patrick D. Lyons 2004 "Prehistoric Demography in the Southwest: Migration, Coalescence, and Hohokam Population Decline." *American Antiquity* 69(4):689–716.

Hill, James N. 1970 "Broken K Pueblo: Prehistoric Social Organization in the American Southwest." *Anthropological Papers of the University of Arizona* No. 18.

Hill, Jane H. 2001 "Proto-Uto-Aztecan: A Community of Cultivators in Central Mexico?" *American Anthropologist* 103(4):913–934.

2002a "Proto-Uto-Aztecan Cultivation and the Northern Devolution." In: *Examining the Farming/Language Dispersal Hypothesis*, Peter Bellwood and Colin Renfrew, eds., pp. 331–340. Cambridge: McDonald Institute for Archaeological Research.

2002b "Toward a Linguistic Prehistory of the Southwest: 'Azteco-Tanoan' and the Arrival of Maize Cultivation." *Journal of Anthropological Research* 58(4):457–475.

2005 "Evaluating Historical Linguistic Evidence for Ancient Human Communities in the Americas." In: *The Settlement of the American Continents*, C. Michael Barton, Geoffrey A. Clark, David R. Yesner, and George A. Pearson, eds, pp. 39–48. Tucson: University of Arizona Press.

Hill, Matthew E., Jr. 2007 "A Movable Feast: Variation in Faunal Resource Use Among Central and Western North American Paleoindian Sites." *American Antiquity* 72(3):417–438.

Hoard, Robert J., and William E. Banks (eds.) 2006 *Kansas Archaeology*. Lawrence: University of Kansas Press.

Hockett, Bryan Scott 1994 "A Descriptive Reanalysis of the Leporid Bones from Hogup Cave, Utah." *Journal of California and Great Basin Anthropology* 16(1):106–117.

1998 "Sociopolitical Meaning of Faunal Remains from Baker Village." *American Antiquity* 63(2):289–302.

2005 "Middle and Late Holocene Hunting in the Great Basin: A Critical Review of the Debate and Future Prospects." *American Antiquity* 70(4):713–731.

Hodder, Ian 1991 *Reading the Past: Current Approaches to Interpretation in Archaeology* (2nd ed.). Cambridge, UK: Cambridge University Press.

1999 *The Archaeological Process: An Introduction*. Oxford, UK: Blackwell Publishers.

Hodgetts, Lisa M., M. A. P. Renouf, Maribeth S. Murray, Darlene McCuaig-Balkwill, and Lesley Howse 2003 "Changing Subsistence Practices at the Dorset Paleoeskimo Site of Phillip's Garden, Newfoundland." *Arctic Anthropology* 40(1):106–120.

Hoffecker, John F. 2001 "Late Pleistocene and Early Holocene Sites in the Nenana River Valley, Central Alaska." *Arctic Anthropology* 38(2):139–153.

Hoffecker, John F., William R. Powers, and Ted Goebel 1993 "The Colonization of Beringia and the Peopling of the New World." *Science* 259:46–53.

Hofman, Jack L. 2002 "High Points in Folsom Archaeology." In: *Folsom Technology and Lifeways*, John E. Clark and Michael B. Collins, eds., pp. 399–412. Lithic Technology Special Publication No. 4.

Hofman, Jack L. and Russell W. Graham 1998 "The Paleo-Indian Cultures of the Great Plains." In: *Archaeology on the Great Plains*, W. Raymond Wood, ed., pp. 87–139. Lawrence: University of Kansas Press.

Hofman, Jack L., Richard O. Rose, Larry D. Martin, and Daniel S. Amick 2000 "Folsom Adornment and Bone Technology." *Current Research in the Pleistocene* 17:42–45.

Holder, Preston 1970 *The Hoe and the Horse on the Plains: A Study of Cultural Development among North American Indians*. Lincoln: University of Nebraska Press.

Holen Steven R. 2005 "Taphonomy of Two Last Glacial Maximum Mammoth Sites in the Central Great Plains of North America: A Preliminary Peport on La Sena and Lovewell." *Quaternary International* 142–143:30–43.

Holliday, Vance T. 1997 *Paleoindian Geoarchaeology of the Southern High Plains*. Austin: University of Texas Press.

Holliday, Vance T., and David J. Meltzer 1996 "Geoarchaeology of the Midland (Paleoindian) Site, Texas." *American Antiquity* 61(4):755–771.

Holliday, Vance T., Eileen Johnson, and Thomas W. Stafford, Jr. 1999 "AMS Radiocarbon Dating of the Type Plainview and Firstview (Paleoindian) Assemblages: The Agony and the Ecstasy." *American Antiquity* 64(3):444–454.

Hollimon, Sandra E. 2000 "Archaeology of the *'Aqi*: Gender and Sexuality in Prehistoric Chumash Society." In: *Archaeologies of Sexuality*, Robert A. Schmidt and Barbara L. Voss, eds., pp.179–196. London: Routledge.

Holly, Donald H., Jr. 2002 "Subarctic 'Prehistory' in the Anthropological Imagination." *Arctic Anthropology* 39(1–2):10–26.

Holmer, Richard N. 1994 "In Search of the Ancestral Shoshone." In: *Across the West: Human Population*

Movement and the Expansion of the Numa, David B. Madsen and David Rhode, eds., pp. 179–178. Salt Lake City: University of Utah Press.

Holmes, Charles E. 1996 "Broken Mammoth." In: *American Beginnings: The Prehistory and Paleoecology of Beringia*, Frederick Hadleigh West, ed., pp. 312–318. Chicago: University of Chicago Press.

Holmes, Charles E., Richard VanderHoek, and Thomas E. Dilley 1996 "Swan Point." In: *American Beginnings: The Prehistory and Paleoecology of Beringia*, Frederick Hadleigh West, ed., pp. 319–323. Chicago: University of Chicago Press.

Holt, Julie Zimmerman 2009 "Rethinking the Ramey State: Was Cahokia the Center of a Theater State?" *American Antiquity* 74(2):231–254.

Honigmann, John J. 1981 "Expressive Aspects of Subarctic Indian Culture." In: *Handbook of North American Indians, Vol. 6, Subarctic*, June Helm, ed., pp. 718–738. Washington, DC: Smithsonian Institution.

Hoover, Robert L. 1973 "Chumash Fishing Equipment." *San Diego Museum of Man, Ethnic Technology Notes* 9.

Hopkins, David M. 1996 "Introduction: The Concept of Beringia." In: *American Beginnings: The Prehistory and Paleoecology of Beringia*, Frederick Hadleigh West, ed., pp. xvii–xxi. Chicago: University of Chicago Press.

1967 (ed.) *The Bering Land Bridge*. Stanford, CA: Stanford University Press.

Horai, Satoshi, Rumi Kondo, Y. Nakagawa-Hattori, S. Hayashi, Shunro Sonoda, and Kazuo Tajima 1993 "Peopling of the Americas, Founded by Four Major Lineages of Mitochondrial DNA." *Molecular Biological Evolution* 10(1):23–47.

Horai, Satoshi, Rumi Kondo, Shunro Sonoda, and Kazuo Tajima 1996 "The First Americans: Different Waves of Migration to the New World Inferred from Mitochondrial DNA Sequence Polymorphisms." In: *Prehistoric Mongoloid Dispersals*, Takeru Akazawa and Emöke J. E. Szathmary, eds., pp. 270–283. Oxford: Oxford University Press.

Hosley, Edward H. 1981 "Environment and Culture in the Alaska Plateau." In: *Handbook of North American Indians, Vol. 6, Subarctic*, June Helm, ed., pp. 533–545. Washington, DC: Smithsonian Institution.

Howard, E. B. 1935 "Evidence of Early Man in North America." *University of Pennsylvania, Museum Journal* 24(2–3):61–175.

Howard, William J., and L. Mark Raab 1993 "*Olivella* Grooved Rectangle Beads as Evidence of an Early-Period Southern Channel Islands Interaction Sphere." *Pacific Coast Archaeological Society Quarterly* 29(3):1–11.

Howse, Lesley 2008 "Late Dorset Caribou Hunters: Zooarchaeology of the Bell Site, Victoria Island." *Arctic Anthropology* 45(1):22–40.

Hubbs, Carl L., Robert Rush Miller, and Laura C. Hubbs 1974 *Hydrographic History and Relict Fishes of the North-Central Great Basin*. San Francisco: California Academy of Sciences.

Huckell, Bruce B. 1996 "The Archaic Prehistory of the North American Southwest." *Journal of World Prehistory* 10(3):305–373.

2004 "Clovis in the Southwestern United States." In: *New Perspectives on the First Americans*, Bradley T. Lepper and Robson Bonnichsen, eds., pp. 93–101. Texas A&M University: Center for the Study of the First Americans.

Huckell, Bruce B., and C. Vance Haynes, Jr. 2003 "The Ventana Complex: New Dates and New Ideas on its Place in Early Holocene Western Prehistory." *American Antiquity* 68(2):353–371.

Hudson, Charles 1976 *The Southeastern Indians*. Knoxville: University of Tennessee Press.

1994 "The Hernando de Soto Expedition, 1539–1543." In: *The Forgotten Centuries: Indians and Europeans in the American South, 1521–1704*, Charles Hudson and Carmen Chaves Tesser, eds., pp. 74–103. Athens: University of Georgia Press.

1997 *Knights of Spain, Warriors of the Sun: Hernando de Soto and the South's Ancient Chiefdoms*. Athens: University of Georgia Press.

Hughes, Richard E. 1994a "Editors's Introduction." In: *Toward a New Taxonomic Framework for Central California Archaeology: Essays by James A. Bennyhoff and David A. Fredrickson*, Richard E. Hughes, ed., pp. 1–5. Berkeley: Contributions of the University of California Archaeological Research Facility No. 52.

1994b "Mosaic Patterning in Prehistoric California-Great Basin Exchange." In: *Prehistoric Exchange Systems in North America*, Timothy G. Baugh and Jonathon E. Ericson, eds., pp. 363–383. New York: Plenum Press.

Hughes, Richard E., and Max G. Pavesic 2009 "Geochemical Analysis of Obsidian from the DeMoss Site, Western Idaho: Implications for the Western Idaho Archaic Burial Complex." *Journal of Northwest Archaeology* 43(1):117–124.

Hull, Kathleen L. 2007 "The Sierra Nevada: Archaeology in the Range of Light." In: *California Prehistory: Colonization, Culture, and Complexity*, Terry L. Jones and Kathryn A. Klar, eds., pp. 177–190. Lanham, MD: AltaMira Press.

Hunn, Eugene S. 1990a "The Plateau Culture Area." In: *Native North Americans: An Ethnohistoric Approach*, Daniel L. Boxberger, ed., pp. 361–385. Dubuque, IA: Kendall Hunt Publishing Company.

1990b *Nch'i-Wána: The Big River: Mid-Columbia Indians and Their Land*. Seattle: University of Washington Press.

Hurlbut, Sharon A. 2000 "The Taphonomy of Cannibalism: A Review of Anthropogenic Bone Modification in the American Southwest." *International Journal of Osteoarchaeology* 10(1):4–26.

Husted, Wilfred M., and Robert Edgar 2002 *The Archeology of Mummy Cave, Wyoming: An Introduction to Shoshonean Prehistory*. Lincoln: National Park Service, Midwest Archeological Center and Southeast Archeological Center, Special Report No. 4, Technical Reports Series No. 9.

Husted, Wilfred M., and Oscar Mallory 1967 "The Fremont Culture: Its Derivation and Ultimate Fate." *Plains Anthropologist* 12(37):222–232.

Hutchinson, Ian, and Alan D. McMillan 1997 "Archaeological Evidence for Village Abandonment Associated with Late Holocene Earthquakes at the Northern Cascadia Subduction Zone." *Quaternary Research* 48(1):79–87.

Hyland, Justin R. 2006 "The Central Sierras." In: *Advances in the Archaeology of the Forgotten Peninsula*, Don Laylander and Jerry D. Moore, eds., pp. 117–134. Gainesville: University Press of Florida.

Ingram, Scott E. 2008 "Streamflow and Population Change in the Lower Salt River Valley of Central Arizona, ca. A.D. 775–1450." *American Antiquity* 73(1):136–165.

Ingstad, Anne Stein 1985 *The Norse Discovery of America, Vol. 1, Excavations of a Norse Settlement at L'Anse aux Meadows, Newfoundland, 1961–1968.* Oslo: Norwegian University Press.

Ingstad, Helga 1985 *The Norse Discovery of America, Vol. 2, Historical Background and the Evidence of the Norse Settlement Discovered in Newfoundland.* Oslo: Norwegian University Press.

Irving, William N. 1987 "New Dates from Old Bones." *Natural History* 96(2):8–14.

Irving, William N., and C. R. Harrington 1973 "Upper Pleistocene Radiocarbon-Dated Artifacts from the Northern Yukon." *Science* 179:335–340.

Irwin-Williams, Cynthia 1973 "The Oshara Tradition: Origins of Anasazi Culture." *University of New Mexico Contributions in Anthropology* 5(1).

Iseminger, William R. 1996 "Mighty Cahokia." *Archaeology* 49(3):30–37.

Iverson, Peter (ed.) 1985 *The Plains Indians of the Twentieth Century.* Norman: University of Oklahoma Press.

Ives, John W. 1990 *A Theory of Northern Athapaskan Prehistory.* Boulder, CO: Westview Press.

2003 "Alberta, Athapaskans and Apachean Origins." In: *Archaeology in Alberta: A View from the New Millennium*, Jack W. Brink and John F. Dormaar, eds., pp. 256–289. Medicine Hat, Alberta: The Archaeological Society of Alberta.

Jablonski, Nina G. (ed.) 2002 "The First Americans: The Pleistocene Colonization of the New World." *Memoirs of the California Academy of Sciences* No. 27.

Jackson, H. Edwin 1991 "The Trade Fair in Hunter-Gatherer Interaction: The Role of Intersocietal Trade in the Evolution of Poverty Point Culture." In: *Between Bands and States*, Susan A. Gregg, ed., pp. 265–286. Southern Illinois University, Carbondale, Center for Archaeological Investigations, Occasional Paper No. 9.

Jackson, H. Edwin, and Susan L. Scott 2003 "Patterns of Elite Faunal Utilization at Moundville, Alabama." *American Antiquity* 68(3):552–572.

Jackson, Lawrence J. 1995 "A Clovis Point from South Coastal Chile." *Current Research in the Pleistocene* 12:21–23.

2006a "Fluted and Fishtail Points from Southern Coastal Chile." In: *Paleoindian Archaeology: A Hemispheric Perspective*, Juliet E. Morrow and Cristóbal Gnecco, eds., pp. 105–120. Gainesville: University Press of Florida.

2006b "Changing Our Views of Late Palaeo-Indian in Southern Ontario." In: *The Late Palaeo-Indian Great Lakes:*

Geological and Archaeological Investigations of Late Pleistocene and Early Holocene Environments, Lawrence J. Jackson and Andrew Hinshelwood, eds., pp. 25–56. Canadian Museum of Civilization, Mercury Series, Archaeological Survey of Canada, Paper 165.

Jackson, Lionel E., and Alejandra Duk-Rodkin 1996 "Quaternary Geology of the Ice-Free Corridor: Glacial Controls on the Peopling of the New World." In: *Prehistoric Mongoloid Dispersals*, Takeru Akazawa and Emöke J. E. Szathmary, eds., pp. 214–227. Oxford, UK: Oxford University Press.

Jackson, Robert H. 1994 *Indian Population Decline: The Missions of Northwestern New Spain, 1687–1840.* Albuquerque: University of New Mexico Press.

2000 *From Savages to Subjects: Missions in the History of the American Southwest.* Armonk, NY: M. E. Sharpe.

Jackson, Thomas L. 1991 "Pounding Acorn: Women's Production as Social and Economic Focus." In: *Engendering Archaeology: Women and Prehistory*, Joan M. Gero and Margaret W. Conkey, eds., pp. 301–325. Oxford, UK: Blackwell Publishers.

Jackson, Thomas L., and Jonathon E. Ericson 1994 "Prehistoric Exchange Systems in California." In: *Prehistoric Exchange Systems in North America*, Timothy G. Baugh and Jonathon E. Ericson, eds., pp. 385–415. New York: Plenum Press.

Jaeger, E. C. 1965 *The California Deserts.* Stanford, CA: Stanford University Press.

James, Steven R. 1983 "Surprise Valley Settlement and Subsistence: A Critical Review of the Faunal Evidence." *Journal of California and Great Basin Anthropology* 5(1 and 2):156–175.

Janetski, Joel C. 1979 "Implications of Snare Bundles in the Great Basin and Southwest." *Journal of California and Great Basin Anthropology* 1(2):306–321.

1990 "Wetlands in Utah Valley Prehistory." In: *Wetlands Adaptation in the Great Basin*, Joel C. Janetski and David B. Madsen, eds., pp 233–257. Provo: Brigham Young University, Museum of Peoples and Cultures, Occasional Paper No. 1.

1994 "Recent Transitions in the Eastern Great Basin: The Archaeological Record." In: *Across the West: Human Population Movement and the Expansion of the Numa*, David B. Madsen and David Rhode, eds., pp. 157–178. Salt Lake City: University of Utah Press.

1997 "Fremont Hunting and Resource Intensification in the Eastern Great Basin." *Journal of Archaeological Science* 24(12):1075–1088.

2002 "Trade in Fremont Society: Contexts and Contrasts." *Journal of Anthropological Anthropology* 21(3):344–370.

2006 "Mosquito Willie (42TO137): A Late Archaic Site on the Western Edge of the Great Salt Lake Desert." *Journal of California and Great Basin Anthropology* 26(1):77–94.

2008 "The Enigmatic Fremont." In: *The Great Basin: People and Place in Ancient Times*, Catherine S. Fowler and Don D. Fowler, eds., pp. 104–115. Santa Fe: School of American Research.

Janetski, Joel C., Karen D. Lupo, John M. McCullough, and Shannon A. Novak 1992 "The Mosida Site: A Middle Archaic Burial from the Eastern Great Basin." *Journal of California and Great Basin Anthropology* 14(2):180–200.

Janetski, Joel C., and David B. Madsen (eds.) 1990 *Wetlands Adaptation in the Great Basin*. Provo, UT: Brigham Young University, Museum of Peoples and Cultures, Occasional Paper No. 1.

Janetski, Joel C., and Grant C. Smith 2007 *Hunter-Gatherer Archaeology in Utah Valley*. Provo, UT: Brigham Young University, Museum of Peoples and Cultures, Occasional Paper No. 12.

Jantz, R. L., and Douglas W. Owsley 1997 "Pathology, Taphonomy, and Cranial Morphometrics of the Spirit Cave Mummy." *Nevada Historical Society Quarterly* 40(1):62–84.

2001 "Variation among Early North American Crania." *American Journal of Physical Anthropology* 114(2):146–155.

2005 "Circumpacific Populations and the Peopling of the New World: Evidence from Cranial Morphometrics." In: *Paleoamerican Origins: Beyond Clovis*, Robson Bonnichsen, Bradley T. Lepper, Dennis Stanford, and Michael R. Waters, eds., pp. 267–275. Texas A&M University: Center for the Study of the First Americans.

Jefferies, Richard W. 1996 "The Emergence of Long-Distance Exchange Networks in the Southeastern United States." In: *Archaeology of the Mid-Holocene Southeast*, Kenneth E. Sassaman and David G. Anderson, eds., pp. 222–234. Gainesville: University Press of Florida.

2004 "Regional Cultures, 700 B.C.–A.D. 1000." In: *Handbook of North American Indians, Vol. 14, Southeast*, Raymond D. Fogelson, ed., pp. 115–127. Washington, D.C.: Smithsonian Institution.

Jefferson, Thomas 1797 *Notes on the State of Virginia*. London: J. Stockdale.

Jelnick, Arthur J. 1992 "Perspectives from the Old World on the Habitation of the New." *American Antiquity* 57(2):345–347.

Jelsma, Johan 2006 "Three Social Status Groups at Port au Chiox: Maritime Archaic Mortuary Practices and Social Structure." In: *The Archaic of the Far Northeast*, David Sanger and M. A. P. Renouf, eds., pp. 83–103. Orono: University of Maine Press.

Jenkins, Dennis L., and Thomas J. Connolly 1994 "Archaeological Excavations at the Paquet Gulch Bridge Site: A Pithouse Village in the Deschutes River Basin, Southwestern Columbian Plateau, Oregon." *University of Oregon Anthropological Papers* No. 49.

Jenkins, Dennis L., Thomas J. Connolly, and C. Melvin Aikens (eds) 2004 "Early and Middle Holocene Archaeology of the Northern Great Basin." *University of Oregon Anthropological Papers* No. 62.

Jenks, A. E. 1937 "Minnesota's Browns Valley Man and Associated Burial Artifacts." *Memoirs of the American Anthropological Association* No. 49.

Jenness, Diamond 1925 "A New Eskimo Culture in Hudson Bay." *Geographical Review* 15(3):428–437.

Jennings, Jesse D. 1957 "Danger Cave." *University of Utah Anthropological Papers* No. 27.

1964 "The Desert West." In: *Prehistoric Man in the New World*, Jesse D. Jennings and Edward Norbeck, eds., pp. 149–174. Chicago: University of Chicago Press.

1973 "The Short Useful Life of a Simple Hypothesis." *Tebiwa* 16(1):1–11.

1978 "Prehistory of Utah and the Eastern Great Basin." *University of Utah Anthropological Papers* No. 98.

1989 *Prehistory of North America* (3rd ed.). Mountain View, CA: Mayfield Publishing.

1998 *Glen Canyon: An Archaeological Summary*. Salt Lake City. University of Utah Press.

Jennings, Jesse D., Alan R. Schroedl, and Richard N. Holmer 1980 "Sudden Shelter." *University of Utah Anthropological Papers* No. 103.

Jensen, Jens Fog 2005 "Palaeo-Eskimo Continuity and Discontinuity in West Greenland." In: "Contributions to the Study of the Dorset Paleoindians," Patricia D. Sutherland, ed., pp. 93–103. Special issue, *Canadian Museum of Civilization, Mercury Series, Archaeological Survey of Canada*, Paper 167.

Johnson, Alfred E. 2001 "Plains Woodland Tradition." In: *Handbook of North American Indians, Vol. 13, Plains*, Raymond J. DeMallie, ed., pp. 159–172. Washington, D.C.: Smithsonian Institution.

Johnson, Ann Mary, and Alfred E. Johnson 1998 "The Plains Woodland." In: *Archaeology on the Great Plains*, W. Raymond Wood, ed., pp. 201–234. Lawrence: University of Kansas Press.

Johnson, Craig M. 1998 "The Coalescent Tradition." In: *Archaeology on the Great Plains*, W. Raymond Wood, ed., pp. 308–344. Lawrence: University of Kansas Press.

2007 *A Chronology of Middle Missouri Plains Village Sites*. Washington, D.C.: Smithsonian Contributions to Anthropology No. 47.

Johnson, Edward C. 1986 "Issues: The Indian Perspective." In: *Handbook of North American Indians, Vol. 11, Great Basin*, Warren L. d'Azevedo, ed., pp. 592–600. Washington, D.C.: Smithsonian Institution.

Johnson, Eileen 1991 "Late Pleistocene Cultural Occupation on the Southern Plains." In: *Clovis: Origins and Adaptations*, Robson Bonnichsen and Karen L. Turnmire, eds., pp. 215–236. Oregon State University: Center for the Study of the First Americans.

Johnson, John R. 2000 "Social Responses to Climate Change among the Chumash Indians of South-Central California." In: *The Way the Wind Blows: Climate, History, and Human Action*, Roderick J. McIntosh, Joseph A. Tainter, and Susan Keech McIntosh, eds., pp. 301–327. New York: Columbia University Press.

Johnson, John R., Thomas W. Stafford, Jr., Henry O. Ajie, and Don P. Morris 2002 "Arlington Springs Revisited." In: *Proceedings of the California Islands Symposium*, David R. Browne, Kathryn L. Mitchell, and Henry W. Chaney, eds., pp. 541–545. U.S. Department of the Interior, Minerals Management Service, and Santa Barbara Museum of Natural History.

Johnson, William C. 2001 "The Protohistoric Monogahela and the Case for an Iroquoian Connection." In: *Societies in Eclipse: Archaeology of the Eastern Woodlands Indians, A.D. 1400–1700*, David S. Brose, C. Wesley Cowan, and Robert C. Mainfort, Jr., eds., pp. 67–82. Washington, D.C.: Smithsonian Institution Press.

Johnston, W. A. 1933 "Quaternary Geology of North America in Relation to the Migration of Man." In: *The American Aborigines: Their Origin and Antiquity,* Diamond Jenness, ed., pp. 11–45. Toronto: University of Toronto Press.

Johnstone, David P. 2003 "Early Architecture from the Southern Georgia Strait Region." In: *Archaeology of Coastal British Columbia: Essays in Honour of Professor Philip M. Hobler,* Roy L. Carlson, ed., pp. 109–112. Burnaby, B.C.: Simon Fraser University, Archaeology Press, Publication No. 30.

Jonaitis, Aldona (ed.) 1991 *Chiefly Feasts: The Enduring Kwakiutl Potlatch.* New York: American Museum of Natural History.

Jones, George T., and Charlotte Beck 1999 "Paleoarchaic Archaeology in the Great Basin." In: *Models for the Millennium: Great Basin Anthropology Today,* Charlotte Beck, ed., pp. 83–95. Salt Lake City: University of Utah Press.

Jones, George T., Charlotte Beck, Eric E. Jones, and Richard E. Hughes 2003 "Lithic Source Use and Paleoarchaic Foraging Territories in the Great Basin." *American Antiquity* 68(1):5–38.

Jones, George T., Charlotte Beck, Fred L. Nials, Joshua J. Neudorfer, Brian J. Brownholtz, and Hallie B. Gilbert 1996 "Recent Archaeological and Geological Investigations at the Sunshine Locality, Long Valley, Nevada." *Journal of California and Great Basin Anthropology* 18(1):48–63.

Jones, Kevin T., and David B. Madsen 1989 "Calculating the Cost of Resource Transportation: A Great Basin Example." *Current Anthropology* 30(4):529–534.

Jones, Scott, and Robson Bonnichsen 1994 "The Anzick Clovis Burial." *Current Research in the Pleistocene* 11:42–44.

Jones, Terry L. 1992 "Settlement Trends Along the California Coast." In: *Essays on the Prehistory of Maritime California,* Terry L. Jones, ed., pp. 1–37. Center for Archaeological Research at Davis, Publication No. 10.

1996 "Mortars, Pestles, and Division of Labor in Prehistoric California: A View from Big Sur." *American Antiquity* 61(2):243–264.

2008 "Culture or Adaptation: Milling Stone Reconsidered." In *Avocados to Millingstones: Papers in Honor of D. L. True,* Georgie Waugh and Mark E. Basgall, eds., pp. 137–153. Monographs in California and Great Basin Anthropology No. 5, Archaeological Research Center, Department of Anthropology, California State University, Sacramento.

Jones, Terry L., Gary M. Brown, L. Mark Raab, Janet L. McVickar, W. Geoffrey Spaulding, Douglas J. Kennett, Andrew York, and Phillip L. Walker 1999 "Environmental Imperatives Reconsidered: Demographic Crises in Western North America During the Medieval Climatic Anomaly." *Current Anthropology* 40(2):137–170.

Jones, Terry L., Richard T. Fitzgerald, Douglas J. Kennett, Charles H. Miksicek, John L. Fagan, John Sharp, and Jon M. Erlandson 2002 "The Cross Creek Site (CA-SLO-1797) and Its Implications for New World Colonization." *American Antiquity* 67(2):213–230.

Jones, Terry L., Richard T. Fitzgerald, and Judith F. Porcasi 2008a "The Cross Creek-Diablo Canyon Complex of South Central California: Mid-latitude Pacific Foragers at the Pleistocene-Holocene Boundary." *North Pacific Prehistory* 2:169–202.

Jones, Terry L., and William R. Hildebrandt 1995 "Reasserting a Prehistoric Tragedy of the Commons: Reply to Lyman." *Journal of Anthropological Archaeology* 14(1):78–98.

Jones, Terry L., and Kathryn A. Klar 2005 "Diffusionism Reconsidered: Linguistic and Archaeological Evidence for Prehistoric Polynesian Contact with Southern California." *American Antiquity* 70(3):457–484.

2007 (eds.) *California Prehistory: Colonization, Culture, and Complexity.* Lanham, MD: AltaMira Press.

Jones, Terry L., Judith F. Porcasi, Jereme W. Gaeta, and Brian F. Codding 2008b "The Diablo Canyon Fauna: A Coarse-Grained Record of Trans-Holocene Foraging from the Central California Mainland Coast." *American Antiquity* 73(2):289–316.

Jones, Terry L., and Georgie Waugh 1997 "Climatic Consequences or Population Pragmatism? Middle Holocene Prehistory of the Central California Coast." In: *Archaeology of the California Coast during the Middle Holocene,* Jon M. Erlandson and Michael A. Glassow, eds., pp. 111–128. University of California Los Angeles, Institute of Archaeology, Perspectives in California Archaeology, Vol. 4.

Jones, Terry L., Nathan E. Stevens, Deborah A. Jones, Richard T. Fitzgerald, and Mark G. Hylkema 2007 "The Central Coast: A Midlatitude Milieu." In: *California Prehistory: Colonization, Culture, and Complexity,* Terry L. Jones and Kathryn A. Klar, eds., pp. 125–146. Lanham, MD: AltaMira Press.

Josenhans, Heiner, Daryl W. Fedje, Reinhard Pienitz, and John Southon 1997 "Early Humans and Rapidly Changing Holocene Sea Levels in the Queen Charlotte Islands-Hecate Straight, British Columbia, Canada." *Science* 277:71–74.

Joyce, Arthur A. 1988 "Early/Middle Holocene Environments in the Middle Atlantic Region: A Revised Reconstruction." In: *Holocene Human Ecology in Northeastern North America,* George P. Nicholas, ed., pp. 185–214. New York: Plenum Press.

Joyce, Daniel J. 2006 "Chronology and New Research on the Schaefer Mammoth (?*Mammuthus primigenius*) Site, Kenosha County, Wisconsin, USA." *Quaternary International* 142–143:44–57.

Judd, Neil M. 1967 *The Bureau of American Ethnology: A Partial History.* Norman: University of Oklahoma Press.

Kaberline, C. Michael 1995 "A Preliminary Study of Tulare Lake Pinto Point Morphology: An Archaeological Application for Cluster Analysis." *Kern County Archaeological Society Journal* 6:101–110.

Kaestle, Frederika A., and David Glenn Smith 2001 "Ancient Mitochondrial DNA Evidence for Prehistoric Population Movement: The Numic Expansion." *American Journal of Physical Anthropology* 115(1):1–12.

Kamp, Kathryn A., and John C. Whittaker 1999 "Surviving Adversity: The Sinagua of Lizard Man Village." *University of Utah Anthropological Papers* No. 120.

Kantner, John 1996 "Political Competition among the Chaco Anasazi of the American Southwest." *Journal of Anthropological Archaeology* 15(1):41–105.

2004 *Ancient Puebloan Southwest.* Cambridge, UK: Cambridge University Press.

Kantner, John, and Nancy M. Mahoney (eds.) 2000 "Great House Communities Across the Chacoan Landscape." *Anthropological Papers of the University of Arizona* No. 64.

Kapches, Mima 1990 "The Spatial Dynamics of Ontario Iroquoian Longhouses." *American Antiquity* 55(1):49–67.

Katzenberg, M. Anne, Henry P. Schwarcz, Martin Knyf, and F. Jerome Melbye 1995 "Stable Isotope Evidence for Maize Horticulture and Paleodiet in Southern Ontario, Canada." *American Antiquity* 60(2):335–350.

Kaufman, Terrence, and Victor Golla 2000 "Language Groupings in the New World: Their Reliability and Usability in Cross-Disciplinary Studies." In: *America Past, America Present: Genes and Languages in the Americas and Beyond*, Colin Renfrew, ed., pp. 47–57. Cambridge, UK: McDonald Institute for Archaeological Research.

Kay, Marvin 1998 "The Central and Southern Plains Archaic." In: *Archaeology on the Great Plains*, W. Raymond Wood, ed., pp. 173–200. Lawrence: University of Kansas Press.

Keefer, David K., Susan D. deFrance, Michael E. Moseley, James B. Richardson III, Dennis R. Satterlee, and Amy Day-Lewis 1998 "Early Maritime Economy and El Niño Events at Quebrada Tacahuay." *Science* 281:1833–1835.

Keenlyside, David L. 1985 "Late Palaeo-Indian Evidence from the Southern Gulf of St. Lawrence." *Archaeology of Eastern North America* 13:79–92.

Kehoe, Alice Beck 1998 *The Land of Prehistory: A Critical History of American Archaeology*. New York: Routedge.

Kelly, John E. 1990 "The Emergence of Mississippian Culture in the American Bottom Region." In: *The Mississippian Emergence*, Bruce D. Smith, ed., pp. 113–152. Washington, D.C.: Smithsonian Institution Press.

2000 "Cahokia and Its Role as a Gateway Center in Interregional Exchange." In: *Cahokia and the Hinterlands: Middle Mississippian Cultures of the Midwest*, Thomas E. Emerson and R. Barry Lewis, eds., pp. 61–80. Chicago: University of Illinois Press.

Kelly, John E., Steven J. Ozuk, Douglas K. Jackson, Dale L. McElrath, Fred A. Finney, and Duane Esarey 1984 "Emergent Mississippian Period." In: *American Bottom Archaeology*, Charles J. Bareis and James W. Porter, eds., pp. 128–157. Urbana: University of Illinois Press.

Kelly, Robert L. 1990 "Marshes and Mobility in the Western Great Basin." In: *Wetlands Adaptation in the Great Basin*, Joel C. Janetski and David B. Madsen, eds., pp 259–276. Provo, UT: Brigham Young University, Museum of Peoples and Cultures, Occasional Paper No. 1.

1997 "Late Holocene Great Basin Prehistory." *Journal of World Prehistory* 11(1):1–49.

1995 *The Foraging Spectrum: Diversity in Hunter-Gatherer Lifeways*. Washington, D.C.: Smithsonian Institution Press.

1996 "Ethnographic Analogy and Migration to the Western Hemisphere." In: *Prehistoric Mongoloid Dispersals*, Takeru Akazawa and Emöke J. E. Szathmary, eds., pp. 228–240. Oxford, UK: Oxford University Press.

1997 "Late Holocene Great Basin Prehistory." *Journal of World Prehistory* 11(1):1–49.

1999 "Theoretical and Archaeological Insights into Foraging Strategies among the Prehistoric Inhabitants of the Stillwater Wetlands." In: *Prehistoric Lifeways in the Great Basin Wetlands: Bioarchaeological Reconstruction and Interpretations*, Brian E. Hemphill and Clark Spencer Larsen, eds., pp. 117–150. Salt Lake City: University of Utah Press.

2001 "Prehistory of the Carson Desert and Stillwater Mountains." *University of Utah Anthropological Papers* No. 123.

2003 "Maybe We Do Know When People First Came into North America: And What Does It Mean if We Do?" *Quaternary International* 109–110:133–145.

Kelly, Robert L., and Lawrence C. Todd 1988 "Coming into the Country: Early Paleoindian Hunting and Mobility." *American Antiquity* 53(2):231–244.

Kemp, Brian M., Ripan S. Malhi, John McDonough, Deborah A. Bolnick, Jason A. Eshleman, Olga Rickards, Cristina Martinez-Labarga, John R. Johnson, Joseph G. Lorenz, E. James Dixon, Terence E. Fifield, Timothy H. Heaton, Rosita Worl, and David Glenn Smith 2007 "Genetic Analysis of Early Holocene Skeletal Remains from Alaska and its Implications for the Settlement of the Americas." *American Journal of Physical Anthropology* 132(4):605–621.

Kennett, Douglas J., and James P. Kennett 2000 "Competitive and Cooperative Responses to Climatic Instability in Coastal Southern California." *American Antiquity* 65(2):379–395.

Kennett, Douglas J., James P. Kennett, A. West, C. Mercer, S. S. Que Hee, L. Bement, T. E. Bunch, M. Sellers, and W. S. Wolbach 2009 "Nanodiamonds in the Younger Dryas Boundary Sediment Layer." *Science* 323:94.

Kennett, James P., and Allen West 2008 "Biostratigraphic Evidence Supports Paleoindian Population Disruption at̄ 12.9 ka." *Proceedings of the National Academy of Sciences* 105(50):E110.

Kessell, John L. 1979 *Kiva, Cross, and Crown: The Pecos Indians and New Mexico*. Washington, DC: National Park Service.

Key, Patrick J. 1994 "Relationships of the Woodland Period on the Northern and Central Plains: The Craniometric Evidence." In: *Skeletal Biology in the Great Plains: Migration, Warfare, Health, and Subsistence*, Douglas W. Owsley and Richard L. Jantz, eds., 179–187. Washington, D.C.: Smithsonian Institution Press.

Keyser. James D. 1986 "The Evidence for McKean Complex Plant Utilization." *Plains Anthropologist* 31(113):225–235.

1992 *Indian Rock Art of the Columbia Plateau*. Seattle: University of Washington Press.

Kidder, Alfred V. 1924 "An Introduction to the Study of Southwestern Archaeology, with a Preliminary Account of the Excavations at Pecos." *Yale University, Papers of the Southwestern Expedition, Phillips Academy*, No. 1.

1927 "Southwestern Archaeological Conference." *Science* 66:486–491.

Kidder, Tristram R. 2006 "Climate Change and the Archaic to Woodland Transition (3000–2500 cal B.P.) in the Mississippi River Basin." *American Antiquity* 71(2):195–231.

Kilby, J. David, and Bruce B. Huckell 2003 "A Comparison of Caches: An Initial Look at Regional Variation in Clovis

Caching." Paper presented at the annual meeting of the Society for American Archaeology, Milwaukee.

King, Adam (ed.) 2003 "Over a Century of Explorations at Etowah." *Journal of Archaeological Research* 11(4):279–306.

2007 (ed.) *Southeastern Ceremonial Complex: Chronology, Content, Context.* Tuscaloosa: University of Alabama Press.

King, Chester D. 1990 *Evolution of Chumash Society: A Comparative Study of Artifacts Used for Social System Maintenance in the Santa Barbara Channel Region Before A.D. 1804.* New York: Garland Publishing, Inc.

King, Francis B. 1993 "Climate, Culture, and Oneota Subsistence in Central Illinois." In: *Farmers and Foragers in the Eastern Woodlands*, C. Margaret Scarry, ed., pp. 232–254. Gainseville: University Press of Florida.

King, James E., and Jeffrey J. Saunders 1984 "Environmental Insularity and the Extinction of the American Mastodont." In: *Quaternary Extinctions: A Prehistoric Revolution*, Paul S. Martin and Richard G. Klein, eds., pp. 315–339. Tucson: University of Arizona Press.

King, Linda B. 1969 *The Medea Creek Cemetery (LAn-243): An Investigation of Social Organization from Mortuary Practices.* Los Angeles: University of California Archaeological Survey Annual Report 1969:27–68.

King, Maureen L., and Sergei B. Slobodin 1996 "A Fluted Point from the Uptar Site, Northeastern Siberia." *Science* 273:634–636.

Kirk, Robert, and Emöke J. E. Szathmary (eds.) 1985 *Out of Asia: Peopling the Americas and the Pacific.* Canberra: Australian National University.

Kivett, M. F., and R. E. Jensen 1976 *Archaeological Investigations at the Crow Creek Site (39BF11).* Lincoln: Nebraska State Historical Society Publications in Anthropology 7.

Knack, Martha C. 1986 "Indian Economies, 1950–1980." In: *Handbook of North American Indians, Vol. 11, Great Basin*, Warren L. d'Azevedo, ed., pp. 573–591. Washington, D.C.: Smithsonian Institution.

Knecht, Richard A., and Richard S. Davis 2007 "The Amaknak Bridge Site: Cultural Change and the Neoglacial in the Eastern Aleutians." *Arctic Anthropology* 45(1):61–78.

Knight, James Vernon, Jr. 1998 "Moundville as a Diagrammatic Ceremonial Center." In: *Archaeology of the Moundville Chiefdom*, Vernon James Knight, Jr., and Vincas P. Steponaitis, eds., pp. 44–62. Washington, D.C.: Smithsonian Institution Press.

2004 "Characterizing Elite Midden Deposits at Moundville." *American Antiquity* 69(2):304–321.

Knight, James Vernon, Jr., and Vincas P. Steponaitis 1998 "A New History of Moundville." In: *Archaeology of the Moundville Chiefdom*, Vernon James Knight, Jr., and Vincas P. Steponaitis, eds., pp. 1–25. Washington, D.C.: Smithsonian Institution Press.

Knuth, Eigil 1954 "The Paleo-Eskimo Culture of Northeast Greenland Elucidated by Three New Sites." *American Antiquity* 19(4):367–381.

Koerper, Henry C., and Ken Hedges 1996 "Patayan Anthropomorphic Figurines from an Orange County Site." *Journal of California and Great Basin Anthropology* 18(2):204–220.

Kohler, Timothy A. 1991 "The Demise of Weeden Island, and Post-Weeden Island Cultural Stability, in Non-Mississippianized Northern Florida." In: *Stability, Transformation, and Variation: The Late Woodland Southeast*, Michael S. Nassaney and Charles R. Cobb, eds., pp. 91–110. New York: Plenum Press.

Kohler, Timothy A., and Meredith H. Matthews 1988 "Long Term Anasazi Land Use and Forest Reduction: A Case Study from Southwest Colorado." *American Antiquity* 53(3):537–564.

Kohler, Timothy A., Matt Pier Glaude, Jean-Pierre Bocquet-Appel, and Brian M. Kemp 2008 "The Neolithic Demographic Transition in the U.S. Southwest." *American Antiquity* 73(4):645–669.

Kononenko, Nina A., and Jim Cassidy 2007 "The Prehistory of Eastern Asia." *North Pacific Prehistory* 1:15–36.

Kooyman, Brian, L. V. Hills, Paul McNeil, and Shayne Tolman 2006 "Late Pleistocene Horse Hunting at the Wally's Beach Site (DhPg-8), Canada." *American Antiquity* 71(1):101–121.

Kooyman, Brian, Margaret E. Newman, Christine Cluney, Murray Lobb, Shayne Tolman, Paul McNeil, and L. V. Hills 2001 "Identification of Horse Exploitation by Clovis Hunters Based on Protein Analysis." *American Antiquity* 66(4):686–691.

Kornfeld, Marcel 2002 "Folsom Technological Organization in the Middle Park of Colorado: A Case for Broad Spectral Foraging." In: *Folsom Technology and Lifeways*, John E. Clark and Michael B. Collins, eds., pp. 47–67. Lithic Technology Special Publication No. 4.

Kornfeld, Marcel, George C. Frison, and Mary Lou Larson 2009 *Prehistory of the Plains and Rockies* (3rd ed). Walnut Creek, CA: Left Coast Press.

Kornfeld, Marcel, Mary Lou Larson, David J. Rapson, and George C. Frison 2001 "10,000 Years in the Rocky Mountains: The Helen Lookingbill Site." *Journal of Field Archaeology* 28(3/4):307–324.

Kowta, Makoto 1984 "The 'Layer Cake' Model of Baja California Prehistory Revisited: An Hypothesis." *Pacific Coast Archaeological Society Quarterly* 20(1):1–16.

Kozuch, Laura 2002 "*Olivella* Beads from Spiro and the Plains." *American Antiquity* 67(4):697–709.

Kraft, J. C., D. F. Belknap, and I. Kayan 1983 "Potential of Discovery of Human Occupation Sites on the Continental Shelves and Nearshore Coastal Zones." In: *Quaternary Coastlines and Marine Archaeology: Towards the Prehistory of Land Bridges and Continental Shelves*, P. M. Masters and N. C. Flemming, eds., pp. 87–120. London: Academic Press.

Krause, Richard A. 1998 "A History of Great Plains Prehistory." In: *Archaeology on the Great Plains*, W. Raymond Wood, ed., pp. 48–86. Lawrence: University of Kansas Press.

1999 "Kinship, Tradition and Settlement Pattern: An Archaeology of Prehistoric Middle Missouri Community Life." In: *Making Places in the Prehistoric World: Themes in Settlement Archaeology*, Joanna Brück and Melissa Goodman, eds., pp. 129–144. London: UCL Press.

2001 "Plains Village Tradition: Coalescent." In: *Handbook of North American Indians, Vol. 13, Plains*, Raymond J. DeMallie, ed., pp. 196–206. Washington, D.C.: Smithsonian Institution.

Krauss, Michael E., and Victor Golla 1981 "Northen Athapaskan Languages." In: *Handbook of North American Indians, Vol. 5, Arctic, David Damas*, ed., pp. 67–85. Washington, D.C.: Smithsonian Institution.

Krech, Shepard (ed.) 1984 *The Subarctic Fur Trade: Native Social and Economic Adaptations.* Vancouver: University of British Columbia Press.

Krieger, Alex D. 1964 "Early Man in the New World." In: *Prehistoric Man in the New World*, Jesse D. Jennings and Edward Norbeck, eds., pp. 23–81. Chicago: University of Chicago Press.

Kroeber, Alfred L. 1925 "Handbook of the Indians of California." *Bureau of American Ethnology Bulletin* 78.

1932 "The Patwin and Their Neighbors." *University of California Publications in American Anchaeology and Ethography* 29.

1939 "Cultural and Natural Areas of Native North America." *University of California Publications in American Archaeology and Ethnology* 38.

Kubler, George 1940 *The Religious Architecture of New Mexico in the Colonial Period and Since the American Occupation.* Colorado Springs, CO: The Taylor Museum.

Kuckelman, Kristin A. 2002 "Thirteenth Century Warfare in the Central Mesa Verde Area." In: *Seeking the Central Place: Archaeology and Ancient Communities in the Mesa Verde Region*, Mark D. Varien and Richard H. Wilshusen, eds., pp. 233–253. Salt Lake City: University of Utah Press.

Kuckelman, Kristin A., Ricky R. Lightfoot, and Debra L. Martin 2002 "The Bioarchaeology and Taphonomy of Violence at Castle Rock and Sand Canyon Pueblos, Southwestern Colorado." *American Antiquity* 67(3):486–513.

Kuehn, Steven R. 1998 "New Evidence for Late Paleoindian-Early Archaic Subsistence Behavior in the Western Great Lakes." *American Antiquity* 63(3):457–476.

Kuijt, Ian 1989 "Subsistence Resource Variability and Culture Change During the Middle-Late Prehistoric Cultural Transition on the Canadian Plateau." *Canadian Journal of Archaeology* 13:97–118.

2001 "Reconsidering the Cause of Cultural Collapse in the Lillooet Area of British Columbia, Canada: A Geoarchaeological Perspective." *American Antiquity* 66(4):692–703.

Kuijt, Ian, and William C. Prentiss 2004 "Villages on the Edge: Pithouses, Cultural Change, and the Abandonment of Aggregate Villages." In: *Complex Hunter-Gatherers: Evolution and Organization of Prehistoric Communities on the Plateau of Northwestern North America*, William C. Prentiss and Ian Kuijt, eds., pp. 155–168. Salt Lake City: University of Utah Press.

Kunz, Michael L., Michael Beaver, and Constance Adkins 2003 *The Mesa Site: Paleoindians Above the Arctic Circle.* Anchorage: Bureau of Land Management-Alaska Open File Report 86.

Kunz, Michael L., and Richard E. Reanier 1994 "Paleoindians in Beringia: Evidence from Arctic Alaska." *Science* 263:660–662.

1996 "The Mesa Site, Iteriak Creek." In: *American Beginnings: The Prehistory and Paleoecology of Beringia*, Frederick Hadleigh West, ed., pp. 497–513. Chicago: University of Chicago Press.

Kuzmin, Yaroslav V. 2000 "Radiocarbon Chronology of the Stone Age Cultures on the Pacific Coast of Northeastern Siberia." *Arctic Anthropology* 37(1):120–131.

Kvamme, Kenneth L., and Stanley A. Ahler 2007 "Integrated Remote Sensing and Excavation at Double Ditch State Historic Site, North Dakota." *American Antiquity* 72(3):539–561.

La Jeunesse, Roger M., and John H. Pryor 1998 "Romer's Rule and the Paleoindian/Archaic Transition." *Current Research in the Pleistocene* 15:29–32.

La Jeunesse, Roger M., John H. Pryor, and Walter A. Dodd, Jr. 2004 "Battered Implements and Milling Slab Rejuvenation from a Paleoindian/Archaic Transition Site." *Current Research in the Pleistocene* 21:55–57.

La Vere, David 1998 *The Caddo Chiefdoms: Caddo Economics and Politics, 700–1835.* Lincoln: University of Nebraska Press.

Lahren, L. L., and Robson Bonnichsen 1974 "Bone Foreshafts from a Clovis Burial in Southwestern Montana." *Science* 186:147–150.

Lahren, Sylvester L., Jr. 1998 "Reservations and Reserves." In: *Handbook of North American Indians, Vol. 12, Plateau*, Deward E. Walker, Jr., ed., pp. 484–498. Washington, D.C.: Smithsonian Institution.

Lamb, Sydney M. 1958 "Linguistic Prehistory in the Great Basin." *International Journal of American Linguistics* 24(2):95–100.

Lambert, Patricia M. 1993 "Health in Prehistoric Populations of the Santa Barbara Channel Islands." *American Antiquity* 58(3):509–522.

1997 "Patterns of Violence in Prehistoric Hunter-gatherer Societies of Coastal Southern California." In: *Troubled Times: Violence and Warfare in the Past*, Debra L. Martin and David W. Frayer, eds., pp. 77–109. Amsterdam: Gordon and Breach.

Lambert, Patricia M., and Philip J. Walker 1991 "Physical Anthropological Evidence for the Evolution of Social Complexity in Coastal Southern California." *Antiquity* 65(249):963–973.

Lambert, Patricia M., Brian R. Billman, and Banks L. Leonard 2000 "Explaining Variability in Mutilated Human Bone Assemblages from the American Southwest: A Case Study from the Southern Piedmont of Sleeping Ute Mountain, Colorado." *International Journal of Osteology* 19(1):49–64.

Lampl, Michelle, and Baruch S. Blumberg 1979 "Blood Polymorphisms and the Origins of New World Populations." In: *The First Americans: Origins, Affinities, and Adaptations*, William S. Laughlin and Albert B. Harper, eds., pp. 107–123. New York: Gustav Fischer.

Lanata, José Luis, Luis Martino, Ana Osella, and Arleen Garcia-Herbst 2008 "Demographic Conditions Necessary to Colonize New Spaces: The Case for Early Human Dispersal in the Americas." *World Archaeology* 40(4):520–537.

Lane, Leon, and David G. Anderson 2001 "Paleoindian Occupations of the Southern Appalachians." In: *Archaeology of the Appalachian Highlands*, Lynne P. Sullivan and Susan C. Prezzano, eds., pp. 88–102. Knoxville, University of Tennessee Press.

Larsen, Clark Spencer, and Dale L. Hutchinsen 1999 "Osteopathology of Carson Desert Foragers: Reconstructing Prehistoric Lifeways in the Western Great Basin." In: *Prehistoric Lifeways in the Great Basin Wetlands: Bioarchaeological Reconstruction and Interpretations*, Brian E. Hemphill and Clark Spencer Larsen, eds., pp. 184–202. Salt Lake City: University of Utah Press.

Larsen, Clark Spencer, and Robert L. Kelly 1995 "Summary and Conclusions." In: *Bioarchaeology of the Stillwater Marsh: Prehistoric Human Adaptation in the Western Great Basin*, Clark Spencer Larsen and Robert L. Kelly, eds., pp. 134–137. *Anthropological Papers of the American Museum of Natural History* 77.

Larsen, Clark Spencer, and George R. Milner (eds.) 1994 *In the Wake of Contact: Biological Responses to Conquest.* New York: Wiley-Liss.

Larsen, Clark Spencer, Mark C. Griffin, Dale L. Huchinson, Vivian E. Nobel, Lynette Noor, Robert F. Pastor, Christopher B. Ruff, Katherine F. Russell, Margaret J. Schoeninger, Michael Schultz, Scott W. Simpson, and Mark F. Teaford 2001 "Frontiers of Contact: Bioarchaeology of Spanish Florida." *Journal of World Prehistory* 15(1):69–123.

Larson, Daniel O., and Joel Michaelsen 1990 "Impacts on Climatic Variability and Population Growth on Virgin Branch Anasazi Cultural Developments." *American Antiquity* 55(2):227–249.

Larson, Mary Lou, Marcel Kornfled, and George C. Frison (eds.) 2009 *Hell Gap: A Stratified Paleoindian Campsite at the Edge of the Rockies.* Salt Lake City: University of Utah Press.

Laughlin, William S. 1967 "Human Migration and Permanent Occupation in the Bering Sea Area." In: *The Bering Land Bridge*, David M. Hopkins, ed., pp. 409–450. Stanford, CA: Stanford University Press.

1975 "Aleuts: Ecosystem, Holocene History, and Siberian Origin." *Science* 189:507–515.

Laughlin, William S., Jørgen B. Jørgensen, and Bruno Frøhlich 1979 "Aleuts and Eskimos: Survivors of the Bering Land Bridge Coast." In: *The First Americans: Origins, Affinities, and Adaptations*, William S. Laughlin and Albert B. Harper, eds., pp. 91–104. New York: Gustav Fischer.

Laughlin, William S., and Albert B. Harper (eds.) 1979 *The First Americans: Origins, Affinities, and Adaptations.* New York: Gustav Fischer.

Lavallée, Danièle 2000 *The First South Americans: The Peopling of a Continent from the Earliest Evidence to High Culture.* Salt Lake City: University of Utah Press.

Lawton, Harry W., Philip J. Wilke, Mary DeDecker, and William M. Mason 1976 "Agriculture among the Paiute of Owens Valley." *Journal of California Anthropology* 3(1):13–50.

Laylander, Don 1992 "The Development of Baja California Prehistoric Archaeology." In: *Essays on the Prehistory of Maritime California*, Terry L. Jones, ed., pp. 231–250. Center for Archaeological Research at Davis, Publication No. 10.

1997a "The Last Days of Lake Cahuilla: The Elmore Site." *Pacific Coast Archaeological Society Quarterly* 33(1 & 2).

1997b "The Linguistic Prehistory of Baja California." In: *Contributions to the Linguistic Prehistory of Central and Baja California*, Gary S. Breschini and Trudy Haversat, eds., pp. 1–94. Salinas: Coyote Press Archives of California Prehistory No. 44.

2006 "Issues in Baja California Prehistory." In: *Advances in the Archaeology of the Forgotten Peninsula*, Don Laylander and Jerry D. Moore, eds., pp. 1–13. Gainesville: University Press of Florida.

2007 "Large Projectiles and the Cultural Distinction of Southern Baja California: A Reexamination." *Pacific Coast Archaeological Society Quarterly* 39(1 & 2):11–21.

Laylander, Don, and Jerry D. Moore (eds.) 2006 *The Prehistory of Baja California: Advances in the Archaeology of the Forgotten Peninsula.* Gainesville: University Press of Florida.

Layton, Thomas N. 1985 "Invaders from the South? Archaeological Discontinuities in the Northwestern Great Basin." *Journal of California and Great Basin Anthropology* 7(2):183–201.

Leach, Melinda 1999 "In Search of Gender in Great Basin Prehistory." In: *Models for the Millennium: Great Basin Anthropology Today*, Charlotte Beck, ed., pp. 182–191. Salt Lake City: University of Utah Press.

LeBlanc, Steven A. 1999 *Prehistoric Warfare in the American Southwest.* Salt Lake City: University of Utah Press.

2008 "The Case for an Early Farmer Migration into the Greater American Southwest." In: *Archaeology Without Borders: Contact, Commerce, and Change in the U. S. Southwest and Northwestern Mexico*, Laurie D. Webster, Maxine E. Brown, and Eduardo Gamboa Carrera, eds., pp. 107–142. Boulder: University Press of Colorado.

Lehmer, Donald J. 1954 "Archaeological Investigations in the Oahe Dam Area, South Dakota, 1950–51." *Bureau of American Ethnology Bulletin* 158.

1971 *Introduction to Middle Missouri Archaeology.* Washington, D.C.: National Park Service, Anthropological Papers No. 1.

2001 "Plains Village Tradition: Postcontact." In: *Handbook of North American Indians, Vol. 13, Plains*, Raymond J. DeMallie, ed., pp. 245–255. Washington, D.C.: Smithsonian Institution.

Lehmer, Donald J., and Warren W. Caldwell 1966 Horizon and Tradition on the Northern Plains. *American Antiquity* 31(4):511–516.

Leigh, R. W. 1928 "Dental Pathology of Aboriginal California." *University of California Publications in American Archaeology and Ethnography* 23(10).

Lekson, Stephen H. 1992 "The Surface Archaeology of Southwestern New Mexico." *Artifact* 30(3):1–35.

1993 "Chaco, Mimbres, and Hohokam: The 11th and 12th Centuries in the American Southwest." *Expedition* 35(1):44–52.

1999 *The Chaco Meridian: Centers of Political Power in the Ancient Southwest.* Walnut Creek, CA: AltaMira Press.

2002a "War in the Southwest, War in the World." *American Antiquity* 67(4):607–624.

2002b "Salado Archaeology of the Upper Gila, New Mexico." *Anthropological Papers of the University of Arizona* No. 67.

2005 "Chaco and Paquimé: Complexity, History, and Landscape." In: *North American Archaeology*, Timothy R. Pauketat and Diana DiPaolo Loren, eds., pp. 235–272. Malden, MA: Blackwell Publishing.

2006a Chaco Matters: An Introduction. In: *The Archaeology of Chaco Canyon: An Eleventh-Century Pueblo Regional Center*, Stephen H. Lekson, ed., pp. 3–44. Santa Fe, NM: School of American Research Press.

2006b (ed.) *The Archaeology of Chaco Canyon: An Eleventh-Century Pueblo Regional Center*. Santa Fe: School of American Research Press.

Lekson, Stephen H., and Catherine M. Cameron 1995 "The Abandonment of Chaco Canyon, the Mesa Verde Migrations, and the Reorganization of the Pueblo World." *Journal of Anthropological Archaeology* 14(2):184–202.

Leland, Joy 1986 "Population." In: *Handbook of North American Indians, Vol. 11, Great Basin*, Warren L. d'Azevedo, ed., pp. 608–619. Washington, D.C.: Smithsonian Institution.

Lell, Jeffrey T., Rem I. Sukernik, Yelena B. Starikovskaya, Bing Su, Li Jin, Theodore G. Schurr, Peter A. Underhill, and Douglas C. Wallace 2002 "The Dual Origin and Siberian Affinities of Native American Y Chromosomes." *American Journal of Human Genetics* 70(1):192–206.

LeMoine, Genevieve 2003 "Woman of the House: Gender, Architecture, and Ideology in Dorset Prehistory." *Arctic Anthropology* 40(1):121–138.

Leonard, N. Nelson III, and Christopher E. Drover 1980 "Prehistoric Turquoise Mining in the Halloran Springs District, San Bernardino County, California." *Journal of California and Great Basin Anthropology* 2(2):245–256

Leonard, Robert D., and Heidi E. Reed 1993 "Population and Aggregation in the Prehistoric American Southwest: A Selectionist Model." *American Antiquity* 58(4):648–661.

Lepofsky, Dana, and Sandra L. Peacock 2004 "A Question of Intensity: Exploring the Role of Plant Foods in Northern Plateau Prehistory." In: *Complex Hunter-Gatherers: Evolution and Organization of Prehistoric Communities on the Plateau of Northwestern North America*, William C. Prentiss and Ian Kuijt, eds., pp. 115–139. Salt Lake City: University of Utah Press.

Lepofsky, Dana, Ken Lertzman, Douglas Hallett, and Rolf Mathewes 2005 "Climate Change and Culture Change on the Southern Coast of British Columbia 2400–1200 Cal. B.P.: An Hypothesis." *American Antiquity* 70(2):267–293.

Lepofsky, Dana, Michael Blake, Douglas Brown, Sandra Morrison, Nicole Oakes, and Natasha Lyons 2000 "The Archaeology of the Scowlitz Site, SW British Columbia." *Journal of Field Archaeology* 27(4):391–416.

Lepofsky, Dana, David M. Schaepe, Anthony P. Graesch, Michael Lenert, Patricia Ormerod, Keith Thor Carlson, Jeanne E. Arnold, Michael Blake, Patrick Moore, and John J. Clague 2009 "Exploring Stó:lōCoast Salish Interaction and Identity in Ancient Houses and Settlements in the Fraser Valley, British Columbia." *American Antiquity* 74(4):595–626.

Lepper, Bradley T. 1995 "Tracking Ohio's Great Hopewell Road." *Archaeology* 48(6):52–56.

1999 "Pleistocene Peoples of Midcontinental North America." In: *Ice Age Peoples of North America: Environments, Origins, and Adaptations of the First Americans*, Robson Bonnichsen and Karen L. Turnmire, eds., pp. 362–394. Oregon State University: Center for the Study of the First Americans.

2005 *Ohio Archaeology: An Illustrated Chronicle of Ohio's Ancient American Indian Cultures*. Wilmington, OH: Orange Frazer Press.

2006 "The Great Hopewell Road and the Role of Pilgrimage in the Hopewell Interaction Sphere." In: *Recreating Hopewell*, Douglas K. Charles and Jane E. Buikstra, eds., pp. 122–133. Gainesville: University Press of Florida.

Lepper, Bradley T., and David J. Meltzer 1991 "Late Pleistocene Human Occupation of the Eastern United States." In: *Clovis: Origins and Adaptations*, Robson Bonnichsen and Karen L. Turnmire, eds., pp. 175–184. Oregon State University: Center for the Study of the First Americans.

Leroux, Odette, Marion E. Jackson, and Minnie Aodla Freeman (eds.) 1994 *Inuit Women Artists: Voices from Cape Dorset.* Seattle: University of Washington Press

Levine, Mary Ann 1999 "Native Copper in the Northeast: An Overview of Potential Sources Available to Indigenous Peoples." In: *The Archaeological Northeast*, Mary Ann Levine, Kenneth E. Sassaman, and Michael S. Nassaney, eds., pp. 183–199. Westport: Bergin & Garvey.

2004 "The Clauson Site: Late Archaic Settlement and Subsistence in the Uplands of Central New York." *Archaeology of Eastern North America* 32:161–181.

2007 "Determining the Provenance of Native Copper Artifacts from Northeastern North America: Evidence from Instrumental Neutron Activation Analysis." *Journal of Archaeological Science* 34(4):572–587.

Liebmann, Matthew, and Robert W. Preucel 2007 "The Archaeology of the Pueblo Revolt and the Formation of the Modern Pueblo World." *Kiva* 73(2):195–217.

Lightfoot, Kent G. 1997 "Cultural Construction of Coastal Landscapes: A Middle Holocene Perspective from San Francisco Bay." In: "Archaeology of the California Coast during the Middle Holocene," Jon M. Erlandson and Michael A. Glassow, eds., pp. 129–141. *University of California Los Angeles, Institute of Archaeology, Perspectives in California Archaeology*, Vol. 4.

2005 *Indians, Missionaries, and Merchants: The Legacy of Colonial Encounters on the California Frontiers*. Berkeley: University of California Press.

Lightfoot, Kent G., and Gary M. Feinman 1982 "Social Differentiation and Leadership Development in Early Pithouse Villages in the Mogollon Region of the American Southwest." *American Antiquity* 47(1):64–86.

Lightfoot, Kent G., and Edward M. Luby 2002 "Late Holocene in the San Francisco Bay Area: Temporal Trends in the Use and Abandonment of Shell Mounds in the East Bay." In:

"Catalysts to Complexity: Late Holocene Societies of the California Coast," Jon M. Erlandson and Terry L. Jones, eds., pp. 263–281. *University of California Los Angeles, Institute of Archaeology, Perspectives in California Archaeology*, Vol. 6.

Lightfoot, Kent G., and Otis Parrish 2009 *California Indians and Their Environment: An Introduction.* Berkeley: University of California Press.

Lightfoot, Kent G., and William S. Simmons 1998 "Culture Contact in Protohistoric California: Social Contexts of Native and European Encounters." *Journal of California and Great Basin Anthropology* 20(2):138–170.

Lightfoot, Kent G. Ann F. Schiff, and Thomas A. Wake (eds.) 1991a *The Archaeology and Ethnohistory of Fort Ross, California: Volume 2, The Native Alaskan Neighborhood: A Multiethnic Community at Colony Ross.* Berkeley: Contributions of the University of California Archaeological Research Facility No. 55.

Lightfoot, Kent G., Thomas A. Wake, and Ann F. Schiff (eds.) 1991b *The Archaeology and Ethnohistory of Fort Ross, California: Volume 1, Introduction.* Berkeley: Contributions of the University of California Archaeological Research Facility No. 49.

Lillard, J. B., Robert F. Heizer, and Franklin F. Fenenga 1939 "An Introduction to the Archaeology of Central California." *Sacramento Junior College, Department of Anthropology Bulletin* 2.

Lindauer, Owen, and John H. Blitz 1996 "Higher Ground: The Archaeology of North American Platform Mounds." *Journal of Archaeological Research* 5(2):169–207.

Lindsey, Roche M., and Richard A. Krause 2007 "Assessing Plains Village Mobility Patterns on the Central High Plains." In: *Plains Village Archaeology: Bison-hunting Farmers in the Central and Northern Plains*, Stanley A. Ahler and Marvin Kay, eds., pp. 96–104. Salt Lake City: University of Utah Press.

Lipe, William D. 1995 "The Depopulation of the Northern San Juan: Conditions in the Turbulent 1200s." *Journal of Anthropological Archaeology* 14(2):143–165.

2002 "Social Power in the Central Mesa Verde Region, A. D. 1150–1290." In: *Seeking the Central Place: Archaeology and Ancient Communities in the Mesa Verde Region*, Mark D. Varien and Richard H. Wilshusen, eds., pp. 203–232. Salt Lake City: University of Utah Press.

Little, Keith J. 1999 "Role of Late Woodland Interactions in the Emergence of Etowah." *Southeastern Archaeology* 18(1):45–56.

Livingston, Stephanie D. 1986 "Archaeology of the Humboldt Lakebed Site." *Journal of California and Great Basin Anthropology* 8(1):99–115.

Lobdell, John E. 1986 "The Kuparuk Pingo Site: A Northern Archaic Hunting Camp of the Arctic Coastal Plain, North America." *Arctic* 39(1):47–51.

Loendorf, Lawrence L., and Stuart W. Conner 1993 "The Pectoral Shields and the Shield-Bearing Warrior Motif." Journal of *California and Great Basin Anthropology* 15(2):216–224.

Logan, Brad 2006 "Woodland Adaptations in Eastern Kansas." In: *Kansas Archaeology*, Robert J. Hoard and William E. Banks, eds., pp. 76–92. Lawrence: University of Kansas Press.

Lohse, E. S., and Roderick Sprague 1998 "History of Research." In: *Handbook of North American Indians, Vol. 12, Plateau*, Deward E. Walker, Jr., ed., pp. 8–28. Washington, D.C.: Smithsonian Institution.

Longacre, William A. 1970 "Archaeology as Anthropology: A Case Study." *Anthropological Papers of the University of Arizona* No. 17.

Loosle, Byron 2000 "The Acquisition of Nonlocal Lithic Material by the Uinta Fremont." *Journal of California and Great Basin Anthropology* 22(2):277–294.

Lopinot, Neal H., and William I. Woods 1993 "Wood Overexploitation and the Collapse of Cahokia." In: *Farmers and Foragers in the Eastern Woodlands*, C. Margaret Scarry, ed., pp. 206–231. Gainesville: University Press of Florida.

Losey, Robert J. 2005a "Earthquakes and Tsunami as Elements of Environmental Disturbance on the Northwest Coast of North America." *Journal of Anthropological Archaeology* 24(2):101–116.

2005b "House Remains at the Netarts Sandspit Village, Oregon." *Journal of Field Archaeology* 30(4):401–417.

Loud, Llewellyn L., and Mark R. Harrington 1929 "Lovelock Cave." *University of California Publications in American Archaeology and Ethnology* 25(1).

Lovis, William A. 2008 "Hunter-gatherer Archaeology and the Upper Great Lakes Archaic." *SAA Archaeological Record* 8(5):27–30.

Lovis, William A., Randolph E. Donahue, and Margaret B. Holman 2005 "Long-Distance Logistic Mobility as an Organizing Principle Among Northern Hunter-Gatherers: A Great Lakes Middle Holocene Settlement System." *American Antiquity* 70(4):669–693.

Lovis, William A., Katheryn C. Egan-Bruhy, Beverly A. Smith, and G. William Monaghan 2001 "Wetlands and Emergent Horticultural Economies in the Upper Great Lakes: A New Perspective from the Schultz Site." *American Antiquity* 66(4):615–632.

Lovisek, Joan A. 2007 "Aboriginal Warfare on the Northwest Coast: Did the Potlatch Replace Warfare?" In: *North American Indigenous Warfare and Ritual Violence*, Richard J. Chacon and Rubén G. Mendoza, eds., pp. 58–73. Tucson: University of Arizona Press.

Lowell, Julia C. 2007 "Women and Men in Warfare and Migration: Implications of Gender Imbalance in the Grasshopper Region of Arizona." *American Antiquity* 72(1):95–123.

Lowery, Darrin, and Jay F. Custer 1990 "Crane Point: An Early Archaic Site in Maryland." *Journal of Middle Atlantic Archaeology* 6:75–120.

Loy, Thomas H., and E. James Dixon 1998 "Blood Residues on Fluted Points from Beringia." *American Antiquity* 63(1):21–46.

Lubinski, Patrick M. 1999 "The Communal Pronghorn Hunt: A Review of the Ethnographic and Archaeological Evidence." *Journal of California and Great Basin Anthropology* 21(2):158–181.

Luby, Edward M., and Mark F. Gruber 1999 "The Dead Must Be Fed: Symbolic Meanings of the Shellmounds of the San Francisco Bay." *Cambridge Archaeological Journal* 9(1):95–108.

Lupo, Karen D., and Dave N. Schmitt 1997 "On Late Holocene Variability in Bison Populations in the Northeastern Great Basin." *Journal of California and Great Basin Anthropology* 19(1):50–69.

Lyman, R. Lee 1991 *Prehistory of the Oregon Coast.* San Diego: Academic Press.

   1995 "On the Evolution of Marine Mammal Hunting on the West Coast of North America." *Journal of Anthropological Archaeology* 14(1):45–77.

   1997 "Assessing a Reassessment of Early 'Pre-Littoral' Radiocarbon Dates from the Oregon Coast." *Journal of California and Great Basin Anthropology* 19(2):260–269.

Lyman, R. Lee, Michael J. O'Brien, and Virgil Hayes 1998 "A Mechanical and Functional Study of Bone Rods from the Richey-Roberts Clovis Cache, Washington, U.S.A." *Journal of Archaeological Science* 25(9):887–906.

Lynch, Thomas F. 1982 "Chronology and Stratigraphy at Guitarreno Cave, Peru." In: *Peopling of the New World,* Jonathon E. Ericson, R. E. Taylor, and Rainer Berger, eds., pp. 263–268. Los Altos, CA: Ballena Press Anthropological Papers No. 23.

   1990 "Glacial-Age Man in South America? A Critical Review." *American Antiquity* 55(1):12–36.

   1991 "Lack of Evidence for Glacial-Age Settlement of South America: Reply to Dillehay and Collins and to Gruhn and Bryan." *American Antiquity* 56(2):348–355.

Lyneis, Margaret M. 1995 "The Virgin Anasazi, Far Western Puebloans." *Journal of World Prehistory* 9(2):199–241.

Lyneis, Margaret M., Mary K. Rusco, and Keith Myhrer 1989 "Investigations at Adam 2 (26Ck 2059): A Mesa House Phase Site in the Moapa Valley, Nevada." *Nevada State Museum Anthropological Papers* No. 22.

Lyons, William H., Scott P. Thomas, and Craig E. Skinner 2001 "Changing Obsidian Sources at the Lost Dune and McCoy Creek Sites, Blitzen Valley, Southeast Oregon." *Journal of California and Great Basin Anthropology* 23(2):273–296.

Mabry, Jonathan B. 2005 "Changing Knowledge and Ideas about the First Farmers in Southeastern Arizona." In: *The Late Archaic Across the Borderlands: From Foraging to Farming,* Bradley J. Vierra, ed., pp. 41–83. Austin: University of Texas Press.

   2008 "What's So Archaic about the Late Archaic?" *SAA Archaeological Record* 8(5):36–40.

Mabry, Jonathan B., John P. Carpenter, and Guadalupe Sanchez 2008 "Archaeological Models of Early Uto-Aztecan Prehistory in the Arizona-Sonora Borderlands." In: *Archaeology Without Borders: Contact, Commerce, and Change in the U. S. Southwest and Northwestern Mexico,* Laurie D. Webster, Maxine E. Brown, and Eduardo Gamboa Carrera, eds., pp. 155–183. Boulder: University Press of Colorado.

MacDonald, Douglas H. 1998 "Substance, Sex, and Cultural Transmission in Folsom Culture." *Journal of Anthropological Archaeology* 17(3):217–239.

MacDonald, George F. 1968 *Debert, A Paleo-Indian Site in Central Nova Scotia.* Ottawa: National Museums of Canada, Anthropology Papers No. 16.

MacDonald, George F., and Jerome S. Cybulski 2001 "Introduction: The Prince Rupert Harbour Project." In: *Perspectives on Northwest Coast Prehistory,* Jerome S. Cybulski, ed., pp. 1–23. Canadian Museum of Civilization, Mercury Series, Archaeological Survey of Canada, Paper 160.

Mackie, Quentin, and Steven Achenson 2005 "The Graham Tradition." In: *Haida Gwaii: Human History and Environment from the Time of Loon to the Time of the Iron People,* Daryl W. Fedje and Rolf W. Mathewes, eds., pp. 274–302. Vancouver: University of British Columbia Press.

MacNeish, Richard S. 1976 "Early Man in the New World." *American Scientist* 64(3):316–327.

Madsen, Carl D. 1997 "Microwear Analysis of the Lithic Assemblage at the Rosenberger Site." *Journal of California and Great Basin Anthropology* 19(1):116–123.

Madsen, David B. 1979 "The Fremont and the Sevier: Defining Prehistoric Agriculturalists North of the Anasazi." *American Antiquity* 44(4):711–722.

   1986a "Great Basin Nuts: A Short Treatise on the Distribution, Productivity, and Prehistoric Use of Pinyon." In: "Anthropology of the Desert West: Essays in Honor of Jesse D. Jennings," Carol J. Condie and Don D. Fowler, eds., pp. 21–42. Special issue, *University of Utah Anthropological Papers* No. 110.

   1986b "Prehistoric Ceramics." In: *Handbook of North American Indians, Vol. 11, Great Basin,* Warren L. d'Azevedo, ed., pp. 206–214. Washington, D.C.: Smithsonian Institution.

   2002 "Great Basin Peoples and Late Quaternary Aquatic History." In: *Great Basin Aquatic Systems History,* Robert Hershler, David B. Madsen, and Donald R. Currey, eds., pp. 387–405. Washington, D.C.: Smithsonian Contributions to the Earth Sciences No. 33.

   2004 "Colonization of the Americas before the Last Glacial Maximum: Issues and Problems." In: *Entering America: Northeast Asia and Beringia Before the Last Glacial Maximum,* David B. Madsen, ed., pp. 1–26. Salt Lake City: University of Utah Press.

Madsen, David B., and James E. Kirkman 1988 "Hunting Hoppers." *American Antiquity* 53(3):593–604.

Madsen, David B., and LaMar W. Lindsay 1977 "Backhoe Village." *Utah State Historical Society Antiquities Section Selected Papers* 4(12).

Madsen, David B., and James F. O'Connell (eds.) 1982 "Man and Environment in the Great Basin." *Society for American Archaeology Papers* No. 2.

Madsen, David B., and David Rhode (eds.) 1994 *Across the West: Human Population Movement and the Expansion of the Numa.* Salt Lake City: University of Utah Press.

Madsen, David B., and Dave N. Schmitt 1998 "Mass Collecting and the Diet Breadth Model: A Great Basin Example." *Journal of Archaeological Science* 25(5):445–455.

   2005 "Buzz-Cut Dune and Fremont Foraging at the Margin of Horticulture." *University of Utah Anthropological Papers* No. 124.

Madsen, David B., and Steven R. Simms 1998 "The Fremont Complex: A Behavioral Perspective." *Journal of World Prehistory* 12(3):255–336.

Mahoney, Nancy M., and John Kantner 2000 "Chacoan Archaeology and Great House Communities." In: *Great House Communities Across the Chacoan Landscape*, John Kantner and Nancy M. Mahoney, eds., pp. 1–15. *Anthropological Papers of the University of Arizona* No. 64.

Mainfort, Robert C., and Lynne P. Sullivan 1998 "Explaining Earthen Enclosures." In: *Ancient Earthen Enclosures of the Eastern Woodland*, Robert C. Mainfort, Jr. and Lynne P. Sullivan, eds., pp. 1–16. Gainesville: University Press of Florida.

Malhi, Ripan S., and David Glenn Smith 2002 "Haplogroup X Confirmed in Prehistoric North America." *American Journal of Physical Anthropology* 119(1):84–86.

Malhi, Ripan S., Brian M. Kemp, Jason A. Eshleman, Jerome Cybulski, David Glenn Smith, Scott Cousins, and Harold Harry 2007 "Mitochondrial Haplogroup M Discovered in Prehistoric North Americans." *Journal of Archaeological Science* 34(4):642–648.

Mancall, Peter C., and James H. Merrell (eds.) 2000 *American Encounters: Natives and Newcomers from European Contact to Indian Removal—1500–1850.* London: Routledge.

Mandryk, Carole A. 1990 "Could Humans Survive the Ice-Free Corridor? Late-Glacial Vegetation and Climate in West Central Alberta." In: *Megafauna & Man: Discovery of America's Heartland*, Larry D. Agenbroad, Jim L. Mead, and Lisa W. Nelson, eds., pp. 67–79. Flagstaff: Northern Arizona University Press.

2005 "Invented Traditions and the Ultimate American Origin Myth: In the Beginning . . . There Was an Ice-Free Corridor." In: *The Settlement of the American Continents*, C. Michael Barton, Geoffrey A. Clark, David R. Yesner, and George A. Pearson, eds, pp. 113–120. Tucson: University of Arizona Press.

Mandryk, Carole A., Heiner Josenhans, Daryl W. Fedje, and Rolf W. Mathewes 2001 "Late Quaternary Paleoenvironments of Northwestern North America: Implications for Inland Versus Coastal Migration Routes." *Quaternary Science Reviews* 20(1–3):301–314.

Mann, Daniel H., Richard E. Reanier, Dorothy M. Peteet, Michael L. Kunz, and Mark Johnson 2001 "Environmental Change and Arctic Paleoindians." *Arctic Anthropology* 38(2):119–138.

Marlar, Richard A., Banks L. Leonard, Brian R. Billman, Patricia M. Lambert, and Jennifer E. Marlar 2000 "Biochemical Evidence of Cannibalism at a Prehistoric Puebloan Site in Southwestern Colorado." *Nature* 407:74–78.

Marquardt, William H. 2001 "The Emergence and Demise of the Calusa." In: *Societies in Eclipse: Archaeology of the Eastern Woodlands Indians, A.D. 1400–1700*, David S. Brose, C. Wesley Cowan, and Robert C. Mainfort, Jr., eds., pp. 157–171. Washington, D.C.: Smithsonian Institution Press.

Marquardt, William H., and Patty Jo Watson 2005 "The Green River Shell Mound Archaic: Conclusions." In: *The Archaeology of the Middle Green River Region, Kentucky*, William H. Marquardt and Patty Jo Watson, eds., pp. 629–647. University of Florida, Gainesville, Florida Museum of Natural History,

Institute of Archaeology and Paleoenvironmental Studies, Monograph No. 5.

Martijn, Charles A. 1964 "Canadian Eskimo Carving in Historical Perspective." *Anthropos* 59(3–4):546–596.

Martin, Paul Schultz 1967a "Pleistocene Overkill." *Natural History* 76(10):32–38.

1967b "Prehistoric Overkill." In: *Pleistocene Extinctions: The Search for a Cause*, Paul S. Martin and H. E. Wright, Jr., eds., pp. 75–120. New Haven: Yale University Press.

1973 "The Discovery of America." *Science* 179:969–974.

1974 "Palaeolithic Players on the American Stage: Man's Impact on the Late Pleistocene Megafauna." In: *Arctic and Alpine Environments*, Jack D. Ives and Roger G. Barry, eds., pp. 669–700. London: Metheun & Co.

1987 "Clovisia the Beautiful!" *Natural History* 96(10):10–13.

2002 "Prehistoric Extinctions: In the Shadow of Man." In: *Wilderness and Political Ecology: Aboriginal Influences and the Original State of Nature*, Charles E. Kay and Randy T. Simmons, eds., pp. 1–27. Salt Lake City: University of Utah Press.

2005 *Twilight of the Mammoths: Ice Age Extinctions and the Rewilding of North America.* Berkeley: University of California Press.

Martin, Paul Sidney 1979 "Prehistory: Mogollon." In: *Handbook of North American Indians, Vol. 9, Southwest*, Alfonzo Ortiz, ed., pp. 61–74. Washington, D. C.: Smithsonian Institution.

Martin, Paul Sidney, John B. Rinaldo, Elaine A. Bluhm, H. C. Cutler, and R. Grange, Jr. 1952 "Mogollon Cultural Continuity and Change: The Stratigraphic Analysis of Tularosa and Cordova Caves." *Fieldiana: Anthropology* 40.

Martin, Scott W. J. 2008 "Languages Past and Present: Archaeological Approaches to the Appearance of Northern Iroquoian Speakers in the Lower Great Lakes Region of North America." *American Antiquity* 73(3):441–363.

Martz, Patricia 1992 "Status Distinctions Reflected in Chumash Mortuary Populations in the Santa Monica Mountains Region." In: *Essays on the Prehistory of Maritime California*, Terry L. Jones, ed., pp. 145–156. Center for Archaeological Research at Davis, Publication No. 10.

Marwitt, John P. 1986 "Fremont Cultures" *Handbook of North American Indians, Vol. 11, Great Basin*, Warren L. d'Azevedo, ed., pp. 161–172. Washington, D.C. Smithsonian Institution.

Maschner, Herbert D. G. 1991 "The Emergence of Cultural Complexity on the Northern Northwest Coast." *Antiquity* 65(249):924–934.

1997 "The Evolution of Northwest Coast Warfare." In: *Troubled Times: Violence and Warfare in the Past*, Debra L. Martin and David W. Frayer, eds., pp. 267–302. Amsterdam: Gordon and Breach.

1999a "Sedentism, Settlement, and Village Organization on the Lower Alaskan Peninsula: A Preliminary Assessment." In: *Settlement Pattern Studies in the Americas: Fifty Years Since Virú*, Brian R. Billman and Gary M. Feinman, eds., pp. 56–76. Washington, D.C.: Smithsonian Institution Press.

1999b "Prologue to the Prehistory of the Lower Alaska Peninsula." *Arctic Anthropology* 36(1–2):84–102.

Maschner, Herbert D. G., and James W. Jordan 2008 "Catastrophic Events and Punctuated Culture Change: The Southern Bering Sea and North Pacific in a Dynamic Global System." In: *Time and Change: Archaeological and Anthropological Perspectives on the Long-Term in Hunter-Gatherer Studies*, Dimitra Papagianni, Robert Layton, and Herbert Maschner, eds., pp. 95–113. Oxford, UK: Oxbow Books.

Maschner, Herbert D. G., and Katherine L. Reedy-Maschner 1998 "Raid, Retreat, Defend (Repeat): The Archaeology and Ethnohistory of Warfare on the North Pacific Rim." *Journal of Anthropological Archaeology* 17(1):19–51.

Mason, Otis 1894 "Technogeography, or the Relation of the Earth to the Industries of Mankind." *American Anthropologist* 7(2):137–161.

Mason, Owen K. 1998 "The Contest Between the Ipiutak, Old Bering Sea, and Birnirk Polities and the Origin of Whaling during the First Millennium A.D. along Bering Strait." *Journal of Anthropological Archaeology* 17(3):240–325.

2009 "Flight from the Bering Straight: Did Siberian Punuk/Thule Military Cadres Conquer Northwest Alaska?" In: *The Northern World: AD 900–1400*, Herbert D. G. Maschner, Owen Mason, and Robert McGhee, eds., pp. 76–128. Salt Lake City: University of Utah Press.

Mason, Owen K., and Nancy H. Bigelow 2008 "The Crucible of Early to Mid-Holocene Climate in Northern Alaska: Does Northern Archaic Represent the People of the Spreading Forest?" *Arctic Anthropology* 45(2):39–70.

Mason, Owen K., and Stefanie L. Ludwig 1990 "Resurrecting Beach Ridge Archaeology: Parallel Depositional Records from St. Lawrence Island and Cape Krusenstern, Western Alaska." *Geoarchaeology* 5(4):349–373.

Mason, Roger D., Henry C. Koerper, and Paul E. Langenwalter II 1997 "Middle Holocene Adaptations on the Newport Coast of Orange County." In: *Archaeology of the California Coast During the Middle Holocene*, Jon M. Erlandson and Michael A. Glassow, eds., pp. 35–60. University of California Los Angeles, Institute of Archaeology, Perspectives in California Archaeology, Vol. 4.

Mason, Ronald J. 1962 "The Paleo-Indian Tradition in Eastern North America." *Current Anthropology* 3(2):227–278.

1981 *Great Lakes Archaeology.* New York: Academic Press.

Massey, William C. 1947 "Brief Report on Archaeological Investigations in Baja California." *Southwestern Journal of Anthropology* 3(4):334–359.

1955 "Culture History of the Cape Region of Baja California." Ph.D. dissertation, University of California, Berkeley.

1961 "The Survival of the Dart-Throwers on the Peninsula of Baja California." *Southwestern Journal of Anthropology* 17(1):81–93.

1966 "Archaeology and Ethnohistory of Lower California." In: *Handbook of Middle American Indians, Vol. 4, Archaeological Frontiers and External Connections*, Gordon F. Ekholm and Gordon R. Willey, eds., pp. 38–58. Austin: University of Texas Press.

Massey, William C., and Carolyn M. Osborne 1961 "A Burial Cave in Baja California: The Palmer Collection, 1887." *University of California Anthropological Records* 16(8).

Masters, Patricia M., and Dennis R. Gallegos 1997 "Environmental Change and Coastal Adaptations in San Diego County during the Middle Holocene." In: *Archaeology of the California Coast during the Middle Holocene*, Jon M. Erlandson and Michael A. Glassow, eds., pp. 11–21. University of California Los Angeles, Institute of Archaeology, Perspectives in California Archaeology, Vol. 4.

Mathes, W. Michael 1989 "Baja California: A Special Area of Contact and Colonization, 1535–1697." In: *Columbian Consequences, Vol. 1, Archaeological and Historical Perspectives on the Spanish Borderlands West*, David Hurst Thomas, ed., pp. 407–422. Washington: Smithsonian Institution Press.

Matson, R. G. 1976 "The Glenrose Cannery Site." *Canadian Museum of Civilization, Mercury Series, Archaeological Survey of Canada*, Paper 52.

1991 *The Origins of Southwestern Agriculture.* Tucson: University of Arizona Press.

2002 "The Spread of Maize Agriculture into the U.S. Southwest." In: *Examining the Farming/Language Dispersal Hypothesis*, Peter Bellwood and Colin Renfrew, eds., pp. 341–356. Cambridge: McDonald Institute for Archaeological Research.

2003 "Introduction: The Northwest Coast in Perspective." In: *Emerging from the Mist: Studies in Northwest Coast Culture History*, R. G. Matson, Gary Coupland, and Quentin Mackie, eds., pp. 1–11. Vancouver: University of British Columbia Press.

2005 "Many Perspectives but a Consistent Pattern: Comments on Contributions." In: *The Late Archaic Across the Borderlands: From Foraging to Farming*, Bradley J. Vierra, ed., pp. 279–299. Austin: University of Texas Press.

Matson, R. G., and Brian Chisholm 1991 "Basketmaker II Subsistence: Carbon Isotopes and Other Dietary Indicators from Cedar Mesa, Utah." *American Antiquity* 56(3):444–459.

Matson, R. G., and Gary Coupland 1995 *The Prehistory of the Northwest Coast.* New York: Academic Press.

Maxwell, Moreau S. 1985 *Prehistory of the Eastern Arctic.* Orlando: Academic Press.

McAvoy, Joseph M. 1997 "Addendum: Excavation of the Cactus Hill Site, 44SX202, Area A-B, Spring 1996." In: *Archaeological Investigations of Site 44SX202, Cactus Hill, Sussex County, Virginia*, Joseph M. McAvoy and Lynn D. McAvoy, pp. 193–228. Virginia Department of Historic Resources, Research Report Series No. 8.

McAvoy, Joseph M., and Lynn D. McAvoy 1997 "Archaeological Investigations of Site 44SX202, Cactus Hill, Sussex County, Virginia." *Virginia Department of Historic Resources, Research Report Series* No. 8.

McCaffrey, Moira T. 2006 "Archaic Period Occupation in Subarctic Quebec: A Review of the Evidence." In: *The Archaic of the Far Northeast*, David Sanger and M. A. P. Renouf, eds., pp. 161–190. Orono: University of Maine Press.

McCartney, Allen P., and Douglas W. Veltre 1999 "Aleutian Island Prehistory: Living in Insular Extremes." *World Archaeology* 30(3):503–515.

McCartney, Peter H. 1990 "Alternative Hunting Strategies in Plains Paleoindian Adaptations." In: *Hunters of the Recent Past*, Leslie B. Davis and Brian O. K. Reeves, eds., pp. 111–121. London: Unwin Hyman.

McClellan, Catharine, and Glenda Denniston 1981 "Environment and Culture in the Cordillera." In: *Handbook of North American Indians, Vol. 6, Subarctic*, June Helm, ed., pp. 372–386. Washington, DC: Smithsonian Institution.

McCutcheon, Sean 1991 *Electric Rivers: The Story of the James Bay Project*. Montreal: Black Rose Books.

McDonald, Jerry N. 1981 *North American Bison: Their Classification and Evolution*. Berkeley: University of California Press.

2000 "Pre-Clovis Archaeology at SV-2, Saltville, Virginia." *Virginia Museum of Natural History, Jeffersoniana Series* 9.

McDonald, Meg 1992 "Indian Hill Rockshelter and Aboriginal Cultural Adaptation in Anza-Borrego Desert State Park, Southeastern California." Ph.D. dissertation, University of California, Riverside.

McElrath, Dale L., Thomas E. Emerson, and Andrew C. Fortier 2000 "Social Evolution or Social Response? A Fresh Look at the 'Good Gray Cultures' after Four Decades of Midwest Research." In: *Late Woodland Societies: Tradition and Transformation Across the Midcontinent*, Thomas E. Emerson, Dale L. McElrath, and Andrew C. Fortier, eds., pp. 3–36. Lincoln: University of Nebraska Press.

McGhee, Robert 1976 "Paleoeskimo Occupations of Central and High Arctic Canada." In: "Eastern Arctic Prehistory: Paleoeskimo Problems," Moreau S. Maxwell, ed., pp. 15–39. Special issue, *Memoirs of the Society for American Archaeology* No. 31.

1984 "Contact Between Native North Americans and the Medieval Norse: A Review of the Evidence." *American Antiquity* 49(1):4–26.

1996 *Ancient People of the Arctic*. Vancouver: University of British Columbia Press.

2009 "When and Why Did the Inuit Move to the Eastern Arctic?" In: *The Northern World: AD 900–1400*, Herbert D. G. Maschner, Owen Mason, and Robert McGhee, eds., pp. 155–163. Salt Lake City: University of Utah Press.

McGinnis, Samuel M. 1984 *Freshwater Fishes of California*. Berkeley: University of California Press.

McGovern, Thomas H. 1980 "The Vinland Adventure: A North Atlantic Perspective." *North American Archaeologist* 2(4):285–308.

1990 "The Archaeology of the Norse North Atlantic." *Annual Review of Anthropology* 19:331–351.

2000 "The Demise of the Norse Greenland." In: *Vikings: The North Atlantic Saga*, William W. Fitzhugh and Elisabeth I. Ward, eds., pp. 327–339. Washington, D.C.: Smithsonian Institution Press.

McGuire, Kelly R. 1995 "Test Excavations at CA-FRE-61, Fresno County, California." California State University, Bakersfield,

Museum of Anthropology, *Occasional Papers in Anthropology* No. 5.

2007 "Models Made of Glass: A Prehistory of Northeastern California." In: *California Prehistory: Colonization, Culture, and Complexity*, Terry L. Jones and Kathryn A. Klar, eds., pp. 165–176. Lanham, MD: AltaMira Press.

McGuire, Kelly R., and Brian W. Hatoff 1991 "A Prehistoric Bighorn Sheep Drive Complex, Clan Alpine Mountains, Central Nevada." *Journal of California and Great Basin Anthropology* 13(1):95–109.

McGuire, Kelly R., and William R. Hildebrandt 2005 "Re-Thinking Great Basin Foragers: Prestige Hunting and Costly Signaling During the Middle Archaic Period." *American Antiquity* 70(4):695–712.

McHenry, Henry M. 1968 "Transverse Lines in Long Bones of Prehistoric California Indians." *American Journal of Physical Anthropology* 29(1):1–29.

McKern, William C. 1939 "The Midwestern Taxonomic Method as an Aid to Archaeological Study." *American Antiquity* 4(4):301–313.

McMillan, Alan D. 2003a "The Early Component at Ts'ishaa, An Outer Coast Site on Western Vancouver Island." In: *Archaeology of Coastal British Columbia: Essays in Honour of Professor Philip M. Hobler*, Roy L. Carlson, ed., pp. 39–44. Burnaby, B.C.: Simon Fraser University, Archaeology Press, Publication No. 30.

2003b "Reviewing the Wakashan Migration Hypothesis." In: *Emerging from the Mist: Studies in Northwest Coast Culture History*, R. G. Matson, Gary Coupland, and Quentin Mackie, eds., pp. 244–259. Vancouver: University of British Columbia Press.

McMillan, Alan D., Iain McKechnie, Denis E. St. Claire, and S. Gay Frederick 2008 "Exploring Variability in Maritime Resource Use on the Northwest Coast: A Case Study from Barkley Sound, Western Vancouver Island." *Canadian Journal of Archaeology* 32(2):214–238.

McNett, Charles W., Jr. 1986 "The Shawnee Minisink Site: An Overview." In: *The Shawnee Minisink Site: A Stratified Paleoindian-Archaic Site in the Upper Delaware Valley of Pennsylvania*, Charles W. McNett, Jr., ed., pp. 321–325. Orlando: Academic Press.

McNutt, Charles H. 1996 "The Central Mississippi Valley: A Summary." In: *Prehistory of the Central Mississippi Valley*, Charles H. McNutt, ed., pp. 187–257. Tuscaloosa: University of Alabama Press.

McWeeney, Lucinda, and Douglas C. Kellogg 2001 "Early and Middle Holocene Climate Changes and Settlement Patterns along the Eastern Coast of North America." *Archaeology of Eastern North America* 29:187–212.

Mead, Jim I., and David J. Meltzer (eds.) 1985 *Environments and Extinctions: Man in Late Glacial North America*. University of Maine, Orono: Center for the Study of Early Man.

Meatte, Daniel S. 1990 "Prehistory of the Western Snake River Basin. Pocatello." *Occasional Papers of the Idaho Museum of Natural History*, No. 35.

Meggers, Betty J. 1972 *Prehistoric America*. Chicago: Aldine-Atherton.

Mehringer, Peter J., Jr. 1986 "Prehistoric Environments." In: *Handbook of North American Indians, Vol. 11, Great Basin,* Warren L. d'Azevedo, ed., pp. 31–50. Washington, D.C.: Smithsonian Institution.

Mehringer, Peter J., Jr., Eric Blinman, and Kenneth L. Petersen 1977 "Pollen Influx and Volcanic Ash." *Science* 198:257–261.

Meighan, Clement W. 1955 "Archaeology of the North Coast Ranges." *University of California (Berkeley) Archaeological Survey Reports* 30:1–39.

1959a "Californian Cultures and the Concept of an Archaic Stage." *American Antiquity* 24(3):289–305.

1959b 'The Little Harbor Site, Catalina Island: An Example of Ecological Interpretation in Archaeology." *American Antiquity* 24(4):383–405.

1983 "Early Man in the New World." In: *Quaternary Coastlines and Marine Archaeology: Towards the Prehistory of Land Bridges and Continental Shelves,* P. M. Masters and N. C. Flemming, eds., pp. 441–462. London: Academic Press.

1987 "Reexamination of the Early Central California Culture." *American Antiquity* 52(1):28–36.

Meldgaard, Jorgen 1952 "A Paleo-Eskimo Culture in West Greenland." *American Antiquity* 17(3):222–230.

Meltzer, David J. 1988 Late Pleistocene Human Adaptations in Eastern North America. *Journal of World Prehistory* 2(1):1–52.

1989 "Why Don't We Know When the First People Came to North America?" *American Antiquity* 54(3):471–490.

1991 "On 'Paradigms' and 'Paradigm Bias' in Controversies Over Human Antiquity in America." In: *The First Americans: Search and Research,* Tom D. Dillehay and David J. Meltzer, eds, pp. 13–49. Boca Raton: CRC Press.

1993a Pleistocene Peopling of the Americas. *Evolutionary Anthropology* 1(5):157–169.

1993b "Is There a Clovis Adaptation?" In: *From Kostenki to Clovis: Upper Paleolithic-Paleo-Indian Adaptations,* Olga Soffer and N. D. Praslov, eds., pp. 293–310. New York: Plenum Press.

1995 "Clocking the First Americans." *Annual Review of Anthropology* 24:21–45.

1999 "Human Responses to Middle Holocene (Altithermal) Climates on the North American Great Plains." *Quaternary Research* 52(3):404–416.

2002 "What Do You Do When No One's Been There Before? Thoughts on the Exploration and Colonization of New Lands." In: "The First Americans: The Pleistocene Colonization of the New World," Nina G. Jablonski, ed., pp. 27–58. Special issue, *Memoirs of the California Academy of Sciences* No. 27.

2006 *Folsom: New Archaeological Investigations of a Classic Paleoindian Bison Kill.* Berkeley: University of California Press.

2009 *First Peoples in a New World: Colonizing Ice Age America.* Berkeley: University of California Press.

Meltzer, David J., James M. Adovasio, and Tom D. Dillehay 1994 "On a Pleistocene Human Occupation at Perda Furada, Brazil." *Antiquity* 68(261):695–714.

Meltzer, David J., and Michael B. Collins 1987 "Prehistoric Water Wells on the Southern High Plains: Clues to Altithermal Climate." *Journal of Field Archaeology* 14(1):9–28.

Meltzer, David J., and Robert C. Dunnell 1987 "Fluted Points from the Pacific Northwest." *Lithic Studies* 4(1):64–67.

Meltzer, David J., Don D. Fowler, and Jeremy A. Sabloff (eds.) 1986 *American Archaeology: Past and Future.* Washington, D.C.: Smithsonian Institution Press.

Meltzer, David J., Donald K. Grayson, Gerardo Ardila, Alex W. Barker, Dena F. Dincauze, C. Vance Haynes, Francisco Mena, Lautaro Núñez, and Dennis J. Standford 1997 "On the Pleistocene Antiquity of Monte Verde, Southern Chile." *American Antiquity* 62(4):659–663.

Meltzer, David J., and Vance T. Holliday 2010 "Would North American Paleoindians Have Noticed Younger Dryas Age Climate Change?" *Journal of World Prehistory* 23(1):1–41.

Meltzer, David J., and Bruce D. Smith 1986 "Paleoindian and Early Archaic Subsistence Strategies in Eastern North America." In: *Foraging, Collecting, and Harvesting: Archaic Period Subsistence and Settlement in the Eastern Woodlands,* Sarah W. Neusius, ed., pp. 3–31. Southern Illinois University, Carbondale, Center for Archaeological Investigations, Occasional Paper No. 6.

Meltzer, David J., Lawrence C. Todd, and Vance T. Holliday 2002 "The Folsom (Paleoindian) Type Site: Past Investigations, Current Studies." *American Antiquity* 67(1):5–36.

Menzies, Galvin 2003 *1421: The Year China Discovered America.* New York: William Morrow.

Menzies, John 2002 "The Pleistocene Legacy: Glaciation." In: *The Physical Geography of North America,* Antony R. Orme, ed., pp. 36–54. Oxford, UK: Oxford University Press.

Merrett, Deborah C. 2003 "Maxillary Sinusitis among the Moatfield People." In: *Bones of the Ancestors: The Archaeology and Osteobiography of the Moatfield Ossuary,* Ronald E. Williamson and Susan Pfeiffer, eds., pp. 241–261. Canadian Museum of Civilization, Mercury Series, Archaeological Survey of Canada, Paper 163.

Merrill, William L., Robert J. Hard, Jonathan B. Mabry, Gayle J. Fritz, Karen R. Adams, John R. Roney, and A. C. MacWilliams 2009 "The Diffusion of Maize to the Southwestern United States and Its Impact." *Proceedings of the National Academy of Sciences* 106(50):21019–21026.

Merriwether, D. Andrew 2002 "A Mitochondrial Perspective on the Peopling of the New World." In: "The First Americans: The Pleistocene Colonization of the New World," Nina G. Jablonski, ed., pp. 295–310. Special issue, *Memoirs of the California Academy of Sciences* No. 27.

Merriwether, D. Andrew, F. Rothhammer, and R. E. Ferrell 1995 "Distribution of the Four Founding Haplotypes in Native Americans Suggests a Single Wave of Migration of the New World." *American Journal of Physical Anthropology* 98(4):411–430.

Metcalfe, Duncan, and Lisa V. Larrabee 1985 "Fremont Irrigation: Evidence from Gooseberry Valley, Central Utah." *Journal of California and Great Basin Anthropology* 7(2):244–254.

Michael, Henry N. 1984 "Absolute Chronologies of Late Pleistocene and Early Holocene Cultures of Northeastern Asia." *Arctic Anthropology* 21(2):1–68.

Mihesuah, Devon A. (ed.) 2000 *Repatriation Reader: Who Owns American Indian Remains?* Lincoln: University of Nebraska Press.

Milanich, Jerald T. 1994 *Archaeology of Precolumbian Florida.* Gainesville: University Press of Florida.

2002 "Weeden Island Cultures." In: *The Woodland Southeast,* David G. Anderson and Robert C. Mainfort, Jr., eds., pp. 352–372. Tuscaloosa: University of Alabama Press.

2004 "Prehistory of Florida After 500 B.C." In: *Handbook of North American Indians, Vol. 14, Southeast,* Raymond D. Fogelson, ed., pp. 191–203. Washington, D.C.: Smithsonian Institution.

Milanich, Jerald T., Ann S. Cordell, Vernon James Knight, Jr., Timothy A. Kohler, and Brenda J. Sigler-Lavelle 1997 *Archaeology of Northern Florida A.D. 200–900: The McKeithen Weeden Island Culture.* Gainesville: University Press of Florida.

Miller, Jay 2001 "Keres: Engendered Key to the Pueblo Puzzle." *Ethnohistory* 48(3):495–514.

Miller, Suzanne J. 1972 "Weston Canyon Rockshelter: Big-Game Hunting in Southeastern Idaho." Master's thesis, Idaho State University.

1982 "The Archaeology and Geology of an Extinct Megafauna/Fluted-Point Association at Owl Cave, the Wasden Site, Idaho: A Preliminary Report." In: *Peopling of the New World,* Jonathon E. Ericson, R. E. Taylor, and Rainer Berger, eds., pp. 81–95. Los Altos, CA: Ballena Press Anthropological Papers No. 23.

Milliken, Randall, Richard T. Fitzgerald, Mark G. Hylkema, Randy Groza, Tom Origer, David G. Bieling, Alan Leventhal, Randy S. Wiberg, Andrew Gottsfield, Donna Gillette, Viviana Bellifemine, Eric Strother, Robert Cartier, and David A. Fredrickson 2007 "Punctuated Culture Change in the San Francisco Bay Area." In: *California Prehistory: Colonization, Culture, and Complexity,* Terry L. Jones and Kathryn A. Klar, eds., pp. 99–123. Lanham, MD: AltaMira Press.

Milne, S. Brooke, and Sarah M. Donnelly 2004 "Going to the Birds: Examining the Importance of Avian Resources to Pre-Dorset Subsistence Strategies on Southern Baffin Island." *Arctic Anthropology* 41(1):90–112.

Milner, George R. 1996 "Development and Dissolution of a Mississippian Society in the American Bottom, Illinois." In: *Political Structure and Change in the Prehistoric Southeastern United States,* John F. Scarry, ed., pp. 27–52. Gainesville: University Press of Florida.

1998 *The Cahokia Chiefdom: The Archaeology of a Mississippian Society.* Washington, D.C.: Smithsonian Institution Press.

1999 "Warfare in Prehistoric and Early Historic Eastern North America." *Journal of Archaeological Research* 7(2):105–151.

2004 *The Moundbuilders: Ancient Peoples of Eastern North America.* London: Thames and Hudson.

2007 "Warfare, Population, and Food Production in Prehistoric Eastern North America." In: *North American Indigenous Warfare and Ritual Violence,* Richard J. Chacon and Rubén G. Mendoza, eds., pp. 182–201. Tucson: University of Arizona Press.

Milner, George R., and James S. Oliver 1999 "Late Prehistoric Settlements and Wetlands in the Central Mississippi Valley." In: *Settlement Patterns in the Americas: Fifty Years Since Virú,* Brian R. Billman and Gary M. Feinman, eds., pp. 79–95. Washington, D.C.: Smithsonian Institution Press.

Milner, George R., Eve Anderson, and Virginia G. Smith 1991a "Warfare in Late Prehistoric West-Central Illinois." *American Antiquity* 56(4):581–603.

Milner, George R., Virginia G. Smith, and Eve Anderson 1991b "Conflict, Mortality, and Community Health in an Illinois Oneota Population." In: *Between Bands and States,* Susan A. Gregg, ed., pp. 245–264. Southern Illinois University, Carbondale, Center for Archaeological Investigations, Occasional Paper No. 9.

Minnis, Paul E. 1979 "Paleoethnobotanical Indicators of Prehistoric Environmental Disturbance." In: "The Nature and Status of Ethnobotany," Richard I. Ford, ed., pp. 347–366. Speicla issue, *University of Michigan, Museum of Anthropology, Anthropological Papers* No. 67.

Minnis, Paul E., Michael E. Whalen, and R. Emerson Howell 2006 "Fields of Power: Upland Farming in the Prehispanic Casas Grandes Polity, Chihuahua, Mexico." *American Antiquity* 71(4):707–722.

Minor, Rick 1995 "A Reassessment of Early 'Pre-Littoral' Radiocarbon Dates from the Southern Northwest Coast." *Journal of California and Great Basin Anthropology* 17(2):267–273.

1997 "Pre-Littoral or Early Archaic? Conceptualizing Early Adaptations on the Southern Northwest Coast." *Journal of California and Great Basin Anthropology* 19(2):269–280.

Minor, Rick, Guy L. Tasa, and George B. Wasson, Jr. 2001 "The Raymond's Dune Site and Its Place in the History of Southern Northwest Coast Archaeology." *Journal of California and Great Basin Anthropology* 23(1):77–92.

Mirau, Neil A. 1995 "Medicine Wheels on the Northern Plains: Contexts, Codes, Symbols." In: *Beyond Subsistence: Plains Archaeology and the Postprocessual Critique,* Philip Duke and Michael C. Wilson, eds., pp. 193–210. Tuscaloosa: University of Alabama Press.

Mitchell, Donald 1990 "Prehistory of the Coasts of Southern British Columbia and Northern Washington." In: *Handbook of North American Indians, Vol. 7, Northwest Coast,* Wayne Suttles, ed., pp. 340–358. Washington, D.C.: Smithsonian Institution.

Mitchell, Douglas R., and Judy L. Brunson-Hadley 2001 "An Evaluation of Classic Period Hohokam Burials and Society: Chiefs, Priests, or Acephalous Complexity?" In: *Ancient Burial Practices in the American Southwest: Archaeology, Physical Anthropology, and Native American Perspectives,* Douglas R. Mitchell and Judy L. Brunson-Hadley, eds., pp. 43–67. Albuquerque: University of New Mexico Press.

Mitchell, Douglas R., and Michael S. Foster 2000 "Hohokam Shell Middens along the Sea of Cortez, Puerto Peñasco, Sonora, Mexico." *Journal of Field Archaeology* 27(1):27–41.

Mitchell, Mark D. 2006 "Research Traditions, Public Policy, and the Underdevelopment of Theory in Plains Archaeology: Tracing the Legacy of the Missouri Basin Project." *American Antiquity* 71(2):381–396.

Møbjerg, Tinna 1999 "New Adaptive Strategies in the Saqqaq Culture of Greenland, c. 1600–1400 BC." *World Archaeology* 30(3):452–465.

Molto, J. Eldon, and Harumi Fujita 1995 "La Matancita: A Las Palmas Mortuary Site from the West Cape Region of Baja California Sur, Mexico." *Pacific Coast Archaeological Society Quarterly* 31(1&2):20–55.

Molto, J. Eldon, and Brenda Kennedy 1991 "Diet of the Las Palmas Culture of the Cape Region, Baja California Sur." *Pacific Coast Archaeological Society Quarterly* 27(4):47–59.

Molto, J. Eldon, Joe D. Stewart, and Paula J. Reimer 1997 "Problems in Radiocarbon Dating Human Remains from Arid Coastal Areas: An Example from the Cape Region of Baja California." *American Antiquity* 62(3):489–507.

Monaghan, G. William, William A. Lovis, and Kathryn C. Egan-Bruhy 2006 "Earliest *Cucurbita* from the Great Lakes, Northern USA." *Quaternary Research* 65(2):216–222.

Moodie, Roy Lee 1929 "Studies in Paleodontology XV: Dental Attrition and its Results among Certain Ancient Indians from Southern California." *Pacific Dental Gazette* 37:217–227.

Moore, Jerry D. 1999 "Archaeology in the Forgotten Peninsula: Prehistoric Settlement and Subsistence Strategies in Northern Baja California." *Journal of California and Great Basin Anthropology* 21(1):17–44.

Moore, Steven, Denise Jurich, and Mark E. Basgall 2003 "Reassessing Archaeology of the Lakebed Locality, Pleistocene Lake China, California." *Current Research in the Pleistocene* 20:54–56.

Moorehead, Warren K. 1913 "The Red-Paint People of Maine." *American Anthropologist* 15(1):33–47.

Moratto, Michael J. 1984 *California Archaeology*. Orlando, FL: Academic Press.

2002 "Culture History of the New Melones Reservoir Area, Calaveras and Tulomne Counties, California." In: *Essays in California Archaeology: A Memorial to Franklin Fenenga*, William J. Wallace and Francis A. Riddell, eds., pp. 25–54. Berkeley: Contributions of the University of California Archaeological Research Facility No. 60.

Moratto, Michael J., Thomas F. King, and Wallace B. Woolfenden 1978 "Archaeology and California's Climate." *Journal of California Anthropology* 5(2):147–161.

Morlan, Richard E. 1977 "Fluted Point Makers and the Extinction of the Arctic-Steppe Biome in Eastern Beringia." *Canadian Journal of Archaeology* 1:95–108.

Morey, Darcy F., and Michael D. Wiant 1992 "Early Holocene Domestic Dog Burials from the North American Midwest." *Current Anthropology* 33(2):224–229.

Morrison, David A. 1987 "The Middle Prehistoric Period and the Archaic Concept in the Mackenzie Valley." *Canadian Journal of Archaeology* 11:49–74.

1990 "Iglulualumiut Prehistory: The Lost Inuit of Franklin Bay." *Canadian Museum of Civilization, Mercury Series, Archaeological Survey of Canada*, Paper 142.

1997 "Caribou Hunters in the Western Arctic: Zooarchaeology of the Rita-Claire and Bison Skull Sites." *Canadian Museum of Civilization, Mercury Series, Archaeological Survey of Canada*, Paper 157.

Morrow, Juliet E., and Stuart J. Fiedel 2006 "New Radiocarbon Dates for the Clovis Component of the Anzick Site, Park County, Montana." In: *Paleoindian Archaeology: A Hemispheric Perspective*, Juliet E. Morrow and Cristóbal Gnecco, eds., pp. 123–138. Gainesville: University Press of Florida.

Morrow, Juliet E., and Toby A. Morrow 1999 "Geographic Variation in Fluted Projectile Points: A Hemispheric Perspective." *American Antiquity* 64(2):215–231.

Morse, Dan F. 1997a "An Overview of the Dalton Period in Northeastern Arkansas and in the Southeastern United States." In: *Sloan: A Paleoindian Dalton Cemetery in Arkansas*, Dan F. Morse, ed., pp. 123–139. Washington, D.C.: Smithsonian Institution Press.

1997b "Description of Artifacts." In: *Sloan: A Paleoindian Dalton Cemetery in Arkansas*, Dan F. Morse, ed., pp. 14–52. Washington, D.C.: Smithsonian Institution Press.

Morse, Dan F., David G. Anderson, and Albert C. Goodyear 1996 "The Pleistocene-Holocene Transition in the Eastern United States." In: *Humans at the End of the Ice Age: The Archaeology of the Pleistocene-Holocene Transition*, Lawrence Guy Straus, Berit Valentin Eriksen, Jon M. Erlandson, and David R. Yesner, eds., pp. 319–338. New York: Plenum Press.

Morse, Dan F., and Phyllis A. Morse 1990 "Emergent Mississippian in the Central Mississippian Valley." In: *The Mississippian Emergence*, Bruce D. Smith, ed., pp. 153–173. Washington, D.C.: Smithsonian Institution Press.

1996 "Northeast Arkansas." In: *Prehistory of the Central Mississippi Valley*, Charles H. McNutt, ed., pp. 119–135. Tuscaloosa: University of Alabama Press.

Morss, Noel 1931 "The Ancient Culture of the Fremont River in Utah." *Papers of the Peabody Museum of American Archaeology and Ethnology* 12(3).

Moss, Madonna L. 1993 "Shellfish, Gender, and Status on the Northwest Coast: Reconciling Archaeological, Ethnographic, and Ethnohistorical Records on the Tlingit." *American Anthropologist* 95(3):631–652.

1998 "Northern Northwest Coast Regional Overview." *Arctic Anthropology* 35(1):88–111.

2004 "Archaeological Investigations of Cape Addington Rockshelter: Human Occupation of the Rugged Seacoast on the Outer Prince of Wales Archipelago, Alaska." *University of Oregon Anthropological Papers* No. 63.

Moss, Madonna L., and Jon M. Erlandson 1995 "Reflections on North American Pacific Coast Prehistory." *Journal of World Prehistory* 9(1):1–45.

1998a "Early Holocene Adaptations on the Southern Northwest Coast." *Journal of California and Great Basin Anthropology* 20(1):13–25.

1998b "A Comparative Chronology of Northwest Coast Fishing Features." In: *Hidden Dimensions: The Cultural Significance of Wetland Archaeology*, Kathryn Bernick, ed., pp. 180–198. Vancouver: University of British Columbia Press.

Moss, Madonna L., Jon M. Erlandson, and Robert Stuckenrath 1989 "The Antiquity of Tlingit Settlement on Admiralty Island, Southeast Alaska." *American Antiquity* 54(3):534–543.

Moss, Madonna L., Dorothy M. Peteet, and Cathy Whitlock 2007 "Mid-Holocene Culture and Climate on the Northwest Coast of North America." In: *Climate Change and Cultural Dynamics: A Global Perspective on Mid-Holocene Transitions*, David G. Anderson, Kirk A. Maasch, and Daniel H. Sandweiss, eds., pp. 491–529. New York: Elsevier Press.

Moss, Madonna L., and Robert Stuckenrath 1990 "Wood Stake Weirs and Salmon Fishing on the Northwest Coast: Evidence from Southeast Alaska." *Canadian Journal of Archaeology* 14:143–158.

Motsinger, Thomas N. 1998 "Hohokam Roads at Snaketown, Arizona." *Journal of Field Archaeology* 25(1):89–96.

Muir, Robert J., and Jonathan C. Driver 2002 "Scale of Analysis and Zooarchaeological Interpretation: Pueblo III Faunal Variation in the Northern San Juan Region." *Journal of Anthropological Archaeology* 21(2):164–199.

Mullen, Grant J., and Robert D. Hoppa 1992 "Rogers Ossuary (AgHb-131): An Early Ontario Iroquois Burial Feature from Brantford Township." *Canadian Journal of Archaeology* 16:32–47.

Muller, Jon 1986 *Archaeology of the Lower Ohio River Valley*. Orlando: Academic Press.

1997 *Mississippian Political Economy*. New York: Plenum Press.

Muller, Jon, and Jeanette E. Stephens 2000 "Mississippian Sociocultural Adaptation." In: *Cahokia and the Hinterlands: Middle Mississippian Cultures of the Midwest*, Thomas E. Emerson and R. Barry Lewis, eds., pp. 297–310. Chicago: University of Illinois Press.

Munson, Marit K. 2000 "Sex, Gender, and Status: Human Images from the Classic Mimbres." *American Antiquity* 65(1):127–143.

Munson, Patrick J. 1990 "Folsom Fluted Projectile Points East of the Great Plains and Their Biogeographical Correlates." *North American Archaeologist* 11(3):255–272.

Musil, Robert R. 1995 "Adaptive Transitions and Environmental Change in the Northern Great Basin: A View from Diamond Swamp." *University of Oregon Anthropological Papers* No. 51.

Nagy, Murielle 1994 "A Critical Review of the Pre-Dorset/Dorset Transition." In: "Threads of Arctic Prehistory, Papers in Honor of William E. Taylor, Jr.," David Morrison and Jean-Luc Pilon, eds., pp. 1–14. *Canadian Museum of Civilization, Mercury Series, Archaeological Survey of Canada*, Paper 149.

Napton, Lyle K. 1970 "Archaeological Investigations in Lovelock Cave, Nevada." Ph.D. dissertation, University of California, Berkeley.

Nash, Stephen Edward 1999 *Time, Trees, and Prehistory: Tree-Ring Dating and the Development of North American Archaeology, 1914 to 1950*. Salt Lake City: University of Utah Press.

Nassaney, Michael S. 2000 "The Late Woodland Southeast." In: *Late Woodland Societies: Tradition and Transformation across the Midcontinent*, Thomas E. Emerson, Dale L. McElrath, and Andrew C. Fortier, eds., pp. 713–730. Lincoln: University of Nebraska Press.

Nassaney, Michael S., and Kendra Pyle 1999 "The Adoption of the Bow and Arrow in Eastern North America: A View from Central Arkansas." *American Antiquity* 64(2):243–263.

Neill, Wilfred T. 1964 "The Association of Suwannee Points and Extinct Animals in Florida." *Florida Anthropologist* 17(1):17–32.

Neitzel, Jill E. (ed.) 2003 *Pueblo Bonito: Center of the Chacoan World*. Washington, D.C.: Smithsonian Books.

2007 "Architectural Studies of Pueblo Bonito: The Past, the Present, and the Future." In: *The Architecture of Chaco Canyon, New Mexico*, Stephen H. Lekson, ed., pp. 127–154. Salt Lake City: University of Utah Press.

Neitzel, Robert S. 1965 "Archeology of the Fatherland Site: The Grand Village of the Natchez." *Anthropological Papers of the American Museum of Natural History* 51(1).

Nelson, D. E., Richard E. Morlan, J. S. Vogel, J. R. Southon, and C. R. Harrington 1986 "New Dates on Northern Yukon Artifacts: Holocene Not Upper Pleistocene." *Science* 232:749–751.

Nelson, James S. 1997 "Interpersonal Violence in Prehistoric Northern California: A Bioarchaeological Approach." Master's Thesis, California State University, Chico.

Nelson, Margaret C., Michelle Hegmon, Stephanie Kulow, and Karen Gust Schollmeyer 2006 "Archaeological and Ecological Perspectives on Reorganization: A Case Study from the Mimbres Region of the U. S. Southwest." *American Antiquity* 71(3):403–432.

Nelson, Sarah Milledge 1997 *Gender in Archaeology: Analyzing Power and Prestige*. Walnut Creek, CA: AltaMira Press.

Nettle, Daniel 1999 "Linguistic Diversity of the Americas Can Be Reconciled with a Recent Colonization." *Proceedings of the National Academy of Sciences* 96(6):3325–3329.

Neusius, Sarah W., and G. Timothy Gross 2007 *Seeking Our Past: An Introduction to North American Archaeology*. New York: Oxford University Press.

Neves, Walter A., and Max Blum 2000 "The Buhl Burial: A Comment on Green et al." *American Antiquity* 65(1):191–193.

2001 "'Luzia' Is Not Alone: Further Evidence of a Non-Mongoloid Settlement of the New World." *Current Research in the Pleistocene* 18:73–77.

Neves, Walter A., Max Blum, and Lyvia Kozameh 1999 "Were the Fuegians Relics of a Paleoindian Nonspecialized Morphology in the Americas?" *Current Research in the Pleistocene* 16:90–92.

Neves, Walter A., D. Munford, and M. C. Zanini 1996 "Cranial Morphological Variation and the Colonization of the New World: Towards a Four Migration Model." *American Journal of Physical Anthropology Supplement* 22:176.

Neves, Walter A., Rolando González-José, Mark Hubbe, Renato Kipis, Astolfo G. M. Araujo, and Oldemar Blasi 2004 "Early Holocene Human Skeletal Remains from Cerca Grande, Lagoa Santa, Central Brazil, and the Origins of the First Americans." *World Archaeology* 36(4):479 501.

Newell Gillian E., and Emiliano Gallaga (eds.) 2004 *Surveying the Archaeology of Northwest Mexico.* Salt Lake City: University of Utah Press.

Nials, Fred L. David A. Gregory, and Donald A. Graybill 1989 "Salt River Streamflow and Hohokam Irrigation Systems." In: *The 1982–1984 Excavations at Las Colinas: Environment and Subsistence,* Donald A. Graybill, ed., pp. 59–76. University of Arizona, Arizona State Museum, Cultural Resources Management Division, Archaeological Series 162, Vol. 5.

Nicholas, George P. 1998 "Wetlands and Hunter-Gatherers: A Global Perspective." *Current Anthropology* 39(5):720–731.

Nichols, Johanna 1990 Linguistic Diversity and the First Settlement of the New World. Language 66(3):475–521.

2002 "The First American Languages." In: "The First Americans: The Pleistocene Colonization of the New World," Nina G. Jablonski, ed., pp. 273–293. Special issue, *Memoirs of the California Academy of Sciences* No. 27.

Nicholson, B. A. 1990 "Ceramic Affiliations and the Case for Incipient Horticulture in Southwestern Manitoba." *Canadian Journal of Archaeology* 14:33–59.

Noble, William C. 1981 "Prehistory of the Great Slave Lake and Great Bear Lake Region." In: *Handbook of North American Indians, Vol. 6, Subarctic,* June Helm, ed., pp. 97–106. Washington, D.C.: Smithsonian Institution.

Novak, Shannon A., and Dana D. Kollmann 2000 "Perimortem Processing of Human Remains Among the Great Basin Fremont." *International Journal of Osteology* 10(1):65–75.

O'Brien, Michael J., and W. Raymond Wood 1998 *The Prehistory of Missouri.* Columbia: University of Missouri Press.

O'Brien, Patricia J. 1989 "Cahokia: The Political Capital of the 'Ramey' State?" *North American Archaeologist* 10(4):275–292.

O'Connell, James F. 1975 *The Prehistory of Surprise Valley.* Ramona, CA: Ballena Press Anthropological Papers No. 4.

O'Connell, James F., and Cari M. Inoway 1994 "Surprise Valley Projectile Points and Their Chronological Implications." *Journal of California and Great Basin Anthropology* 16(2):162–198.

O'Donnell, James H. 2004 *Ohio's First Peoples.* Athens: Ohio University Press.

Oetting, Albert C. 1992 "Lake and Marsh-Edge Settlements on Malheur Lake, Harney County, Oregon." *Journal of California and Great Basin Anthropology* 14(1):110–129.

Olsen, Stanley J. 1990 "Was Early Man in North America a Big Game Hunter?" In: *Hunters of the Recent Past,* Leslie B. Davis and Brian O. K. Reeves, eds., pp. 103–110. London: Unwin Hyman.

Orme, Antony R. 2002 "The Pleistocene Legacy: Beyond the Ice Front." In: *The Physical Geography of North America,* Antony R. Orme, ed., pp. 55–85. Oxford, UK: Oxford University Press.

O'Rourke, Dennis H., Ryan L. Parr, and Shawn W. Carlyle 1999 "Molecular Genetic Variation in Prehistoric Inhabitants of the Eastern Great Basin." In: *Prehistoric Lifeways in the Great Basin Wetlands: Bioarchaeological Reconstruction and Interpretations,* Brian E. Hemphill and Clark Spencer Larsen, eds., pp. 84–102. Salt Lake City: University of Utah Press.

Orr, Philip C. 1968 *Prehistory of Santa Rosa Island.* Santa Barbara: Santa Barbara Museum of Natural History.

Orser, Charles E., and Brian M. Fagan 1995 *Historical Archaeology.* New York: HarperCollins.

Ortiz, Alfonso (ed.) 1979 *Handbook of North American Indians, Vol. 9, Southwest.* Washington, D.C.: Smithsonian Institution.

1983 *Handbook of North American Indians, Vol. 10, Southwest.* Washington, D.C.: Smithsonian Institution.

Ossenberg, Nancy S. 1994 "Origins and Affinities of the Native Peoples of Northwestern North America: The Evidence of Cranial Nonmetric Traits." In: *Method and Theory for Investigating the Peopling of the Americas,* Robson Bonnichsen, and D. Gentry Steele, eds., pp. 79–115. Oregon State University: Center for the Study of the First Americans.

2005 "Ethnogenesis in the Central and Eastern Arctic: A Reconstruction Based on Cranial Nonmetric Traits." In: *Contributions to the Study of the Dorset Paleoindians,* Patricia D. Sutherland, ed., pp. 33–56. Canadian Museum of Civilization, Mercury Series, Archaeological Survey of Canada, Paper 167.

Overstreet, David F. 2005 "Late-Glacial Ice-Marginal Adaptations in Southeastern Wisconsin." In: *Paleoamerican Origins: Beyond Clovis,* Robson Bonnichsen, Bradley T. Lepper, Dennis Stanford, and Michael R. Waters, eds., pp. 183–195. Texas A&M University: Center for the Study of the First Americans.

Owen, Roger C. 1984 "The Americas: The Case Against an Ice-Age Human Population." In: *The Origins of Modern Humans: A World Survey of the Fossil Evidence,* Fred H. Smith and Frank Spencer, eds., pp. 517–563. New York: Alan R. Liss.

Owsley, Douglas W., and Richard L. Jantz 2001 "Archaeological Politics and Public Interest in Paleoamerican Studies: Lessons from Gordon Creek Woman and Kennewick Man." *American Antiquity* 66(4):565–575.

Pääbo, Svante, K. Dew, B. S. Frazier, and R. H. Ward 1990 "Mitochondrial Evolution and the Peopling of the Americas." *American Journal of Physical Anthropology* 81(2):277.

Pacheco, Paul J., and William S. Dancey 2006 "Integrating Mortuary and Settlement Data on Ohio Hopewell Society." In: *Recreating Hopewell,* Douglas K. Charles and Jane E. Buikstra, eds., pp. 3–25. Gainesville: University Press of Florida.

Parenti, Fabio, Michel Fontugue, and Claude Guérin 1996 "Pedra Furada in Brazil and Its 'Presumed' Evidence: Limitations and Potential of the Available Data." *Antiquity* 70(268):416–421.

Park, Robert W. 1993 "The Dorset-Thule Succession in Arctic North America: Assessing Claims for Culture Contact." *American Antiquity* 58(2):203–234.

1997 Thule Winter Site Demography in the High Arctic. *American Antiquity* 62(2):273–284.

Parr, Ryan L., Shawn W. Carlyle, and Dennis H. O'Rourke
1996 Ancient DNA Analysis of Fremont Amerindians of the Great Salt Lake Wetlands. *American Journal of Physical Anthropology* 99(4):507–518.

Patterson, Thomas C. 1995 *Toward a Social History of Archaeology in the United States*. Fort Worth, TX: Harcourt Brace.

Pauketat, Timothy R. 1994 *The Ascent of Chiefs: Cahokia and Mississippian Politics in Native North America*. Tuscaloosa: University of Alabama Press.

1998 "Refiguring the Archaeology of Greater Cahokia." *Journal of Archaeological Research* 6(1):45–89.

2003 "Resettled Farmers and the Making of a Mississippian Polity." *American Antiquity* 68(1):39–66.

2004 *Ancient Cahokia and the Mississippians*. Cambridge, UK: Cambridge University Press.

2007 *Chiefdoms and Other Archaeological Delusions*. Lanham, MD: AltaMira Press.

Pauketat, Timothy R., and Neal H. Lopinot 1997 "Cahokian Population Dynamics." In: *Cahokia: Domination and Ideology in the Mississippian World*, Timothy R. Pauketat and Thomas E. Emerson, eds., pp. 103–123. Lincoln: University of Nebraska Press.

Pavesic, Max G. 1985 "Blade Caches and Turkey Tails: Piecing Together the Western Idaho Archaic Burial Complex." In: *Stone Tool Analysis: Essays in Honor of Don E. Crabtree*, Mark G. Plew, James C. Woods, and Max G. Pavesic, eds., pp. 55–89. Albuquerque: University of New Mexico Press.

2000 "Prehistoric Pipes from the Olds Ferry Dunes Site (10-WN-557), Western Idaho." *Journal of California and Great Basin Anthropology* 22(2):321–331.

2007 "The Bonneville Flood Debris Field as Sacred Landscape." *Journal of California and Great Basin Anthropology* 27(1):15–27.

Pavesic, Max G., and William Studebaker 1993 *Backtracking: Ancient Art of Southern Idaho*. Pocatello: Idaho Museum of Natural History.

Peebles, Christopher S., and Glenn A. Black 1987 "Moundville from 1000 to 1500 AD as Seen from 1840 to 1985 AD." In: *Chiefdoms in the Americas*, Robert D. Drennan and Carlos A. Uribe, eds., pp. 21–42. Lanham, MD: University Press of America.

Peebles, Christopher S., and Susan M. Kus 1977 "Some Archaeological Correlates of Ranked Societies." *American Antiquity* 42(3):421–448.

Pendergast, David M., and Clement W. Meighan 1959 *The Greasy Creek Site, Tulare County, California*. Los Angeles: University of California Archaeological Survey Annual Report 1958–1959:1–12.

Penders, Thomas 2002 "Bone, Antler, Dentary, and Lithic Artifacts." In: *Windover: Multidisciplinary Investigations of an Early Archaic Florida Cemetery*, Glen H. Doran, ed., pp. 97–120. Gainesville: University Press of Florida.

Pendleton, Lorann S. A., and David Hurst Thomas 1983 "The Fort Sage Drift Fence, Washoe County, Nevada." *Anthropological Papers of the American Museum of Natural History* 58(2).

Peregory, Robert M. 1999 "Nebraska's Landmark Repatriation Law: A Case Study of Cross-Cultural Conflict and Resolution." In: *Contemporary Native American Political Issues*, Troy R. Johnson, ed., pp. 229–274. Walnut Creek, CA: AltaMira Press.

Peros, Matthew C., Samuel E. Munoz, Konrad Gajewski, and André E. Viau 2010 "Prehistoric Demography of North America Inferred from Radiocarbon Data." *Journal of Archaeological Science* 37(3):656–664.

Perttula, Timothy K. 1991 "European Contact and Its Effects on Aboriginal Caddoan Populations Between A.D. 1520 and A.D. 1680." In: *Columbian Consequences, Vol. 3, The Spanish Borderlands in Pan-American Perspective*, David Hurst Thomas, ed., pp. 501–518. Washington, D.C.: Smithsonian Institution Press.

1992 "*The Caddo Nation*": *Archaeological and Ethnohistoric Perspectives*. Austin: University of Texas Press.

1993 "*Kee-Oh-Na-Wah'-Wah*: The Effects of European Contact on the Caddoan Indians of Texas, Louisiana, Arkansas, and Oklahoma." In: *Ethnohistory and Archaeology: Approaches to Postcontact Change in the Americas*, J. Daniel Rogers and Samuel M. Wilson, eds., pp. 89–109. New York: Plenum Press.

1996 "Caddoan Area Archaeology Since 1990." *Journal of Archaeological Research* 4(4):295–348.

Peterson, James B., and Nancy Asch Sidell 1996 "Mid-Holocene Evidence of *Cucurbita* Sp. from Central Maine." *American Antiquity* 61(4):685–698.

Petersen, James B., Robert N. Bartone, and Belinda J. Cox 2000 "The Varney Farm Site and the Late Paleoindian Period in Northeastern North America." *Archaeology of Eastern North America* 28:113–140.

Petersen, James B., Brian S. Robinson, Daniel F. Belcamp, James Stark, and Lawrence K. Kaplan 1994 "An Archaic and Woodland Period Fish Weir Complex in Central Maine." *Archaeology of Eastern North America* 22:197–222.

Pettigrew, Richard M. 1984 "Prehistoric Human Land-use Patterns in the Alvord Basin, Southeastern Oregon." *Journal of California and Great Basin Anthropology* 6(1):61–90.

1990 "Prehistory of the Lower Columbia and Willamette Valley." In: *Handbook of North American Indians, Vol. 7, Northwest Coast*, Wayne Suttles, ed., pp. 518–529. Washington, D.C.: Smithsonian Institution.

Pfeiffer, Susan 2003 "The Health of the Moatfield People as Reflected in Paleopathological Features." In: *Bones of the Ancestors: The Archaeology and Osteobiography of the Moatfield Ossuary*, Ronald E. Williamson and Susan Pfeiffer, eds., pp. 189–204. Canadian Museum of Civilization, Mercury Series, Archaeological Survey of Canada, Paper 163.

Phillips, David A., Jr. 1989 "Prehistory of Chihuahua and Sonora, Mexico." *Journal of World Prehistory* 3(4):373–401.

2009 "Adoption and Intensification of Agriculture in the North American Southwest: Notes Toward a Quantitative Approach." *American Antiquity* 74(4):691–707.

Pilles, Peter J., Jr. 1979 "Sunset Crater and the Sinagua: A New Interpretation." In: *Volcanic Activity and Human Ecology*,

Payson D. Sheets and Donald K. Grayson, eds., pp. 459–485. New York: Academic Press.

1996 "The Pueblo III Period along the Mogollon Rim: The Honanki, Elden, and Turkey Hill Phases of the Sinagua." In: *The Prehistoric Pueblo World, A.D. 1150–1350,* Michael A. Adler, ed., pp. 59–72. Tucson: University of Arizona Press.

Pisias, Nicklas G. 1978 "Paleoceanography of the Santa Barbara Basin During the Last 8000 Years." *Quaternary Research* 10(3):366–384.

Pitul'ko, Vladimir V. 1999 "Ancient Humans in Eurasian Arctic Ecosystems: Environmental Dynamics and Changing Subsistence." *World Archaeology* 39(3):421–436.

2001 "Terminal Pleistocene—Early Holocene Occupation in Northeast Asia and the Zhokhov Assemblage." *Quaternary Science Reviews* 20(1–3):267–275.

Pitul'ko, Vladimir V., P. A. Nikolsky, E. Yu. Girya, A. E. Basilyan, V. E. Tumskoy, S. A. Koulakov, S. N. Astakhov, E. Yu. Pavlova, and M. A. Anisimov 2004 "The Yana RHS Site: Humans in the Arctic Before the Last Glacial Maximum." *Science* 303:52–56.

Pleger, Thomas C. 2000 "Old Copper and Red Ochre Social Complexity." *Midcontinental Journal of Archaeology* 25(2):169–190.

Plew, Mark G. 1983 "Implications of Nutritional Potential of Anadromous Fish Resources of the Western Snake River Plain." *Journal of California and Great Basin Anthropology* 5(1 and 2):58–65.

2000 *The Archaeology of the Snake River Plain.* Boise, ID: Boise State University.

Plog, Fred 1979 "Prehistory: Western Anasazi." In: *Handbook of North American Indians, Vol. 9, Southwest,* Alfonzo Ortiz, ed., pp. 108–130. Washington, D.C.: Smithsonian Institution.

1989 "The Sinagua and Their Relations." In: *Dynamics of Southwestern Prehistory,* Linda S. Cordell and George J. Gumerman, eds., pp. 263–291. Washington, D.C.: Smithsonian Institution Press.

Plog, Stephen 1997 *Ancient Peoples of the American Southwest.* London: Thames and Hudson.

Plog, Stephen, and Shirley Powell (eds.) 1984 *Papers on the Archaeology of Black Mesa, Arizona, Volume II.* Carbondale: Southern Illinois University Press.

Pokotylo, David L., and Donald Mitchell 1998 "Prehistory of the Northern Plateau." In: *Handbook of North American Indians, Vol. 12, Plateau,* Deward E. Walker, Jr., ed., pp. 81–102. Washington, D.C.: Smithsonian Institution.

Pollack, David, and A. Gwynn Henderson 1992 "Toward a Model of Fort Ancient Society." In: *Fort Ancient Cultural Dynamics in the Middle Ohio Valley,* A. Gwynn Henderson, ed., pp. 281–294. Madison, WI: Prehistory Press, Monographs in World Archaeology No. 8.

Polzer, Charles W., Thomas H. Naylor, Thomas E. Sheridan, and Diana Hadley (eds.) 1991 *The Jesuit Missions of Northern Mexico, Spanish Borderlands Sourcebooks, Vol. 19.* New York: Garland Publishing.

Popson, Colleen C. 2003 "Vintage Skulls." *Archaeology Magazine* 56(2):15.

Porcasi, Judith F. 2008 "Dietary Patterns of Paleocoastal California: A Regional Synthesis of Terminal Pleistocene Archaeofaunas." *North Pacific Prehistory* 2:203–232.

Porcasi, Judith F., and Harumi Fujita 2000 "The Dolphin Hunters: A Specialized Prehistoric Maritime Adaptation in the Southern California Channel Islands and Baja California." *American Antiquity* 65(3):543–566.

Powell, Joseph F., and Walter A. Neves 1999 "Craniofacial Morphology of the First Americans: Pattern and Process in the Peopling of the New World." *Yearbook of Physical Anthropology* 42:153–198.

Powell, Joseph F., and D. Gentry Steele 1992 "A Multivariate Crainometric Analysis of North American Paleoindian Remains." *Current Research in the Pleistocene* 9:59–62.

Powell, Mary Lucas 1992 "Health and Disease in the Late Prehistoric Southeast." In: *Disease and Demography in the Americas,* John W. Verano and Douglas H. Ubelaker, eds., pp. 41–53. Washington, D.C.: Smithsonian Institution Press.

Powell, Shirley, and Francis E. Smiley (eds.) 2002 *Prehistoric Culture Change on the Colorado Plateau: Ten Thousand Years on Black Mesa.* Tucson: University of Arizona Press.

Powell-Marti, Valli S., and Patricia A. Gilman (eds.) 2006 *Mimbres Society.* Tucson: University of Arizona Press.

Powers, William R., and John F. Hoffecker 1989 "Late Pleistocene Settlement in the Nenana Valley, Central Alaska." *American Antiquity* 54(2):263–287.

Prentiss, Anna M., Natasha Lyons, Lucille E. Harris, Melisse R. P. Burns, and Terrence M. Godin 2007 "The Emergence of Status Inequality in Intermediate Scale Societies: A Demographic and Socio-Economic History of the Keatley Creek Site, British Columbia." *Journal of Anthropological Archaeology* 26(2):299–327.

Prentiss, Anne M., Guy Cross, Thomas A. Foor, Mathew Hogan, Dirk Markle, and David S. Clarke 2008 "Evolution of a Late Prehistoric Winter Village on the Interior Plateau of British Columbia: Geophysical Investigations, Radiocarbon Dating, and Spatial Analysis of the Bridge River Site." *American Antiquity* 73(1):59–81.

Prentiss, William C., and Ian Kuijt 2004a "The Evolution of Collector Systems on the Canadian Plateau." In: *Complex Hunter-Gatherers: Evolution and Organization of Prehistoric Communities on the Plateau of Northwestern North America,* William C. Prentiss and Ian Kuijt, eds., pp. 49–63. Salt Lake City: University of Utah Press.

Prentiss, William C., and Ian Kuijt (eds.) 2004b *Complex Hunter-Gatherers: Evolution and Organization of Prehistoric Communities on the Plateau of Northwestern North America.* Salt Lake City: University of Utah Press.

Prentiss, William C., James C. Chatters, Michael Lenert, David S. Clarke, and Robert C. O'Boyle 2005b "The Archaeology of the Plateau of Northwestern North America During the Late Prehistoric Period (3500-200 B.P.): Evolution of Hunting and Gathering Societies." *Journal of World Prehistory* 19(1):47–118.

Prentiss, William C., Michael Lenert, Thomas A. Foor, and Nathan B. Goodale 2005a "The Emergence of Complex

Hunter-Gatherers on the Canadian Plateau: A Response to Hayden." *American Antiquity* 70(1):175–180.

Prentiss, William C., Michael Lenert, Thomas A. Foor, Nathan B. Goodale, and Trinity Schlegel 2003 "Calibrated Radiocarbon Dating at Keatley Creek: The Chronology of Occupation at a Complex Hunter-Gatherer Village." *American Antiquity* 68(4):719–735.

Preston, William L. 2002 "Post-Columbian Wildlife Irruptions in California." In: *Wilderness and Political Ecology: Aboriginal Influences and the Original State of Nature*, Charles E. Kay and Randy T. Simmons, eds., pp. 111–140. Salt Lake City: University of Utah Press.

Prine, Elizabeth 2000 "Searching for Third Genders: Towards a Prehistory of Domestic Space in Middle Missouri Villages." In: *Archaeologies of Sexuality*, Robert A. Schmidt and Barbara L. Voss, eds., pp.197–219. London: Routledge.

Purdy, Barbara A. 2008 *Florida's People during the Last Ice Age.* Gainesville: University Press of Florida.

Quinn, David B. 1974 *England and the Discovery of America, 1481–1620.* New York: Alfred A. Knopf.

Raab, L. Mark 1996 "Debating Prehistory in Coastal Southern California: Political Economy versus Resource Intensification." *Journal of California and Great Basin Anthropology* 18(1):64–80.

1997 "The Southern Channel Islands during the Middle Holocene." In: *Archaeology of the California Coast During the Middle Holocene*, Jon M. Erlandson and Michael A. Glassow, eds., pp. 23–34. University of California Los Angeles, Institute of Archaeology, Perspectives in California Archaeology, Vol. 4.

2009 "The Dolphin Hunters." In: *California Maritime Archaeology: A San Clemente Perspective*, L. Mark Raab, Jim Cassidy, Andrew Yatsko, and William J. Howard, eds., pp. 93–106. Lanham, MD: AltaMira Press.

Raab, L. Mark, and Jim Cassidy 2009 "The Ancient Mariners of Eel Point." In: *California Maritime Archaeology: A San Clemente Perspective*, L. Mark Raab, Jim Cassidy, Andrew Yatsko, and William J. Howard, eds., pp. 67–92. Lanham, MD: AltaMira Press.

Raab, L. Mark, and Terry L. Jones 2004 "The Rediscovery of California Prehistory. In: *Prehistoric California: Archaeology and the Myth of Paradise*, L. Mark Raab and Terry L. Jones, eds., pp. 1–9. Salt Lake City: University of Utah Press.

Raab, L. Mark, and Daniel O. Larson 1997 "Medieval Climatic Anomaly and Punctuated Cultural Evolution in Coastal Southern California." *American Antiquity* 62(2):319–336.

Raab, L. Mark, Katherine Bradford, and Andy Yatsko 1994 "Advances in Southern Channel Islands Archaeology: 1983–1993." *Journal of California and Great Basin Anthropology* 16(2):243–270.

Raab, L. Mark, Katherine Bradford, Judith F. Porcasi, and William J. Howard 1995a "Return to Little Harbor, Santa Catalina Island, California: A Critique of the Marine Paleotemperature Model." *American Antiquity* 60(2):287–308.

Raab, L. Mark, Judith F. Porcasi, Katherine Bradford, and Andy Yatsko 1995b "Debating Cultural Evolution: Regional Implications of Fishing Intensification at Eel Point, San Clemente Island." *Pacific Coast Archaeological Society Quarterly* 31(3):3–27.

Rafferty, Sean M. 2006 "Evidence of Early Tobacco in Northeastern North America?" *Journal of Archaeological Science* 33(4):453–458.

Ragir, Sonja 1972 *The Early Horizon in Central California Prehistory*. Berkeley: Contributions of the University of California Archaeological Research Facility No. 15.

Ramenofsky, Ann F. 1987 *Vectors of Death: The Archaeology of European Contact.* Albuquerque: University of New Mexico Press.

Ramsden, Peter, and Maribeth S. Murray 1995 "Identifying Seasonality in Pre-Dorset Structures in Back Bay, Prince of Wales Island, NWT." *Arctic Anthropology* 32(2):106–117.

Randall, Asa R. 2008 "Archaic Shell Mounds of the St. Johns River, Florida." *SAA Archaeological Record* 8(5):13–17.

Ranere, Anthony J. 2006 "The Clovis Colonization of Central America." In: *Paleoindian Archaeology: A Hemispheric Perspective*, Juliet E. Morrow and Cristóbal Gnecco, eds., pp. 69–85. Gainesville: University Press of Florida.

Rasic, Jeffrey T., and Natalia S. Slobodina 2008 "Weapons Systems and Assemblage Variability during the Northern Archaic Period in Northern Alaska." *Arctic Anthropology* 45(1):71–88.

Rasmussen, Morten, Yingrui Li, Stinus Lindgreen, Jakob Skou Pedersen, Anders Albrechtsen, Ida Moltke, Mait Metspalu, Ene Metspalu, Toomas Kivisild, Ramneek Gupta, Marcelo Bertalan, Kasper Nielsen, M. Thomas P. Gilbert, Yong Wang, Maanasa Raghavan, Paula F. Campos, Hanne Munkholm Kemp, Andrew S. Wilson, Andrew Gledhill, Silvana Tridico, Michael Bunce, Eline D. Lorenzen, Jonas Binladen, Xiaosen Guo, Jing Zhao, Xiuqing Zhang, Hao Zhang, Zhuo Li, Minfeng Chen, Ludovic Orlando, Karsten Kristainsen, Mads Bak, Niels Tommerup, Christian Bendixen, Tracey L. Pierra, Bjarne Grønnow, Morten Meldgaard, Claus Andreasen, Sardana A. Fedorova, Ludmila P. Osipova, Thomas F. G. Higham, Christopher Bronk Ramsey, Thomas v. O. Hansen, Finn C. Nielsen, Michael H. Crawford, Søren Brunak, Thomas Sicheritz-Pontén, Richard Villems, Rasmus Nielsen, Anders Krogh, Jun Wang, and Eske Willerslev 2010 "Ancient Human Genome Sequence of an Extinct Palaeo-Eskimo." *Nature* 463:757–762.

Rautman, Alison E., and Todd W. Fenton 2005 "A Case of Historic Cannibalism in the American West: Implications for Southwestern Archaeology." *American Antiquity* 70(2):321–341.

Ravesloot, John C. 2008 "Changing Views of Snaketown in a Larger Landscape." In: *The Hohokam Millennium*, Suzanne K. Fish and Paul R. Fish, eds., pp. 90–97. Santa Fe, NM: School for Advanced Research Press.

Ray, Dorothy J. 1967 *Eskimo Masks: Art and Ceremony.* Seattle: University of Washington Press.

Raymond, Anan W. 1982 "Two Historic Aboriginal Game-Drive Enclosures in the Eastern Great Basin." *Journal of California and Great Basin Anthropology* 4(2):23–33.

Raymond, Anan W., and Virginia M. Parks 1990
"Archaeological Sites Exposed by Recent Flooding of
Stillwater Marsh, Carson Desert, Churchill County, Nevada."
In: *Wetlands Adaptation in the Great Basin*, Joel C. Janetski
and David B. Madsen, eds., pp 33–61. Provo, UT: Brigham
Young University, Museum of Peoples and Cultures,
Occasional Paper No. 1.

Raymond, Anan W., and Elizabeth Sobel 1990 "The Use of Tui
Chub as a Food by Indians of the Western Great Basin."
Journal of California and Great Basin Anthropology
12(1):2–18.

Reanier, Richard E. 1995 "The Antiquity of Paleoindian Materials
in Northern Alaska." *Arctic Anthropology* 32(1):31–50.

Reddy, Marlita A. (ed.) 1995 *Statistical Record of Native North
Americans* (2nd ed.). Detroit: Gale Research Inc.

Reed, Paul F. 2000 "Fundamental Issues in Basketmaker
Archaeology." In: *Foundations of Anasazi Culture: The
Basketmaker-Pueblo Transition*, Paul F. Reed, ed., pp. 3–16.
Salt Lake City: University of Utah Press.

Reeves, Brian O. K. 1978 "Head-Smashed-In: 5500 Years of
Bison Jumping in the Alberta Plains." In: "Bison Procurement
and Utilization: A symposium," L. B. Davis and M. Wilson,
eds., pp. 63–78. *Plains Anthropologist Memoir* 14.

1990 "Communal Bison Hunters of the Northern Plains." In:
Hunters of the Recent Past, Leslie B. Davis and Brian O. K.
Reeves, eds., pp. 168–194. London: Unwin Hyman.

Reid, C. S., and Grace Rajnovich 1991 "Laurel: A Re-evaluation of
the Spatial, Social and Temporal Paradigms." *Canadian
Journal of Archaeology* 15:193–234.

Reid, Jefferson, and Stephanie Whittlesey 1997 *The Archaeology
of Ancient Arizona*. Tucson: University of Arizona Press.

1999 *Grasshopper Pueblo: A Story of Archaeology and Ancient
Life*. Tucson: University of Arizona Press.

2005 *Thirty Years into Yesterday: A History of Archaeology at
Grasshopper Pueblo*. Tucson: University of Arizona
Press.

Reinhard, Karl J. 2006 "A Coprological View of Ancestral Pueblo
Cannibalism." *American Scientist* 94(3):254–261.

Renfrew, Colin 1994 "Towards a Cognitive Archaeology." In: *The
Ancient Mind: Elements of Cognitive Archaeology*, Colin
Renfrew and Ezra B. W. Zubrow, eds., pp. 3–12. Cambridge:
Cambridge University Press.

1998 "Applications of DNA in Archaeology: A Review of the
DNA Studies of the Ancient Biomolecules Initiative."
Ancient Biomolecules 2(2/3):107–117.

2000 "Genetics and Languages in the Americas and Beyond:
Variations at the Micro and the Macro Level." In: *America
Past, America Present: Genes and Languages in the
Americas and Beyond*, Colin Renfrew, ed., pp. 3–15.
Cambridge, UK: McDonald Institute for Archaeological
Research.

Renouf, M. A. P. 1999 "Prehistory of Newfoundland Hunter-
Gatherers: Extinctions or Adaptations?" *World Archaeology*
30(3):403–420.

Renouf, M. A. P., and Trevor Bell 2006 "Maritime Archaic Site
Locations on the Island of Newfoundland." In: *The Archaic of*
the Far Northeast, David Sanger and M. A. P. Renouf, eds., pp.
1–46. Orono: University of Maine Press.

2008 "Dorset Paleoeskimo Skin Processing at Phillip's
Garden, Port au Choix, Northwestern Newfoundland."
Arctic 61(1):35–47.

2009 "Contraction and Expansion in Newfoundland
Prehistory, AD 900–1500." In: *The Northern World: AD
900–1400*, Herbert D. G. Maschner, Owen Mason, and
Robert McGhee, eds., pp. 263–278. Salt Lake City:
University of Utah Press.

Renouf, M. A. P., and Maribeth S. Murray 1999 "Two Winter
Dwellings at Phillip's Garden, A Dorset Site in Northwestern
Newfoundland." *Arctic Anthropology* 36(1–2):118–132.

**Reynolds, Amanda C., Julio L. Betancourt, Jay Quade, P.
Jonathan Patchett, Jeffrey S. Dean, and John Stein** 2005
"^{87}Sr/^{86}Sr Sourcing of Ponderosa Pine Used in Anasazi Great
House Construction at Chaco Canyon, New Mexico."
Journal of Archaeological Science 32(7):1061–1075.

Rhode, David 2003 "Coprolites from Hidden Cave,
Revisited: Evidence for Site Occupation History,
Diet and Sex of Occupants. *Journal of Archaeological
Science* 30(7):909–922.

Rhode, David, and David B. Madsen 1998 "Pine Nut Use in the
Early Holocene and Beyond: The Danger Cave
Archaeobotanical Record." *Journal of Archaeological Science*
25(12):1199–1210.

**Rhode, David, David B. Madsen, P. Jeffrey Brantingham, and
Ted Geobel** 2003 "Human Occupation in the Beringian
'Mammoth Steppe': Starved for Fuel, or Dung-Burner's
Paradise?" *Current Research in the Pleistocene* 20:68–70.

Rhode, David, David B. Madsen, and Kevin T. Jones 2006
"Antiquity of Early Holocene Small-seed Consumption and
Processing at Danger Cave." *Antiquity* 80(309):328–339.

Rice, David G. 1972 *The Windust Phase in Lower Snake River
Prehistory*. Pullman: Washington State University, Department
of Anthropology Reports of Investigations 50.

Rice, Glen E., and Steven A. LeBlanc 2001 *Deadly Landscapes:
Case Studies in Prehistoric Southwestern Warfare*. Salt Lake
City: University of Utah Press.

Richards, Thomas H., and Mike K. Rousseau 1987 *Late
Prehistoric Cultural Horizons on the Canadian Plateau*.
Burnaby, B.C.: Simon Fraser University, Department of
Archaeology, Publication No. 16.

**Richardson, James B. III, David A. Anderson, and Edward R.
Cook** 2003 "The Disappearance of the Monongahela: Solved?"
Archaeology of Eastern North America 30:81–96.

Rick, Torben C., and Jon M. Erlandson 2001 "Late Holocene
Subsistence Strategies on the South Coast of Santa Barbara
Island, California." *Journal of California and Great Basin
Anthropology* 23(1):297–307.

Rick, Torben C., Jon M. Erlandson, and René L. Vellanoweth
2001 "Paleocoastal Marine Fishing on the Pacific Coast of the
Americas: Perspectives from Daisy Cave, California."
American Antiquity 66(4):595–613.

**Rick, Torben C., Jon M. Erlandson, René L. Vellanoweth, and
Todd J. Braje** 2005 "From Pleistocene Mariners to Complex

Hunter-Gatherers: The Archaeology of the California Channel Islands." *Journal of World Prehistory* 19(3):169–228.

Rick, Torben C., and Michael A. Glassow 1999 "Middle Holocene Fisheries of the Central Santa Barbara Channel, California: Investigations at CA-SBA-53." *Journal of California and Great Basin Anthropology* 21(2):236–256.

Riddell, Francis A., and William H. Olsen 1969 "An Early Man Site in the San Joaquin Valley." *American Antiquity* 34(2):121–130.

Riggs, Charles R. 2007 "Architecture and Identity at Grasshopper Pueblo, Arizona." *Journal of Anthropological Research* 63(4):489–513.

Riley, Carroll L. 2005 *Becoming Aztlan: Mesoamerican Influence in the Greater Southwest, AD 1200–1500.* Salt Lake City: University of Utah Press.

Ritchie, William A. 1938 "A Perspective on Northeastern Archaeology." *American Antiquity* 4(2):94–112.

1980 *The Archaeology of New York State.* Harrison, NY: Harbor Hill Books.

Ritchie, William A., and Don W. Dragoo 1959 "The Eastern Dispersal of Adena." *American Antiquity* 25(1):43–50.

Ritter, Eric W. 1979 "An Archaeological Study of South-Central Baja California, Mexico." Ph.D. dissertation, University of California, Davis.

1981 "The Description and Significance of Some Prehistoric Stone Features, South-Central Baja California." *Pacific Coast Archaeological Society Quarterly* 17(1):25–42.

2006a "South-Central Baja California." In: *Advances in the Archaeology of the Forgotten Peninsula*, Don Laylander and Jerry D. Moore, eds., pp. 99–116. Gainesville: University Press of Florida.

2006b "The Vizcaíno Desert." In: *Advances in the Archaeology of the Forgotten Peninsula*, Don Laylander and Jerry D. Moore, eds., pp. 135–152. Gainesville: University Press of Florida.

Ritter, Eric W., and Peter D. Schulz 1975 "Mortuary Practices and Health Conditions Among a Small Prehistoric Population from Baja California Sur." *Pacific Coast Archaeological Society Quarterly* 11(1):43–53.

Ritterbush, Lauren W. 2006 "Late Prehistoric Oneota in the Central Plains." In: *Kansas Archaeology*, Robert J. Hoard and William E. Banks, eds., pp. 151–164. Lawrence, University of Kansas Press.

Robinson, Brian S. 1996 "A Regional Analysis of the Moorehead Burial Tradition: 8500-3700 B.P." *Archaeology of Eastern North America* 24:95–148.

2006 "Burial Ritual, Technology, and Cultural Landscape in the Far Northeast: 8600–3700 B.P." In: *The Archaic of the Far Northeast*, David Sanger and M. A. P. Renouf, eds., pp. 341–381. Orono: University of Maine Press.

2008 "'Archaic Period' Traditions of New England and the Northeast." *SAA Archaeological Record* 8(5):23–26, 46.

Robinson, Brian S., Jennifer C. Ort, William A. Eldridge, Adrian L. Burke, and Bertrand G. Pelletier 2009 "Paleoindian Aggregation and Social Context at Bull Brook." *American Antiquity* 74(3):423–447.

Roca, Paul M. 1979 *Spanish Jesuit Churches in Mexico's Tarahumara.* Tucson: University of Arizona Press.

Rogers, David B. 1929 *Prehistoric Man of the Santa Barbara Coast.* Santa Barbara: Santa Barbara Museum of Natural History.

Rogers, Edward S., and James G. E. Smith 1981 "Environment and Culture in the Shield and Mackenzie Borderlands." In: *Handbook of North American Indians, Vol. 6, Subarctic,* June Helm, ed., pp. 130–145. Washington, DC: Smithsonian Institution.

Rogers, J. Daniel 1996 "Markers of Social Integration: The Development of Political Authority in the Spiro Region." In: *Political Structure and Change in the Prehistoric Southeastern United States*, John F. Scarry, ed., pp. 53–68. Gainesville: University Press of Florida.

Rogers, Malcolm J. 1939 "Early Lithic Industries of the Lower Basin of the Colorado River and Adjacent Desert Areas." *San Diego Museum of Man Papers* No. 3.

1945 "An Outline of Yuman Prehistory." *Southwestern Journal of Anthropology* 1(2):167–198.

Rogers, R. A., L. A. Rogers, and L. D. Martin 1992 "How the Door Was Opened: The Peopling of the New World." *Human Biology* 64(3):281–302.

Roll, Tom E., and Steven Hackenberger 1998 "Prehistory of the Eastern Plateau." In: *Handbook of North American Indians, Vol. 12, Plateau*, Deward E. Walker, Jr., ed., pp. 120–137. Washington, D.C.: Smithsonian Institution.

Rondeau, Micahel F., Jim Cassidy, and Terry L. Jones 2007 "Colonization Technologies: Fluted Projectile Points and the San Clemente Island Woodworking/Microblade Complex." In: *California Prehistory: Colonization, Culture, and Complexity*, Terry L. Jones and Kathryn A. Klar, eds., pp. 63–70. Lanham, MD: AltaMira Press.

Rondeau, Michael F., and Jerry N. Hopkins 2008 "A Reevaluation of Reported Clovis Points from Tulare Lake, California." In: *Ice-Age Stone Tools from the San Joaquin Valley*, Jerry N. Hopkins and Alan P. Garfinkel, eds., pp. 99–108. Redondo Beach, CA: Tulare Lake Archaeological Research Group, Contributions to Tulare Lake Archaeology IV.

Roney, John R., and Robert J. Hard 2004 "A Review of Cerros de Trincheras in Northwest Chihuahua." In: *Surveying the Archaeology of Northwest Mexico*, Gillian E. Newell and Emiliano Gallaga, eds., pp. 127–147. Salt Lake City: University of Utah Press.

Roosevelt, Anna C., John Douglas, and Linda Brown 2002 "The Migrations and Adaptations of the First Americans: Clovis and Pre-Clovis Viewed from South America." In: "The First Americans: The Pleistocene Colonization of the New World," Nina G. Jablonski, ed., pp. 159–235. Special issue, *Memoirs of the California Academy of Sciences* No. 27.

Roosevelt, Anna C., M. Lima da Costa, C. Lopes Machado, M. Michab, N. Mercier, H. Valladas, J. Feathers, W. Barnett, M. Imazio de Silveria, A. Henderson, J. Silva, B. Chernoff, D. S. Reese, J. A. Holman, N. Toth, and K. Schick 1996 "Paleoindian Cave Dwellers in the Amazon: The Peopling of the Americas." *Science* 272:373–384.

Roper, Donna C. 1996 "Variability in the Use of Ochre During the Paleoindian Period." *Current Research in the Pleistocene* 13:40–42.

2006 "The Central Plains Tradition." In: *Kansas Archaeology*, Robert J. Hoard and William E. Banks, eds., pp. 105–132. Lawrence: University of Kansas Press.

2007 "The Origins and Expansion of the Central Plains Tradition." In: *Plains Village Archaeology: Bison-hunting Farmers in the Central and Northern Plains*, Stanley A. Ahler and Marvin Kay, eds., pp. 53–63. Salt Lake City: University of Utah Press.

Roper, Donna C., and Elizabeth Pauls (eds.) 2005 *Plains Earthlodges: Ethnographic and Archaeological Perspectives.* Tuscaloosa: University of Alabama Press.

Roscoe, James 1995 *CA-HUM-513/H, A Borax Lake Pattern Site Located in a Coastal Setting.* Paper presented at the annual meetings of the Society for California Archaeology, Eureka.

Rose, Fionnuala 2008 "Inter-Community Variation in Diet during the Adoption of a New Staple Crop in the Eastern Woodlands." *American Antiquity* 73(3):413–439.

Rosenthal, Jeffrey S. 2002 "Projectile Point Typology and Chronology in the North Central Sierra Nevada." *North American Archaeologist* 23(2):157–183.

Rosenthal, Jeffrey S., William R. Hildebrandt, and Jerome King 2001 "Donax Don't Tell: Reassessing Late Holocene Land Use in Northern San Diego County." *Journal of California and Great Basin Anthropology* 23(1):179–214.

Rosenthal, Jeffrey S., Gregory G. White, and Mark Q. Sutton 2007 "The Central Valley: A View from the Catbird's Seat." In: *California Prehistory: Colonization, Culture, and Complexity*, Terry L. Jones and Kathryn A. Klar, eds., pp. 147–163. Lanham, MD: AltaMira Press.

Roth, Barbara J. 2000 "Households at a Rincon Phase Hohokam Site in the Tucson Basin of Southern Arizona." *Journal of Field Archaeology* 27(3):285–294.

Rousseau, Mike K. 2004 "A Culture Historic Synthesis and Changes in Human Mobility, Sedentism, Subsistence, Settlement, and Population on the Canadian Plateau, 7000–200 BP." In: *Complex Hunter-Gatherers: Evolution and Organization of Prehistoric Communities on the Plateau of Northwestern North America*, William C. Prentiss and Ian Kuijt, eds., pp. 3–22. Salt Lake City: University of Utah Press.

Rousseau, Mike K., and Thomas H. Richards 1988 "The Oregon Jack Creek Site (EdRi-6): A Lehman Phase Site in the Thompson River Valley, British Columbia." *Canadian Journal of Archaeology* 12:39–63.

Rowlands, Peter, Hyrum Johnson, Eric Ritter, and Albert Endo 1982 "The Mojave Desert." In: *Reference Handbook on the Deserts of North America*, Gordon L. Bender, ed., pp. 103–162. Westport, CT: Greenwood Press.

Rowley, Susan 1994 "The Sadlermiut: Mysterious or Misunderstood?" In: "Threads of Arctic Prehistory, Papers in Honor of William E. Taylor, Jr.," David Morrison and Jean-Luc Pilon, eds., pp. 361–384. *Canadian Museum of Civilization, Mercury Series, Archaeological Survey of Canada*, Paper 149.

Rowley-Conwy, Peter 1999 "Introduction: Human Occupation of the Arctic." *World Archaeology* 30(3):349–353.

Rubertone, Patricia E. 2000 "The Historical Archaeology of Native Americans." *Annual Review of Anthropology* 29:425–446.

Ruhlen, Merrit 1994 "Linguistic Evidence for Peopling of the Americas." In: *Method and Theory for Investigating the Peopling of the Americas*, Robson Bonnichsen, and D. Gentry Steele, eds., pp. 177–188. Oregon State University: Center for the Study of the First Americans.

Rusco, Elmer R., and Mary K. Rusco 1986 "Tribal Politics." In: *Handbook of North American Indians, Vol. 11, Great Basin*, Warren L. d'Azevedo, ed., pp. 558–572. Washington, D.C.: Smithsonian Institution.

Russo, Michael 1996a "Southeastern Mid-Holocene Coastal Settlements." In: *Archaeology of the Mid-Holocene Southeast*, Kenneth E. Sassaman and David G. Anderson, eds., pp. 177–199. Gainesville: University Press of Florida.

1996b "Southeastern Archaic Mounds." In: *Archaeology of the Mid-Holocene Southeast*, Kenneth E. Sassaman and David G. Anderson, eds., pp. 259–287. Gainesville: University Press of Florida.

2008 "Late Archaic Shell Rings and Society in the Southeast U.S." *SAA Archaeological Record* 8(5):18–22.

Rutherford, Douglas F. 1990 "Reconsidering the Middlesex Burial Phase in the Maine-Maritimes Region." *Canadian Journal of Archaeology* 14:169–181.

Salls, Roy A. 1991 "Early Holocene Maritime Adaptation at Eel Point, San Clemente Island." In: *Hunter-Gatherers of Early Holocene Coastal California*, Jon M. Erlandson and Roger H. Colten, eds., pp. 63–80. University of California Los Angeles, Institute of Archaeology, Perspectives in California Archaeology, Vol. 1.

Salls, Roy A., L. Mark Raab, and Katherine Bradford 1993 "A San Clemente Island Perspective on Coastal Residential Structures and the Emergence of Sedentism." *Journal of California and Great Basin Anthropology* 15(2):176–194.

Samuels, Michael L., and Julio L. Betancourt 1982 "Modeling the Long-Term Effects of Fuelwood Harvesting on Pinon-Juniper Woodlands." *Environmental Management* 6(6):505–515.

Samuels, Stephan R. 1991 (ed.) *Ozette Archaeological Project Research Reports, Volume 1, House Structure and Floor Midden.* Pullman: Washington State University, Department of Anthropology Reports of Investigations 63.

2006 "Ozette Household Production." In: *Household Archaeology on the Northwest Coast*, Elizabeth A. Sobel, D. Ann Trieu Gahr, and Kenneth M. Ames, eds., pp. 200–232. Ann Arbor: International Monographs in Prehistory, Archaeological Series 16.

Sandweiss, Daniel H. 2005a "Early Maritime Adaptations in Western South America: Part I." *Mammoth Trumpet* 20(4):14–20.

2005b "Early Maritime Adaptations in Western South America: Conclusion." *Mammoth Trumpet* 21(1):14–17.

Sandweiss, Daniel H., Heather McInnis, Richard L. Berger, Asunción Cano, Bernardino Ojeda, Rolando Paredes, María del Carmen Sandweiss, and

Michael D. Glassock 1998 "Quebrada Jaguay: Early South American Maritime Adaptations." *Science* 281:1830–1832.

Sanger, David 1967 "Prehistory of the Pacific Northwest Plateau as Seen from the Interior of British Columbia." *American Antiquity* 32(2):186–197.

2006 "An Introduction to the Archaic of the Maritime Peninsula: The View from Central Maine." In: *The Archaic of the Far Northeast*, David Sanger and M. A. P. Renouf, eds., pp. 221–252. Orono: University of Maine Press.

Sanger, David, Heather Almquist, and Ann Dieffenbacher-Krall 2007 "Mid-Holocene Cultural Adaptations to Central Maine." In: *Climate Change and Cultural Dynamics: A Global Perspective on Mid-Holocene Transitions*, David G. Anderson, Kirk A. Maasch, and Daniel H. Sandweiss, eds., pp. 435–456. New York: Elsevier Press.

Santos, G. M., M. I. Bird, F. Parenti, L. K. Fifield, N. Guidon, and P. A. Hausladen 2003 "A Revised Chronology of the Lowest Occupation Layer of Pedra Furada Rock Shelter, Piauí, Brazil: The Pleistocene Peopling of the Americas." *Quaternary Science Reviews* 22(21–22):2303–2310.

Sassaman, Kenneth E. 2001 "Articulating Hidden Histories of the Mid-Holocene in the Southern Appalachians." In: *Archaeology of the Appalachian Highlands*, Lynne P. Sullivan and Susan C. Prezzano, eds., pp. 103–120. Knoxville, University of Tennessee Press.

2002 "Woodland Ceramic Beginnings." In: *The Woodland Southeast*, David G. Anderson and Robert C. Mainfort, Jr., eds., pp. 398–420. Tuscaloosa: University of Alabama Press.

2005 "Poverty Point as Structure, Event, Process." *Journal of Archaeological Method and Theory* 12(4):335–364.

2008 "The New Archaic, It Ain't What It Used to Be." *SAA Archaeological Record* 8(5):6–8, 12.

Sassaman, Kenneth E., and David G. Anderson (eds.) 1996 *Archaeology of the Mid-Holocene Southeast.* Gainesville: University Press of Florida.

Sassaman, Kenneth E., and David G. Anderson 2004 "Late Holocene Period, 3750 to 650 B.C." In: *Handbook of North American Indians, Vol. 14, Southeast*, Raymond D. Fogelson, ed., pp. 101–114. Washington, D.C.: Smithsonian Institution.

Sassaman, Kenneth E., Meggan E. Blessing, and Asa R. Randall 2006 "Stallings Island Revisited: New Evidence for Occupational History, Community Pattern, and Subsistence Technology." *American Antiquity* 71(3):539–565.

Saunders, Joe W., Rolfe D. Mandel, C. Garth Sampson, Charles M. Allen, E. Thurman Allen, Daniel A. Bush, James K. Feathers, Kristen J. Gremillion, C. T. Hallmark, H. Edwin Jackson, Jay K. Johnson, Reca Jones, Roger T. Saucier, Gary L. Stringer, and Malcolm F. Vidrine 2005 "Watson Brake: A Middle Archaic Mound Complex in Northeast Louisiana." *American Antiquity* 70(4):631–668.

Savelle, James M. 2002 "Logistical Organization, Social Complexity, and the Collapse of Prehistoric Thule Whaling Societies in the Central Canadian Arctic Archipelago." In: *Beyond Foraging and Collecting: Evolutionary Change in Hunter-Gatherer Settlement Systems*, Ben Fitzhugh and Junko Habu, eds., pp. 73–90. New York: Kluwer Academic/Plenum Publishers.

Savelle, James M., and Authur S. Dyke 2002 "Variability in Palaeoeskimo Occupation on South-Western Victoria Island, Arctic Canada: Causes and Consequences." *World Archaeology* 33(3):508–522.

Scarry, C. Margaret 1993a "Variability in Mississippian Crop Production Strategies." In: *Farmers and Foragers in the Eastern Woodlands*, C. Margaret Scarry, ed., pp. 78–90. Gainesville: University Press of Florida.

1993b "Agricultural Risk and the Development of the Moundville Chiefdom." In: *Farmers and Foragers in the Eastern Woodlands*, C. Margaret Scarry, ed., pp. 157–181. Gainesville: University Press of Florida.

2003 "Patterns of Wild Plant Utilization in the Prehistoric Eastern Woodlands." In: *People and Plants in Ancient Eastern North America*, Paul E. Minnis, ed., pp. 50–104. Washington, D.C.: Smithsonian Books.

Scarry, John F. 1996a (ed.) *Political Structure and Change in the Prehistoric Southeastern United States.* Gainesville: University Press of Florida.

1996b "The Nature of Mississippian Societies." In: *Political Structure and Change in the Prehistoric Southeastern United States*, John F. Scarry, ed., pp. 12–24. Gainesville: University Press of Florida.

Schaasfsma, Curtis F., and Carroll L. Riley 1999 "The Casas Grandes World: Analysis and Conclusion." In: *The Casas Grandes World*, Curtis F. Schaafsma and Carroll L. Riley, eds., pp. 237–249. Salt Lake City: University of Utah Press.

Schaafsma, Polly 1971 "The Rock Art of Utah." *Papers of the Peabody Museum of American Archaeology and Ethnology* 65.

2008 "Shamans, Shields, and Stories on Stone." In: *The Great Basin: People and Place in Ancient Times*, Catherine S. Fowler and Don D. Fowler, eds., pp. 144–151. Santa Fe, NM: School of American Research.

Schachner, Gregson 2001 "Ritual Control and Transformation in Middle-Range Societies: An Example from the American Southwest." *Journal of Anthropological Archaeology* 20(2):168–194.

Schaefer, Jerry 1994 "The Challenge of Archaeological Research in the Colorado Desert: Recent Approaches and Discoveries." *Journal of California and Great Basin Anthropology* 16(1):60–80.

Schaefer, Jerry, and Don Laylander 2007 "The Colorado Desert: Ancient Adaptations to Wetlands and Wastelands." In: *California Prehistory: Colonization, Culture, and Complexity*, Terry L. Jones and Kathryn A. Klar, eds., pp. 247–257. Lanham, MD: AltaMira Press.

Schaepe, David M. 2003 "Validating the Maurer House." In: *Archaeology of Coastal British Columbia: Essays in Honour of Professor Philip M. Hobler*, Roy L. Carlson, ed., pp. 113–152. Burnaby, B.C., Canada: Simon Fraser University, Archaeology Press, Publication No. 30.

2006 "Rock Fortifications: Archaeological Insights into Pre-contact Warfare and Sociopolitical Organization Among the Stó:Lo of the Lower Fraser River Canyon, B.C." *American Antiquity* 71(4):671–705.

Schambach, Frank F. 1988 "The Archaeology of Oklahoma." *Quarterly Review of Archaeology* 9(4):5–9.

1993 "Some New Interpretations of Spiroan Culture History." In: *Archaeology of Eastern North America: Papers in Honor of Stephen Williams*, James B. Stoltman, ed., pp. 187–230. Jackson: Mississippi Department of Archives and History, Archaeological Report No. 25.

Scharf, Elizabeth A. 2009 "Foraging and Prehistoric Use of High Elevations in the Western Great Basin: Evidence from Seed Assemblages at Midway (CA-MNO-2196), California." *Journal of California and Great Basin Anthropology* 29(1):11–27.

Scheiber, Laura L. 2006 "The Late Prehistoric on the High Plains of Western Kansas: High Plains Upper Republican and Dismal River." In: *Kansas Archaeology*, Robert J. Hoard and William E. Banks, eds., pp. 133–150. Lawrence, University of Kansas Press.

Schiffer, Michael B. 1975 "An Alternative to Morse's Dalton Settlement Pattern Hypothesis." *Plains Anthropologist* 20(70):253–266.

Schlesier, Karl H. (ed.) 1994 *Plains Indians: A.D. 500–1500: The Archaeological Past of Historic Groups*. Norman: University of Oklahoma Press.

Schmitt, Dave N., and David B. Madsen 2005 "Camels Back Cave." *University of Utah Anthropological Papers* No. 125.

Schoenberg, Kenneth M. 1995 "The Post-Paleoarctic Interval in the Central Brooks Range." *Arctic Anthropology* 32(1):51–61.

Schoeninger, Margaret M. 1999 "Prehistoric Subsistence Strategies in the Stillwater Marsh Region of the Carson Desert." In: *Prehistoric Lifeways in the Great Basin Wetlands: Bioarchaeological Reconstruction and Interpretations*, Brian E. Hemphill and Clark Spencer Larsen, eds., pp. 151–166. Salt Lake City: University of Utah Press.

Schollmeyer, Karen Gust, and Christy G. Turner II 2004 "Dental Caries, Prehistoric Diet, and the Pithouse to Pueblo Transition in Southwestern Colorado." *American Antiquity* 69(3):569–582.

Schroeder, Albert H. 1957 "The Hakataya Cultural Tradition." *American Antiquity* 23(2):176–178.

1979 "Prehistory: Hakataya." In: *Handbook of North American Indians, Vol. 9, Southwest*, Alfonzo Ortiz, ed., pp. 100–107. Washington, D.C.: Smithsonian Institution.

Schroeder, Sissel 2004 "Current Research on Late Precontact Societies of the Midcontinental United States." *Journal of Archeological Research* 12(2):311–372.

Schroedl, Alan R. 1976 "The Grand Canyon Figurine Complex." *American Antiquity* 42(2):254–265.

Schroedl, Gerald F., and C. Clifford Boyd, Jr. 1991 "Late Woodland Period Culture in East Tennessee." In: *Stability, Transformation, and Variation: The Late Woodland Southeast*, Michael S. Nassaney and Charles R. Cobb, eds., pp. 69–90. New York: Plenum Press.

Schulz, Peter D. 1970 "Solar Burial Orientation and Paleodemography in the Central California Windmiller Tradition." In: *Papers on California and Great Basin Prehistory*, Eric W. Ritter, Peter D. Schulz, and Robert Kautz, eds.,

pp. 185–198. Center for Archaeological Research at Davis, Publication No. 2.

1981 "Osteoarchaeology and Subsistence Change in Prehistoric Central California." Ph.D. dissertation, University of California, Davis.

Schurr, Theodore G. 2002 "A Molecular Perspective on the Peopling of the Americas." *Athena Review* 3(2):62–75, 104–108.

2004a "Molecular Genetic Diversity in Siberians and Native American Suggests and Early Colonization of the New World." In: *Entering America: Northeast Asia and Beringia before the Last Glacial Maximum*, David B. Madsen, ed., pp. 187–238. Salt Lake City: University of Utah Press.

2004b "The Peopling of the New World: Perspectives from Molecular Anthropology." *Annual Review of Anthropology* 33:551–583.

2005 "Tracking Genes through Time and Space: Changing Perspectives on New World Origins." In: *Paleoamerican Origins: Beyond Clovis*, Robson Bonnichsen, Bradley T. Lepper, Dennis Stanford, and Michael R. Waters, eds., pp. 221–2242. Texas A&M University: Center for the Study of the First Americans.

Schurr, Mark R., and Margaret J. Schoeninger 1995 "Associations between Agricultural Intensification and Social Complexity: An Example from the Prehistoric Ohio Valley." *Journal of Anthropological Archaeology* 14(3):315–339.

Schurr, Theodore G., and Douglas C. Wallace 1999 "mtDNA Variation in Native Americans and Its Implications for the Peopling of the New World." In: *Who Were the First Americans?*, Robson Bonnichsen, ed., pp. 41–77. Oregon State University: Center for the Study of the First Americans.

Schwaderer, Rae 1992 "Archaeological Test Excavations at the Duncans Point Cave, CA-SON-348/H." In: *Essays on the Prehistory of Maritime California*, Terry L. Jones, ed., pp. 55–71. Center for Archaeological Research at Davis, Publication No. 10.

Scuderi, Louis A. 2002 "The Holocene Environment." In: *The Physical Geography of North America*, Antony R. Orme, ed., pp. 86–97. Oxford, UK: Oxford University Press.

Sears, William H. 1982 *Fort Center. An Archeological Site in the Lake Okeechobee Basin*. Gainesville: University Press of Florida.

Sebastian, Lynne 1992 *The Chaco Anasazi: Sociopolitical Evolution in the Prehistoric Southwest*. Cambridge, UK: Cambridge University Press.

Secoy, Frank R. 1953 "Changing Military Patterns on the Great Plains." *Monographs of the American Ethnological Society* No. 21.

Seeman, Mark F. 1979 *The Hopewell Interaction Sphere: The Evidence for Interregional Trade and Structural Complexity*. Indiana Historical Society Prehistory Research Series 5(2).

1988 "Ohio Hopewell Trophy-Skull Artifacts as Evidence for Competition in Middle Woodland Societies circa 50 B.C.–A.D. 350." *American Antiquity* 53(3):565–577.

1992 "Woodland Traditions in the Midcontinent: A Comparison of Three Regional Sequences." In: *Long-Term Subsistence Change in Prehistoric North America*, Dale R. Croes, Rebecca A. Hawkins, and Barry L. Isaac, eds., pp. 3–46. Research in Economic Anthropology, Supplement 6. Greenwich, CT: JAI Press.

Settipane, Guy A. (ed.) 1995 *Columbus and the New World: Medical Implications*. Providence, RI: OceanSide Publications.

Shanks, Michael, and Christopher Tilley 1987 *Re-Constructing Archaeology: Theory and Practice*. Cambridge, UK: Cambridge University Press.

Shaul David L., and Jane H. Hill 1998 "Tepimans, Yumans, and Other Hohokam." *American Antiquity* 63(3):375–396.

Shaw, Robert D. 1998 "An Archaeology of the Central Yupik: A Regional Overview for the Yukon-Kuskokwim Delta, Northern Bristol Bay, and Nunivak Island." *Arctic Anthropology* 35(1):234–246.

Sheehan, Glenn W. 1985 "Whaling as an Organizing Focus in Northwestern Alaska Eskimo Societies." In: *Prehistoric Hunter-Gatherers: The Emergence of Cultural Complexity*, T. Douglas Price and James A. Brown, eds., pp. 123–154. Orlando: Academic Press.

Sheppard, John C., Peter E. Wigand, Carl E. Gustafson, and Meyer Rubin 1987 "A Reevaluation of the Marmes Rockshelter Radiocarbon Chronology." *American Antiquity* 52(1):118–125.

Sheridan, Thomas E., Charles W. Polzer, Thomas H. Naylor, and Diana Hadley (eds.) 1991 *The Franciscan Missions of Northern Mexico*. New York: Garland Publishing.

Sherwood, Sarah H., Boyce N. Driskell, Asa R. Randall, and Scott C. Meeks 2004 "Chronology and Stratigraphy at Dust Cave, Alabama." *American Antiquity* 69(3):533–554.

Shields, Edward D., and Gregory Jones 1998 "Dorset and Thule Divergence from East Central Asian Roots." *American Journal of Physical Anthropology* 106(2):207–218.

Shields, Gerald F., Andrea M. Schmiechen, Barbara L. Frazier, Alan Reed, Mikhail I. Voevoda, Judy K. Reed, and R. H. Ward 1993 "mtDNA Sequences Suggest a Recent Evolutionary Divergence for Berigian and Northern North American Populations." *American Journal of Human Genetics* 53(3):549–562.

Shipley, William F. 1978 "Native Languages of California." In: *Handbook of North American Indians, Vol. 8, California*, Robert F. Heizer, ed., pp. 80–90. Washington, D.C.: Smithsonian Institution.

Shutler, Richard, Jr. 1961 "Lost City: Pueblo Grande de Nevada." *Nevada State Museum Anthropological Papers* No. 5.

1983 (ed.) *Early Man in the New World*. Beverly Hills: Sage Publications.

Sillman, Stephen W. 2005 "Culture Contact of Colonialism? Challenges in the Archaeology of Native North America." *American Antiquity* 70(1):55–74.

Silverberg, Robert 1968 *Mound Builders of Ancient America: The Archaeology of a Myth*. Greenwich, CT: New York Graphic Society.

Simms, Steven R. 1984 "Aboriginal Great Basin Foraging Strategies: An Evolutionary Analysis." Ph.D. dissertation, University of Utah.

1985 "Pine Nut Use in Three Great Basin Cases: Data, Theory, and a Fragmentary Material Record." *Journal of California and Great Basin Anthropology* 7(2):166–175.

1986 "New Evidence for Fremont Adaptive Diversity." *Journal of California and Great Basin Anthropology* 8(2):204–216.

1988 "Conceptualizing the Paleoindian and Archaic in the Great Basin." In: "Early Human Occupation in Far Western North America: The Clovis-Archaic Interface," Judith A. Willig, C. Melvin Aikens, and John L. Fagan, eds., pp. 41–52. Special issue, *Nevada State Museum Anthropological Papers* No. 21.

1999 "Farmers, Foragers, and Adaptive Diversity: The Great Salt Lake Wetlands Project." In: *Prehistoric Lifeways in the Great Basin Wetlands: Bioarchaeological Reconstruction and Interpretations*, Brian E. Hemphill and Clark Spencer Larsen, eds., pp. 21–54. Salt Lake City: University of Utah Press.

2008 *Ancient Peoples of the Great Basin & Colorado Plateau*. Walnut Creek, CA: Left Coast Press.

Sjøvold, Torstein 1992 "The Stone Age Iceman from the Alps: The Find and the Current Status of Investigation." *Evolutionary Anthropology* 1(4):117–124.

Skibo, James M., Eugene B. McCluney, and William H. Walker 2002 *The Joyce Well Site: On the Frontier of the Cases Grandes World*. Salt Lake City: University of Utah Press.

Slobodin, Sergei B. 1999 "Northeast Asia in the Late Pleistocene and Early Holocene." *World Archaeology* 30(3):484–502.

2001 "Western Beringia at the End of the Ice Age." *Arctic Anthropology* 38(2):31–47.

2006 "The Paleolithic of Western Beringia: A Summary of Research." In: *Archaeology in Northeast Asia: On the Pathway to Bering Straight*, Don E. Dumond and Richard L. Bland, eds., pp. 9–23. *University of Oregon Anthropological Papers* No. 65.

Smith, Bruce D. 1986 "The Archaeology of the Southeastern United States: From Dalton to de Soto, 10,500-500 B.P." In: *Advances in World Archaeology, Vol. 5*, Fred Wendorf and Angela E. Close, eds., pp. 1–92. Orlando, FL: Academic Press.

1987 "Independent Domestication of Indigenous Seed-Bearing Plants in Eastern North America." In: "Emergent Horticultural Economies of the Eastern Woodlands," William F. Keegan, ed., pp. 3–47. *Southern Illinois University, Carbondale, Center for Archaeological Investigations, Occasional Paper* No. 7.

1989 "Origins of Agriculture in the Eastern United States." *Science* 246:1566–1571.

1990 (ed.) *The Mississippian Emergence*. Washington, D.C.: Smithsonian Institution Press.

1992 "The Floodplain Weed Theory of Plant Domestication in Eastern North America." In: *Rivers of Change: Essays on Early Agriculture in Eastern North America*, Bruce D. Smith, ed., pp. 19–34. Washington, D.C.: Smithsonian Institution Press.

1993 "Reconciling the Gender-Credit Critique and the Floodplain Weed Theory of Plant Domestication." In: *Archaeology of Eastern North America: Papers in Honor of*

Stephen Williams, James B. Stoltman, ed., pp. 111–125. Jackson: Mississippi Department of Archives and History, Archaeological Report No. 25.

1996 "Agricultural Chiefdoms of the Eastern Woodlands." In: *The Cambridge History of Native Peoples of the Americas, Vol. 1, North America*, Bruce G. Trigger and Wilcomb E. Washburn, eds., pp. 267–323. Cambridge: Cambridge University Press.

Smith, Bruce D., and C. Wesley Cowan 2003 "Domesticated Crop Plants and the Evolution of Food Production Economies in Eastern North America." In: *People and Plants in Ancient Eastern North America*, Paul E. Minnis, ed., pp. 105–125. Washington, D.C.: Smithsonian Books.

Smith, Brian F. 1987 "A Reinterpretation of the Transitional Phase." In: *San Dieguito-La Jolla: Chronology and Controversy*, Dennis R. Gallegos, ed., pp. 61–71. San Diego County Archaeological Society Research Paper No. 1.

Smith, Craig S. 2003 "Hunter-Gatherer Mobility, Storage, and Houses in a Marginal Environment: An Example from the Mid-Holocene of Wyoming." *Journal of Anthropological Archaeology* 22(2):162–189.

Smith, Craig S., and Thomas P. Reust 1995 "The Dry Susie Creek Site: Site Structure of Middle Archaic Habitation Features from the Upper Humboldt River Area, Nevada." *Journal of California and Great Basin Anthropology* 17(2):244–266.

Smith, David Glenn, Becky K. Rolfs, Frederika A. Kaestle, Ripan S. Malhi, and Glen H. Doran 2002 "Serum Albumin Phenotypes and a Preliminary Study of the Windover mtDNA Haplogroups and Their Anthropological Significance." In: *Windover: Multidisciplinary Investigations of an Early Archaic Florida Cemetery*, Glen H. Doran, ed., pp. 241–249. Gainesville: University Press of Florida.

Smith, David Glenn, Ripan S. Malhi, Jason A. Eshleman, Frederika A. Kaestle, and Brian M. Kemp 2005 "Mitochondrial DNA Haplogroups of Paleoamericans in North America." In: *Paleoamerican Origins: Beyond Clovis*, Robson Bonnichsen, Bradley T. Lepper, Dennis Stanford, and Michael R. Waters, eds., pp. 243–254. Texas A&M University: Center for the Study of the First Americans.

Smith, Kevin P., and Richard S. Laub 2000 "The Late-Pleistocene/Early-Holocene Transition in Western New York: A Reexamination of the Ritchie-Fitting Hypothesis." *Current Research in the Pleistocene* 17:75–78.

Smith, Larry N. 2006 "Stratigraphic Evidence for Multiple Drainings of Glacial Lake Missoula along the Clark Fork River, Montana, USA." *Quaternary Research* 66(2):311–322.

Smith, Marvin T. 2000 *Coosa: The Rise and Fall of a Southeastern Mississippian Chiefdom*. Gainesville: University Press of Florida.

2001 "The Rise and Fall of the Coosa, A.D. 1350-1700." In: *Societies in Eclipse: Archaeology of the Eastern Woodlands Indians, A.D. 1400–1700*, David S. Brose, C. Wesley Cowan, and Robert C. Mainfort, Jr., eds., pp. 143–155. Washington, D.C.: Smithsonian Institution Press.

Smith, F. Todd 1995 *The Caddo Indians: Tribes at the Convergence of Empires, 1542–1854*. College Station: Texas A & M University Press.

Snow, Dean 1976 *The Archaeology of North America*. New York: Viking Press.

1980 *The Archaeology of New England*. New York: Academic Press.

1981 (ed.) *Foundations of Northeastern Archaeology*. New York: Academic Press.

1995 Migrations in Prehistory: The Northern Iroquoian Case. *American Antiquity* 60(1):59–79.

2009 *Archaeology of Native North America*. Upper Saddle River, NJ: Prentice Hall.

Sobolik, Kristin D. (ed.) 1994 "Paleonutrition: The Diet and Health of Prehistoric Americans." *Southern Illinois University, Carbondale, Center for Archaeological Investigations, Occasional Paper* No. 22.

Sobolik, Kristin D., Kristen J. Gremillion, Patricia L. Whitten, and Patty Jo Watson 1996 "Technical Note: Sex Determination of Prehistoric Human Paleofeces." *American Journal of Physical Anthropology* 101(2):283–290.

Sofaer, Anna 2007 "The Primary Architecture of the Chacoan Culture: A Cosmological Expression." In: *The Architecture of Chaco Canyon, New Mexico*, Stephen H. Lekson, ed., pp. 225–254. Salt Lake City: University of Utah Press.

Soffer, Olga, and N. D. Praslov (eds.) 1993 *From Kostenki to Clovis: Upper Paleolithic—Paleo-Indian Adaptations*. New York: Plenum Press.

Spector, Janet D. 1991 "What This Awl Means: Toward a Feminist Archaeology." In: *Engendering Archaeology: Women and Prehistory*, Joan M. Gero and Margaret W. Conkey, eds., pp. 388–406. Cambridge, UK: Basil Blackwell, Inc.

1993 *What This Awl Means: Feminist Archaeology at a Wahpeton Dakota Village*. St. Paul: Minnesota Historical Society Press.

Speller, Camilla F., Dongya Y. Yang, and Brian Hayden 2005 "Ancient DNA Investigation of Prehistoric Salmon Resource Utilization at Keatley Creek, British Columbia, Canada." *Journal of Archaeological Science* 32(9):1378–1389.

Speth, John D. 1983 *Bison Kills and Bone Counts: Decision Making by Ancient Hunters*. Chicago: University of Chicago Press.

Spicer, Edward H. 1962 *Cycles of Conquest: The Impact of Spain, Mexico, and the United States on the Indians of the Southwest, 1533–1960*. Tucson: University of Arizona Press.

Spielmann, Katherine A. 2002 "Feasting, Craft Specialization, and the Ritual Mode of Production in Small-Scale Societies." *American Anthropologist* 104(1):195–207.

Spiess, Arthur E. 1993 "Caribou, Walrus and Seals: Maritime Archaic Subsistence in Labrador and Newfoundland." In: *Archaeology of Eastern North America: Papers in Honor of Stephen Williams*, James B. Stoltman, ed., pp. 43–100. Jackson: Mississippi Department of Archives and History, Archaeological Report No. 25.

Spiess, Authur E., and John Mosher 2006 "Archaic Period Hunting and Fishing around the Gulf of Maine." In: *The Archaic of the Far Northeast*, David Sanger and M. A. P. Renouf, eds., pp. 383–408. Orono: University of Maine Press.

Spiess, Authur E., Deborah Wilson, and James W. Bradley 1998 "Paleoindian Occupation in the New England-Maritimes

Region: Beyond Cultural Ecology." *Archaeology of Eastern North America* 26:201–264.

Squier, Ephraim G., and Edwin U. Davis 1848 *Ancient Monuments of the Mississippi Valley.* Washington, D.C.: Smithsonian Contributions to Knowledge 1.

Stahl. Peter W. 1996 "Holocene Biodiversity: An Archaeological Perspective from the Americas." *Annual Review of Anthropology* 25:105–126

Stanford, Dennis J. 1999 "Paleoindian Archaeology and Late Pleistocene Environments in the Plains and Southwestern United States." In: *Ice Age Peoples of North America: Environments, Origins, and Adaptations of the First Americans*, Robson Bonnichsen and Karen L. Turnmire, eds., pp. 281–339. Oregon State University: Center for the Study of the First Americans.

Stanford, Dennis J., and Bruce Bradley 2002 "Ocean Trails and Prairie Paths? Thoughts about Clovis Origins." In: "First Americans: The Pleistocene Colonization of the New World," Nina G. Jablonski, ed., pp. 255–271. Special issue, *Memoirs of the California Academy of Sciences* No. 27.

Stanford, Dennis J., Margaret Jodry, and Robson Bonnichsen 1999 "Clovis and Non-Clovis Traditions West of the Mississippi." Paper presented at the Clovis and Beyond Conference, Santa Fe.

Stannard, David E. 1992 *American Holocaust: Columbus and the Conquest of the New World.* Oxford, UK: Oxford University Press.

Steele, D. Gentry 1989 "Recently Recovered Paleoindian Skeletal Remains from Texas and the Southwest." *American Journal of Physical Anthropology* 78(2):307.

Steele, D. Gentry, and Joseph F. Powell 1993 "Paleobiology of the First Americans." *Evolutionary Anthropology* 2(4):138–146.

   1994 "Paleobiological Evidence of the Peopling of the Americas: A Morphometric View." In: *Method and Theory for Investigating the Peopling of the Americas*, Robson Bonnichsen and D. Gentry Steele, eds., pp. 141–163. Oregon State University: Center for the Study of the First Americans.

   1999 "Peopling of the Americas: A Historical and Comparative Perspective." In: *Who Were the First Americans?*, Robson Bonnichsen, ed., pp. 97–126. Oregon State University: Center for the Study of the First Americans.

   2002 "Facing the Past: A View of the North American Human Fossil Record." In: "First Americans: The Pleistocene Colonization of the New World," Nina G. Jablonski, ed., pp. 93–122. Special issue, *Memoirs of the California Academy of Sciences* No. 27.

Steele, James, Jonathan Adams, and Tim Sluckin 1998 "Modelling Paleoindian Dispersals." *World Archaeology* 30(2):286–305.

Stein, John, Richard Friedman, Taft Blackhorse, and Richard Loose 2007 "Revisiting Downtown Chaco." In: *The Architecture of Chaco Canyon, New Mexico*, Stephen H. Lekson, ed., pp. 199–223. Salt Lake City: University of Utah Press.

Stein, Scott 1994 "Extreme and Persistent Drought in California and Patagonia During Medieval Time." *Nature* 369:546–549.

Steinacher, Terry L., and Gayle F. Carlson 1998 "The Central Plains Tradition." In: *Archaeology on the Great Plains*, W. Raymond Wood, ed., pp. 235–268. Lawrence: University of Kansas Press.

Steward, Julian H. 1938 "Basin-Plateau Aboriginal Sociopolitical Groups." *Bureau of American Ethnology Bulletin* 120.

Stewart, Francis L., and Peter W. Stahl 1977 "Cautionary Note on Edible Meat Poundage Figures." *American Antiquity* 42(2):267–270.

Stewart, Kathlyn M., and Francis L. Stewart 2001 "Prehistoric Subsistence and Seasonality at Prince Rupert Harbour: History and Synthesis of Zooarchaeological Research." In: *Perspectives on Northwest Coast Prehistory*, Jerome S. Cybulski, ed., pp. 173–202. Canadian Museum of Civilization, Mercury Series, Archaeological Survey of Canada, Paper 160.

Stewart, R. Michael 1993 "Comparison of Late Woodland Cultures: Delaware, Potomac, and Susquehanna River Valleys, Middle Atlantic Region." *Archaeology of Eastern North America* 21:163–178.

   1994a "Late Archaic through Late Woodland Exchange in the Middle Atlantic Region." In: *Prehistoric Exchange Systems in North America*, Timothy G. Baugh and Jonathon E. Ericson, eds., pp. 73–98. New York: Plenum Press.

   1994b "Prehistoric Farmers of the Susquehanna Valley: Clemson Island Culture and the St. Anthony Site." *Occasional Publications in Northeastern Anthropology* No. 13.

Stewart, Tamara 2003 "Mexican Skull Is Nearly 13,000 Years Old." *American Archaeology* 7(1):8.

Stine, Scott 1994 "Extreme and Persistent Drought in California and Patagonia During Mediaeval Time." *Nature* 369:546–549.

Stiger, Mark 2006 "A Folsom Structure in the Colorado Mountains." *American Antiquity* 71(2):321–351.

Stoffle, Richard W., and Maria Nieves Zedeño 2001 "Historical Memory and Ethnographic Perspectives on the Southern Paiute Homeland." *Journal of California and Great Basin Anthropology* 23(2):229–248.

Stoltman, James B. 1997 "The Archaic Tradition." *Wisconsin Archaeologist* 78(1–2):112–139.

   2004 "History of Archaeological Research." In: *Handbook of North American Indians, Vol. 14, Southeast*, Raymond D. Fogelson, ed., pp. 14–30. Washington, D.C.: Smithsonian Institution.

Stone, Anne C., and Mark Stoneking 1998 "MtDNA Analysis of a Prehistoric Oneota Population: Implications for the Peopling of the New World." *American Journal of Human Genetics* 62(5):1153–1170.

Stopp, Marianne P. 2002 "Ethnohistoric Analogues for Storage as an Adaptive Strategy in Northeastern Subarctic Prehistory." *Journal of Anthropological Archaeology* 21(3):301–328.

Stothers, David M. 1996 "Resource Procurement and Band Territories: A Model for Lower Great Lakes Paleoindian and Early Archaic Settlement Systems." *Archaeology of Eastern North America* 24:173–216.

Stothers, David M., and Timothy J. Abel 1991 "Earliest Man in the Southwestern Lake Erie Basin: A 1990 Perspective." *North American Archaeologist* 12(3):195–242.

Straus, Lawrence Guy 2000 "Solutrean Settlement of North America? A Review of Reality." *American Antiquity* 65(2):219–226.

Straus, Lawrence Guy, David J. Meltzer, and Ted Goebel 2005 "Ice Age Atlantis? Exploring the Solutrean-Clovis 'Connection.'" *World Archaeology* 37(4):507–532.

Strong, William Duncan 1935 "An Introduction to Nebraska Archaeology." *Smithsonian Miscellaneous Collections* 93(10).

1936 "Anthropological Theory and Archaeological Fact." In: *Essays in Anthropology*, Robert H. Lowie, ed., pp. 359–368. Berkeley: University of California Press.

Struever, Stuart, and Felicia Antonelli Holton 1979 *Koster: Americans in Search of Their Prehistoric Past.* Garden City, NY: Anchor Press.

Struever, Stuart, and Gail L. Houart 1972 "An Analysis of the Hopewell Interaction Sphere." In: "Social Exchange and Interaction," E. N. Wilmsen, ed., pp. 47–79. Special issue, *University of Michigan, Museum of Anthropology, Anthropological Papers* No. 46.

Stuart, David E. 2000 *Anasazi America.* Albuquerque: University of New Mexico Press.

Stuiver, Minze, and Thomas F. Braziunas 1993a "Sun, Ocean, Climate and Atmospheric 14CO$_2$: An Evaluation of Causal and Spectral Relationships." *The Holocene* 3(4):289–305.

Stuiver, Minze, and Thomas F. Braziunas 1993b "Modeling Atmospheric ^{14}C Influences and ^{14}C Ages of Marine Samples to 10,000 BC." *Radiocarbon* 35(1):137–189.

Stuiver, Minze, and Paula J. Reimer 1993 "Extended 14C Data Base and Revised Calib 3.0 14C Calibration Program." *Radiocarbon* 35(1):215–230.

Stuiver, Minze, Paula J. Reimer, Edouard Bard, J. Warren Beck, G. S. Burr, Konrad A. Hughen, Bernd Kromer, Gerry McCormac, Johannes van der Plicht, and Marco Spurk 1998a "INTCAL98 Radiocarbon Age Calibration, 24,000-0 cal BP." *Radiocarbon* 40(3):1041–1083.

Stuiver Minze, Paula J. Reimer, and Thomas F. Braziunas 1998b "High-Precision Radiocarbon Age Calibration for Terrestrial and Marine Samples, 1998." *Radiocarbon* 40(3):1127–1151.

Styles, Bonnie W., and Walter E. Klippel 1996 "Mid-Holocene Faunal Exploitation in the Southeastern United States." In: *Archaeology of the Mid-Holocene Southeast*, Kenneth E. Sassaman and David G. Anderson, eds., pp. 115–133. Gainesville: University Press of Florida.

Styrd, Arnoud R. 1982 "Prehistoric Mobile Art from the Mid-Fraser and Thompson River Areas." In: *Indian Art Traditions of the Northwest Coast*, Roy L. Carlson, ed., pp. 167–181. Burnaby, B.C.: Simon Fraser University, Archaeology Press.

Stryd, Arnoud R., and Mike K. Rousseau 1996 "The Early Prehistory of the Mid Fraser-Thompson River Area." In: *Early Human Occupation in British Columbia*, Roy L. Carlson and Luke Dalla Bona, eds., pp. 177–204. Vancouver: University of British Columbia Press.

Sundahl, Elaine 1992 "Cultural Patterns and Chronology in the Northern Sacramento River Drainage." In: *Proceedings of the Society for California Archaeology, Vol. 5*, Martin D. Rosen, Lynne E. Christenson, and Don Laylander, eds., pp. 89–112. San Diego: Society for California Archaeology.

Sundahl, Elaine, and Winfield Henn 1993 "Borax Lake Pattern Assemblages on the Shasta-Trinity National Forests, North-Central California." *Journal of California and Great Basin Anthropology* 15(1):73–90.

Surovell, Todd A. 2000 "Early Paleoindian Women, Children, Mobility, and Fertility." *American Antiquity* 65(3):493–508.

Surovell, Todd A., and Niclole M. Waguespack 2009 "Human Prey Choice in the Late Pleistocene and Its Relation to Megafaunal Extinction." In: *American Megafaunal Extinctions at the End of the Pleistocene*, Gary Haynes, ed., pp. 77–105. New York: Springer.

Surovell, Todd A., Vance T. Holliday, Joseph A. M. Gingerich, Caroline Ketron, C. Vance Haynes, Jr., Ilene Hilman, Daniel P. Wagner, Eileen Johnson, and Philippe Claeys 2009 "An Independent Evaluation of the Younger Dryas Extraterrestrial Impact Hypothesis." *Proceedings of the National Academy of Sciences* 106(43):18155–18158.

Sutherland, Patricia D. 2001 "Shamanism and the Iconography of Palaeo-Eskimo Art." In: *The Archaeology of Shamanism*, Neil Price, ed., pp. 135–145. London: Routledge.

2009 "The Question of Contact between Dorset Paleo-Eskimos and Early Europeans in the Eastern Arctic." In: *The Northern World: AD 900-1400*, Herbert D. G. Maschner, Owen Mason, and Robert McGhee, eds., pp. 279–299. Salt Lake City: University of Utah Press.

Suttles, Wayne 1990a "Environment." In: *Handbook of North American Indians, Vol. 7, Northwest Coast*, Wayne Suttles, ed., pp. 16–29. Washington, D.C.: Smithsonian Institution.

1990b (ed.) *Handbook of North American Indians, Vol. 7, Northwest Coast*. Washington, D.C.: Smithsonian Institution.

Sutton, Mark Q. 1982 "Kawaiisu Mythology and Rock Art: One Example." *Journal of California and Great Basin Anthropology* 4(1):148–154.

1984 "The Productivity of *Pinus monophylla* and Modeling Great Basin Subsistence Strategies." *Journal of California and Great Basin Anthropology* 6(2):240–246.

1986 "Warfare and Expansion: An Ethnohistoric Perspective on the Numic Spread." *Journal of California and Great Basin Anthropology* 8(1):65–82.

1988 *Insects as Food: Aboriginal Entomophagy in the Great Basin.* Menlo Park, CA: Ballena Press Anthropological Papers No. 33.

1989 "Late Prehistoric Interaction Spheres in the Mojave Desert, California." *North American Archaeologist* 10(2):95–121.

1993a "On the Subsistence Ecology of the "Late Inland Millingstone Horizon" in Southern California." *Journal of California and Great Basin Anthropology* 15(1):134–140.

1993b "Midden and Coprolite Derived Subsistence Evidence: An Analysis of Data from the La Quinta Site, Salton Basin, California." *Journal of Ethnobiology* 13(1):1–15.

1995 "Archaeological Aspects of Insect Use." *Journal of Archaeological Method and Theory* 2(3):253–298.

1996 "The Current Status of the Archaeology of the Mojave Desert." *Journal of California and Great Basin Anthropology* 18(2):221–257.

1997 A Background for Archaeological Investigations at Buena Vista Lake, Southern San Joaquin Valley, California. Kern County Archaeological Society Journal 8:3–21.

1998 "Cluster Analysis of Paleofecal Data Sets: A Test of Late Prehistoric Settlement and Subsistence Patterns in the Northern Coachella Valley, California." *American Antiquity* 63(1):86–107.

2000 "Strategy and Tactic in the Analysis of Archaeological Hunter-Gatherer Systems." *North American Archaeologist* 21(3):217–231.

2008 *An Introduction to Native North America* (3rd ed.). Boston: Allyn and Bacon.

2009 "People and Language: Defining the Takic Expansion into Southern California." *Pacific Coast Archaeological Society Quarterly* 41(2 & 3):31–93.

2010a "A Reevaluation of Early Northern Uto-Aztecan Prehistory in Alta California." *California Archaeology* 2(1):3–30.

2010b "The Del Rey Tradition and its Place in Southern California Prehistory." *Pacific Coast Archaeological Society Quarterly* 44(2):1–54.

Sutton, Mark Q., and E. N. Anderson 2010 *Introduction to Cultural Ecology* (2nd ed). Lanham, MD: AltaMira Press.

Sutton, Mark Q., Mark E. Basgall, Jill K. Gardner, and Mark W. Allen 2007 "Advances in Understanding Mojave Desert Prehistory." In: *California Prehistory: Colonization, Culture, and Complexity*, Terry L. Jones and Kathryn A. Klar, eds., pp. 229–245. Lanham, MD: AltaMira Press.

Sutton, Mark Q., and Jill K. Gardner 2010 "Reconceptualizing the Encinitas Tradition of Southern California." *Pacific Coast Archaeological Society Quarterly* 42(4):1–64.

Sutton, Mark Q., and Henry C. Koerper 2009 "The Middle Holocene Western Nexus: An Interaction Sphere Between Southern California and the Northwestern Great Basin." *Pacific Coast Archaeological Society Quarterly* 41(2&3):1–29.

Sutton, Mark Q., and Rebecca S. Orfila 2003 "A Radiocarbon Correction Factor for Freshwater Shell for the Lower Kern River/Northern Buena Vista Lake Area, Southern San Joaquin Valley, California." *Society for California Archaeology Newsletter* 37(2):23–24.

Sutton, Mark Q., and Karl J. Reinhard 1995 "Cluster Analysis of the Coprolites from Antelope House: Implications for Anasazi Diet and Cuisine." *Journal of Archaeological Science* 22(6):741–750.

Sutton, Mark Q., and David Rhode 1994 "Background to the Numic Problem." In: *Across the West: Human Population Movement and the Expansion of the Numa*, David B. Madsen and David Rhode, eds., pp. 6–15. Salt Lake City: University of Utah Press.

Sutton, Mark Q., Joan S. Schneider, and Robert M. Yohe II 1993 "The Siphon Site (CA-SBR-6580): A Millingstone Horizon Site in Summit Valley, California." *San Bernardino County Museum Association Quarterly* 40(3).

Sutton, Mark Q., Kristin D. Sobolik, and Jill K. Gardner 2010 *Paleonutrition*. Tucson: University of Arizona Press.

Sutton, Mark Q., and Philip J. Wilke (eds.) 1988 *Archaeological Investigations at CA-RIV-1179, CA-RIV-2823, and CA-RIV-2827, La Quinta, Riverside County, California*. Salinas: Coyote Press Archives of California Prehistory No. 20.

Svingen, Orlan J. 1992 "The Pawnee of Nebraska: Twice Removed." American Indian Culture and Research Journal 16(2):121–137.

Swagerty, William R. 2001 "History of the United States Plains Until 1850." In: *Handbook of North American Indians, Vol. 13, Plains*, Raymond J. DeMallie, ed., pp. 256–279. Washington, D.C.: Smithsonian Institution.

Swanton, John R. 1942 "Source Material on the History and Ethnology of the Caddo Indians." *Bureau of American Ethnology Bulletin* 132.

Swedlund, Alan C., and Duane C. Anderson 1999 "Gordon Creek Woman Meets Kennewick Man: New Interpretations and Protocols Regarding the Peopling of the Americas." *American Antiquity* 64(4):569–576.

Swidler, Nina, Kurt E. Dongoske, Roger Anyon, and Alan S. Downer (eds.) 1997 *Native Americans and Archaeologists: Stepping Stones to Common Ground*. Walnut Creek, CA: AltaMira Press.

Swinton, George 1992 *Sculpture of the Inuit*. Toronto: McClelland and Stewart, Inc.

Szathmary, Emöke J. E. 1979 "Blood Groups of Siberians, Eskimos, Subarctic, and Northwest Coast Indians: the Problem of Origin and Genetic Relationships." In: *The First Americans: Origins, Affinities, and Adaptations*, William S. Laughlin and Albert B. Harper, eds., pp. 185–209. New York: Gustav Fischer.

1993 "Genetics of Aboriginal North Americans." *Evolutionary Anthropology* 1(6):202–220.

1994 "Modelling Ancient Population Relationships from Modern Population Genetics." In: *Method and Theory for Investigating the Peopling of the Americas*, Robson Bonnichsen, and D. Gentry Steele, eds., pp. 117–130. Oregon State University: Center for the Study of the First Americans.

Talbot, Richard K. 2000 "Fremont Farmers." In: *The Archaeology of Regional Interaction: Religion, Warfare, and Exchange across the American Southwest and Beyond*, Michelle Hegmon, ed., pp. 275–293. Boulder: University of Colorado Press.

Talbot, Richard K., and James D. Wilde 1989 "Giving Form to the Formative: Shifting Settlement Patterns in the Eastern Great Basin and Northern Colorado Plateau." *Utah Archaeology* 2(1):3–18.

Tankersley, Kenneth B. 1995 "Seasonality of Stone Procurement: An Early Paleoindian Example in Northwestern New York State." *North American Archaeologist* 16(1):1–16.

1998 "Variation in the Early Paleoindian Economies of Late Pleistocene Eastern North America." *American Antiquity* 63(1):7–20.

2002 *In Search of Ice Age Americans*. Salt Lake City: Gibbs Smith.

Tankersley, Kenneth B., and Yaroslav V. Kuzmin 1998 "Patterns of Culture Change in Eastern Siberia During the Pleistocene-Holocene Transition." *Quaternary International* 49/50:129–139.

Tankersley, Kenneth B., Cheryl Ann Munson, and Donald Smith 1987 "Recognition of Bituminous Coal Contaminants in Radiocarbon Samples." *American Antiquity* 52(2):318–330.

Tankersley, Kenneth B., Michael R. Waters, and Thomas W. Stafford, Jr. 2009 "Clovis and the American Mastodont at Big Bone Lick, Kentucky." *American Antiquity* 74(3):558–567.

Tankersley, Kenneth B., David G. Anderson, Christopher Ellis, and Bradley T. Lepper 1999 "Are We Sure Its Clovis?" Paper presented at the Clovis and Beyond Conference, Santa Fe.

Taylor, Amanda K. 2003 "Results of a Great Basin Fluted-Point Survey." *Current Research in the Pleistocene* 20:77–79.

Taylor, R. E. 1987 *Radiocarbon Dating: An Archaeological Perspective*. Orlando: Academic Press.

1991 "Frameworks for Dating the Late Pleistocene Peopling of the Americas." In: *The First Americans: Search and Research*, Tom D. Dillehay and David J. Meltzer, eds, pp. 77–111. Boca Raton: CRC Press.

Taylor, R. E., and Martin Aitken (eds.) 1997 *Chronometric Dating in Archaeology*. New York: Plenum Press.

Taylor, R. E., C. Vance Haynes, Jr., Donna L. Kerner, and John R. Southon 1999 "Radiocarbon Analyses of Modern Organics at Monte Verde, Chile: No Evidence for a Local Reservoir Effect." *American Antiquity* 64(3):455–460.

Taylor, R. E., C. Vance Haynes, Jr., and Minze Stuiver 1996 "Clovis and Folsom Age Estimates: Stratigraphic Context and Radiocarbon Calibration." *Antiquity* 70(269):515–525.

Taylor, R. E., Donna L. Kerner, John R. Southon, and James C. Chatters 1998 "Radiocarbon Dates of Kennewick Man." *Science* 280:1171–1172.

Taylor, R. E., L. A. Payen, C. Pryor, P. J. Slota Jr., R. Gillespie, J. A. J. Gowlett, R. E. B. Hedges, A. J. T. Jull, T. H. Zable, D. J. Donahue, and R. Berger 1985 "Major Revisions in the Pleistocene Age Assignments for North American Human Skeletons by ^{14}C Accelerator Mass Spectrometry: None Older than 11,000 ^{14}C Years B.P." *American Antiquity* 50(1):136–140.

Taylor, Walter W. 1948 *A Study of Archaeology*. Menasha, WI: American Anthropological Association.

1961 "Archaeology and Language in Western North America." *American Antiquity* 27(1):71–81.

Taylor, William E. 1968 "The Arnapik and Tyara Sites: An Archaeological Study of Dorset Cultural Origins." *Memoirs of the Society for American Archaeology* No. 22.

Teller, James T., and Lee Clayton (eds.) 1983 *Glacial Lake Agassiz*. Toronto: Geological Association of Canada Special Paper 26.

Theler, James L., and Robert F. Boszhardt 2003 *Twelve Millennia: Archaeology of the Upper Mississippi River Valley*. Iowa City: University of Iowa Press.

2006 "Collapse of Crucial Resources and Culture Change: A Model for the Woodland to Oneota Transformation in the Upper Midwest." *American Antiquity* 71(3):433–472.

Thomas, Chad R., Christopher Carr, and Cynthia Keller 2006 "Animal-Totemic Clans of Ohio Hopewellian Peoples." In: *Gathering Hopewell: Society, Ritual, and Ritual Interaction*, Christopher Carr and D. Troy Case, eds., pp. 339–385. New York: Springer.

Thomas, Cyrus 1894 *Report of the Mound Explorations of the Bureau of Ethnology. Twelfth Annual Report of the Bureau of Ethnology, 1890–91*. Washington, D.C.: Government Printing Office.

1898 *Introduction to the Study of North American Archaeology*. Cincinnati, OH: The Robert Clarke Company.

Thomas, David Hurst 1973 An Empirical Test for Steward's Model of Great Basin Settlement Patterns. *American Antiquity* 38(2):155–176.

1981 "How to Classify the Projectile Points from Monitor Valley, Nevada." *Journal of California and Great Basin Anthropology* 3(1):7–43.

1983a "The Archaeology of Monitor Valley 1: Epistemology." *Anthropological Papers of the American Museum of Natural History* 58(1).

1983b "The Archaeology of Monitor Valley 2, Gatecliff Shelter." *Anthropological Papers of the American Museum of Natural History* 59(1).

1985 "The Archaeology of Hidden Cave, Nevada." *Anthropological Papers of the American Museum of Natural History* 61(1).

1990 "The Spanish Missions of La Florida: An Overview." In: *Columbian Consequences, Vol. 2, Archaeological and Historical Perspectives on the Spanish Borderlands East*, David Hurst Thomas, ed., pp. 357–397. Washington, D.C.: Smithsonian Institution Press.

1991 "Harvesting Ramona's Garden: Life in California's Mythical Mission Past." In: *Columbian Consequences, Vol. 3, The Spanish Borderlands in Pan-American Perspective*, David Hurst Thomas, ed., pp. 119–157. Washington, D.C.: Smithsonian Institution Press.

1994 *Exploring Ancient Native America*. New York: Macmillan.

2000 *Skull Wars: Kennewick Man, Archaeology, and the Battle for Native American Identity*. New York: Basic Books.

2008 "Native American Landscapes of St. Catherines Island, Georgia" (3 vols.). *Anthropological Papers of the American Museum of Natural History* 88.

Thompson, Victor D., and John A. Turck 2009 "Adaptive Cycles of Coastal Hunter-Gatherers." *American Antiquity* 74(2):255–278.

Thornton, Russell 1997 "Aboriginal North American Population and Rates of Decline, ca. A.D. 1500–1900." *Current Anthropology* 38(2):310–315.

2000 "Population History of Native North Americans." In: *A Population History of North America*, Michael R. Haines and Richard H. Steckel, eds., pp. 9–50. Cambridge: Cambridge University Press.

Thornton, Russell, Jonathan Warren, and Tim Miller 1992 "Depopulation in the Southeast after 1492." In: *Disease and Demography in the Americas*, John W. Verano and Douglas H. Ubelaker, eds., pp. 187–195. Washington, D.C.: Smithsonian Institution Press.

Tiffany, Joseph A. 2007 "Examining the Origins of the Middle Missouri Tradition." In: *Plains Village Archaeology: Bison-hunting Farmers in the Central and Northern Plains*, Stanley A. Ahler and Marvin Kay, eds., pp. 3–14. Salt Lake City: University of Utah Press.

Tinker, George E. 1993 *Missionary Conquest: The Gospel and Native American Cultural Genocide.* Minneapolis: Fortress Press.

Titmus, Gene L., and James C. Woods 1991a "A Closer Look at Margin 'Grinding' on Folsom and Clovis Points." *Journal of California and Great Basin Anthropology* 13(2):194–203.

1991b "Fluted Points from the Snake River Plain." In: *Clovis: Origins and Adaptations*, Robson Bonnichsen and Karen L. Turnmire, eds., pp. 119–132. Oregon State University: Center for the Study of the First Americans.

Todd, Lawrence C. 1991 "Seasonality Studies and Paleoindian Subsistence Strategies." In: *Human Predators and Prey Mortality*, Mary C. Stiner, ed., pp. 217–276. Boulder, CO: Westview Press.

Todd, Lawrence C., Jack L. Hofman, and C. Bertrand Schultz 1990 "Seasonality of the Scottsbluff and Lipscomb Bison Bonebeds: Implications for Modeling Paleoindian Subsistence." *American Antiquity* 55(4):813–827.

Tomczak, Paula D., and Joseph F. Powell 2003 "Postmarital Residence Practices in the Windover Population: Sex-Based Dental Variation as an Indicator of Patrilocality." *American Antiquity* 68(1):93–108.

Tooker, Elisabeth 1978 "History of Research." In: *Handbook of North American Indians, Vol. 15, Northeast*, Bruce Trigger, ed., pp. 4–15. Washington, D.C.: Smithsonian Institution.

Torbenson, Micahel, Authur Aufderheide, and Elden Johnson 1992 "Punctured Human Bones of the Laurel Culture from Smith Mound Four, Minnesota." *American Antiquity* 57(3):506–514.

Torroni, Antonio 2000 "Mitochondrial DNA and the Origin of Native Americans." In: *America Past, America Present: Genes and Languages in the Americas and Beyond*, Colin Renfrew, ed., pp. 77–87. Cambridge: McDonald Institute for Archaeological Research.

Torroni, Antonio, J. V. Neel, R. Barrantes, Theodore G. Schurr, and Douglas C. Wallace 1994 "Mitochondrial DNA 'Clock' for the Amerinds and its Implications for Timing Their Entry into North America." *Proceedings of the National Academy of Sciences* 91(3):1158–1162.

Torroni, Antonio, Theodore G. Schurr, M. F. Cabell, Michael D. Brown, J. V. Neel, M. Larsen, D. G. Smith, C. M. Vullo, and Douglas C. Wallace 1993 "Asian Affinities and Continental Radiation of the Four Founding Native American Mitochrondrial DNAs." *American Journal of Human Genetics* 53(3):563–590.

Torroni, Antonio, Theodore G. Schurr, C. C. Yang, Emöke J. E. Szathmary, R. C. Williams, M. S. Schanfield, G. A. Troup, W. C. Knowler, D. N. Lawrence, K. M. Weiss, and Douglas C. Wallace 1992 "Native American Mitochrondrial DNA Analysis Indicates That the Amerind and the Nadene Populations Were Founded by Two Independent Migrations." *Genetics* 130(1):153–162.

Toth, Nicholas 1991 "The Material Record." In: *The First Americans: Search and Research*, Tom D. Dillehay and David J. Meltzer, eds, pp. 53–76. Boca Raton: CRC Press.

Treganza, Adan E. 1946 *California Clay Artifacts.* Berkeley: Robert E. Schenk Archives of California Archaeology, Paper No. 22.

Trigger, Bruce G. 1978 (ed.) *Handbook of North American Indians, Vol. 15, Northeast.* Washington, D.C.: Smithsonian Institution.

1989 *A History of Archaeological Thought.* Cambridge, UK: Cambridge University Press.

True, D. L., and Martin A. Baumhoff 1985 "Archaeological Investigations at Lake Berryessa, California, Berryessa II." *Journal of California and Great Basin Anthropology* 7(1):21–45.

True, D. L., Martin A. Baumhoff, and J. E. Hellen 1979 "Milling Stone Cultures in Northern California: Berryessa I." *Journal of California and Great Basin Anthropology* 1(1):124–154.

Tuck, James A. 1974 "Early Archaic Horizons in Eastern North America." *Archaeology of Eastern North America* 2(1):72–80.

1976 "Ancient People of Port au Choix: The Excavation of an Archaic Indian Cemetery in Newfoundland." St. John's: Memorial University, Social and Economic Series 17.

1978 "Regional Cultural Development, 3,000 to 300 B.C." In: *Handbook of North American Indians, Vol. 15, Northeast*, Bruce Trigger, ed., pp. 28–43. Washington, D.C.: Smithsonian Institution.

1982 "Prehistoric Archaeology in Atlantic Canada Since 1975." *Canadian Journal of Archaeology* 6:201–218.

1984 *Maritime Provinces Prehistory.* Ottawa: National Museums of Canada, Canadian Prehistory Series.

Tuck, James A., and Robert McGhee 1976 "An Archaic Indian Burial Mound in Labrador." *Scientific American* 235(5):122–129.

Tuohy, Donald R., and Amy J. Dansie 1997 "New Information Regarding Early Holocene Manifestations in the Western Great Basin." *Nevada Historical Society Quarterly* 40(1):24–53.

Turnbull, Christopher J. 1976 "The Augustine Site: A Mound from the Maritimes." *Archaeology of Eastern North America* 4:50–62.

Turner, Christy G. II 1983 "Taphonomic Reconstructions of Human Violence and Cannibalism Based on Mass Burials in the American Southwest." In: *Carnivores, Human Scavengers, and Predators: A Question of Bone Technology,*

G. M. LeMoine and A. S. MacEachern, eds., pp. 219–240. Calgary: Archaeological Association of the University of Calgary.

1985 "The Dental Search for American Origins." In: *Out of Asia: Peopling the Americas and the Pacific*, Robert Kirk and Emöke J. E. Szathmary, eds., pp. 31–78. Canberra: Australian National University.

1987 "Telltale Teeth." *Natural History* 96(1):6–10.

1993 "Southwest Indian Teeth." *National Geographic Research and Exploration* 9(1):32–53.

1994 "Relating Eurasian and Native American Populations Through Dental Morphology." In: *Method and Theory for Investigating the Peopling of the Americas*, Robson Bonnichsen, and D. Gentry Steele, eds., pp. 131–140. Oregon State University: Center for the Study of the First Americans.

2002 "Teeth, Needles, Dogs, and Siberia: Bioarchaeological Evidence for the Colonization of the New World." In: "The First Americans: The Pleistocene Colonization of the New World," Nina G. Jablonski, ed., pp. 123–158. Special issue, *Memoirs of the California Academy of Sciences* No. 27.

2003 "Three Ounces of Sea Shells and One Fish Bone Do Not a Coastal Migration Make." *American Antiquity* 68(2):391–395.

Turner, Christy G. II, and Nancy T. Morris 1970 "A Massacre at Hopi." *American Antiquity* 35(3):320–331.

Turner, Christy G. II, and Jacqueline A. Turner 1999 *Man Corn: Cannibalism and Violence in the Prehistoric American Southwest.* Salt Lake City: University of Utah Press.

Tushingham, Shannon, Jane Hill, and Charles H. McNutt (eds.) 2002 *Histories of Southeastern Archaeology.* Tuscaloosa: University of Alabama Press.

Ugan, A. 2005 "Climate, Bone Density, and Resource Depression: What Is Driving Variation in Large and Small Game in Fremont Archaeofaunas?" *Journal of Anthropological Archaeology* 24(3):227–251.

Uhle, Max 1907 "The Emeryville Shellmound." *University of California Publications in American Anchaeology and Ethography* 7.

Upham, Steadman 1988 "Archaeological Visibility and the Underclass of Southwestern Prehistory." *American Antiquity* 53(2):245–261.

1992 "Population and Spanish Contact in the Southwest." In: *Disease and Demography in the Americas*, John W. Verano and Douglas H. Ubelaker, eds., pp. 223–236. Washington, D.C.: Smithsonian Institution Press.

1994 "Nomads of the Desert West: A Shifting Continuum in Prehistory." *Journal of World Prehistory* 8(2):113–167.

Van der Merwe, Nikolaas J., Ronald F. Williamson, Susan Pfeiffer, Stephen Cox Thomas, and Kim Oakberg Allegretto 2003 "The Moatfield Ossuary: Isotopic Dietary Analysis of an Iroquoian Community, Using Dental Tissue." *Journal of Anthropological Archaeology* 22(3):245–261.

Van Dyke, Ruth M. 1999 "The Chaco Connection: Evaluating Bonito-Style Architecture in Outlier Communities." *Journal of Anthropological Archaeology* 18(4):471–506.

2004 "Memory, Meaning, and Masonry: The Late Bonito Chacoan Landscape." *American Antiquity* 69(3):413–431.

2007a *The Chaco Experience: Landscape and Ideology at the Center Place.* Santa Fe: School for Advanced Research Press.

2007b "Great Kivas in Time, Space, and Society." In: *The Architecture of Chaco Canyon, New Mexico*, Stephen H. Lekson, ed., pp. 93–126. Salt Lake City: University of Utah Press.

Van Nest, Julieanne 2006 "Rediscovering This Earth: Some Ethnogeological Aspects of the Illinois Valley Hopewell Mounds." In: *Recreating Hopewell*, Douglas K. Charles and Jane E. Buikstra, eds., pp. 402–426. Gainesville: University Press of Florida.

Van West, Carla R. 1996 "Agricultural Potential and Carrying Capacity in Southwestern Colorado, A.D. 901 to 1300." In: *The Prehistoric Pueblo World, A.D. 1150–1350*, Michael A. Adler, ed., pp. 214–227. Tucson: University of Arizona Press.

Van West, Carla R., and Jeffrey S. Dean 2000 "Environmental Characteristics of the A.D. 900–1300 Period in the Central Mesa Verde Region." *Kiva* 66(1):19–44.

Van West, Carla R., and Timothy A. Kohler 1996 "A Time to Rend, a Time to Sew: New Perspectives on Northern Anasazi Sociopolitical Development in Later Prehistory." In: *Anthropology, Space, and Geographic Information Systems*, Mark Aldenderfer and Herbert D. G. Maschner, eds., pp. 107–131. New York: Oxford University Press.

VanPool, Todd L., and Robert D. Leonard 2002 "Specialized Ground Stone Production in the Casas Grandes Region of Northern Chihuahua, Mexico." *American Antiquity* 67(4):710–730.

VanPool, Christine S., and Todd L. VanPool 2006 "Gender in Middle Range Societies: A Case Study in Casas Grandes Iconography." *American Antiquity* 71(1):53–75.

2007 *Signs of the Casas Grandes Shamans.* Salt Lake City: University of Utah Press.

Vansina, Jan 1985 *Oral Tradition as History.* Madison: University of Wisconsin Press.

Varien, Mark D., Scott G. Ortman, Timothy A. Kohler, Donna M. Glowacki, and C. David Johnson 2007 "Historical Ecology in the Mesa Verde Region: Results from the Village Ecodynamics Project." *American Antiquity* 72(2):273–299.

Vehik, Susan C. 2001 "Hunting and Gathering Tradition: Southern Plains." In: *Handbook of North American Indians, Vol. 13, Plains*, Raymond J. DeMallie, ed., pp. 146–158. Washington, D.C.: Smithsonian Institution.

Vehik, Susan C., and Timothy G. Baugh 1994 "Prehistoric Plains Trade." In: *Prehistoric Exchange Systems in North America*, Timothy G. Baugh and Jonathon E. Ericson, eds., pp. 249–274. New York: Plenum Press.

Vellanoweth, René L., and Jon M Erlandson 1999 "Middle Holocene Fishing and Maritime Adaptations at CA-SNI-161, San Nicolas Island, California." *Journal of California and Great Basin Anthropology* 21(2):257–274.

Veltre, Douglas W. 1998 "Prehistoric Maritime Adaptations in the Western and Central Aleutian Islands, Alaska." *Arctic Anthropology* 35(1):223–233.

Vernon, William W. 1990 "New Archaeometallurgical Perspectives on the Old Copper Industry of North America." In: *Archaeological Geology of North America*, Norman P. Lasca and Jack Donahue, eds., pp. 499–512. Boulder: Geological Society of America, Centennial Special Volume 4.

Versaggi, Nina M., LouAnn Wurst, T. Cregg Madrigal, and Andrea Lain 2001 "Adding Complexity to Late Archaic Research in the Northeastern Appalachians." In: *Archaeology of the Appalachian Highlands*, Lynne P. Sullivan and Susan C. Prezzano, eds., pp. 121–133. Knoxville: University of Tennessee Press.

Vierra, Bradley J., and Richard I. Ford 2007 "Foragers and Farmers in the Northern Rio Grande Valley, New Mexico." *Kiva* 73(2):117–130.

Vivian, R. Gwinn 1990 *The Chacoan Prehistory of the San Juan Basin, New Mexico.* San Diego: Academic Press.

1997a "Chacoan Roads: Morphology." *Kiva* 63(1):7–34.

1997b "Chacoan Roads: Function." *Kiva* 63(1):35–67.

2000 "Basketmaker Archaeology at the Millennium." In: *Foundations of Anasazi Culture: The Basketmaker–Pueblo Transition,* Paul F. Reed, ed., pp. 251–257. Salt Lake City: University of Utah Press.

Vivian, R. Gwinn, and Bruce Hilpert 2002 *The Chaco Handbook: An Encyclopedic Guide.* Salt Lake City: University of Utah Press.

von Werlhof, Jay 1961 "Archaeological Investigations at Tul-145 (Cobble Lodge)." Report on file at the Southern San Joaquin Valley Archaeological Information Center, California State University, Bakersfield.

1987 *Spirits of the Earth: A Study of Earthen Art in the North American Deserts, Vol. 1, The Northern Desert.* El Centro, CA: Imperial Valley College Museum Society.

2004 *Spirits of the Earth: That They May Know and Remember, Vol. 2.* El Centro, CA: Imperial Valley College Museum Society.

Waguespack, Nicole M., and Todd A. Surovell 2003 "Clovis Hunting Strategies, or How to Make Out on Plentiful Resources." *American Antiquity* 68(2):333–352.

Wake, Thomas A. 2003 "New Insight into Mammal Exploitation at the Emeryville Shellmound, Alameda County, California." Paper presented at the annual meeting of the Society for American Archaeology, Milwaukee.

Wake, Thomas A., and Dwight D. Simons 2000 "Trans-Holocene Subsistence Strategies and Topographic Change on the Northern California Coast: The Fauna from Duncans Point Cave." *Journal of California and Great Basin Anthropology* 22(2):295–320.

Walker, Deward E., Jr. 1998a (ed.) *Handbook of North American Indians, Vol. 12, Plateau.* Washington, D.C.: Smithsonian Institution.

1998b Introduction. In: *Handbook of North American Indians, Vol. 12, Plateau,* Deward E. Walker, Jr., ed., pp. 1–7. Washington, D.C.: Smithsonian Institution.

Walker, Ernest G. 1984 The Graham Site: A McKean Cremation from Southern Saskatchewan. *Plains Anthropologist* 29(104):139–150.

Walker, William H. 2002 "Stratigraphy and Practical Reason." *American Anthropologist* 104(1):159–177.

Wallace, Douglas C., and Antonio Torroni 1992 "American Indian Prehistory as Written in the Mitochondrial DNA: A Review." *Human Biology* 64(3):403–416.

Wallace, Henry D. (ed.) 2003 *Roots of Sedentism: Archaeological Excavations at Valencia Vieja, a Founding Village in the Tucson Basin of Southern Arizona.* Tucson: Center for Desert Archaeology, Anthropological Papers No. 29.

Wallace, Henry D., James M. Heidke, and William H. Doelle 1995 "Hohokam Origins." *Kiva* 60(4):575–618.

Wallace, William J. 1955 "A Suggested Chronology for Southern California Coastal Archaeology." *Southwestern Journal of Anthropology* 11(3):214–230.

1991 "Tulare Lake's Archaeological Past." In: *Background to a Study of Tulare Lake's Archaeological Past,* William J. Wallace and Francis A. Riddell, eds., pp. 23–33. Redondo Beach, CA: Tulare Lake Archaeological Research Group, Contributions to Tulare Lake Archaeology I.

1993 "A Lost Opportunity? A Brief History of Archaeological Research in the Tulare Lake Basin." In: *Finding the Evidence: The Quest for Tulare Lake's Archaeological Past,* William J. Wallace and Francis A. Riddell, eds., pp. 1–11. Redondo Beach: Tulare Lake Archaeological Research Group, Contributions to Tulare Lake Archaeology II.

Wallace, William J., and Francis A. Riddell 1988 "Archaeological Background of Tulare Lake, California." In: "Early Occupation in Far Western North America: The Clovis-Archaic Interface," Judith A. Willig, C. Melvin Aikens, and John L. Fagan, eds., pp. 87–101. Special issue, *Nevada State Museum Anthropological Papers* No. 21.

Walthall, John A. 1998 "Rockshelters and Hunter-Gatherer Adaptation to the Pleistocene/Holocene Transition." *American Antiquity* 63(2):223–238.

Wang, Sijia, Cecil M. Lewis Jr., Mattias Jakobsson, Sohini Ramachandran, Nicolas Ray, Gabriel Bedoya, Winston Rojas, Maria V. Parra, Julio A. Molina, Carla Gallo, Guido Mazzotti, Giovanni Poletti, Kim Hill, Ana M. Hurtado, Damian Labuda, William Klitz, Ramiro Barrantes, Maria Cá tira Bortolini, Francisco M. Salzano, Maria Luiza Petzl-Erler, Luiza T. Tsuneto, Elena Llop, Francisco Rothhammer, Laurent Excoffier, Marcus W. Feldman, Noah A. Rosenberg, and Andrés Ruiz-Linares 2007 "Genetic Variation and Population Structure in Native Americans." *PLoS Genetics* 3(11):2049–2067.

Ward, H. Trawick, and R. P. Stephen Davis, Jr. 1999 *Time before History: The Archaeology of North Carolina.* Chapel Hill: University of North Carolina Press.

Warren, Claude N. 1966 "The San Dieguito Type Site: M. J. Rogers' 1938 Excavation on the San Dieguito River." *San Diego Museum Papers* 5.

1967 "The San Dieguito Complex: A Review and Hypothesis." *American Antiquity* 32(2):168–185.

1968a *The View from Wenas: A Study in Plateau Prehistory.* Pocatello: Occasional Papers of the Idaho State University Museum, No. 24.

1968b "Cultural Tradition and Ecological Adaptation on the Southern California Coast." In: "Archaic Prehistory in the Western United States," C. Irwin-Williams, ed., pp. 1–14. *Eastern New Mexico University Contributions in Anthropology* 1(3).

1980 "Pinto Points and Problems in Mojave Desert Archaeology." In: *Anthropological Papers in Memory of Earl H. Swanson, Jr.*, L. B. Harton, Claude N. Warren, and Donald R. Tuohy, eds., pp. 67–76. Pocatello: Idaho Museum of Natural History.

1984 "The Desert Region." In: *California Archaeology*, Michael J. Moratto, pp. 339–430. Orlando: Academic Press.

1991 Archaeological Investigations at Nelson Wash, Fort Irwin, California. *Fort Irwin Archaeological Project Research Report No. 23* (2 vols.). San Bernardino County Museum, Redlands.

Warren, Claude N., and Robert H. Crabtree 1986 "Prehistory of the Southwestern Area." In: *Handbook of North American Indians, Vol. 11, Great Basin*, Warren L. d'Azevedo, ed., pp. 183–193. Washington, D.C.: Smithsonian Institution.

Warren, Claude N., and Carl Phagan 1988 "Fluted Points in the Mojave Desert: Their Technology and Cultural Context." In: "Early Human Occupation in Far Western North America: The Clovis-Archaic Interface," Judith A. Willig, C. Melvin Aikens, and John L. Fagan, eds., pp. 121–130. Special issue *Nevada State Museum Anthropological Papers* No. 21.

Warren Claude N., and D. L. True 1961 *The San Dieguito Complex and Its Place in California Prehistory*. Los Angeles: University of California Archaeological Survey Annual Report 1960–1961:246–338.

Warrick, Gary 1996 "Evolution of the Iroquoian Longhouse." In: *People Who Lived in Big Houses*, Gary Coupland and E. B. Banning, eds., pp. 11–26. Madison, WI: Prehistory Press, Monographs in World Archaeology No. 27.

2000 "The Precontact Iroquoian Occupation of Southern Ontario." *Journal of World Prehistory* 14(4):415–466.

Watanabe, Shigueo, Walter Elias Feria Ayta, Henrique Hamaguchi, Niède Guidon, Eliany S. La Salvia, Silvia Maranca, and Oswaldo Baffa Filho 2003 "Some Evidence of a Date of First Humans to Arrive in Brazil." *Journal of Archaeological Science* 30(4):351–354.

Watchman, Alan, Maria de la Luz Gutiérrez Martínez, and M. Hernandéz Llosas 2002 "Giant Murals of Baja California: New Regional Archaeological Perspectives." *Antiquity* 76(294):947–948.

Waters, Michael R. 1982 "The Lowland Patayan Ceramic Tradition." In: *Hohokam and Patayan: Prehistory of Southwestern Arizona*, Randall H. McGuire and Michael B. Schiffer, eds., pp. 275–297. New York: Academic Press.

1983 "Late Holocene Lacustrine Chronology and Archaeology of Ancient Lake Cahuilla, California." *Quaternary Research* 19(3):373–387.

1986a "Sulphur Springs Woman: An Early Human Skeleton from Southeastern Arizona." *American Antiquity* 51(2):361–365.

1986b "The Sulphur Spring Stage and Its Place in New World Prehistory." *Quaternary Research* 25(2):251–256.

Waters Michael R., Steven L. Forman, Thomas W. Stafford, Jr., and John Foss 2009 "Geoarchaeological investigations at the Topper and Big Pine Tree Sites, Allendale County, South Carolina." *Journal of Archaeological Science* 36(7):1300–1311.

Waters, Michael R., and Thomas W. Stafford, Jr. 2007a "Redefining the Age of Clovis: Implications for the Peopling of the Americas." *Science* 315:1122–1126.

2007b "Response to Comment on 'Redefining the Age of Clovis: Implications for the Peopling of the Americas.'" *Science* 317:320c.

Waters, Michael R., Thomas W. Stafford, Jr., Brian G. Redmond, and Kenneth B. Tankersley 2009 "The Age of the Paleoindian Assemblage at Sheriden Cave, Ohio." *American Antiquity* 74(1):107–111.

Watkins, Joe 2005 "Through Wary Eyes: Indigenous Perspectives on Archaeology." *Annual Review of Anthropology* 34:429–449.

Watson, Patty Jo, and Mary C. Kennedy 1991 "The Development of Horticulture in the Eastern Woodlands of North America: Women's Role." In: *Engendering Archaeology: Women and Prehistory*, Joan M. Gero and Margaret W. Conkey, eds., pp. 255–275. Oxford, UK: Basil Blackwell.

Wauchope, Robert 1962 *Lost Tribes & Sunken Continents: Myth and Method in the Study of American Indians*. Chicago: University of Chicago Press.

Webb, David S. (ed.) 2005 *First Floridians and Last Mastodons: The Page-Ladson Site in the Aucilla River*. New York: Springer.

Wedel, Waldo R. 1936 "An Introduction to Pawnee Archaeology." *Bureau of American Ethnology Bulletin* 112.

1938 "The Direct-Historical Approach in Pawnee Archaeology." *Smithsonian Miscellaneous Collections* 97(7).

1940 "Culture Sequences in the Central Great Plains." *Smithsonian Miscellaneous Collections* 100:291–352.

1941a "Environment and Native Subsistence Economies in the Central Great Plains." *Smithsonian Miscellaneous Collections* 100(3).

1961 *Prehistoric Man on the Great Plains*. Norman: University of Oklahoma Press.

1986 *Central Plains Prehistory: Holocene Environments and Culture Change in the Republican River Basin*. Lincoln: University of Nebraska Press.

2001 "Plains Village Tradition: Central." In: *Handbook of North American Indians, Vol. 13, Plains*, Raymond J. DeMallie, ed., pp. 173–185. Washington, D.C.: Smithsonian Institution.

Wedel, Waldo R., and Richard A. Krause 2001 "History of Archaeological Research." In: *Handbook of North American Indians, Vol. 13, Plains*, Raymond J. DeMallie, ed., pp. 14–22. Washington, D.C.: Smithsonian Institution.

Wedel, Waldo R., Wilfred M. Husted, and John H. Moss 1968 "Mummy Cave: Prehistoric Record from Rocky Mountains of Wyoming." *Science* 160:184–186.

Weide, David L. 1976 "Summary of Radiometric Dates for the Salton Sink Region." In: *Background to Prehistory of the Yuha Desert Region*, Philip J. Wilke, ed., pp. 95–97. Ramona, CA: Ballena Press Anthropological Papers No. 5.

Welch, Paul D. 1996 "Control over Goods and the Political Stability of the Moundville Chiefdom." In: *Political Structure and Change in the Prehistoric Southeastern United States*,

John F. Scarry, ed., pp. 69–91. Gainseville: University Press of Florida.

Wells, E. Christian, Glen E. Rice, and John C. Ravesloot 2004 "Peopling the Landscapes between Villages in the Middle Gila River of Central Arizona." *American Antiquity* 69(4):627–652.

Wendorf, Fred, Alex D. Krieger, C. C. Albritton, Jr., and T. D. Stewart 1955 *The Midland Discovery*. Austin: University of Texas Press.

Wesler, Kit W. 1981 "Models for Pleistocene Extinction." *North American Archaeologist* 2(2):85–100.

Wessen, Gary C. 1988 "The Use of Shellfish Resources on the Northwest Coast: The View from Ozette." In: *Research in Economic Anthropology, Supplement 3, Prehistoric Economies of the Pacific Northwest Coast*, Barry L. Isaac, ed., pp. 179–207. Greenwich, CT: JAI Press.

1990 "Prehistory of the Ocean Coast of Washington." In: *Handbook of North American Indians, Vol. 7, Northwest Coast*, Wayne Suttles, ed., pp. 412–421. Washington, D.C.: Smithsonian Institution.

Wesson, Cameron B. 1999 "Chiefly Power and Food Storage in Southeastern North America." *World Archaeology* 31(1):145–164.

West, Constance F. 1996 "Trial Creek Caves, Steward Peninsula." In: *American Beginnings: The Prehistory and Paleoecology of Beringia*, Frederick Hadleigh West, ed., pp. 482–484. Chicago: University of Chicago Press.

West, Frederick Hadleigh 1967 "The Donnelly Ridge Site and the Definition of an Early Core and Blade Complex in Central Alaska." *American Antiquity* 32(3):360–382.

1996 (ed.) *American Beginnings: The Prehistory and Paleoecology of Beringia*. Chicago: University of Chicago Press.

West, G. James, Owen K. Davis, and William J. Wallace 1991 "Fluted Points at Tulare Lake, California: Environmental Background." In: *Background to a Study of Tulare Lake's Archaeological Past*, William J. Wallace and Francis A. Riddell, eds., pp. 1–10. Redondo Beach, CA: Tulare Lake Archaeological Research Group, Contributions to Tulare Lake Archaeology I.

Whalen, Michael E., and Paul E. Minnis 2000 "Leadership at Casas Grandes, Chihuahua, Mexico." In: *Alternative Leadership Strategies in the Prehispanic Southwest*, Barbara J. Mills, ed., pp. 168–179. Tucson: University of Arizona Press.

2001a *Casas Grandes and Its Hinterlands: Prehistoric Regional Organization in Northwest Mexico*. Tucson: University of Arizona Press.

2001b "Architecture and Authority in the Casas Grandes Area, Chihuahua, Mexico." *American Antiquity* 66(4):651–668.

2001c "The Cases Grandes Regional System: A Late Prehistoric Polity of Northwestern Mexico." *Journal of World Prehistory* 15(3):313–364.

2003 "The Local and The Distant in the Origin of Casas Grandes, Chihuahua, Mexico." *American Antiquity* 68(2):314–332.

Wheat, Joe Ben 1955 "Mogollon Culture Prior to A.D. 1000." *Memoirs of the American Anthropological Association* No. 82.

1972 "The Olsen-Chubbuck Site: A Paleo-Indian Bison Kill." *Memoirs of the Society for American Archaeology* No. 26.

Wheeler, S. M. 1997 "Cave Burials Near Fallon, Nevada." *Nevada Historical Society Quarterly* 40(1):15–23.

White, Greg, and Ronald F. King 1993 "Rethinking the Mostin Site." In: *There Grows a Green Tree: Papers in Honor of David A. Fredrickson*, Greg White, Pat Mikkelsen, William R. Hildebrandt, and Mark E. Basgall, eds., pp. 121–140. Center for Archaeological Research at Davis, Publication No. 11.

White, James M., Rolf W. Mathewes, and W. H. Mathews 1985 "Late Pleistocene Chronology and Environment of the 'Ice-Free Corridor' of Northwestern Alberta." *Quaternary Research* 24(2):173–186.

White, Max E. 2002 *The Archaeology and History of the Native Georgia Tribes*. Gainesville: University Press of Florida.

White, Tim D. 1992 *Prehistoric Cannibalism at Mancos 5MTUMR-2346*. Princeton, NJ: Princeton University Press.

Whitley, David S. 1994 "By the Hunter, for the Gatherer: Art, Social Relations and Subsistence Change in the Prehistoric Great Basin." *World Archaeology* 25(3):356–373.

Whitley, David S., and Ronald I. Dorn 1993 "New Perspectives on the Clovis vs. Pre-Clovis Controversy." *American Antiquity* 58(4):626–647.

Whitridge, Peter 2000 "The Prehistory of Yupik and Inuit Whale Use." *Revista de Arqueología Americana* 16(1):99–154.

2001 "Zen Fish: A Consideration of the Discordance between Artifactual and Zooarchaeological Indicators of Thule Inuit Fish Use." *Journal of Anthropological Archaeology* 20(1):3–72.

Whittlesey, Stephanie M. 1997 "Rethinking the Core-Periphery Model of the Pre-Classic Period Hohokam." In: *Vanishing River: Landscapes and Lives of the Lower Verde Valley*, Stephanie M. Whittlesey, Richard Ciolek-Torrello, and Jeffrey H. Altschul, eds., pp. 597–628. Tucson: SRI Press.

Whittlesey, Stephanie M., and Richard Ciolek-Torrello 1996 "The Archaic-Formative Transition in the Tucson Basin." In: *Early Formative Adaptations in the Southern Southwest*, Barbara J. Roth ed., pp. 49–64. Madison, WI: Prehistory Press, Monographs in World Archaeology No. 25.

Whittlesey, Stephanie M., Richard Ciolek-Torrello, and Jeffrey H. Altschul (eds.) 1997 *Vanishing River: Landscapes and Lives of the Lower Verde Valley*. Tucson, AZ: SRI Press.

Wilcox, David R. 1995 "A Processual Model of Charles C. Di Peso's Babocomari Site and Related Systems." In: *The Gran Chichimeca: Essays on the Archaeology and Ethnohistory of Northern Mesoamerica*, Jonathan E. Reyman, ed., pp. 281–319. Aldershot, UK: Avebury.

1996 "Pueblo III People and Polity in Regional Context." In: *The Prehistoric Pueblo World, A.D. 1150–1350*, Michael A. Adler, ed., pp. 241–254. Tucson: University of Arizona Press.

Wilde, James D., and Guy L. Tasa 1991 "A Woman at the Edge of Agriculture: Skeletal Remains from the Elsinore Burial Site,

Sevier Valley, Utah." *Journal of California and Great Basin Anthropology* 13(1):60–76.

Wilke, Phillip J. 1978 *Late Prehistoric Human Ecology at Lake Cahuilla, Coachella Valley, California.* Berkeley: University of California Archaeological Research Facility Contributions No. 38.

——— 1991 "Lanceolate Projectile Points from Tulare Lake, California." In: *Background to a Study of Tulare Lake's Archaeological Past,* William J. Wallace and Francis A. Riddell, eds., pp. 41–52. Redondo Beach: Tulare Lake Archaeological Research Group, Contributions to Tulare Lake Archaeology I.

Wilke, Philip J., and J. Jeffrey Flenniken 1991 "Missing the Point: Rebuttal to Bettinger, O'Connell, and Thomas." *American Anthropologist* 93(1):172–173.

Wilke, Philip J., J. Jeffrey Flenniken, and Terry L. Ozbun 1991 "Clovis Technology at the Anzick Site, Montana." *Journal of California and Great Basin Anthropology* 13(2):242–272.

Wilke, Philip J., and Meg McDonald 1989 "Prehistoric Use of Rock-Lined Cache Pits: California Deserts and Southwest." *Journal of California and Great Basin Anthropology* 11(1):50–73.

Will, G. F., and H. J. Spinden 1906 "The Mandans: A Study of Their Culture, Archaeology and Language." *Papers of the Peabody Museum of Archaeology and Ethnology* 3(4).

Willey, Gordon R. 1945 "The Weeden Island Culture: A Preliminary Definition." *American Antiquity* 10(3):225–254.

——— 1949 "Archaeology of the Florida Gulf Coast." *Smithsonian Miscellaneous Collections* 113.

——— 1953 "Prehistoric Settlement Patterns in the Virú Valley, Peru." *Bureau of American Ethnology Bulletin* 155.

——— 1966 *An Introduction to American Archaeology, Vol. One, North and Middle America.* Englewood Cliffs, NJ: Prentice Hall, Inc.

Willey, Gordon R., and Philip Phillips 1958 *Method and Theory in American Archaeology.* Chicago: University of Chicago Press.

Willey, Gordon R., and Jeremy A. Sabloff 1993 *A History of American Archaeology* (3rd ed.). New York: W. H. Freeman and Co.

Willey, P. 1990 *Prehistoric Warfare on the Great Plains: Skeletal Analysis of the Crow Creek Massacre Victims.* New York: Garland Publishing, Inc.

Willey, P., and Thomas E. Emerson 1993 "The Osteology and Archaeology of the Crow Creek Massacre." In: "Prehistory and Human Ecology of the Western Prairies and Northern Plains," Joseph A. Tiffany, ed., pp. 227–269. *Plains Anthropologist Memoir* 27, *Plains Anthropologist* 38(145).

Williams, Stephen 1990 The Vacant Quarter and Other Late Events in the Lower Valley. In: *Towns and Temples Along the Mississippi,* David H. Dye and Cheryl Anne Cox, eds, pp. 170–180. Tuscaloosa: University of Alabama Press.

——— 2001 "The Vacant Quarter Hypothesis and the Yazoo Delta." In: *Societies in Eclipse: Archaeology of the Eastern Woodlands Indians, A.D. 1400–1700,* David S. Brose, C. Wesley Cowan, and Robert C. Mainfort, Jr., eds., pp.

191–203. Washington, D.C.: Smithsonian Institution Press.

Williamson, Ronald F., and Susan Pfeiffer (eds.) 2003 "Bones of the Ancestors: The Archaeology and Osteobiography of the Moatfield Ossuary." *Canadian Museum of Civilization, Mercury Series, Archaeological Survey of Canada,* Paper 163.

Williamson, Ronald F., Stephen Cox Thomas, and Robert I. MacDonald 2003 "The Archaeology of the Moatfield Village Site." In: *Bones of the Ancestors: The Archaeology and Osteobiography of the Moatfield Ossuary,* Ronald E. Williamson and Susan Pfeiffer, eds., pp. 19–88. Canadian Museum of Civilization, Mercury Series, Archaeological Survey of Canada, Paper 163.

Williamson, Ronald F., Shaun J. Austin and David A. Robertson (eds.) 2006 *In The Shadow of the Bridge II: The Archaeology of the Peace Bridge Site (AfGr-9), 1997–2000 Investigations.* Toronto: Occasional Publications of Archaeological Services, Inc., Vol. 2.

Willig, Judith A. 1988 "Paleo-Archaic Adaptations and Lakeside Settlement Patterns in the Northern Great Basin." In: *Early Human Occupation in Far Western North America: The Clovis-Archaic Interface,* Judith A. Willig, C. Melvin Aikens, and John L. Fagan, eds., pp. 417–482. *Nevada State Museum Anthropological Papers* No. 21.

——— 1990 "Western Clovis Occupation at the Dietz Site, Northern Alkali Lake Basin, Oregon." *Current Research in the Pleistocene* 7:52–56.

——— 1991 "Clovis Technology and Adaptation in Far Western North America: Regional Pattern and Environmental Context." In: *Clovis: Origins and Adaptations,* Robson Bonnichsen and Karen L. Turnmire, eds., pp. 91–118. Oregon State University: Center for the Study of the First Americans.

——— 1996 "Environmental Context for Early Human Occupation in Western North America." In: *Prehistoric Mongoloid Dispersals,* Takeru Akazawa and Emöke J. E. Szathmary, eds., pp. 241–253. Oxford, UK: Oxford University Press.

Willig, Judith A., and C. Melvin Aikens 1988 "The Clovis-Archaic Interface in Far Western North America." In: "Early Human Occupation in Far Western North America: The Clovis-Archaic Interface," Judith A. Willig, C. Melvin Aikens, and John L. Fagan, eds., pp. 1–40. Special issue, *Nevada State Museum Anthropological Papers* No. 21.

Wills, W. H. 1995 "Archaic Foraging and the Beginnings of Food Production in the American Southwest." In: *Last Hunters-First Farmers: New Perspectives on the Prehistoric Transition to Agriculture,* T. Douglas Price and Anne Birgitte Gebauer, eds., pp. 215–242. Santa Fe, NM: School of American Research.

——— 2000 "Political Leadership and the Construction of Chacoan Great Houses, A.D. 1020–1140." In: *Alternative Leadership Strategies in the Prehispanic Southwest,* Barbara J. Mills, ed., pp. 19–44. Tucson: University of Arizona Press.

Wills, W. H., and Thomas C. Windes 1989 "Evidence for Population Aggregation and Dispersal During the Basketmaker III Period in Chaco Canyon, New Mexico." *American Antiquity* 54(2):347–369.

Wilmsen, Edwin N., and Frank H. H. Roberts 1978 *Lindenmeier, 1934–1974: Concluding Report on Investigations.* Washington, D.C.: Smithsonian Contributions to Anthropology No. 24.

Wilson, Gregory D. 2008 *The Archaeology of Everyday Life at Moundville.* Tuscaloosa: University of Alabama Press.

2010 "Community, Identity, and Social Memory at Moundville." *American Antiquity* 75(1):3–18.

Windes, Thomas C. 2007 "Gearing Up and Piling On: Early Great Houses in the Interior San Juan Basin." In: *The Architecture of Chaco Canyon, New Mexico*, Stephen H. Lekson, ed., pp. 45–92. Salt Lake City: University of Utah Press.

Wingard, George F. 2001 "Carlon Village: Land, Water, Subsistence, and Sedentism in the Northern Great Basin." *University of Oregon Anthropological Papers* No. 57.

Wingerson, Lois 2009 "High Life in the High Mountains?" *American Archaeology* 13(4):12–18.

Winham, R. Peter, and F. A. Calabrese 1998 "The Middle Missouri Tradition." In: *Archaeology on the Great Plains*, W. Raymond Wood, ed., pp. 269–307. Lawrence: University of Kansas Press.

Wohlgemuth, Eric 1996 "Resource Intensification in Prehistoric Central California: Evidence from Archaeobotanical Data." *Journal of California and Great Basin Anthropology* 18(1):81–103.

Wood, W. Raymond 1974 "Northern Plains Village Cultures: Internal Stability and External Relationships." *Journal of Anthropological Research* 30(1):1–16.

1998 (ed.) *Archaeology on the Great Plains.* Lawrence: University of Kansas Press.

2001 "Plains Village Tradition: Middle Missouri." In: *Handbook of North American Indians, Vol. 13, Plains*, Raymond J. DeMallie, ed., pp. 186–195. Washington, D.C.: Smithsonian Institution.

Woody, Alanah, and Angus Quinlan 2008 "Rock at in the Western Great Basin." In: *The Great Basin: People and Place in Ancient Times*, Catherine S. Fowler and Don D. Fowler, eds., pp. 136–143. Santa Fe: School of American Research.

Woosley, Anne I., and Michael R. Waters 1990 "Reevaluation of Early Holocene Cochise Artifact Associations with Pleistocene Lake Cochise, Southeastern Arizona." *American Antiquity* 55(2):360–366.

Wormington, H. M. 1959 "Ancient Man in North America." *Denver Museum of Natural History Popular Series* No. 4

Wright, H. E., Jr. 1991 "Environmental Conditions for Paleoindian Immigration." In: *The First Americans: Search and Research*, Tom D. Dillehay and David J. Meltzer, eds, pp. 113–136. Boca Raton: CRC Press.

Wright, James V. 1981 "Prehistory of the Canadian Shield." In: *Handbook of North American Indians, Vol. 6, Subarctic*, June Helm, ed., pp. 86–96. Washington, D.C.: Smithsonian Institution.

1994 "The Prehistoric Transportation of Goods in the St. Lawrence River Basin." In: *Prehistoric Exchange Systems in North America*, Timothy G. Baugh and Jonathon E. Ericson, eds., pp. 47–71. New York: Plenum Press.

1995 "A History of the Native People of Canada" (3 vols.). *Canadian Museum of Civilization, Mercury Series, Archaeological Survey of Canada*, Paper 152.

Wyckoff, Don G. 1999 "The Burnham Site and Pleistocene Human Occupation of the Southern Plains of the United States." In: *Ice Age Peoples of North America: Environments, Origins, and Adaptations of the First Americans*, Robson Bonnichsen and Karen L. Turnmire, eds., pp. 340–362. Oregon State University: Center for the Study of the First Americans.

Yarnell, Richard A., and M. Jean Black 1985 "Temporal Trends Indicated by a Survey of Archaic and Woodland Plant Food Remains from Southeastern North America." *Southeastern Archaeology* 4:93–106.

Yatsko, Andrew, and L. Mark Raab 2009 "Medieval Climatic Crisis." In: *California Maritime Archaeology: A San Clemente Perspective*, L. Mark Raab, Jim Cassidy, Andrew Yatsko, and William J. Howard, eds., pp. 163–178. Lanham, MD: AltaMira Press.

Yerkes, Richard W. 1988 "The Woodland and Mississippian Traditions in the Prehistory of the Midwestern United States." *Journal of World Prehistory* 2(3):307–358.

2005 "Bone Chemistry, Body Parts, and Growth Marks: Evaluating Ohio Hopewell and Cahokia Mississippian Seasonality, Subsistence, Ritual, and Feasting." *American Antiquity* 70(2):241–265.

2006 "Middle Woodland Settlements and Social Organizations in the Central Ohio Valley: Were the Hopewell Really Farmers?" In: *Recreating Hopewell*, Douglas K. Charles and Jane E. Buikstra, eds., pp. 50–61. Gainesville: University Press of Florida.

Yesner, David R. 1980 "Maritime Hunter-Gatherers: Ecology and Prehistory." *Current Anthropology* 21(6):727–735.

1989 "Moose Hunters of the Boreal Forest? A Re-examination of Subsistence Patterns in the Western Subarctic." *Arctic* 42(2):97–108.

1996 "Human Adaptation at the Pleistocene-Holocene Boundary (circa 13,000 to 8,000 BP) in Eastern Beringia." In: *Humans at the End of the Ice Age: The Archaeology of the Pleistocene-Holocene Transition*, Lawrence Guy Straus, Berit Valentin Eriksen, Jon M. Erlandson, and David R. Yesner, eds., pp. 255–276. New York: Plenum Press.

1998 "Origins and Development of Maritime Adaptations in the Northwest Pacific Region of North America: A Zooarchaeological Perspective." *Arctic Anthropology* 35(1):204–222.

2001 "Human Dispersal into Interior Alaska: Antecedent Conditions, Mode of Colonization, and Adaptations." *Quaternary Science Reviews* 20(1–3):315–327.

Yesner, David R., Charles E. Holmes, and Kristine J. Crossen 1992 "Archaeology and Paleoecology of the Broken Mammoth Site, Central Tanana Valley, Interior Alaska, USA." *Current Research in the Pleistocene* 9:53–57.

Yi, Seonbok, and Geoffrey A. Clark 1985 "The 'Dyuktai Culture' and New World Origins." *Current Anthropology* 26(1):1–20.

Yohe, Robert M. II 1998 "The Introduction of the Bow and Arrow and Lithic Resource Use at Rose Spring (CA-INY-372)."

Journal of California and Great Basin Anthropology 20(1):26–52.

2000 "A New Radiocarbon Date on a Maize Cob from Diversion Dam Cave (10-AA-99)." *Idaho Archaeologist* 23(2):23–24.

Yohe, Robert M. II, Margaret E. Newman, and Joan S. Schneider 1991 "Immunological Identification of Small-Mammal Proteins on Aboriginal Milling Equipment." *American Antiquity* 56(4):659–666.

Yohe, Robert M., II, and Max G. Pavesic 1997 "*Olivella* Beads from the Braden Site (10-WN-117), Southwestern Idaho." *Tebiwa* 26(2):225–232.

2000 "Early Archaic Domestic Dogs from Western Idaho, U.S.A." In: *Dogs through Time: An Archaeological Perspective*, Susan Crockford, ed., pp. 93–104. Oxford, UK: British Archaeological Reports International Series 889.

2002 "Recent Isotopic Studies of Human Remains Attributable to the Western Idaho Archaic Burial Complex." Paper presented at the Great Basin Anthropological Conference, Boise.

Yohe, Robert M. II, and James C. Woods 2002 *The First Idahoans: A Paleoindian Context for Idaho*. Bosie: Idaho State Historical Society.

Young, Biloine Whiting, and Melvin L. Fowler 2000 *Cahokia: The Great American Metropolis*. Urbana: University of Illinois Press.

Young, Diane 1988 "An Osteological Analysis of the Paleoindian Double Burial at Horn Shelter, Number 2." *Central Texas Archaeologist* 11:11–115.

Zdanowicz, C. M., G. A. Zielinski, and M. S. Germani 1999 "Mount Mazama Eruption: Calendrical Age Verified and Atmospheric Impact Assessed." *Geology* 27(7):621–624.

Zeanah, David W. 2002 "Central Place Foraging and Prehistoric Pinyon Utilization in the Great Basin." In: *Beyond Foraging and Collecting: Evolutionary Change in Hunter-Gatherer Settlement Systems*, Ben Fitzhugh and Junko Habu, eds., pp. 231–256. New York: Kluwer Academic/Plenum Publishers.

2004 "Sexual Division of Labor and Central Place Foraging: A Model for the Carson Desert of Western Nevada." *Journal of Anthropological Archaeology* 23(1):1–32.

Zeanah, David W., and Robert G. Elston 2001 "Testing a Simple Hypothesis Concerning the Resilience of Dart Point Styles to Hafting Element Repair." *Journal of California and Great Basin Anthropology* 23(1):93–124.

Zimmerman, Larry J. 1985 *Peoples of Prehistoric South Dakota*. Lincoln: University of Nebraska Press.

Zimmerman, Larry J., and Lawrence E. Bradley 1993 "The Crow Creek Massacre: Initial Coalescent Warfare and Speculations about the Genesis of Extended Coalescent." In: "Prehistory and Human Ecology of the Western Prairies and Northern Plains," Joseph A. Tiffany, ed., pp. 215–226. *Plains Anthropologist Memoir 27, Plains Anthropologist* 38(145).

Zimmerman, Larry J., Anne M. Jensen, and Glenn W. Sheehan 2000 "Agnaiyaaq: The Autopsy of a Frozen Thule Mummy." *Arctic Anthropology* 37(2):52–59.

CREDITS

Chapter 1: Page 2: CORBIS-NY   **Chapter 2:** Page 32: Tri-City Herald Library; page 40: Nigel Bean, Nature Picture Library; page 41: Kunz & Reanier, Science Magazine; page 43: Kenneth Garrett, Kenneth Garrett Photograph; page 47: Kenneth Garrett, National Geographic Image Collection   **Chapter 3:** Page 63: Denver Museum of Nature and Science; page 64: Joe Ben Wheat, University of Colorado Museum—Boulder   **Chapter 4:** Page 88: Washington State Historical Society   **Chapter 5:** Page 108 (top): Pearson Education—Addison-Wesley; page 108 (bottom): Harvey Rise, Library of Congress   **Chapter 8:** Page 176: Utah Museum of Natural History   **Chapter 9:** Page 184: Werner Forman, Art Resource, N.Y.; page 186: Christian Williams, Rough Guides Dorling Kindersley; page 202: Walter Rawlings, Robert Harding World Imagery; page 206: National Geographic Image Collection   **Chapter 10:** Page 231 (top): Denver Museum of Nature and Science; page 231 (bottom): Library of Congress; page 233: Walter Bibikow, Danita Delimont Photography; page 235: U.S. Forestry Service; page 241: Fred Armstrong, United States Department of the Interior; page 242: Pawnee Earth Lodges, Nebraska, National Anthropological Archives
Chapter 11: Page 256: Del Baston, Center for American Archeology; page 267: Pictures of Record, Inc.; page 269 (top): Werner Forman, Art Resource, N.Y.; page 269 (bottom): The Field Museum; page 271: The Ohio Historical Society   **Chapter 12:** Page 281: University of Tennessee; page 287: Jon L. Gibson; page 297: National Geographic Image Collection; page 300: The Ohio Historical Society; page 302: Gordan Gahan, National Geographic Image Collection; page 303: Alabama Museum of Natural History   **Chapter Art** 3drenderings, Shutterstock

INDEX